THE BIRDS

OF INDIANA

by Russell E. Mumford and Charles E. Keller

Original Paintings by William Zimmerman

Indiana University Press, Bloomington

Manufactured in Japan

Library of Congress Cataloging in Publication Data

Mumford, Russell E.
    The birds of Indiana.

    Bibliography: p.
    Includes index.
    1. Birds—Indiana.   I. Keller, Charles E., 1929–
II. Zimmerman, William.   III. Title.
QL684.I5M86   1984   598.29772   83-49454
ISBN 0-253-10736-9

1 2 3 4 5 88 87 86 85 84

to our wives—

Vivian, Shirley, and Judy

CONTENTS

As must always be the case with a work of this kind, the authors have relied heavily on both past and contemporary observers. Amos W. Butler did likewise when he wrote *Birds of Indiana,* published in 1898. In some ways his task was easier than ours, for there were relatively few regular correspondents sending him information, and he had a much smaller volume of data to organize. On the other hand, because of the dearth of observers, several sections of the state were poorly represented by his published records. We have had the benefit of the unpublished notes and observations of the hundreds of birdwatchers, naturalists, bird banders, trained biologists, and professional zoologists whom we have come to know during the past forty years as well as the mass of published data now available to the birder or ornithologist.

We were denied (by our relative youth) the opportunity to know personally most of those who cooperated with Amos Butler. Too many generations have appeared in the interim, and practically all of the old guard is gone (an exception is Henry A. Link, now ninety-nine years old, with whom Mumford became acquainted nearly thirty years ago). These pioneers left their legacies in carefully taken notes, journals, and publications. Unfortunately, the years between our involvement with Indiana birds and that of Butler took their toll of collected specimens (which often graced the households of avid birdwatchers), letters, and other notes which would have proved invaluable to us. We can only marvel that some observers were able to gather so much information, given the constraints of travel, visual equipment, and inadequate identification guides of their day. We salute these early bird-lovers, most of whom are mentioned by Butler in his book.

To the many who have aided our work and helped to benefit and expand the knowledge of Indiana's birdlife, we owe a great debt of gratitude. We suppose it is inevitable that in attempting to list those who have been of some service in the past forty years we will, unintentionally, miss someone. We only trust that this book reflects the same dedication and perseverance these observers have shown. They have truly made it possible to produce this book. Many of them, if not mentioned here, are recognized throughout the text. Among this group are numerous friends, acquaintances, and colleagues now deceased. We learned from each and we were saddened by their deaths. Paramount among these was Herbert L. Stoddard, Sr. We recall, with much pleasure, visiting him at Sherwood Plantation in Georgia and birding with him at the St. Marks Refuge and Wakulla Springs areas in Florida. During these visits, he made his extensive notes and journals available to us and recounted some of his exploits along Lake Michigan, where he conducted field work principally from 1914 to 1921. It was Herb who once strapped his old Parker shotgun onto a log, then climbed up on the log and paddled it into Lake Michigan to determine what interesting birds might be found offshore. He made many significant contributions to our knowledge of the birdlife in the three counties bordering Lake Michigan.

We have been aided in various ways by the following: Kenneth P. Able, John M. Allen, Larry L. Allsop, Delano Z. Arvin (and his sons Kevin D., Kyle W., Mark C., and Scott B., some of the best bird's nest finders in the state), Richard C. Banks, William B. Barnes, James E. Bergens, Charles S. Berriman, Laurence C. Binford, Emmet R. Blake, Alex J. Bognar, Louis Bognar, Donald H. Boyd, Leonard C. Brecher, Kenneth J. Brock, Earl A. Brooks, Michael R. Brown, Alan W. Bruner, Harold D. Bruner, John P. and Dorthy Buck, Anthony D. Burnside, Irving W. Burr, Robert F. Buskirk, William H. Buskirk, Ted T. Cable, James H. Campbell, Arline L. Carter, Larry Carter, Lee A. Casebere, John S. Castrale, Theodore A. Chandik, Roy Chansler, Mary A. Cincotta, Charles T. Clark, Robert H. Cooper, James B. Cope, Noel J. Cutright, Hubert O. Davis, W. Marvin Davis, David L. Drury, Allan J. Duvall, David A. Easterla, William R. Eberly, Jackie and Diane Elmore, Ruth Erickson, Sidney R. Esten, Bruce A. Fall, John W. Fitzpatrick, Max A. Forsyth, Raymond J. Fleetwood, Billie E. Gahl, Boyd Gill, Steven H. Glass, William E. Ginn, John D. Goodman, Willard R. Gray, Raymond and Nora Grow, Peter B., Brendan, Kristin, and Nila Grube, Frank D. Haller, C. Leroy Harrison, James A. Haw, Harold Hawkins, Charles Heiser, Dick D. Heller, Jr., Irene Herlocker, Geoffrey E.

Hill, Edward M. Hopkins, David Howell, Richard H. Hudson, Russell R. Hyer, Virgil and Marcie Inman, G. Christopher Iverson, Scott F. Jackson, Bradley K. Jackson, Merle E. Jacobs, Dennis W. Jones, Gwilym S. Jones, Williard H. Kaehler, M. Philip Kahl, Jr., James R. Karr, Timothy C. Keller, Emerson Kemsies, Charles M. Kirkpatrick, Ralph D. Kirkpatrick, Michael N. Kochert, Michael P. Kowalski, Robert Krol, James E. Landing, Roxie C. Laybourne, Lynn Lightfoot, John M. Louis, Dorothy (Hobson) Luther, Will E. Madden, Floyd and Thelma Maffitt, Timothy D. Manolis, David A. Manuwal, Dale N. Martin, James and Amy Mason, Brother Edwin Mattingly, James D. McCall, Charles and Dorothy Meek, Morris Mercer, Peter E. Meyer, Charles E. Mills, Edward L. Mockford, Burt L. Monroe, Sr., Burt L. Monroe, Jr., Jeff S. Moore, Daniel Mosher, Eugene V. Muench, Jimmy F. New, Val Nolan Jr., Theodore J. Nork, Brainard Palmer-Ball, Jr., Larry L. Parker, Jerome Parrot, Temple D. Pearson, Lawrence Peavler, Richard E. Phillips, Emma B. Pitcher, Thomas A. Potter, George W. Pyle, Nancy E. Rea, Scott Rea, Maurice C. Reeves, Virginia Reuter-skiold, Victor and Marjorie Riemenschneider, Mark C. Rhodes, Dale W. Rice, Warren S. Rowe, Charles E. Scheffe, Simon and Jean Segal, Randy Shedd, Duane L. Shroufe, Litha Smith, Marietta Smith, Phillip R. Smith, Donald T. Sporre, Anne L. Stamm, Thomas and Lavetta Stankus, Alfred Starling, Nathalee D. Stocks, Herbert L. Stoddard, Sr., David and Myra Styer, Merrill Sweet, Frederick H. Test, James M. Tucker, Robert C. Tweit, Dolph E. and Susan Ulrich, Francis and Katherine Van Hufel, Mr. and Mrs. John W. Visher, Edward Wagner, Lawrence H. Walkinshaw, Gertrude L. Ward, Dwain W. Warner, Helen J. Weber, J. Dan Webster, Merritt S. Webster, Harmon P. Weeks, Jr. (another super nest finder), Mark A. Weldon, Henry C. West, Nixon A. Wilson, Samuel W. Witmer, Donald Whitehead, Bret Whitney, Clayton E. Wiggins, Vernon L. Wright, David C. Zumeta, Richard L. Zusi.

Zimmerman is particularly grateful to Ruth and Dick Johnson, without whom his part of the project would have been impossible; Jay Shuler, for his constant support and advice; DeVere Burt, Director, and Richard A. Davis, Curator of Collections, for allowing him unlimited access to the bird collection at the Cincinnati Museum of Natural History; Jenny and Art Wiseman, for their assistance in selecting bird skins used; Lorin I. Nevling, Jr., Director, and John W. Fitzpatrick, Assistant Curator of Birds, for the privilege of borrowing eggs and nests from Chicago's Field Museum of Natural History; and David E. Willard, Collection Manager, for selecting many nest and egg specimens that were used.

We thank Melanie Boes and Naomi Homan for typing early versions of the manuscript.

We have had access to the unpublished notes of Donald H. Boyd, Amos W. Butler, Sidney R. Esten, William B. Van Gorder, Virginia Reuter-skiold, Charles A. Stockbridge, Herbert L. Stoddard, Sr., and Howard F. Wright. Data compiled by Esten during the 1930s, when he anticipated writing a book on the birds of Indiana, have been valuable to us.

In preparing this manuscript, we have had the cooperation of the Indiana Department of Natural Resources (formerly Department of Conservation) and its following divisions: Fish and Wildlife, Forestry, Nature Preserves, State Parks. The Nature Conservancy has allowed us to work on their properties, as have the U.S. Forest Service and personnel of the Muscatatuck National Wildlife Refuge. Personnel of the Northern Indiana Public Service Generating Station, Michigan City (especially John Nichols and B. J. Komasinski), allowed us access to their grounds to observe and collect rare birds. The U.S. Coast Guard came to our aid at Michigan City one cold winter day.

Mumford's initial interest in birds (and nature in general) was fostered and encouraged by his parents, Charles E. and Cecile Floe. He also wishes to acknowledge the inspiration of Irving W. Burr and Charles M. Kirkpatrick at Purdue University. Keller especially remembers the sage advice and counsel of Scott Calvert, Mildred Campbell, Dorothy White, and Howard F. Wright, who patiently answered the questions of a curious teenager.

All three of our families became involved either directly or indirectly in our efforts. To our wives, Vivian, Shirley, and Judy, we owe a debt of gratitude for their sacrifices while their husbands were totally absorbed in this project. They have also aided materially in field work, record keeping, and typing throughout the years. The Mumford children, James Lee, Jean Lynne, and Russell, Jr., assisted in various ways. The Kellers' son, Timothy C., has made significant contributions through his field work and photography, and their daughter, Bernadette, also contributed in many ways, as did Matthew and Martha Zimmerman. Their father is grateful for their patience and understanding during the time he worked on this book.

We received much assistance from the employees of the Indiana University Press while this work was in progress, especially the copy editor, Bobbi Diehl. Our special thank-you is reserved for John Gallman, Director of the Press, for his urging, untiring support, and dedication during all phases of this project. Without him it would not have been possible.

Russell E. Mumford
Charles E. Keller
William Zimmerman

It is impossible to write about Indiana birds without frequent mention of Amos William Butler, born October 1, 1860, in Brookville, Franklin County, Indiana. He had a keen curiosity about nature, especially the wild creatures that lived near his home, an interest encouraged by his father and mother. Butler later wrote, "From my parents I acquired the habit of observing and noting what I saw. . . . My father was well acquainted with the common animals and plants, the birds and the trees of his region. According to recollection or tradition, I was introduced to birds at an early age." Later he attended Indiana University and there continued his studies in zoology. The contributions of this excellent naturalist to ornithology (and mammalogy) in Indiana cannot be overemphasized.

When Butler was a boy, identification of birds was far from easy. There were no field guides, and relatively few farm youths owned a pair of binoculars—primitive instruments at best, compared with those of today. To identify an unfamiliar bird, it was usually necessary to kill it. Like many other boys, Butler killed his share of birds. He also had an egg collection—this was a popular hobby in his day. But unlike many others, he also kept meticulous records of the birds' migrations, numbers, habits, habitats, and behavior. Later he kept up a large correspondence with other birders, both in Indiana and in surrounding states. At first, his personal collection of specimens probably consisted mostly of birds he found near Brookville, to which were added those he brought back from a trip to Mexico in 1879. Then he began exchanging specimens with other collectors across the United States and in many foreign countries. His *Birds of Indiana*, published in 1898, was the single most important ornithological milestone for the state, and it is inevitable that anyone writing seriously about the birdlife of Indiana today must refer constantly to this book. In the text that follows, whenever we mention Butler it should be understood that we mean Butler, *Birds of Indiana* (1898a). He was the author of numerous other publications, and these we have cited in the usual fashion for scientific works—last name and date. Full citations can be found in the Reference List.

In the early days of Indiana, a few men who traveled through the state were interested in nature and left us some published notes concerning its birdlife. John James Audubon, the famous bird painter, arrived in Louisville, Kentucky, in September 1807. He moved to Henderson, Kentucky, in 1810; to Cincinnati, Ohio, in 1819, and back to Louisville for the winter of 1823–24. Some of Audubon's observations can be found in our species accounts, for he spent some time in southern Indiana. Alexander Wilson, who might be called the father of American ornithology, visited Louisville on March 18, 1810, and evidently was briefly in Indiana, but recorded little of note from the Hoosier State. The first extensive published notes on Indiana birds are those of Prince Maximilian of Wied (Prussia), who spent the period from October 19, 1832, to March 16, 1833, at New Harmony (Posey County). Butler evidently was unfamiliar with his writings. In those days, the showy Carolina parakeet could still be seen in the southern part of the state, and passenger pigeons were still abundant and received a great deal of attention. In northern Indiana, the greater prairie-chicken and whooping crane occurred, though perhaps rarely. But no one mentioned the ivory-billed woodpecker. One can only presume that it was either quite rare even by then or so secretive that casual travelers had scant opportunity to see it.

The first checklist for the state was Brayton's *Catalogue of the Birds of Indiana*, published in 1880, a hastily prepared list of the birds thought to occur in the state. Rumor has it that it was originally supposed to have been a checklist of Ohio birds, but was changed to Indiana; we have been unable to confirm this. Brayton, a physician, wrote in his Introduction: ". . . as an apology for errors and omissions that may be in this list, to the naturalist I would say that it has been prepared on only two weeks' notice, and that while the writer has been daily engaged in professional duties." The list was compiled mostly from the literature, especially the works of E. W. Nelson

(1877) and F. W. Langdon (1877), and is of limited value. For a bibliography of papers published on Indiana birds before 1898, the reader is encouraged to consult Butler. Evermann (1917) updated Butler's bibliography, and Butler himself continued publishing notes on Indiana birds until his death in 1937.

In the late 1920s, Sidney R. Esten began collecting data on a systematic basis with the preparation of a *Birds of Indiana* in mind. The project was not completed; all the information he had collected (most of it in the 1930s) was given to Mumford about 1956. In this book we have made use of much of Esten's data.

An updated and definitive work on the birds of Indiana has long been a goal for both of us. We began our observations of birdlife in the state in the 1940s, and started seriously collecting specimens and photographs and compiling data about 1946. These efforts resulted in the publication of an annotated checklist of Indiana birds in 1975. Keller, his wife, Shirley, and his son, Timothy C. Keller, updated this checklist in 1979. Both publications elicited additional information from students of birds throughout Indiana. We feel that with the publication of the current work, birding in the state has come of age.

About the Species Accounts

So much has been published about birds that it was a major problem deciding what to include in this volume. The decision was made to omit most physical descriptions and information on total distribution. These subjects are covered admirably in several excellent field guides that are readily obtainable. *Birds of North America* by Robbins et al. (1966) is a good example. Similar works are Roger Tory Peterson's *A Field Guide to the Birds East of the Rockies*, *A Field Guide to Western Birds*, and others, and Richard H. Pough's *Audubon Land Bird Guide*, *Audubon Water Bird Guide*, and *Audubon Western Bird Guide*.

The current names of birds and their taxonomic order of listing follow the *Sixth Check-list of North American Birds*, published by the American Ornithologists' Union in 1983. For the most part, vernacular names listed for various species were taken from publications dealing with Indiana. Such names may be quite local in usage, but sometimes are colorful and/or of historical interest. We have determined that possibly 390 species of birds have been recorded in Indiana. In addition, an unidentified hummingbird and flycatcher have been reported in recent years. Butler listed 303 species of birds from the state (based on names currently accepted by the A.O.U., which appear on the 1983 Check-list). Forty-six of the eighty-one species on Butler's hypothetical list have now been seen in Indiana.

In earlier years, authors of regional works usually included only those species considered to be on the "official" state list that were represented by a specimen collected in the area. There was considerable justification for this procedure. Field identification had not then been refined to its current state. A museum specimen is indisputable proof of the occurrence of some unusual species far out of its normal range, and can make it possible to distinguish between species that might look similar in the field. Even today there is occasional need for taking a specimen. A case in point is the flycatcher (probably of the genus *Myiarchus*) that was seen and photographed in color in Allen County in 1978. Although the photographs were examined by several flycatcher experts, the species could not be identified and will always remain a mystery. The same is true of an unusual gull photographed in color at Gary in 1978. There are also four recent sightings of hummingbirds, which were probably rufous; none could be identified with certainty as to species.

On the other hand, it has been possible for many species to be added to the state list on the basis of recognizable photographs. This practice is to be lauded when the birds in question can readily be identified from photographs; there is then no necessity to collect specimens. Several states have instituted a documentation procedure by which birds observed may be added to the "official" state list if certain criteria are satisfied by the documentation process. Criteria for inclusion on such lists vary from state to state. Although the requirements for documentation currently in effect in Indiana are generally satisfactory, there is still a chance for error in identification. One must take into account the competence of observers, attempt to separate what they really saw from what they thought they saw, consider viewing conditions, experience with the species in question, influence of other observers on the identification, and other factors. In short, no documentation system of sight observations is foolproof. In light of this, we have decided to include unsubstantiated sightings, but to place the names of these species in brackets. Some of our own sightings fall into this category. We are not implying that any observation is unreliable (although some are certainly quite unusual), but simply feel that sightings of such species must be treated differently from those species for which we have knowledge of a specimen or a recognizable photograph. In short, the bracketed species are not necessarily "hypothetical," but are considered uncorroborated. We feel that the term *uncorroborated* should be used as stated below.

In the species accounts, under the discussion of status, we use a number of terms in a very particular way. Most of these are well known and have been widely used by other authors, but some definitions may nonetheless be in order here.

Permanent resident: A species present throughout the year.

Summer resident: A species that nests in the state and is present primarily in the summer.

Winter resident or visitant: A species that occurs primarily in winter.

Summer visitant: A species that occurs primarily in summer but does not nest in the state.

Migrant: A species that regularly arrives in spring and leaves in fall. Some are summer residents, others not.

Local: A species of limited distribution (usually in specific habitat).

Irregular: A species that does not occur each year and may show cyclic eruptions.

Ideally, status encompasses both frequency of occurrence and numbers. All too often, however, we lack sufficient data to estimate the population of a species with very much accuracy. But in general, we believe our indications of status give a fairly good idea of relative abundance as well as frequency of occurrence.

Abundant: A species found in very large numbers in suitable habitat at the correct season.

Common: A species found in large numbers in suitable habitat at the correct season.

Fairly common: A species found in moderate numbers in suitable habitat at the correct season.

Uncommon: A species found in small numbers in suitable habitat at the correct season.

Rare: A species found in very small numbers in suitable habitat at the correct season.

Very Rare: A species found infrequently (absent some years) and in small numbers in suitable habitat at the correct season.

Casual: A species somewhat outside its usual range, found at widely spaced intervals in very small numbers.

Accidental: A species outside its usual range generally found only once or twice in the state.

Hypothetical: A species that on the basis of its occurrence in adjacent areas might be found in the state, but has not been reported to date.

Extinct: A species believed or known to be extinct.

Extirpated: A species once present in Indiana but no longer found here, although still present in other areas and may possibly occur here again.

Exotic: A species believed to have escaped from captivity that has not yet become established (i.e., no nesting population) in a feral state.

Uncorroborated: A species that does not meet the criteria for inclusion on official state checklists.

The color plates by William Zimmerman depict, with a few exceptions, species that nest in Indiana: birds that are known to have nested in the state at least twice and continue to do so. We have stretched the point for the bald eagle, which has not nested in Indiana for many years.

The solitary vireo is not included, although there are two recent nesting records, the second one having been obtained too late for it to be painted. Numerous species are known to have nested in the state at least once; these have not been painted. An example is the scissor-tailed flycatcher.

We think that Bill Zimmerman's paintings add a dimension to the current work that makes it unique among state bird books. It was Bill's idea to depict each species in a scene showing the nest and eggs in typical habitat, often with a native wildflower in bloom, and his care, skill, and knowledge of his subjects are beautifully evident. We have attempted to identify the more interesting and dominant plants and trees pictured, for the most part only those in leaf or bloom. Whenever the eggs are not visible in the nest, as in the case of woodpeckers, they are shown on the Egg Plate following the species accounts.

A map of the state showing the names of the 92 counties is included to facilitate a grasp of the distribution of species (Fig. 1). Although birds do not recognize political

boundaries, the counties of the state make convenient units for which to record data.

The species accounts all follow the same general outline. Common name, Latin name, and vernacular names by which the birds have been known in Indiana lead off, followed by a short essay that more or less fits each species into its niche in the state. Past status (based on Butler, 1898a) and current status, habitat, migration, and nesting information follow, and then, where applicable, a few miscellaneous notes (on food, song, etc.). Space constraints have made it necessary to keep these species accounts as brief as possible, but we have attempted to include all the salient points. Extreme dates of both spring and fall occurrence have been included, as are the maximum numbers recorded in these two seasons, which give some indication of when the bulk of each species passes through Indiana. It is evident that many migration peaks are reported on weekends, the time when birdwatchers tend to be afield. Because seasonal abundance may vary greatly from locality to locality both with regard to time and numbers of birds, it is often rather difficult to make a generalization about it that is valid for all parts of the state. The Occurrence Chart, which follows the species accounts, shows the times of year each species is present and gives a general idea of its abundance in Indiana.

Much remains to be learned about the distribution of many nesting species. Some may have nested in the state and gone undetected; the black rail is an example. And to our knowledge, no one has ever found the nest of an alder flycatcher or western meadowlark, although both are widespread during the nesting season and certainly must nest. Nesting birds are often restricted to small remnants of habitat, widely scattered and perhaps not often visited by birders. Nesting ranges are subject to rapid change. For example, the creation of a new reservoir and the nearly immediate presence of a new aquatic habitat where none was present before enables some species to expand their breeding ranges very quickly. Conversely, the draining of a small, isolated wetland may mark the disappearance of the sole nesting site for a particular species in a county.

Over the past forty-odd years of living in Indiana, we have learned much about its native flora, fauna, geography, climate, and people. Hoosierland is a wonderful place to work and to play, and to anyone who gets to know its birdlife, a day in the field nearly anywhere in the state will have its rewards. Such pleasures come in various forms—large and small, subtle and dramatic, expected and unexpected. It is these changing experiences that whet one's appetite for more field work, trips to new areas, rechecking of birding spots that are personal favorites, and birdwatching trips with friends. The joy of simply being out of doors also enters into the equation. It goes without saying that we enjoy the changing seasons and the various eccentricities of Indiana's unpredictable weather, at times in itself an unforgettable experience. We hope that in this book some of our enthusiasm for birding and living in the state communicates itself to the reader.

Description of the State

Indiana is situated in the middle-eastern part of the United States, although in the general region called the Midwest. It lies near the eastern border of the great interior plains. The total area of the state is 36,555 square miles; the Indiana portion of Lake Michigan occupies 230 square miles of this, interior lakes and rivers 280 square miles. The average elevation above sea level is about 715 feet, with extremes of 1,285 feet (Randolph County) and 313 feet (mouth of the Wabash River, Posey County). About five-sixths of Indiana is covered with glacial drift, while about 6,000 square miles in the south-central portion are unglaciated. Nearly nine-tenths of the state is drained by rivers flowing southwestward and westward into the Mississippi Basin; the remainder, in the northeastern corner, drains into the St. Lawrence Basin. The Ohio River forms the southern boundary of the state.

Physiographic features. Wayne (1956) and Schneider (1966) have discussed the glacial history and detailed the physiographic areas of Indiana. According to Schneider, the state can be divided roughly into three broad physiographic zones situated in a general east-west direction. The central zone of about 12,000 square miles is a depositional plain of low relief modified only slightly by postglacial stream erosion. This region, covering roughly the central one-third of the state, has long been called the Tipton Till Plain. The northern zone, roughly the northern one-fourth of the state, characterized by greater relief, contains areas that are quite hilly. But the hilly uplands are frequently broken by lowlands and plains of little relief. The northern zone is mostly of glacial origin and contains end moraines, outwash plains, kames, lake plains and kettle holes, along with lakes, sand dunes, and peat bogs. Most of the natural lakes in the state are in this zone, of about 8,500 square miles, called the Northern Moraine and Lake Region. The southern zone of about 15,500 square miles is divided into seven physiographic units, all trending north-northwest, and occupies about the southern third of the state. The middle part of this zone was not glaciated during the Pleistocene epoch and is thus the most rugged terrain in the state. Landforms in the southern zone are the result of normal degradational processes—weathering, stream erosion, and mass movement. The lateral parts of the southern zone were glaciated. From west to east across southern Indiana, these seven units are the Wabash Lowland, Crawford Upland,

Mitchell Plain, Norman Upland, Scottsburg Lowland, Muscatatuck Regional Slope, and Dearborn Upland. The northern boundary of this zone is nearly the southern edge of the Wisconsin glacial boundary.

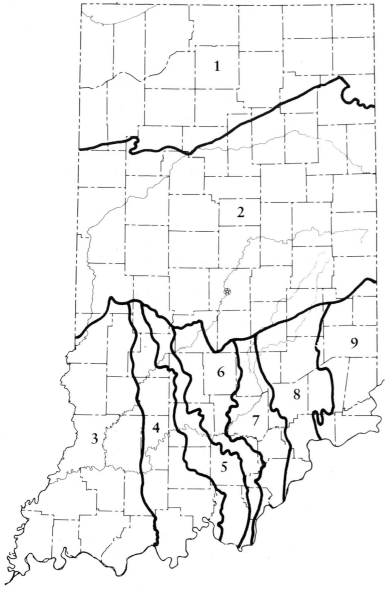

In general, the physiography of Indiana has little effect on the distribution of nesting birds. Species currently or formerly (*) restricted to nesting mainly south of the Tipton Till Plain are: double-crested cormorant,* snowy egret,* little blue heron,* yellow-crowned night heron, black vulture, Mississippi kite, American avocet,* chuckwill's-widow, common raven,* blue grosbeak, Bachman's sparrow.

Species currently restricted primarily to nesting in the Northern Moraine and Lake Region, or formerly (*) thought to have been restricted, or mainly restricted, to that region are: common loon, trumpeter swan, Canada goose, green-winged teal, American black duck,* mallard,* northern pintail, blue-winged teal,* northern shoveler, American wigeon, redhead, ring-necked duck, lesser scaup, ruddy duck, greater prairie-chicken, Virginia rail,* sora,* common moorhen,* American coot,* sandhill crane, whooping crane, piping plover, common snipe, Wilson's phalarope, common tern, Forster's tern, black tern, short-eared owl,* northern saw-whet owl, yellow-bellied sapsucker, alder flycatcher, least flycatcher,* black-capped chickadee, veery,* chestnut-sided warbler, northern waterthrush, Canada warbler, swamp sparrow, western meadowlark, yellow-headed blackbird, Brewer's blackbird.

Vegetation. The plants that grow in an area determine in great part what animals will be found there. There is a basic natural relationship between plants and animals. The absence of certain plants may result in the absence of certain birds. About 160 years ago, 87 percent of Indiana was covered by deciduous forests, the remainder (in the northwestern portion) with tall grass prairie. Small prairie outliers were also probably present all along the western edge of the state. Lindsey et al. (1965) analyzed the presettlement vegetation of Indiana by means of original land survey records and modern soil surveys. Gordon (1936) prepared a vegetation map of Indiana based on his reconnaissance by automobile in 1928. Deam (1940) included a map of the plant communities of the state in his monumental work on Indiana flora. Petty and Jackson (1966) have more recently discussed the plant communities of the state.

It is quite clear that birds that were adapted to life in the deciduous forest were more common in Indiana before settlement by the white man. Although much of the state was extensively forested, there would have been some openings along streams, around lakes and marshes, and near the prairies. Other openings were no doubt created (and maintained) by fires, both natural and those set by the Indians when hunting. It is difficult today for us to visualize what the great forests of Indiana once looked like, but an English farmer, Morris Birkbeck, gave us his impression when crossing Indiana in 1818.

It is a feeling of confinement which begins to damp the spirits, from this complete exclusion of distant objects. To travel day after day among trees of a hundred feet high, without a glimpse of the surrounding country, is oppressive to a degree which those cannot conceive who have not experienced it; and it must depress the spirits of the solitary settler to pass years in this state. His visible horizon extends no farther than the tops of the trees which bound his plantation—perhaps, five hundred yards. Upwards he sees the sun, and sky, and stars; but around him an eternal forest from which he can never hope to emerge. . . .

It is quite possible that the large, unbroken tracts of dense forests harbored relatively few birds at certain seasons. Some travelers remarked that when passing through the southern Indiana woodlands in the early 1800s they saw and heard few birds. This might be partially explained by the season of the year they made their trips, for in midsummer and midwinter birdlife of the forests may be scant.

There is little doubt that when the forests were lumbered near the turn of the century (and openings were created by settlers long before that), the numbers of species of nesting birds increased because of the new habitats. More species of birds nest in brushy or scrubby areas and openings than in climax forests. As woodlands continued to be decreased in size or totally eliminated, birds adapted to nesting in them also decreased. Today, in certain sections of the state, some land is reverting back to forests and will, to some extent, reverse this trend.

The prairies of presettlement Indiana were mostly quite wet, as pointed out by Lindsey (1961). The preponderance of marshes, swamps, ponds, and other wetlands was quite important to waterbirds. Benton County, where the original tall-grass prairie in Indiana was probably best developed, was 69 percent wetlands in 1830, and about 12,000 acres were permanently ponded. Nearly 55 percent (108,000 acres) of Starke County was permanently ponded at this time, as were more than 20 percent of Kosciusko, Lake, LaPorte, Newton, Porter, St. Joseph, and White Counties. Beaver Lake (Newton County), now drained, was a large, shallow body of water where the trumpeter swan probably once occurred; it used to be visited by hordes of geese, ducks, and other waterbirds. English Lake, really an enlargement of the Kankakee River, was a large lake bordering Starke and LaPorte Counties. It was attractive to ducks and other waterbirds that were sought by hunters, and for years was a famous hunting site. It was also probably of great importance to breeding birds.

The greater prairie-chicken must have been present on the prairies of northwestern Indiana in great numbers. Judge James Hall described prairie-chickens in Benton County in 1848: "The number of these fowls is astonishing. The plain is covered with them; and when they have been driven from the ground by deep snow, I have seen thousands—or more probably tens of thousands—thickly clustered in the tops of the trees surrounding the prairies" (Birch, 1928). William F. Swan, an old hunter, stated that "the numbers of these birds were simply incalculable" near Swanington, Benton County, in April 1865 (Barce and Swan, 1930). These same authors also wrote that "thousands and tens of thousands of these birds were slain before and for many years after the Civil War," and that "Hunters from Louisville, Cincinnati, and other points often came with their guns, dogs and Negro servants to the tavern of Robert Alexander at Parish Grove in the fall season and would hunt for days and weeks." In the late 1840s, Mark J. Brier is said to have shot 144 prairie-chickens in a single day. Hunting parties frequently were composed of several men, who walked across the prairies in a line and flushed the birds. They usually took a team of horses and a wagon along to haul the birds and made these trips all-day affairs.

That the duck hunting was fabulous in the Grand Marsh of the Kankakee River has also been well documented. This marsh once covered about 1,000 square miles along the Kankakee River and was attractive to untold numbers of ducks, geese, swans, cranes, rails, shorebirds, and other species. But efforts to drain it began as early as 1873; the region had been effectively drained by 1917. There are few data concerning the numbers of birds that nested there, and we suspect that many of the popular accounts are exaggerated. But it was, without question, a favorite staging area for waterfowl and other aquatic birds to gather in spring and fall. Much of the hunting took place in spring (before federal regulations stopped this practice) and probably most of the ducks and geese found there at that season went farther north to nest.

The extensive swamps in Gibson and Knox Counties must have been impressive too. Robert Ridgway, who visited some of them in the late 1870s and early 1880s and published accounts of the nesting of herons and other birds there, reported finding stumps of felled baldcypress trees that were nine to ten feet in diameter. It is estimated that there used to be 20,000 acres of cypress stands in southern Knox County. Not much remains of the famous Little Cypress Swamp today. Smaller cypress forests were present in other southwestern Indiana counties bordering the Ohio and Wabash Rivers. One of these was an oxbow annually flooded by the Ohio River called Hovey Lake, where osprey and double-crested cormorants nested, that supported a huge population of wintering mallards, American black ducks, and other waterfowl into the 1950s. Limited data are available regarding the former abundance and species composition of breeding birds of the cypress swamps, and it is now too late to remedy that situation. Of interest, however, is the recent discovery of a brown creeper's nest in such a site.

Climate. Indiana has a humid, continental climate. There are no definite dry seasons or periods with an average humidity of less than 50 percent; it is humid throughout the year. A given locality may be extremely hot in summer and extremely cold in winter. Southern Indiana has a warm temperate climate resembling that to the south and east. Northern Indiana has a cool temperate climate, more like that to the north and east. Lake Michigan has the greatest influence on local climate. The normal frost-free growing season is thirty days longer near its shoreline than at the Kankakee River basin about twenty miles south. The lake also affects summer temperatures, cloudiness, and winter snowfall. The "snowbelt" area south and east of the lake is well known.

Major stream valleys, shores of larger lakes, and the highest plateaus of Indiana are landforms that may influence local climatic conditions. Cities and large artificial bodies of water have some effect, also. Such local effects may be important to certain birds which require some specific habitat. Such habitats are normally determined by the prevailing vegetation. Certain plant associations grow best on slopes facing a specific direction (north versus south, for example) and steep slopes may support different vegetation than level terrain nearby. These micro-habitats may be of more importance to certain nesting birds than we realize. One need only visit Turkey Run State Park in mid-summer to experience a good example. The deep sandstone canyons remain relatively cool, while in the surrounding forests temperatures may be considerably higher. Newman (1966) has discussed the bioclimate of the state.

Visher (1944) published a detailed study of the climate of Indiana and included much data on temperature. The average annual temperature of Indiana is about 52° Fahrenheit. July, the hottest month, averages slightly more than 75°; January, the coldest, averages about 30°. In July 1936, the temperature reached 116° F at Rensselaer (Jasper County); on January 2, 1887, the temperature at Lafayette (Tippecanoe County) was −33° F.

Annual precipitation averages about 45 inches in southern Indiana, 40 inches in central Indiana, and 35 inches in northern Indiana. Precipitation is rather evenly distributed throughout the year, with the wettest months normally in late spring. Snowfall is variable from north to south. Northern Indiana receives an average of 30 inches annually (but more than 50 inches in some years), most of central Indiana gets about 20 inches, and part of southwestern Indiana receives less than 15 inches. More than 50 inches is the normal amount just east of the southern tip of Lake Michigan. More than 100 inches are occasionally recorded in that region, and in the winter of 1977–78 nearly 200 inches fell at South Bend (St. Joseph County).

Land Use

In an agricultural state such as Indiana, there are large acreages of land under cultivation. The average numbers of acres planted to various crops from 1979 to 1981 were as follows: corn, 6,300,000; soybeans, 4,510,000; wheat, 1,183,000; oats, rye, sorghum, 280,000; all hay, 802,000. Many other crops could be included in this list.

It has been estimated that presettlement Indiana had about 23,000,000 acres of forest land (roughly 87 percent of the land area). As of 1981, there were about 4,000,000 acres. The major forested areas are in southern Indiana, especially in the unglaciated, hilly, south-central portion. Forested areas in the northern half of the state are small. They consist mainly of woodlots, riparian woodlands, and forest tracts on state or private lands, but

make up an insignificant portion (in general, less than 10 percent) of the total land of this portion of Indiana.

About 13 percent of Indiana was at one time prairie, which extended into the northwestern part of the state. Much of the original prairie of Indiana, because it was ponded for at least six months of the year, was considered worthless by early farmers. Once drained, however, the prairie soils proved to be among the most fertile in the state and practically all former prairie land today is under intense cultivation. This fact finally led to the demise of the greater prairie-chicken.

Land use and the resultant habitat alterations are constantly changing. We can anticipate that these changes will continue indefinitely and be constant factors in dictating the birdlife of a particular area.

Many natural wetlands have been drained, not only the 500,000 acres of the Kankakee Marsh but thousands of smaller sites. Thus, good aquatic habitats (some of considerable size) have been lost to birds. Over the years, more and more impoundments have been constructed. Most of these provide an aquatic habitat, but usually the resulting wetlands are far different from the natural ones that were drained. Given time and good management (such as on fish and wildlife areas), some marsh habitats resembling those of early years may be created. The total acreage, however, will be much less. As of 1981, an estimated 275,000 acres of non-flowing waters in the state were available for fishing. Half of this acreage is in Lake Michigan. Much of the remainder represents impoundments and, of course, natural lakes. We do not know if farm ponds are included in the figure. One cannot dismiss the great importance of impoundments to birds; a birder need only visit Lake Monroe, Lake Gibson, Eagle Creek Reservoir, Geist Reservoir, and many others at various seasons to observe the large numbers and variety of waterbirds they attract. Even the presence of a small farm pond may result in the addition of numerous new species of birds to a given locality if no such water area was previously available to them.

The general aspect of Indiana since its settlement has changed from a forested region to farmland. Only the unglaciated section retains much of its original form and even here extensive forest was long ago broken by logging, cultivation, and other practices. A considerable acreage of formerly forested land in this region is now included within the Hoosier National Forest, but it is mostly composed of abandoned agricultural land that has been allowed to revert naturally to forests or has been planted to pines.

Throughout most of the northern two-thirds of the state, there has been a continual decrease in forest since the late 1800s. As the land became more open and placed under cultivation, some tree growth was replaced by the extensive planting of "living fences" (hedgerows) of osage orange. But in recent years, most of these hedgerows have been eliminated. Farm boundaries were formerly mostly marked by hedgerows or wire fences, many of which are also now gone. Such fencerows often supported weedy, shrubby, or tree growth of considerable importance to birds. The removal of wire fences allows cultivation closer to roadsides, with further depletion of habitat. Woodlots, once present on nearly every farm in Indiana, have greatly decreased in numbers. Many have been ravaged by old age, grazing, windstorms, and other factors, but others have been altered (or removed) for human housing, pastures, or cultivation. The result has been most evident in the large Tipton Till Plain, where from year to year the aspect of the countryside has become more open and more like that of the northwestern section, originally prairie.

It is inevitable that such habitat changes cause changes in the birdlife. Regions originally supporting forest lands, where birds characteristic of the eastern deciduous woods were formerly found, now support habitats more suitable to birds that live in fields or field borders. As the forests were removed, species of birds formerly restricted more or less to the prairies of Indiana have been able to expand their ranges over long distances (especially to the south and east). Some western birds, such as Bell's vireo, western meadowlark, and Brewer's blackbird, invaded the state from the west and became part of Indiana's nesting bird fauna.

The following birds no doubt benefited from the clearing of forests and were able to expand their nesting ranges and increase in numbers: mallard, blue-winged teal, northern harrier, killdeer, spotted sandpiper, upland sandpiper, American woodcock, common nighthawk, eastern kingbird, horned lark, Carolina wren, Bewick's wren, house wren, eastern bluebird, American robin, gray catbird, northern mockingbird, brown thrasher, cedar waxwing, loggerhead shrike, white-eyed vireo, warbling vireo, blue-winged warbler, golden-winged warbler, yellow warbler, chestnut-sided warbler, prairie warbler, common yellowthroat, yellow-brested chat, northern cardinal, indigo bunting, dickcissel, rufous-sided towhee, Bachman's sparrow, chipping sparrow, field sparrow, vesper sparrow, lark sparrow, savannah sparrow, grasshopper sparrow, Henslow's sparrow, song sparrow, bobolink, red-winged blackbird, eastern meadowlark, western meadowlark, common grackle, brown-headed cowbird,

orchard oriole, American goldfinch. Other species could probably be added to this list.

Large-scale lumbering, additional disturbance by man, and probably other factors brought about the extirpation of the wild turkey, passenger pigeon, Carolina parakeet, ivory-billed woodpecker, and common raven.

In the prairie region, the trumpeter swan, greater prairie-chicken, and whooping crane were eliminated.

The bald eagle ceased to be an important member of the nesting birds of the state by 1900 or shortly thereafter. The peregrine falcon and double-crested cormorant, although probably never common as nesting species in Indiana, held on as local nesters for some time—the cormorant until recently.

Since Butler's day, there has been a dramatic movement of "southern" birds northward across the state. Some of these species include the tufted titmouse, Carolina wren, northern mockingbird, northern cardinal, and blue grosbeak.

The number of species of birds that nest in Indiana (about 170) is slightly more than nest in Illinois or Kentucky and fewer than nest in Michigan or Ohio. The number of nesting species per state for all states east of the Mississippi River ranged from about 130 to 225 as of 1963.

Finally, it will be noticed that most species of birds included in this book are discussed only in a Hoosier context. For the most part, Indiana is where we first saw the birds, and where we know them best. In this way, in addition, we have been able to take advantage of the great amount of data that scores of excellent Indiana birders past and present were kind enough to share. For record keeping alone is not enough. No doubt much fascinating and useful information about Indiana birds remains in the possession of people who do not realize the importance of their records or what they could contribute to our knowledge of the state and its avifauna. We cannot imagine a world—or a state—without birds, and nothing would make us happier than to think that, as a result of the publication of this work, some of that information might be preserved and eventually find its way to us or to others who can put it to good use.

If in addition *The Birds of Indiana* adds to the enjoyment of those who live in or travel through the state, we shall have been amply rewarded for our efforts.

SPECIES ACCOUNTS

RED-THROATED LOON

Gavia stellata

Anyone who birds regularly along Lake Michigan should sooner or later encounter a red-throated mingled in with the more abundant common loons. Many undoubtedly go undetected however, despite the fact that they are smaller than common loons and exhibit other field characteristics that enable trained birdwatchers to identify them.

Before 1900 there were only four records for the red-throated loon in Indiana. There are now several dozen, and it should be considered a rare to casual migrant and casual winter resident. More observations (16 in all) were made in the 1950s than in any other decade, with sight records spanning the months October to May. Most records are of singles, but nine were seen in Lake County on October 12, 1966. Although more than half of the red-throated loons observed in Indiana were on Lake Michigan, the species probably occurs throughout the state.

Most of the birds were found on the larger lakes and reservoirs. Spring migrants pass through mostly in April (the peak month) and May. Fall migration spans October to December, with the bulk of the birds being recorded in November. Red-throated loons seen in Indiana are normally in winter plumage, although three May migrants showed signs of molting into spring plumage and one had reddish tinges on its throat. The habits of this loon are similar to those of other loons.

ARCTIC LOON

Gavia arctica

Pacific Loon

This loon was first added to the Indiana list by Cope (1951), who reported a specimen (Joseph Moore Museum, Earlham College) found in April 1949 by a Henry County farmer in his cornfield. It is smaller than the common loon and slightly larger than the red-throated, but identification in the field requires extreme care. The arctic loon is still considered accidental in Indiana, although there have been several additional sight records, all of single birds: Indiana Dunes, May 6, 1950; Tippecanoe County, May 20–21, 1961; Huntington County, May 15–16, 1974; Lake Waveland (Montgomery County), November 7–14, 1979; Hurshtown Reservoir (Allen County), October 28–November 25, 1980; Geist Reservoir, Indianapolis, November 15, 1982. Habitats and habits of the three species of loons that occur in Indiana are similar, and common loons were present with arctic loons on three sightings. Alan W. Bruner noted that the arctic held the beak horizontal to the water when feeding or relaxing, but might elevate the beak at an angle of about thirty degrees when nearby duck hunters began shooting; this was interpreted as an alert posture.

COMMON LOON

Gavia immer

Most Hoosiers seldom see the common loon. Only people who live near the larger bodies of water in the state, or can visit them, have much opportunity to observe this bird. And, since it is usually silent except in nesting season and does not currently nest in Indiana, there is little likelihood of our hearing its unforgettably wild, ringing, mournful calls.

A loon is marvelously adapted for moving in water but almost helpless on land. Its legs cannot support the bird in a walking position; it must propel itself by pushing with both feet and lunging forward, often with its belly bumping along the ground. Nor can it take flight from land. This is why loons are frequently found stranded ashore after severe storms. Take-off from the water also requires a great deal of effort. There is much splashing and running along the surface and flailing of wings before the loon gets up enough speed to become airborne. But it is a strong swimmer and a superb diver.

Butler wrote that this loon was "a regular migrant throughout the State in some numbers," sometimes remained through the winter, and formerly nested across northern Indiana. It is now a fairly common spring and fall migrant, but more abundant in fall, casual in summer, and casual to regular in winter in small numbers (fourteen were seen on the Lake Monroe Christmas bird count December 19, 1982). We have records for every month of the year, but no reports of nesting since 1893.

Although larger lakes and reservoirs are most likely to attract groups of loons, singles and small numbers are found on ponds, rivers, and other smaller water areas.

Spring migration generally begins about the first half of March, reaches its peak in April, and tapers off in early May, with stragglers lingering until late May or longer. Fall migration in some years begins before mid-August, but the major migration period is from late October to early November. More loons are seen in April and November than in any other months, especially away from Lake Michigan.

Raymond Grow, James E. Landing, and others have observed fall migration at the south end of Lake Michigan. On October 17, 1952, they saw twenty-one flying westward; on October 28, 1953, ninety-five flew past; on October 26, 1957, seventy passed overhead in several flights; on October 25, 1958, there were fifty-eight; on the morning of October 25, 1959, five hundred passed in two hours (one flock contained a hundred); from October 7 to November 18, 1961, there was "steady migration"; on November 15, 1964, a "fairly large westward movement" was seen.

Butler reported that nests and eggs had been found at Lake James and Crooked Lake (Steuben County), and noted the presence of loons "in the breeding season" at Hamilton Lake and Golden Lake (Steuben County), Turkey Lake (Steuben-Lagrange County line), and Bear Lake (Noble County). He had other reports of nesting at Twin Lakes of the Wood and Big Turkey Lake (Steuben County) and in Noble County. William B. Van Gorder reported this loon nesting at Bear Lake

(Noble County) in July 1890, and his last nesting record for this county was June 11, 1893 (Esten, 1931). It may formerly have nested around Wolf Lake (Lake County). One common loon remained "all summer" on Shriner Lake (Whitley County) in 1896 (Williamson, 1900), and there are numerous recent (1945 to 1979) records of loons present in June through early August.

Primarily fish eaters, loons also consume other aquatic animals, such as insects, leeches, and frogs, as well as plants, and may dive to considerable depths to obtain food. The speed of a swimming loon is reasonably swift and it may travel several hundred feet underwater before surfacing to breathe. The best way to appreciate these facts is to attempt to keep pace with a submerged bird by rowing a boat or paddling a canoe in pursuit. Donald H. Boyd (personal communication) found that a feeding loon remained submerged on four consecutive dives for 58, 50, 47, and 48 seconds and above water preceding dives for 17, 10, 18, and 17 seconds respectively.

Nolan (1949) described the largest assemblage of common loons reported in Indiana (at Geist Reservoir on November 23, 1948), as follows:

Standing just before dusk on a small hill at the water's edge at a point on the west side of the lake on the county line, I saw well over three hundred loons spread out before me. The birds seemed to form a large, loose flock one-half mile square, and within the general gathering were more compact groupings. Immediately in front of me and quite near the shore were 118 birds drawn together as tightly as a similar number of Canada geese might be. Smaller similar flocks comprised the remainder of the total. That the flock migrated together might be inferred from the fact that early next morning only fifteen scattered loons were to be seen on the entire lake.

There appear to be few reports of migrating flocks in the spring, but Virginia Reuter-skiold saw flocks of six, fifteen, and fifty flying past on March 11, 1957 (Lake County).

PIED-BILLED GREBE

Podilymbus podiceps

Helldiver, Water Witch, Dabchick, Didipper, Dipper, Diedapper, Thick-billed Grebe

To the experienced listener, loud *cow, cow, cow, cow . . . uh* calls coming from a marsh on a warm spring morning signal that a male pied-billed grebe is back on its nesting grounds and courting the females. It is one of those sounds that, along with the yelps, grunts, and whinnies of rails, the pumping of bitterns, and the incessant gabbling of coots, make marshes such pleasant places in spring and early summer. The grebe is so secretive that, at many sites, if it remained silent one would scarcely know it was present.

Around 1900 this grebe was a regular but uncommon migrant and bred across the northern half of the state and south to Knox County. It had never been reported as wintering, according to Butler. Its status has certainly changed, for now it is a permanent resident in mild winters and a common spring and fall migrant. It is rare to uncommon locally in winter but has been recorded on more than 150 Christmas bird counts. Nesting is confined primarily to the northern third of the state, where this grebe may be locally common or very rare. There are few nesting records for the central and southern sections of Indiana, where marshy habitats are few or lacking. Pied-billed grebes are observed in greatest numbers in the fall, when there appears to be more of a flocking tendency than in the spring. A flock of 216 was seen at the Willow

Slough Fish and Wildlife Area on September 20, 1952, and on September 2, 1952, in Marion County, a flock of 118 was observed closely packed in a space about ten feet square. The largest group in the spring records was a flock of fifty.

The relatively few birds present in February (which have probably overwintered) are augmented in March by migrants. Spring migration peaks the last half of March in southern, about a week later in central, and around mid-April in northern Indiana. The start of fall migration is most evident in September and in some areas numbers reach their peak late in that month. Peaks are also reported in October, with records for an individual lake revealing peaks for successive years in different months. There are fewer data for fall than for spring, but it appears that fall flights are not as predictable as spring flights, and prevailing weather is apparently a major factor.

Although pied-billed grebes may be present anywhere in the state throughout the summer, the lack of suitable habitat over much of the southern third is reflected in the scarcity of summer or nesting records. One may find as many as five nests on a relatively small marsh. Nests with eggs have been found from May 6 to July 11, but these dates could probably be extended at both ends by more intensive field work. In forty nests containing eggs, clutch size ranged from one to ten. We did not calculate average clutch size, as we could not determine which nests held complete clutches. For the twenty-six nests that contained more than six eggs, the average number of eggs per clutch was 7.5; twelve of these nests contained seven eggs each. Pied-billed grebes almost invariably nest on the water in patches of emergent vegetation, such as cattail, smart-weed, bulrush, sedges, bur-reed, or some combination. One nest-building adult was diving in water two feet deep and bringing up decayed vegetation (presumably off the bottom) in its beak to add to the nest. One nest held a single egg and a newly hatched young on May 22. When the nest was approached the young left it, dived, and hid in the surrounding vegetation.

Feeding grebes have been observed catching small unidentified minnows, a carp six inches long, a six-inch bullhead, red-eared sunfish, tadpoles, and skipjacks.

Twenty-five dazed pied-billed grebes were found at dawn on November 4, 1944, on a wet highway that they had evidently mistaken for a stream when forced down by a driving rain. After a severe windstorm in early September, five dead pied-billed grebes were found along highways between Brownstown and Wabash.

Depicted plant: Spatterdock (*Nuphar advena*)

PIED-BILLED GREBE

HORNED GREBE
Podiceps auritus

In mid-April it is possible to see this handsome bird in breeding plumage as it glides, seemingly without effort, among the emergent vegetation of a marsh with the sunlight emphasizing the rich colors of its head and neck. At close range, or in the hand, the beautiful multicolored eye is evident. Most horned grebes seen in Indiana are in winter plumage, a pleasing combination of white, gray, and black. Although singles are most common, especially in spring, at certain seasons large numbers of horned grebes are present on the larger lakes, in particular Lake Michigan.

Butler considered this grebe a regular migrant, noting that at some localities it wintered, and that it bred in the northern part of the state, but that it was never abundant. The only satisfactory nesting record is that of a specimen "in downy plumage," taken at Sheffield on May 24, 1878. An 1876 map of Lake County does not show a town called Sheffield, but the name Sheffield Bay is printed on the eastern side of what is now Wolf Lake (on the Illinois-Indiana state line). Perhaps this is the location mentioned by Butler. Today this grebe is an uncommon spring migrant statewide and a fairly common fall migrant. It is uncommon to rare in winter and recorded at that season most often on Lake Michigan. Since 1900, we know of a single record for June (1901), none for July, and three for August.

Almost any body of water sufficiently large to enable the birds to take flight from the surface may be frequented by horned grebes. Our records indicate a preference for larger lakes and reservoirs, but individuals are seen occasionally on small ponds and marshes and along streams.

Statewide, spring migration apparently begins around mid-March and ends about the first week of May, with peak numbers in April. The largest spring numbers have been recorded in Marion County: 50 on March 28, 1964, and 50 on March 29, 1970. Early fall migrants enter Indiana during the first half of August; their numbers steadily increase throughout September, then reach their peak from early October to mid-November. By far the largest numbers are observed along the southern end of Lake Michigan. For example, on November 15, 1964, 500 were recorded in LaPorte County. There were 225 in Porter County on October 6, 1957, and 200 in Lake County on November 17, 1955. Such aggregations are not an entirely recent phenomenon on this lake, for Herbert L. Stoddard reported seeing literally hundreds of horned grebes between Millers and the Indiana Dunes State Park November 9, 1919. Although most migration occurs at night, Raymond Grow watched ten flights (a total of 69 birds) flying west about two feet above the water of Lake Michigan (Lake County) on November 6, 1955.

In common with the other species of grebes that do not nest in Indiana, the horned grebe is silent while here. Small flocks appear to migrate as a group, appearing overnight at a particular spot.

RED-NECKED GREBE
Podiceps grisegena

Holboell's Grebe

The reported sighting of a red-necked grebe usually causes Indiana birdwatchers from miles around to converge on the site. We have records of only about forty sightings since 1940 and only three before that date. Butler considered it a rare migrant and possible winter resident, but was able to cite just one record, for 1883. We have found two reports for the following fifty-seven years, one in 1913 (Lake Maxinkuckee) and another in 1938 (Marion County). The red-necked grebe may have become more numerous over the years, and this, coupled with the fact that more and more experienced birders are now afield, means it is recorded more frequently. It now appears to be a casual migrant and winter resident. We have at least one record for each month except July.

Red-necked grebes have been observed along rivers, on reservoirs and lakes, and (occasionally) on smaller bodies of water such as gravel pits. Relatively few have been recorded on Lake Michigan.

Spring migration evidently peaks in March and early April, although a few birds are seen in February and May. Fall migration begins in September, reaches its peak in October, and a few birds linger into November and throughout the winter. It is impossible to distinguish clearly between early spring and late fall birds and wintering individuals because of the overlap in dates.

Red-necked grebes are usually seen singly, but there are a few reports of as many as three. They have been found swimming with wood ducks, common goldeneyes, mallards, northern pintails, American black ducks, and red-breasted mergansers. Like loons and other grebes, some apparently are forced down on land by storms. Such a grounded bird was found at Marion on February 19, 1979. Others that were disabled by oil slicks have been found on Lake Michigan.

EARED GREBE
Podiceps nigricollis

A group of birdwatchers carefully make their way along the breakwater at the Michigan City harbor. It is late fall or early winter, and a cold northwest wind drives the waves pounding against the breakwater, sending spray over it. Riding the waves at the entrance to the harbor is a small gray and black grebe with white markings on the head. It dives, but soon reappears not far from shore. The thin, upturned lower mandible and reddish eye are plainly seen. It is under such conditions that most birders record their first eared grebe in Indiana.

Specimens were collected at Brookville in 1883 and 1886, but the species was considered an accidental visitor or perhaps a rare migrant by Butler. We now have more than fifty records of this grebe from Indiana and they are for every month but February. We consider it a casual migrant and winter resident that is considerably more common than the red-necked grebe. About twice as many eared grebes are seen in fall as in spring. Many of the spring observations and practically all of the fall sightings were made along the southern end of Lake Michigan, but the species sometimes occurs on smaller bodies of water. The number at each sighting ranged from one to seven, but most records are for individuals. Eared grebes are about equally abundant in the state in March, April, and May, but quite rare or absent from June through August. Fall migration begins in late September, and reaches its peak in November; some birds remain into December or January.

Otto D. McKeever observed and photographed an eared grebe that stayed at the Jasper-Pulaski Fish and Wildlife Area from spring until at least July 28, 1944. Birds in breeding plumage have been recorded between April 12 and 27 and on August 19 and September 20. The one seen August 19 remained until November 25, by which time it had molted into its winter plumage. David A. Easterla and Mumford found an individual that seemed quite curious about them; the observers had been standing, watching the bird at a distance, but when they crouched down, the grebe swam directly toward them to within about twenty yards.

WESTERN GREBE
Aechmophorus occidentalis

This spectacular grebe was first reported from Indiana on October 27, 1945, when it was seen at Indiana Dunes State Park (DuMont and Smith, 1946). It was next reported in 1953, and an additional twenty sightings have been made since then. Most were seen from October to December; there is one record for January, two for April, and two for May. We consider it a casual migrant and winter visitor.

All sightings to date have been of birds on larger bodies of water, such as reservoirs and Lake Michigan, where more than half of the observations were made. Most records are of single birds, but Harold Fetter and Helen Lane watched three for many hours on October 9 and 11, 1960, at Millers (Lake County). Although there is no preserved specimen of this grebe from the state, good photographs were obtained of one in January 1980 and on May 31, 1982.

BAND-RUMPED STORM-PETREL
Oceanodroma castro

Butler (1906) recorded the only occurrence of this accidental species in Indiana. N. H. Gano found one "fluttering in a wheelbarrow" at Martinsville (Morgan County) on June 15, 1902. He captured the bird, which soon died. Alden H. Hadley obtained the dead bird and preserved its skin (now in the National Museum of Natural History), noting that the stomach was empty.

NORTHERN GANNET
Sula bassanus

This gannet, an accidental visitor to Indiana, has been recorded only three times. An immature was killed on Lake Michigan about two miles from Michigan City in November 1904, the mounted specimen was displayed in a Michigan City store, and a photograph was published in *Proc. Ind. Acad. Sci.* (1907). We do not know whether this specimen is extant. An immature male was found dead along the road about three miles northwest of Portland (Jay County) on December 5, 1947. It had probably flown into a wire. The specimen is in the Purdue University Wildlife Laboratory Collection. A gannet in adult plumage was seen April 18, 1981, on Lake Monroe (Monroe County) by Thomas Alexander, Deborah Alexander, and Pamela Powers.

AMERICAN WHITE PELICAN
Pelecanus erythrorhynchos

Rough-billed Pelican, White Pelican

The idea of a white pelican at Willow Slough Fish and Wildlife Area may seem incongruous, but in 1953 one stayed there from late August until early October, and many of us saw it. Over the years other birders have occasionally been startled to encounter this interesting bird in Indiana.

In the years before 1900, most records for this pelican were of birds either shot or found dead. Butler noted in 1898 that almost every year one or more were seen somewhere in Indiana. Nonetheless, he considered it a rare migrant. The white pelican is currently a very rare migrant and has been recorded in more than a third of the state's counties.

Most white pelicans have been observed on larger lakes or along the larger rivers. Except for a single bird seen on the Ohio River in February, all records are for the months April through November. More birds were seen in May and October than in any other months.

Although most current reports involve single birds or small groups, there are earlier records of fairly good numbers of white pelicans. Large numbers were noted in Knox County in 1850. A flock of thirty-seven was seen near Laurel (Franklin County) on September 29, 1902. There were reportedly more than one hundred at Bass Lake (Starke County) in the fall of either 1926 or 1927.

BROWN PELICAN
Pelecanus occidentalis

This accidental visitor has seldom been found in Indiana. Audubon saw three along the Ohio River, three miles south of Evansville, in the fall of 1820. A specimen taken in Marion County on March 28, 1907, and deposited in the Indiana State Museum, was seen by Mumford in 1958. Thomas R. Micetich observed an adult brown pelican at Fish Lake, LaPorte County, on June 11, 1978. In late November 1981, one was obtained on Lake Monroe near Bloomington but there is good reason to suspect that this bird had escaped from the Indianapolis Zoo.

DOUBLE-CRESTED CORMORANT

DOUBLE-CRESTED CORMORANT

Phalacrocorax auritus

Common Cormorant, Florida Cormorant, Water Turkey

There is something almost prehistoric-looking about cormorants, especially cormorants perched in cypress trees. Even when they are in the water they have a somehow unbirdlike air. Dozens of cormorants used to visit Hovey Lake every spring and fall and their presence added to the exotic—for Indiana—ambience of this large, shallow, muddy oxbow lake, surrounded by huge cypress, silver maple, sycamore, and other swamp-loving trees and shrubs. Visiting Hovey Lake when the cormorants were there was like going back many millennia in time. Cormorants no longer nest at Hovey Lake and the large cypresses are all dead or dying since construction of the dam that raised the water level about seven feet.

Butler considered the double-crested cormorant a regular migrant, more or less common along the larger rivers, and thought that some wintered. He noted that Robert Ridgway thought the species probably bred in Gibson and Knox Counties. There has been a great decrease in numbers of double-crested cormorants in the past two decades, which is thought to be mostly the result of their eating fish contaminated with pesticides. Today it is a rare to very rare migrant and casual in summer and winter. Our latest breeding record is 1953.

Most of the larger bodies of water and larger rivers are used by cormorants, but they are also occasionally seen on small ponds. Spring migration begins about mid-March in the southern region, and migrants reach the central and northern regions shortly thereafter. Most have left the state by June 1. Recent records of summering birds are as follows: Gibson County, June 23, 1980 (1); LaPorte County, June 20, 1980 (1); Posey County, June 2, 1966 (1); Vermillion County, June 16, 1978 (1). There are two records for July and one for August since 1953. Fall migration is under way in early September in the northern half of the state, and (judging from available records) a few weeks later in the southern region. The largest fall numbers recorded include 100 in Marion County on October 24, 1951, and 200 at Hovey Lake on November 15, 1928. One to two cormorants have been recorded on each of eight Christmas bird counts (four times on Lake Michigan). There are eight records for January and early February, but the maximum seen was three.

The first circumstantial evidence that this cormorant might nest in Indiana was obtained by Samuel E. Perkins III, who visited Hovey Lake on September 9, 1929. Cormorants were "present in considerable numbers"; he collected two, and saw a nest he believed to be that of a cormorant. He visited Hovey Lake again on June 16, 1934, and observed two cormorants "little more than half grown" out of the nest being fed by adults. He did not mention seeing a nest (Perkins, 1935). Mumford examined four cormorant nests at Hovey Lake in May 1949. One was empty; three contained three eggs each. These nests were gone by August 1949. On June 4, 1950, Val Nolan Jr., Charles F. Marks, and Vivian and Russell Mumford found two cormorant nests at Hovey Lake. One held three and the other four eggs. The nests were about 45 feet above the water in the same clump of cypresses where the birds had nested in 1949. On October 28, 1952, nine old nests were noted. Edward J. Javorka and Mumford found five nests (four appeared complete) on July 8, 1953. One of the two examined was empty; the other contained only a dead adult cormorant. Gerald L. Brody and Mumford found no cormorants and only one old nest at the lake on May 24, 1957. On June 2, 1966, Gwilym S. Jones and Mumford saw one adult cormorant flying over Hovey Lake, but found no nests.

The only other known nesting locality in Indiana is Willow Slough Fish and Wildlife Area (Newton County), where Will E. Madden observed adults carrying nesting material on May 18, 1953. On July 5, 1953, Mumford examined eight nests in a huge black willow tree standing in the lake some distance from shore (Madden had counted nine nests in this tree earlier). All nests were empty and no traces of eggs could be found in any of them. The birds may have abandoned this location because of disturbance by fishermen. In mid-May 1954, Madden saw sixty-six cormorants at Willow Slough, but there were no known further nesting attempts.

The nesting site at Hovey Lake consisted of a small clump of cypress trees forty-five to fifty feet tall on the east side of the lake, at the mouth of the "drain," a channel leading to the Dry Lake and Pirogue Slough sections of the area. The nest trees were in an isolated cluster in the water a short distance from shore and were shorter than the many huge cypress that ringed this section of the lake. The stick nests were rather bulky and each contained a smooth, deep cup, lined with cypress bark and cypress leaves (some of which were still green).

During the November 1948 waterfowl hunting season at Hovey Lake, the numerous cormorants using the lake were usually absent during the day, but returned at dusk to roost. They may have fed along the nearby Ohio or Wabash Rivers during the daytime, thus avoiding the disturbance from duck hunters at the lake.

ANHINGA

Anhinga anhinga

This more southern species can only be considered accidental in Indiana. There is a report of two killed just north of Indianapolis in 1858, and Fletcher M. Noe claimed to have received one obtained "two miles south" of Indianapolis (no date). We question this record, as well as many of Noe's other bird and mammal records for Indiana, for it is known that he passed off specimens from other states as having been taken in Indiana (Mumford and Whitaker 1982). Floyd S. Carpenter (1964) observed an anhinga on the Ohio River about five miles above Jeffersonville on June 4, 1964. Keller et al. (1979) mention a possible sighting of two anhingas near Franklin on August 14, 1976.

MAGNIFICENT FRIGATEBIRD

Fregata magnificens

Man-o-War Bird, Frigate Bird

This is another accidental wanderer to Indiana. Butler reported that he had examined an immature male of this species in a Lebanon taxidermy shop in 1896. It had reportedly been killed near Shelbyville on July 14, 1896. The only other record is of an immature seen at Michigan City on April 27 and 28, 1957, by Dorthy Buck, Nora Grow, Raymond Grow, James E. Landing, Jean Segal, and Simon Segal. On both days the frigatebird was being harassed by gulls.

AMERICAN BITTERN

Botaurus lentiginosus

Thunder-Pumper, Plum Puddin', Stake-Driver, Indian Hen, Bittern

The American bittern is usually heard before it is seen, if it is seen at all. It is another of those marsh inhabitants that lead a secretive and usually quiet life. During its most vocal season, at courting time, the male displays and utters his unbirdlike, thunder-pumper call. We are sure many people who hear this sound never associate it with a bird. Courting males frequently make themselves more conspicuous than at other seasons; lucky birders may then see them displaying their whitish plumes—not usually visible—or actually performing their pumping calls. On cool, clear early spring mornings bitterns may be seen standing in the sunshine along the edge of dense cover.

Around the turn of the century this bittern was considered a fairly common regular migrant that frequently nested in suitable places in northern Indiana. Some were said to be present in mild winters in the lower Wabash River valley. Except for the fact that considerably fewer bitterns now breed in Indiana due to loss of nesting habitat, that status holds fairly well today. The secretive nature of the species allows it to go undetected, even in localities where it may be fairly common and breeding. It is also a nocturnal migrant, which contributes to its lack of visibility.

Marshes with large stands of cattail, bulrush, or bur-reed are the favored haunts and only known nesting habitat, but migrants may appear in relatively small wet sites on occasion. Such locations include roadside ditches, old fields, ponds, and along rivers.

American bitterns arrive in central Indiana during the last half of March and in northern Indiana by the first week of April. Numerous birds remain into November, but except for the few that occasionally winter most have left the state by December 1. There are six records for December, three for January, and two for February, from areas as far north as Jasper and Porter Counties.

Nests are constructed in emergent vegetation, of whatever materials are close by, on the surface of the water. Enough nesting material is used to keep the eggs dry and above the water. From four to seven eggs may be laid per clutch, but most Indiana nests we have examined held three or (usually) four. Unlike the eggs of other herons that nest in Indiana, they are not blue. Eggs have been observed in nests from May 19 to June 14, but young already half grown were noted in one nest on the latter date. Since incubation commences as soon as the egg is laid, nestlings, having hatched on different days, are of different sizes. When we neared a nest containing two young, the larger climbed out and swam away. When we came within six feet of another nest, one that contained three young and an adult, all four birds stretched their necks upward, beaks pointing straight up, and froze in characteristic bittern position. Full-grown young have

AMERICAN BITTERN

been observed by July 19. Adults of both species of bitterns are frequently reluctant to leave their nests when attending young. Most of our nesting records are of single nests, but in one marsh two nests only fifty yards apart were found in a stand of softstem bulrushes.

This bittern eats a variety of aquatic foods, but we have little Indiana data on its food habits. One was seen holding a bullhead in its beak. Virginia Reuter-skiold watched a wintering American bittern that was standing at a small open air hole on an otherwise frozen lake, catching the small fish that came to the opening to gulp air.

American bitterns normally perch on the ground, usually in shallow water among vegetation, but Irving W. Burr saw one perched in a tree. Although one normally sees single bitterns, one spring we observed four in view at one time in a marsh; at least two were displaying. Bitterns are slow, somewhat awkward-looking flyers. When flushed, they usually fly a short distance at no great height, then drop back into the marsh. Occasionally one will squawk when flushed.

Depicted plants: Broad-leaved arrowhead (*Sagittaria latifolia*), Common cattail (*Typha latifolia*)

LEAST BITTERN

Ixobrychus exilis

Dwarf Bittern

The surest way to see a least bittern is to wade suitable cattail marshes in spring or summer. Seldom does the bird show itself unless flushed from cover. Birders almost have to make an extra effort to locate it on its home ground in order to be successful. When flushed, the bird flies a short distance with dangling legs just above the top of the vegetation and then suddenly and rather awkwardly drops back out of sight. At times it will permit an observer to get very close, relying on its camouflaging colors and ability to stay motionless to avoid detection. Some birds have been captured by hand. Because of their secretive and retiring habits and relative silence at most seasons, the presence of least bitterns in an area is often totally unsuspected.

Butler considered the least bittern a regular but generally rare migrant and a summer resident (locally common) in suitable habitat, in northern Indiana. Today it is a rare to casual (southern region) migrant and locally uncommon to casual summer resident. It is evidently mostly absent, because of lack of habitat, from the southern region. The drainage of marshes throughout the state has decreased the numbers of least bitterns now found at all seasons. Practically all available data about the numbers of this species are inferred from nest counts.

Least bitterns prefer habitat similar to that of the American bittern: large marshes with emergent vegetation. Except for a bird found dead that had probably struck some wires, all records were obtained from marshes.

Like the American bittern, the least is a nocturnal migrant, so arrival dates are difficult to ascertain. Some

birds probably actually arrive earlier than our records indicate, but known dates range from April 5 to November 14. "First" spring records of many observers probably reflect more accurately their first visits to the bittern's habitat than actual arrival, for most such reports are for late April and early May. Fall migration is even less well known, for the birds apparently slip away mostly undetected from their breeding grounds. There are numerous records for August and September, two for October, and one for November. Since the highest counts were all obtained on the breeding grounds, those numbers will be given below.

Some notion of the former abundance of this little bittern can be gained from the fact that Earl A. Brooks found twenty-six nests containing eggs on June 14, 1925, at Lake Webster (Kosciusko County). Barton W. Evermann located twelve nests with eggs on May 31, 1890, at Goose Pond (now drained) in Vigo County.

Adult least bitterns occasionally remain at the nest with young even when an observer is near. Like the American bittern, they may freeze in position facing the observer, beak pointed skyward, and watch him with their peculiarly positioned eyes that can peer around the sides of the beak.

Most known nesting localities of this bittern in Indiana are in the northern third of the state, where most of the suitable nesting habitat is (and was) present. The southernmost nesting records in Indiana are for Sullivan County (1973) and Jackson County (1954). We suspect that least bitterns may breed locally almost anywhere in the state,

LEAST BITTERN

especially in areas where new impoundments supporting adequate nesting vegetation have been established.

Nests are usually over water in emergent vegetation, anywhere from water level to about four feet above it. They are rather loosely constructed of vegetation found at the site, often cattails. Nests containing eggs have been observed from May 21 to July 30, but fully fledged young have been seen by May 28. Young in the nest were noted until July 18. It is obvious that the nesting season is quite long; possibly some renesting occurs. Eggs per nest for forty-four nests ranged from one to six (average 4.1). The usual complete clutch contains four to six eggs.

Bitterns have long, very flexible toes and are adept at scrambling about among the plants surrounding the nests. Partially grown young may leave the nest and hide in the area when disturbed. Once, when we approached a nest containing downy young, the adult flew, uttering a short *keck* or *kuck* note. A fresh, decapitated green sunfish two inches long was lying on the edge of the nest.

Depicted plant: Pickerelweed (*Pontederia cordata*)

GREAT BLUE HERON

GREAT BLUE HERON

Ardea herodias

Blue Crane, Crane

It was dawn in mid-April and a mist hung over the Muscatatuck River. Our canoe drifted along with the sluggish current. In the distance, a barred owl was calling. As we came around a sharp bend we startled a large, grayish heron at its feeding site in a shallow bay behind a sandbar. The great bird gave a hoarse squawk and with a few slow, deliberate strokes of its huge wings disappeared around the next bend. Many have observed the great blue heron under similar circumstances. The popularly known "blue crane" is a skulker that silently wades about in shallow, often weedy, water areas in search of aquatic animals on which to feed. The sudden forward thrust of the head and neck as it strikes its prey is a startling sight.

Around the turn of the century this heron was a common migrant and summer resident in Indiana and it rarely wintered in the southern part of the state. Butler noted that it was an abundant breeder in the northern half of Indiana in suitable localities, and also bred in Gibson and Knox Counties. Today it is a fairly common migrant and a rare to casual winter resident throughout the state, especially in the central portion. It is not nearly as abundant a nesting species as in former years and probably should now be classified as a rare nester.

Great blue herons frequent a variety of water areas: ditches, ponds, lakes, streams, marshes, swamps, flooded fields, and other sites providing food. Shallow marshes with emergent vegetation are preferred for feeding. Nesting colonies (rookeries, heronries) may be in woodlots or wooded areas some distance from water or in trees standing in water.

Spring migrants appear about the first week of March. Fall migration occurs from mid-September to early November, usually peaking sometime in October. Judging from Christmas bird counts, the number of great blue herons wintering in the state has dramatically increased over the past two or three decades, possibly as the result of more and more impoundments being available to them. Between 1943 and 1979, the species has failed to appear on the Indianapolis count in only seven years.

One requirement for nesting appears to be tall trees in which to construct the large, bulky stick nests—sometimes more than a dozen of them to a tree. In woodlots, large beech trees are (or were) frequently used for nesting, and along rivers and streams, sycamore and elm trees provided the best sites. The nests may be added on to and reused over the years, and can become enormous. The one shown is a rather small, flimsy first-year nest. Nesting colonies may be composed entirely of great blue herons or be mixed assemblages of great blues, black-crowned night-herons, great egrets, or perhaps other herons. The average number of nests in 44 recent rookeries was 29; the largest contained 130. Long ago, much larger nesting colonies were apparently common in Indiana. Butler wrote of one "crane heaven" along the Kankakee River in Lake County that occupied a site of "thirty or forty acres" as late as May 1886 and must have contained hundreds if not thousands of nests. The majority of the birds were great blue herons and black-crowned night-herons, but there were "numerous" great egrets as well. Another "crane heaven" was located in Starke County near English Lake in March 1894. In Jasper County was another huge rookery where in 1887 "thousands of Great Blue Herons" nested. Still another was in Steuben County, in "an almost inaccessible bayou, covered for the most part by very large elm trees."

Even in 1898, Butler noted the year-to-year decrease in heronries, and the trend has continued. Many birds were shot for sport, and countless eggs were destroyed in windstorms or forest fires or taken by collectors. A further factor in the general decline of heron populations has probably been the increased use of pesticides and the deaths of birds from eating contaminated fish. Undoubtedly the cutting of timber, reclamation of marsh and swamplands, and other habitat alterations and destruction have taken the greatest toll of all.

Some rookeries were evidently used for many years and well known to several generations of humans living in the area. One such heronry, in Decatur County, was said to have been in use for eighty years. Another in Montgomery County may have been active for a century. Luther (1973) mentioned a rookery that declined from ninety-six nests in 1924 to three nests in 1972.

A nest in Lagrange County contained five fresh eggs on April 15, 1934 (Harris, 1936). Harmon P. Weeks, Jr., examined seven nests (Martin County) on May 4, 1971. Three held four, five, and five eggs each; one held four young; two each contained two eggs and one young, and the other contained two eggs and two young. Large young were seen out of the nests (Newton County) on July 4, 1953.

Great blue herons feed primarily on fish, the remains of which can always be found in and beneath the nests in a rookery, including bullheads, sunfishes, carp, suckers, and other species, as well as frogs and crayfish.

GREAT EGRET

GREAT EGRET

Casmerodius albus

Common Egret, Great White Egret, Great White Heron, American Egret, White Crane, White Heron, Egret

In those infrequent summers when large numbers of "white herons" come to Indiana, we have occasionally been treated to the sight of fifteen to twenty or more great egrets feeding in a shallow marsh. In silhouette against the green vegetation, with their graceful lines and snowy whiteness, they make a beautiful picture. One evening at Hovey Lake we watched dozens of them silently feeding as they waded among the buttonbush and swamp privet and the buttressed trunks of cypress. In this oxbow lake were small fish, crayfish, and even fresh-water shrimp—plenty of food to attract the egrets. Then they began to gather in a clump of tall cypress trees to roost. In the dusk, it was as if the trees had suddenly burst into bloom with huge, white flowers.

Butler considered the great egret a regular migrant and summer resident, formerly fairly common but becoming rare. He wrote that it bred "in some numbers" locally in northern Indiana and in the lower Wabash River valley, specifically in Daviess, DeKalb, Gibson, Jasper, Knox, Noble, and Porter Counties. There were questionable reports from Jasper and Steuben Counties. In a later paper (Butler, 1898b) he added Marshall and Vigo Counties to the nesting range. Evidently most of the great egrets nesting at that time in Indiana were in rookeries along the Kankakee River, where they usually were associated with great blue herons and black-crowned night-herons in the breeding colonies. A terrible fire that swept through the Kankakee River valley in the fall of 1895 destroyed at least some of these rookeries. Great egrets were seen at other great blue heron rookeries in the late 1890s, but with no proof of nesting. Unfortunately, we have almost no egg laying dates or fledgling dates from these early nesting records, except for a report that at least one egret and some eggs were collected at Kouts (Porter County) in May 1895 (Woodruff, 1907). After 1897 we have no records of nesting by this egret until 1953.

In the spring of that year, a heron rookery was established at the Willow Slough Fish and Wildlife Area (Newton County), in a patch of trees flooded the previous year by the creation of a lake. Among the 125 nests—mostly of great blue herons and black-crowned night-herons—were at least seven egret nests containing two to five eggs each on May 28, 1953 (Ginn, 1954). By July 4, at least one large young was noted out of the nest by Mumford. The following spring, about forty adult great egrets were present at the rookery, but before it could be checked for egret nests a severe windstorm destroyed it, blowing down practically all of the nesting trees. On July 10, 1954, no birds were left. Our next report of possible nesting of great egrets is for 1980, in Brown County, and is unverified.

This egret is usually found foraging or associating with great blue herons and little blue herons, primarily in marshes. Shallow overflow areas also appear to be attractive, for forty-three egrets and ten great blue herons were noted feeding at one of these in Sullivan County on August 5, 1957. But individual birds may be seen almost anywhere there is water. Great egrets have been found at small ponds, lakes, and sloughs, in cypress swamps, along rivers, and at fish hatcheries and a sewage disposal plant.

Spring migrants usually arrive in April or early May, but there are several records of birds present in the last half of March. All but one of the March sightings were in the northern region. The buildup in numbers follows the pattern for the little blue heron, with a peak in July or August. In early August of 1952—a good flight year—there were about five hundred great egrets at Willow Slough, and two hundred remained at Hovey Lake until October 5. By December 1 they have usually left the state. We have only three winter records for great egrets, two for January and one for February.

Depicted tree: Baldcypress (*Taxodium distichum*)

SNOWY EGRET

Egretta thula

Little White Egret, Snowy Heron, Snow Heron

This small, relatively rare white heron has never been common in Indiana and is seldom seen. That is a shame, for it is an attractive bird with its golden feet and black legs. Males in courting plumage sport spectacular lacy plumes called aigrettes, once avidly sought to decorate women's hats. Snowy egrets do appear periodically in the state, usually in the company of other herons, especially little blues. Since they are similar in size and color to immature little blues, the two can best be differentiated in flight by the yellow feet of the snowy. Habitat is similar to that of other herons.

Butler noted that the snowy egret was not common, but was a migrant and summer resident in southern Indiana, and that according to Robert Ridgway it bred in Gibson and Knox Counties, but gave no details. It should now be considered a casual to rare summer visitor; there are only eight recorded sightings since 1971.

Spring migrants have been seen as early as April 2. Most are encountered in April or May. Most fall records are for July and August, with occasional sightings in October and the latest on November 2. Since 1900 there have been forty recorded observations in twenty-five different years. Most records were for single birds, but frequently two or three were reported. Eight were recorded at Geist Reservoir on August 24, 1952 (a good "white heron" flight year). Monroe and Monroe (1961) mentioned seeing fifty at the Falls of the Ohio on August 28, 1949.

LITTLE BLUE HERON

Egretta caerulea

Little White Heron, White Heron

In the summer and early fall of 1930, Indiana birdwatchers were treated to an unprecedented ornithological event: thousands of "white herons" appeared throughout the state in the course of their northward post-breeding wanderings. Evidently many were great egrets, but most—as many as 25,000—were immature little blue herons. Nothing like it had ever happened before; several papers were published on the phenomenon, and for years Indiana residents recalled the spectacle. Since then there have been a few other such flight years, notably 1952 and, to a lesser extent, 1954. In other years, the species can be virtually absent. It appears to prefer marshes, but also congregates at overflows along streams, and at sloughs and ponds, and along rivers. They can be quite conspicuous at dusk, when they gather after feeding to roost in trees.

Butler mentioned that the little blue heron was a summer resident in the lower Wabash River valley. He quoted Robert Ridgway as saying that as of about 1889 the species was nesting in Gibson and Knox Counties and was abundant each summer in that region. E. J. Chansler also told Butler that the little blue nested in Indiana (but did not state the county). We have no other details, no actual mention of nests seen here, and no nesting records later than 1896. We now consider it a casual to rare spring migrant and summer visitor, except in flight years.

It has been recorded in Indiana as early as April 1; most birds appear throughout April and May. Numbers peak in August (Will E. Madden saw 200 in early August 1952 at Willow Slough), then dwindle as the birds withdraw. Most have left the state by the end of October. A bird was collected in Tippecanoe County on November 14, 1903. One remained in Posey County until November 12, 1949; one was seen in Union County on November 27, 1965; one was reported near Westville (LaPorte County) on December 17, 1982.

Little blue herons are often seen with great egrets and great blue herons; all three species utilize similar habitats, especially when feeding.

Relatively few little blue herons in adult plumage are seen in Indiana; we have only about thirty records. Occasionally a molting individual in intermediate plumage between the white immature and the bluish mature is seen. One such bird looked like an adult except for two white feathers in each wing.

TRICOLORED HERON

Egretta tricolor

There are at least nine Indiana reports of this southern heron: two nineteenth-century records, and seven since then. Don C. Erman and Nancy Erman saw one along the Wabash River (Tippecanoe County) on July 26, 1964; Irving W. Burr and Ben Trimble found it again two days later. Two tricoloreds were recorded in Vigo County from May 5 to 8, 1971, by James H. Mason and Amy Mason. The next sighting was of one in Gibson County on July 2 and 9, 1978, by Dennis W. Jones, C. Leroy Harrison, and Charles E. Mills. John W. McCain and Gail McCain observed one along the Wabash River at West Lafayette from May 24 to 27, 1976. A bird at Eagle Creek Reservoir (Marion County) was seen from July 2 to July 9, 1979, by Kenneth J. Brock, Michael R. Brown, Alan W. Bruner, Ted T. Cable, Edward M. Hopkins, Timothy C. Keller, and Alfred Starling. One was also seen (and photographed) on May 17, 1981, in Gibson County by Jones and Harrison. It was feeding in a pond along a road at the edge of a lake and busily running about. The most recent record is one seen by David Styer and Myra Styer in Dearborn County on May 21, 1983.

CATTLE EGRET

Bubulcus ibis

On May 1, 1964, in Pulaski County, a boy named Gayland Brettman captured a white heron with an injured wing. The bird was taken to Kenneth C. Nettles for identification and later brought to our attention. It was subsequently prepared as a museum specimen and became the first record of a cattle egret for Indiana (Mumford, 1964). It was probably inevitable that this Old World species would eventually appear in Indiana, given the history of its immigration to South America and gradual movement northward across the North American continent.

Since its first known appearance in Indiana in 1964, it has been increasing in numbers. By 1968 there were six records; between 1969 and 1973, twelve; 1974 and 1978, twenty-six; 1979 and 1981, twenty-six. Although we know of no nesting in the state as yet, we feel that it is simply a matter of time before it does nest. We consider it to be a rare migrant, more common in spring than in fall. It has been seen in each month except December to February.

Cattle egrets spend a considerable amount of time feeding on land, where they hunt insects and associate with some of the larger mammals (usually sheep and cattle in Indiana). In other states they are frequently seen foraging along the grassy strips of interstate highways. They have also been observed in overflow ponds along rivers, in marshes, on a flooded golf course, near ponds, and in pastures.

Spring migrants arrive as early as March 21 and are mostly gone by June 1. There are three June records (Gibson, Hancock, Lake Counties), two July reports (Gibson County), and three August records (Dearborn, Marion, Warrick Counties). Fall migrants (possibly some summer residents) have been observed from August 10 to early December. The largest groups encountered were as follows: May 12, 1982 (40), at Merom; April 26, 1980 (flock of 38), Lake Monroe; May 8, 1983 (28), Dearborn County.

Cattle egrets have been observed with little blue herons and with American crows. One egret was in a farmer's hoglot.

GREEN-BACKED HERON

Butorides striatus

Green Heron, Fly-up-the-Creek, Shitepoke, Poke, Shikepoke

There was once a dense thicket of wild plum trees just inside a beech-maple woods near Brazil, Indiana, where green-backed herons nested. Since the site was several hundred yards from the nearest water, it seemed an unlikely place to find a nesting heron unless one was familiar with the habits of the bird. One day in mid-June, Mumford happened to walk past this thicket and flushed an adult from its nest. The nest contained young; the broken shell of one of the eggs was on the ground beneath it. As he tried to penetrate the thicket to get a better view an adult heron came near and uttered a clucking call. Mumford then made a squeaking sound and both adults approached closely to investigate.

Amos W. Butler considered the green-backed heron the

commonest and best known of the herons that occurred in Indiana. He classified it as a summer resident throughout Indiana, but noted that in some localities it was becoming less common than formerly. It is currently a fairly common migrant, fairly common to rare summer resident, and casual winter resident in suitable habitat.

The green-backed heron may be found in nearly all aquatic habitats, including small ponds and drainage ditches. Some available data regarding birds seen on float trips along various Indiana streams suggest that at some seasons this heron may be most abundant along such watercourses. During the nesting season, green-backed herons may be seen in upland pastures, orchards, woodlots, and other nonaquatic areas where they also nest.

Birds usually arrive in the southern region the first half of April and appear throughout the state within a week or so. Early migrants have been reported in late March. The fall migration usually peaks in October and most migrants have left the state by mid-November. Green-backed herons have been reported on Christmas bird counts at South Bend, Columbus, Vigo County, Evansville, and Spring Mill State Park. There are two sightings for January and one for February. The maximum number recorded in spring was for Gibson County, April 18, 1972, when fifteen to twenty were noted in various places. In the fall, the largest numbers have been observed from mid-August to early September, as follows: August 13, 1964 (30), Franklin County; August 13, 1965 (30), Geist Reservoir; August 14, 22, and 29, 1953 (30 to 35 each), Falls of the Ohio.

Green-backed herons build their nests relatively low in rather dense vegetation, either over water or land. Nests have been observed in willow, locust, and hawthorn trees, an elm, and a clump of swamp rose at the edge of a pond or marsh. Others were placed in wild plum thickets in a deciduous woods, pine plantations, a small clump of cedar trees, a box elder thicket, orchards, hawthorn thickets along a creek, slender maple saplings in a deciduous woods, dense thickets of wild crabapple, and buttonbush trees in the middle of a pond or along a slough. One usually finds only a single nest in such locations, but there are at least two records of colonial nesting in Indiana. In one instance ten to twelve nests were in a clump of cedar trees. Donald H. Boyd found twenty-one nests in the tops of buttonbush trees growing in the water of a slough. The slough was isolated, about one hundred feet in diameter, and completely surrounded by black oak and white oak woodland. The nests were all within six feet of the water. All of the nests for which we have details were constructed within twenty-five feet of the ground (or water). The average height of thirty-two nests was 8.6 feet.

Eggs have been found in nests from May 8 to July 1 and young in some nests were hatched by May 29. In fifteen nests the number of eggs per nest varied from 3 to 6 and averaged 4.3. Five nests each held 5 eggs and 4 eggs. Adults were seen feeding young as late as September 7. After young are half grown they may climb about in the nest tree, especially if disturbed by an observer.

The green-backed heron feeds on a variety of aquatic and semiaquatic animals. Most feeding is done at the water's edge; the birds wade in or perch just above the surface and watch for prey. This heron can take flight from the water; we once watched one being pursued by an eastern kingbird forced to land on the water, from which it easily flew after the kingbird gave up the chase. When flushed or alarmed it may give a hoarse squawk as it flies, and Evermann and Clark (1920) mentioned the "loud sneeze-like call."

Depicted tree: Northern catalpa, Catawba-tree (*Catalpa speciosa*)

BLACK-CROWNED NIGHT-HERON

Nycticorax nycticorax

Squawk, Night Heron, Quawk, Qua-bird

An encounter with a black-crowned night-heron is apt to take place at dusk, and to be aural rather than visual. Typically, the unseen bird, as it flies overhead on its way to the evening feeding grounds, utters its single *wok* call. This call may also be heard any time during the night, for the birds remain active throughout the hours of darkness. As with most other more or less nocturnal animals, an unwarranted air of mystery surrounds it.

Around 1900, this heron was a regular migrant and summer resident that bred locally "in some numbers" in the northern part of the state, according to Butler. It had been recorded from April 10 to November 24. Keller (1966) considered it a locally abundant summer resident and irregular to very rare winter resident. Later (Keller et al., 1979), its status was changed to rare migrant, casual in winter, and only known to breed in one Indiana

BLACK-CROWNED NIGHT-HERON

locality. Obviously, we have witnessed a drastic change in status in Indiana during the past eighty years.

Marshes, lakes, rivers, sloughs, and ponds are all utilized as feeding sites by the black-crowned night-heron, which seems to favor marshes more or less surrounded by trees. Val Nolan Jr. noted that it sometimes roosted in pine plantations during the day. Rookeries are usually established in deciduous trees near or in water in company with other species of herons.

Although a small number of black-crowned night-herons occasionally winter in the state, spring migrants arrive in southern and central Indiana from mid-March through April and reach northern Indiana by late March. Most spring records from all regions are for April. On April 18, 1952, there were 120 in Marion County; thirty were noted in Porter County on April 24, 1960. Fall migration data are sparse, but 821 were seen at the Falls of the Ohio on September 18, 1949. Most black-crowned night-herons have left Indiana by mid-November, except for stragglers and wintering birds, which have been recorded on at least twenty Christmas bird counts. In winter this heron has occurred most consistently in the Indianapolis area, where it was observed on eleven consecutive counts (1952 to 1962). The average number per count during this period was nine, and numbers ranged from one to twenty-seven. Eighteen or more were recorded three times (1954, 1956, 1959). None has been seen on Indianapolis area counts since 1972.

The black-crowned night-heron used to be a fairly common (probably locally common) breeding bird in the northern two-thirds of Indiana, nesting at least as far south as Hancock, Henry, Marion, and Wayne Counties. In the large rookeries along the Kankakee River observers noted "great numbers" nesting in 1886, but cited no precise figures or nest counts, probably because other species of herons were nesting in the same colonies. We do have nest counts from 1928 to 1980 for nineteen rookeries of black-crowned night-herons, most of which evidently were not nesting with other species. Colony size ranged from 8 to 244 and averaged 90 nests. Three rookeries contained 200 or more nests. Since the black-crowned has decreased so drastically in numbers in the past twenty years, all of the known Indiana colonies have been abandoned. The last one was active in 1980 (Lake County).

Rookeries were situated in a flooded stand of oaks, hickories, and aspens at the edge of a lake; in a grove of box elder trees along a creek; in a tract of woods consisting mainly of oaks, ash, and butternut trees; in a stand of tall cottonwoods; and in deciduous timber along rivers. When one colony on a golf course was abandoned, a few pairs of birds nested nearby in a stand of conifers. We have been unable to find a single reference to dates that eggs were observed in nests. At one rookery, young were heard in nests on May 13. At another, some young were out of the nest by July 5. One observer noted that grackles at a rookery were killing the young herons in the nest and dropping them to the ground (Sieber, 1932).

Depicted tree: Red maple (*Acer rubrum*)

YELLOW-CROWNED NIGHT-HERON

Nycticorax violaceus

White-crowned Night Heron, Squawk

This striking but retiring heron was a common nester in the lower Wabash River valley in the early 1880s, but after that the species apparently declined rapidly in our area and for the next seventy years there were few records. In the late 1940s and early 1950s, however, a censusing technique for wood ducks was worked out that involved exploration by canoe of fifteen-mile segments of many of Indiana's major streams. In the course of these census expeditions, yellow-crowned night-herons began to be seen as far north as the Iroquois River (Newton County) and the Salamonie River (Wells County). It is quite likely that they were there all along, and that Indiana birdwatchers simply were not visiting the correct habitats—muddy sloughs and temporary shallow overflow ponds along rivers.

Butler considered this heron a locally common summer resident in the lower Wabash River valley; Robert Ridgway visited a rookery near Vincennes (Knox County) in the spring of 1881 that contained "perhaps a hundred pairs," plus other herons. Butler noted that this colony was the most northern known for the species. The next Indiana nesting record was obtained in 1958 (Delaware County) by Harold A. Zimmerman; eight more nesting localities had been reported by 1981. Today this heron is probably a casual to rare migrant and summer resident, but appears to be becoming more common, especially in

YELLOW-CROWNED NIGHT-HERON

the southern half of the state. It appears to be absent in winter.

In Indiana the yellow-crowned is fairly closely associated with rivers and sloughs, overflows, and ponds near rivers. There are a few observations from marshes, reservoirs, sewage disposal plants, and lakes. Most nests were along rivers. Some nests were isolated, but there seems to be a tendency for this heron to nest in "colonies" of two or three nests fairly close together. We have observed one nest at a great blue heron rookery. Twelve of the seventeen recent nests observed were constructed on horizontal tree branches over a stream. Three were over land in a woodlot, and two others were along a creek, but whether they were over water was not reported. Distance from the ground ranged from 25 to 40 feet and averaged 31 feet. Preferred trees for nesting were red birch, silver maple, sycamore, ash, sweet gum, and white oak. There

were two or three eggs per nest; eggs were found in nests from May 4 to June 9. At least one of the clutch was pipped on this latter date.

Spring migrants apparently arrive in late March and probably go directly to the breeding areas. Birds have been observed on nests by April 8. They remain in the northern region until at least late September and in central Indiana until October 10. No doubt they linger longer in the southern region, from which we need more data. Maximum numbers reported at favored feeding sites include about a dozen in Posey County from June 4 to 6, 1950; 11 in the Patoka River bottoms on July 11, 1973; 4 on April 24, 1960, in Porter County; 4 on April 21, 1955, in Marion County. Usually the bird is alone. An adult collected on May 24 while feeding in a temporary pond in a plowed field near a river had 15 crayfish in its gullet.

Depicted tree: Umbrella magnolia (*M. tripetala*)

WHITE IBIS
Eudocimus albus

An accidental visitor, this showy species has seldom been reported from Indiana. Most of those observed in the state were evidently immatures that had wandered northward from their usual haunts. Butler noted that all three of the then-known Indiana records for this ibis were for Knox County: one "over fifty years ago," another in 1864, and a third for 1878. Gordon (1931) reported two sightings in 1925: a flock of twenty or more seen at New Albany (Floyd County), and two birds between Henderson, Kentucky, and Mount Vernon, Indiana. We doubt the accuracy of the first of these sightings; the birds may have been wood storks.

As far as we know, the next occurrence was not until 1980, when, from May 15 to August 30, the species was observed in Daviess, Delaware, Gibson, Lake, Marion, and Warrick Counties and at Lake Monroe. The largest number—five—was seen in Warrick County between August 2 and August 30. At two localities, photographs of the ibises were obtained. Some of the birds were found in an area of cattails, grass, and willows bordering a soybean field and creek bottom woods. At another site they were observed with yellowlegs and killdeer in a wet, muddy soybean field. They were also noted in a cattail marsh and a grassy area that had recently been flooded and in which several small ponds remained. At one site they were associating with little blue herons.

The glossy ibis was considered hypothetical until an adult was seen May 20, 1962, at the Indianapolis Sewage Disposal Plant by at least five competent observers. Larry E. Lehman and others saw two, feeding in a small pond in a cow pasture near farm buildings, in Pulaski County on April 17 and 18, 1968. One was collected (Mumford and Lehman, 1969).

Individual ibises of the genus *Plegadis* not definitely determined as to species have been reported in Indiana as follows: August 21, 1966, Lake County, Lawrence G. Balch and Howard Bloom; weekend of October 1–2, 1966, Warren County, Mr. and Mrs. Thomas C. Doody; September 26, 1976, Tippecanoe County, Paul Pilch and others; May 9, 1977, Marion County, Timothy C. Keller; October 27, 1979, Porter County, Kenneth J. Brock, Donald Coslet, Sonya D. Coslet, and Scott F. Jackson. Keller thought that the bird he saw was a white-faced ibis, which it may well have been.

[WHITE-FACED IBIS]
Plegadis chihi

Our only reason for including the white-faced ibis (even as uncorroborated) is the observation of a bird by Timothy C. Keller on May 9, 1977. The ibis in question was seen in flight only, but under good viewing conditions. Unfortunately, the record does not meet our criteria for inclusion on the state list.

GLOSSY IBIS
Plegadis falcinellus

The glossy ibis is an accidental wanderer to Indiana that has been reported here infrequently and only within the past twenty-five years. Positive identification of this and the similar white-faced ibis in the field can be tricky. In fact, some authors consider the two conspecific.

ROSEATE SPOONBILL
Ajaia ajaja

This spectacular waterbird is accidental in Indiana, to which it evidently wandered a few times from its Gulf Coast habitat many years ago. We can add nothing to the account of the species written by Butler in 1898, from which the following information was taken. E. J. Chansler wrote Butler that in the spring of 1856, a collector had shot two roseate spoonbills "in a swampy place a few miles east of Vincennes" (Knox County). Barton W. Evermann obtained information that led him to believe that spoonbills were seen and one was killed near Terre Haute (Vigo County) several years before 1897. The third record is that of a bird killed near Portland (Jay County) on July 14, 1889. This specimen was preserved and in the possession of a man at Bryant, Indiana, according to R. E. Kirkman, who related the data to Butler.

WOOD STORK

Mycteria americana

Wood Ibis, Bald Ibis, Wood Groo

When John James Audubon was traveling down the Ohio River below Evansville on November 4, 1820, he saw some "wood groos" at Diamond Island, thus providing us with the first recorded sighting of the wood stork in the state. The species was recorded from Indiana seven more times prior to 1900, ranging as far north as Allen County in 1890. All other sightings and specimens came from that part of Indiana south of a line connecting Parke, Carroll, and Jay Counties.

Butler listed it as a more or less irregular summer visitor or summer resident in the lower Wabash River valley and a rare summer visitor throughout the remaining southern two-thirds of the state. He noted that all dated records were for the period July 30–October 30 (evidently he was unaware of Audubon's sighting). Since 1900, wood storks have been reported in only eleven years, most recently in 1944 (we do not include a queried sighting in 1976). Except for one sighting in mid-June, all occurrences were for the months cited by Butler above. Today this stork should be considered an accidental visitor to Indiana.

Sightings of wood storks have most frequently been along rivers (up which they possibly migrated), about ponds, along smaller streams, and around cypress swamps.

Flocks of from 150 to 200 were seen in Parke County between August 10 and September 28, 1901, and flocks of 40 or more were reported from other localities. In some cases, birds remained at a given locality for as long as three months. Although there are at least fifteen reports of wood storks killed in the state, scarcely any specimens can be found in museums.

[FULVOUS WHISTLING-DUCK]

Dendrocygna bicolor

Fulvous Tree Duck

This accidental species has been recorded twice in Indiana, although there is no preserved specimen or photograph. One was present at Lake Sullivan, Indianapolis, from May 28 to early September, 1960, and many observers saw it. John M. Louis found two at Jasper-Pulaski Fish and Wildlife Area on May 16, 1964. There is a possibility that one or both of these records involved escaped birds.

TUNDRA SWAN

Cygnus columbianus

Whistling Swan, American Swan

It is especially thrilling to be afield on a frosty, crisp late October or early November day when a sizable flock of tundra swans passes overhead. Silhouetted against a blue sky, they move silently, with purposeful flight, and are gone so suddenly that you wonder if you really saw them. These great birds migrate across Indiana in spring and fall, but since our state is on the western fringe of their usual route we do not see many of them.

Butler reported the tundra swan to be an uncommon migrant and rare winter resident, but the trumpeter swan was then still present in Indiana, so there was undoubtedly confusion in attempting to separate the two species in the field. Today the tundra swan is a rare but regular migrant in both spring and fall throughout the state. We have the fewest records for the southern region, where in the past suitable habitat may have been lacking. Also, swans are capable of long, nonstop flights and undoubtedly many pass over undetected. It is casual in winter, in small numbers.

This swan has been seen on lakes and reservoirs, small ponds, in marshes, along the Ohio River, at gravel pits, and in flooded fields along some of the larger rivers (especially the Kankakee). In other parts of its range, it congregates by the thousands in staging areas, often larger lakes. At times small flocks have been found on relatively small bodies of water.

Spring migration occurs mainly from the end of the first week of March to April 1, with peak numbers during the fourth week of March. A few stragglers have been reported until about mid-May; an immature was recorded on June 10, 1978, in Johnson County. Fall migrants pass through from about October 20 to mid-November, with the bulk of the larger flocks being noted from late October to early November. Spring and fall numbers are about the same. Eight flocks of twenty to ninety birds have been observed in spring; nine flocks of twenty-two to fifty-two have been recorded in fall. On October 29, 1966, in Steuben County, Phillip R. Smith saw one hundred passing overhead; only one small group stopped. The length of time swans remain varies from a day to several weeks. Nine groups remained for periods of from eight to twenty-three days and averaged about two weeks. Eleven of the fourteen records of wintering birds were for singles; one was of two birds; and two reports were of three birds each.

TRUMPETER SWAN

Cygnus buccinator

This impressive waterfowl was probably once a permanent resident of Indiana, but it passed from the Hoosier scene with scant details of its existence being known. It is now impossible to reconstruct the history of this grand bird in the state, for most of what we know is only hearsay or conjecture. Amos W. Butler was in much the same situation in 1897 when he prepared his *Birds of Indiana*. A few additional reports have accumulated since 1900 as the result of research of the literature and interviews with early settlers in northwestern Indiana.

Butler considered this swan a rare migrant and probable winter resident, noting that it formerly bred in the state. He did not cite an actual nesting record, however, or a sighting during the nesting season. Although there were listings of sightings of the trumpeter swan as late as 1913 (Esten, 1931), we cannot be sure how well the observers could distinguish between trumpeters and tundra swans, and some of the observations are very doubtful. To our knowledge, the only extant Indiana specimens are one shot on the Ohio River, twelve miles below Cincinnati, in December 1876, and one shot February 22, 1894, near Valparaiso (Field Museum of Natural History).

A. W. Schorger (1964) concluded that the trumpeter had indeed once nested in the northwestern corner of the state. According to published interviews with several early residents of Newton County, the birds nested at what was then Black Marsh in the Beaver Lake area as late as 1872 or 1873. The settlers told of taking the eggs from these nests and hatching them under a domestic goose or hen. Swans reared this way were reputedly easily tamed. They said the swans laid from five to seven eggs per nest. These nests were on floating bogs in the marsh, very treacherous quagmires of moss or turf. One could easily sink down into the ooze and slime and decayed vegetation beneath, which was eight to ten feet in depth. According to one resident, "The nest of the swan was always in a position where the water could seep up through the soil from below. Occasionally the mother bird would thoroughly drench her feathers, stand up over the nest and shake herself, so as to sprinkle the eggs." It has been assumed that the trumpeter swan nested in this region because of the submerged aquatic plants called "swan celery" that grew in Beaver Lake. The drainage of this lake, initiated in the 1850s, was practically completed thirty years later, and may have been an important factor in the disappearance of this swan as a nesting bird in Indiana.

A dead trumpeter swan was found near the Indiana line, in southwestern Ohio, in February 1982. Since trumpeters are now being raised at various places, it could have been an escape from captivity.

MUTE SWAN

Cygnus olor

This showy, Old World swan has been kept captive on lakes, in parks, zoos, and private estates, and probably in other places throughout Indiana for many years. Frank C. Evans of Crawfordsville successfully raised mute swans which bred in captivity. We cannot establish when he acquired the birds, but it may have been between 1921 and 1925 (Indiana Audubon Society Year Book, 1931). Birders paid little attention to this domestic species until free-flying birds began to attract their attention.

Butler did not mention it. A lineman found one entangled in telephone wires near Fort Wayne (probably in the 1950s); we have been unable to confirm the date. Six each were recorded on New Castle Christmas bird counts in 1955 and 1956 (and periodically to 1981). Two were seen on the Bloomington Christmas count in 1957 and four in 1958. From 1961 to 1966, birds were observed in Bartholomew, Delaware, Elkhart, Hamilton, Henry, and Jefferson Counties. Relatively few were observed from 1967 to 1972 and most of those were seen on the New Castle Christmas bird counts. Since 1974, free-flying mute swans have been reported each year in Indiana and the frequency of sightings has increased. One can expect to see the mute swan in any part of the state throughout the year. It is probably best considered a casual to very rare migrant and casual nester.

Almost any body of water large enough to allow the birds to land and take off may attract this swan. Some sightings have involved birds in passage. Although some authorities do not consider the North American mute swans truly migratory, they do fly considerable distances. Perhaps some of the longer flights could indeed be termed migration. Bellrose (1976) wrote that the nesting mute swans in Michigan resulted from a release of birds there in 1919. This population was said to consist of forty-seven birds in the mid-1940s and of five hundred by 1974. The increased frequency of sightings in Indiana since 1973 may be partially the result of movements of the Michigan birds.

Although this swan readily breeds in captivity, it is desirable to obtain records of nesting in the wild before it is considered a true "breeding" species in the state. Val Nolan Jr. noted that the mute swan was "now breeding locally" in the Bloomington area when he submitted his 1958 Christmas bird count. From 1954 through 1959, Lynn Cross lived at Lake Tippecanoe (Kosciusko County) in the summers. Every summer a wild mute swan built a nest at the water's edge in the marsh at the western end of the lake. People who had lived at the lake before 1954 remembered the summers when its mate was alive. Two swans appeared at Grass Lake (Steuben County) in the fall of 1974, remained for a week, then left. Two returned to the lake in the spring of 1975, constructed a nest, but produced no young. Observers did not examine the nest to determine whether eggs were laid. We expect other nestings to occur in the near future.

Most sightings have been of singles or two birds together, but groups of three to eight have been recorded several times. As many as eleven remained near South Bend from December 8, 1976, to February 20, 1977, and fourteen were seen on the Columbus Christmas bird count on December 19, 1981.

GREATER WHITE-FRONTED GOOSE

Anser albifrons

Laughing Goose, Gray Brant, American White-fronted Goose, Wild Goose, Specklebelly

This western species is rarely seen east of the Mississippi River. Its principal migratory route across the United States is from the Dakotas to Texas and Louisiana. Evidently the birds that appear in Indiana in spring and fall are migrating on the eastern edge of this corridor. Waterfowl hunters shot white-fronted geese at English Lake along the Kankakee River as early as 1874; three specimens shot at old Beaver Lake (Newton County) between 1881 and 1889 are in the collection of the Ohio State Museum. Although both of these large lakes have long since been drained, this goose still migrates through the region, stopping at Jasper-Pulaski, Kankakee, and Willow Slough Fish and Wildlife Areas, which were all created since 1930. Within the past thirty years, there have been an increasing number of sightings of white-fronted geese in Indiana.

Butler considered it a rare migrant and listed only five records for the state. According to Bellrose (1976) the midcontinent portion of the white-fronted goose population (that which crosses Indiana) steadily increased from 1955 to 1970, and since 1968 the segment that winters in Louisiana has shown a consistent upward trend in numbers. No doubt this explains why Indiana birders have been seeing this once-rare goose more frequently during the past thirty years. From 1949 to 1981, the species was recorded in the state in all but ten years. From 1968 to 1981, we lack reports only for 1973. This goose was seen in the spring in twenty-six years and recorded in fall only six years. Today it is probably a rare spring migrant and casual fall migrant. There are at least ten December records, none for January, and only two for February. It has occurred in both spring and fall in only four years, all since 1969.

Most of the birds were seen in comparatively large marshy habitats, but a few were noted about ponds, lakes, or reservoirs. One flock of forty-eight was observed in late March in a wheatfield near a marsh.

Spring migrants have been reported from February 18 (early) to April 23, with the largest numbers recorded between March 20 and the first week of April. For example, in late March 1970, there were fifty-seven at the Willow Slough Fish and Wildlife Area. Forty-eight were noted in Tippecanoe County on March 26, 1970, and forty-one at Willow Slough on April 6, 1954. There are relatively few data on fall flights, but observations ranged from mid-September to the second week of November, excluding the few birds reported in winter. During the week of October 7 to 14, 1977, sixty-five were seen at Willow Slough. Eleven were present at the Pigeon River Fish and Wildlife Area on October 11, 1977.

SNOW GOOSE
Chen caerulescens

Blue Goose, Blue Brant, Blue-winged Goose, Alaska Goose, White Brant, Brant, White-headed Goose, Lesser Snow Goose, Greater Snow Goose

No doubt many of us first became aware of snow geese from hearing their yelping cries as they migrated high overhead in late October. The call is so different from the honking of the commoner and better-known Canada goose that it is easily detected. The behavior of migrating snow geese can be quite variable from year to year. They may travel with Canada geese or alone. They may stop off during their journey, but they are also perfectly capable of performing their entire fall migration nonstop, and in some years scarcely any are reported on the ground. Their migration can be diurnal or nocturnal (but even at night, their characteristic calls can often still be heard).

Butler included the lesser snow goose, greater snow goose, and blue goose in his list of Indiana birds as rare migrants, and more common in spring than in fall. Scientists now consider these three birds a single species—the snow goose. It is a regular and uncommon migrant throughout the state, and, interestingly, we now have many more records for fall than for spring, apparently because its current migration patterns take it over Indiana in fall and mostly to the west in spring.

Snow geese usually congregate in greatest numbers in fish and wildlife areas where there are marshes, open fields, and other waterfowl. Flocks of resting birds are frequently seen on reservoirs, lakes, or ponds. Snow geese may sometimes be seen feeding in picked cornfields or other open fields, often with Canada geese.

In some years, there are wintering birds throughout the state, but they are found in greatest numbers in the southwest corner in the Hovey Lake area. About three hundred wintered there in 1949–50, an unusually large number even for that part of the state. Spring migrants usually appear the first half of March, with stragglers as late as the first week of May in southern Indiana. Normally, however, the spring flight passes through rather quickly, and most are gone by the end of March. The maximum numbers recorded in spring are for Lake County on March 21, 1959 (745), and Willow Slough on March 23, 1953 (200). The few summering birds reported are thought to have been captives or cripples.

Early fall migrants appear in northern Indiana in the first week of October, and most pass through the state during the remainder of that month. By mid-December few remain. We suspect that at least some of those that spend the winter are casualties of the hunting season, unable to complete their migration. Peak numbers during fall migration are as follows: Willow Slough, November 28, 1960 (7,000); Starke County, November 2, 1961 (4,000); Jasper-Pulaski, November 7, 1976 (3,000); Greene-Sullivan Counties, October 21–27, 1949 (2,200).

When large flocks do stop off, they are sometimes quite tame and can be observed at relatively close range. The birds may appear fatigued or sleepy; perhaps inclement weather or adverse headwinds tired them and caused them to stop off prematurely. We have analyzed the ratio of white morph to blue morph snow geese in fifty-five flocks, totaling more than 10,000 birds, as reported in Indiana. The blue morph outnumbered the white five to one.

Hunters and birders of earlier years often incorrectly called snow geese "brant." The rare brant is of course a different species.

[ROSS' GOOSE]
Chen rossii

The only record of this goose in Indiana is that published by Mumford (1966): "On 30 December 1965, at the Willow Slough Fish and Game Area, Newton County, Indiana, several of us watched for some time a bird that was undoubtedly a Ross' Goose (Chen rossii). Although we did not see the bird at close enough range to check all diagnostic features, Charles M. Kirkpatrick, Will E. Madden, and I did observe it with binoculars at 200 yards. This small goose always associated with mallards and other dabbling ducks, rather than with several hundred Canada Geese that were not far away. On the water, it appeared slightly larger than a mallard; in flight, the goose appeared relatively larger in comparison with the mallards than it did when swimming with them. Its beak was very stubby. According to Glenn A. Baker and other personnel of the area, this goose had been present several weeks."

BRANT
Branta bernicla

This coastal species is seldom found in the interior of the United States and is an accidental to casual visitor to Indiana, where it has been reported at least seven times since 1957. Butler listed it as accidental, based on an 1870 report that it was "occasionally seen flying over when migrating" in Franklin County. We question the validity of this record, and have pointed out that the name "brant" was widely used for both color morphs of the snow goose.

On October 19, 1957, three brant were seen at Michigan City by August Verhoestra, Raymond Grow, and others. Seven days later one, unable to fly, was captured there (specimen in National Museum of Natural History). Six other sightings have been made along Lake Michigan and one in Gibson County. On five occasions a single bird was observed, but Kenneth J. Brock and Joy Underborn reported a large flock on Lake Michigan at Beverly Shores on December 14, 1975. There were from seventy-five to one hundred in a densely packed group, which the observers first took to be a large floating log. Dates of observation of this brant in Indiana range from October 16 to February 26, with a single "spring" date from May 13 to 27, 1983, at Michigan City.

CANADA GOOSE

Branta canadensis

Common Wild Goose, Lesser Canada Goose, Little Wild Goose, Honker, Hutchins' Goose, Canadian Goose

The Canada goose has probably caught the fancy of Hoosiers more than any other species of waterfowl. The Canada is synonymous with the call of the wild. Especially after a particularly severe winter, the spring flights —signaling the approach of warmer weather—are a welcome sight. In the fall, southbound flocks stir the waterfowl hunter and remind us all that autumn is nearly over. On foggy nights we sometimes hear flocks of geese flying lower than usual and calling more frequently to keep their bearings.

Around 1900 the Canada goose was considered a common migrant and permanent resident. It was said to winter in northern Indiana sometimes and often to breed in the state. Butler noted that it was much more abundant formerly and still bred "in some numbers" in the Kankakee River region and a few other sites across northern Indiana. This goose is still a common migrant and permanent resident in Indiana, but determining the true breeding distributions of wild birds is virtually impossible. So many geese are kept captive or semicaptive throughout the state that breeding may occur anywhere. We wonder if any of the nesting Canada geese in the state are truly wild stock, free of manipulation by man. In some years, large numbers spend the winter, especially in the southwestern corner, near the junction of the Wabash and Ohio Rivers. About 15,000 wintered in Posey County in 1948–49. Smaller numbers may winter throughout the state.

Canada geese are likely to be found on nearly any water habitat, but the largest numbers occur on or near refuges, where the birds have suitable feeding and resting areas and protection. Larger bodies of water adjacent to extensive marsh are favored, but the birds also utilize reservoirs, smaller lakes and ponds, rivers, and fields (especially those that are inundated). Flooded or dry harvested cornfields and wheatfields are choice feeding habitat during migration and winter. There is no doubt that the switch to mechanical corn harvesting methods has had a tremendous influence on the habits of Canada geese and other waterfowl species. After harvest much food is left in open fields with short stubble, where waterfowl can feed and feel secure. The creation of more and more reservoirs and other fairly large impoundments has also benefited waterfowl, especially geese.

Spring migration begins as soon as food and open water are available, thus arrival dates vary for any particular area from year to year, depending upon the climatic conditions. The hardy geese push northward on the heels of the breakup of ice. Although migrants have been seen in southern Indiana in late January, most spring migration takes place in the latter half of February and early March. Fall migration is usually under way by the first week of October, reaching peaks between mid-October and mid-November. The heaviest concentration of geese in the fall in Indiana migrate down the western side of the state en route to their southern Illinois wintering area. There were 9,000 at the Kankakee Fish and Wildlife Area on February 28, 1974. An estimated 11,000 were present at the Jasper-Pulaski Fish and Wildlife Area from November 20 to 25, 1951.

Butler mentioned nesting "in the Kankakee region" and in DeKalb, Lake, LaPorte, and Steuben Counties. Although the Kankakee River valley was reputedly a haven for waterfowl and there have been reports of large numbers of geese nesting there, we have no real evidence to support this claim. Canada geese have now been reintroduced throughout most of the state in order to increase their numbers. In many cases the adults are pinioned to render them incapable of flight, but the offspring are allowed to go free. Captives kept by parks, zoos, and individuals frequently escape and nest in the vicinity, rearing young that become free flying and depart before they can be captured and pinioned.

For many years the breeding population at the Jasper-Pulaski Fish and Wildlife Area was the only significant nesting aggregation in Indiana. Two pairs of Canada geese, released on the marsh there in either 1935 or 1937 (reports in the literature conflict), nested successfully. More birds were released there through the years, and their offspring remained to breed; by 1978 this flock totalled more than 150 pairs. Similar breeding flocks were established on other state-owned areas. Since this goose has adapted well to this type of management, Indiana now has a large population of nesting birds.

Canada geese seem to prefer to nest in marshy areas, but captives will nest in a variety of sites, either dry or wet. At Jasper-Pulaski the free-roaming geese in the marshes formerly nested on muskrat houses, piles of debris over the water, islands, or levees, and in the edge of the oak-hickory woods bordering the marsh. Most of the land nests were within a few feet of the water, often at the base of a stump or tree. In later years, after various experimental structures were erected for the geese to nest in, the birds readily took to building their nests in steel "baskets" on poles over water.

Practically all of our nesting data were gathered at

CANADA GOOSE

Jasper-Pulaski. Egg laying usually begins at about April 1 and continues for about two weeks. Evidently a few eggs are laid in late March, for our earliest observation of a newly hatched brood is April 27. Hatching normally occurs during the first half of May. Clutch size ranged from four to six (average 5.4) and more than half of the nests contained six eggs. Migrant geese sometimes deposit eggs on areas where they stop to rest, some distance from their breeding grounds.

Depicted plant: Golden Alexanders (*Zizia aurea*)

WOOD DUCK

Aix sponsa

Summer Duck, Tree Duck, Woodie

One evening in late September more than thirty years ago, Mumford happened to be at a pond overgrown with buttonbush near Lake Manitou in Fulton County. Suddenly through the twilight came small groups of wood ducks, twisting and turning as they approached, flying fairly close to the ground. With little hesitation, group after group pitched into the buttonbushes and noisily plunged through the branches down to the water. Some of the females gave squealing calls, but mostly the birds were silent. As the dusk deepened and more and more birds arrived, the noise level increased. It became difficult to see the birds, except against the sky. By dark, at least two hundred were present; as they milled about getting settled for the night, they called from time to time. At many other roosting sites in Indiana this scenario is repeated each fall, for this beautiful duck is a common nesting species in the state. Individual sites are used year after year, as long as they remain suitable.

Wood ducks were once plentiful in the eastern half of the United States, but by the early 1900s the population was declining rapidly. A ban on hunting from 1918 to 1938 and strict regulations thereafter may have saved the bird from extinction. The species suffered another setback in Indiana and the rest of the Mississippi Flyway during the 1950s, but since then has enjoyed a safe level of population.

Today the wood duck is a common spring and fall migrant and summer resident, probably breeding in every county of the state. It is casual in winter, except at Muscatatuck National Wildlife Refuge, where on four Christmas bird counts between 1974 and 1980 numbers from 40 to 125 have been recorded. Sutherland (1971) estimated the Indiana breeding population of wood ducks to be about 40,000.

During spring, summer, and fall, nearly every sizable stream or drainage ditch with large trees nearby harbors wood ducks. They also inhabit the sloughs and overflows along rivers. Wood ducks may use nearly any water area; females with broods have been observed on tiny temporary ponds. Wood ducks are especially attracted to lakes, marshes, sloughs, and streams where there are drifts, trees, and logs lying in the water and overhanging vegetation along the banks. The birds like to rest and loaf out of the water in such sites. Good rearing cover is often a pond or marsh where yellow water lily, American lotus, cattail, or other emergent aquatic plants form dense stands in summer. As we mentioned above, ponds with buttonbush are a favorite roosting area. Large numbers of woodies also congregate in marshes to roost. During spring and fall, flooded timberlands along streams are used extensively by this duck.

By the last half of February wood ducks are present throughout Indiana. Peak numbers are probably reached from late March to early April. On March 20, 1981, there were 100 at Jasper-Pulaski Fish and Wildlife Area. Summer residents with that year's young begin to flock by late July, and numbers steadily increase at favorite roosting sites while the adults undergo their eclipse molt. The largest numbers of wood ducks are usually found at Jasper-Pulaski and Willow Slough in October, but some years the peak has been the first week of September. There were 2,000 at Willow Slough the week of September 2 to 8, 1978, and 2,500 at Jasper-Pulaski between August 28 and September 3, 1976. By mid-November most wood ducks have left the state, but some linger into December and a relatively small number winter here.

Since wood ducks nest primarily in natural cavities high in trees, data on egg laying and hatching dates from such sites are difficult to obtain. Practically all the nesting information we have was derived from inspections of nesting boxes. Soon after their arrival, pairs of birds—the males in their spectacular breeding plumage—begin searching for suitable nesting sites. Dorthy Buck watched a pair looking at a prospective nesting box on February 22 in LaPorte County. Subsequently, this box was selected. The male, like other ducks, then goes off to moult into his eclipse plumage, leaving the female to incubate the eggs and raise the young. It is known that egg laying begins in southern Indiana by the first half of March. Since two to five females will sometimes lay eggs in the same nest,

WOOD DUCK

clutch size is difficult to determine; such nests, termed dump nests, are frequently found in nesting boxes. In nearly fifty nests examined, clutch size varied from six eggs to thirty-three. Fifteen is thought to be about the maximum number for a single female. The incubation period averages about thirty days. Downy young ducklings have been seen with females as early as April 19 and as late as August 7.

Young wood ducks consume a variety of insects. We have seen day-old woodies snatching flying insects with their beaks. As the ducks grow older their diet becomes increasingly vegetarian. A favorite food of adults is acorns, especially those of the pin oak and white oak. Waste grain is also eaten; this duck can sometimes be seen feeding in picked cornfields.

GREEN-WINGED TEAL

Anas crecca

This tiny dabbling duck is usually not seen in large numbers except in the fall at certain marshes, such as those at the Willow Slough Fish and Wildlife Area. In spring, small numbers are usually observed: pairs or groups containing three to eight. Single drakes are frequently encountered on small ponds in spring and a male in full breeding plumage is a striking and dainty duck. Green-winged teal are fast flyers, darting and wheeling about in closely packed flocks, with swift wingbeats. When greenwings are present in their greatest numbers, during fall migration, they are mostly in rather drab plumage, the males having molted their bright breeding plumage for a more somber fall and winter one. An occasional male retains much of its spring color into the fall. Mixed flocks of greenwings and blue-winged teal are commonplace, and the two species are difficult to distinguish in the water. In flight, however, the large blue wing patches of the bluewing are conspicuous.

The green-winged teal was formerly classed as a common migrant and a winter resident. Butler thought it might be a rare summer resident locally in northern Indiana. Today it seems to be a fairly common migrant and regular winter resident, usually in small numbers. It is a casual nesting species in the northern region.

This little duck prefers shallow marshes, overflows, and ponds. Bellrose mentioned its preference for feeding on mudflats. In these habitats it finds its varied diet of seeds, insects, grain, and mollusks. The large fall congregations of greenwings at Willow Slough are in the rather extensive marshes, where in some years the water levels are low and mudflats abound.

Because they winter throughout the state, the first spring migrants may be missed. Peak flights occur in southern Indiana in mid-March, but during April in the northern part. There were seventy at the Kankakee Fish and Wildlife Area on April 22, 1962. Birds linger into May in central and northern Indiana, and there are numerous records for June and July.

Fall migration normally begins the last half of August, but there is a record of one greenwing at the Falls of the Ohio on August 1. The peak of fall migration is usually between mid-October and mid-November, perhaps a week later in southern Indiana. Fall migrants greatly outnumber spring migrants. For example, during the week of

November 5 through 11, 1977, there were 1,500 at Willow Slough, and 600 were recorded around November 1, 1977, and from October 14 through 20, 1978, at Jasper-Pulaski.

From 1943 to 1981, the greenwing was reported on seventy-nine Christmas bird counts from seventeen counties throughout the state, thirty-one of them taken in Monroe County. The largest number reported on a Christmas count was 450 at Lake Monroe in 1969.

Although we have only three nesting records for the state, there is the distinct possibility that more green-wings nest and go undetected, especially in northern Indiana where blue-winged teal nest. Female teal with broods on the water are not easy to identify as to species. Two pairs of greenwings nested at Jasper-Pulaski in the summer of 1967, according to Russell R. Hyer. James E. Savery reported a brood at the Winamac Fish and Wildlife Area in 1974. The other record is of a brood observed near Decatur on July 24, 1978, by Larry L. Parker.

Depicted plant: Hoary puccoon (*Lithospermum canescens*)

AMERICAN BLACK DUCK

Anas rubripes

Black Mallard, Dusky Duck, Red-legged Black Duck, Black Duck

This large, handsome duck is a favorite of duck hunters and birdwatchers alike: hunters for its wariness and the sport it provides them—not to mention the fact that it makes very good eating; birders because it is fun to watch and easily identified even at long distances by the combination of blackish body and silvery white wing linings, so conspicuous in flight.

Butler designated the black duck as an uncommon migrant, occasional winter resident, and rare summer resident, and felt sure that proof of nesting in the state would eventually be obtained. Since 1900, this duck has become much more abundant in Indiana, although in the Mississippi Flyway as a whole there was a steady decline between 1952 and 1974. This decrease was evident in Indiana too, as we can tell from censuses of wintering birds and Christmas bird counts. We consider the black duck a permanent resident, fairly common migrant, and casual nesting species, primarily across northern Indiana. It winters in greatest numbers in southwestern Indiana, where it is fairly common; elsewhere it is generally a rare winter resident, locally more abundant under certain conditions.

Black ducks and mallards utilize much the same kinds of habitat at all seasons and are common associates, and there is considerable hybridization. The black duck's migration patterns are also similar to those of the mallard; it moves northward in spring as soon as the ice breaks up. Spring migration peaks are sometimes reached the first week of March in central and northern Indiana. Examples of peak numbers are as follows: Jasper-Pulaski, April 1, 1938 (1,000); Willow Slough, February 26–March 2, 1952 (800). By far the largest numbers of black ducks in the state occur during fall and winter. Movement begins in early September, but most years the bulk of the fall migration takes place in November. At Hovey Lake, where large numbers may winter, there is a rather steady increase of birds throughout November and much of December. The largest concentrations there were recorded in the winters of 1949–50 and 1950–51: more than twenty thousand each year.

Like the mallard, the black duck pairs during the winter. This was quite evident at Hovey Lake, where nearly all of the black ducks we saw after early January were in pairs. As we drove along the road bordering the west side of the lake, these pairs were scattered among the huge cypress trees. Looking down on the birds from the road, it was easy to distinguish the males from the females; the males had prominent, silver-colored tertials. (A female is shown in our illustration.)

Some black ducks nest across the northern end of the state, but probably most nest in the northeastern corner. In 1951 Lester G. Harding showed Mumford several black duck nests along the Pigeon River in Lagrange County. The earliest record of an Indiana nest of the black duck was at Jasper-Pulaski in 1943. It reportedly also bred in Steuben County the same year. Between 1945 and 1954, this duck is known to have nested in nine counties; all but one of these sites were in the northern third of Indiana, the other was in Shelby County. Broods of black ducks were seen nearly every year from 1956 to 1963 at the Indianapolis Sewage Disposal Plant. Our next (and latest) nesting record was obtained in 1974, when this duck nested at Atterbury Fish and Wildlife Area. The current summer status of the black duck needs reevaluation; many of the former nesting areas may now be deserted, and there are records of its presence during nesting season from other counties.

Specific nesting sites include an unplowed red clover field containing briers and weeds; a small patch of wet prairie; and an alfalfa field. Seventeen black duck nests were reportedly destroyed in one 24-acre alfalfa field in Lagrange County.

The number of eggs per clutch in four nests ranged from 9 to 13, averaging 10. Eggs were observed in nests from April 15 to June 2, but one nest that was watched rather closely (and was destroyed) was due to hatch on June 19. We would expect the black duck's nesting chronology to be about the same as the mallard's. It, like many other species of duck, will renest if its first nest is destroyed.

Although mallards and black ducks mingle freely to feed on waste corn and other grains, black ducks consume more animal matter than mallards do. A black duck shot in fall along the Tippecanoe River contained five gizzard shad 3 to 3.7 inches long in its digestive tract. No other food was present.

Depicted plant: Moccasin-flower (*Cypripedium acaule*)

MALLARD

Anas platyrhynchos

Greenhead, Greenhead Mallard, Susie (female)

When most people hear the word "duck," the mental picture they form is apt to be of a mallard, the showy bird that is the ancestor of various strains of domestic ducks. There are more mallards in the Mississippi Flyway (which includes Indiana) than anywhere else in the United States, and they have always been held in high esteem by wildfowl hunters here. During migration sometimes thousands of the birds will gather at choice staging areas. We will never forget several fall and winter days back in the late forties and early fifties when we rowed a boat into the Dry Lake refuge section of Hovey Lake Fish and Wildlife Area and gazed out over thirty acres of mallards that completely covered the water. Because the birds were mostly males, Dry Lake was a living, moving carpet of green. It was impossible to estimate their numbers to within fifty thousand, much less make an accurate count.

As the birds took alarm and flushed, the many thousands in the flooded brush surrounding the open water would also take wing, in successive waves, until the sky from horizon to horizon was filled with them. Sadly, today's birders—and tomorrow's—may never have a chance to see such a spectacular sight; the numbers of mallards in the Mississippi Flyway have declined drastically in the past twenty years.

The mallard has probably always been a permanent resident in Indiana, but is especially abundant during migration. The major wintering concentrations have historically been in the southwestern corner. Today it is a common migrant and winter resident throughout the state and an uncommon summer resident in the northern quarter. It breeds sparingly in the center portion of the state, and less frequently still in the southern region, where

MALLARD

suitable habitat is scarce. Winter numbers vary with the depth of snow cover and the amount of open water; the greatest numbers are still regularly found in winter in the southwestern section.

Mallards are likely to be found wherever there is water, from ditches and tiny ponds to Lake Michigan. The greatest concentrations are normally found at the various fish and wildlife areas, which provide adequate protection, favorable habitat, and a nearby food supply. For many years the two most important of these areas in terms of total numbers of birds, have been Willow Slough and Hovey Lake, both of which are situated along a major fall migration corridor down the western side of Indiana. Since the advent of mechanical crop harvesters, mallards and other waterfowl have adapted well to feeding in picked cornfields and other grain fields. They also eat the seeds or leaves of pondweed, smartweed, wild celery, and other plants.

The mallard is an early spring migrant: wintering birds begin pushing north as soon as weather permits, sometimes in early February. The bulk of the spring migrants probably cross the state between late February and April 1, usually peaking sometime in March. By far the largest number of spring migrants—15,000—was recorded at Willow Slough on March 24, 1953.

There are many more mallards in Indiana during the fall migration, although in northern Indiana in early fall it is difficult to determine whether local increases are due to arriving migrants or to local post-breeding congregations. Such flocks are noticeable by late August. During the first week of September we can see what are evidently migrants arriving at Jasper-Pulaski and Willow Slough. Small numbers of migrating mallards reach Hovey Lake by the first week of October.

During fall migration, the number of birds present in an area after the first major flight usually increases until the wintering group has stabilized or inclement weather triggers further migration. More mallards are usually present in Indiana in November than any other month. During the week ending November 12, 1976, there were 27,000 at Willow Slough. The largest congregations of mallards occur throughout December and January; these are mostly wintering flocks. About a quarter of a million mallards were recorded each year during the 1950, 1952, and 1954 Hovey Lake Christmas bird counts. On December 31, 1955, there were 150,000 at Willow Slough. On December 29, 1956, an estimated 200,000 mallards were counted there. By contrast, the largest numbers seen on a Willow Slough Christmas count from 1973 to 1982 were 2,000 (in 1973) and 1,500 (in 1979).

During the nesting season, mallards have always been most numerous across the northern three tiers of counties. Nowadays so many domestic and semidomestic birds are kept throughout the state that things get a bit confused, and we have never had much data on the mallard's abundance in the state as a breeding bird. Mallards engage in courtship in winter and usually pair up by January. Most mallard nests found in Indiana have been on the ground, at no great distance from water, in habitats that included a red clover field, a field of oats, a grassy border of marsh, old pasture, sedge/grass meadow, fallow field, a grassy depression between sand dunes, on muskrat houses over water, and about the brushy/weedy edges of potholes. Nests in low-lying areas subject to seasonal flooding are usually constructed on top of a grass hummock. In some of the larger marshes, the birds nest on levees and along roads.

Nests examined contained eggs as early as March 25 and as late as June 29. Clutch size for 36 nests ranged from 7 to 14 eggs (average 10), but some of the smaller clutches may have been incomplete.

The familiar quacking calls associated with the mallard are made by the female; it is these calls that are imitated by hunters when attempting to coax birds close enough for shooting. Male mallards utter a soft *quek* call. As the birds fly out to feed, one often hears the rapidly repeated *tik-tik-tik-tik-tik* feeding call.

Mallards hybridize with other ducks, especially the black duck. We have seen numerous mallard/black duck crosses and examined several mallard/northern pintail hybrids taken in Indiana.

Depicted tree: Pin cherry (*Prunus pensylvanica*)

NORTHERN PINTAIL

Anas acuta

Sprig, Pintail, Pintailed Duck, Sprigtail, Sea Pheasant

A spring flight of streamlined pintails, passing swiftly overhead and uttering their short whistles, delights the eye and pleases the ear of birder and hunter alike. It is especially interesting to watch several males courting a lone female. Erratically and at great speed the birds fly over the marshes, each male attempting to reach a point in front of the female where he can best display his fine plumage. Such flights are normally noisy, since the drakes call while performing their acrobatics. Birds sitting on the water appear quite buoyant, and when alarmed or alert stretch their long necks upward and hold their heads high. When the Kankakee River was flooded during early spring in the late 1940s, hundreds and hundreds of pintails were sometimes found there in the flooded cornfields near Shelby and Thayer.

Butler called the pintail an abundant spring migrant and uncommon fall migrant and thought perhaps a few occasionally wintered, although he had no winter records. We consider it a regular and fairly common migrant, but less numerous in fall than in spring. It winters throughout the state in small numbers, with the largest concentrations being recorded from the Hovey Lake area. There is a single nesting record, but pintails have been seen during the nesting season in various northern Indiana counties. They prefer extensive, shallow marshes and flooded fields, but use many different kinds of water areas.

The hardy pintail is one of the first ducks to migrate north in the spring, often appearing as soon as open water is available. Spring migrants usually pass through the state rather quickly. James D. McCall mentioned the species' "moving back north" in early January in Posey County, where as many as 3,000 were known to winter in the late 1940s. Migrants usually reach their peak in early March; by April 1 relatively few remain. A pair was noted April 28, 1949, in Posey County; a female was seen until May 26, 1981, at Atterbury Fish and Wildlife Area. A few birds have been observed in June in Dearborn, Newton, Tippecanoe, and Whitley Counties, and there are July records for Lake, Newton, and Warren Counties. During the summer of 1979, as many as five were seen at Willow Slough until August 15 by Ted T. Cable. Fall migration begins early, normally in August, and migrants have reached Gibson County by August 16.

The major peaks of fall migration, however, are as follows: Jasper-Pulaski and Willow Slough, last half of October; Marion County, November; Posey County, last half of November.

The maximum number of spring migrants has been observed in the southern region: 5,000 were noted in Posey County; 5,000 in Warrick County. They have not been seen elsewhere in the state in such numbers; perhaps the birds take northward routes that bypass Indiana, or overfly the remainder of the state in their migrations. The maximum number for the Willow Slough area is 2,500 from March 2–8, 1952. Except for the Hovey Lake area, fall migrants are not nearly so abundant. For example, the maximum for Willow Slough is 700 (October 7–14, 1977). There were 3,000 at Hovey Lake the week of November 21–28, 1948, and 5,000 on December 12, 1948.

Since there are numerous records of pintails' presence in the state during nesting season, it was long suspected that a few might breed here. The single published record is of a female seen with six young in Whitley County in June 1958 (Nolan, 1958).

Pintails feed on a variety of seeds of moisture-loving plants, and on small grains (corn is not favored). We have noticed that pintails sometimes accompany mallards and black ducks feeding in picked cornfields.

BLUE-WINGED TEAL

Anas discors

Bluewing

The blue-winged teal is one of the best-known ducks in Indiana, for it is relatively tame, widespread, and readily observed during spring and fall migrations. The male in spring is particularly striking in color, but the large "teal blue" wing patches of both sexes at all seasons simplify identification in flight and make it instantly possible to distinguish between blue-winged and green-winged teal in the field. Blue-winged teal sometimes fly in tightly packed flocks, twisting and turning as a single bird, the blue wing patches now in view, now hidden, as all the birds simultaneously turn their bodies. Amos W. Butler marveled at these aerial maneuvers, remarking that their speed and method of flight reminded him of the flight of the passenger pigeon.

Around 1900 this teal was a common migrant and local summer resident, known to nest in Gibson, Knox, Lake, Porter, and Starke Counties. Butler noted that it was most abundant in the fall. It is still a common migrant and found in largest numbers in the fall migration period. There are now nesting records for twenty-six counties throughout the state, but most nest in the northern three tiers of counties. There are several records of

wintering birds, but we cannot verify all of them. Normally no blue-winged teal remain in Indiana during the winter, but there is always the possibility of injured or sick birds being found at that season. It should probably be considered a casual winter resident until further data are at hand.

Blue-winged teal are likely to be found in much the same habitat as green-winged teal: shallow marshes, potholes, ponds, flooded fields, along ditches or streams, and on borrow pits. Some of the largest congregations of bluewings reported in Indiana were observed in flooded river bottoms during the fall.

This teal is a late spring or early fall migrant that shuns cold weather for the most part. For the state as a whole, spring migrants arrive around mid-March. An occasional bird has been reported in late February. Peak numbers are usually encountered in the southern region the last half of March, in central Indiana about a week later, and in northern Indiana the last week of March or first half of April. Five hundred were seen in Gibson County on March 20, 1976, and the same number in Marion County on March 29, 1970. About 400 were recorded in St.

Joseph County on March 28, 1980. Summering birds have been observed throughout the state, but tend to be mostly concentrated in the northern third, where the major nesting habitats are located. It is interesting that in the past decade there have been nesting records in six counties in the southern half of the state—before 1968 none was known to have nested since 1897.

In northern Indiana it is hard to tell fall migrants from the locally reared young, which gather at staging areas quite early. Peak numbers of from 1,000 to 1,500 are at Willow Slough the last half of August and migration peaks of from 150 to 600 have been noted at Jasper-Pulaski from late August to the first week of September. On September 23, 1979, there were 2,000 blue-winged teals in the Patoka River bottoms. Most bluewings have departed from Indiana by mid-November. All are normally gone by December 1, but we have at least five records for this teal in Indiana during December. Four of these reports resulted from Christmas bird counts and in-

volved from one to four birds each. But on December 21, 1980, there were twelve bluewings at Eagle Creek Reservoir, Indianapolis.

Favored habitat for nesting is weedy and grassy old fields or marsh borders, not far from water. At Lafayette there were at least six nests in an alfalfa field next to a shallow marsh in May. Most of the nests we have examined were quite well hidden in dense bluegrass or other ground cover. Incubating females are difficult to flush from their nests, permitting humans to walk very close. The clutch size in twenty nests ranged from four to thirteen and averaged nine, but the several small clutches included in this sample may have been incomplete. Eggs were observed in nests from April 24 to July 17. Number of young per brood with females averaged nine and ranged from five to twelve. Some of these broods were probably incomplete. Females with accompanying young were noted from May 13 to August 29.

Depicted plant: Yellow stargrass (*Hypoxis hirsuta*)

BLUE-WINGED TEAL

CINNAMON TEAL

Anas cyanoptera

This showy western species is an accidental to casual migrant, mostly in the spring, that has been reported in the state at least seven times. We cannot vouch for the authenticity of all of these sightings, but all may be valid. Adult males in spring, with their reddish bodies and blue wing patches, are of course unmistakable. Accurately distinguishing female cinnamon teals from female blue-winged teals in the field, however, is virtually impossible.

The first record is of ten or twelve cinnamon teal, two of them adult males, seen near Hammond (Brodkorb, 1926b). If valid, this is quite remarkable, since all other Indiana sightings involved single birds. A male was collected from a flock of blue-winged teals near Mitchell (Lawrence County) on May 4, 1940. A male was observed at Kankakee Fish and Wildlife Area on February 29, 1944, and another at Jasper-Pulaski from March 26 to April 1, 1944 (McKeever, 1944). Another was photographed at Muscatatuck National Wildlife Refuge in April 1972. Charles E. Mills found a male near Oakland City (Gibson County) on April 7, 1977. Timothy C. Keller, Daniel Mosher, and Mark C. Rhodes identified a molting male in Lake County on August 23, 1980.

NORTHERN SHOVELER

Anas clypeata

Shoveler, Shoveler Duck, Spoonbill, Spoony

This bird is known to duck hunters as the spoonbill or spoony. The drake is frequently mistaken for the larger but somewhat similar male mallard. Male shovelers in breeding plumage are very showy indeed, although some think the outsized beak detracts from their beauty. One should really find a male shoveler at sunup on a small marshy pond in late April to see him at his best: floating on the mirrorlike surface of the water with the sun's low rays highlighting his nuptial finery.

Butler listed this duck as a "not uncommon" migrant, a rare summer resident, and a possible winter resident in southern Indiana. Today it is a fairly common spring migrant, an uncommon fall migrant, and casual in winter.

We tend to associate the shoveler with the small, shallow marshes, potholes, and ponds in which it is usually seen during migration. The largest concentrations have been found in the more extensive marshes, but fairly large groups may sometimes be seen in flooded cultivated fields.

Although small numbers of shovelers winter throughout the state, spring migrants are usually evident about mid-March. There are records from all regions for the

NORTHERN SHOVELER

last week of February, but these were undoubtedly early migrants or wintering birds. The numbers of shovelers passing through Indiana in spring are much greater than in fall. Migration peaks have been detected in central and northern Indiana from the last half of March to mid-April. There were 400 shovelers at Willow Slough April 7 to 13, 1952, and on March 26, 1969, a reported 175 were present in Marion County. Most migrants have left the state by May 1, although some linger through May and a very small number may be present throughout the summer. A pair occasionally nests in northern Indiana. Fall migration is evident mostly during the first half of September, but some shovelers have reached Wayne County by August 16 and Gibson County by August 17. The peak flights occur in the northern region during October. Maximum numbers observed in the fall at Jasper-Pulaski and Willow Slough were fifty and one hundred respectively. By December 1 there are relatively few shovelers left in the state, but the species has been recorded on twenty-two Christmas bird counts. The maximum number seen during one of these was thirty at Eagle Creek Reservoir (Marion County) on December 17, 1978. On twenty-one other Christmas counts the number varied from one to ten.

There are at least six nesting records for the state, all from three counties in the northwestern corner. Butler noted that the shoveler nested in Lake County (no date given) and Starke County (May 4, 1890). Nests with eggs were found in Lake County in 1935 and 1936, and a female with a brood was seen there in 1965. A female and brood were seen at Willow Slough (Newton County) in 1979. Three nests for which there were egg counts contained eight, nine, and nine each, from May 4 to July 14. One brood of very small young was seen on June 11. One nest was reportedly on the ground in a clump of willows near the edge of a meadow.

Shovelers like to feed on surface plankton, busily moving about on the surface of the water with their beaks partially submerged, taking in food and water and expelling the water through the lamellae along the sides of their beaks. We have watched a small group of shovelers that were feeding in this manner, spinning around in circles on the water, probably to stir up food. In shallow feeding areas, the birds usually feed by immersing their heads and swimming along slowly. They also eat aquatic animals and seeds of various plants.

When shovelers flush from the water, their wings make a characteristic clattering sound by which a knowledgeable observer can identify them. We have noticed in spring a tendency for shovelers to occur in groups composed of two males and a female.

Depicted plant: Blue-eyed grass (*Sisyrinchium angustifolium*)

GADWALL

Anas strepera

Gray Duck

The somber gray gadwall is generally inconspicuous and quiet. It is present in small numbers during spring and fall migrations, but because of its retiring nature and unspectacular coloring many birders probably fail to recognize it until it flushes and the white speculum—a good field identification mark—becomes evident. We have noticed that gadwalls seem to prefer quiet, shallow bays around the border of marshes or lakes. At Hovey Lake this species could usually be found on Pirogue Slough, a narrow, shallow area sheltered from the wind. The bulk of the gadwall population and most of the major migration corridors are west of Indiana.

In 1898, the gadwall was classified as a rare migrant in Indiana: there were "but few records of its occurrence." Bellrose (1976) noted that gadwalls had increased steadily in number since the late 1950s; this increase seems to be borne out by recent weekly fall migration counts for the Jasper-Pulaski and Willow Slough Fish and Wildlife Areas by Donald T. Sporre. The gadwall is a regular but rare to uncommon migrant in Indiana, being considerably more abundant in fall than in spring. It winters throughout Indiana, but normally in small numbers.

The largest numbers of gadwalls have been observed in marshy habitats, mostly at fish and wildlife areas, where there is considerable marshland. Gadwalls feed primarily on submerged aquatic plants and their seeds, often in company with American wigeons or American coots. For several years in the late 1940s and early 1950s gadwalls frequented Indian Lake (Marion County) in some numbers in late winter and early spring. No doubt some choice food was available there during that period.

Much of the migration of gadwalls occurs at night. The maximum numbers of birds are seen during spring migration in late March and early April. Stragglers remain until about mid-May. One bird was present until June 1, 1944, at Jasper-Pulaski; two were seen in Porter County in early June 1978; and five were noted at Willow Slough as late as June 23, 1974, by Edward M. Hopkins. The spring maximum, eighty, was at Eagle Creek Reservoir, Indianapolis, April 3, 1969. We have no records for July and only one for August. On August 17, 1952, Mumford and Val Nolan Jr. observed two gadwalls at Willow Slough. Fall migrants begin arriving the first half of September and generally reach a peak of abundance in northern Indiana from the last half of October to mid-November, or, in some years, slightly later. Peak fall migration dates for the rest of the state are about the same. Peak numbers at both Willow Slough and Jasper-Pulaski reached five hundred during the years 1976 to 1978.

The gadwall has been recorded on Christmas bird counts throughout the state. Two hundred were seen at Lake Monroe December 28, 1969, and 150 in Indianapolis during the winter of 1948–49.

EURASIAN WIGEON

Anas penelope

European Widgeon, Widgeon

This Old-World counterpart of the familiar American wigeon is a rare visitor to Indiana, where it has been recorded at least twenty-one times. In 1903 Ruthven Deane reported that there were only seventeen records of this showy duck in the interior of the United States, nine of which were for Indiana. All nine had evidently been shot by hunters along a thirty-mile stretch of the Kankakee River. It would be interesting to know what conditions caused this species to occur with such frequency in that location. Most of the Indiana sightings have been in seven counties in the northwestern corner, but one was at Geist Reservoir near Indianapolis, one in Wayne County, and one in Henry County.

Eighteen of the observations were made from March 9 to May 9; one was on September 23 and one October 30–31; the remaining record was not dated except to year. In many cases the Eurasian wigeons were in the company of American wigeons, with which they often associate. It was stated that one of the Eurasian wigeons shot at English Lake came to the duck decoys alone, although there were American wigeons in the area that day. All but one of the sightings are of single birds (possibly all males), but on April 21, 1930, two were reported at Hobart. At least one of the birds killed by a duck hunter was a female; where known, the remainder of those shot were males.

The Eurasian wigeon frequents the same habitats as its American cousin, being found on lakes, ponds, marshes, and flooded fields.

There were three reports from 1902 to 1943, and there have been ten observations since 1943, the most recent being April 3, 1982.

AMERICAN WIGEON

Anas americana

Baldpate

The presence of this duck is often made known by its mellow, piping three-note whistle, given both in flight and on the water. The males are especially vocal toward the end of the mating season, when as many as ten of them may be courting a single female. There is much competition, for most of the females have already mated and some of the males will probably have to go without a mate for the season. The courting behavior consists mostly of aerial chases over the marshes in twisting, turning, erratic flight, each male attempting to position himself for optimum display of his fine plumage. During these flights they keep up their whistling calls. It is a colorful performance.

Butler considered this wigeon a common migrant and rare summer resident in northern Indiana but made no mention of wintering birds. He reported the sighting of two broods (Starke and Steuben Counties). Today this duck is a fairly common spring migrant and uncommon fall migrant. We know of no additional breeding records. The species winters throughout the state, usually in small numbers.

American wigeons congregate on reservoirs and in large marshes and overflow areas, usually with other ducks. Small numbers may be found on nearly any type of aquatic habitat, including small ponds, streams, and drainage ditches.

Migrants arrive in southern Indiana by mid-February (possibly earlier) and by the last week of that month have reached the northern portion. The dates of peak numbers fluctuate somewhat from year to year; for example, in Marion County flight waves have been recorded between March 18 and April 16 for nine different years. The greatest numbers observed there have been 200 to 300, all the first half of April. There were 1,000 wigeons at the Kankakee Fish and Wildlife Area on March 22, 1964, and 945 in Newton County March 13, 1952. Migrants have largely left southern Indiana by mid-April and the remainder of the state by June 1. A few individuals, mostly males, are present throughout the summer in northern Indiana. We have June and July records for Jasper, Kosciusko, Lake, Newton, Tippecanoe, and Wayne Counties.

By mid-August fall migrants are arriving in northwestern Indiana. Shortly after mid-September (possibly earlier) migrants appear in southwestern Indiana. Migration peaks in northern Indiana during the last half of October, and in central Indiana at about the same time or in November. We have little information for the southern region. At Jasper-Pulaski, a fall maximum of 700 was reached the week of October 8 to 14, 1951. During the last half of October 1977, there were 2,000 at Willow Slough.

Although there are many records of American wigeons on Christmas bird counts, we have relatively few from the first week of January to the first week of February. Whether this is because the birds depart in early January or because observers are not afield during that month is not certain. The largest number of birds reported on a Christmas count was on December 28, 1969, when 1,100 were at Lake Monroe. By late December, the majority of the wigeons present are in the southern half of the state.

Unlike most other dabbling ducks that occur in Indiana, the American wigeon feeds heavily on the leaves and stems of submerged aquatic plants. If this vegetation is growing in shallow water the birds can reach it themselves, but in deeper water they appear to rely on diving ducks and coots, which can reach the more deeply submerged plants, to bring their favorite foods to the surface. Thus, wigeons are quite frequently seen on the water in rafts of coots or flocks of diving ducks. When these birds surface, the wigeon quickly moves in and either attempts to take the food or feeds on plant fragments that are dropped. Small numbers of wigeons have been observed feeding with mallards and black ducks in picked cornfields, and three wigeons were once observed feeding in a wheatfield with mallards in early April.

CANVASBACK

Aythya valisineria

Canvas-back Duck, Can

To a duck hunter, the driving flight of a string of canvasbacks "working" the decoys time and time again, circling warily, swinging in, swinging out, circling, and repeating the performance several times, is a heart-stopping sight. The great birds are capable of flying at considerable speed, often rushing over the decoys with a swoosh of wings audible for some distance. Frequently, evidently sensing that something is amiss, they will not come in to the decoys; instead with one last pass out of gunshot range, they disappear from sight, leaving the hunter simultaneously deflated and thrilled.

We see all too few canvasbacks in Indiana these days, and they are less numerous in fall than in spring. In the early part of the century large numbers of them congregated to feed on the

wild celery at Wolf Lake, Lake Wawasee, Lake Maxinkuckee, and probably other lakes in northern Indiana. According to Woodruff (1907), in the 1870s the "water-celery beds in Calumet and Wolf lakes fairly swarmed" with them, and sportsmen came from "the east and even from Europe to bag them." Evermann and Clark (1920) remarked that coots and ducks were especially fond of the wild celery's white stolons (winter buds) put out by the rootstock in autumn; since these stolons were the starters for the next season's growth, the ducks themselves restricted the abundance and distribution of this plant: "Soon after the waterfowl arrive, torn up plants of this species are washed up in great rolls along shore, probably having been pulled up by these birds."

Butler wrote that the canvasback was a regular migrant, but was uncommon in some years, even in the lake district. He considered it quite rare throughout the greater part of the state, and knew of no winter or summer records. The canvasback has fallen on hard times and in 1936 and 1937 it was given complete protection from hunting. Since 1958 there have been restrictions on the hunting of the canvasback, but its populations are not faring well. Brodkorb (1926a) reported 5,000 canvasbacks on Wolf Lake (on the Illinois-Indiana state line) on April 3, 1926. This is the last record of such a large assemblage. In the late 1940s and early 1950s, fairly large numbers—1,000 to 3,000 birds—were observed in southwestern Indiana (primarily at Hovey Lake). Since 1955 the largest congregation has not exceeded 400. The canvasback today is an uncommon to rare migrant throughout the state, but it occurs locally in fair numbers. It winters in small numbers in all sections, but most wintering birds are now found on Lake Monroe and in Gibson County.

The canvasback is an early spring migrant, sometimes reaching northern Indiana by mid-February. Most of them pass through during March and are generally present in the greatest numbers in late March or early April. There were 1,500 at Hovey Lake on March 8, 1949, and only 22 ten days later. The largest number reported from Willow Slough was 100, on March 29, 1952. Stragglers (most of them males) remain in small numbers throughout May and an occasional bird is present in June or July. There is one August record (possibly a cripple) and no reports for September.

Fall migrants, which are relatively scarce, begin entering northern Indiana the first week of October. The week of November 4–11, 1943, there were 500 at Lake Maxinkuckee. There were 130 in Steuben County on November 24, 1978.

At Hovey Lake, where the largest wintering concentrations were formerly observed, 3,500 were present January 9, 1952, and 2,000 each on December 23, 1951, and from February 13 to 16, 1949. With the recent impoundment of a new, large lake (Northern Indiana Public Service Company) in western Gibson County, this area has become one of the current major wintering sites. On December 28, 1976, there were 386 canvasbacks there. From 200 to 330 wintered on Lake Monroe during 1969–70, 1974–75, and 1975–76.

Other than Lake Michigan, the canvasback seems to prefer the larger lakes and reservoirs. Small numbers may be also seen along rivers, on ponds, small marshes, gravel pits, and borrow pits. The birds may feed in relatively deep water. They frequently form rafts, usually with other divers, and loaf by day well offshore on the larger bodies of water.

Though famed for feeding on wild celery (as indicated by the species name, valisineria), canvasbacks consume numerous other plant parts and take a considerable amount of animal life. A male collected along the Wabash River in mid-March had nothing but dragonfly larvae in its gullet. During a Christmas bird count in Gibson County, a group of canvasbacks was seen feeding on gizzard shad. To keep the turbines of the power plant from being fouled by fish, screens had been placed in the warm water outlets. The canvasbacks were swimming along this wire screen and diving beneath the surface every few seconds to catch the shad, which averaged about four inches in length.

REDHEAD

Aythya americana

Pochard, Red Head

This handsome duck is unfortunately not nearly as common now in the state as it used to be. Redheads and canvasbacks evidently find the same habitats to their liking and are often seen together, particularly when feeding on some favored submerged aquatic plant. Both species will form large flocks on occasion, but redheads in Indiana are usually seen in small groups. It is a memorable experience to witness the courtship behavior of redheads, as we once did at Starve Hollow Lake in early March. There were twenty-six birds in the group and several of the males were displaying and giving their catlike *meow* calls. (When there are large mixed flocks of diving ducks rafted far offshore in spring, one can frequently detect whether there are redheads in the group by listening for the meowing calls.) Many more redheads migrate across Indiana in spring than in fall, when the state is essentially bypassed. The continental redhead population has undergone considerable fluctuation during the past fifty years, and at various times it has been necessary to protect the redhead with hunting restrictions. There appear to be nearly one-third more males than females in the population and the species has a high annual mortality rate. In view of this, the observation of two thousand redheads in Gibson County on March 9, 1980, by Dennis W. Jones and C. Leroy Harrison is significant.

Butler called the redhead a common migrant and thought it might occasionally breed in the state; he cited no winter records. Today this duck is a fairly common and regular spring migrant and a regular but fairly rare fall migrant. There are two breeding records. For most of the state, the redhead is a casual to rare winter resident, usually in small numbers.

Redheads are commonly observed on marshes, ponds, borrow pits, and lakes. Formerly they congregated on some of Indiana's larger natural lakes (Lake Maxinkuckee, Lake Wawasee) where wild celery, a favorite food, was plentiful. They feed mainly in relatively shallow water, but may raft in the open water far offshore to rest. To date, there seems to be little use of Lake Michigan by redheads.

Spring migration appears to begin early, usually the last half of February, but, since some redheads overwinter, in some areas spring migrants may not be evident. Migration peaks usually occur in southern Indiana in early March, the central section around mid-March, and the northern zone the last half of March. There were 500 at Willow Slough on March 24, 1953. Most migrants have left the state by mid-April, but a few stragglers linger through most of May, and there are a few records for June and July. Most of the stragglers are probably males that did not find mates. During the first week of October redheads move into northern Indiana (there is one September 6 date for Allen County) and some reach Monroe and Lawrence Counties the first week of October and Hovey Lake at least by October 25. According to L. G. Walker, an old duck hunter on Lake Maxinkuckee, there were about five hundred redheads on that lake the week of November 4 to 11, 1943. This is by far the largest number reported during the fall. On December 28, 1969, there were 105 on Lake Monroe. We have winter records from throughout Indiana.

It is possible that a small number of redheads have nested in Indiana, but we have only two records. Jimmy F. New told us that he observed a brood of redheads at

Kingsbury Fish and Wildlife Area during the summer of 1967. Cable (1981) published an account of the first redhead nest found in the state, at Willow Slough. This nest contained four eggs on May 16, 1979, when first found, and ten eggs on May 21 and 22. On the latter date, a thick layer of down covered the eggs. The next visit to the nest was on July 3, and there were indications that it had hatched successfully. This nest was on the surface of the water in a clump of cattails growing in 12.5 inches of water and was constructed entirely of cattails. The general area was a rather extensive cattail marsh and the nest was adjacent to a large area of open water.

Redheads feed to a large extent on plants. Woodruff (1907) had this to say about an area in extreme north-western Indiana: "Wolf and George lakes in Indiana were the favorite feeding grounds of this and [the Canvas-

back]. However, because of the draining of this region, the beds of water-celery and wild rice have been destroyed, thus removing the food supply of these ducks and causing them to seek new feeding grounds." It appears that one of the reasons the redhead was formerly so common at lake Maxinkuckee in the fall was because of the food supply there. Evermann and Clark (1920) wrote that "The Redhead is one of the most abundant ducks at the lake. . . . They are often seen associated with the little bluebills, canvasbacks and coots; most often, perhaps, with the canvasbacks, which it much resembles. . . . It is often seen in Outlet Bay, coming in near shore on fine mornings and quiet afternoons to feed on the wild celery which there abounds." They noted that it also ate pondweed and other aquatics.

Depicted plant: Common cattail (*Typha latifolia*)

REDHEAD

RING-NECKED DUCK

Aythya collaris

Ringneck, Blackjack, Ringbill, Marsh Bluebill, Ring-billed Blackhead, Ring-necked Scaup Duck

In early April when the shallow, temporary ponds in the vicinity of Chalmers (White County) are full, ring-necked ducks are sometimes present by the hundreds. This area was once a famous duck hunting ground during the spring, and migrants traditionally swarmed over the region. Today few such ponds are left undrained, but those that remain are at times nearly covered with ducks. One small puddle contained 120 ringnecks on March 24, 1949. These spring flocks are frequently mixed with lesser scaups and small numbers of redheads. A significant number of ringnecks also migrate across Indiana in autumn en route to their Florida wintering grounds. The largest congregations are observed, however, in the spring.

Around 1900, the ringneck was considered a common spring and fall migrant in northern Indiana and a "tolerably common" migrant in general. There were no nesting records or reports of birds present during the winter. It is still a common spring migrant but uncommon to rare locally in the fall. There are three nesting records for northern Indiana; the ringneck winters, usually in small numbers, throughout the state.

This duck favors shallow marshes, ponds, borrow pits, and flooded fields, but also occurs along rivers and on larger lakes and reservoirs. It is a shallow water feeder and much of its diet consists of vegetable matter (seeds and leaves). Snails, insect larvae, and small clams are also eaten. Some temporary ponds in northwestern Indiana hold water into the summer in some years, allowing damp-soil species of plants such as smartweeds to grow in abundance. No doubt this type of food attracts the ducks during their spring migration.

Migrants begin arriving by late February and peak numbers are reached in March. On March 13–14, 1950, there were 2,500 ring-necked ducks on Hovey Lake, and

from 1,500 to 2,000 were recorded on Lake Monroe in March 1980. For the state as a whole, peak numbers are usually present during the last half of March, but in some years maximum numbers may be present locally about the first week of April. There are numerous records for May and a few each for June and July; many of these stragglers are males. It is possible that more ringnecks breed in the state than is currently known. A few birds, possibly migrants, have been observed in September, but the peak of fall migration occurs in late October and the first half of November. There were 500 ringnecks at Willow Slough the week of October 22–28, 1977. Although the ring-necked duck has been reported on Christmas bird counts from much of the state, the largest numbers were all found in the southern third. The maximum was 700 at Hovey Lake, December 27, 1950.

On June 17, 1949, Charles M. Kirkpatrick and Donald E. Stullken observed a female ringneck at the Purdue Wildlife Area, Tippecanoe County. They revisited the marsh on July 2, 1949, and located a nest with four eggs (two other broken eggs were nearby). The nest was composed mostly of bur-reeds and was in a clump of floating cattail debris, in about three feet of water, twenty-five to thirty yards from shore. In the summer of 1953, James D. McCall observed a ringneck brood at Lake George, Whiting. Conservation officer Robert Thomas and Dale N. Martin saw a brood of ringnecks on a marsh two miles east of Ligonier (Noble County) in July 1957.

One sometimes hears a rather soft *p-r-r-r-t* note given by ringnecks as they flush or as they are in flight. We have heard this note when the birds were "working" decoys.

Depicted plant: Marsh-marigold (*Caltha palustris*)

RING-NECKED DUCK

[TUFTED DUCK]

Aythya fuligula

This Eurasian species is a straggler to North America, where the number of sight observations has increased over the past decade. It would be quite easy to overlook tufted ducks in mixed flocks of scaups and ringnecks because of the similarities of these species. There are three recent records of the tufted duck in the Chicago area, and two for Indiana.

On November 29, 1978, Kenneth J. Brock found one at the Port of Indiana, Porter County. Later that day Mumford and Ted T. Cable met Brock at the site and spent considerable time watching the bird, finally determining that it was an immature male. It was with a small group of lesser scaups, swimming and flying about and resting on the water (Brock et al., 1979). Timothy C. Keller photographed an adult male that may have been a zoo escapee at the Willow Slough Fish and Wildlife Area on May 6, 1982. No doubt other tufted ducks will be found in the state.

GREATER SCAUP

Aythya marila

Big Bluebill, Broadbill, Scaup Duck, Big Black Head Duck, Raft-duck, American Scaup Duck, Blue-bill

It is not surprising that the greater scaup is relatively little known in Indiana. Most people simply assume that any scaup they see is the much more abundant lesser, making no effort to separate the two species. Admittedly it is not an easy task to distinguish between lesser and greater scaups in the field, but with sufficient practice well-marked birds can be identifed. In Indiana, we tend to associate the greater scaup with Lake Michigan, where it is most abundant and most regularly recorded during migration and in winter. The only significant fall migration route that crosses the state is along the Illinois-Indiana state line, lending support to Amos W. Butler's observation that this duck was most often noted in the Wabash River valley before 1900.

Butler considered it a rare migrant. He had no fall records for the state. Although there is a real need for additional migration data, we consider the greater scaup today to be an uncommon to rare but probably regular migrant. Away from Lake Michigan it is seldom seen except in small numbers, and more often in spring than in fall. The largest winter concentrations on Lake Michigan are at Calumet Harbor (one-half mile east of the Illinois-Indiana state line) and at Michigan City. Most greater scaups have been observed on the larger lakes and reservoirs, which appear to be its favored habitat and probably provide its major foods.

Since this duck winters quite commonly and is reported so infrequently from most locations, details of migration are not clear. It seems to migrate mainly in March and early April. A few birds linger into May. Fall migrants have been reported on Lake Michigan in October. There is evidently a rather steady fall increase in the Lake Michigan population, which reaches a peak in late December. In late December 1960, a large raft of greater scaup frequented the Calumet Harbor area and a num-

ber of them were shot by duck hunters. On a December 31, 1977, Christmas bird count in this area, 289 were reported, mostly at Calumet Harbor. Lesser numbers occur around the south end of the lake and as many as 100 have been seen at Michigan City (January 27, 1955). Single greater scaup were shot by hunters at Hovey Lake on December 16, 1953, and December 29, 1955. Practically all wintering birds have thus far been recorded in the western half of Indiana, no farther east than Geist Reservoir.

In January 1982 Harmon P. Weeks, Jr., and Mumford observed a few greater scaups along Trail Creek, Michigan City. The scaups were feeding with a group of mallards by dabbling, submerging only their heads and necks; they were not diving. The water appeared to be quite shallow at the feeding site.

LESSER SCAUP

Aythya affinis

Bluebill, Little Bluebill, Little Black-head, Little Black Head Duck, Lesser Scaup Duck

When Mumford arrived at Hovey Lake on the morning of February 16, 1949, and looked out from the boat dock, he was hardly prepared for the waterfowl spectacle he found: more than 6,000 newly arrived diving ducks. About 4,000 of this congregation were lesser scaups and 2,000 were canvasbacks, but there was a sprinkling of redheads, ring-necked ducks, American goldeneyes, common mergansers, ruddy ducks, buffleheads, and others.

Butler regarded the lesser scaup as an abundant migrant and rare summer resident, noting that it was the most common of all ducks in Indiana. He mentioned the possibility that some might remain in mild winters. Although the numbers of lesser scaups that migrate across the state have drastically decreased since 1900, it is still a common spring migrant, but is now less common during the fall. Numerous birds do winter, but as a rule not in large numbers. It is not unusual to see single lesser scaups throughout the summer. A pair may breed occasionally. There are three nesting records for the state, the most recent in 1952, when James D. McCall observed a female with six young at Lake George, Whiting, on June 25. We have little doubt that others have nested from time to time but gone undetected.

The largest concentrations of lesser scaups are usually seen on the larger lakes and reservoirs. It is not unusual, however, to find birds along roadside ditches, on small ponds or marshes, on gravel and borrow pits, and along rivers. They also congregate in flooded fields and overflows along major rivers.

The spring migration period is quite long, normally beginning in February and ending in May. The bulk of migrants are present during the last half of March and first half of April. There were 5,000 at Geist Reservoir on April 3, 1969. At Willow Slough 2,700 were present from March 13 to 29, 1952, and 2,500 on March 26, 1977. Butler noted that there were "thousands" on Wolf Lake March 20, 1886. Fall migrants usually appear in early October; a female was observed in Fulton County on September 8. Peak numbers are reached during the last half of October and the first half of November. On November 7, 1948, 4,400 lesser scaups were recorded in Marion County. At Michigan City, 1,350 were seen on October 30, 1954. This duck winters throughout the state, but numbers at any locality vary considerably. For example, there appear to be relatively few in winter on Lake Michigan, although from 200 to 300 have been recorded at Michigan City on several Christmas bird counts. About 800 were at Hovey Lake on December 27, 1950. In recent years, lesser scaups have frequented Lake Monroe in large numbers. On December 28, 1969, 4,000 were there. Fair-sized groups may winter locally on the open water of rivers. There were 500 on the Tippecanoe River near Warsaw on January 14–15, 1950.

Evermann and Clark (1920) made extensive observations of the lesser scaup at Lake Maxinkuckee, where in the early 1900s it was the most abundant duck. On April 12, 1901, they wrote, ". . . the whole lake off east side of Long Point [was] nearly black with them." On October 15, 1903, many were killed by "pot hunters" who sold them six for a dollar. The ducks' feeding habits at Lake Maxinkuckee were studied:

When unmolested and in calm weather, they usually stay not far from shore and in rather shallow water where they feed upon the wild celery. They mix freely with the coots with which they appear to be on the best of terms. They delight, perhaps more than any other duck, to gather in great flocks, hence the name Flocking-fowl which Audubon says was in his day applied to them in the lower Mississippi valley. During fair days in the fall they may be seen in great numbers near shore at Lake Maxinkuckee, diving and feeding in shallow water, 3 to 15 feet deep, all the time keeping up rather low, subdued conversations quite unlike the quacking of the mallard; it is more conversational, like that of the coots. . . . In stormy weather, or when disturbed, they move farther out on the lake or seek the quiet protected places. . . . At night, especially in foggy weather, they frequently come ashore.

Evermann and Clark examined "a good many" stomachs of these birds and found that their food consisted mainly of small mollusks (mostly *Vivipara contectoides*) and vegetation. One bird, shot December 1, 1904, contained about 1,000 very small shells, thought to be young *Vivipara*. The ducks fed on wild celery, and when it became scarce ate pondweed leaves, chara, water-milfoil, and hornwort.

saw this (or another) eider there in the following ten days were also unable to reach agreement as to its species. In retrospect, Mumford thinks this bird was indeed a common eider, a determination upheld by his detailed notes taken the day the bird was first seen. James E. Landing reported observing a common eider repeatedly at Michigan City from November 30, 1957, to January 27, 1958.

KING EIDER
Somateria spectabilis

This eider duck is a casual winter visitor on Lake Michigan, where it was reported from Indiana most frequently in the late 1950s. We have one record since 1959.

The species was on Butler's hypothetical list, on the basis of its being recorded in Michigan and Illinois. The earliest Indiana record we have found is that of one shot at Lake George, Whiting, on November 6, 1936 (Smith, 1950). Another was shot by a hunter along the southern end of Lake Michigan on December 16, 1956; the specimen was preserved by Dale N. Martin. Single birds were observed at Michigan City on November 30, 1957, October 22, 1959, and November 25–26, 1981. Between November 26 and December 24, 1959, duck hunters Gerald Brown and Willard H. Kaehler shot at least five king eiders at Calumet Harbor, a half mile east of the Illinois-Indiana state line. All five specimens were preserved. Kaehler wrote (letter of December 27, 1959) that he had seen about 20 eiders at that site while duck hunting during the past thirty years. An eider seen at Michigan City from December 26, 1956, to January 12, 1957, and identified as a common eider by some was reported as a king eider by others, and is the only eider reported on an Indiana Christmas bird count. All other king eiders were found between October 22 and December 24.

[COMMON EIDER]
Somateria mollissima

This duck of the more northern and Arctic latitudes is an accidental winter visitor to Indiana. There are only a handful of reports from the state, all from Lake Michigan or a short distance inland (Lake George, Whiting), and, because they are difficult to identify in the field, some of these sightings are open to question. Aside from a single specimen formerly said to be from Indiana in the Field Museum of Natural History, we have seen no physical evidence of its occurrence.

Butler considered the common eider hypothetical, noting that it had been recorded in Illinois and Michigan. On December 26, 1956, William J. Barmore, Richard E. Phillips, and Mumford found what they believed to be a female eider at Michigan City, but not being entirely familiar with eiders they declined to make a positive identification. Other persons who

HARLEQUIN DUCK
Histrionicus histrionicus

Finding the first harlequin duck ever sighted in Indiana was an event that Richard E. Phillips and Mumford will never forget. The morning of January 27, 1955, it was 13 below zero at Michigan City harbor with an SSW wind of about 15 miles per hour. Birders familiar with this site in winter know what we are describing—normal weather. The only sizable patch of open water was an area of about one acre where warm water from the Northern Indiana Public Service Plant flowed into the lake. In this patch of open water were mallards, American black ducks, greater and lesser scaups, buffleheads, oldsquaws, redheads, canvasbacks, two unidentifed scoters, three cormorants, and the harlequin. It was Phillips who first noticed the harlequin; we crawled across the ice on our bellies to get a closer look. There was no mistaking the field marks—stubby beak and three whitish spots on either side of the head. The warmth of the car felt good after this experience and over hot coffee we savored our discovery.

Butler suspected that the harlequin duck might one day be found in Indiana because it was known from Illinois and Michigan, and included it on his hypothetical list. Three specimens have been collected from Indiana since that first sighting and there are at least twenty other records of this interesting duck. All but five of them were on Lake Michigan, where the harlequin has been observed in fourteen years between 1955 and 1980. One was seen at Morse Reservoir near Noblesville on December 24 and 25, 1961. There was one on the St. Joseph River in the Mishawaka–South Bend area in January and February 1973 and another on February 26, 1978. On December 17, 1978, Thomas W. Butler shot one on the Wabash River between Attica and Covington while duck hunting. Two were seen at the Brookville Reservoir on December 7, 1977.

All observations were made between November 6 and March 27. Along Lake Michigan the harlequin is frequently seen feeding at the shoreline where large blocks of concrete have been placed along breakwaters. Apparently some favored food is present in these situations, but we do not know what it is. The harlequin duck observed at Morse Reservoir also frequented the rocky slopes of the dam, where riprap had been placed.

Most of the birds recorded in Indiana have been immatures or females, but several were adult males. Kenneth J. Brock noted that at Michigan City two birds first thought to be females on November 13 remained until the lake froze on December 26. By the latter date, both had molted sufficiently that it could be determined they were males.

the Wabash River bridges between Lafayette and West Lafayette and watch the ducks diving, feeding, and resting among the ice floes. Oldsquaws were most numerous there in March 1947; about thirty spent several weeks in the area that spring.

Butler noted that this duck was a very common winter resident on Lake Michigan and was "exceedingly rare" in winter elsewhere in Indiana. Unfortunately, he made no mention of actual numbers observed, only referring to "several enormous flocks" in February 1897 at Millers (Lake County), and as "very abundant" at Michigan City on December 12, 1887. It was also "very abundant" at Lake Michigan the winter of 1894–95 and "quite common" the winter of 1896–97.

The oldsquaw remained a common to abundant winter visitor to Lake Michigan through the winter of 1957–58. Since then there has been a dramatic decrease and the species has become rare. We now consider it rare to very rare throughout Indiana, especially away from Lake Michigan.

The first fall arrivals have been recorded along Lake Michigan the last half of October; the earliest date is October 19, 1952, when twenty were seen at Millers. On seven Michigan City Christmas bird counts from 1951 to 1957, numbers of oldsquaws recorded ranged from 250 to 31,539 per count and averaged about 5,600. The 1955–56 count of more than 31,000 seems quite remarkable, in view of the 1957–58 count, 750, and the 1958–59 count, 1! This sharp decrease in numbers over such a short period may be related to a decrease in the food supply. Another explanation might be some change in this ducks' fall migration route. Whatever the cause, Indiana lost a desirable species of her winter avifauna with the virtual disappearance of the oldsquaw. So far no significant recovery has been made by this duck; the numbers of oldsquaws seen on Christmas bird counts at the Indiana Dunes National Lakeshore from 1976 to 1982 were 0, 0, 0, 10, 13, 1, and 1, respectively. Our latest spring date is May 12 (Delaware and Warren Counties).

OLDSQUAW
Clangula hyemalis

Old Wife Duck, Old Wife, South Southerly, Long-tailed Duck

Except at Lake Michigan, the oldsquaw has always been relatively unknown in Indiana. The Great Lakes are one of its major wintering grounds, and evidently not many birds migrate across the state. The larger lakes are attractive, for they provide deep water and favored foods. Oldsquaws are noted for their ability to dive deeper than any other species of duck, sometimes reaching depths of 180 feet (where they have been captured in fish nets). In fact, becoming entangled in nets was one of the major causes of mortality for oldsquaws on the Great Lakes before the decline of fish populations and the resultant decrease in commercial fishing. In the years when this duck was still common on Lake Michigan in winter the large, noisy flocks could easily be seen from points along the lakeshore. Long lines of flying oldsquaws traded back and forth at no great distance from shore, and numerous birds fed at the mouth of Trail Creek and even in the yacht basin at Michigan City. In those rare years when some birds chose to winter on the Wabash River at Lafayette and the White River at Indianapolis they attracted considerable attention from local birders, who could stand on one of

BLACK SCOTER
Melanitta nigra

American Scoter, Velvet Duck

Away from Lake Michigan, this is the rarest scoter in Indiana, but individuals or small groups have been observed in all sections of the state except the southwestern. Birdwatchers who visit Lake Michigan in mid-October may see all three species of scoters on the same day, for at this season fall flights occur. From shore one can sometimes look out over the lake and see sizable flocks of black scoters flying past.

The black scoter was only on Butler's hypothetical list, although there were early records from Illinois, Michigan, and Ohio. In those times apparently relatively little birding was done in winter along the southern end of Lake Michigan, so bird reports from that region and era are scant. This scoter today is probably a rare but regular fall migrant in northern Indiana, and casual elsewhere in the state. Only a handful have been recorded on Christmas bird counts—six total, all along Lake Michigan—but there are numerous January sightings along the lake between Gary and Michigan City.

Fall migrants arrive along Lake Michigan around the first week of October. There were fourteen near Gary on October 6, 1956, and nine on Lake Michigan, October 13, 1952. It was during the period from 1953 to 1960 that most of the biggest flocks were seen. The largest number of birds recorded was forty-three, on October 17, 1959, by Raymond Grow. Since that time the largest flocks recorded on Lake Michigan have numbered twenty-five (on October 14, 1978), and twenty (on October 23, 1965). Alan W. Bruner and Mark C. Rhodes saw more than 100 along Lake Michigan on November 13, 1982. The three fall records away from Lake Michigan are for the period 1973 to 1977; all were found on manmade lakes and reservoirs.

Away from Lake Michigan, recorded sightings of black scoter tend to be more frequent in spring than in fall. Even so, there are relatively few spring records and all involve single birds or small groups. The latest record from the lake is April 6. But from other sites birds have been recorded as follows: Brookville Reservoir, May 1, 1977 (1); St. Joseph County, May 21, 1977 (1).

A female collected November 11 at Michigan City contained snails in the digestive tract. This bird was observed feeding near shore in the yacht basin.

SURF SCOTER
Melanitta perspicillata
Surf Duck, Sea Coot

Although this may be the rarest of the three scoters that occur in Indiana on Lake Michigan, it is one of the two most likely to be seen elsewhere in the state as it moves from its breeding grounds to its wintering areas. One sees surf scoters in Indiana more frequently and in larger numbers in fall than in spring, especially on Lake Michigan. Butler considered this duck a rare winter resident on Lake Michigan and of occasional occurrence elsewhere, and its status is much the same today.

Fall migrants have been observed along the south end of Lake Michigan as early as October 5. Individuals have reached Jackson County by October 9, Lake Waveland by October 15, and Hovey Lake by October 28. The largest fall flocks have been seen in mid-October. Populations decrease throughout November; only a few overwinter. On October 19, 1980, there were forty-four at Michigan City. One surf scoter has been reported on each of four Christmas bird counts, all along Lake Michigan, in 1953, 1955, 1956, and 1977. There are several records for each month from January to May. The latest spring date we have found is May 13, 1978 (Lagrange County).

One surf scoter was seen in spring with a group of 112 red-breasted mergansers. Scott F. Jackson saw one eating Cheerios. Dark-winged scoters (sometimes in sizable flocks) are occasionally seen offshore over Lake Michigan but cannot be identified with certainty to species.

WHITE-WINGED SCOTER
Melanitta fusca
Velvet Scoter

The majority of the white-winged scoters seen in Indiana are along Lake Michigan, but individuals and small groups occur throughout the state. For the most part they frequent the larger lakes and reservoirs, but occasionally they are reported from smaller bodies of water. In the fall, flocks of as many as fifty have been observed along Lake Michigan between Michigan City and Gary. This scoter is one of the largest native ducks, and adult males are impressive-looking birds.

Around the turn of the century the white-winged scoter was considered a rare winter visitor to Indiana, being more numerous on Lake Michigan. It is more commonly seen today, and is an uncommon fall migrant in the northern portion of the state. For the remainder of Indiana, it is probably best considered rare to casual as a fall migrant. In general, the species is a rare winter resident. Relatively few birds are seen anywhere in the state after January.

In the southern region of Indiana, this scoter has been reported only from Hovey Lake and Dearborn County in spring. One was seen in the former location on February 17, 1949, and two on March 9, 1949. A late spring departure date is May 17, 1956 (1), Lake County. Early fall migrants arrive along Lake Michigan around mid-October; early dates are October 5, 1980, October 7, 1978, and October 13, 1979. Numbers reach a peak during the last half of October. For example, on October 30, 1954, seventy-two were counted between Gary and Michigan City. The largest flock—fifty—was seen on November 11, 1980, at Michigan City. Throughout the winter a few white-winged scoters remain on Lake Michigan (and elsewhere).

They have been reported on fourteen Christmas bird counts between 1941 and 1980. Twenty-six was the largest number recorded on a Christmas count; this was the 1975 Indiana Dunes National Lakeshore count.

COMMON GOLDENEYE
Bucephala clangula
Whistler, Whistle-wing

On the evening of February 15, 1949, William B. Barnes and Mumford stood in a cornfield east of Hovey Lake censusing waterfowl. The evening was clear and calm and thousands of dabbling ducks were returning to the lake to roost. There were also small flocks of common goldeneyes passing over. The characteristic whistle of their wings could be heard for a considerable distance in the cold air. During the day the birds had been feeding on the Ohio River; they now were returning to the lake to spend the night. The total count of goldeneyes that evening was 534. During mid-winter, hundreds of goldeneyes remain on flowing streams throughout the state and such rivers as the St.

Joseph, Tippecanoe, and Wabash may harbor large numbers. These rivers evidently provide good supplies of animal foods—crustaceans, small fish, and insects—upon which the birds like to feed. Because of their diet many hunters consider them unfit for consumption, and they make up only a small proportion of the annual waterfowl kill in Indiana.

Butler listed this goldeneye as a common migrant and winter resident. In the northern two-thirds of Indiana it is generally a fairly common migrant, and may be common locally on choice feeding or wintering areas. It is less common in the southern one-third, except in the southwestern portion. Winter numbers fluctuate depending on available open water.

In general the common goldeneye is a bird of the larger lakes, reservoirs, and rivers. Relatively few are observed on small ponds, no doubt in part due to the lack of food there. When major streams freeze, the birds concentrate in open water below dams. At Michigan City, goldeneyes move up into Trail Creek when Lake Michigan becomes icebound. We do not know whether the birds remain on the lake beyond the ice packs, which sometimes extend a great distance from shore.

A few goldeneyes begin moving into northern Indiana in October. These records include Steuben County, October 2; Porter County, October 15; Lake Maxinkuckee, October 21. Numbers increase throughout November and December and probably peak in late December or January, depending upon the area and prevailing weather. The largest numbers have been reported on Christmas bird counts, but ordinarily this is the major period of the winter when many birders are in the field. Some maximums for these counts are: Western Gibson County, 8,061 on January 2, 1982; Lake Monroe, 1,935 on December 28, 1969; South Bend, 1,229 on January 1, 1970; Hovey Lake, 1,000 on December 27, 1950. These are the only areas where a thousand or more have been seen. More than 500 birds per count have been tallied at South Bend ten times, twice at Lake Monroe, and once each at Hovey Lake, Gibson County, and northern Lake County. The consistent numbers at South Bend each winter inhabit the St. Joseph River in the South Bend–Mishawaka area.

Small numbers of goldeneyes linger into May (ten records) and there are two June reports of single birds. Most depart during or before April, depending upon the locality; in general, after mid-April relatively few are noted. There were seventy reported in Kosciusko County the week of May 1–8, 1947, but this is unusual.

Courtship is frequently observed among the wintering birds and this behavior has been recorded at least from December 30 to March 10. At Michigan City, both goldeneyes and buffleheads (which occur commonly in mixed flocks) have been observed courting at the same time.

BARROW'S GOLDENEYE

Bucephala islandica

Whistler

It is difficult to know to what extent we can rely on sight records for this duck in Indiana because female and immature Bar-

row's goldeneyes and common goldeneyes are so similar. Adult males of the two species have field marks that allow them to be separated more easily. Butler considered the Barrow's goldeneye a rare visitor in winter and spring, citing two specimens collected in the state as his only records. We do not know where these specimens are, if still extant, and know of no others from Indiana. The species should probably be classified as a casual winter visitor.

Butler referred to a specimen taken on the Wabash River, Gibson County, in 1874 and another taken in Carroll County, March 19, 1885. There are eight sight records for the St. Joseph River, Mishawaka–South Bend area, from 1945 to 1980. Most of the sightings involve males, which were photographed by James Taylor on March 3, 1962 (*Ind. Aud. Quart.* 40, No. 1, cover) and in March 1963. A pair was reported there in April 1980. In addition, there are eight other sight records for the state. We do not feel that we can vouch for all of the sightings of this duck in Indiana, but include them for the sake of completeness. All observations were made between December 3 and April 9.

BUFFLEHEAD

Bucephala albeola

Butterball, Dipper, Butter Duck, Spirit Duck

There is little doubt that the best place to see these beautiful little ducks in numbers is along Lake Michigan. Here from the first of November until the first of April buffleheads are in evidence—in late winter, by the hundreds—at the Michigan City harbor in the yacht basin, along Trail Creek, or along the lake shore. They often associate closely with common goldeneyes, their close relatives.

Around 1900 the bufflehead was considered a common migrant and winter resident. Butler noted that in southern Indiana it was better known than the common goldeneye. Today it is a fairly common migrant and winters in varying numbers throughout the state. Two minor migration routes cross Indiana; along these corridors buffleheads pass southeastward in the fall en route to their wintering grounds along the Atlantic coast. On the average, about 500 winter along Lake Michigan and another 100 elsewhere in the state.

Spring migration evidently begins in late February, when birds have arrived at locations in northern Indiana where they were absent in winter. Peak numbers are reached in late March and early April. On April 3, 1969, there were 100 in Marion County. Groups of thirty to forty have been observed elsewhere in the state during the last half of March. By mid-April, buffleheads have departed from the southern third of the state and most are gone by May 1 elsewhere. There are several May sightings and three or four June records. A male remained at Willow Slough from June 13 to July 21, 1952, and a female was observed in LaPorte County from June 20 to July 3, 1981. Early fall migrants sometimes appear by October 10 in the northern section of the state. A mounted female in the University of Michigan collection was taken September 30, 1899, in Porter

County. Away from Lake Michigan there are insufficient records for fall migrants to determine when peak numbers are present. In some areas there seems to be a population peak in late October, but at many localities the maximum numbers of birds are recorded on the Christmas bird counts. Small numbers may winter almost anywhere in the state, but by far the greatest concentrations are on Lake Michigan. All of the ten Christmas counts that tallied 200 or more buffleheads were taken in counties bordering the lake. Other wintering areas of some significance are the St. Joseph River, South Bend–Mishawaka (24 to 120 on four counts), and Lake Monroe (20 to 56 on three counts). From 10 to 30 have been observed in Gibson, Marion, Posey, Steuben, and Union Counties.

Buffleheads examined by Evermann and Clark at Lake Maxinkuckee had been feeding mainly on small mollusks, vegetation, and small fish. These authors noted that the birds came near shore to feed in shallow water. At this lake the bufflehead was popular with hunters, especially in fall when it was fat.

Courtship evidently occurs from at least the observed dates of December 6 to March 9. We have observed courting behavior on several occasions. This often involves chases, especially between rival males. One will rush at another on the water; the one being attacked will dive, followed by its pursuer; the birds quickly surface, literally flying from the water, continue the chase in flight, then abruptly dive underwater again. This duck is capable of swift flight and its wingbeats are quite rapid.

HOODED MERGANSER

Lophodytes cucullatus

Fish Duck, Sawbill, Wood Duck

Early one February we had an opportunity to watch courtship behavior of two male and two female hooded mergansers at Lake Greenwood (Martin County). There were about a thousand ducks and geese on the only open water, an acre-sized patch. The hooded mergansers were there with 850 mallards, 60 American black ducks, 3 northern pintails, 5 green-winged teals, a ring-necked duck, 5 lesser scaup, a bufflehead, a common merganser, 170 Canada geese, and a pied-billed grebe. There was considerable milling about, but the male hooded mergansers, intent on their rivalry, were oblivious to the other birds. Rapidly one would spurt through the water, puffing out his head feathers; the other would do the same. One male chased the other; the pursued one dived. The other followed it underwater. When one bird broke the surface, the other emerged directly beneath it; the first had to put on a burst of speed to avoid being collided with. This behavior continued for some time, until the birds became alarmed by our presence.

This beautiful, shy duck is seldom seen by the average birdwatcher. Although it occurs throughout the state and evidently breeds in all sections, its secluded habitat and retiring ways make it seem rarer than it actually is. During breeding season it is most likely to be found along streams and about swamps, where it is frequently mistaken for the wood duck, which prefers the same sort of habitat; both species also like to nest in tree cavities and nesting boxes.

Butler listed the hooded merganser as an abundant migrant, a less common winter resident, and a local permanent resident. Robert Ridgway found hooded mergansers breeding at Monteur's Pond, Knox County, in 1881, and reported that they were more numerous than the wood duck there. Today it certainly is not abundant; we would consider it an uncommon migrant throughout Indiana. Before 1970 relatively few hoodeds were found on Christmas bird counts. Since then their numbers have increased, probably due in part to the construction of new reservoirs in southern Indiana that provide suitable wintering grounds. There are breeding records from more than twenty counties, and the species probably breeds rarely in favorable habitat throughout the state.

Spring migrants reach a peak in late March. The week of March 16–22, 1952, there were 61 at Willow Slough. This is the largest assemblage on record for spring, although not as large as some wintering groups. As many as 100 (Lake Monroe, November 22 and 29, 1975) have been seen in the fall, and single flocks of up to 45 have been reported. Hooded mergansers were reported on nearly sixty different Christmas bird counts between 1940 and 1980. More than 25 per count were found at the Lake Greenwood, Gibson County, Indianapolis, Kosciusko County, Lake Monroe, and South Bend counts. That the birds were widely distributed over the state is clear from the locations of these counts.

Although there are at least twenty-five records of breeding in Indiana, relatively little is known of the nesting chronology, for most of the breeding records are based on observations of broods. Only Peter E. Meyer appears to have seen nests of the hooded merganser in Indiana. When he worked at Hovey Lake, several nested in wood duck nesting boxes. He photographed a female in one box and young in the nest. Meyer told us he had seen six female hooded mergansers at one time at a single nesting box. It was reported to Butler that "quite a few" hoodeds nested along the Kankakee River near Kouts. Many of the most recent sightings of broods were made along rivers during wood duck surveys.

Some birds must nest quite early, for the calculated hatching date for a brood observed on April 22 was April 16. Since the incubation period is about 32 days, egg laying would have begun around mid-March. Perhaps, like wood ducks, this merganser wastes little time finding nesting cavities upon arrival at the breeding grounds. On a float trip down the Muscatatuck River, between Jackson and Washington Counties, on April 19, 1950, we saw a female hooded merganser taking flight from a tall sycamore standing at the edge of the water; the tree contained numerous cavities that seemed suitable for nesting. On our next trip along this same stream, on May 25, a female (presumably the same one) again flushed from this tree.

We have no records of clutch size. Most broods for which there was a complete count contained from six to eight young. For some reason, in some instances only one to three young were found with a female. A brood of seven young, about six or seven weeks old, was observed with a female on July 7. Some of the young were diving and feeding. When frightened, they grouped together and swam behind their mother into cover.

HOODED MERGANSER

HOODED MERGANSER

COMMON MERGANSER

Mergus merganser

American Merganser, Fish Duck, Merganser, Sheldrake

A hardy bird, this big, colorful merganser may be seen swimming about and feeding among the ice floes throughout the winter. Males in breeding plumage are strikingly beautiful ducks; especially in good light, one can sometimes see in the field the delicate peach-colored "bloom" on the breast. It is the largest of the mergansers, with a heavy body that rides low in the water.

Butler considered it a common migrant and winter resident, noting that numbers present during the winter varied with the amount of open water. He reported it as being one of the commonest ducks on Lake Michigan in winter. There has been sufficient decline in this species through the years to reduce it to the status of uncommon migrant and winter resident in Indiana today. Numbers may vary considerably with locality, however. As many as 500 have been recorded on a single Christmas bird count. It is more abundant in spring than in fall.

Most of the larger congregations have been observed on lakes and reservoirs, but when these freeze over, this merganser frequents the larger rivers that are free of ice, especially the Tippecanoe, St. Joseph, and Wabash.

The largest numbers recorded in the southern third of the state have been noted in early February; there were 400 in Gibson County on February 3, 1980. In central Indiana, 800 were seen on March 17, 1951. There were 600 on Lake Freeman, in northern Indiana, on March 18, 1950. It may be significant that most of the large spring flocks were reported between 1946 and 1951, since which time there has been a decline. Wintering birds are supplemented by spring migrants in most areas, making it difficult to determine just when spring migration begins. Most have left the state by mid-May, but a few linger until the last week of that month. One, thought to be a cripple, was seen near Indianapolis on July 7 and 25, 1948. Another was present in Warren County from July 14 to August 3, 1963. A male was observed at Gary on August 4, 1980. Fall migrants begin arriving in late October, but throughout the state most fall arrivals appear in November, even reaching Hovey Lake the first week of that month. There are few data regarding the peak of the fall migration, but on November 11, 1945, there were 500 on Geist Reservoir. Most of the wintering birds have been recorded in the northern region of Indiana, with decreasing numbers wintering in central and even fewer in southern Indiana.

RED-BREASTED MERGANSER

Mergus serrator

Fish Duck, Sawbill

When migrating red-breasted mergansers congregate along the southern end of Lake Michigan it is possible to see 1,500 at a time, as Lawrence H. Walkinshaw did on November 4, 1951. This area is definitely the most likely place to see large numbers of this interesting duck. Observers who visit the lake regularly in fall and early winter are sometimes treated to spectacular movements of birds. For example, on October 24, 1959, Raymond Grow watched for three hours as 24,000 ducks, fleeing from a storm in the northwest, passed by from west to east. About 95 percent of them were scaups and red-breasted mergansers. Such storm flights probably occur with some regularity, but few are witnessed except by luck.

About 1900, this merganser was a generally rare migrant and winter visitor throughout the state, but was "rather common" on the larger bodies of water. Butler considered it by far the least common of the mergansers in Indiana. Today it is a fairly common migrant (especially in spring) and generally rare winter resident, being more abundant on Lake Michigan in fall and winter. Flocks containing more than a hundred birds have been reported there. No large flocks appear to stop off elsewhere in the state during this season. In contrast, hundreds are recorded throughout Indiana each spring; these are undoubtedly migrants on their return flight.

In central and northern Indiana the peak of the spring flight occurs around the first of April. There were 1,000 at Eagle Creek Reservoir on March 29, 1970. On March 27, 1948, about 800 were at Michigan City, and 500 were observed at Wolf Lake on March 25, 1979. There are at least six records of one or two red-breasted mergansers in the state during June, July, and August. One pair spent most of the summer of 1972 on the Tippecanoe River (White County).

RUDDY DUCK

Oxyura jamaicensis

Black Jack, Bristle-Tail, Fool Duck, Brown Teal

The thick-necked, stiff-tailed little ruddy duck is seen all too infrequently by birdwatchers. It is an interesting species, often identified on the water solely by the way it holds its relatively long tail up at an angle, creating a silhouette that is unmistakable even in poor light or at a distance. With their unbelievably blue beaks and reddish-chestnut bodies, male ruddies in full nuptial plumage are a treat for the eyes, but the spring molt is sometimes quite protracted and relatively few males that pass through Indiana in the spring exhibit their finest plumage. Numerous stragglers linger here during June and into July, however, and the adult males among them may attain their brightest colors before departing. Ruddy ducks frequently dive rather than fly in attempting to escape impending danger, even when pursued by hunters in boats—an ill-advised and dangerous ploy that has earned them the scornful nickname "fool duck."

Butler considered this duck only a migrant and stated that it was "usually not common." He did write that it might be found breeding in Indiana. Throughout the state today it is an uncommon migrant and has been recorded on thirty-six Christmas bird counts from various portions of the state between 1949 and 1979. From time to time a brood of ruddy ducks has been observed in Lake County, but the species has also been seen in June, July, and August in nine other counties where it is not known to breed. It may do so in some of these areas.

Since wintering birds in small numbers may be present nearly everywhere in the state, determining when the earliest migrants arrive is sometimes impossible. At Hovey Lake, the greatest number of spring migrants were seen March 10 and March 14, for two years. The largest number recorded in Gibson County was on March 27. There are few additional records for the southern region of the state. In central Indiana, peaks have been anywhere from March 29 to April 20; for the northern section, April 14 to 22. The numbers reported during the spring are usually small, but as many as fifty birds may be present at a particular site.

In the northwestern corner of the state, where the ruddy duck is known to breed and there is also more of a possibility of summering birds, fall migration appears to be underway by September. Two ruddies were found in Tippecanoe County on August 2, 1952, but this is probably unseasonably early for migration. Birds arrive in central Indiana by mid-September and in the extreme southwestern corner of the state by the last week of October. Peak numbers of fall migrants have been recorded at

Jasper-Pulaski between October 22 and 28; the highest count for Willow Slough was December 5. Flights have peaked on Geist Reservoir from November 6 to 24 in four different years. At Lake Waveland, the largest count was on December 1. There are few data for the southern region, but November 11, 1948, was the date of the largest number (28) reported at Hovey Lake. Dennis W. Jones recorded 150 at Merom (Sullivan County) November 28, 1982.

Of the thirty-six Christmas counts on which the ruddy duck was seen, the maximum number for a single count was 122, at Lake Monroe on December 28, 1969, one of only four counts on which 16 or more were tallied. Thir-teen counts reported one; fourteen, from 2 to 6; and five counts, 7 to 15.

Although the largest numbers of ruddies have been on lakes and reservoirs, this little duck can be found on ponds, small marshes, borrow pits, and other small bodies of water.

No nest of the ruddy duck has been reported in Indiana, but there are six observations of broods, all from Lake County, where it bred in 1953, 1959, 1961, 1962, 1965, and 1980. Female ruddies with their broods can be quite secretive, and we suspect that breeding has taken place more times than records indicate.

Depicted plant: Great bulrush (*Scirpus validus*)

RUDDY DUCK

BLACK VULTURE

Coragyps atratus

Carrion Crow, Buzzard, Black Buzzard

There are relatively few Indiana records for this vulture north of the Old National Road (U.S. Route 40). Some years ago there was a poultry farm along the Blue River at the west entrance to Harrison State Forest, west of Corydon. Here both black vultures and turkey vultures gathered to feed on discarded dead chickens in the adjacent woods. Birders could usually depend upon finding at least a few black vultures at this site. About the only other locality in the state where black vultures have occurred with regularity is Clifty Falls State Park.

According to Audubon, the black vulture was a permanent resident of Indiana in 1834. For the next fifty years there were no records. Then, from 1879 to 1935, the black vulture was reported nearly every year from the state. Butler (1935) wondered whether it had withdrawn from its former range only to reoccupy it later. There were few breeding records before 1940, and there have been even fewer since. Throughout the northern two-thirds of the state today the black vulture is a casual spring or summer visitor; in the remainder it is a rare summer resident and is casual in winter. In the vicinity of Clifty Falls State Park, it is virtually a permanent resident.

Black vultures and turkey vultures often occur together in mixed flocks when foraging, migrating, or roosting. Black vulture roosts are usually in rocky areas in woodlands, the same type of habitat where they usually nest. There is little information regarding the migration of the black vulture but records accumulated over the years suggest that it occasionally wanders to the northern border of Indiana sometime during the late summer, for it has been observed migrating southward with turkey vultures and hawks in Franklin County the last half of September. Migration has also been observed in Lawrence, Owen, and Parke Counties in late August and September. Floyd S. Carpenter made an interesting observation at about 4:00 P.M. on October 19, 1954: fifty vultures (both blacks and turkeys) flying northward across the Ohio River into Indiana, near Laconia. Vultures are powerful fliers, and it is not inconceivable that some of these fall "migrations" are simply movements back to a roosting site after the birds have foraged far from the roosts during the day.

Most of the winter records for black vultures in Indiana are for counties either bordering the Ohio River or not far from it. The best-known winter roost of black vultures in recent years, as we have said, is in Clifty Falls State Park. In the 1920s, as many as 500 used this roost. Butler observed about 150 vultures at this roost on November 12, 1934; he estimated that about three-fourths of them were black vultures. Thereafter the population seems to have declined again. An average number of 48 black vultures were observed at Clifty Falls on five Christmas bird counts from 1974 to 1981. The maximum number recorded was 97, on January 2, 1982.

Relatively few black vulture nests have been found during the past forty years in Indiana, and we are not sure some of the older "breeding" records are valid. Butler cited breeding records for Franklin and Lawrence Counties before 1927. Nests were subsequently observed at Clifty Falls in three different years in the late 1920s, in 1933, 1937, 1976, 1977, and 1979. William P. Allyn discovered at least five nests at "Hoosier Highlands" about six miles south of Manhattan (Putnam County) from 1931 to 1934. A pair nested in McCormick's Creek State Park in 1935. In 1973 and 1974, nests were found at the same site three miles north of Sulphur (Crawford County). No doubt they also nest elsewhere in southern Indiana.

At Hoosier Highlands, the birds nested in "caves about the rock cliffs." The nest at Clifty Falls was "among a pile of rocks near the falls," and the nest at McCormick's Creek was "among the rocks." The Crawford County nest was likewise in a rocky site—a grottolike recess among some huge limestone boulders. Of the nests described in print, only that found by Butler was not in a rocky place. It was on the ground inside a hollow tree snag. The earliest and latest dates we have for eggs are April 2 and May 22. Two small young were found in a nest on May 1. Young have been observed in the nest until at least June 23.

Depicted plant: Liverwort (*Marchantia* sp.)

BLACK VULTURE

TURKEY VULTURE

Cathartes aura

Turkey Buzzard, Buzzard

It was a cool, foggy early morning in April. Along the White River near Waverly, a dozen turkey vultures perched motionless in the top of a tall dead tree, their wings spread to catch the warmth from the rising sun. They had roosted there all through the chilly, damp night, and did not move until the sun had generated enough heat to create the thermals they like to ride. Once in the air, the birds no longer looked awkward or ugly. Effortlessly they glided and maneuvered, making the merest, almost imperceptible adjustments of their wings and tails. When the updrafts are right, turkey vultures may not flap their wings for long periods. Holding them in a slight dihedral, they glide, circle, swoop, and perform other aerial movements merely by flexing the primaries or shearing the tail. In buoyant, slightly rocking flight, they may forage for miles away from the roosting site.

About a hundred years ago, this vulture was a permanent resident as far north as Vincennes and Brookville. In northwestern Indiana it evidently seldom ranged farther north than the Kankakee River valley, but it occurred throughout northeastern Indiana. Today the turkey vulture is a common migrant and uncommon summer resident over the southern two-thirds of the state, generally rare as a migrant and summer resident in the northern portion (especially the unforested extreme northwest). Individuals have been recorded on Christmas bird counts as far north as Adams, Allen, Kosciusko, and Tippecanoe Counties, but the farthest north known winter concentration of the species is in Montgomery-Parke Counties. This vulture probably nests throughout its summer range, but there are relatively few Indiana nesting records.

Turkey vultures forage over all types of habitats in search of food, but usually roost in wooded areas, frequently about rock outcrops. Some Indiana roosts have been used for decades and are well known, such as those in Clifty Falls, Shades, and Turkey Run State Parks. Here groups of turkey vultures are likely to be seen perched in tall dead trees, especially early in the morning, or sitting on gravel bars along the rivers. They also make use of manmade structures for perching: buildings, water towers, and the like. Nesting sites are normally in wooded areas.

There is considerable migratory movement of turkey vultures in southern Indiana the first week of February; individuals reach the northern border of the state by the last week of that month. For the state as a whole, March is the major month of migration. At times, notable spring congregations of birds are reported. Alfred Starling observed 550 turkey vultures milling about at a site in Ripley County on March 9, 1970.

Sizable flocks are formed by the last part of August; 80 turkey vultures were noted in Franklin County on August 22, 1956. Flocks of from 50 to 100 birds are not unusual during September and October, sometimes migrating with hawks. The most notable migrations of turkey vultures on record to date were observed by James B. Cope, Jay Schnell, and others in the Brookville (Franklin County) area in September 1953: 125 on the 19th; 202 on the 20th; 252 on the 26th; 199 on the 27th. It would be interesting to know the origin of these flights. Surprisingly, 100 vultures were recorded in Allen County (where one might not expect such abundance) on September 23, 1979.

Turkey vultures have been seen in winter throughout Indiana except for the extreme northeastern corner, but at this season most are in the southern half of the state, returning year after year to favored roosts. One such site, now within Shades State Park, has been a winter roost for turkey vultures since before the turn of the century. As many as 164 were there on December 28, 1964. We do not know when these vultures began using the winter roost at Turkey Run State Park, but more than 100 were there on January 2, 1954. Some of the maximum numbers of birds recorded there on various Christmas bird counts are as follows: 266 (December 23, 1965); 265 (December 20, 1976); 235 (December 21, 1966). Considerable numbers of turkey vultures and black vultures have roosted in the rocky canyons of Clifty Falls State Park since at least the mid-1920s. In some years, as many as 500 were present. The tally on the Hanover-Madison Christmas bird count on January 2, 1982, was 210.

There are at least thirty nesting records for turkey vultures in the state. Eggs have been found in nests from March 7 to May 27. The turkey vulture almost invariably lays two eggs per clutch. There is one record of young leaving the nest as late as the third week of September. Several nests were located in hollow logs lying on the ground and in large cavities of standing trees. Others were in small rocky grottoes or caves, or under or beside a log. Large hollow sycamores and other trees along streams seem to be favorite nesting sites. Most nests were situated in or at the edge of deciduous woods. One nesting site was used for six and others for at least three consecutive years. Newly hatched turkey vultures are covered with white down; baby black vultures have tan down.

Depicted plant: Drooping trillium (*T. flexipes*)

TURKEY VULTURE

OSPREY

Pandion haliaetus

Fish Hawk

Our canoe drifted along Raccoon Creek below Mansfield shortly after sunup on a late April morning. At several places the stream was so narrow and shallow that we were forced to leave the canoe and drag it to deeper water. Suddenly a large bird, giving a weak, repeated chirping call, came flying along the creek and passed not far above our heads. It was an osprey, apparently fishing, and seeming quite out of place on such a small body of water. Many of the larger pools were completely overhung by the tree canopy. We had always associated this hawk with larger expanses of water, where it could hunt more easily in the open.

About 1898 the osprey was considered to be a local summer resident, a regular migrant, and, in some years, a rare winter resident in the southern part of the state. Evidently one such winter was that of 1880–81, in the Whitewater River valley. Butler listed one winter record for Lafayette. Spring migrants began to appear in February, but most were seen in April. It was reportedly abundant along Lake Michigan in the vicinity of Michigan City during the summer. Today the osprey is a rare to uncommon migrant throughout Indiana. Relatively few nests have been reported since 1900, but we think it possible that from time to time a pair still nests in the state, for there are several recent sightings for June and July. It is very rare in winter, according to the Christmas bird counts and other data.

The osprey inhabits nearly any place where it can find fish, its principal food. Ponds, marshes, lakes, reservoirs, and streams of all sizes attract this interesting hawk. Nesting sites are usually the tops of dead or living trees standing in the water.

Spring migration begins in February and reaches its peak in April. Quite a few birds linger throughout the first half of May, some even later. We doubt that all of those seen in June and July are breeding. Fall migrants appear about mid-August and most pass through in the last half of September. Relatively few are still here in November.

The osprey is known to have nested in at least eleven counties. It is rather surprising that Butler knew of only a few breeding records. Since 1960 the osprey has evidently nested in Bradford Woods, near Martinsville (fairly large young were seen in the nest August 20, 1962); at Sylvan Lake, Noble County, "for several years" before about 1975; Raccoon Lake, Parke County, in the summer of 1971; and Hovey Lake Fish and Wildlife Area, Posey County, into the late 1970s.

The most interesting nesting site of the osprey in Indiana is Hovey Lake, where ospreys are known to have nested intermittently since at least 1933. The reports give no particulars except for a note that incubation was in progress by early May in 1959. The lack of data is due in part to the inaccessibility of the nesting sites, which are often in the tops of dead, isolated cypresses and impossible to reach without serious risk of bodily harm. Once a nest is constructed, it may be used year after year, as long as it is suitable. The adults normally show considerable concern when a human intruder comes near the nest and will call loudly and circle low over the observer.

The osprey feeds mostly on fish, primarily live ones, which it catches by hovering over the water, then diving into it to capture its prey with its feet, which are specially designed for handling live, slippery fish. These headlong dives into the water are spectacular, but frequently unsuccessful. Because of their method of feeding, ospreys are limited to catching fish near the surface of the water or in shallow water. One bird was observed catching a carp. Another, seen in flight along the White River near Martinsville, was carrying a 12-inch goldfish in its talons—it had evidently just paid a visit to the goldfish hatchery there. One osprey, seen in migration over the hills in Jackson County in late September, was carrying a fish. Alfred Starling observed an osprey at Eagle Creek Reservoir for about three weeks that seemed to have a fishing lure embedded in its chest.

The osprey's usual call is a *cheep, cheep, cheep* noise like that of a baby chicken—an incongruous sound to be coming from such a large and noble bird. When disturbed near their nests, ospreys utter louder calls, including high-pitched screams.

While Mumford and Gerald L. Brody were watching ospreys at a nest at Hovey Lake in 1957, they noticed several house sparrows entering and leaving the bulky stick nest, in which they too were evidently nesting.

AMERICAN SWALLOW-TAILED KITE

Elanoides forficatus

Although all the kites are graceful birds in flight, the swallow-tailed is the most beautiful of the group. It has also occurred more frequently in Indiana than the other two kites.

Butler called it a rare summer resident in the southwestern part of the state, rare and irregular in occurrence elsewhere. Alexander Wilson (1812) reported that this kite was abundant on the prairies of Ohio and the Indiana territory, but we do not know which portion of the Indiana territory he was referring to. John James Audubon found a nest at the Falls of the Ohio in 1820. E. J. Chansler (1912) reported nesting in Knox County "in early days." Before 1900, there were records from the following counties: Allen, Clinton, Decatur, Franklin, Knox, Monroe, and Vigo. It has been observed in the state six times since 1900. Dates of observation range from April 5 to September 3. The most recent sighting was on May 31 and June 1, 1982, near Battle Ground in Tippecanoe County, by Edward M. Hopkins and Ted T. Cable.

BLACK-SHOULDERED KITE

Elanus caeruleus

This kite is an accidental visitor to Indiana and its inclusion on the state list is based on a bird seen and photographed April 18, 1981, at Lake Monroe in Monroe County. Geoffrey E. Hill discovered this bird and shortly thereafter Steven H. Glass and Thomas Alexander also observed and photographed it.

MISSISSIPPI KITE

Ictinia mississippiensis

This beautiful hawk evidently once nested in southwestern Indiana and occasionally wandered farther north in the state. Robert Ridgway noted that the species bred at the cypress ponds in Knox County from May 15 to September, and he also saw them at Washburne Pond, Cypress Swamp, in the spring of 1878. Butler mentioned a specimen received by Charles Dury from the Lafayette area "several years ago." E. J. Chansler (1912) observed one in Knox County on September 18, 1911.

The next report was by Floyd S. Carpenter, who saw a Mississippi kite at the Tunnel Mill Boy Scout Camp four miles west of Charlestown (Clark County) on June 26, 1937. Val Nolan Jr. saw one at Bloomington on May 1, 1959. Between 1967 and 1976 there were five additional sight records for this kite in the state. All sightings to date have been between April 24 and September 18. A casual summer visitor to Indiana, the Mississippi kite may be increasing its rate of occurrence. It is becoming more common in parts of Kentucky and is extending its range there. The most northerly sightings in Indiana were at the Dunes in 1967 and 1973.

BALD EAGLE

Haliaeetus leucocephalus

White-headed Eagle, Southern Bald Eagle, Washington Sea Eagle

Amos Butler considered the bald eagle a local resident "generally distributed in fall, winter, and spring," and formerly a common resident throughout the state. There are old nesting records from English Lake (Starke County); DeKalb County; Knox County; near Kouts (Porter County); and in Carroll and Franklin Counties. One well-known nest, occupied for many years, was at Eagle Ford, about five miles west of Brookville on the Whitewater River. The latest confirmed Indiana record for a bald eagle nest was 1897. This nest was near Millers, in Lake County.

Eagles are still a part of the avifauna of Indiana, even though none has nested in the state for about eight decades. It is understandable that these large raptors would attract attention, for they are spectacular birds that in closeup views present an inspiring sight. In the past many of these great birds were shot, but an enlightened public and conservation efforts by many organizations have resulted in better protection for eagles in general.

An analysis of bald eagle sightings in Indiana from 1975 to the present reveals that there are records for every month of the year, but it is most frequently seen in November and December. In general, most are seen from October through March. These are no doubt the major migration periods. There are single records for June and July, two for May, and three for August. Wintering birds are most likely to be seen in the southern third of the state, although Christmas bird count data contain observations from nearly every part of Indiana.

The bald eagle is most often seen near water where it usually feeds, but it may be found in nearly any habitat during migration.

Much of the bald eagle's food consists of fish, both living and dead. It also occasionally takes small livestock

OSPREY

BALD EAGLE

and poultry. There are reports of this eagle killing small pigs and lambs. It also preys on flocks of geese, ducks, and especially coots. At the Crane Naval Weapons Support Center (Martin County), wintering eagles have been observed feeding on the offal left in the woods by deer hunters who partially dress their game kills in the field. We once saw an eagle carrying a dead mallard, which it dropped into the water; a second eagle immediately swooped down and retrieved the duck. Another bald eagle picked up from the water a dead oldsquaw that had just been shot by a hunter. At the Jasper-Pulaski Fish and Wildlife Area, a bald eagle killed a captive Canada goose. Steven H. Glass and Thomas Alexander saw bald eagles extract small fish from the ice into which they had been frozen. Glass also watched an eagle leave its perch, swoop, and break off the tree branch, then fly low with the branch over a group of coots, scattering the birds.

Bands of crows sometimes harass bald eagles; John P. Buck observed an adult eagle surrounded by crows sitting in a cornfield.

NORTHERN HARRIER

Circus cyaneus

Marsh Hawk, Harrier, Mouse Hawk

In the early light of a foggy morning a long-winged, long-tailed pale gray hawk quarters back and forth over a fallow lowland field. Its color and manner of flight suggest a foraging gull, but it is a splendid adult male northern harrier. As he banks and swerves just above the tops of the weeds, watching for a meadow vole, the white rump patch is visible. Silently he disappears into the mist. The harrier has less often been seen in Indiana in recent years, for much of the bird's hunting habitat has decreased because of drainage, fall plowing, and more intensive farming practices, but there are indications that this hawk is taking advantage of the extensive, grassland-type habitat now being provided in southern Indiana by the reclamation of old stripmined land.

Butler considered this hawk a resident in northern Indiana and a winter resident farther south. He wrote, "Its residence is confined more or less closely to the original prairie region. There, in the northern part of the State, it is a common, well known bird, and breeds. It is probable that it also breeds southward along the western side of the State." He further noted that it was of rare or irregular occurrence in fall, winter, and spring in the southeastern part of Indiana. Twenty years ago the northern harrier was considerably more common in the state than it is today: an uncommon migrant and rare permanent resident throughout Indiana. We are aware of only five nesting records since 1965, but not many birders frequent the nesting habitats of northern harriers, so that the species may well be more common than our breeding records indicate.

It is most frequently observed quartering back and forth over open fields or about ponds, potholes, and marshes. Favored fall and winter feeding sites in years past were stubble fields, fallow fields, hayfields, and what native grasslands remained in the state. Nesting cover was sometimes provided by the same types of fields over which the birds hunted, especially if there were swales and other low areas supporting tall weedy growth.

Many northern harriers migrate great distances in the fall. Most spring migrants are seen in the state in March and April, and most fall migrants from September to November, with early movements being detected in August.

The courtship behavior of the northern harrier is a spectacular aerial display that includes swooping dives and looping or barrel-rolling, quite different from its rather deliberate, leisurely flight when feeding. Nests are usually constructed in marshes, old pastures, or rather large grassy or weedy fields. It is not unusual for the birds to nest in damp sites, placing the nest on a hummock to keep it out of the water, but drier sites are also used; one nest was near the middle of a large field planted with Reed canary grass. Eggs have been found in nests from April 30 to June 17. The number of eggs per clutch in seventeen nests ranged from three to nine (average 5.2), and five was the most common clutch size. Two clutches were partially hatched on May 25 and five others hatched between June 6 and June 17. Four large young were seen in one nest until August 2. Since the young hatch at different times, siblings can vary considerably in size. Occasionally, the larger nestlings will kill and eat the smaller ones. Adults can be quite aggressive toward humans at the nest, especially when young are present.

NORTHERN HARRIER

Butler wrote that in the Whitewater River valley of southeastern Indiana, this hawk fed chiefly on "meadow mice, rabbits, squirrels and ground squirrels, lizards, snakes, frogs and birds, grasshoppers, locusts and other meadow insects." Birds eaten were principally those of the open field. Carrion is also eaten. Undigested portions of the food are regurgitated in the form of pellets, consisting mainly of bones, hair, and feathers. Mumford and Danner (1974) examined the contents of 344 pellets gathered in January and February at a roosting area in Ripley County. By far the most abundant prey items were the prairie vole and the meadow vole. Northern harriers have been observed attempting to catch coots and ducks.

Mumford and Danner (1974) also described a commu-nal roost of this harrier in Ripley County, Indiana, that was located in a forty-acre field of fescue (*Festuca* sp.). A few inches of standing water were present in some parts of the field and the fescue was from 2 to 3.5 feet tall. At least sixty birds were present on January 24; Marvin Doyle, a local landowner, told Danner the birds had been there for "a few weeks." The roost was in use until at least February 27 (when only four birds were seen). Smaller communal roosts have been observed in April and December in a stubble field and a field of switch grass.

Depicted plant: Northern pitcher plant (*Sarracenia purpurea*)

SHARP-SHINNED HAWK

Accipiter striatus

Little Blue Tail, Darter, Little Blue-tailed Hawk, Dart, Blue Darter

This secretive little hawk is unfamiliar to many because it is not easily found or identified. Its habits are similar to those of the larger Cooper's hawk, in that it spends considerable time perched quietly in dense cover, watching for small birds, on which it preys. Possibly more sharp-shins are observed in migration than at any other time, for then the birds are in the open and provide an observer more time to check field marks and make identifications.

This species was considered most abundant throughout Indiana during migrations by Butler, who reported that in southern Indiana it was more often found in winter than in summer. It is difficult to assign any status to this hawk, for we have little population information about it. Apparently it is an uncommon migrant and a very rare permanent resident. It is rare in winter and summer. Sharp-shinned hawks have been reported on 191 Christmas bird counts; only one hawk was recorded on 138 of these. Two were observed on thirty-nine, and three or more on only thirteen. The greatest abundance on such counts has been at the Muscatatuck National Wildlife Refuge, where seven each were noted on December 31, 1977, and December 20, 1980. Otherwise it appears about equally distributed throughout the state in winter.

Spring migration occurs mainly from late March to late April. Most of the scant spring migration data were gathered by Virginia Reuter-skiold at Baileytown (Porter County) in 1960 and 1961. In 1960, she observed migra-tion from March 29 (10 birds) to April 27 (4 birds). She saw 30 on April 10 and 57 on April 15. Sharp-shinned hawks moved through the area in 1961 from March 26 to April 20, the maximum being 8 on the former date. On April 19, 1957, 10 sharp-shinned and 11 Cooper's hawks were noted at Beverly Shores (Porter County). Elsewhere in the state, the meager records indicate movements during April. Sharp-shins usually migrate with other hawks, especially in the fall. Fall movements have been detected from the last half of September through October, and generally involved small numbers of birds.

Butler reported nesting records for DeKalb, Lake, and Vigo Counties. Before 1935, nesting was reported in Delaware and Kosciusko Counties. Only one record is dated: a nest with two eggs found April 17, 1886, in Lake County by LeGrand T. Meyer. We know of two nesting reports (1982, Monroe County; 1983, Marshall County) since about 1935, although this hawk is present, at least locally, during the breeding season. Diligent search is required, however, before we can correctly assign it a summer status.

Most of the food of the sharp-shinned hawk consists of small birds ranging in size from sparrows and juncos to mourning doves. This species is frequently attracted to bird feeding stations or bird banding sites where small birds congregate to feed. On at least four occasions we have been witness to interaction between blue jays and

SHARP-SHINNED HAWK

sharp-shinned hawks. On one of these occasions, a hawk was perched in a dead tree over a pond and eight blue jays were scolding it. Whenever the hawk made short flights from tree to tree, the jays all followed and perched as close as two feet away. The hawk usually sat quietly, but the jays called excitedly and moved about. It would then fly toward the jays and all birds would take flight, only to repeat the entire performance.

Dorthy Buck watched a sharp-shinned hawk at her feeding station. Some sparrows were taking cover from the hawk in a bush. The hawk alighted on the ground and walked around and around the bush, probably attempting to flush the sparrows. But the sparrows did not fly, and occasionally the hawk would fly into the bush in unsuccessful attempts to capture them.

Depicted plant: Northern white cedar (*Thuja occidentalis*)

COOPER'S HAWK

Accipiter cooperii

Big Blue-tailed Hawk, Big Blue Hawk, Long-tailed Dart, Darter, Blue Darter, Chicken Hawk

Many rural people who maintain bird feeding stations become familiar with these hawks, for they often visit the feeders to harass and try to capture small birds, and are usually so intent on making a kill that they are quite unself-conscious about being observed. If the prey eludes the hawk, it may perch close by and await another opportunity to give chase. We know of several instances when Cooper's hawks in pursuit of their prey flew into windowpanes, and of others when the prey crashed into a window or against the side of the house. The Cooper's hawk can also be seen at times soaring about fairly high in the sky, but more often it is in low flight, moving swiftly from one thick patch of cover to another. Like the sharp-shinned hawk, its main hunting tactic is to perch quietly inside the crown of a tree or shrub, then dart out to seize a bird. Captured prey is usually taken to a plucking station—a log, stump, tree branch, or even the ground —where it is divested of its larger feathers before being consumed. We once saw three such plucking stations within a hundred yards on a narrow, grassy pond dam. At each was a pile of the larger wing feathers and tail feathers, plus a few body feathers—the remains of two blue jays and a robin.

Butler considered the Cooper's hawk a resident, but rare in winter, noting that it was most numerous during migrations and in summer. The current status of this hawk is similar to that of the smaller sharp-shinned hawk: uncommon in migration and rare in winter and summer. Tallies of Cooper's hawks and sharp-shinned hawks seen on all Christmas bird counts taken in Indiana through the 1980–81 season are, respectively, 562 and 270. Single Cooper's were seen on 197 counts and 2 each were noted on 76. Three or more were recorded on 56 counts. The maximum number seen on a count was 7, on December 31, 1960, at Indianapolis.

Migration data are sparse, but seem to indicate that spring migrants pass through in some numbers the last half of April. For example, on April 19, 1957, eleven Cooper's hawks were seen at Beverly Shores (Porter County) along with ten sharp-shinned hawks. A single Cooper's hawk was migrating with other hawks at Indianapolis on April 22, 1961. Lawrence E. Hicks counted sixty-four Cooper's and twelve unidentified accipiters as he was driving from Fort Wayne, Indiana, to Danville, Illinois, on October 21, 1934.

Cooper's hawks no doubt breed throughout Indiana, but specific nesting records are mainly for the northern two-thirds of the state. Nests are usually in a hardwood tree thirty to sixty feet from the ground. One nest was in a large tamarack tree. Eggs have been found in nests from April 18 to June 5. Large young, nearly ready to leave the nest, have been observed as late as July 13. This hawk sometimes nests along roadsides and fairly close to buildings.

The major food of the Cooper's hawk is birds. On the average, avian prey taken by Cooper's hawks is larger in size than that taken by sharp-shinned hawks: among the birds known to have been killed or eaten by Cooper's hawks are blue jay, mourning dove, American robin, eastern meadowlark, and American kestrel. One hawk was observed pursuing a little blue heron. Harmon P. Weeks, Jr., saw a Cooper's hawk carrying an eastern chipmunk. We once saw a Cooper's hawk dive at three green-winged teal and an American black duck that were sitting on the water. The ducks did not fly and the hawk did not strike them, but landed on a tree limb just above the water and about ten feet from the ducks. The ducks remained sitting and one, with partially extended wings, made what appeared to be a threat display toward the hawk.

A flock of starlings will frequently "mob" Cooper's hawks in flight, forming a rather dense mass and circling about and following the hawk.

NORTHERN GOSHAWK

Accipiter gentilis

Big Blue Hen Hawk, American Goshawk

In certain years, this large, spectacular accipiter makes southward flights in the fall to Indiana, where it spends the winter. Positive field identification is often difficult or impossible, because the observer frequently gets only a brief glimpse of a large accipitrene hawk in flight. Under such conditions, telling a goshawk from a large Cooper's hawk in the field can be quite difficult. Most birders who have spent considerable time in the field in Indiana have seen hawks that they "thought," but could not be certain, were goshawks.

Butler considered the goshawk a rare winter visitor; he knew of only three records of its occurrence in the state. It is still a

COOPER'S HAWK

rare, irregular winter resident, although there are now numerous records. There is an indication that it has become more abundant in Indiana since about 1977. This hawk has been recorded most frequently in the northern one-quarter of the state, especially in the western portion of that region.

Goshawks, like other accipiters, prefer wooded areas where their avian prey is available and sufficient cover is present. They may be found in deciduous or coniferous woodlands, especially pine plantings. During some flight years, it appears that the goshawk has been attracted to the penned ring-necked pheasants at the Jasper-Pulaski Fish and Wildlife Area.

The earliest fall sighting of this hawk for Indiana is September 18, but most arrivals are detected in October. It has been recorded on at least twenty-two Christmas bird counts. Three were observed on the Willow Slough count, December 16, 1973; otherwise, all other sightings are of single birds. Late stragglers were seen May 13 in LaPorte County and May 14 in St. Joseph County.

One bird, while chasing a ring-necked pheasant, flew into a building and killed itself. Another killed itself by flying into a window at a backyard bird feeding station. One was observed picking up a cottontail from the road.

RED-SHOULDERED HAWK

Buteo lineatus

Red-shouldered Buzzard, Northern Red-shouldered Hawk

In the floodplains and sweet gum—pin oak flats along the winding Muscatatuck and other southern Indiana rivers, this fine hawk can usually be found throughout the year. In adult plumage, it is a striking bird.

From all reports, the red-shouldered hawk once was more abundant than the red-tailed hawk in much of Indiana, but there has been a drastic decrease in its numbers since 1900. Today it is an uncommon migrant, rare to very rare summer resident, and rare to very rare winter resident.

The relative abundance of the red-shouldered hawk and the red-tailed hawk in winter is best shown by Christmas bird count data. Red-tails were recorded on 616 counts, red-shoulders on only 295. The largest number of red-shoulders noted on a single count was 14, at Terre Haute on December 27, 1962. The average numbers of red-tails and red-shoulders, respectively, recorded per count for five selected localities were as follows: 5.7 and 2, Evansville; 4.6 and 2.3, Indianapolis; 17 and 1.8, Lafayette; 4.9 and 1.3, Richmond; 11.1 and 1.8, South Bend.

Migration of the red-shouldered hawk in Indiana has evidently escaped the attention of most observers, for there are few published data pertaining to flights. Migrants were observed at the southern end of Lake Michigan from March 3 to April 20. Fall migrants were recorded from September 4 to October 28. In all cases, small numbers of birds were involved. Seven were seen in the Indiana Dunes on March 22, 1980, and eight passed over Hovey Lake on October 28, 1952.

This hawk shows an interest in potential nesting sites early in the spring. Henry C. West watched one "on and around a nest" on February 4 in central Indiana. Nests are often constructed in trees along rivers and in swampy woodlands, but some birds nest in non-riparian habitats. Clutches of eggs have been recorded in nests from March 20 to June 20, but most records are for April. In sixteen nests for which clutch size was known, there were ten clutches of four eggs each, four of three, and one each of two and five. Thus, clutch size for the red-shouldered hawk is on the average larger than for the red-tailed hawk. In some cases, some of the eggs were buried in the soft nest lining. Lining materials included wool from

sheep and an old northern oriole nest. Twigs with green leaves attached or clusters of pine needles are sometimes used to decorate the nests.

Much of our knowledge of nesting was obtained from the records of those who collected eggs before 1940. H. Wesley McBride and his father collected about eighty sets of eggs near Waterloo from 1884 to 1897 and "examined several hundred nests." Between 1900 and 1917 Edward B. Williamson collected twenty-five sets of eggs of this hawk in Wells County. Homer F. Price took eleven sets of eggs in Allen County before 1934. These data confirm the reported former abundance of this hawk in northeastern Indiana. Williamson (1913) rationalized his egg collecting ventures as follows:

The Red-shoulder has endured persecution here in Wells County, Indiana, better than the Red-tail, which has almost disappeared, and every year I am able to locate a few nests. To take the eggs and cause the birds to nest a second time when leaves are on the trees and nests less readily discovered gives the birds and their offspring a better chance of escaping the constant warfare waged on them. Birds once robbed of their eggs are more wary and have a better chance of escaping the guns of irate chicken owners.

The red-shouldered hawk feeds on much the same foods as the red-tailed hawk, primarily small rodents. Red-shoulders perhaps eat more crayfish, fish, earthworms, insects, snakes, and the like than red-tails. One observer found a dead garter snake in a nest. Steven H. Glass watched a red-shoulder jumping up and down on the ice in an apparent attempt to get at a frozen fish, and another was seen feeding on fish discarded by an ice fisherman on a frozen borrow pit. James H. Mason and Amy Mason watched a red-shouldered hawk come to their feeding station and eat suet during the winter.

Individual birds are quite aggressive in defense of their nest and may strike a human who comes too near. Quite often one or both of the parents will remain in the vicinity when a human intruder approaches, circle overhead, and scream loudly and persistently. At other times, the birds will simply slip away and remain hidden until the intruder leaves. Blue jays often mimic one of the regular calls of the red-shouldered hawk, and inexperienced observers are hard pressed to distinguish between the calls.

RED-SHOULDERED HAWK

BROAD-WINGED HAWK

Buteo platypterus

From the top of a fire lookout near Houston, in Jackson County, one morning during the last half of September, we watched a large, milling, circling flight of hawks moving southward across the sky. They had come into view over the wooded hills some distance away. As they neared us, still swirling high in the air, we could see that they were, as we had suspected, broad-wings. Such flights are frequent throughout Indiana during the usual fall migration period of the broad-winged hawk in September. It is interesting to watch: the groups of birds circle and "kettle," riding the air currents, always steadily moving along their invisible route. The broad-winged in adult plumage is an attractive little buteo hawk with a distinctive tail pattern.

Butler reported that this hawk was "not common" in Indiana, but was a summer resident in the northern portion and "resident in southern Indiana." He cited no specific winter records and we suspect that, as today, this little hawk very seldom if ever remained in Indiana throughout the winter. It was known to have nested in three counties (Gibson, Knox, and Lake) by 1900. The broad-wing is currently a fairly common spring and fall migrant and rare to very rare summer resident throughout the state. It is probably most abundant in the wooded hills of the unglaciated portion of south-central Indiana during the summer. Although there have been several winter sightings of this hawk, we feel that most (if not all) of them are erroneous; most broad-wings winter far south of the United States.

Broad-wings tend to nest in the more extensive stands of forest or the larger woodlots, especially those that are ungrazed and relatively free from daily disturbance from man. During migration these hawks are frequently seen perched on fence posts, telephone poles, or trees along roadsides. They are somewhat tamer than the larger buteos. Some years ago, when it was popular to shoot hawks, squirrel hunters took their toll of them because many hunters were in the woodlands during the September peak of hawk migration.

A few migrants reach northern Indiana during the first week of March, but most spring migration occurs in April and are first seen in spring throughout the state during that month. The largest spring flights have been observed in the dunes region along Lake Michigan. On April 23, 1955, about 275 hawks (most of them broad-wings) passed over that area. About 290 broad-wings migrated past Baileytown (Porter County) on April 23, 1961. Evidently there is some flocking and movement of birds during June. On June 10, 1977, seven broad-wings (all appearing to be immatures or subadults) were noted flying over the Pigeon River Fish and Wildlife Area. All of these birds were molting, and had missing wing and tail features, according to Lee A. Casebere. Kenneth J. Brock, Brendan Grube, and Peter B. Grube observed a migration of broad-wings westward along Lake Michigan (Porter County) on June 20, 1981. Between 9:00 and 11:00 A.M. they counted 110 broad-wings, including groups of 17, 21, and 36. It was determined that some were adults, but most appeared to be immatures, and most were molting their flight feathers.

In general, fall migration begins in late August, continues most heavily throughout September, then decreases (and occurs more erratically) during October. Most broad-wings have left the state by mid-November. Virginia Reuter-skiold observed one in Porter County on November 22, 1958 and Howard F. Wright and Val Nolan Jr. saw one at Geist Reservoir, near Indianapolis, on November 29, 1947. Some large fall migrations include the following: Wayne County, September 23, 1977 (about 800 passed); Bloomington, September 18, 1960 (321); Franklin County, September 24, 1955 (166); Allen County, September 10, 1979 (150 in forty-five minutes).

Although there are nesting records from more than a dozen counties, few reports mention numbers of eggs or young in the nests. Five nests containing eggs were examined from April 11, to June 12. These nests held 1, 2, 2, 3, and 5 eggs respectively. Young have been observed in the nest until at least July 1. A nest on the Pigeon River Fish and Wildlife Area was used by this species for four consecutive years, according to Mark A. Weldon and Lee A. Casebere. Broad-winged hawks were present, and presumably nesting, in nineteen additional counties during the nesting season.

Broad-winged hawks eat much the same foods as the other buteos that occur in Indiana, but perhaps take more insects, reptiles, and amphibians than most. We once saw one carrying a lizard and another had the remains of a Fowler's toad in its gullet when shot.

Depicted tree: American basswood (*Tilia americana*)

BROAD-WINGED HAWK

[SWAINSON'S HAWK]

Buteo swainsoni

This buteo is at best a casual visitor to Indiana. Although there have been several reported sightings, not all of them are satisfactory for positive identification. We hope that someone will eventually obtain a suitable photograph or specimen. James E. Landing observed a hawk he thought was a Swainson's on May 3, 1958, in Porter County. On July 24, 1977, Jackie B. Elmore, Diane Elmore, and Lene Rauth had a rather brief view of a buteo they identified as a Swainson's hawk at Lake Monroe. William H. Buskirk and Bret Whitney saw an adult on October 22, 1977, in Union County.

RED-TAILED HAWK

RED-TAILED HAWK

Buteo jamaicensis

Hen Hawk, Chicken Hawk, Red-tailed Buzzard, Black Hawk, Eastern Red-tailed Hawk

Snow covered the ground and blew in drifts against the shrubby fencerow. In the cold wind of an overcast winter day, few creatures were moving about. A tall dead tree in the fencerow towered above the surrounding vegetation. Close to the top sat a large-bodied hawk, slightly hunched as it peered at the ground, waiting for a small rodent or bird to appear. Suddenly the hawk glided to the ground at least a hundred yards from its perch and seized a meadow vole in its talons. In flight, the broad, rounded rufous tail was clearly visible. Many Hoosier birders first identified a red-tailed hawk in similar conditions. Or our attention may have been focused on a large hawk soaring overhead on broad wings, its reddish tail fully spread. This beautiful hawk is a familiar part of the Indiana scene throughout the year.

A hundred years ago it was a common resident, but considered more numerous in the southern two-thirds of the state. Today it is a fairly common migrant and rare to uncommon summer resident (locally more abundant). It is generally uncommon in winter. More information is needed to assess migration patterns. Winter populations are best indicated by Christmas bird counts. At Lafayette, an average of seventeen red-tailed hawks per count has been reported on thirty-eight counts; numbers per count ranged from 1 to 43. In the South Bend area, 11.1 per count were recorded on thirty-three counts. The range was from 1 to 29. An average of only 4.6 red-tails were found at Indianapolis on thirty-one counts; the largest number was 16. Twenty-eight counts in the Richmond area averaged 4.9, with ranges from 1 to 12. There was an average of 5.7 on twenty-seven counts in the Evansville area.

In general the red-tailed hawk is a bird of the woodlands, but foraging birds venture into more open areas. During the nesting season, it (like many other hawks) is more difficult to find. The birds tend to be more retiring and evidently confine their time spent in relatively open areas to the early morning or late evening. Nesting sites are usually in extensive wooded areas or woodlots (frequently near human dwellings). Nests are also present along stream valleys and occasionally are placed in isolated large trees in open areas. At Willow Slough, a pair of red-tailed hawks nested in the middle of a large heron rookery. During the winter, this hawk may be found in nearly any type of habitat.

Spring migration is evident from about the first of March throughout April. Most of the available spring migration data are from the counties bordering Lake Michigan. From March 27 to April 18, 1960, five flights totaling about 700 hawks (85% redtails) passed at Baileytown (Porter County), according to Raymond Grow and Virginia Reuter-skiold. Other migrations were observed in this general region on March 3, 26, 30, and 31 and April 14 and 20. Robert S. Gregory reported migrants passing over the Mooresville area (Morgan County) during the first half of March. Southbound migrants have been recorded as early as August 7 at Baileytown and August 15 in LaPorte and Porter Counties. Fall migration appears to be quite prolonged, with birds reported moving through the state until at least November 18. There appears to be a significant influx of red-tailed hawks from the west and northwest into Indiana during the winter, for very dark plumaged and very pale plumaged birds are noted quite regularly. Such birds probably represent two other races of red-tailed hawk other than the race that breeds in Indiana.

Nests are usually conspicuous in early spring because the birds begin nesting activities before leaves appear on the trees. Eggs have been found in nests from March 17 to April 30. The usual number of eggs per clutch is two, but three (and even four) are sometimes reported. Young have been observed in a nest as late as June 3. Butler mentioned a particular nest he knew had been used "for nearly twenty years." Reuse of nests in succeeding years is quite common and an aid to locating breeding hawks. From time to time, a nest used by a red-tailed hawk one year will be taken over by a great horned owl the next year, or vice versa. Squirrels may construct a nest on top of a hawk's nest, and raccoons probably utilize nests for sunning and sleeping at times. Nests normally require refurbishing each spring, which may entail adding fresh sprigs of greenery. We once watched a red-tailed hawk taking nesting material for its nest from what appeared to be an old squirrel's nest.

Red-tailed hawks eat a variety of foods: birds, mammals, reptiles, insects, and carrion. Specific prey found at nests includes muskrat, cottontail, rats, mice, squirrel, domestic chicken, northern flicker, and screech-owl. The stomach of an immature we examined contained only insects; another had a short-tailed shrew (*Blarina brevicauda*) in the gullet. One was seen carrying a fox squirrel and Coffin (1906) reported seeing one feeding on the still warm carcass of another red-tailed hawk. Mr. and Mrs. Fredrick H. Montague, Jr., watched a red-tailed hawk capture a muskrat, take it into a tree, and spend several hours feeding on it.

FERRUGINOUS HAWK

Buteo regalis

Ferruginous Rough-legged Hawk

This beautiful hawk is an accidental visitor to Indiana. More study is required to determine its true status. Butler placed it on his hypothetical list, but later reported that he examined one trapped in Boone County on January 6, 1909. The whereabouts of this mounted specimen are unknown. Arthur C. Bent (1937) reported the taking of two ferruginous hawks near Richmond on April 12, 1917, and November 13, 1930; but we do not know if they were preserved. An injured one found in Porter County on September 25, 1934, was banded and released (Ford, 1956). Virginia Reuter-skiold observed a hawk she identified as this species from November 30, 1952, to January 8, 1953, in Porter County. John D. Goodman reported the sighting of a ferruginous hawk in Madison County in May 1976.

ROUGH-LEGGED HAWK

Buteo lagopus

American Rough-legged Hawk, Black Hawk

From time to time the wintering population of rough-legged hawks in the region of northwestern Indiana that was originally prairieland is quite large and the great, quiet birds, which can be seen perched on telephone poles, fenceposts, in treetops, or hovering while foraging over waste areas are quite conspicuous. Before fall plowing became common in this section of the state, one might see as many as six rough-legged hawks feeding in a single field. But fall plowing dramatically decreased the grain stubble that harbored mice and voles, eliminating most of the hawks' good winter foraging habitat. They now must find odd patches of fallow field, ditch banks, railroad and highway rights-of-ways, and the very few remaining brushy fencerows to search for prey. These wintering birds show considerable variation in color and there are certain years when a larger than usual percentage of them are of the black color phase. Of the eighteen rough-legged hawks seen by Irving W. Burr in the Lafayette area on January 29, 1961, five were in the black phase; likewise, four of seventeen observed by Burr in the same area, February 10, 1962, were black-phased birds. One seen recently was chocolate brown all over.

Butler noted that the rough-legged hawk was an irregular winter visitor and was usually rare except along the western side of the state, where it was "more or less common." He further stated that it was "very abundant throughout the State" in some winters. The current Indiana range and occurrence are much the same as formerly, but numbers have evidently decreased considerably. The species is found throughout the state, but still tends to be most abundant in the northwestern portion. Data from Christmas bird counts substantiate Butler's statement that it is present in greatest numbers in western Indiana. All the Christmas counts that reported a maximum of fifteen or more rough-legged hawks on a single count were in the western third of the state. There is considerable fluctuation in numbers from year to year. In northwestern Indiana, an average of seven rough-legged hawks per count was recorded on thirty-two Christmas bird counts at Lafayette and an average of 7.2 per count was found on twenty-four counts in southeastern LaPorte County.

Rough-legged hawks begin appearing in northern Indiana in late September; our earliest date is September 12 (Porter County). However, the largest influx occurs in October. Available habitat, snow cover, and food supply probably determine to some extent how far south the birds go during a particular year. Migrants were in evidence in LaPorte County on October 26, 1958, when eight flew over from east to west in one hour. Sixteen were observed flying west in Porter County on November 8, 1952 and twelve on November 18, 1956. Wintering birds have mostly left the southern third of the state by the last week of April. A few have lingered at scattered locations throughout the remainder of Indiana through the first half of May. Howard F. Wright and Val Nolan Jr. observed one in Marion County on May 18, 1946. Our latest record for Indiana is that of one noted June 1, 1971 in LaPorte County by Dorthy Buck.

Cope (1949) reported that he found twenty-seven least shrews (*Cryptotis parva*) and a short-tailed shrew (*Blarina brevicauda*) in the digestive tract of a rough-legged hawk killed in Wayne County. Another, shot in early November, was holding a vole (*Microtus* sp.) in its talons. Amos W. Butler examined six hawks of this species and found they had eaten mice and cottontails. Other rough-legged hawks were observed feeding on the carcasses of a lamb and a striped skunk. Foraging rough-legged hawks frequently hover as they scan the ground below, but we have also seen red-tailed hawks hover on several occasions. Thus, one should not assume that any large buteo hawk seen hovering is a rough-leg.

GOLDEN EAGLE

Aquila chrysaetos

Field identification of both golden and bald eagles has long been a problem because of species and individual variations in plumages. Thus, in evaluating observations of eagles in Indiana, we cannot be certain how many of the birds reported (especially immatures) were correctly identified. A number of earlier state records (for example, some of those cited by Butler in 1898) were substantiated by the examination of birds killed. Many Indiana residents who have never seen one outside of a zoo are surprised to learn that wild eagles are still found in the state.

Butler noted that the golden eagle was a regular but uncommon winter resident that was said to have formerly been more abundant. He mentioned that the greatest numbers were seen from December to February. Today, this eagle is rare to very rare in most parts of the state, but is seen most frequently at Lake Monroe, Jasper-Pulaski Fish and Wildlife Area, Willow Slough Fish and Wildlife Area, and Crane Naval Weapons Support Center. There are records from throughout the state and for all months of the year except June (there is a single July record).

The golden eagle appears to be attracted to larger bodies of water, where it is frequently seen with the bald eagle. Such areas probably are favored sites because of the concentration of waterfowl and other birds about the lakes and marshes.

Although there is no noticeable migration of golden eagles, most birds are seen during March and April in the spring and from October to December in the fall. These data indicate that migration takes place during these periods. The species evidently wanders erratically, so may appear at any season. Relatively few have been recorded on Christmas bird counts.

AMERICAN KESTREL

Falco sparverius

Sparrow Hawk, Eastern Sparrow Hawk

In the extensive, relatively flat cultivated fields that were formerly upper terraces of the Wabash and White Rivers in southwestern Indiana, American kestrels find winter habitat to their liking. Fairly large numbers can be found there at that season, hovering in the air or perched on telephone poles and wires, usually facing the roadways. The birds become accustomed to passing motor vehicles, and afford good views to birdwatchers who drive slowly.

Even though much cover is lost by fall plowing and the

harvesting of crops, there are still grassy and weedy ditch banks, roadsides, railroad rights-of-way, and fencerows where small rodents thrive. Birders who live in the northern part of the state are often surprised to find this beautiful little kestrel so common in southern Indiana in winter.

Butler wrote that the American kestrel was a regular resident north to Wabash, Tippecanoe, and Carroll Counties, rare north of there in winter, but more numerous southward, and common throughout the state in summer. It is currently a common migrant and uncommon summer resident throughout the state. We consider it common in winter in the southern two-thirds of Indiana and locally it may be common in the northern third.

In addition to open areas along roadsides, the kestrel also inhabits vacant lots and waste areas in towns and may be found on university campuses and in cemeteries and open residential areas. Roosting sites include tree cavities and holes in buildings.

Butler reported that American kestrels began to leave the northern part of the state in September and "in some winters all leave." He further noted that in more open winters there was an increase in numbers in the southern part of the state in February, with migration continuing throughout March. Smith (1936) wrote that the average arrival date for this kestrel in the Calumet region of northwestern Indiana was about March 4 and the average departure date September 14. There is practically nothing in the literature concerning American kestrel migration in the state. They are found throughout the year in all parts and migrants are not easily detected. Keller observed a flight of hawks at Indianapolis on April 22 that included two of these kestrels.

There are relatively few data on nesting, for the birds build their nests in tree cavities and nesting boxes where examination of nests is usually difficult or impossible. Dorthy Buck and John P. Buck have watched nesting kestrels in a nest box at their home for many years and have amassed considerable data regarding the breeding cycle there. Birds were noted at the nest box on February 20 and copulation was observed as early as February 28 and on March 22. Nests are usually constructed in a tree cavity or old woodpecker nesting hole, but the kestrels readily nest in boxes provided for them or other birds. One nest was found about thirty feet up in a dead cottonwood. Another was in an old woodpecker nesting hole. One was in the top of a dead snag, in which a pair of red-headed woodpeckers were also nesting. This kestrel has also nested in crevices in brick and stone buildings on the Purdue University campus for many years.

Eggs have been found in nests as early as about April 10 and as late as July 19. Our sample is small, thus these dates could no doubt be extended on both ends. Clutch size for five nests ranged from four to six eggs and averaged five. The number of young per nest, for six nests, was three to five (average 4.5). Adults have been observed feeding young in the nest by April 29, and young have been reported leaving the nest from May 17 to July 6. One of five young in one nest box was evidently eaten by its nestmates.

The food of the American kestrel includes small mammals (mice, shrews, voles) and birds, insects, snakes, earthworms, and carrion. One was observed trying to catch an American goldfinch in a bird banding trap. Another was feeding an unidentified sparrow to its young and a third was eating a house sparrow. One kestrel was seen eating a garter snake. Buskirk (1962) reported two instances of this hawk's feeding on earthworms. We have observed a kestrel feeding on a dead eastern cottontail killed by a motor vehicle on the road.

It is this hawk's *kee kee kee* or *killy killy killy* call, rapidly repeated several times, that often draws our attention to it. The birds are especially noisy in spring during the courtship period. During the nesting season, this kestrel is much less conspicuous, but by August it is again seen along roadsides.

MERLIN

Falco columbarius

Pigeon Hawk, Eastern Pigeon Hawk

We had rowed our boat across Hovey Lake to watch for birds along the shoreline, where large baldcypress, buttonbush, and other swamp-inhabiting trees grew. There was quite a commotion in a nearby clump of smaller cypress and it soon became apparent that three merlins and a small group of blue jays were involved in a fracas. The jays were calling and scolding the hawks, while the latter were perched. Then a hawk would fly out toward the jays, causing them to retreat, still screaming, into cover. The hawk would again perch, the jays would return, and the process would be repeated. We watched this performance for several minutes, and no harm came to the jays. Perhaps they were lucky in evading the merlins, or perhaps the hawks were not really intent on making a kill just then, and it was only a game. This happened during mid-October, at the height of both species' fall migration southward through Indiana.

Butler considered the merlin a regular migrant and irregular winter resident, noting that it was not common. He thought (erroneously) that it might nest in northern Indiana. It is difficult to determine accurately the change of status of this species in the state since 1900. It is now thought to be a very rare migrant and casual winter resident. The number of fall sightings totals a bit more than twice the number of spring observations. Most of the two dozen winter records are the results of sightings within the past twenty years. Birdwatchers may be becoming more and more aware of the possibility of seeing this falcon at that season.

Although merlins have been observed in various open habitats, the majority of them were seen about or over water areas. At the Jasper-Pulaski Fish and Wildlife Area, they have been noted perched in the tops of dead trees bordering swampy sites; the same sort of habitat was used at the Hovey Lake Fish and Wildlife Area. A number have been found along the Lake Michigan shore, around the borders of reservoirs, marshes, and lakes, and along rivers. Birds in passage may occur nearly anywhere there is rather open terrain. Individuals may hunt at bird feeding stations, on campuses, and in residential areas, or along roadsides. During the winter of 1913–14, one lived in the tower of the high school in Lyons (Greene County) and fed on rock doves (domestic pigeons), according to William B. Van Gorder (Esten, 1931).

Spring migrants probably appear in March, although some wintering individuals are also present into that month. April is the month with the largest number of sightings, followed by March; a few birds are present in May, and there is one observation for June. Fall migration evidently begins in late August and peaks in September and October, with a few more sightings in the latter than in the former month. There are relatively few November and early December records. Merlins are usually seen alone, but on rare occasions two or three may be found together. James B. Cope saw three pass in migration in one day with other hawks.

Haymond (1870) wrote that merlins were "occasionally seen following the flight of [passenger] pigeons in their migrations" and were "very rarely seen at other times" in Franklin County.

Most of the food of this hawk consists of birds ranging in size from sparrows to pigeons. Among the known prey in Indiana are unidentified sparrows, house sparrow, blue jay, red-winged blackbird, and rock dove. In addition, merlins have been observed swooping at (and possibly catching) European starlings. One was seen chasing a northern flicker. At times the hawks seem to indulge in play and have been seen harassing shorebirds and a belted kingfisher. Henry C. West saw one calling as it was being pursued by four blue jays and a northern flicker.

PEREGRINE FALCON

Falco peregrinus

Duck Hawk, Great-footed Hawk

To see this magnificent predator in action is to understand why it has fascinated men from time immemorial. Its power, grace, and swiftness inspire awe tinged with terror.

About half a dozen of us were birding at a marsh when several blue-winged teal hurtled past about twenty-five feet over our heads. Out of nowhere came a peregrine falcon. It struck one of the teal, which plummeted into the cattails. Making no attempt to retrieve its kill, the hawk shot upward, then stooped on an American black duck, sending it tumbling end over end— quite dead—to the ground. Again disdaining to retrieve its prey, the falcon swiftly flew out of sight. On another occasion, while watching shorebirds on a pond, we were startled by the sound of air rushing through wings. A peregrine suddenly stooped on the birds, leveled off about ten feet above them (they did not flush), then climbed steadily and flew about a hundred yards farther to dive on a turkey vulture that was lazily rocking in the thermals. It did not appear to be attempting a kill, for it veered off at the last second and disappeared into the distance.

Butler reported that the peregrine was resident and "not rare" in the lower Wabash River valley, a rare migrant elsewhere in the state. On the authority of Robert Ridgway it was listed as breeding in Gibson and Knox Counties, but we know of no actual nest found there. Ridgway did find three nests near Mount Carmel, Illinois, in the spring of 1878. They were all in cavities in the tops of very large sycamore trees and were inaccessible. One nest was eighty-nine feet from the ground. Peregrine falcons possibly also nested in similar sites across the border in Indiana. Today it appears to be a very rare to casual migrant and winter resident, and no additional reports of nesting have appeared in the literature.

The peregrine falcon frequents water areas, for much of its food consists of waterfowl, shorebirds, and other birds found in aquatic habitats. Thus, many sightings have been near reservoirs, at fish and wildlife areas, and along Lake Michigan. Birds in migration, however, may occur nearly anywhere.

This falcon is occasionally seen in winter. Spring migrants begin to arrive in March, and most of them are observed in April and May. There are three sightings for June, one for July, and four for August—evidently the month that fall migration begins. The bulk of the falcons pass through from September to November. More are seen in October than in any other month; the smallest numbers are seen in November. There are few records for early December, then from eight to ten sightings on Christmas bird counts (two of them for the first week of January). Single peregrines are most commonly seen, but—rarely— two are reported together. In some years, more than the usual number are seen along Lake Michigan. For example, on October 8, 1983, there were at least ten (and possibly as many as twenty-three). The birds are often seen as they fly along parallel to the shore, sometimes within three or four feet of the water and at other times as much as a hundred feet in the air. When wind currents are suitable, they engage in considerable soaring as they move along the sand dunes.

The peregrine falcon feeds mainly on other birds; its propensity for killing waterfowl was no doubt responsible for its vernacular name of duck hawk. Evidently birds from the size of warblers to ducks are taken. In Indiana, peregrines have been observed to kill American black duck, blue-winged teal, black tern, American coot, European starling and meadowlark. In addition, they have been seen pursuing mourning doves, rock doves, American crows, mallards, and shorebirds. We have seen one kill an American coot and spotted another that was carrying a black tern to a feeding perch. Thomas Alexander once watched a peregrine take a meadowlark from its perch on a telephone wire; the hawk had attacked from the front, but the meadowlark would not flush. Peregrines frequently stoop down on birds they have no intention of killing.

In Indiana, peregrines are normally silent, but Edwin R. Larson heard one give its *chew chew chew* call.

PRAIRIE FALCON
Falco mexicanus

The prairie falcon has occurred in Indiana on at least two occasions. Esten (1933) reported that one "was found in late December, 1931, west of Terre Haute by Dr. Allyn of Terre Haute Normal School [now Indiana State University]." Butler (1936) reported that "a Prairie Falcon was captured in Sullivan County, Indiana, about thirty miles south of Terre Haute, January 9, 1932, by a student of State Teacher's College. It was brought alive to Prof. William P. Allyn of the Zoology department. . . . He kept it about a month when it died, after a treatment of sodium fluoride for lice. He gave it to Mr. Sidney R. Esten, then of the Indiana State Department of Conservation, Indianapolis. Mr. Esten made a skin of it and preserved the specimen. I know of no other record of this species for Indiana. At Prof. Allyn's request I am making this record." We have been unable to locate this specimen.

On January 13, 1980, James H. Campbell and Willard N. Gray observed a prairie falcon south of Boonville (Warrick County) on a utility pole in an open area of tilled fields. It was seen again on January 18 and 19 and was subsequently trapped by a falconer (photographs were obtained of the captive bird).

GRAY PARTRIDGE

Perdix perdix

Hungarian Partridge, European Partridge, Hun, Hunky

If the gray partridge became extinct in Indiana, we would be saddened, but not surprised. Since World War II drastic changes in agricultural and other land-use patterns have eliminated most of its habitat—and very nearly succeeded in eliminating this European game bird as well.

Thousands of gray partridges were released throughout the state around 1910, and by 1938 the birds had established themselves in east-central Indiana, in a range bounded by Dearborn, Jennings, Boone, Fulton, Whitley, and DeKalb Counties. Wright (1966), a graduate student at Purdue University, studied the species in the mid-sixties and found it had withdrawn along the eastern side of the state and had moved about one county westward into Hendricks, Montgomery, and Tippecanoe Counties. Since 1965 there have been only eight sightings of this partridge in the state. The four latest reports (1975 to 1977) were from Adams, Allen, Lagrange, and Noble Counties. We think there may still be a small number of partridges left in northeastern Indiana.

Wright found that the gray partridge in Indiana used three main types of habitats—row crops (corn and soybeans), small grains (wheat and oats), and meadows (hay, pasture, idle land, other cover that allows a sod to form). Cornfields were an especially important habitat during January and February; thus the relatively new practice of fall plowing has been very detrimental. Few gray partridge nests have been discovered in Indiana, and we have been unable to find dates for the few nests reported. Baker (1955) found a nest with twenty-two eggs in a hayfield, and Wright located three nests, all in hayfields. A farmer reported another nest with sixteen eggs in a roadside ditch. William B. Barnes (1941) mentioned a nest in a hayfield, two in fencerows, and one in a roadside ditch. Three of these nests contained 15, 16, and 24 eggs on June 25, August 3, and May 28. Partridges nesting in hayfields are of course vulnerable to mowing operations.

Wright observed a partridge brood estimated to be about three days old on June 10. Eggs in one nest hatched on August 8. Several of the broods observed by Wright contained from ten to fourteen young. Broods seemed to prefer wheat or oats for cover, but after these grains were harvested the birds fed and roosted in stubble or meadows. Cornfields provided the major escape cover after the young were capable of strong flight. Wright compiled data on thirty-four coveys, which averaged ten birds per covey and varied from three to eighteen.

The food habits of the gray partridge in Indiana were determined by examination of birds shot during the fall hunting season. Corn was by far the most important food. Other food items were soybeans, wheat, crabgrass, witchgrass, panic grass sp., yellow foxtail, green foxtail, bulrush, Pennsylvania smartweed, black bindweed, lamb's-quarters, pigweed, spurge, wild grape, giant ragweed, lesser ragweed, and unknown weeds and grasses. During the winter, the birds dug through three feet of snow to reach corn; one farmer saw a covey feeding with his cattle when the snow was deep.

Our illustration shows a female partridge. The sexes are very similar.

Depicted plant: Red clover (Trifolium pratense), like the gray partridge an alien.

GRAY PARTRIDGE

RING-NECKED PHEASANT

Phasianus colchicus

Pheasant, Ringneck, English Ringneck, Chinese Ringneck

Heavy dew coated everything in the mid-April landscape, and a spider's web strung across one of the larger openings in a woven wire fence had been transformed into strands of water droplets that shone silver in the rays of the rising sun. It was cool and calm that morning in Benton County and one could see for long distances in nearly every direction, for this region was formerly prairie land. An upland sandpiper, which had probably just arrived from its wintering grounds, called as he flew by. A flock of pectoral sandpipers wheeled past in their typical precision flight and immediately dropped into a low spot where rainwater had collected. Suddenly we heard a peculiar, two-syllable screech, followed by a rapid flapping of wings. It was a male ring-necked pheasant, standing alertly less than fifty yards away at the corner of a patch of rank weeds along a brushy ditch bank. The sun glistened on his feathers as he stood in the open, avoiding the dew-laden vegetation. Again he uttered the raspy call, and we were surprised at its unmusical quality. The cock pheasant was on his territory, sending out his challenge to any rival males in the area, warning them that this was his "turf," and letting hens know that he was ready to mate with them.

Several very ambitious attempts have been made, beginning in 1899, to establish this exotic game bird in the state. Between the turn of the century and 1962 some two million ring-necked pheasants were released here, in virtually every county. It soon became apparent that optimal

pheasant range was of two distinct types, one the flat, black fertile soils of the western prairie, the other the pothole and lake region of northeastern Indiana. There were several setbacks, but the population in general was on the increase as of 1960. Then came the almost universal change to fall plowing, followed in the late 1970s by three very severe winters in a row. The effect was disastrous. So far, the ring-necked pheasant population has not recovered.

Although this pheasant may exhibit local seasonal movements, it is not highly migratory. Ginn (1947) analyzed the movements of 325 pheasants banded at release. Eleven percent were recovered on the farms where they had been released. Sixty-eight percent were recovered within one to five miles from the release sites. Of the twenty-one percent recovered more than five miles away, many traveled twenty miles and one moved ninety-seven miles.

Males begin to select their territories in late February and remain on them throughout April or later. Each male attempts to obtain a harem of females, and may mate with ten or more, depending partly upon the hen population. In Indiana this is usually not possible. One nest has been observed as early as March 18, but this is probably unusually early. Most nests are probably begun in April, but nesting continues into September. Nest sites include alfalfa and clover fields, weedy and brushy fencerows, ditch banks, roadsides and railroad rights-of-way, pastured woodlot, fallow fields, and grassy marsh borders. The number of eggs in eight recent nests averaged 14.5 and ranged from 6 to 22. William E. Ginn reported that twenty-eight nests contained a total of 257 eggs, but gave no breakdown per nest. Two or more females may lay eggs in the same nest. Most young are hatched in May or June, and some as late as September.

The ring-necked pheasant feeds on a wide variety of plant foods (mainly seeds) and during the summer consumes considerable animal life (especially grasshoppers). An analysis of the food present in fourteen crops and twenty-one gizzards revealed that corn was by far the most important food on the basis of amount consumed. Various smartweeds, ragweeds, and foxtails were also important, as were insects. In all, thirty-two different plant seeds or leaves had been eaten by these birds.

Depicted plant: Hedge bindweed (*Convolvulus sepium*)

RUFFED GROUSE

Bonasa umbellus

Pheasant, Wood Pheasant, Partridge, Heathcock, Ruffled Grouse, Drumming Pheasant

The wooded hill country around Maumee in Jackson County, one of the places we used to visit in the early fifties while conducting ruffed grouse drumming counts, contains an interesting variety of birds around the middle of April, and to us it was a special place. We would stand along the roadside on those calm, cool mornings at sunrise and listen as the forest-inhabiting birds woke up. Visibility was limited by tree growth to only the road and its borders, but scattered patches of old fields and young pine plantations were interspersed with thick woodland. The whip-poor-will chorus had ceased and a red bat that had lingered to feed until the sky brightened disappeared into the treetops to roost for the day. A Bachman's sparrow sang nearby, and a northern cardinal in the distance had been singing for some time. From the woods we could hear black-and-white warblers, worm-eating warblers, and Louisiana waterthrushes, all newly arrived on their breeding grounds. A yellow-throated warbler was singing from some tall sycamores along a small stream. Other early migrants that were quite active were the blue-gray gnatcatchers and scarlet tanagers. While listening to these bird songs, we would suddenly become aware of a peculiar dull, distant thumping sound, like the beating of a giant heart, that one seemed to feel more than hear. It was, of course, a male ruffed grouse in the forest, drumming on his favorite log. When it was time to drive to the next stop, we always went reluctantly back to the car.

Butler reported the ruffed grouse as a permanent resident in varying abundance in suitable forested areas throughout the state. It was common in Brown and DeKalb Counties, while in the lower Whitewater River valley it still occurred "in some numbers." Aldo Leopold reported the presence of this grouse in the following counties in 1931: Bartholomew, Brown, Clark, Jackson, Lake, Lawrence, Marshall, Monroe, Porter, Scott, Washington, and Wayne. When the occupied range was mapped by Mumford in 1954, it was found to be restricted to the unglaciated section of the state. The contiguous range was thought to include Monroe, Brown, Jackson, Lawrence, Bartholomew, Washington, Morgan, Orange, Clark,

RUFFED GROUSE

Johnson, Crawford, and Harrison Counties. Smaller occupied areas were present in Perry, Owen, Greene, and
Martin Counties. Grouse were purchased from Wisconsin and released in Harrison, Perry, and Pike Counties in
1952 and in Martin County in 1957. After this date the
Indiana Department of Natural Resources began restock-
ing ruffed grouse into other sections of the state with
birds that had been trapped in Indiana. From 1968 to
1982 birds were recorded from twenty-eight counties.

P. Decker Major obtained the best data concerning
grouse numbers, most of it for the Nebo Ridge area
(Brown–Jackson Counties), which he studied from 1969
to 1980. Spring drumming counts and walking censuses
resulted in population estimates ranging from two to five
birds per hundred acres. Summer densities were calcu-

lated to range from seven to fourteen birds per hundred
acres for the years 1976 to 1978.

The ruffed grouse is found in woods, woods borders,
and brushy areas or openings. Formerly it was probably
present in all of Indiana except for the prairie and other
open lands. Obviously it has best been able to sustain
itself in the rugged, heavily forested hills of the south-
central region, from which it was never extirpated. Brushy
areas, woody, brushy fields or creek valleys, and pine
plantations are utilized by this grouse at certain seasons.
Dusting sites, such as those along woods roads, or patches
of barren soil, are used heavily by the birds. They may
roost on the ground, in trees, or (in winter) beneath
the snow.

The ruffed grouse is not a migratory bird, but there is

considerable local movement, especially during the fall, and to a lesser extent in the spring. Audubon reported the movements of grouse from Indiana across the Ohio River into Kentucky during the fall.

In early spring, male ruffed grouse select drumming sites (usually a partially rotten log lying on the ground) and perform their interesting drumming to attract females. Drumming has been heard in nearly every month of the year, but it occurs mostly in March and April. Nests are mainly leaf and grass-lined depressions in the ground, often at the base of a stump or tree. Eggs have been found in nests from at least April 3 to June 7. There are few data on clutch size for nests found in Indiana. Eight clutches thought to be complete contained from ten

to fifteen eggs and averaged twelve. In two nests the eggs hatched on May 14 and June 7.

Adults and young feed heavily on insects and, to some extent, other invertebrates during the warmer weather. But the staple diet throughout the year consists of seeds, leaves, twigs, fruits, and buds of various plants. Some important fall foods are wild grape (*Vitis* spp.), greenbrier (*Smilax*) fruits and leaves, treefoils (*Desmodium*), fern leaves, hazelnut (*Corylus*) catkins, and miscellaneous green material and buds (Johnson, 1965, 1966).

Males and females are similar. The male is slightly larger and the black band on the tail is more pronounced. The female is illustrated here, along with crested dwarf iris (*Iris cristata*).

GREATER PRAIRIE-CHICKEN

Tympanuchus cupido

Prairie Chicken, Prairie Hen, Pinnated Grouse, Chicken

A few miles north of Enos (Newton County), it was possible in the spring of 1950 to stand in one spot and listen to greater prairie-chickens booming simultaneously on at least four different booming grounds. North, south, and east of Bogus Island was some of the best remaining prairie-chicken habitat in Indiana and birdwatchers would flock to the region each April to watch (and listen to) the birds perform their distinctive courtship display—one of Nature's prize shows. On a cold, cloudy, windy morning in April 1950 (not unusual for Newton County at this season), Mumford was fortunate enough to witness the last large gathering of prairie-chickens on an Indiana booming ground. The site had been original prairie, first plowed in 1949 and planted to wheat. Seventy-five male prairie-chickens were performing on the courting grounds—strutting, giving their low, moaning calls, cackling, squabbling, jumping into the air, and otherwise engaged in their ritual dance. The following spring, less than half this number returned to the booming ground, and later the site was abandoned altogether as the birds disappeared from the region. Those early April mornings were memorable, for there were shorebirds and waterfowl on the wetter prairie sites, and Smith's longspurs and Lapland longspurs in huge flocks. Once, when we were watching prairie-chickens booming from a nearby blind, a large flock of lesser golden-plover alighted amidst the courting birds and remained feeding with them for a short time.

Butler listed the prairie-chicken as a resident and "formerly very abundant over the original prairie district and now approximately confined to that district." He further stated, "In most places becoming scarce, in some very rare." It was evidently an abundant species in the mid-1800s, for one shipment from Michigan City to Chicago in 1851 contained 6,000 birds. About the same time, 20,000 were shipped from Lake County, Indiana, to Detroit, within six weeks (Schorger, 1944). It formerly occurred in at least forty-four counties.

The hunting season on prairie-chickens was closed in 1909; hunting was again allowed (on a limited basis) in 1915. The Commissioner of Fisheries and Game wrote that in 1912 there

were certainly more than 100,000 greater prairie-chickens in the state. We suspect that this number was considerably larger than the actual population. In any event, it was found necessary to close the hunting season again in 1937 for a five-year period. But there were only about 1,000 birds left in Indiana by 1941, and the hunting season was never reopened. Personnel of the Indiana Division of Fish and Game, as it was then called, began an annual census of all known prairie-chicken booming grounds in the spring of 1942 and continued it until 1973, when no more courting birds could be found.

The prairie-chicken throve on native prairie grasslands, which provided food, cover, and open spots with low vegetation for booming grounds. The original prairies of Indiana were well suited to the birds, but unfortunately the rich prairie soils were found capable of producing high yields of corn, soybeans, and other crops. For a time, the establishment of pastures of Reed canary grass postponed the extirpation of the prairie-chicken on some lands, but changes of farm ownership and land use and the eventual elimination of virtually every acre of original prairie eventually spelled doom. Even the fences, telephone wires, power lines, windmills, and buildings that sprang up on the flat prairies were hazards; many birds were killed when they flew into such new obstacles.

There were evidently seasonal movements of prairie chickens, although the species is not generally considered migratory. During the winter of 1832–33, Prince Maximilian of Wied lived at New Harmony (Posey County), where he studied the natural history of the region. He wrote, ". . . the prairie hen comes in large flocks to the New Harmony neighborhood as soon as the cold weather and snow sets in." The implication was that the birds were absent in summer.

We have little information regarding the nesting of this grouse in Indiana. Nests were on the ground and in eight nests for which we have records the clutch size ranged from ten to eighteen and averaged thirteen. Eggs were observed in nests from about April 26 to July 4. Nest sites included prairie grasses, railroad rights-of-way, and clover fields. The birds evidently nested about marsh borders, for on June 5, 1892, Ruthven Deane found seven prairie-chicken nests under water due to flooding at English Lake (Starke County). The last recorded prairie-chicken nest in Indiana was found on June 13, 1964, in Newton County. Several of us examined it, and the fourteen eggs it contained were pipping. The last brood observed, to our knowledge, was by Russell R. Hyer, who saw a hen with nine chicks along the Jasper–Newton County line on May 25, 1970.

[SHARP-TAILED GROUSE]

Tympanuchus phasianellus

Prairie Sharp-tailed Grouse

The principal basis for considering this an accidental visitor to Indiana is an observation by Brennan (1918), who reported one in the Dunes region in April 1915. He had also talked to old residents in the area, two of whom told him they had occasionally shot this grouse in former years. The sharp-tail used to be found in northern Illinois, so stragglers might conceivably have reached the Indiana Dunes. Butler included the species on his hypothetical list. Between 1939 and 1941, 275 sharp-tails were released in Newton County and in Lake County, in attempts to establish them in the prairie-chicken habitat of northwestern Indiana. Little is known of the fate of these introductions. Whether earlier attempts had been made to introduce the sharp-tailed grouse into Indiana, we do not know. If so, it could well have been during the period just before 1915, when there were widespread releases of gray partridges and ring-necked pheasants throughout the state.

WILD TURKEY

Mealeagris gallopavo

This wonderful bird must have been common in most of Indiana in the early years. No doubt it was rare or absent in some northwestern counties that were predominantly prairie, but it evidently did occur in wooded sections of that region. According to Prince Maximilian of Wied, who spent the winter of 1832–33 at New Harmony (Posey County), the wild turkey was "formerly extremely numerous" and "still pretty common" there. This appears to be the first reference to a decreasing turkey population in the state. He also noted that a large "cock" turkey sold at New Harmony for a quarter of a dollar (Thwaites, 1906).

As more and more of the state was settled, habitat destruction and increased trapping and hunting began to take their toll. As the turkeys were forced into more remote habitats away from man, they managed to survive for a time. But eventually they were unable to exist; most disappeared from the state by about 1900. It is impossible to determine just when the wild turkey was extirpated, for domestic turkeys were brought in by settlers before 1900, but it appears certain that very few, if any, wild birds survived after the early 1920s.

There are numerous anecdotes about turkeys in many county histories and published recollections of persons who lived in Indiana between 1840 and 1900. Audubon was in a boat on the Ohio River below Cincinnati on October 17, 1820, when he noted that turkeys were extremely plentiful and were crossing the river hourly from the north (Indiana) side. He added that a "great number," unable to make the flight across the river, were drowned. Wilson (1910), writing about early Dubois County, mentioned that "if needed, a pioneer could kill a dozen or more wild turkeys in a day," and "Often a load of them would be taken, on foot, to Vincennes, and exchanged for a bag of salt, which would be carried back home." It was said that early settlers could stand at their cabin doors and shoot a turkey. But the great numbers began to dwindle quite rapidly from 1810 to 1860 and by 1880 the species was gone or rare in many counties, virtually extinct in northern Indiana, but still present in small numbers in southern Indiana.

About fifty years ago the Indiana Department of Conservation began attempts to reintroduce turkeys into the state, with releases in Brown County and other areas. These introductions were not successful. U.S. Navy personnel released five Arkansas turkeys on land of the Crane Naval Weapons Support Center (Martin County) in 1956, and this introduction resulted in the establishment of a turkey population of from 100 to 200 birds on the naval base by the winter of 1960–61. In the spring of 1961, what is now the Indiana Division of Fish and Wildlife, began trapping turkeys at Crane for release in other Indiana counties. Additional turkeys were brought in from Missouri. Turkeys became established in several other sites and were released in additional counties so that now they are found in about twenty-three counties, mostly in south-central Indiana, according to the Division of Fish and Wildlife.

The courtship of the turkey is a spectacular sight, especially when several males and females come together on the courting grounds. The males display and strut, feathers fluffed, tails spread, wattles shining, and wings drooping.

The nest is placed on the ground, often at the base of a

shrub or tree. A nest found recently in a Perry County pine plantation was at the base of a pine tree among the honeysuckle, according to George R. Parker. Roosts are usually in trees, and particular roosts may be used for considerable periods of time.

Kirkpatrick et al. (1972) reported on the food items found in 207 droppings of adults and 84 droppings of juvenile turkeys collected in Indiana. Foods found in order of decreasing volume were grass (Gramineae) seeds, soil and organic matter (including grit), unidentified leaves and stems of plants, insects, seeds of oaks, dog-

woods, and greenbrier. Additional foods were pine, ash, redbud, rose, sumac, honeysuckle, *Lespedeza*, and miscellaneous (snails, reptile scales, feathers, nightshade, buttercup, dock, hair, sedge, wild grape, *Desmodium*, *Sida*).

In turkeys, the sexes are similar, but the hen is generally smaller with a less brilliantly colored head and feathers bordered a light tan. The male is shown; since his association with the female stops once incubation begins, the nest is on the facing page.

Depicted plant: Trout lily (*Erythronium americanum*)

WILD TURKEY

NORTHERN BOBWHITE

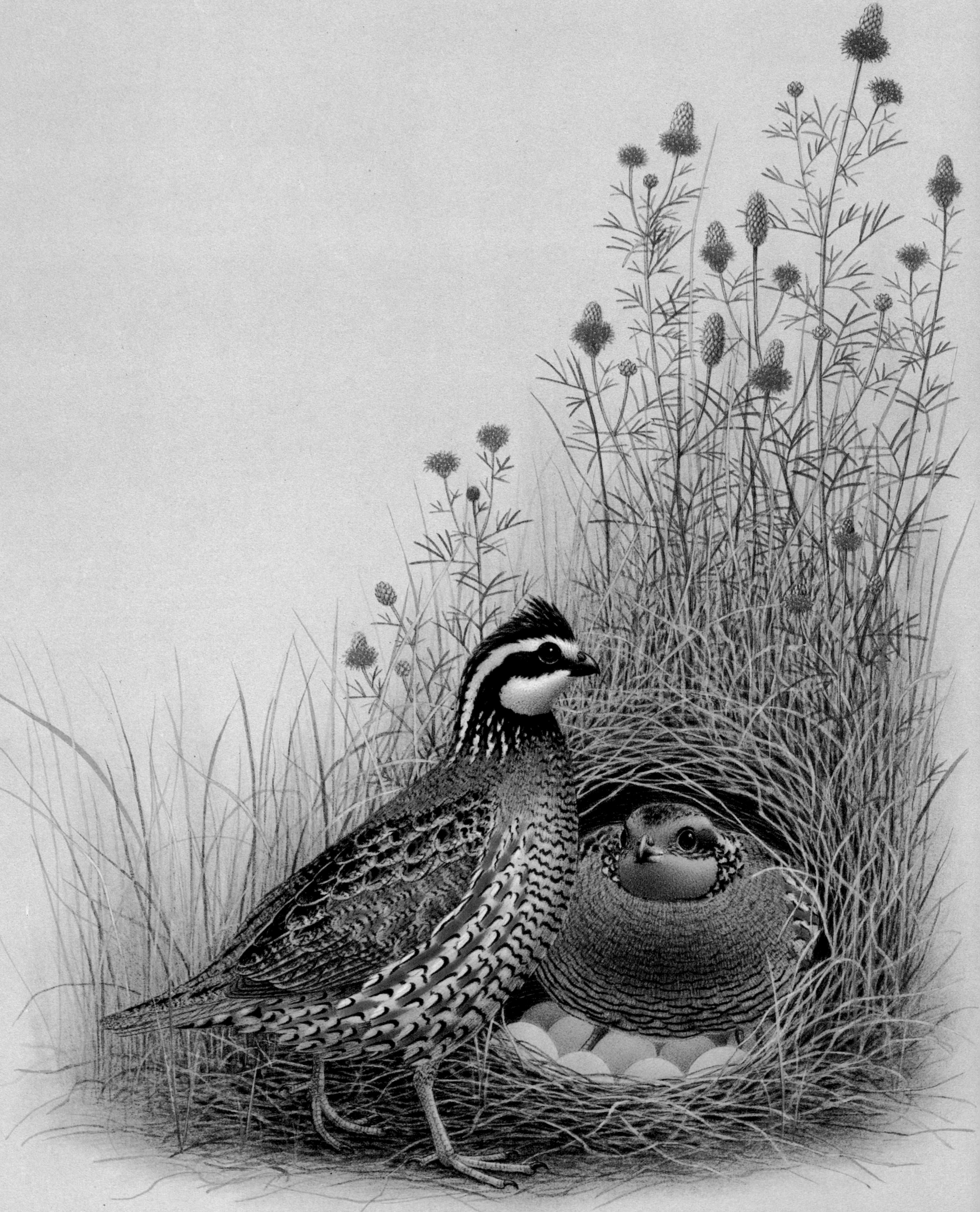

NORTHERN BOBWHITE

Colinus virginianus

Quail, Bobwhite, Bobwhite-partridge, Bobwhite Quail

This quail, a familiar bird to the rural residents of Indiana, is often seen in spring and summer perched on a fencepost along a country road, giving its clear *bobwhite* call to attract a mate. It undoubtedly benefited greatly from the cutting of the forests and the creation of more openings and cultivated land, and probably expanded its range and increased in numbers after Indiana was settled. The bobwhite is susceptible to wholesale dieoffs during severe winters when ice or crusted snow remain on the ground for extended periods. The winter of 1878–79 was such a time, and Butler noted that the species was "almost exterminated." The same phenomenon occurred during the winter of 1892–93, and several successive severe winters from 1976 to 1981 virtually eliminated bobwhites from northern Indiana.

Butler considered the bobwhite a generally common resident. Reeves (1955), who studied the bobwhite intensively near Washington (Daviess County), thought the period of greatest abundance for the bobwhite in Indiana was shortly after the Civil War. For the period 1940 to 1954, he estimated that about 800,000 bobwhites were killed by hunters each year, with as many as 1,500,000 being harvested in 1940. Barnes (1947) mapped the distribution of this quail in Indiana based on the average number of birds shot per hunter from 1940 to 1945. The kill was highest in the southern third of the state, and Brown County topped the list. Over the northern two-thirds of Indiana, only Clay, Putnam, Starke, and Vermillion Counties were considered good for hunting. Intensive land use and habitat destruction had taken a heavy toll of the bobwhite by this period, and the trend continues today, exacerbated by the severe winters in the late 1970s. The estimated annual harvest by hunters during the 1977–78 season was down to 313,503; only 90,985 were killed in 1979–80, and 76,812 in 1980–81.

The bobwhite thrives in old fields and waste areas with fencerows where there is an abundance of weed seed and nesting cover. It also frequents brushy areas and uses woodlots and forests in some seasons. Such habitat has always been most abundant in southern Indiana, where the land is generally more broken and less intensively cultivated. But even here much bobwhite habitat has been put to other uses, fencerows have been taken out, marginal farm land has been put back into cultivation or supports real estate developments, and the bobwhite has suffered as a result. In fact, the future of this native quail in the state is not very bright.

Seasonal movements of bobwhites have been recorded for some time, but such wanderings do not constitute true migrations. Butler wrote:

About the middle of October I have noticed the Bobwhites of southern Indiana begin to change their habits. From the cheerful, matter-of-fact bird about the farm, they become erratic. Hunters say they are crazy. They seem possessed with a desire to migrate, coming into towns and cities in some numbers. They, at such times, are lost and bewildered. They are found in trees and among the shrubbery of gardens, in outbuildings and among lumber piles. I have seen them in the cellar window-boxes and over the transoms of the front doors of houses. They fly into stores and dash against their glass fronts. . . . Some years they appear to desert the uplands and seek the river valleys. . . . The Ohio River bottoms contained immense numbers of Bobwhites, and many crossed the river into Kentucky, others were killed in attempting to cross.

Nesting activity usually begins in April and eggs are laid from at least late April to September. Nests are on the ground in old fields, along fencerows, roadsides, and ditches, in overgrown pastures, weedy cemeteries, marsh borders, uncultivated fields and similar places. In thirteen nests with full clutches there were on the average nineteen eggs per nest. As many as twenty-seven eggs have been found in a single nest. Although the nesting season is quite extended, the peak of hatching usually occurs from about the last week of June to mid-July, depending upon prevailing weather. Some young are known to have hatched as late as October 24.

The bobwhite eats a wide variety of vegetable foods, including seeds of native plants and agricultural crops, and insects. Reeves (1955) reported on the fall foods found in 831 bobwhite crops during two hunting seasons. He found 69 different food items, but the twelve most important were corn, sassafras, Korean lespedeza, ragweed, touch-me-not, insects, soybeans, wheat, acorns, ash, foxtail, and tickclovers.

During the fall and winter bobwhites form coveys and remain in these groups until the spring breeding season. These coveys average about fifteen birds, but much larger coveys have been reported. The covey roosts on the ground in weedy or grassy fields where there is usually considerable cover. The birds form a closed circle, each facing outward and touching the bird on either side. Such a formation allows each individual a clear flight path when danger threatens.

Depicted plant: Purple prairie clover (*Petalostemum purpureum*)

YELLOW RAIL
Coturnicops noveboracensis

Yellow Crake, Little Yellow Rail

By late September, the sumac has turned bright red, and woolly bear caterpillars are much in evidence. Each morning a heavy dew bows down the mature seed heads of foxtail grasses. At this season, we expect migrant rails to be returning to their usual haunts; so, in certain low, poorly drained fields on the Willow Slough Fish and Wildlife Area, birders congregate for a yellow rail hunt. Walking close together in a line back and forth across likely areas bordering the marsh, sometimes dragging long ropes or heavy chains, they attempt to flush one of the secretive birds. Infrequently, their efforts result in a brief look at this elusive rail as it flushes, flies weakly for a short distance, then drops back into the vegetation, from which it often cannot be flushed a second time.

We know little about the yellow rail in Indiana. Butler considered the species a rare migrant and a very local summer resident; he also stated that it probably bred in the state, according to J. A. Balmer, who had written Butler that he had seen this rail "in the breeding season" in Knox County. Audubon wrote that he observed "young broods" on the Wabash River, near Vincennes, in summer. Today the yellow rail is a rare spring migrant and casual fall migrant. Most spring sightings are for April, but a few were made in March and May. On June 3, 1976, a yellow rail was heard in response to the playing of a taped call in St. Joseph County. There are half a dozen sightings for September and two for November. Spring records range from March 3 to June 3 and fall observations were made from September 1 to November 22. Most records are of single birds, but on occasion two or three have been found. There is every reason to suspect that this rail is much more abundant in the state than records indicate, for its secretive habits render it difficult to find. After the severe windstorm, with hail, over Lake Michigan on April 16, 1960, at least fourteen dead yellow rails were found along the shore of the lake with hundreds of other dead birds.

Yellow rails prefer drier habitats than some of the other rails found in Indiana. Damp sedge meadows, upland pastures, and cultivated fields are used, especially if there are wet depressions. The birds also are found about marsh borders, in mixed vegetation of weeds, bushes, and small trees.

J. A. Balmer wrote about his experiences with yellow rail in Indiana, as follows:

While in Knox County, snipe hunting, each spring, especially in April, I used to find (on particular swamps only) an abundance of this tiny Rail. My old Gordon setter would point by a tussock, and as I walked up to flush, he would nose into the grass and bring out a Yellow Rail, always quite unharmed. I have seen him repeat this act as many as a half dozen times in a single day.

They were always abundant in spring in this particular part of Males Prairie. I have found them in the fall while quail hunting, but this rarely. [in Butler, 1898a]

Another hunter who shot rails in an undetermined part of the Kankakee River marsh from about 1876 to 1885 was William S. Perry. Ruthven Deane supplied Butler (1898a) with Perry's comments concerning yellow rails:

I consider them quite rare. I hunted every day for six weeks, especially for Rails, and probably started 1,500 Virginia, 1,500 Sora, 200 King and 5 Yellow. I think that is about the proportion they occur, although with the experience I had, I could probably find more if I should try again. I found the Yellow Rail in a very small part of the marsh, say 50 acres in extent, rather high ground that is not so boggy and wet as where the other species of Rail were plenty. They come very late in April and possibly late in March. The five I have I got between April 2 and 13.

BLACK RAIL
Laterallus jamaicensis

Little Black Rail

One of the dearest wishes of many serious Indiana birdwatchers is to add the black rail to their life list of birds observed in the state. This shy, sparrow-sized marsh-dweller evidently prefers walking and running to flying—it very rarely flushes—so even where it is present, it is seldom seen.

By 1898 there were only two records for Indiana, and Butler listed it as a rare, local summer resident. Ruthven Deane had identified it at English Lake on April 22, 1888. A black rail was seen near Greencastle (Putnam County) the last week of July 1894 on several occasions, and on August 1 Jesse Earlle and Alexander Black, with the aid of a dog, captured an immature rail unable to fly and an adult male. Only a few additional records of this species were accumulated during the next forty years. Cox (1937) recorded the "nesting" of the black rail near Windfall (Tipton County) in June 1936, although no nest was found. Two rails (presumably a pair) were captured, and one laid an egg while captive.

At least nine black rails have been reported from Indiana from 1941 to 1982, but this rail is still a rare spring migrant and casual fall migrant. There is a possibility that it still breeds, for two were found at the Willow Slough Fish and Wildlife Area on July 6, 1976. Most spring records are for April (three) and May (six), and fall sightings were made in August (one) and September (three). Dates of occurrence fall between April 8 and September 29.

It appears that the black rail utilizes much the same habitat as the yellow rail, being found in seasonably wet, overgrown fields with marshy areas. Two were found in June along the marshy edge of an alfalfa field and the two collected at Greencastle were in the "saw grass" near a pond.

KING RAIL

Rallus elegans

Red-breasted Rail, Marsh Hen

This, the largest of the rails found in Indiana, sometimes appears to be as much chickenlike as raillike, for it may be seen in dry terrain scratching about for food along fencerows, and it may nest some distance from water. It is quite vocal, especially near its nest, and will frequently remain close to a nest being examined by human observers and call persistently. This big rail is more apt to be seen than the black or yellow rail, but is much rarer than the Virginia or sora.

Butler noted that the king rail was a migrant, rare in southern Indiana (but locally a summer resident), and common "among the lakes and marshes in the northern part of the State," where it bred "in some numbers." Today, it is still an uncommon migrant and summer resident, probably nesting in suitable habitat throughout Indiana. A few evidently winter. It is difficult to obtain population data regarding rails, for their habits do not lend themselves to easy censusing. Most sightings are of

KING RAIL

single birds (or adults with young), but as many as four adults have been found at a single location in spring.

King rails are usually seen at cattail marshes and ponds and along ditch banks. At times, they wander some distance from water and may be found along brushy fence-rows or along overgrown roadsides and in sedge meadows. Spring migrants have been recorded as early as March 30; most arrive in April. The latest fall departure date is October 31. One was found dead in Lake County on February 4, 1935, and another was observed in LaPorte County on February 10, 1956.

Nests with eggs have been found by May 10, but since young have also been reported in May, some nesting may occur earlier. The latest date for eggs in the nest is July 5. Nests are usually near marshes or ponds, in fairly good cover, but often situated in drier parts of the habitat. Nests have also been seen on grass tussocks in flooded meadows, and one nest was in a wheatfield, 100 feet from the edge and 300 feet from water. The number of eggs in nine nests ranged from eight to twelve and averaged ten. A considerable proportion of our breeding records consists of sightings of adults with their black, downy young.

The king rail readily responds in spring to the playing of its recorded calls and this may prove to be the best method for determining its presence at that season.

Depicted plant: Water arum (*Calla palustris*)

VIRGINIA RAIL

Rallus limicola

Among the strange noises that emanate from the marshes in the spring is the piglike grunting of the Virginia rail. Since the caller is seldom seen, many who hear the sound probably never connect it with a bird. In fact, the various calls given by rails are still being studied in an effort to determine which species are responsible for certain mysterious sounds regularly heard in marshlands.

The Virginia rail was formerly listed as a rather common migrant, most numerous in the spring, and a summer resident (locally, in "some numbers"), principally in northern Indiana. It was evidently abundant during April 1885 in a section of the Kankakee River marsh, where William S. Perry flushed 1,500 in six weeks of daily hunting. This rail is currently an uncommon spring and fall migrant, but may be locally common. There are more spring records than fall records. Birdwatchers from South Bend found an estimated 200 Virginia rails at Sousley's Lake, St. Joseph County, on September 3, 1949, but we do not know how they arrived at that figure. Much smaller numbers are normally reported and many sightings are of single birds. Twenty-one were found dead along Lake Michigan after the April 16, 1960, storm.

This rail inhabits cattail marshes and wet, grassy areas, ditch banks, and the borders of nearly all water areas, especially where marsh vegetation is present. Some observers have pointed out that the Virginia rail and sora choose different habitats, but in our experience the two are frequently found together.

Spring migrants begin arriving in March, but most are seen in April. Some March sightings may be of birds that overwintered. The fall migrants are evidently most abundant in September, but there are few data on rail populations for the state. Stragglers are found in November and a small number of birds spend the winter at sites where

they can find food and open water. Some wintering birds have been detected because they called in a response to the playing of their taped vocalizations. One was captured in a trap set for muskrats. Another was observed on December 24 as it floated across a small creek on a chunk of ice. The sixteen observations made in December, January, and February are all since 1958, most of them since 1975.

Data on nesting of the Virginia rail in Indiana are rather sparse, for there are relatively few published observations concerning nests and eggs. First eggs are laid at least by April 30 (probably earlier) and clutches have been recorded until May 30. The average number of eggs in ten nests was eight (six to eleven). Nests were situated in a recently dried-up brushy marsh with scattered clumps of quaking aspen, in shallow cattail marshes, in patches of grasses and sedges in shallow water, and in a wet meadow with scattered bushes. A study area at the Willow Slough Fish and Wildlife Area contained a minimum of 0.52 pairs of nesting Virginia rails per hectare in the summer of 1979 (Cable, 1980).

Depicted plant: Water willow (*Justicia americana*)

SORA

Porzana carolina

Sora Rail, Carolina Rail, Crake, Common Rail, Ortolan

The rail most often observed in Indiana is the sora, which during migration may become abundant in the marshes. Its rapid, whinnying call is characteristic, and any sudden loud sound—clapping one's hands, throwing a stone in the water, or thumping an oar against the boat—will evoke a chorus from soras in the area. One will call, followed immediately by another, then another and another, until it sounds as if the marsh must be teeming with rails. Many more are heard than seen, because like most rallids the sora is a skulker and prefers running to flying when disturbed. In the early morning and the late evening, however, it sometimes feeds in the open, usually not too far from dense cover, and can be observed for prolonged periods.

Butler wrote that this rail was a common migrant throughout Indiana and a common breeder in the northern part of the state. It is interesting that he did not cite even one nesting record for Indiana! References to large numbers of soras in the Kankakee River marshes are mainly for migrants. The sora is still considered a common spring and fall migrant and it breeds at least throughout the northern half of Indiana. It may be rare locally in migration and in summer due to the lack of suitable habitat. Soras have been recorded during the nesting season far to the south of the principal breeding range and isolated pockets of good cover may prove to harbor nesting birds in these regions. A nest was found in Warrick County in 1983. There appears to be no midwinter record for the sora in the state. The greatest numbers have been reported in spring between mid-April and mid-May. For example, 104 were found in Marion County on May 7, 1950. Soras reach their greatest abundance in the fall from September to early October, and 100 were recorded at Sousley's Lake (St. Joseph County) on September 3, 1949. During the fall of 1976, the peak of fifty-two was reached at Lake Waveland (Montgomery County).

Although the sora is primarily a bird of shallow cattail and sedge marshes, during migration it may appear in damp meadows, clover fields, wheat stubble, and cornfields. Individuals also have been found in cities and at farm ponds; possibly some of these birds were forced down by inclement weather. Several soras have been found dead on city streets and underneath power lines and telephone wires.

There is an early spring migration date of March 6 for Frankfort (Clinton County), and a few records for the

SORA

last week of March, but most soras arrive in April. During mid-May many are evidently still in migration while others are nesting. This situation may have given rise to the notion that many more soras nest in the state than is actually the case. It appears that fall migration is under way before the end of August and is mostly completed by November. There are a few November sightings and one late observation of one bird at Lake Maxinkuckee (Marshall County) on December 11, 1900 (Evermann and Clark, 1920). Butler wrote about fall migration of this rail as follows: "Throughout the latter part of August and most of September they are passing. Meanwhile the great numbers of old and young are collecting in northern Indiana and other States until the marshes fairly swarm with them. This is the season for Rail shooting. They are very sensitive to cold. A sudden heavy frost comes, and the myriad voices of the marsh one day are silenced and their owners flown when the sun of the morrow rises."

Eggs have been found in nests from May 6 to July 1. The average number of eggs per nest, in cases where it was believed the clutches were complete, was nine (eight to twelve). Nests are normally placed in shallow water in emergent vegetation such as cattails, sedges, smartweeds, grasses, and the like. Some nests are quite well concealed while others may be in fairly open sites. On a study area at the Willow Slough Fish and Wildlife Area, a minimum density of 0.47 pairs of soras per hectare was found (Cable, 1980). Three or four nests found in 1979 were in cattails and smartweed and another in grasses and sedges (where most of the Virginia rail nests were found).

We need to learn much more about the biology of the sora and other rails in Indiana, for this group of birds is not well known at present. Of particular interest would be an evaluation of their abundance, breeding distribution, migration, and other behavior. Evidently the sora at times performs an evening flight similar to that of the American coot. On the evening of October 13, 1952, Mumford watched a sora fly up out of a marsh, fly about high in the air in several wide circles, then alight again.

Depicted plant: Sessile-fruited arrowhead (*Sagittaria rigida*)

PURPLE GALLINULE
Porphyrula martinica

This showy gallinule is a casual visitor to Indiana, and there are only twelve records of its occurrence in the state, the first in 1880, the most recent in 1973. Butler considered it to be a rare visitor in spring and perhaps a summer resident. He knew of no sightings north of the latitude of Indianapolis, but Ford (1956) mentioned a specimen taken in Lake County about 1868.

There are eight dated reports from six counties of the purple gallinule. All eight were between March 27 and June 23 (one in March, one in April, three in May, and three in June). Of the four undated sightings, one was clearly in the spring, and the other three probably also were.

Purple gallinules frequent the same habitats as common moorhens, American coots, and rails. The two birds reported in 1973 were found in a marsh in Tippecanoe County and a marshy pond overgrown with spatterdock on the Willow Slough Fish and Wildlife Area. Some authors attribute the periodic occurrence of such birds north of their normal range to overflights during the spring migration.

COMMON MOORHEN

Gallinula chloropus

Common Gallinule, Florida Gallinule, Mud Hen

Although the common moorhen is widely distributed throughout Indiana, it is relatively little known because of its secretive habits, choice of marshy habitat, and comparatively small numbers. Except for their striking candy-corn beaks, moorhens closely resemble American coots, and the casual observer may fail to distinguish between the two species, which are frequently found feeding and nesting together.

Butler described the moorhen as a regular migrant and summer resident, noting that it was locally common to abundant, and nested in the state. It is still a regular spring and fall migrant and found nesting (usually in unknown numbers) over the northern half of Indiana where it can find the correct habitat. It was nesting as far south as Sullivan County (Merom) in 1975, and may breed in other southern Indiana localities in isolated marshy sites.

The common moorhen is usually found where there is emergent marsh vegetation. Some of its favorite nesting sites in northeastern Indiana are potholes and small lakes with dense stands of spatterdock and/or buttonbush growing in the centers. During migration moorhens frequently appear in residential areas, cities, barnyards, chickenyards, and other nonaquatic places.

Spring migrants are usually first recorded in April and early May, but the secretive nature of this marsh dweller makes it difficult to determine when the "first" birds arrive. Some reach the northernmost counties during the first week of April. Our earliest record is for March 17. Fall migration probably begins in August, but there are few data on movements at this season. A few moorhens linger into November, but this is unusual. Two, seen in Lake County on December 1, 1981, were extremely late migrants. Numbers seen in the spring are small, with maxima of four to six being recorded. Larger congregations are observed in the fall, many the result of numerous families reared on a single marsh. Kenneth J. Brock reported the phenomenal number of ninety at Roxana Pond, Hammond, on September 4, 1980. No other Indiana record even approaches that number, although Butler was told by J. G. Parker and G. L. Toppan that "the boys collect hundreds of their eggs every year" at Wolf Lake and Lake George (Lake County).

Nests are located in clumps of emergent vegetation (frequently cattails), usually in shallow water, but where nests are placed in spatterdock the water may be quite deep. Moorhen nests and American coot nests are quite similar in construction and both species choose the same nesting sites. Nests containing eggs have been found from May 15 to July 24, but downy young estimated to be not more than two days old were found on August 5. Clutch size in thirty-one nests averaged 9.3 and ranged from 7 to 20. Not all eggs of a clutch hatch the same day and one frequently finds eggs and small young in a nest. In many cases, the precocial young will leave the nest and swim away when a human observer approaches. We have noticed the same behavior in American coots and soras.

Depicted plant: American lotus (*Nelumbo lutea*)

AMERICAN COOT

Fulica americana

Mud Hen, Coot, Crow-duck

Coots are noisy, chickenlike birds of the marshes, sometimes found in large flocks during migration. Groups of American coots are seldom quiet, but maintain a rather constant "conversational" gabbling regardless of their activities, day and night. As with other rallids, migration occurs at night; suddenly one fall morning the marsh, deserted the day before, is full of coots. They are good swimmers and divers, sometimes reaching depths of twenty-five feet or more to obtain the water plants they feed on. Their curious lobed toes enable them to dive and swim with ease. Various ducks frequently accompany flocks of feeding coots. American wigeons, lesser scaups, and canvasbacks have been observed trying to take aquatic vegetation from coots as they surface after a dive, and coots frequently take food from one another in a like manner. They also sometimes turn the tables and try to steal food from feeding diving ducks. Coots spend some time out of the water and may walk about on dry, grassy areas or rest there in the sun.

Butler listed the American coot as a common migrant and a summer resident in the northern part of Indiana. He noted that it was very common locally and some wintered, during favorable years, in southern portions of the state. He wrote that they were sometimes found on some of the smaller lakes by the thousands, but were rarely observed on Lake Michigan. Evermann and Clark reported "not fewer than 10,000" on Lake Maxinkuckee on October 25, 1904, and Donald H. Boyd found 5,000 at LaPorte on November 4, 1928. Today, the American coot is a common to abundant migrant and winters in varying numbers throughout Indiana. It still nests in suitable habitat over the northern half of the state and locally (usually in isolated marshes) in small numbers in the southern half. The maximum numbers observed on Christmas bird counts in recent years are as follows: 1,280 (Nashville, 1974); 928 (Nashville, 1975); 656 (Indianapolis, 1972); 545 (Lake Monroe, 1969); 533 (Tippecanoe [Warsaw area], 1978).

American coots are marsh dwellers during the nesting season, but also congregate on reservoirs and lakes during migration. They tend to frequent those lakes that provide an abundance of submerged vegetation upon which they like to feed. Individuals and small groups of coots may be found on nearly any type or size of water area in spring and fall.

Butler noted that spring migration usually began in March, but during the period he wrote about few coots were known to winter in the state. The birds were most abundant during April and arrival dates for a particular locality varied considerably from year to year. Fall migrants were most numerous in October and Butler had no records for December or January. Although he wrote that "they again become very abundant" in the fall, no details of numbers observed were mentioned. Recent data reveal that spring migrants reach their greatest abundance in southern Indiana in late March and generally peak in numbers farther north during April. Some recent maxima include 2,000 at the Jasper-Pulaski Fish and Wildlife Area on April 12, 1980 and 1,456 at Prairie Creek Reservoir on April 16, 1972. There were 1,500 at the Willow Slough Fish and Wildlife Area on April 21 and 22, 1979. It appears that the coot has increased considerably in numbers throughout the past few decades. Fall migrants reach their peaks of abundance during October and early November. There were 6,000 at the Jasper-Pulaski Fish and Wildlife Area on October 25, 1969, and 4,000 in Marion County on November 7, 1948. American coots were evidently extremely abundant on Lake Monroe on November 1, 1971, since "a zillion" were reported there.

Butler's only definite nesting record was for English Lake (Starke County), but he had been told that coots also nested in Boone, DeKalb, LaPorte and Lake Counties. Coots still nest rather commonly across the northern one-third of the state, where most of the remaining habitat is located today, and they may be locally abundant. For example, during the summer of 1979 Ted T. Cable and Mumford found 154 nests at the Willow Slough Fish and Wildlife Area. Laying apparently begins at least by the last week of April and eggs have been found in nests until July 24. Nests are situated on the water in emergent vegetation such as cattails, bulrushes, bur-reed, and the like. The average clutch size for thirty-eight nests was 8.6, but several of these nests may have contained incomplete clutches. The number of eggs per nest ranged from six to fifteen. Like all nests at ground level, they are vulnerable to predators, including some species of snakes. In the illustration, the coot is attempting to intimidate a marauding fox snake.

Coot shooting used to be a popular sport on certain northern Indiana lakes. Evermann and Clark (1920), who intensively studied coots at Lake Maxinkuckee (Marshall County), have a long account of coot shooting on that lake during the period 1885 through 1913. Practically all of the information we have on the feeding habits of Indiana coots was obtained by Evermann and Clark as well. They reported that coots fed actively on clear moonlight nights as well as during the day. Plant materials found in the birds included chara, *Ceratophyllum, Potamogeton*, wild celery, and *Naias*. They also contained snails (*Vivipara contectoides*). When the coots were feeding in water from four to ten feet in depth, the average length of their dives was about nine seconds, but dives lasting sixteen seconds were recorded in deeper water.

AMERICAN COOT

SANDHILL CRANE

Grus canadensis

Sandy Hill Crane

We heard them in the distance long before we saw them; then the great birds came flying across the wooded sand ridges to their roosting marsh at the Jasper-Pulaski Fish and Wildlife Area. In the quiet, cool evening air, their loud, gutteral croaks echoed across the marshes as they milled about before settling down for the night in a shallow marsh within the refuge. Even after dark, and from time to time during the night, the wary cranes could be heard if anything disturbed them. They were up and away a long time before the sun came up, flying out in small groups, individual families and congregations of families, to feed in the cornfields surrounding the wildlife area. At dusk they returned to their usual roost.

Butler reported that the sandhill crane was a regular migrant, sometimes common, and an occasional summer resident and visitor in northwestern Indiana. He noted that it formerly was an abundant nester in the large marshes of the state. To his knowledge, it occurred mostly in the Wabash River valley and northward, being very rare elsewhere. Some were reputedly nesting as of 1897. Little was then recorded regarding this fascinating crane until it began using the Jasper-Pulaski Fish and Wildlife Area as a spring and fall staging area in the late 1930s. A pair nested near Parr (Jasper County) in 1929. E. F. Pullins had found the nest and described it and the behavior of the cranes to Lawrence H. Walkinshaw and Mumford on April 29, 1950. In April 1935, John Gottschalk observed twenty-four cranes at Jasper-Pulaski. Their numbers rather steadily increased (with some fluctuations): 700 were present in 1944, 1,800 in 1956, 4,000 in 1963, 8,000 in 1973, and a peak of 12,928 in 1978. There was a slight decrease between 1979 and 1981. Away from Jasper-Pulaski, the sandhill crane is a regular migrant, but may be absent in most years, except for birds observed flying over. It is hoped that satellite staging areas can be developed along the flyways through Indiana so that the concentration at Jasper-Pulaski may be reduced, thus cutting down on the chances of some epidemic's spreading through the entire crane population. Adults with very young cranes were seen in northeastern Indiana for several years before 1982, when the first sandhill crane nest seen in the state for fifty-three years was found there.

Cranes rest, roost, feed, and nest in marshy or swampy habitats, but also spend considerable time feeding and resting in drier marshes, pastures, and dry, upland fields, both cultivated and uncultivated. During migration, they frequently alight in cornfields for various lengths of time or frequent various water areas which provide safe resting or feeding sites. Small numbers may be seen on the ground in nearly any type of open habitat.

Spring migrants usually arrive during the last half of February and normally reach their greatest abundance in northwestern Indiana about the third week of March. Practically all have gone by May 1, but stragglers (probably mostly non-breeders) and a very few breeding individuals remain during the summer, mostly in extreme northern Indiana. Fall migration is most apparent in September, when the birds begin to gather on the staging grounds at Jasper-Pulaski. Most are gone by mid-December, but in some years dozens of birds remain until the last week of December. Prevailing weather apparently determines when the last lingerers depart. There are very few records for January and early February. T. H. Ball (1900) wrote that during the "open winter" of 1863–64, a few cranes were seen in Lake County all winter. Over the past five years, single sandhill cranes have been seen in January at Jasper-Pulaski and Mishawaka, and the unusual number of sixty passed over toward the southeast near Buck Creek (Tippecanoe County), on January 11, 1982, according to Delano Z. Arvin and his family.

There are relatively few nesting records for this crane in Indiana, despite the statements that it was formerly an abundant nesting bird in the northern portion. Butler noted that it still nested in Starke County in 1892 and in Lake County in 1897. He also wrote that "in recent years" it nested in Carroll and Fulton Counties. Two eggs were collected from a nest at North Judson (Starke County) on May 5, 1890. A sandhill crane egg in the collection of Donald H. Boyd was taken from a nest at Lemon's Bridge, on the Kankakee River, LaPorte County, in 1895. Patricia Pichon and her family observed young cranes with adults and adults throughout the summer in Lagrange and Steuben Counties in the mid-1970s. Field work in the area since 1977 finally resulted in the finding of a nest on April 23, 1982, in Steuben County, by Lee A. Casebere, S. Christopher Iverson, and Mark A. Weldon.

Modern-day cranes appear to feed mainly on corn or wheat, but no doubt insects are also taken in the same fields. In former years the birds at Jasper-Pulaski were observed feeding in the marshes, probing the mucky soils with their beaks and creating many funnel-shaped depressions. The birds were probably obtaining plant tubers. Butler mentioned that the cranes ate field mice, grasshopppers, and potatoes (especially sweet potatoes).

SANDHILL CRANE

Three sora eggs were found in the gullet of a crane shot in the Kankakee marshes (Forbush, 1916). T. H. Ball wrote the following about Lake County: "In the fall they would come from the marshes into our cornfields, forty or fifty, perhaps a hundred, at a time, and tear the corn almost as bad as a drove of hogs. Then I shot them. They were fat, and considered, when properly cooked, superior to wild geese."

Many of the old-time hunters shot cranes along with ducks, geese, shorebirds, and other marsh birds, especially in northwestern Indiana. Birch (1928) quoted William F. Swan, who hunted for the market in Benton County from August until Christmas, in 1868. Swan reportedly killed some "old cranes" and noted that "I cut their breasts out and then fried them, which made mighty good feed for a tired hunter."

One of the most interesting behavior patterns of the sandhill crane is its courtship dancing, sometimes engaged in simultaneously by many members of a flock. Such performances include bowing, leaping high into the air, hopping and skipping about with dropping wings, and croaking vocalizations. B. T. Gault described such dances in Starke County as "cotillions." One can witness these courtship antics at Jasper-Pulaski and other places in Indiana today.

WHOOPING CRANE

Grus americana

This splendid crane, once reputedly present in unknown numbers in Indiana, passed from the Hoosier scene before much was recorded concerning it. Many an old-time market hunter must have seen whooping cranes in the hordes of waterbirds that formerly inhabited the great Kankakee River marshes, listened to their wild, trumpeting calls, and no doubt tried to shoot them. The plight of the whooping crane throughout its range is well known, but with the management practices being used today, perhaps it can be saved from extinction.

By 1897 the whooping crane was a rare migrant, but Butler thought that it had formerly been more common. It reportedly was a summer resident in the Kankakee River marshes, where Timothy H. Ball and L. T. Meyer reported it from Lake County. Ball thought that it nested in the region, but there is no proof of this. The last Indiana sighting was April 4, 1907, at Waterloo (DeKalb County). Butler mentioned a specimen in the Cuvier Club collection, Cincinnati, Ohio, that was taken near Bloomington (no date). A mounted whooping crane in the Charles A. Stockbridge collection at Fort Wayne was probably from Indiana, according to Stockbridge's daughter. Perhaps the specimen now in the Purdue University Wildlife Laboratory Collection is from Indiana, but there is no label with it.

Most general references to this crane in the state involve its presence in marshland. The two dated sightings were in April; R. B. Trouslot reported three at Valparaiso on April 25, 1887.

Frank Baczkowski (1955), who remembered the whooping crane, supplied the following:

A mile west of Chesterton, Indiana, in Porter Co. . . . is a small cattail bog. . . . Some 50 years ago the bog had an open water surface, the area around it being cleared and in grass. It served as a migration stop for many species of water birds, including geese, ducks and at times Whooping Cranes, those giant white birds with some black feathers, a species now almost extinct. The birds usually stopped in the evening, at night or on rainy or cloudy days, when no one was seen in the vicinity.

As this location seemed to be on the southward migration route of the whoopers, we often heard their wild cries but could seldom see them as they passed overhead in a southwesterly direction. Flying overhead in the early evening about dusk, occasionally they were somewhat lower and we could then distinguish their outlines. There never were very many, and they always headed southwest. . . .

The evening that my friend and I still remember was something out of the ordinary. Soon after dark, about 8 or 8:30 p.m., while my father, mother and I were in the house, my father said, "I hear whoopers." (He was familiar with this family of birds from having seen them on the small lakes and marshes of Poland.) Soon we all heard them, and their calls seemed very plain as they flew lower than ordinarily, but on their usual course.

As we waited for them to pass over, we noticed that their wild cries seemed to linger in one area. Realizing that they apparently had seen the water of the bog, we continued to wait. They had started circling while still high; their cries and the noise of their wings could be heard coming closer and closer. When finally they were quite low, the commotion of their wings, mingled with wild calls, was terrific. Soon they seemed to be all around us, their very wings brushing the house and small fruit trees in the yard. Before they flew low we had put out the light so as not to frighten them. As soon as they landed, things quieted down.

Next morning at daybreak we went out to look from the nearest point of vantage. Two large birds, mostly white with bodies resembling those of geese, were clearly visible. A little farther back and between the first two we saw a small light tan bird. Still farther back there seemed to be another of the same color.

We never knew how many there were in the entire flock. When daylight came they were gone and I did not see them any more.

During the spring of 1983 we received word of three different sightings in the northwestern section of the state of from nine to twelve birds believed to be whooping cranes. Although this would seem most unlikely, all of the observers stressed that the sightings involved large white, long-legged and long-necked birds with black wingtips. One group was in a field with sandhill cranes.

BLACK-BELLIED PLOVER

Pluvialis squatarola

Grey Plover, Ox-Eye, Bull-head

The Lake Michigan shoreline in Indiana extends from just north of Michigan City to Whiting. Except for a few highly industrialized areas, this strip is characterized by long, wide sandy beaches. Despite the fact that these beaches support a heavy concentration of human activity (jogging, sunbathing, hiking) during the warmer parts of the year, the black-bellied plover finds this region to its liking. A larger cousin of the lesser golden-plover, it is a striking bird in its handsome breeding plumage. In the spring, some early migrants are in the more somber winter plumage, hence the European name grey plover.

Butler considered the black-belly a rare migrant, more numerous in the northwestern part of the state. Its status today is in general the same. It is an uncommon spring and fall migrant except near Lake Michigan, where it may at times be fairly common. On October 12, 1953, W. Marvin Davis saw sixty-five in Lake County.

This plover is found in spring in stubble fields, plowed fields, sod farms, and other places with low vegetation. In this respect it is similar to the lesser golden-plover, which it sometimes accompanies while feeding. In the fall, black-bellies are more likely to be seen at mudflats, beaches, and sewage lagoons.

Generally thought of as late spring migrants, most birds reach southern Indiana early in May, but because of a protracted migration they may be seen throughout the state until about the first week of June. During the southbound migration, some return by mid-July or early August and remain in suitable areas into November. Extreme spring dates are April 1 and June 30. Butler mentioned a Knox County record for March 30, 1888, but we wonder if this might be erroneous. Fall migration dates range from July 15 to December 6.

LESSER GOLDEN-PLOVER

Pluvialis dominica

Prairie Pigeon, American Golden Plover, Field Plover,
Bullhead, Whistling Plover

Reading the accounts of John J. Audubon or Elliott Coues of the spring abundance of this species in the prairie states, one is left with a sense of awe. These birds must have been present in incredible numbers; for example, Audubon (1840–1844 [1967]) calculated that French hunters killed nearly 48,000 near New Orleans on a single day—March 16, 1821. That the golden-plover was able to survive such large-scale slaughter for so many decades is truly remarkable. Even so, its numbers declined drastically until protective legislation enabled it to stage a comeback. Today, in the former prairie region of northwestern Indiana in April, it is again possible to see long, uneven strings, vees, or dense flocks of these strong-flying birds, or to watch more than a thousand scattered about, feeding, in a freshly plowed field.

In 1898, the golden-plover was considered a common migrant "over the original prairie region" of the state, but quite rare to the south and east. By Butler's time, its numbers were already greatly reduced, but sometimes hundreds, or even thousands, were seen in a spring flock. Butler made little mention of fall migration. This is not surprising, for most golden-plovers migrate southward off the eastern seaboard to the Argentine pampas. In spring, their route to their Arctic nesting grounds is mainly through the Mississippi River valley, and far greater numbers can be seen in Indiana. Most are in flocks of from ten to fifty birds, but flocks of as many as one thousand may be seen, and as many as three thousand birds have been seen in a single field.

When they are here in the spring, golden-plovers prefer pastures, meadows, airports, golf courses, crop stubble, and sod farms. They will often congregate around small temporary ponds in cultivated fields. Freshly plowed fields are quite attractive to them, no doubt because of the abundance of food uncovered by the plow, and the birds will feed along behind the farm equipment on insects, worms, and other invertebrate animals. In earlier years, farmers learned to capitalize on this habit and carried a shotgun on the tractor while they were working in the fields. It was thus easy to shoot enough plovers for a meal. During the fall migration the birds are likely to be found in similar habitat but are perhaps a bit more inclined to feed at sewage lagoons and mudflats.

Early spring migrants appear in Indiana in March, but the bulk of migration occurs in April. At this season in Indiana, the species is probably nowhere so abundant as on the flat farmlands in Benton County. There the members of the Sycamore Audubon Society (Lafayette, Indiana) conducted a one-day census of golden-plovers each April from 1980 to 1982; between 7,217 and 8,260 birds were observed on each count. Extreme dates are March 8 to June 5. Practically all early spring migrants are in their drab winter plumage, but by mid-May many are in nearly full breeding plumage.

In general, this plover is a relatively late fall migrant, although a few birds return in July. Most do not appear before early September, then stragglers occur into November. Extreme dates are July 15 to November 25. Keller found 100 in Marion County on September 28, 1960, but fall numbers are usually much smaller.

[SNOWY PLOVER]

Charadrius alexandrinus

Snowy Ring Plover

The snowy plover, a bird of more southern and western distribution, is considered accidental in Indiana. Charles Brandler reportedly collected the first specimen for the state on September 4, 1887, at Millers (Lake County) and donated it to the Field Museum. Butler did not mention this record in 1898. Keller wrote to the museum in 1956 and was informed that the specimen could not be found and was presumed to have been lost. Albert Franzen recalled seeing the specimen and was sure of its identification. Naturally, the sighting of a snowy plover at Millers on May 19, 1980, by Raymond Grow, was a noteworthy event. Kenneth J. Brock, Ted T. Cable, and Edward M. Hopkins also observed this bird and all concurred on its identification.

SEMIPALMATED PLOVER

Charadrius semipalmatus

Ring Plover, Ring-neck, Red-eye, Beach Bird, Ring-necked Plover

This diminutive plover generally resembles the larger and more familiar killdeer and, like its larger relative, uses the characteristic "hunt and peck" method of feeding. Because of its small size, the habitats where it is found, and the camouflage provided by its color (that of wet sand) and markings, it can be surprisingly difficult to see when foraging or sitting quietly.

Butler noted that the semipalmated plover was a generally rare migrant, which at times was uncommon in the vicinity of Lake Michigan, sometimes found in flocks containing as many as twenty-five birds. Today we consider it a fairly common spring migrant and an uncommon fall migrant. There were 600 in Allen County on May 11, 1980. Thirty-two were observed in Marion County on September 4, 1954.

This little plover is often found in wet, newly disked fields or at fish hatchery ponds and sewage lagoons in the spring. In addition, in the fall, it is especially attracted to extensive mudflats caused by the lowered water levels of lakes, marshes, reservoirs and ponds and also occurs on sand beaches.

Spring migrants have been detected as early as April 3, but most of them arrive the latter part of April and peak in numbers during the first half of May. Lingering individuals remain until June 22. Some have been at the Falls of the Ohio on June 23 and 24. Fall migration begins as early as July 8, but the greatest numbers have been recorded during the first half of September. Our latest departure date is October 29. Semipalmated plovers (like some other shorebirds) usually have two peaks of fall migration.

At the Indianapolis Sewage Disposal Plant, where shorebirds have been intensively studied by Keller and others for many years, semipalmated plovers and many other species of shorebirds feed in the several ponds. The semipalmateds have been observed to eat small earthworms, leeches, and unidentified small insect larvae.

Keller has also noticed that these plovers are quite noisy in the spring. When a new flock of birds arrived on the feeding grounds and joined others already there, it often did so to the accompaniment of sharp, staccato whistles, displaying, active courtship, and aerial chases. During the fall migration, the birds are relatively silent, except for their familiar call notes, which sound like *co-eep*.

PIPING PLOVER
Charadrius melodus

Pale Ringneck, Clam Bird, Belted Piping Plover

This little plover, whose ghostly pale plumage blends so well with the sand beaches where it is most often found, once nested along some sections of the Indiana shore of Lake Michigan. Here it attracted a great deal of attention from ornithologists and collectors between 1896 and 1921. Its extirpation as a breeding bird in the state is another of those unfortunate stories of habitat destruction, disturbance, and possibly over-zealous collecting of specimens.

Butler wrote that it was a migrant over most of the state and summer resident "in considerable numbers along Lake Michigan," where it was known to breed. It is possible that Butler overestimated the numbers of breeding birds in that region, for Herbert L. Stoddard conducted considerable field work along the Lake Michigan border from about 1914 to 1921. A manuscript of his, written in 1923 and found in Butler's files, is illuminating:

The early writers left us an erroneous impression of the abundance of this species in their day. . . . In the first place, on the whole western shore of Lake Michigan, only a small part was ever suitable for the breeding of these birds. The wide, flat, pebbly beaches back of the storm beach, which they demand, occurring only here and there, the long stretches of narrow sand shore, or steep clay bluff being entirely unsuitable. As far as I know, they are now breeding on a few miles of Indiana beach only, one spot having five or six pair.

Although Russell (1973) claims that sporadic breeding occurred in the Wolf Lake and dunes region of Indiana into the 1960s, we have seen nothing to substantiate this. W. Marvin Davis saw two adults with a downy chick at Wolf Lake on June 6, 1955. The species no longer breeds in the state and has been reduced to a casual spring and fall migrant, most often seen in the northwestern corner.

Although the piping plover is primarily a bird of the beach, it has also been observed at sewage ponds, overflows in fields, on a sandbar along a river, in the dried-up bed of a lake, on a cinder fill that was formerly marshland, and about lakes and ponds.

Spring migration is under way in April, with our earliest date being April 4. Most birds are observed in April and May, but in the past twenty-five years none has been reported in June. Fall migration dates range from July 20 to October 28, which is very late; the peak is in August. Most sightings are of single birds, but four were reported at Wolf Lake on April 19, 1951. The largest fall group recorded was two (only twice).

Stoddard, who knew the piping plover on its Indiana breeding grounds better than anyone, recorded most of what is known about its nesting in the state. Many of his notes were unpublished, but were obtained from Butler's files and from Stoddard's own notebooks. There are records of nine nests with eggs found between 1905 and 1920. The average number of eggs per clutch was 3.4, but five of the nests contained four eggs each. Eggs were pipped in one nest on June 1 and downy young were reported on August 1. Little was recorded concerning the nesting sites, but reference was made to "pebbly beaches," cinder fill, and the myriad tracks in the sand radiating out from the nests. All nests found in Indiana were in Lake and Porter Counties. One nest was "among the small stone and cinder 'rubble' about 10–15 rods back from the beach." Edward R. Ford (in a letter to A. C. Bent) wrote:

At Dune Park, Ind., the piping plover, to the number of five or six pairs, has taken advantage of the widening of the beach (through the operations of a sand company which has removed part of the dunes) and lays its eggs at a considerable distance from the water's edge. The old ridges formed by the tramway beds, from which the rails have been, for the most part, removed; the old cinder heaps, bits of scrap iron and other odds and ends of human labor, with here and there patches of vetch and coarse grass, seem well suited to its requirements. [quoted in Bent, 1929]

Bent considered this an unusual environment for nesting piping plovers.

C.W.G. Eifrig (1919) supports Stoddard's opinion that the piping plover was not abundant during the nesting season along the Indiana section of the Lake Michigan shore. He wrote, "In a walk along the beach from Millers to Mineral Spring, Ind., a distance of twelve miles, one may see two or three pairs of these diminutive plovers, as on April 22, 1917." It is interesting that Stoddard's notes mention seeing ten to twelve along this stretch on the same date as above (no doubt he and Eifrig were together).

KILLDEER

Charadrius vociferus

Killdeer Plover, Killdee, Noisy Plover, Chattering Plover

The familiar killdeer is the American ecological counterpart of the European lapwing, both of them common species, conspicuous and readily observable by man about his habitations. The birds follow the plow in spring, feeding on the abundance of food it turns out of the ground. Killdeers are often seen in freshly plowed fields, actively feeding, running quickly here and there, stopping abruptly, picking at the loose soil, and remaining alert for possible danger. In mixed flocks of shorebirds, killdeers are usually the first birds to take alarm and flush, noisily calling at times. Old-time hunters as a result often had difficulty getting within shooting range of such flocks and held no love for the killdeer, which they gave the name noisy plover. Even the Latin name *vociferus* refers to this trait.

The killdeer was formerly a common summer resident throughout the state and in some years remained in southern Indiana all winter. There has evidently been a substantial increase in the numbers of killdeers in Indiana, for today they are abundant during migration and during the summer. They winter throughout the state, but are more common at that season in the southern half, least numerous in the northwestern corner. As many as thirty-seven were recorded on a Christmas count at Lafayette and twenty-three at the Pigeon River Fish and Wildlife Area. Twenty or more have been observed on several Christmas counts in the southern part of the state, with seventy-six at Bloomington being the largest number. The clearing of more land and the removal of most of the Indiana forests have benefited the killdeer.

The killdeer is found in a variety of open areas, even concrete or asphalt parking lots at shopping malls and drive-in movie theaters, as well as fields and beaches,

water of a small woodland pond, bobbing and jerking in characteristic fashion and often uttering its diagnostic *peet-tweet* call when flushed.

Butler wrote that it was a common migrant, a summer resident "in some numbers" northward, and bred in the state. There is no valid breeding record. We know now that the species nests mainly in Canada, but non-breeding birds still occupy Indiana during the breeding season. It is still a common migrant, usually being encountered singly or in small groups, and often with other shorebirds. Among the maximum numbers recorded in spring are twenty-seven found on an all-day count in St. Joseph County on May 10, 1980, and twenty-one in Marion County by Keller on May 7, 1960. The largest number of birds in the fall was recorded by Keller, who saw sixty-eight in Marion County on July 26, 1961.

The solitary sandpiper is most commonly seen about small woodland ponds, along streams and roadside ditches, around wet weather ponds in woodlots, gravel pits, sewage lagoons, and small rainpools (some scarcely ten feet in diameter). It seldom occurs on beaches or extensive mudflats. It appears to be quite common on streams in spring, where it is usually found feeding in the sluggish backwaters.

It appears in southern Indiana about the second week of April and reaches the northern region five to ten days later. The bulk of the migrants leave by mid-May, although for much of the northern two-thirds of the state, there are June records, which were no doubt responsible for several erroneous reports that this species breeds in Indiana. It should never be assumed that birds present during the breeding season are indeed nesting. Extreme dates are March 15 to the end of June. Some June dates could be returning fall migrants or birds which remained throughout the summer. Fall movements are evident in early July and the numbers of migrants quickly reaches a peak during the latter part of that month or the first week of August. Most birds have left by mid-September except for a few October stragglers. Recent extreme dates are July 5 to October 29. There is one November 15 sighting (Bent, 1927) which may be erroneous.

WILLET

Catoptrophorus semipalmatus

Semipalmated Tattler, Western Willet, Semipalmated Snipe, Stone Curlew, Humility

Occasionally in late summer Indiana birders are treated to the sight of a flock of this large shorebird so characteristic of Gulf and Atlantic Coast beaches. It appears drab when at rest, but a flock of them in flight, with their bold black and white wing patterns, is spectacular. At times, especially in spring, the willet will call when flushed—the loud, distinctive *pill-will-willet* from which it got its name.

Butler noted that the willet was a rare migrant and possible summer resident. As with the solitary sandpiper, the presence of birds during the breeding season was mistaken for a sign of nesting. Presently the willet is an uncommon spring and fall migrant except in the vicinity of Lake Michigan, where it is fairly common, particularly in early summer. Most of our records are for the western half of Indiana and few sightings have been made east of a line connecting LaPorte and Jefferson Counties. On April 28, 1956, nineteen willets were seen in Marion County, and Burt Monroe, Jr., reported thirty-seven at the Falls of the Ohio, Clark County, on May 5, 1976. The maximum number recorded in the fall was a flock of forty-three at Michigan City on July 14, 1979.

The willet is primarily a bird of the beaches, at least in the Lake Michigan area. Inland it seems to prefer the edges of reservoirs, ponds, sewage lagoons, fish hatcheries, and flooded fields. Butler mentioned one that was shot from its perch atop a barn—a most unusual place to find a willet!

Spring migration occurs mainly from late April to mid-May; extreme dates are April 16 and May 20. Birds on their way south appear in early July and migration is mostly over by the last of August, but an occasional bird remains until mid-September. Extreme dates are June 26 and October 29.

SPOTTED SANDPIPER

Actitis macularia

Peet-weet, Teeter-tail, Teeter Snipe, River Snipe, Spotted Tattler, Tip-up, Sandsnipe

The little "spotty," often seen as it teeters on a conspicuous rock or log in the middle of a stream, is a favorite of many birders. The best way to observe it in its favorite haunts is to make a float trip down one of Indiana's larger rivers in May or June. Such a trip should reveal many of these interesting birds as they flush ahead of the canoe and fly downstream, close to the water, with shallow, quivering wingbeats, uttering their *preet-weet-weet* calls.

Butler called the spotted sandpiper a common summer resident throughout the state, present from March to October. The status of this familiar shorebird is much the same today; in fact, it may have increased in numbers because of the increased amount of nesting habitat furnished by borrow pits, gravel pits, and other open areas of rocky or sandy substrate. Herbert L. Stoddard reported that the species was abundant along Lake Michigan between about 1914 and 1920. Except for family groups, the spotted sandpiper does not occur in flocks. Some of the largest counts for the species were the results of float trips down various rivers from April to August. For example, on April 27, 1950, along a twenty-mile stretch of the White River between Waverly and Martinsville, sixty-four were counted. Forty-two were seen along thirteen miles of the Mississinewa River (Grant and Wabash Counties) on May 9, 1950. On August 13, 1964, sixty spotties were recorded in Franklin County along a five-mile stretch of the Whitewater River.

Although the spotted sandpiper shows a decided preference for watercourses, especially those with gravel bars and sandbars, it also occurs about ponds, borrow pits, gravel pits, sewage ponds, lakes, reservoirs, and the borders of marshes.

Spring migration usually begins the last half of April and reaches its peak in late April or early May. We have a very early arrival record of March 18. The average arrival date in Marion County over a thirty-year period is April 28. Most spotted sandpipers have left Indiana on their fall migration by mid-October, but a few linger into early November; our latest date is November 24. Two that were recorded on the 1959 Christmas bird count at Hanover (Jefferson County) constitute our only winter record.

Nesting sites are usually not far from water (there are some exceptions). The nest is on the ground in a shallow scrape lined with grasses, usually in or at the base of a clump of taller plants. Nesting sites are normally gravelly or sandy with considerable barren ground. Herbert L. Stoddard found nests of this sandpiper "40 rods back from the lake shore" along Lake Michigan. Keller found a nest in the middle of an overgrown road. The usual clutch contains four eggs, but the number may vary from two to five. Of twenty nests for which we have records, fourteen contained four eggs each and two nests each contained two, three, and five eggs. Eggs have been seen in nests from May 16 to July 15, and eggs in one nest were hatching on June 7.

Evermann and Clark (1920) mentioned that spotted sandpipers feeding along the shores of Lake Maxinkuckee ate small crustaceans, mollusks, insects, and other small bits of dead or live animal matter. Keller watched the species actively pursuing and capturing flying grasshoppers.

Depicted plants: Marsh fern (*Thelypteris palustris*); Round-leaved sundew (*Drosera rotundifolia*)

SPOTTED SANDPIPER

UPLAND SANDPIPER

UPLAND SANDPIPER

Bartramia longicauda

Grass Plover, Upland Plover, Bartram's Tattler, Bartramian Sandpiper, Field Plover, Prairie Plover, Prairie Pigeon, Bartram's Sandpiper

Sometimes on an early April day in some abandoned or close-cropped pasture it is possible to hear the clear, far-carrying territorial call of a newly arrived upland sandpiper. The upland is another of those so-called shorebirds that choose to nest in grassy fields and prairie remnants, some distance from water, mingling with meadowlarks, sparrows, bobolinks, and other upland field birds. Today this fine sandpiper is at the mercy of changing land use and resultant habitat destruction that could virtually eliminate it as a breeding bird in our state.

Nearly a hundred years ago, the upland sandpiper was considered common in northwestern Indiana and evidently nested throughout the former prairie region and southward in the lower Wabash River valley. Throughout the remainder of southern Indiana it was (and still is) a very rare migrant. It is currently a fairly common migrant except in the southeastern portion of Indiana and is widely distributed but generally found in small numbers during the nesting season. When habitat is suitable, there can be a fair number of nesting pairs, and the species seems to be maintaining itself mainly at airports and abandoned farmlands.

The upland sandpiper is at home on original prairie grasslands, old fields in early stages of plant succession, pastures, and hayfields. At various times of the year it may be observed in plowed fields, on sod farms and golf courses. In Indiana, any large shorebird seen standing on a fence post along the roadside bordering an open, grassy area is likely to be an upland sandpiper. It occasionally perches on telephone poles and one was observed on a telephone wire. One was seen on a corn stalk. Another was seen by Keller on the gravel rooftop of a downtown Indianapolis building.

Spring migrants are usually first seen in early April, but there is an arrival date of March 13 in Knox County. James B. Cope witnessed an unusually large migration of upland sandpipers in Wayne County in the spring of 1948; the incredible number of 190 were present on April 30. Most southbound migrants have left the state by September 10, but John Gottschalk observed one very late in Starke County in October (no date). As many as twenty or more have been noted in LaPorte County (sod farm), Marion County (Stout Field), and Gibson County during August.

The presence of upland sandpipers on their potential nesting grounds can sometimes be detected in spring by the males' characteristic "towering" courtship performance. A bird will circle upward into the sky until it is practically out of sight, then emit a series of long-drawn-out whistles. It then descends to the ground and alights, holding its wings cocked straight up over its back for some time before folding them into place.

Nests are on the ground in open areas but may be quite well concealed in tufts of grasses or weeds. Nest sites described in the literature include a pasture and clover field with scattered tree stumps, meadow, hay meadow, abandoned fields maintained in early successional stages by burning, airports, native prairie grasslands, hayfields, and planted cornfields. Of six nests containing full clutches, found between April 26 and June 10, five contained four eggs each, the other three. An adult was seen with young on May 30 and young estimated to be one to two days old were found with a parent on June 10.

Depicted plant: Wild lupine (*Lupinus perennis*)

ESKIMO CURLEW

Numenius borealis

Doughbird, Doebird, Prairie Pigeon, Little Curlew, Esquimaux Curlew

In March 1879, a party of hunters from Cincinnati, Ohio, shot some shorebirds near Chalmers (White County), Indiana, then a famous hunting ground. Charles Dury, examining the tied-up bunches of common snipes brought home by the hunters, recognized an Eskimo curlew among them, obtained the bird, and mounted it for the collection of the Cuvier Club. This proved to be one of the very few definite records of the occurrence of this extirpated species for Indiana. The Cuvier Club also possessed two specimens simply labeled "Indiana" and another taken at Vincennes (Knox County). The only other Indiana specimen, to our knowledge, is one mentioned by Butler (1906) as being taken at Chalmers, on April 19, 1890(?). This sums up our knowledge of this much-publicized bird for the state. It may well now be extinct. Butler called it a rare migrant that was formerly found in company with lesser golden-plovers. It used to be considered a rather common migrant in Illinois and no doubt many birds once graced the prairies of northwestern Indiana.

The literature has always considered it a foregone conclusion that the near-extinction of the Eskimo curlew was due to excessive market hunting. A new and interesting speculation by Banks (1977) is that a combination of climatic events took place that primarily affected the southbound migration and may have been more of a contributory cause for extinction than shooting.

WHIMBREL

Numenius phaeopus

Hudsonian Curlew, Jack Curlew, Striped Head

Although Brayton (1880) mentioned this curlew along with the long-billed curlew as being a rare migrant in Indiana, he presented no definite records for the state, and Butler merely quoted Brayton. The earliest Indiana record we have found for it is August 3, 1902 (Lake County). It was next reported from Porter County on September 15, 1923. It appears to be a casual spring migrant, observed from May 10 to June 2, and a very rare fall migrant, recorded from July 13 to November 1. In all there are three spring records and seventeen fall records. One is from Allen County. The others are from the three counties bordering Lake Michigan, and most of those sightings were at the lake front, where the species is sometimes simply recorded during passing flights. Most sightings are of single birds, rarely two to five, but on October 31 and November 1, 1958, eight were recorded by Raymond Grow, James E. Landing, and others.

The whimbrel is an impressive bird and a very powerful flier; some of the population winter on the Argentinian pampas. It is usually quite alert and difficult to approach, but Kenneth J. Brock obtained a fine photograph of one at Michigan City.

LONG-BILLED CURLEW
Numenius americanus

Big Curlew, Sickle Bill, Sabre-bill

The spectacular long-billed curlew was evidently found with some regularity throughout most if not all of Indiana up until 1900, and may well have been a regular visitor to the wet prairies and Kankakee River marshes more than a hundred years ago. Amos W. Butler considered it a rare migrant and a possible nester in the northern part of the state. John J. Audubon wrote that he had shot this curlew in Indiana, but gave no specifics. Butler reported specimens in collections from Clinton, Dubois, Knox, Lake, Starke, and White Counties. In addition, he mentioned sightings from several other counties. Today it is an accidental visitor to the state, and we know of a single modern-day record, August 31, 1963, when James E. Landing observed one in Porter County.

HUDSONIAN GODWIT
Limosa haemastica

Spot-rump, Goose-bird, Red-breasted Godwit

This rather large shorebird has apparently never been common in North America and its pre-1900 status in Indiana cannot be accurately determined because of conflicting statements, mostly dealing with its status in Illinois and about Lake Michigan. Butler did not list a definite Indiana record, and Indiana is not located within the major migration corridors of this godwit. It appears to be a very rare spring migrant and casual fall migrant primarily in northwestern Indiana. It has been reported elsewhere in Clay, Dearborn, Delaware, and Johnson Counties. There are only thirteen records for the state.

The nine spring migration dates fall between April 23 and June 7 and the four fall dates range from August 26 to September 6 (possibly September 15; conflicting dates in the literature). This godwit has been reported about shallow ponds and marshes, on mudflats, and in a flooded, grassy field, but not on the Lake Michigan beaches. The species is usually recorded as a single individual, but the remarkable number of eight was observed on May 11, 1978, by Ted T. Cable, Edward M. Hopkins, and Joy Underborn at Roxana Pond, Lake County.

MARBLED GODWIT
Limosa fedoa

Brant-bird, Red Marlin, Marlin, Spike-bill

The marbled godwit is larger than the Hudsonian godwit and a bit more likely to be seen in Indiana than its smaller cousin.

Although now more typically a bird of the western states, it was once suspected of breeding in Indiana and before the great Kankakee River marshes were drained hunters sometimes shot the marbled godwit. Charles Dury reported that it was an abundant species more than one hundred years ago on the wet prairies near Chalmers (White County), where market hunters and sportsmen once found excellent shooting for waterbirds of all types.

Butler considered the marbled godwit to be a rare migrant by 1898 and his most recent record for the state was for 1883. Today it is generally a very rare to casual spring migrant in northwestern Indiana and a very rare fall migrant, probably throughout the state. The seven recent spring sightings are for the period April 22 to June 5 (1947 to 1980) and all are from a four-county area immediately south of Lake Michigan. Fall observations total fifteen beween July 12 and October 3 (1936 to 1982) and were made along a broad band running southeast from Lake Michigan to the Falls of the Ohio River. All records, with the exception of one for Allen and Sullivan Counties, are from this general area. It appears that all sightings were of single individuals. Most of the birds were found on mudflats, along beaches and about the margins of ponds, lakes, reservoirs, or marshes.

RUDDY TURNSTONE
Arenaria interpres

Calico-bird, Sea Quail, Stone-pecker, Turnstone

In its breeding plumage the so-called calico-bird is one of the most delightful of shorebirds. Small groups feed amid various other sandpipers and plovers, but tend to forage in the rockier spots. Here, deftly flipping and turning small stones and pebbles, bits of shells, or other beach debris with their uniquely designed beaks, turnstones actively search for food. At Michigan City they can frequently be found on the concrete jetties, exploring cracks and crevices for possible food, and are often remarkably tame; they will feed within a few feet of birders or fishermen.

The ruddy turnstone, formerly considered a rare migrant, was virtually unknown in the state except along Lake Michigan in 1898. It is still most abundant there, but occurs as a spring and fall migrant throughout the state. Laurence C. Binford observed sixty at Wolf Lake (Lake County) on June 2, 1951; and 125 were seen in Porter County, October 15, 1976, by Noel J. Cutright. There are two winter records.

Turnstones are usually found on sandy or gravelly beaches, cinder flats, mudflats, in fields with temporary rainpools, at sewage disposal plant ponds, and around the borders of ponds, lakes, and marshes. One was found feeding on garbage on February 2, 1980, at a large garbage dump in Gary.

Spring migration begins relatively late; the earliest arrival date is May 9. Many birds are present throughout May and some linger into June. In fact, it is difficult to determine whether a bird seen on June 28 should be considered a late spring migrant or an early fall migrant. Southbound migrants appear as early as July 7 and turnstones have remained until November 24. One was seen on the 1975 Indiana Dunes Christmas count.

This turnstone feeds mainly on insects and other invertebrates it gleans from the ground. Loftin and Sutton (1979) discovered that it feeds on the eggs of the royal tern and possibly caused the abandonment of an active tern colony in Florida.

RED KNOT
Calidris canutus
Red-breasted Sandpiper

The red knot is a circumpolar species whose nesting and behavior patterns are only now beginning to be understood. Called the robin snipe in some areas because of its handsome contrasting breeding plumage of pink breast and whitish, scaly back, it is one of the showier and more attractive shorebirds that migrate across the state in spring and fall. Birders who frequent the Lake Michigan beaches have the best opportunity to see this large sandpiper in Indiana.

Butler considered it a rare migrant, remarking that in the interior of the United States the knot was found mostly around the Great Lakes. His only two Indiana records for the species were both from Lake County in late August. It is currently a casual spring migrant, not yet recorded from the southern one-third of the state at this season. As a fall migrant it is regular, but usually rare, in northern Indiana and rare to very rare (and local) elsewhere. There are now more than seventy sightings of knots in Indiana, but only five of them are for the spring migration. More than fifty are for August and September, the two months this shorebird is most abundant in the state. Three were seen on May 23, 1976, in LaPorte County and a flock of about eighteen was observed on August 21, 1920, between Gary and Indiana Dunes State Park.

The usual habitat is a beach, but birds also occur on mudflats, at ponds, lakes, reservoirs, and sewage lagoons, and on the concrete breakwaters along Lake Michigan.

Spring migrants have been recorded from May 23 to June 2. Fall migrants have been seen as early as July 30 and as late as November 1. Knots are normally seen as single individuals or in small groups, often in the company of other shorebirds.

SANDERLING
Calidris alba
Ruddy Plover

The rapid, almost mechanical advance and retreat of a small flock of sanderlings from the wave action along the beaches of Lake Michigan is a familiar sight to those who birdwatch there. Exploring a habitat that is for the most part ignored by other sandpipers, they hunt for whatever food is cast ashore or partially buried in the sand. The sanderling is highly social; if one finds itself some distance from the flock it will hastily run or fly to rejoin it. Sanderlings can be remarkably tame, as they are when searching for food on the concrete breakwaters at Michigan City. Oblivious to birders and fishermen, they scurry about, finally taking wing when someone approaches too closely.

Butler knew the sanderling as a migrant that was rare in most places in Indiana other than along Lake Michigan, where it was very common in late summer and fall. He thought the species might also be common along the Ohio River, but that has not proved to be the case. The status of this shorebird has actually changed little since 1900, except that there are now many more records from throughout the state. It is still a fairly common to common fall migrant, an uncommon spring migrant, and casual in winter around Lake Michigan. Elsewhere, it is very rare to uncommon locally in spring, but more frequent in fall.

At Lake Michigan it is usually found on the sand beaches; inland it may be seen at ponds, lakes, reservoirs, sewage lagoons, and flooded river bottoms along rivers and mudflats.

The first spring migrants are normally seen in May, but four were found on April 24 and 27, 1940, in Lake County. There were fifty at Wolf Lake on May 27, 1951, and thirty-one in Marion County on May 29, 1951. Stragglers remain into the first week of June, or even later. There is a fall migration record for July 4 and numerous other July sightings, but most are present in August and September, especially in the latter month. The earliest fall migrants are usually adults, some of which are still in breeding plumage. Raymond Grow found the phenomenal number of 535 in the West Beach area of the Indiana Dunes National Lakeshore on September 23, 1980; he reported one flock of 440 birds. Herbert L. Stoddard walked the beach from Millers to Indiana Dunes State Park on September 24, 1919, and observed more than 200 sanderlings on one two-mile stretch of the route.

SEMIPALMATED SANDPIPER
Calidris pusilla
Peep

At the height of the southbound shorebird migrations, usually from mid-August to the first week of September, it is not unusual to see large numbers of semipalmated sandpipers and other shorebirds on the mudflats of partially dried up reservoirs and lakes in Indiana. From a distance the birds look like small, scurrying mice as they run here and dart there, probing the soft mud with their beaks for some choice, hapless morsel.

Occasionally, as if by some common signal, or if a predator should appear, this group will flush en masse, banking and wheeling, showing first dark backs and then white undersides, like dark and light confetti thrown into the wind or perhaps blowing silver maple leaves, except that instead of being widely spaced, the birds are compacted into a dense, tight, unified flock. Such maneuvers are characteristic not only of this species but of the other small sandpipers that are collectively known as "peeps."

Butler knew this sandpiper as a generally uncommon migrant, often common and perhaps a summer resident in the vicinity of Lake Michigan, more numerous than the least sandpiper, which often occurred with it in spring. Today, the semipalmated sandpiper is a fairly common to common spring and fall migrant throughout the state.

It utilizes much the same habitats as other small shorebirds, being found on mudflats, in wet fields, sewage ponds, temporary overflow pools, and occasionally along beaches. The muddy areas remaining when ponds or lakes have been drained or have dried up are especially attractive to this and other shorebirds.

Spring migration occurs mainly in May, but there are sightings of this sandpiper as early as April 18. Maxima of 200 were found May 27, 1961, and May 15–18, 1963, in Marion County. Edward M. Hopkins recorded more than 250 at the Willow Slough Fish and Wildlife Area on June 2, 1977. Birds have lingered until at least June 15, but most have departed by early June. Fall migrants appear as early as July 10 and the species is usually common in September. The largest fall population was 150, in Marion County on September 1, 1950. Stragglers have been recorded as late as November 3. There is an observation of one in Hamilton County on December 5, 1953, by M. Philip Kahl, Jr.

The semipalmated sandpiper is one of North America's most abundant shorebirds, and huge flocks migrate along the eastern coast of Canada and the United States each year. Keller watched a group of thousands feeding on mudflats in the Bay of Fundy, in Nova Scotia, in early August 1974.

WESTERN SANDPIPER
Calidris mauri

Peep

The history of the western sandpiper in Indiana is a comparatively recent one. Butler listed it as hypothetical and Keller (1958) called it a very rare spring and fall migrant. A specimen (now lost) was supposedly collected August 10, 1940, at Wolf Lake (Indiana or Illinois?) by A. J. Franzen. The next reported observation for the state was August 24–31, 1941, at the Indianapolis Sewage Disposal Plant (Marion County). A specimen was collected at Geist Reservoir (Hamilton County) September 8, 1952.

This species is now a rare to very rare spring migrant recorded in twelve of the last thirty-three springs. It is considerably more abundant in the fall, having been observed in thirty-four of the past forty-two years. There are about twenty spring sightings and about ninety fall sightings from throughout the state. Most spring records are of single birds, but three were found near Lafayette on May 15, 1979. A flock of six was seen at Hammond on July 18, 1982, and six were present at Indianapolis on September 12, 1962, and September 26, 1961. We cannot vouch for the authenticity of all of these records, but it appears that the western sandpiper may have become a regular spring and fall migrant within the past decade.

The western sandpiper may be found on mudflats, cinder flats, inundated fields and concrete jetties; or around borrow pits and small marshy ponds. When feeding it generally prefers to wade in deeper water than the least or semipalmated sandpipers that often accompany it.

Spring migrants have been recorded from May 3 to June 12, but there are only two June sightings; most birds are seen during the last half of May. Fall records range from July 11 to November 5, but the majority are for August. Many fall records were obtained at the Indianapolis Sewage Disposal Plant, evidently a favored site for western sandpipers.

Distinguishing between the several small similar-looking sandpipers often referred to as peeps can be very difficult. There are reliable field marks if the birds are in "typical" plumage or relative beak length and shape are clearly evident. But if not, the sharp *jit jit* notes of the western will separate it from the *cherk cherk* of the semipalmated or the *scree-reet* of the least.

LEAST SANDPIPER
Calidris minutilla

Peep, Stint

The least sandpiper looks much like a miniature pectoral sandpiper and prefers the same type of habitat. Unlike its close rela-

tives the semipalmated and western, the least sandpiper likes to forage amid grass tussocks that grow farther away from the water, where it blends in so well with the surroundings that it can be very difficult to see until it takes flight.

Butler knew this sandpiper as a spring and fall migrant; it was "not common" in spring, but "much more numerous" in the fall, often being common in the vicinity of Lake Michigan. It is now a common spring and fall migrant and casual in the winter. There were 211 at the Indianapolis Sewage Disposal Plant on May 29, 1955, and 230 in Gibson County, May 10, 1972. The maximum number recorded in the fall is 80; at Indianapolis on July 15, 1961, and September 5, 1945.

The least sandpiper seeks much the same habitats as the other peeps: mudflats, temporary pools of water in fields, and the fringes of ponds, lakes, reservoirs, and borrow pits. At the Indianapolis Sewage Disposal Plant they foraged among clumps of grasses growing from the sludge in the settling ponds.

Spring migrants begin to arrive in April. Our earliest date is April 5, at Jeffersonville, but this is quite early. Some have lingered until June 6. The earliest date for the arrival of fall migrants is June 28 and there are several early July sightings. A few remain until November or later. Three were seen in Warren County on December 5, 1965, and one was at the Prairie Creek Reservoir on December 19, 1970. There is a December 22 sighting at the Falls of the Ohio River, Jeffersonville.

WHITE-RUMPED SANDPIPER
Calidris fuscicollis

Peep

Among the groups of small shorebirds foraging in shallow water, there will sometimes be a white-rumped sandpiper. It looks a bit "different" from the others, for its folded wings extend beyond the tip of the tail, and when it is flushed it is seen to have a completely white rump, a distinctive field mark in flight. If you listen carefully you may be able to hear its high-pitched, batlike note, often given in flight or while foraging: a thin, squeaking *zeet*.

It was carried on the hypothetical list by Butler, but Mumford (1953) summarized Indiana records and reported the collection of the first specimen in the state on July 20, 1950, at Wolf Lake (Lake County). The species today is probably a rare spring migrant and very rare to rare fall migrant throughout the state. The largest numbers and the most frequent occurrences are reported during spring. There were about 55 at the Muncie Airport on May 16, 1978. The maximum number seen in the fall was nine, at Geist Reservoir, on October 13, 1953.

The white-rump is found in shallow rain pools or overflows in muddy fields, on cinder flats, or at airports. It can also be seen on the sandy or muddy borders of lakes, ponds, reservoirs, or marshes, near sewage ponds, drained fish hatchery ponds, and the like.

The earliest reported spring sighting is April 10, but this (if correct) is unusually early, and most birds are present in May. Some have remained until June 12. By July 14, fall migrants have appeared in northern Indiana and the latest sighting was made on November 9. Migrants are nearly always in the company of other shorebirds, and we believe that in earlier years the white-rumped sandpiper was largely overlooked by Indiana birders. It appears to be a highly social species.

BAIRD'S SANDPIPER
Calidris bairdii

To many birding neophytes, and even to some experienced birders, distinguishing among migrating sandpipers during August and September can be quite perplexing. Careful scrutiny, however, will reveal the subtle differences—the presence or absence of streaks, eye-stripes, and wingbars, variations in body size, and call notes. In learning to separate these confusing species, there is no substitute for a great deal of careful field work, because it gives one a "feel" about what to watch for. For example, veteran birder Charles T. Clark has made the apt observation that Baird's sandpiper resembles a sandpiper that someone has held by the beak and tail, then stretched.

There were only two records for this shorebird in Indiana in 1900, and Butler listed it as a rare migrant. A good many records have accumulated since then, and now it appears that it is a casual spring migrant and rare to uncommon (locally) fall migrant statewide. Fifteen were seen in Monroe County on May 13, 1978, and twenty in Lake County on September 2, 1951. Much more field work by competent observers is required before we can determine its true status.

Although many of the same habitats used by other shorebirds are favored by Baird's sandpiper, it seems to prefer to forage in the drier portions of shorelines and mudflats. It often feeds more or less alone, away from other species. Other habitats include flooded grassy fields, sand beaches, sod farms, and the edges of borrow pits, ponds, lakes, reservoirs, and sewage pits.

Practically all of the spring sightings are for May, but extremes are April 18 and June 4. Around mid-May seems to be the average time of arrival. Southbound migrants appear as early as July 22, but reach their peak in August or September. Stragglers have been observed as late as November 4.

5,000 was found in Lake County. Fall groups are much smaller. The maximum number recorded was 500, on August 1, 1961, at Indianapolis.

The favored grassy habitat can be either wet or dry. It includes sod farms, airports, pastures, clover fields, and similar habitats with short vegetation. The birds also frequent plowed fields, overflows, and rainpools along rivers, sewage ponds, fish hatchery ponds, mudflats, and the borders of many other types of water areas. Pectoral sandpipers, lesser golden-plovers, and killdeers are frequently seen together.

The pectoral sandpiper is an early spring migrant, arriving in the state as early as March 8, but the greatest numbers are usually present during April. A few birds linger into June. One collected June 21, 1965, in Steuben County may have been an early fall migrant, but one was seen June 12 to 19, 1977, at Willow Slough. Fall migrants have reached Gibson County by July 2, and there are other July sightings. Individuals may remain quite late in the fall. One was present until November 29, 1975, in Delaware County. Sightings were also made in Delaware County on December 19, 1970, and at the Falls of the Ohio, on December 18, 1949. There is a record for February 19 (no year) in Greene County, but we feel this is most likely the result of an error in note keeping.

Aggressive feeding behavior is sometimes observed, especially among adult birds in July and early August. Typically, an individual crouches low and runs toward another that has encroached upon its feeding area. Pectoral sandpipers were seen feeding on insects and their larvae at one site. They forage in dry areas, as well as in wet ones, where they often wade up to their bellies. We once saw a flock of this sandpiper feeding on a sodded lake dam along with red-winged blackbirds and European starlings. Another group was feeding in a strip of unmowed grass between a road and a plowed field.

PECTORAL SANDPIPER
Calidris melanotos

Grass Snipe

The pectoral sandpiper was aptly called the grass snipe by early hunters and authors because of its preference for wet, grassy areas. Judging from the numbers seen in both spring and fall, Indiana apparently lies in the main migratory route of this species. Old-time market hunters must have shot untold numbers in the spring in the Kankakee River valley and on the wet prairies of northwestern Indiana, where pectoral sandpipers are still common at that season. The hunters shot many kinds of "snipe," a term they used for nearly all species of shorebirds with the possible exception of the plovers and other larger species.

Butler wrote that the pectoral sandpiper was a common, sometimes abundant, migrant; he thought a few might be summer residents. This in general describes its current status, for it is common in spring and fall throughout the state, being most abundant in northwestern Indiana, especially in the spring. There are several recent records for June and July, but these are probably migrants. On April 22, 1978, about 5,000 pectoral sandpipers were seen in LaPorte and Starke Counties and a flock of around 4,000 was reported in Newton County on April 3, 1977. On April 29, 1981, a flock containing from 3,000 to

PURPLE SANDPIPER
Calidris maritima

Those who know something about the distribution and habits of the purple sandpiper in North America normally associate it with the rocky, storm-battered Atlantic coast, particularly from Maine to Nova Scotia. Why this circumpolar arctic species has become a winter visitor to Indiana is one of the many mysteries in the avian world that add to the excitement and enjoyment of studying birds. The best way to see a purple sandpiper in Indiana is to visit the harbor at Michigan City between fall and early spring and search the jetties, beaches, and breakwaters. Here, along Lake Michigan, this tame sandpiper has found a suitable winter home for nearly forty years.

Butler put the purple sandpiper on his hypothetical list in 1898 on the basis of records from Illinois and Ohio. William E. Ricker (1942) reported the sighting of a purple sandpiper at Lake Wawasee (Kosciusko County) on December 13, 1941, but there is some doubt that this bird was correctly identified. Hubert O. Davis and W. Marvin Davis found one at Michigan City on November 26, 1948. Other observers recorded the species there in 1950 and 1954, and in the latter year Charles T. Clark obtained movies of one, thus adding it to the official Indiana list. There are now about thirty sightings and it appears that this sandpiper is a rare fall migrant and winter resident on the southern shores of Lake Michigan (particularly at Michigan City). It has been found at Indiana Harbor and Beverly Shores (Porter County). It may also be a casual spring migrant, but some of the "spring" sightings may involve birds that have actually remained in the region throughout the winter.

Nearly all the birds reported were found on jetties, breakwaters, or riprap—jumbled piles of concrete—along the Lake Michigan shoreline. A few sightings have also been made on the nearby beaches, where it was once found feeding with ruddy turnstones. It was seen picking some rather large, unidentified food items from the water-soaked algae growing near the waterline on the concrete slabs. Most sightings are of single birds, but two were at Michigan City in the spring of 1977 and November 23, 1973, and three were reported on May 13, 1978. Early fall sightings are August 21, 1977, and August 26, 1978. The next earliest date is October 9. The latest spring date is May 25.

DUNLIN

Calidris alpina

Red-backed Sandpiper, American Dunlin, Black Breast

In full breeding plumage the showy dunlin is certainly one of the most brightly colored of the sandpipers found in Indiana. Many people prefer its older name, red-backed sandpiper, even though fall migrants are mainly in the grayish winter plumage so strikingly different from that of spring. This is another circumpolar species that Indiana birders may have a chance to see during its migrations across the state.

Around 1900, the dunlin was considered a migrant that was present during the latter part of May, early June, and October. Butler noted that it was sometimes abundant around the southern end of Lake Michigan and small lakes near there, rare elsewhere in the state. Today it appears to be a rare to uncommon migrant locally throughout Indiana. It is most regularly seen and most abundant in the northwestern part of the state. On May 13, 1977, an estimated 250 were recorded at the Willow Slough Fish and Wildlife Area. There were 60 in Marion County on October 15, 1966. Seventy-one birds were seen on the 1980 Lake Monroe Christmas bird count, a remarkable number for that time of year.

This sandpiper frequents mudflats, rain pools on cinder flats and in muddy fields, drained fish hatchery ponds and lake beds, sewage lagoons, and (occasionally) rocky or concrete breakwaters. In these habitats, it is frequently in the company of other species of shorebirds.

Most spring migrants are first recorded around mid-May, but a few birds are sometimes present in March and April. Our earliest date is March 25, 1977, when Ted T. Cable saw one at Willow Slough. Three birds were still present in Lake County on June 13, 1952, and one was there July 4, 1952. The earliest date of fall arrival is August 23, for Lake Monroe, but most birds are present in October. Stragglers then remain into December.

Several groups of dunlins are often seen feeding in an area. The birds tend to be quite active, vigorously probing the mud or sand and flying about from group to group. Sometimes they utter their distinctive call, which sounds somewhat like the word *cheese*.

CURLEW SANDPIPER

Calidris ferruginea

This European species, whose occurrence in Indiana is accidental, has been recorded only once in the state. On May 23, 1980, Kenneth J. Brock and Raymond Grow found one along the east edge of Wolf Lake, an industrialized area on the Indiana-Illinois state line. Brock (1980) obtained excellent photographs of the bird and at least eight other persons also saw it that day.

It was with dunlins, ruddy turnstones, western sandpipers, semipalmated sandpipers and white-rumped sandpipers, feeding along the lake shore and a dike road. When disturbed, it tended to fly with the dunlins. The curlew sandpiper was seen to feed on insect larvae floating on the water's surface.

STILT SANDPIPER

Calidris himantopus

The stilt sandpiper is apparently not well known to Indiana birdwatchers and for many years was evidently largely overlooked among the other shorebirds during migration. Adults in breeding plumage are striking birds, but unfortunately the few we see in Indiana, are usually late spring stragglers or early fall arrivals—most however are in a duller, inconspicuous plumage, and can easily be confused with other, similar species.

Butler knew of a single record of this sandpiper, a specimen collected October 10, 1892, near Lafayette. It appears that through the years the species has become considerably more common, for it is now generally a rare spring migrant and uncommon to fairly common fall migrant locally. The maximum number recorded at any locality in spring is five, all during the first half of May in central Indiana. A flock of 45 was seen at Gary, on July 23, 1978, and 42 were observed in Hamilton County on September 1, 1952.

The stilt sandpiper has been found about shallow ponds and marshes, in flooded fields, ponds, or rainpools in pastures, and at airports and sewage lagoons. It prefers to feed in one or two inches of water, where it probes into the bottom with rapid up-and-down (dowitcherlike) head movements, and is often in the company of lesser yellowlegs.

Extreme spring migration dates range from April 18 to June 2, but most birds pass through in the last three weeks of May. Southbound birds appear as early as July 4. Most have departed by mid-October. The latest fall record is November 7.

BUFF-BREASTED SANDPIPER

Tryngites subruficollis

The delicate-looking buff-breasted sandpiper, which resembles a small upland sandpiper, is still comparatively less well known than the majority of other shorebirds in the state. Whether it was simply very rare or was overlooked in the heyday of Amos W. Butler and other naturalists working in Indiana before 1900, we cannot say. Since most of the market hunting and shorebird shooting in northwestern Indiana took place in the spring, a time of year when the buff-breasted sandpiper today is almost absent, it is not surprising that we have found no specimens taken by hunters. It is indeed encouraging to have the opportunity to observe this fine shorebird in Indiana today.

Butler knew of a single specimen, collected near Lafayette, on September 10, 1892. There are only three spring records for this sandpiper in the state, thus it is casual at that season. It is more commonly seen in the fall, when it should probably be considered rare. All spring sightings were of single birds. Seventeen were seen in Knox County on August 31, 1980, twenty-seven in Lake County, on September 10, 1980.

The buff-breasted sandpiper prefers open, grassy areas, like those used by the upland sandpiper—grassy fields, pastures, sod farms, golf courses, and airports. It has also been found in plowed fields and on cinder flats, beaches and mudflats, in flooded fields, about sewage lagoons, on a drained lake bottom and (once) on a concrete jetty.

Birds have been seen in spring between May 6 and June 1. Fall sightings were recorded from August 2 to October 11. Most have been seen from late August to mid-September. Spring migrants crossing North America are most abundant within a narrow flyway through the Great Plains states, where there are traditional stopover sites. Such known staging areas should be closely monitored to ensure that they remain suitable for the birds. Fall migrants cross the country on a wide front and some birds even reach Europe and Africa.

As buff-breasted sandpipers walk, they often bob their heads back and forth. This characteristic movement, which is called head lagging, can be used, even at a long distance, to identify the species. Sometimes, however, the movements of feeding buff-breasted sandpipers are more ploverlike. Nancy E. Rea described nine that she watched, moving single file, about four to five feet apart, "walking across mowed grass moving their heads forward and backward like chickens."

Keller (1962) remarked that at the Indianapolis Sewage Disposal Plant the buff-breasted sandpipers were generally found "on the cinder road which leads back to the pit area." He approached to within twenty feet of a bird on several occasions, but the bird lazily sauntered away a few paces and resumed feeding. He also found that when the birds crouched down in the cinders they became nearly invisible among the surrounding vegetation.

RUFF

Philomachus pugnax

The showy and interesting ruff is an Old World bird, its occurrence in Indiana is accidental and limited to seven records. Male ruffs are adorned in the breeding season with variegated head and neck tufts, called ruffs, which vary in color from nearly white to nearly black. Each male displays to females from a small, defended territory, adjacent to numerous other defended territories occupied by other males. Such a courtship arena is called a lek. Some of the grouse (one being the greater prairie-chicken) and other birds exhibit similar behavior, as do some mammals.

The first record of the ruff for Indiana was obtained by Ruthven Deane (1905), who described the event:

The celebrated Kankakee Marshes at English Lake, Indiana, have yielded records of several specimens of the English Widgeon, but I can now record the capture of a still rarer visitor from the Old World, the Ruff. While visiting the English Lake Shooting and Fishing Club on April 12, 1905, I examined a number of ducks and shore birds which had been killed that day by Mr. Wm. M. Derby, Jr., of Chicago. The latter consisted principally of Summer Yellow-legs and Pectoral Sandpipers, but there was one specimen in the bag which puzzled me. Mr. Derby had been hunting ducks in the marsh, and while moving from one point to another he fired into a flock of shore birds which flew past his boat, killing several "Grass birds" and the specimen in question.

A bird suspected of being a ruff was seen October 17, 1949, at the Indianapolis Sewage Disposal Plant by Palmer D. Skaar and Henry C. West. There are four sightings from 1976 to 1982 for Porter, Vigo, and Wabash Counties. The birds were found from April 10 to May 5, and three of them were photographed. Charles E. Mills et al. found a ruff near Fort Branch, Gibson County, on June 26, 1982.

Ruffs seen in Indiana have been in flooded corn stubble or soybean fields, at sewage lagoons, and on a flooded baseball diamond. They were in company with lesser yellowlegs, pectoral sandpipers, and lesser golden-plovers. One ruff, behaving as though on territory, was displaying to two lesser yellowlegs. Another's behavior was described by Ruth Erickson: "It seemed to be courting the other shorebirds there. It would put its head down and run forward, then squat down in a crouching position. When it ran it spread the ruff out."

SHORT-BILLED DOWITCHER

Limnodromus griseus

Gray Snipe, Gray Back, Red-breasted Snipe

Dowitchers are long-billed, medium-sized shorebirds that seem to prefer much the same habitat as the yellowlegs and common snipe. The two species (short-billed, long-billed) that occur in Indiana have long been confused because of the difficulty in separating them by sight in the field. Indeed, for many years they were considered to be the same species. Within the past thirty years we have been able to obtain much more data and refine our field identifications, since each does exhibit individual characteristics that may be used to identify it.

Butler had little information regarding the short-billed dowitcher, but was of the opinion that it was much rarer than the long-billed dowitcher here. It is now evident that the short-billed is the more common of the two in Indiana. Available records indicate that it is an uncommon spring and fall migrant that may be fairly common in favorable habitat in certain years. Two hundred were reported in Dearborn County on May 11, 1980. Kenneth J. Brock reported eighty-one at Gary on July 17, 1978.

Dowitchers are often seen in overflow ponds or rainpools in fields, on mudflats about ponds, marshes, lakes, and borrow pits, or about fish hatchery ponds and sewage lagoons. They feed in shallow water, usually wading about and moving their beaks up and down with rapid movements while probing the bottom.

The spring migration appears to be rather short, with birds present from April 15 to May 23. Most are present about mid-May. Fall migrants begin to appear by June 28 and the last stragglers were found November 7. Most have departed by October 1.

The usual call note of the short-billed dowitcher is a *tu tu tu*, often uttered when the birds are flushed. The corresponding call of the long-billed dowitcher is a *keek* or *peep* note. A single *tu* note is reportedly given by either species on occasion. We suggest that call notes be used as an aid in field identification.

LONG-BILLED DOWITCHER

Limnodromus scolopaceus

Greater Gray-back, Red-bellied Snipe, Gray Snipe

Recent study has shown that the long-billed dowitcher is less common in Indiana than the short-billed dowitcher. Whether this was true in Butler's time we cannot say, but he considered the long-billed more common. Numerous records he cited were of birds collected in spring on the famous hunting grounds of northwestern Indiana. We find it surprising that more short-billed dowitchers were not represented by these hunting records, unless there has actually been a reversal of the numerical status of the two species within the past hundred years. We have been unable to use many sightings of "dowitchers," either be-cause they were not identified as to species or, in many cases, were probably misidentified.

Butler knew the long-billed dowitcher as a rare migrant. To-day it appears to be a casual spring migrant and a local, rare to very rare fall migrant. Twenty-five were seen March 27, 1976, in Gibson County, and thirty-four on October 23, 1982, in Lake County.

Habitats used by the two dowitchers are the same except that the long-billed tends to feed in deeper water.

Although there are numerous spring records for the long-billed dowitcher in the state, many of them cannot be considered reliable. Butler mentioned a specimen collected at English Lake on March 11, 1889, a very early spring date for a mi-grant. May 21 is the latest date for a lingerer. Fall records are hopelessly confused. Numerous observers reported long-billed dowitchers in July and August, but it now appears that most of the birds appear in September and October, in general later than the short-billed. Long-bills have been recorded as late as November 18.

Obviously, much more information needs to be gathered in order to correctly assess the relative abundance and migration dates of the two species in the state.

COMMON SNIPE

Gallinago gallinago

Jack Snipe, Wilson's Snipe

We associate the familiar *scape scape* call of a flushing snipe with early spring walks in wet meadows, along ditches, or near borders of shallow marshes. Flushing birds are quite swift of wing; they fly up and away in a zigzag fashion, sometimes reaching a considerable height before pitching back down on set wings into a nearby wet spot. Here they crouch, practically invisible, blending into the surroundings. We have sometimes witnessed their distinctive courtship flight and heard the nonvocal, hollow *who who who who who* ("winnowing") sounds caused by wind rushing through feathers as the bird dives downward at an angle, twisting its body.

Before 1900, this snipe was an abundant migrant and in northern Indiana was considered a summer resident. A few remained in some winters in suitable localities. Butler noted that migration dates and abundance varied greatly from year to year. The snipe is still a common spring and fall migrant and rare to very rare winter resident locally. It is casual as a nesting bird in northern Indiana, but more information is desirable concerning the occurrence and distribution of nesting. It was recorded on 113 Christmas bird counts throughout the state from 1925 to 1980. One each was seen on 45 counts and two each on 27 counts. Maxima of sixteen were seen at Evansville on December 15, 1979, and in Delaware County on December 26, 1974.

The common snipe is found in many types of wet places, wherever the soil is soft. It occurs about the mar-gins of ponds, lakes, borrow pits, rainpools, and over-flows, and along ditches and streams. Flooded fields and pastures and wet meadows are favored habitats. Birds have also been found at fish hatchery ponds, sewage la-goons, and springs or seeps (especially in winter). Three birds were once flushed from a dry, grassy field, but this is unusual, as is their appearance on open mudflats.

Since wintering birds may be present nearly anywhere in the state, determining when spring migration begins is difficult. There is a considerable movement of snipes through the state from about the second week of March throughout April and into May. Most have departed by June 1. Some remain during the summer and may be nest-ing. Fall migrants begin to appear as early as late June;

COMMON SNIPE

most have left the state by December 1. Will E. Madden reported hundreds at Willow Slough about April 1, 1955, and on August 22, 1953. Those present in winter frequently stay near an open spring or seepage area such as that used for years by wintering snipes near West Lafayette. A sizable spring flowed practically all winter, unless it was an extremely cold one, and there was considerable open water in which watercress grew abundantly. The common snipe was found there winter after winter until the spring dried up.

The courtship flight, accompanied by winnowing or bleating, can be seen and heard each spring. It is quite evident that many birds engage in courtship at sites where

they do not nest. Winnowing has been heard at least as early as April 1. Butler reported that this snipe nested at English Lake (Starke County) every year, according to Ruthven Deane. Nesting was also reported from Lake and Miami Counties, with no details. Anthony Hush (1934) recorded downy young found in St. Joseph County on May 5, 1934. Jimmy F. New found a nest he considered to be that of a common snipe at the Kingsbury Fish and Wildlife Area in the summer of 1968. Birds have also been observed during the nesting season in several other counties across northern Indiana, south to Miami and Wabash Counties.

Depicted plant: Marsh blue violet (*Viola cucullata*)

AMERICAN WOODCOCK

Scolopax minor

Timber Doodle, Bogsucker

Except when performing its spectacular courtship display, the nocturnal woodcock is secretive and inconspicuous, resting by day in some damp thicket, where as evidence of its presence one may find splashes of whitewash and holes made in the mud by the bird's probing beak as it seeks earthworms. It becomes more active at dusk, and it is the aerial courtship of the male woodcock that attracts the birdwatcher. This performance often takes place in an old field where there are scattered small sprouts and trees, brier patches, weeds, and (at times) bare soil. A male woodcock sitting on the ground will begin giving a nasal *bzeep* or *peent* call at dusk and after numerous (sometimes one hundred or more) repetitions of the call, will fly up, spiraling on whistling wings, until it reaches a great height in the sky. Then it descends, uttering a rapid, chippering call, often alighting near the spot from which it took flight. It sits there, giving more *bzeep* calls, then repeats the aerial performance. This behavior may continue after it is too dark to watch the bird.

The status of the American woodcock in Indiana has evidently remained about the same for the past one hundred years. It is still a common migrant and nests throughout the state. It is also a casual winter resident, the largest number reported at that season being three, at Indianapolis, on December 27, 1958. Large numbers are not usually encountered, for the birds do not flock. In good habitat, however, woodcocks tend to congregate during migration. Twenty each were found in Marion County on May 17, 1947, and at Willow Slough on March 30, 1968.

This woodcock is usually found in areas where the soil is moist, but it has been observed in open woods on a dry ridge, some three hundred feet above the river valley (Butler, 1898a) and in cornfields or damp meadows. Thickets of sprouts, small trees, giant ragweeds, and the like in boggy or wet areas are the best places to find it, especially during its daytime resting period. Courtship often takes place in dry, upland fields that have been overgrown. Crankshaw et al. (1969) described the singing grounds at some Indiana sites. There are several observations of woodcocks coming to heavily sprinkled lawns at night to feed on earthworms.

Spring migrants normally first appear in late February, but there are earlier records (some of which may have been wintering birds). Courtship appears to begin soon after the birds arrive. Most fall migrants have left the state by mid-November. We suspect more spend the winter in the state than now indicated by the relatively few records.

Nests are on the ground, usually in a relatively dry site, but some nests are inundated by spring rains. The normal clutch size is four; this number was found in twenty-one of twenty-four nests. Full clutches have been observed in nests from March 13 to May 30 (which seems to be late).

Twelve broods found out of the nest ranged in number from one to five (unusual), but eight of them contained four young each. The earliest date for young being found out of the nest is April 13, and young capable of flight have been seen as early as April 22. Adults sometimes carry a young bird while flying.

Courtship flights have been recorded mostly from February 21 through May. However, individual birds occasionally perform throughout the summer, and we have reports for August 6 and October 14. Most remarkable is the courtship activity of a male on December 21, 1982, during the Christmas bird count in Martin County, but the day was relatively warm, mostly clear, and calm. Most courtship flights occur at dusk, but the birds also perform at dawn. Harmon P. Weeks, Jr. (1970) gathered interesting data on courtship and territorial behavior of the woodcock in Indiana. He wrote,

Several aggressive reactions of territorial birds to the presence of the investigator were encountered. On May 1, I was lying about 100 feet from the usual landing site of the bird on Area 1. The taped peenting was played to test the bird's reaction to it. The territorial bird cackled, flew toward the sound and lit within 20 feet of the recorder, which was on the ground about 3 feet from my head. After flying closer to the recorder and peenting several times, it flushed and returned to its usual landing site. The complete approach process was repeated twice more. On the third approach, the bird landed 5 feet from the recorder and approached it on foot. It stood silently next to it for a few seconds and then began searching through the grass around the recorder. Suddenly it moved through the weeds and appeared about a foot from my face. Almost immediately the woodcock lunged toward me and struck my eye with its bill and then grabbed a tuft of hair in its bill and yanked vigorously several times. The bird then released its hold, jumped back about a foot, and stood watching me. I remained as still as possible. The whole attack was then repeated with the bird first striking my eye and then yanking my hair. After this attack an attempt was made to catch the bird by hand, but its reactions were much too quick and it flushed. However, it immediately responded again to the peenting tape and attacked my hand several times as I shuffled it in the grass. These attacks indicate how strong a role peenting plays in the territorial behavior of the woodcock.

WILSON'S PHALAROPE

Phalaropus tricolor

Web-footed Snipe

The roles of the sexes in the three species of phalaropes are substantially reversed. The female is the more brightly plumaged, performs the courtship ritual, and leaves the nesting area after she has laid the eggs. The male constructs the nest, incubates the eggs, and rears the young. Hohn (1969) thought that this turnabout in behavior might be due to a significantly high proportion of the male hormone testosterone in the female. Whatever the reason, it is an interesting phenomenon, shared by relatively few other species of birds. Several of us found a group of twelve Wilson's phalaropes in a wet pasture at Willow Slough on May 10, 1953. The females in the group were exhibiting courtship behavior and from time to time one chased another. A female that was collected here five days later contained an egg ready to be laid in her oviduct. It is interesting that on May 14, 1959, there were nine females and two males at the same site.

Butler reported that this phalarope was a rare migrant in

general, but was common in extreme northwestern Indiana, where it nested (Lake County). It is now uncommon in northwestern Indiana and we know of no nesting record since 1941. It is a spring and fall migrant throughout the state, but still found in the greatest numbers in the northwestern corner. There are June sightings from four counties, and we think it quite likely the species has nested since 1941 in Newton and Lake Counties.

The Wilson's phalarope frequents wet pastures and grassy fields with pools of standing water, sewage lagoons, mudflats, cinder flats, sod (turf) farms, and the edges of ponds, lakes, reservoirs, overflows and marshes. It occasionally wanders onto dry land to feed.

The earliest spring arrival date is April 6 (Lawrence County) and the latest departure is October 16 (Marion County). There are numerous sightings for May, evidently the month when it is most common. William B. Barnes reportedly saw many females, "perhaps 100," at Willow Slough in June 1958 and Will E. Madden observed about forty there in May 1977. Smaller numbers are found in the fall. Kenneth J. Brock visited the Burr Street dump (Gary) and Long Lake (Porter County) on August 24, 1977, and saw a total of ten birds.

The last nesting record we know about was for 1941. Donald H. Boyd found several nests in 1924 at Wolf Lake, Whiting (Lake County). He described them as follows:

These nests were rather well made of dried rush stems and grasses. They were built off or on top of the ground rather than in a depression as in the Spotted Sandpiper. The eggs appeared to be nicely packed in these nests, points down and a little toward the center. The nests were just large enough and no larger. . . . [They] were all placed on the beach not far from the water's edge in the sparse rush growth. The beach is long and flat here—when there is considerable rain as has been the case this season this beach is covered with water and many nests destroyed. Even hard rains cause these nests to become so badly soaked that the eggs chill and addle.

While Boyd examined these nests, several adult birds circling about "uttering their creepy croak, stretching out their necks at each croak."

The only six nests we have knowledge of were all near Whiting (Lake County). Five contained four eggs each, the other three (possibly this nest had been deserted). Eggs were observed in nests from May 30 to July 5.

The feeding behavior of this phalarope is interesting to watch. One will spin around while sitting on the water, evidently stirring up food, and pick objects from on or near the surface. At other times the birds probe about in shallow water with the tips of their beaks or make erratic, jerky sweeps with the beak through the water. Keller watched one awkwardly chasing flying insects on dry land, making delicate stabs at the prey with its beak and moving jerkily like a clockwork toy. A group that Charles E. Mills watched feeding on a mudflat held their heads near the ground, with their beaks parallel to the surface.

RED-NECKED PHALAROPE

Phalaropus lobatus

Northern Phalarope, Web-footed Snipe

The late afternoon of October 7, 1949, in Posey County was cloudless, warm, and completely calm. Hovey Lake was perfectly smooth; the low angle of the sun illuminated the tall cypress trees growing on the eastern side of the lake and their reflections were mirrored in the still water. Two small birds swimming not far offshore caught our eye and we rowed our boat toward them to obtain a better view. They permitted us to get fairly near and even to photograph them at close range, allowing Mumford to add the red-necked phalarope to his list of birds seen in Indiana.

As of 1897, there were only two Indiana records of this phalarope, and Butler considered it a rare migrant. Two had been collected on June 7, 1889, in Boone County and deposited in the State Museum at Indianapolis and Charles A. Stockbridge had observed the species at Fort Wayne. Relatively few were recorded between 1900 and 1950. It is now a very rare spring migrant and a rare fall migrant in small numbers throughout Indiana. Maxima are four, on May 13, 1972 (Wells County), and five, on September 15–18, 1976 (Clay County).

The red-necked phalarope is found in flooded pastures, near shallow ponds and sewage lagoons, on the mucky, muddy bottoms of drained ponds and lakes, and around pools of water on cinder flats and mudflats. The birds frequently alight on the water to feed and swim.

The earliest spring date is April 2 and individuals have lingered until June 7. Most of the spring sightings took place in May. Fall migrants have appeared as early as July 15. There are more records for September than for any other month, and the next largest number is for August. The latest date for a straggler is November 1 (a bird seen November 18 may have been this species).

This phalarope may swim about and pick food from the surface of the water, or feed on the mud. One was seen feeding on the mud of a drained fish hatchery pond with semipalmated sandpipers and a dunlin. A red-necked phalarope collected on September 1 had numerous fat, white larvae resembling maggots in its digestive tract.

In early August on the Bay of Fundy, near New Brunswick, Keller watched a flock of red-necked phalaropes estimated to contain 200,000 birds. They would fly up in front of the boat, alight, spin and twirl, and resume feeding. Small groups kept flying to the edge of the flock to feed. When they had drifted some distance away from the main flock, they would fly back to their starting point. Constant repetition of these maneuvers by thousands upon thousands of birds was an awe-inspiring sight.

RED PHALAROPE

Phalaropus fulicaria

The red phalarope is essentially a bird of the open sea except during the nesting season; its occurrences in Indiana are irregular and mostly confined to Lake Michigan. Hoosier birders usually see their first red phalarope on the breakwater at Michigan City harbor in late fall. When the "whale birds" appear, birders from far and wide come to see them. These cold-weather trips to Lake Michigan quite often resulted in the sighting of other rare or unusual birds, and we have frequently found an excuse to go to Michigan City sometime in November.

Butler considered the red phalarope to be a rare straggler during migration, and cited only two records for the state. One, a specimen collected in Jasper County on April 10, 1885, by R. R. Moffitt, is the only spring record for Indiana. Unfortunately, the specimen cannot now be found in any museum. Today the species is a very rare and local fall migrant in the vicinity of the southern tip of Lake Michigan; elsewhere in the state it is a casual fall migrant. There is one winter record.

This phalarope seems to prefer quiet bays, coves, and yacht basins, where it can more easily feed by picking insects and perhaps other invertebrates from the water's surface. Along Lake Michigan, where it most often occurs, it frequents places near the shore that are more or less protected from the wind by jetties and breakwaters. Habitats where it has been seen away from the lake include a marsh border, a cove along the shoreline of a reservoir, and the Falls of the Ohio River.

The earliest record for a fall arrival is September 12; most fall dates are for October and November, when the species appears to be equally abundant. There is only one December sighting, in 1953—a straggler that remained for most of the month. Maximum numbers seen were fifteen on October 27, 1959, in Lake County and twenty-seven on October 27, 1980, in LaPorte County.

Seven birds were seen at Michigan City on October 30, 1959. On the sandy beach east of the breakwater long wind-rows of dead leaves rolled in the waves. The phalaropes were feeding at the edge of these leaf masses. One bird collected that day had eaten midge larvae (the most numerous food item), an amphipod, mayfly nymphs, and an isopod, according to William R. Eberly, who identified the contents of the digestive tract. Steven H. Glass saw a red phalarope at Monroe Reservoir feeding at the edge of floating masses of algae.

[POMARINE JAEGER]

Stercorarius pomarinus

Gullchaser, Pirate, Sea Hawk

When the cold fronts move into northwestern Indiana around the first of October, jaeger-watchers gather at various points along the Lake Michigan shore on stormy days in hopes of seeing these interesting birds offshore. From time to time, the pomarine—largest of the three species of jaegers that visit this region—is reported. To date there is no collected specimen or photograph of any Indiana birds, but we believe that most (if not all) of these identifications can be relied on.

Butler reported the sighting of a pomarine jaeger near the Indiana-Illinois state line on October 9, 1876, but later authors stated that this bird was actually seen in Illinois. The first pomarine jaeger seen in the state was an adult in the pale color phase, found on June 1, 1946, at Geist Reservoir, near Indianapolis, by Val Nolan Jr., Howard F. Wright, and Keller. Many others saw the bird the following day. The eight other sight records are all for the three counties bordering Lake Michigan and range from August 8 to December 15. Most were for October. It appears that the pomarine jaeger is a casual fall migrant, but it may be more common offshore in Lake Michigan. Most sightings are of single birds, but on October 9, 1965, five were observed by James E. Landing et al.

PARASITIC JAEGER

Stercorarius parasiticus

All the jaegers are known for their habit of harassing gulls, terns, and other birds, and forcing them to give up their food, which the jaeger then eats. This "parasitic" habit is responsible for the common name of this species. Many of the jaegers that appear along the southern tip of Lake Michigan in the fall go unidentified; most are probably immature parasitic jaegers. After they reach the Great Lakes, these birds, hatched and fledged in the tundra during the Arctic summer, still have thousands of miles to fly to reach summer in the southern hemisphere. At Lake Michigan on stormy October days one can often see large numbers of these "hawk gulls" in action.

The parasitic jaeger was on the Indiana hypothetical list for a long time. In light of the relative abundance of the three species of jaegers in the state today this seems quite odd to us. Ford (1956) refers to a specimen of this jaeger taken near Miller (Lake County) on November 30, 1918, according to the notes of Colin C. Sanborn. A parasitic jaeger was collected in Porter County on October 5, 1929, and other specimens have been obtained. Today the species is a rare to uncommon fall migrant that occurs every year on Lake Michigan. It has been reported nowhere else in the state. Raymond Grow observed forty to sixty jaegers per day in the late 1950s and flocks containing as many as fifteen were observed. Laurence C. Binford and Grow saw sixty-one on October 6, 1957.

Fall migration takes place from September 13 to December 21, but most birds are present in October. In 1980, for the first time in some thirty years, there were no October sightings, according to Grow.

LONG-TAILED JAEGER

Stercorarius longicaudus

This graceful jaeger is only an accidental visitor to Indiana. It was first added to the state list by Herbert L. Stoddard (1916), who collected an adult male on the beach east of Millers on September 21, 1915. The bird, Stoddard reported, was in the vicinity of a small flock of ring-billed and herring gulls. Two other specimens were taken in the same area soon after—on September 1, 1917, and November 30, 1918. The species was not reported again until James A. Haw found one at Michigan City on June 21, 1982. Its presence in the state in June, August, and September suggests that it may migrate earlier in the fall than the other jaegers.

LAUGHING GULL

Larus atricilla

The laughing gull, a familiar bird in the southern and southeastern coastal regions of the United States, is like many other species of gulls a wanderer. In the late 1950s, birders began seeing this gull along Lake Michigan. Since the initial observations involved immature birds, there was some concern about whether they had been correctly identified. However, there have been numerous sightings of adult birds during the past twenty years and the laughing gull has become an established member of Indiana's avifauna.

Butler knew of no Indiana records and carried the species on his hypothetical list. Raymond Grow reported an immature in LaPorte County on September 6, 1957, and Virginia Reuterskiold saw what was probably the same bird there on October 15, 1957. There are now about twenty additional sightings for the state and Peter B. Grube obtained a fine photograph of an adult on July 15, 1978. Others have been photographed since then. It appears that the laughing gull is a rare to a very rare visitor to Indiana in the vicinity of Lake Michigan; elsewhere in the state, it is a casual visitor. Birds were seen from May 8 to October 15; six of the sightings were in June. Except for two seen on June 2, 1979, all records are of single birds.

The Lake Michigan shore, especially at Michigan City, is evidently a favored habitat. Laughing gulls have also been found at Lake Monroe, Lake Waveland, Falls of the Ohio, and in Dearborn County.

FRANKLIN'S GULL

Larus pipixcan

Franklin's gull, a bird of the interior of North America, performs a fall migration that takes it as far as the Argentine pampas. Because it nests on the prairies of the United States and Canada, it is sometimes called the "prairie dove." It is not a familiar bird to many Indiana birders, although there is a high probability that many Franklin's gulls pass through the state on migration during certain years. Anyone fortunate enough to see adult birds in spring plumage, with the delicate, rosy "blush" of color on their breasts, will understand why a former name for this beautiful bird was Franklin's rosy gull.

In 1898, Butler was able to cite only two rather vague records for this gull in Indiana and listed it as an occasional migrant. A specimen was collected at Liverpool (Lake County) on May 3, 1898. Another was collected in Putnam County on June 16, 1958. This gull now appears to be a casual spring and rare fall migrant throughout the state. In some years, a large number has been reported in the fall. For example, Val Nolan Jr. found 600 Franklin's gulls at Geist Reservoir, near Indianapolis, and wrote:

November 6, 1948, was a rainy and very windy day following a week of fine autumn weather. At 7:30 a.m. I stood on the dam . . . and strained to see a large number of birds resting on the water nearly beyond my range of vision to the northward. Suddenly the birds began to rise in flight, lifting from the surface, and soaring lightly about over the water until some six hundred or so were in the air. Forming a great cloud, this flock began circling slowly about in a vast funnel-shaped formation that towered from the water to a height of over one hundred feet. Very gradually this funnel began moving in my direction and individual birds within the mass could be discerned. For perhaps ten minutes the formation continued toward me, surprisingly well-disciplined in its continuously circling movements. Occasionally some ten to fifty birds would break from the flock and fly in a long tenuous straight or V-shaped line off on a tangent of its own, but always such stragglers would merge again with the parent mass, the breadth of which was about 1/4 mile across.

A number of Franklin's gulls have been seen over the lake and on the beach or breakwaters along Lake Michigan. Others were found at reservoirs, lakes, and sewage lagoons. They have been recorded along the Wabash River and a small group was found at a small overflow pond in a cultivated field along a creek.

There are sightings of this gull in Indiana for every month of the year except January. Most spring migrants evidently appear from late April to June. There are several summer and early fall records, but migrants are usually most numerous during fall migration in late October and early November. A few linger into late December along the Ohio River. The largest number reported in spring was a flock of twenty, on April 21, 1957, in Tippecanoe County.

The Franklin's gull is usually found in the company of other gulls, but at times small groups composed only of Franklin's are reported. Although on its breeding grounds it is known as an avid insect eater, most of the birds observed in Indiana were scavenging along beaches or over the water.

LITTLE GULL

Larus minutus

This tiny, graceful gull, a comparative newcomer to Indiana, has most often been seen along Lake Michigan at Michigan City. It is frequently in the company of Bonaparte's gulls, so when large flocks of Bonaparte's arrive along the lake, birdwatchers come out to search for the little gull. It has been a member of the North American bird fauna for a relatively short period of years, but now breeds on this continent, which it invaded from Europe.

The first sighting for Indiana was by Amy G. Baldwin at Michigan City in the fall of 1950 (exact date unavailable) Robert D. Nuner and others saw this bird on November 5, 1950. A specimen was collected there on December 22, 1955 (Mumford, 1956). The species was seen nearly every winter from 1951 to 1960, but only once from 1961 to 1975. The number of sightings increased during the late 1970s. This gull is probably now a very rare fall migrant and winter resident along Lake Michigan. It is casual there in spring, but there are observations for every month of the year except April and June. There is a single sighting (Dearborn County) elsewhere in the state. Most records are of single birds, but two were seen on several occasions. Based on plumage differences, as many as three birds may have been present in the fall of 1978.

Virtually all of the many observations were made at the Michigan City harbor. It is possible that some food attracts the birds to this location. We do know that during the mid-1950s huge schools of minnows could be seen just below the surface in the harbor area at Michigan City. These schools measured eight to ten feet in diameter or more. The single sighting away from Lake Michigan is for an oxbow area at the mouth of the Miami River, in southeastern Indiana.

Late October and November is the time most fall migrants appear. They frequently remain throughout the winter. The relatively few spring records do not indicate any pattern of migration and since wandering is so common among gulls of various species it is difficult to set limits for spring migrants.

The little gull evidently obtains much of its food from the water surface or slightly below it. Some birds were observed swimming about and picking food from the surface. Other birds were diving and probably catching small fish. Laurence C. Binford described the behavior of two adults found together in late December:

The birds flew together always and once both birds landed side by side several inches apart, raised their rear ends slightly and stretched their necks, heads and bills at a 45 degree angle; both were facing the same direction. . . . When fishing, when one bird would dive, the second would hover above until the diving bird caught its fish, and then both would fly off together.

The one seen on December 22, 1955, was diving for small

fish among the large chunks of floating ice in the entrance to the yacht basin. The gullet of this bird contained three small minnows, two of which were identified as emerald shiners.

[COMMON BLACK-HEADED GULL]
Larus ridibundus

This is another Old World gull that used to breed as far westward as Iceland. It began to appear along the northeastern coast of the United States and in other areas in North America around 1957. More recently it has been found nesting in Newfoundland and appears to be increasing in numbers along the St. Lawrence Seaway and the Great Lakes. It should be identified with extreme caution, for it closely resembles the Bonaparte's gull.

There are three sightings for Indiana, all from Michigan City. On August 20, 1977, an adult in winter plumage was seen by Kenneth J. Brock, Edward M. Hopkins, Peter B. Grube, and Kristin Grube (Brock et al., 1978). Other observers reported two black-headed gulls there later in the day. A subadult bird was observed on July 18, 1979, by Alan W. Bruner, Charles E. Keller, and Timothy C. Keller. On August 16, 1980, a first-year bird was found by Bruner, Timothy C. Keller, and Mark C. Rhodes. It would be desirable to obtain a photograph or specimen of this gull from Indiana.

BONAPARTE'S GULL
Larus philadelphia

Small flocks of diminutive gulls with black heads and characteristic white-streaked primaries are often seen on our larger rivers and lakes during the spring. At a distance sometimes confused with terns because of their buoyant flight, Bonaparte's gulls are active feeders, diving down to the water and picking food from its surface. Occasionally one will alight on a floating piece of wood or other debris. At times these gulls rest on the water, sometimes in flocks of considerable size.

It was considered a common migrant and a rare winter visitor by Butler. The Bonaparte's gull is now an uncommon migrant in Indiana except in the vicinity of Lake Michigan where it is common (and sometimes, especially in earlier years, abundant). It is very rare during the winter, although it used to be common at Michigan City at that season. There were an estimated 2,000 along Lake Michigan from late December 1954 until January 22, 1955, when they all left because of severe weather. Between 1949 and 1956, more than 600 per count were recorded on four Christmas bird counts in Lake and LaPorte Counties. Since 1957 the maximum number found on any Christmas bird count in those counties was seventeen. This dramatic decrease may be due to the disappearance of some food source.

In addition to being attracted to the shoreline of Lake Michigan, this gull may be seen near other bodies of water and in both flooded and (occasionally) dry fields.

Although some birds may be present throughout the winter, spring migration usually begins in southern Indiana the latter half of March. John M. Louis observed 8,000 at Gary Harbor on April 26, 1955. Non-breeding birds may linger in northern Indiana throughout the summer. Fall migrants begin moving into northwestern Indiana during August, but most are present during October. There were between 3,000 and 4,000 at Lake Michigan on October 30, 1953, according to Raymond Grow. Herbert L. Stoddard walked from Millers to the Indiana Dunes State Park on November 2, 1919 and found Bonaparte's gulls "more numerous than I ever saw them before." He wrote, "They sat on the lake in white windrows, hundreds to a row. Other hundreds fluttering over the water and still others circling high in the air like hawks."

Bonaparte's gull spends much time on the wing while feeding and has been observed harassing shorebirds, apparently in an attempt to force them to relinquish food (a behavior pattern termed kleptoparasitism), as described by Grow (1978). On April 27, 1957, when a magnificent frigatebird was at Michigan City, observers remarked that 800 to 900 Bonaparte's gulls were swarming around it. One flock of Bonaparte's was seen flying about over a field catching flying insects.

RING-BILLED GULL
Larus delawarensis

Sea Gull

The ring-billed gull is the familiar "seagull" that is found around the larger lakes and reservoirs and along major rivers, especially during migration. It used to be considered less abundant than the larger herring gull, and in some parts of the state people automatically misidentify any large gull as a herring gull.

Butler reported this gull as a regular migrant and local winter resident, especially along Lake Michigan and the Ohio River. Today it is a permanent resident at Lake Michigan, where it is common to abundant except in summer, when it is generally fairly common. Elsewhere in the state, it is a common migrant and winter resident, but casual in summer. On the 1960 Christmas count in northern Lake County 2,234 were seen. Flocks of about 200 birds were found at Michigan City on June 20, 1978, and July 31, 1980.

Nearly any large body of water (lake, reservoir, river), will attract this gull, and it has also been seen feeding at fish hatchery ponds, in dry as well as flooded fields, and at garbage dumps.

Most spring migrants are apparently present from mid-March to late May. Raymond Grow found about 1,000 at Gary on May 15, 1978, but only two were there four days later, which indicates a fairly quick passage through the state. Although we know of no nesting records for Indiana, a breeding colony of about 800 adults was found just west of the Indiana state line, at Lake Calumet, Illinois, in 1975. Fall migration is most easily noted away from Lake Michigan. Some ring-billed gulls appear in southern Indiana in early August. A maximum for Geist Reservoir is 200 on November 23, 1962, by Keller. There was a maximum of 400 in Gibson County on December 3, 1978, according to C. Leroy Harrison and Dennis W. Jones. The maximum number recorded on any Christmas bird count away from Lake Michigan is about 200.

Ring-billed gulls obtain much of their food by scavenging. They feed in spring on dead fishes that collect along the shoreline after a winter kill beneath the ice. One bird flying three feet above the surface of a fish hatchery pond suddenly dove into the water and captured a sunfish about four inches long. In fields, the ring-billed gull evidently feeds on insects and other invertebrates.

CALIFORNIA GULL

Larus californicus

This gull has been reported only twice from Indiana. Timothy C. Keller (1983) discovered and photographed one at Eagle Creek Reservoir (Marion County) on July 19, 1980. An adult California gull, first seen by James A. Haw on November 10, 1983, was seen by several other observers that day and the following day at Michigan City. In Salt Lake City there is a statue erected to this gull by the Mormons. California gulls were given credit for destroying insect pests and thus saving the crops of early settler Brigham Young and his followers, and the statue commemorates their appreciation. This species is becoming more frequent in the eastern United States, with sightings from the adjacent states of Illinois and Ohio, a breeding record for Ontario, and other observations from the East Coast.

HERRING GULL

Larus argentatus

Sea Gull, American Herring Gull, Silvery Gull, European Herring Gull

Widely distributed and common over most of its range, the herring gull, like some other gulls, has benefited from the activities of man. This ability to adapt to changing circumstances has allowed it to inhabit new areas and to increase its numbers. It is an aggressive bird, consumes a wide variety of foods, and competes well with other species that have much the same ecological requirements.

About 1900, the herring gull was a common migrant throughout the state and locally a winter visitor or winter resident. Butler noted that it occasionally remained "in great numbers" at Lake Michigan in winter. He added, "This is the most common gull found in the State, and is known popularly as 'Sea Gull.'" Like the ring-billed gull, the herring gull today is a permanent resident along Lake Michigan. Elsewhere in the state, it is a generally uncommon migrant and winter resident, sometimes locally common in winter, at which season it outnumbers the ring-billed gull. Non-breeding birds have been reported from various parts of Indiana in summer, but are by far most abundant near Lake Michigan. On December 23, 1956, 3,400 herring gulls were tallied on the Michigan City Christmas bird count, and more than 1,000 per count have been found at the Indiana Dunes and northern Lake County. The maximum number observed elsewhere in the state on the counts was 306, at New Albany, on December 24, 1952. There were 91 in Gibson County on December 31, 1978. The habitat of the herring gull is almost identical to that of the ring-billed gull, and the two species are quite often found together.

Spring migrants appear from late February to roughly mid-May (some birds remain all summer). On May 12, 1979, 531 were seen in LaPorte County. It appears that some fall migrants reach Indiana during July, and 300 were in LaPorte County on August 30, 1950. In general, there is a gradual buildup of numbers from fall until midwinter on the major wintering grounds. During this season, large numbers can sometimes be found at favorite feeding sites, such as the Burr Street garbage dump in Gary.

Like other gulls, herring gulls feed in shopping mall parking lots, at drive-in movie theaters, along beaches, and in other locations where humans discard garbage, as well as in freshly plowed fields, at sewage outlets, and around locks and dams along rivers. They may travel considerable distances each day between feeding and loafing areas, which are often on sandbars, beaches, and breakwaters. Along Lake Michigan, herring gulls have been found—some dead, others still alive—with their heads or beaks entangled in the plastic rings used to hold a six-pack of beer or soft-drink cans together. Some mortality also results when the gulls become entangled in fishing lines or when they swallow fish hooks attached to lines. Hundreds of gulls of several species were found dead along Lake Michigan beaches in the late fall of 1963; type E botulism was the suspected killer.

On April 7, 1956, Mumford and Paul Slud watched a flock of twenty-five immature herring gulls on the beach at the water's edge that were engaged in a kind of game, repeatedly picking up in their beaks bits of driftwood four to ten inches long, flying up two to ten feet, and dropping the sticks. Occasionally one bird chased another briefly as it flew.

THAYER'S GULL

Larus thayeri

Thayer's gull was long considered to be a subspecies of the herring gull, but is now considered a separate species. There seems little doubt that it has been in Indiana for a long time, for a specimen was collected at Chicago in 1876, and birders have reported others in the general area since at least 1939 (Ford, 1956). Until it was elevated to full species rank, relatively few birders paid much attention to it, especially in Indiana. A first-year bird seen at the Falls of the Ohio River on February 26, 1978, may have been a Thayer's gull; if so, that was the first sighting for the state. Alan W. Bruner, Timothy C. Keller, Burt L. Monroe, Jr., and Brainard Palmer-Ball, Jr. (and possibly others), saw this bird. Ted T. Cable observed a Thayer's gull at the Burr Street garbage dump (Gary) March 14, 1978, and on January 29, 1980, Kenneth C. Brock photographed an adult there.

There are now about twenty sightings of this gull from Indiana. Most of the birds were found either at the Burr Street dump or at Michigan City. There is also a single record for Allen County. All observations were made during the period September 28 to June 20, but most birds were seen between October 14 and March 21. It appears that this gull is a casual migrant and winter resident about Lake Michigan. Elsewhere in the state it is apparently accidental. At least three are believed to have spent the winter of 1979–80 in Lake County.

ICELAND GULL

Larus glaucoides

White-winged Gull

The Iceland gull resembles a small glaucous gull, and there has been a great deal of confusion regarding the taxonomy and field identification of these two and other species of gulls. Therefore, it is difficult to determine which Indiana sightings of the Iceland gull represent correctly identified birds. Butler thought that it was an occasional winter visitor to the northern part of the state, but had no physical evidence of its occurrence in Indiana. Timothy C. Keller photographed one on March 1, 1980, in Lake County (cover, *Indiana Audubon Quarterly*, 58, No. 4).

It has now been reported some fifteen times from the state, mostly in the vicinity of Lake Michigan, where it appears to be a casual migrant and winter visitor. It is accidental in other parts of Indiana. The sightings to date range from October 12 to May 10 and most were made at Michigan City or in Gary at the Burr Street garbage dump. One was seen in Dearborn County from March 26 to 30, 1978.

LESSER BLACK-BACKED GULL

Larus fuscus

This gull is considered to be an accidental visitor to Indiana on the basis of the following records. Mr. and Mrs. Albert Campbell and others observed one at Michigan City on October 2, 1948 (Brock, 1979a). On April 7, 1962, Kenneth P. Able, Theodore A. Chandik, Richard Rosche, and Scott Rea found another at the Willow Slough Fish and Wildlife Area. The bird was collected on April 9 and ultimately determined to be the subspecies *graellsii* (Mumford and Rowe, 1963). Edward M. Hopkins and Scott F. Jackson saw one at Michigan City on December 28, 1979, and what was probably the same bird was seen there January 6, 1980, by Kenneth J. Brock and Brendan, Kristin, and Peter B. Grube. Timothy C. Keller and many other observers studied one at Raccoon Lake State Park (Parke County) between December 20 and 27, 1980.

GLAUCOUS GULL

Larus hyperboreus

Burgomaster

This is a large, powerful gull that often exhibits its dominance over smaller gulls, hence the name "burgomaster." It is a showy species, most apt to be seen in winter along Lake Michigan and at nearby garbage dumps, where birders scan the masses of birds milling about in hopes of picking out a "white-winger"—a glaucous or an Iceland gull. The two species can be quite difficult to separate in the field and identifications must be made with extreme caution.

Butler knew of two records for this gull in Indiana, on the basis of which he listed it as an occasional visitor along Lake Michigan. One was collected at Millers (Lake County) on August 8, 1897, by Frank M. Woodruff. The second was reported by J. W. Byrkit (without details) near Michigan City. The glaucous gull today appears to be a rare to uncommon winter visitor along Lake Michigan, casual elsewhere in the state. It has been reported each year since 1977. Kenneth J. Brock observed five in Gary at the Burr Street dump on March 1, 1980. Two were in first-year plumage, one in second-year, one in third-year, and the other was an adult.

The habitat of this gull is like that of most wintering gulls in the state. The birds spend considerable time loafing on breakwaters, beaches, or other open areas when not foraging for food.

Except for the bird collected by Woodruff in August, all sightings are within the period of November 9 to May 10.

GREAT BLACK-BACKED GULL

Larus marinus

As the amount of food waste discarded by man increases, certain gull populations seem to be growing larger. The many species of gulls that depend to a great extent on garbage dumps for food at certain times of the year have greatly increased in numbers and spread into new areas. One of these is the once-rare great black-backed gull, which invaded the Great Lakes via the St. Lawrence Seaway and has been seen in Indiana almost every year since 1974.

It was of hypothetical occurrence in the state at the turn of the century; the first report from Indiana was by C. W. G. Eifrig (1927), who saw three on a Lake Michigan beach (Porter County) on September 26, 1925. Timothy C. Keller obtained a photograph of an adult on October 26, 1980, in Lake County. It has now reached the status of a casual to very rare migrant and winter resident near Lake Michigan. Throughout the rest of the state, it is accidental. Individuals are usually seen, but two were seen in Dearborn County on February 27, 1982.

Its habitat is the same as that of many other gulls. It is aggressive toward smaller gulls and other birds with which it associates on its wintering and nesting grounds. Kenneth J. Brock saw a great black-backed gull stealing food from herring gulls at a dump.

Indiana sightings range from August 21 to April 29. The maximum number of observations per month was three, for November, December, March, and April. We expect the number of sightings to increase in the coming years, if this gull continues its westward invasion of the Midwest.

BLACK-LEGGED KITTIWAKE

Rissa tridactyla

Kittiwake Gull

This gull is typically a bird of the North Atlantic Ocean and seldom appears inland. It was, therefore, with considerable surprise that Mumford and a group of birders from South Bend observed one at Michigan City on March 11, 1950 (Nuner, 1950). This was yet another example of an "out-of-place" waterbird visiting the southern end of Lake Michigan.

Butler included the kittiwake on his hypothetical list of birds of the state. A specimen was collected on January 27, 1955, at Michigan City, and another, found dead along the lake by Raymond Grow on January 11, 1956, was also preserved. There have now been about thirty sightings of this gull in Indiana, mostly along Lake Michigan, where it is a very rare migrant and winter resident. It is casual to accidental elsewhere in the state, having been found at the Falls of the Ohio, in Clark County, and near Indianapolis.

In Indiana, this gull's habitat is much the same as other wintering gulls. Kittiwakes observed at Michigan City harbor were sometimes feeding at the mouth of Trail Creek, where huge schools of minnows used to be present during the winter. The gullet of the specimen collected at Michigan City contained an emerald shiner about three inches long. One gull was seen inland from Lake Michigan, flying over cornfields.

Dates of observations range from August 17 to May 7, but more have been seen in November than in any other month.

[ROSS' GULL]

Rhodostethia rosea

On April 6, 1982, Nancy J. Gruse observed a pigeon-sized, pinkish gull at Michigan City. She described its wedged tail, black necklace, and gray underwings. It was flying about near domestic pigeons so that size comparisons could be made. Four days later, what was evidently the same bird was again seen flying with Bonaparte's gulls. Gruse was alone the first time she saw the bird, but the second observation was made after a friend she was with commented on "a pink bird" flying overhead.

SABINE'S GULL

Xema sabini

Fork-tailed Gull

The handsome and graceful Sabine's gull is comparatively little known. Its behavior is ternlike and includes hovering and descending to the surface of the water to feed. When foraging on shore, it runs and abruptly stops, in the manner of a plover. The first Indiana record was obtained by Raymond Grow, who saw one in Lake County on December 5, 1954. Other sightings have subsequently been made, and on October 14, 1979, Kenneth J. Brock obtained a fine photograph of a bird in near-adult plumage standing on the beach at Beverly Shores (Porter County).

This interesting gull was long considered hypothetical in Indiana, and birders were delighted when it was found here in actuality. It appears to be a casual fall migrant and to date has only been recorded in the three counties along Lake Michigan. The sightings have been of birds in flight, except for the bird Brock photographed.

There are about a dozen records of the Sabine's gull for the state. Dates of observations range from September 26 to December 12. Nine of them were made in October. Three birds were seen along the lake on September 26, 1958, October 25, 1959, and again on October 26, 1980. At least seven of the birds recorded were in immature plumage and two were in adult or near-adult plumage.

CASPIAN TERN

Sterna caspia

This, the largest of the terns that occur in Indiana, is a striking bird, especially in breeding plumage. Feeding birds hover above the water and often dive into it from some height, striking the surface with considerable force. In spring and fall, numbers of the great birds can be seen feeding offshore in Lake Michigan.

It seems curious, considering the numbers of present-day records, that this tern was on the hypothetical list for the state in 1898. A specimen taken at Calumet Heights on September 27, 1895, may have been collected in either Illinois or Indiana. However, another was secured at Millers (Lake County) on September 27, 1898, by Frank M. Woodruff. J. Grafton Parker, Jr., observed five Caspian terns along Lake Michigan in August 1898. Woodruff (1907) wrote, "A few are seen and captured each fall at Millers, Indiana," and Eifrig (1919) mentioned

"large numbers" at Millers and "the south end of Lake Michigan." From August 4 to September 13, 1980, Raymond Grow observed seventy-five on the beaches at Gary.

Terns inhabit much the same water areas as gulls, and Caspian terns have been found at lakes, ponds, reservoirs, sewage lagoons, and the larger rivers. Migrating birds are sometimes attracted to relatively small water areas, such as abandoned, water-filled pits left after stripmining of coal.

It is a regular and sometimes fairly common spring and fall migrant about Lake Michigan. Throughout the remainder of the state it is generally rare to casual and of irregular occurrence during spring and fall migrations. More Caspian terns are recorded in the fall than in the spring. Small numbers of non-breeding birds may remain throughout the summer. Spring migration occurs from April 1 to about June 15. A report of nine on March 19, 1970, is quite early, if the birds were correctly identified. About equal numbers of birds are seen in April and May, the period of greatest abundance in spring. The maximum number recorded at that season is eight, on May 1, 1949, in Marion County. Fall migrants appear from July 4 to October 22. More are seen in September than in any other month, but nearly as many are observed in August. Most have departed by the end of the first week of October. A crippled specimen was found at New Harmony (Posey County) on December 11, 1926. The maximum number noted in the fall was sixty-two at Michigan City, on August 7, 1982, and more than twenty per day have been reported several times from Lake County.

Once or twice immature Caspian terns have been mistaken for royal terns, for during the fall young and adult Caspian terns exhibit different plumages and give different calls.

[ROYAL TERN]

Sterna maxima

This large tern has a more southerly distribution than the Caspian tern and its occurrence in Indiana would be strictly accidental. Butler considered its presence in the state as hypothetical. What may have been a royal tern was observed in Jefferson County on April 15, 1960, by J. Dan Webster (1980), who is familiar with both Caspian terns and royal terns outside Indiana. He wrote, "I noted five differentiating field marks (small size, slender shape, ragged crest, orange bill, deeply-forked tail)."

ROSEATE TERN

Sterna dougallii

This is another species that is an accidental visitor to Indiana. Butler included the roseate tern on his list of Indiana birds only on the authority of Rufus Haymond (1870). However, Haymond, in writing about the birds of Franklin County, undoubtedly misidentified this species, since the rare roseate was the only species of tern on his list, and he wrote, "I have frequently seen this tern along the river and canal." The first trustworthy record is probably that of Herbert L. Stoddard, who collected a roseate tern along Lake Michigan between Millers and Indiana Dunes State Park on August 14, 1916. Butler (1917), who published a note about this specimen, quoted Stoddard as follows: "The bird was alone on the beach (Lake Michigan) and attracted my attention from this action as I never remember having seen either of our species of white terns on the sand. They almost invariably use the fishermen's net stakes out in the lake. On studying the bird through binoculars I thought I noticed a difference so the specimen was collected. No other was seen, though Forster's and Common Terns as well as the Black Terns were there by the hundred. The specimen is in perfect breeding plumage, the breast being quite rosy in color."

COMMON TERN

Sterna hirundo

Sea Swallow, Wilson's Tern

Two species of terns, the common tern and the Forster's tern, are similar in size and general appearance, and have long given Hoosier birdwatchers problems with field identifications. They are probably still misidentified on numerous occasions. The possibility of erroneous reports in the past therefore makes it difficult to evaluate the relative abundance of both species throughout the years. Both occur along Lake Michigan in large numbers, as they evidently did one hundred years ago, and much of our recent data was obtained in that region.

Butler considered the common tern a migrant that was abundant in some localities. He noted that some remained throughout the summer in northern Indiana and suggested that it might nest there. This assumption was later borne out when nests were found in Lake County in the 1930s. There are no nesting records since 1936. Today, this tern is a common to abundant migrant in the vicinity of Lake Michigan; elsewhere in the state it is uncommon to fairly common locally.

Common terns frequent a variety of water areas, from small ponds to the larger lakes and reservoirs, and they also move along the larger rivers such as the Ohio and Wabash. The major focal point for migrants, however, is along the shore of Lake Michigan.

The earliest spring arrivals are usually seen during the first week of April but one was reported at Geist Reservoir on March 5, 1944, by Scott Calvert and others. Most migrants have departed by the first week of June, but there are several exceptions and individuals or small groups may be present throughout June and July. Fall migration is underway in July and birds have reached Sullivan County by July 15. Few remain into November and there is a very late record for December 5, 1943, at Geist Reservoir. John M. Louis reported 10,000 in Lake County on May 20, 1957. About 2,000 terns, mostly common terns, were at Michigan City September 5, 1980.

Archie F. Wilson located the first Indiana nest of a common tern at the Edison Generating Plant in Lake County on June 13, 1934. Five eggs found in a nest there on June 23, 1935, were collected; the pair of terns apparently renested, for two eggs were found in another nest on July 2. Wilson found a nest at the same site on June 2, 1936; it contained two eggs. Amos W. Butler, Samuel E. Perkins, III, Harry M. Smith, and Wilson visited this nest on June 13 and collected the adult female and, subsequently, the eggs (Butler, 1937; Smith, 1950). Butler noted that the 1936 nest was "on a gravelly fill at the end of a railroad spur."

Much of the food of the common tern consists of small fishes. Kenneth J. Brock et al. watched an adult tern feeding an immature a small fish on October 16, 1981.

[ARCTIC TERN]

Sterna paradisaea

The Arctic Tern is the champion of long-distance migration, spending its summer near the Arctic and its winter in Antarctica. Butler listed it as hypothetical for Indiana, and Keller et al. (1979) considered it accidental on the basis of a sight record on April 30, 1978, at Michigan City, by Michael R. Brown, Alan W. Bruner, and Timothy C. Keller.

FORSTER'S TERN

Sterna forsteri

Sea Swallow

Not far from the old Riverside Park area in Indianapolis, along a four-mile stretch of the White River between Emmericksville Dam and 38th Street, small groups of terns can be seen in late April and early May. Although there is an occasional common tern, most of the birds are Forster's; with their long pointed wings and deeply forked tails, they are graceful creatures that certainly deserve the name sea swallow. Before resuming their northward journey, they spend from one to three days resting and foraging along the river. As they fly over the shallows, they will suddenly compress their wings against their sides and dive from a moderate height into the water with a resounding "smack," as often as not emerging with a small fish.

Butler regarded the Forster's tern as a rare migrant throughout most of Indiana, but remarked that during the fall it was exceedingly abundant on Lake Michigan. Today, this tern appears to be an uncommon migrant except in the vicinity of Lake Michigan, where it is often abundant. In general, it seems to be less common than the common tern. It formerly nested in Lake County, at Gary, in 1957, 1958, and 1962.

The habitat of the Forster's tern is nearly the same as that of the common tern, except that the Forster's nests in marshes rather than on cinder or gravel flats. The species are often observed together during migration.

The earliest date of spring arrival is March 27. Several birds have been reported during June and July, when fall migrants become more numerous. The latest fall date is November 21. There were 120 Forster's terns in LaPorte County on April 29, 1978. About 200 were reported in Lake County on August 30, 1916. During fall migration, the Forster's tern often outnumbers the common tern along the southern tip of Lake Michigan.

Raymond Grow reported the first nesting of the Forster's tern in the state when he found two pairs nesting at a small marsh at Gary (Lake County) in the summer of 1957. The birds nested on muskrat houses; Grow saw one brood of three and another of two young. One pair nested there in 1958. This marsh was partially filled in before 1961, but two pairs again nested in 1962 and produced five young. Human disturbance finally caused the birds to desert the area and we know of no nesting records since that time.

Flocks composed of from sixty to a hundred Forster's terns can sometimes be found resting on the outer breakwater at Michigan City when the lake is calm. The birds travel in small groups to feeding areas well out from shore. When the water is rough at the breakwater and the wind is blowing in off the lake, they may congregate in protected places about the harbor, where they rest on the beach facing the wind.

LEAST TERN

Sterna antillarum

Little Tern

There are many Indiana birdwatchers who have never seen a least tern in the state, where it has never been common. Before the enactment of the Migratory Bird Treaty, the numbers of terns in general, and the least tern in particular, were drastically depleted in North America. Milliners sought the feathers of these birds for adorning women's hats, and this little tern was nearly exterminated by hunting before it received protection. The National Audubon Society and other conservation agencies are to be commended for their efforts to aid in preventing the destruction of migratory birds.

Butler knew it as a rare migrant throughout most of the state. A few were said to be summer residents in the northern part. A nest with eggs, reportedly found at Wolf Lake (Lake County) on June 5, 1882, by J. L. Hancock, was probably not of this species (see below). It is currently a casual migrant.

The least tern is primarily a beach bird, preferring sandy or gravelly beaches and shoreline areas. It has been found in Indiana along Lake Michigan, about marshes, ponds, reservoirs, and lakes, and along the Ohio and Wabash Rivers. One was seen over a small pond, another in flooded fields beside a river.

The earliest spring migration date is June 3 and the latest observation made in the fall was on September 13. Slightly more birds were reported in August than in any other month. The largest number was seventeen, at Hovey Lake (Posey County) on June 3, 1950. On that date, Charles F. Marks, Russell and Vivian Mumford, and Val Nolan Jr. observed this group actively fishing in this cypress-bordered oxbow lake, not far from the junction of the Wabash and Ohio Rivers. There is an unverified report of a "large flock" seen at Waverly Beach (Porter County) in late August 1933.

The least tern nested at the Falls of the Ohio in 1967. Although this is generally considered a Kentucky nesting record (since until recently the Indiana state line had been fixed at the low water level on the north shore of the river), we include it here. It is possible that other least terns have nested on the sandbars or gravel bars along the Ohio and Wabash Rivers. The relatively large number at Hovey Lake on June 3, 1950, indicates the possible presence of a nearby breeding colony. The description of the nest found at Wolf Lake in 1882 does not fit that of the least tern, reminding one instead of a black tern's nest. Butler wrote, "The nest was simply a depression on a pile of reeds in an almost inaccessible portion of a small inlet of water." Hancock reported seeing four least terns the day he found this nest. Woodruff (1907) did not mention this "nesting" record.

[WHITE-WINGED TERN]

Chlidonias leucopterus

A bird believed to be this species was seen July 17, 1979, at Hammond (Lake County), by Kenneth J. Brock. It was first observed flying with a loose flock of eight black terns. Several other observers who saw it clearly concurred on the identification (Brock, 1982a,1983).

BLACK TERN

Chlidonias niger

Short-tailed Tern

Occasionally, at the height of the swallow migration in late April or early May, these large blackish terns with long, pointed wings are found hawking insects over small ponds and marshes with swallows. As the terns weave about, one or two will dip down to the water and skim the surface for a distance of ten feet or so, either for a drink or perhaps to snatch up some aquatic animal for food. During migration, the birds may appear one day and be gone the next, to the consternation of birders who enjoy watching this unique tern in action.

About 1900 the black tern was a regular migrant in southern Indiana, a summer resident at least from the Kankakee River northward, and a common nesting bird at some locations. It is currently an uncommon migrant throughout most of Indiana, but at times is quite common about Lake Michigan. Many of the sites where it nested thirty years ago no longer support breeding colonies and if the trend continues, the species may soon occupy few nesting areas in the state.

The black tern may be found on all types of water areas, wherever there are small fish or other aquatic animals upon which it feeds. Some migration is noted along rivers. It nests in marshes or the borders of ponds and lakes in emergent vegetation.

Spring migrants generally appear in late April, but there is an early record for April 10. Birds remain throughout the summer and probably a few still nest annually. Flocking is evident in late August along Lake Michigan and the latest date for a straggler in the fall is October 18. A hundred black terns were found in Lake County on May 20, 1943. On August 27, 1980, there were 600 in LaPorte County.

Most nesting records are for the two northernmost tiers of counties across the state. Butler mentioned that "two young" were collected in White County on May 17, 1886. These specimens were no doubt immature-plumaged migrants, for this is too early for young of the year to be found. John J. Audubon observed nests with eggs of the black tern in a pond near Vincennes (Knox County), possibly at the site where he found the American avocet nesting in June 1814.

Donald H. Boyd visited black tern nesting grounds at Wolf Lake (Lake County) several times and noted: "They have been increasing each year since 1911. In July of that year two pairs were found on the east shore of the lake. In 1924 ten nests were found, while this year [1926] forty nests were located. . . ." Of his 1924 visit to Wolf Lake, Boyd wrote:

Black Terns were very abundant. Many birds were seen bathing in the shallow water. Some of these were quite gray looking possibly moulting or young birds. Nests were quite abundant. For the most part they were found in the top of a mass of floating or permanent dead rush stems in the shallow (6″ to 12″) water among the growing rushes. Two nests with three dark eggs each were of this nature. It was difficult to tell whether the nest had been made by arranging the material at hand or whether the bird had simply rounded and hollowed a place in the mass of dead rushes. The diameter (about 3″) and depth (about 1¼″) was just enough to contain the eggs. The birds hovered about screaming constantly, at times they would swoop at us coming quite close. Two other nests containing 3 eggs each were placed on floating . . . planks. . . . [On one] the nest was fairly well made of dried rushes built up in a slight cone. The board was held in place by the growing rushes. . . . [On the other,] the eggs were laid on the bare surface of the board with a few loose pieces of dried rushes around them but none underneath.

The eggs of the black tern are quite dark in color and often match perfectly the color of the sodden, decaying nesting material. In thirty-nine nests, there were eleven clutches of two, twenty-six of three, and two of four eggs. Eggs were found in nests from May 31 to July 27. Mumford examined a nesting colony of forty-five adults at Dewart Lake (Kosciusko County) on May 18, 1949. Homer F. Price found about twenty nesting pairs at Jimerson Lake (Steuben County) on July 7, 1940. It is interesting that the most recent nests of this tern (three) were also found at Jimerson Lake, in the spring of 1983.

Depicted plant: Fragrant water-lily (*Nymphaea odorata*)

BLACK TERN

[BLACK SKIMMER]

Rynchops niger

Esther A. Craigmile and Mrs. Charles Raymond reported the only sighting of this accidental species for Indiana. Craigmile (1935) described the event.

August 23, 1913, Mrs. Raymond and I were on the beach near Miller, Indiana. Being quite familiar with the shore birds, we were greatly astonished to see a large black bird rapidly skimming just above the surface of the water, flying eastward. From pictures we had with us we identified it immediately as a Black Skimmer. Mrs. Raymond later verified our record as she studied Skimmers by the acre in Florida. December 29, 1931, it was my pleasure to see large flocks of Black Skimmers on the Gulf off the coast of Biloxi, Mississippi.

THICK-BILLED MURRE

Uria lomvia

Brünnich's Murre

Between December 10 and 31, 1896, a number of thick-billed murres unexpectedly appeared in Indiana and other places in the Midwest. The earliest record appears to be one collected near Pickard on December 10. That specimen was mounted and for some time was in the State Geologist's office at the Indiana Capitol building. Five other birds were obtained, mostly by taxidermists, from Benton, Boone, Marion, Newton, and Wells Counties. One of these, taken in Newton County, was in the collection of Frank M. Woodruff. A specimen taken near Zanesville (Wells County) was reputedly in the collection of Amos W. Butler (1898a), but the specimen was not in that collection when examined by Mumford in 1948. Butler made mention of a report of a bird thought to have been this species found near Reynolds (White County) in March 1869. This murre is strictly an accidental visitor to Indiana.

MARBLED MURRELET

Brachyramphus marmoratus

There is a single record of this accidental visitor (Mumford, 1982). Paul L. Jamison and Michael Jamison obtained a crippled bird while duck hunting on Lake Lemon (Monroe County) on November 29, 1981. Through the efforts of William R. Adams and Donald Whitehead, the specimen was obtained, preserved, and identified by Spencer G. Sealy as the Asiatic race (*B. m. perdix*) of this murrelet. It is in the National Museum of Natural History, Washington, D.C.

The digestive tract of this specimen contained eleven fishes ranging in length from 2.5 to 5 inches. Eight of them were gizzard shads and three were unidentified minnows.

[KITTLITZ'S MURRELET]

Brachyramphus brevirostris

A bird identified as this species was seen at Michigan City on January 16, 1983, by Mr. and Mrs. Robert H. Pease, Jr., and Mr. and Mrs. Owen McCaffrey. It was studied for approximately forty-five minutes and a detailed sketch was made. Available evidence suggests that this accidental visitor was correctly identified by the observers.

ANCIENT MURRELET

Synthliboramphus antiquus

A dead ancient murrelet was found along Lake Michigan at Marquette Park (Lake County) on November 8, 1976, by David Sobal. The specimen is in the Joseph Moore Museum, Earlham College, Richmond, Indiana. The occurrence of this alcid in Indiana is accidental, and Butler carried it on the hypothetical list.

ROCK DOVE

Columba livia

Pigeon

The common "pigeon" is an introduced exotic from the Old World derived from the wild rock dove of Eurasia. Finding structures built by man to its liking, it has become widespread and in many places abundant. Although most people tend to think of the rock dove as a domesticated species, it sometimes nests in rocky cliffs, on bridges, and at stone quarries away from humans. Many city dwellers delight in feeding rock doves in parks and other public places and want them protected. Others consider them a dirty nuisance because of the danger of contracting histoplasmosis or other diseases from the unsightly and abundant droppings.

Butler did not include the rock dove in his *Birds of Indiana*, and it was generally ignored by subsequent authors. Thus we have little information regarding former numbers, distribution, or life history. Today, it is an abun-

ROCK DOVE

dant permanent resident throughout the state. More than 1,000 per count have been recorded on Christmas bird counts at Columbus, Evansville, and South Bend. The largest numbers have consistently been reported from South Bend, where the maximum was 2,024 on December 26, 1982.

The resourceful rock dove coexists very successfully with humans. Among the many manmade structures it uses for nesting, roosting, or resting are inhabited and abandoned buildings, bridges, and underpasses. Some of the bridges spanning the Wabash River at Lafayette sustain a perennial rock dove population, which forages in cultivated fields and at other sites in the vicinity. Irving W. Burr estimated 2,000 using the Brown Street Bridge in Lafayette on September 6, 1964. Public buildings are favorite gathering places for the birds. When feeding or moving to and from feeding grounds, rock doves may be seen nearly anywhere. Grain fields, barnlots, grain elevators, roadsides, city streets, and city parks are all used as feeding sites.

We know nothing about migration or movements of this species in Indiana. No doubt local seasonal movements occur, but the rock dove is generally considered a sedentary, permanent resident where found.

Surprisingly little has been published concerning the nesting of this bird in Indiana. It is highly possible that rock doves nest throughout most of the year. Young were seen in a nest at Lafayette on February 6 and young were in another nest on August 9. The usual clutch size is two. Although most nests have been reported in and about buildings or bridges, we once saw a nest in a large cavity of a partially hollow tree. Alan W. Bruner found rock doves nesting in the rocky ledges along Sugar Creek in Shades State Park in 1979, and we flushed birds from holes in the sandstone cliffs at Portland Arch Nature Preserve (Fountain County) on August 15, 1977. The birds may have been nesting there, but no search was made for nests.

Rock doves frequently fly in compact flocks of several hundred birds. Sometimes one can view such flocks from above, as when the birds are flying about high bridges. There is much variation in coloration of individual rock doves, and as they wheel, soar, and fly, all turning at once, they make an attractive picture. Flight is accomplished by a strong "rowing" motion of the wings and an individual rock dove at a distance has sometimes been mistaken for a peregrine falcon or a jaeger. Concentrations of rock doves have been known to attract peregrine falcons or other hawks that feed on birds, and snowy owls, which sometimes take up a brief winter residence in a city, may feed heavily on rock doves.

BAND-TAILED PIGEON

Columba fasciata

This western North American species occasionally appears far east of its normal range, but has been reported only once in Indiana. John H. Meyer observed one at his feeding station at Beverly Shores (Porter County) on the weekend of January 10, 1981 (Brock and Cable, 1981). It was subsequently seen by scores of birders and photographed before it departed January 31. Meyer noticed that this bird frequently perched in the tall coniferous and deciduous trees in his yard.

RINGED TURTLE-DOVE

Streptopelia risoria

We are a bit hesitant to include this exotic species, but it appears that it is in the process of becoming established. Ringed turtle-doves are kept as cage birds and for avian studies of various kinds at colleges and universities. Escapes are probably not uncommon and the species may be able to maintain itself in a feral state in Indiana, where it has been seen throughout the year.

The ringed turtle-dove was observed at Evansville on April 30, 1971, and was reported there in 1972, 1979, and 1982. One appeared at Munster (Lake County) on November 12, 1974, and a single bird has subsequently been seen there in 1975, 1976, 1977, 1979, and 1981. At South Bend, one was observed April 18, 1976, June 1976, and March 1977. Another was recorded at Berne (Adams County) on January 2 and May 13, 1978. In the summer of 1978, one was reported from Fort Wayne. Another was seen there in 1979 and three were present in August 1980. The last record is of one found August 20, 1983, at Marion (Grant County). Practically all of the observations were made at bird feeders or near human habitations. One was seen flying with a mourning dove in a marsh near Munster.

At the Fort Wayne site, a bird visited a feeder in the summer of 1978. It left for the winter, but it (or perhaps another bird) returned in the spring of 1979 and remained into the fall. Again, it left for the winter. In the summer of 1980, two birds were regularly present and three were seen on one occasion.

No nest has been reported, but Robert Krol watched a ringed turtle-dove court (and attempt to copulate with) mourning doves on several occasions. At two locations, turtle-doves associated with mourning doves.

MOURNING DOVE

Zenaida macroura

Turtle Dove, Carolina Dove, Dove

The familiar mourning dove is one of the best-known birds in Indiana, for it frequents areas near man and is conspicuous nearly everywhere in the state. It is likely to nest on a window ledge, perch on top of the house and sing, or come to the bird feeder in the yard. Doves are often considered symbols of peace; consequently there is much sentiment among humans for them, and in general people like having the birds near their homes and enjoy hearing their mournful song.

It is interesting to read about the status of this dove in Indiana at the turn of the century. It was a common resident in southern Indiana and a common summer resident in northern Indiana. It often remained in winter in the lower Wabash River and Whitewater River valleys, and in

1845. Those who wrote about the parakeets often used such words and phrases as abundant, numerous, in great numbers, and the like. When specific numbers were given, however, the birds were usually seen in flocks of from twenty to fifty. Butler mentioned having heard of flocks ranging from six to a hundred or more. Return Richmond of Lodi (Parke County) cut down a hollow sycamore tree in the winter of 1842 and found "hundreds" of parakeets in a quiescent or semi-torpid condition inside. He kept a dozen of them for some time, using a cut-off section of the hollow tree as their cage. He noted that they slept by suspending themselves from the sides of the cage by their beaks and feet. There are other winter records from southern Indiana; one observer remarked that in January the birds would perch, side by side, in rows on tree branches sunning themselves.

This parakeet seemed to prefer stream valleys and floodplains and the vicinity of ponds. It was also attracted to the springs and salt licks near French Lick, and to wheatfields, cornfields, and orchards, where it fed. The parakeets were quite destructive to orchards, eating leaf buds, blossoms, young fruits, and tearing apart apples to get the seeds. They also ate grapes, wheat, corn, sycamore seeds, cherries, persimmons, black gum fruits, beechnuts, acorns, pecans, and the fruit of haws.

Butler mentioned that one reason the parakeets preferred stream valleys was because their favorite food of all—cockleburrs—grew there in abundance. He wrote: "For these it is said they would leave any other food. Sometimes they would gather —numbers of them—upon a stump and shell out the kernel, leaving instead a pile of empty burrs. Wherever they were found, the universal testimony is, they preferably ate this food. Next to cockle-burrs they preferred hackberries."

BLACK-BILLED CUCKOO

Coccyzus erythropthalmus

Rain Crow, Cow Cow, Wood Pigeon

Many spring seasons in Indiana are notable for outbreaks of tent caterpillars, whose unsightly webs may be seen by the hundreds, especially on black cherry or black walnut trees, which the caterpillars heavily defoliate. The presence of these tent caterpillars often signals the appearance of an increased number of cuckoos, both species of which feed on the hairy larvae that most other birds shun. In mid-May we watched a black-billed cuckoo perched at one of these webs, quietly devouring the larvae as they crawled on the outside of the large web. Cuckoos are skulkers that hide in the tree foliage, and may be quite inconspicuous. It is usually their mournful songs and calls (said to foretell rain) that one first notices. Despite their long migrations, cuckoos look awkward in flight and do not appear to be strong fliers.

Around 1900, the black-billed cuckoo was considered a common migrant throughout the state and a common summer resident in northern Indiana. It is now a locally uncommon to common summer resident in northern Indiana, and is still less abundant at that season in the southern half. It remains a common spring and fall migrant throughout the state.

Habitats include overgrown old fields and pastures and other shrubby places, such as thickly vegetated fencerows, forests and woodlots, the borders of marshes, ponds and lakes, tree nurseries, and plantings of small pines.

The first spring arrivals are normally found during the last week of April. There is an April 5 sighting for Dearborn County; if correct, this is an early date. The birds arrive during May at most places throughout the state. There are no reports of large numbers. Daniel Mosher observed twenty at Lake Waveland on May 10, 1979; Alan W. Bruner reported that eight pairs nested at Shades State Park that summer. Most birds have left the state by mid-October, but there are several records for early November, the latest being November 16 (Vanderburgh County). The largest number recorded in the fall was four, at Jasper-Pulaski Fish and Wildlife Area, on September 7, 1975.

Both cuckoos construct similar looking nests: relatively small platforms of sticks. Black-billed cuckoo nests have been found in elm thickets, *Crataegus* trees, and blackberry canes in old fields. The birds also nest in brushy fencerows, in willows and buttonbushes at the edges of ponds, and in multiflora rose plantings and elderberry bushes. One nest was found in a Norway spruce and one in a Scotch pine in a nursery. Reported distances from the ground ranged from two to seven feet.

The number of eggs per clutch ranges from one to five.

BLACK-BILLED CUCKOO

Of twenty nests examined, six contained two eggs and six three eggs. After an egg is laid, incubation commences; the next egg may not be laid for three days. Thus, in clutches of several eggs, the young in the nest (if they all hatch) are usually of different ages and sizes. The European cuckoo (of cuckoo clock fame) lays its eggs in the nests of other birds. The two species of cuckoos in Indiana may lay their eggs in each other's nests, but normally do not parasitize other birds. Eggs of the black-billed have been found in nests from May 21 to August 25.

While we were examining two young with feather quills just ready to burst, one of them made a clucking sound. One of the parents came near the nest, perched with its tail partly spread and cocked upward and with drooping, spread wings, and gave a whining call.

Most of this cuckoo's summer food consists of insect larvae, but other insects and invertebrates (spiders) are also eaten.

Depicted plant: Northern prickly-ash (*Zanthoxylum americanum*)

YELLOW-BILLED CUCKOO

Coccyzus americanus

Rain Crow, Cow Cow, Wood Pigeon

Like its near relative the black-billed cuckoo, the yellow-billed cuckoo is a very beneficial bird, appearing in numbers when there are infestations of tent caterpillars and other leaf-eating caterpillars. The habits of the two species are quite similar, as are some of the calls, and no doubt the average person finds them difficult to tell apart.

In our experience, neither of the cuckoos is apt to be recognized on sight in Indiana, but the calls of the "rain crow," especially to people living in the country, are familiar.

Butler reported the yellow-billed cuckoo as a common summer resident that was less numerous in the northern part of the state, a status that the species may hold today. It is a common spring and fall migrant and may have increased in numbers in the northern part of the state since 1900.

The habitat of this cuckoo is much the same as for the black-billed, but the yellow-billed is possibly seen more often in orchards, backyards, and other more cultivated areas.

An extremely early date of arrival for a spring migrant is April 13 (March 23 and April 3, 1946, sightings for Lake County may have been an error in notekeeping). In general, early arrivals appear the last half of April and become most numerous during May. There is sometimes considerable variation in the dates of first arrival for a given locality. Irving W. Burr found twenty in Tippecanoe County on May 30, 1963. Birds begin moving from the nesting grounds in August, although some are still nesting throughout that month. No peak of fall migration is revealed by our records. Six birds seen September 6, 1969, and August 9, 1959 (both in Marion County), represent maxima reported at that season. There are several records for October and the last autumn date is for November 4 (when one flew into a window).

Nests and nesting habitats appear to be much the same for both cuckoos. We have found both species nesting together in about equal numbers in a tree nursery at West Lafayette. Shrubby old fields and pastures with scattered trees are attractive nesting sites. We have numerous records of yellow-billed cuckoos nesting in elms, hawthorn, locust, and other trees in such fields. At least seven nests were placed in trees that had been overgrown with wild grapevines. Other nests were in orchards and multiflora rose plantings, and in Scotch pines, hemlocks, and spruces in nurseries or pine plantations. The birds conceal their nests well in thickets or dense clumps of bushes or small trees. Nests have also been noted in open woods, along streams, and at woods borders.

The number of eggs per nest ranged from one (possibly an incomplete clutch) to six. Nineteen of thirty-nine nests contained three eggs each, and eleven held two each. There was a single clutch of six and two of five. Nests were anywhere from two to thirty feet above the ground; the average was about seven. Eggs were observed in nests from May 20 to September 3. An adult cuckoo was seen sitting on a nest on September 4 and again a few days later, but no eggs were found in the nest, according to Susan H. Ulrich. We would not be surprised to learn that some birds nest even later in the fall. On June 2, 1979, Kenneth J. Brock and others counted thirty-two yellow-billed cuckoos along the Kankakee River in Lake and Porter Counties. Alan W. Bruner estimated that fifty-five pairs nested at the Pine Hills Nature Preserve and Shades State Park in 1979.

One adult cuckoo was seen to eat twenty-four tent caterpillar larvae without pausing. Other foods known to be eaten include periodical cicadas, catalpa sphinx larvae, caterpillars from cabbage plants, beetles, and unidentified orthopteran insects. We once watched a cuckoo pull a huge green caterpillar (possibly a tomato sphinx larva) from the limb of a Chinese elm with great difficulty. In late September and early October, yellow-billed cuckoos were eating chironomus insects (midges) as they emerged from the water at Lake Maxinkuckee (Evermann and Clark, 1920).

The familar *kowp kowp kowp kowp* call of this cuckoo is frequently heard, as are other vocalizations, some of which may be mistaken for those of the black-billed cuckoo. Yellow-bills have been heard singing at least as late as September 15. Singing at night is not unusual; we have at least half a dozen reports, from May to August. On the night of August 22–23, 1974, one or more called periodically throughout the night, at Wyandotte Cave.

Depicted plants: Garden phlox (*P. paniculata*); Virginia creeper (*Parthenocissus quinquefolia*)

[SMOOTH-BILLED ANI]

Crotophaga ani

The occurrence of this blackish cuckoo in Indiana is strictly accidental. James E. Landing observed an ani at Michigan City on October 27, 1957, that he was convinced was this species. He carefully observed it for a half hour from a distance of thirty feet with binoculars, aware of the possibility of its being a groove-billed ani. On November 23, Landing and Scott Rea flushed an ani (but were able to view it only for seconds) from the same sumac grove where Landing had seen one on October 27.

GROOVE-BILLED ANI

Crotophaga sulcirostris

Of the two species of anis in North America, this is the species most likely to appear as an accidental visitor in Indiana, based on previous sightings in the Midwest. Norman P. Keammerer and Laura Keammerer first observed this ani on November 16, 1981, among other birds attracted to the bird feeders at their home near Valparaiso (Porter County). They could see the grooves on the beak and were able to observe the bird from a distance of six feet. Two subsequent sightings were made by the Keammerers during the next few days.

Official addition to the state list, however, occurred just recently with an observation on or about October 16, 1983, when Lora Trout found a bird of this species on the maintenance grounds of Taylor University, Upland, Indiana. Mr. Trout had a rudimentary interest in birds and knew it was unusual but could not identify it. Identification was subsequently made by a student, Mark Breederland, several days later. In the following two week scores of birders were able to observe and photograph the bird. Copies of these photos are in our files. It was last seen on November 1.

It is interesting that this bird had more pronounced grooves on one side of its beak than the other. Some observers, viewing the side with faint grooves, reported no grooves.

COMMON BARN-OWL

Tyto alba

Monkey-faced Owl, American Barn Owl, Barn Owl

Owls—even more than other nocturnal (and therefore little-known) animals—have universally been the subject of much superstition and folklore and frequently even been associated with witchcraft, evil spirits, and the occult. This is especially true of the pale, sinister-looking barn-owl, which is found in many parts of the world and is equally at home in an Indiana silo, an Egyptian pyramid, or an English castle.

A little more than a hundred years ago there were no records for the barn-owl in the state. The first was reported after 1879. In 1883 there were additional sightings in southern Ohio and southern Indiana. By 1898 the species was present throughout Indiana, although it was considered rare in the northern portions. It was locally a resident and nested, but remained most numerous in the Wabash River valley and southward. We have no explanation for this sudden increase in the barn-owl population north of the Ohio River. The barn-owl is a difficult bird to census, but there seems little doubt that it continued to expand its range and increase in numbers in Indiana until at least 1960. In the fall of 1958, fourteen were trapped on one farm near Fairmount (Grant County), where rabbits were being raised in open-topped pens.

Within the past twenty years the barn-owl population throughout the state has sharply declined. Pesticides, shooting, and loss of habitat are probably all factors in the decrease. We believe that it is still found in all regions as a permanent resident, but only in very small numbers.

Christmas count data on barn-owls do not give us the whole story—their daytime roosts are virtually impossible to find—but are nonetheless interesting: no barn-owls were observed on any count before 1945; since 1945 twenty have been seen; since 1971 only four have been counted.

During the day barn-owls roost in the cavities of large trees, in buildings or other structures, and (at times) in the branches of conifers. They have an apparent preference for huge sycamore trees along streams. It is in such sites as barns, silos, church belfries, schools, and deserted buildings that roosting barn-owls are most likely to be encountered by humans.

Barn-owls have nested in natural cavities in large trees, the wooden framework of a water tower, a school belfry, silos, barns, on the floor of an open-topped metal grain bin, and in city courthouses. One silo nest was placed atop the dry ensilage, which almost filled the structure. Eggs were observed in nests from March 7 through the month of May, but there are scant Indiana nesting data. Clutch size ranged from three to six for four nests. The number of young per nest, for six nests, varied from three to eight. Barn-owls nested in the Greensburg (Decatur County) courthouse until 1950 and in the Rochester (Fulton County) courthouse in 1959. This owl shows no reluctance to live in cities.

Like some other groups of birds, owls regurgitate the undigested portions of their food in the form of compact

COMMON BARN-OWL

pellets. An analysis of bones, hair, and feathers found in 252 barn-owl pellets collected at three sites in Indiana revealed that prairie voles, meadow voles, short-tailed shrews, deer mice, and white-footed mice comprised the bulk of their food. Other prey included southern bog lemmings, house mice, Norway rats, meadow jumping mice, least shrews, eastern cottontails, and birds.

Except at the nest, especially where young are present, the barn-owl is relatively silent. But a family at the nest will hiss loudly and snap their beaks at an intruder. The regular call of this owl, always heard at night, while the birds are moving about and foraging, is a peculiar, rather long, raspy shriek, which at times sounds like cloth tearing. Such calls may be the first indication of the presence of barn-owls in an area.

EASTERN SCREECH-OWL

Otus asio

Gray Owl, Red Owl, Screech Owl

This misnamed (its calls do not sound like screeches) little owl is common in the state wherever there are large trees it can use for nesting and roosting. It is sometimes much more abundant in cities and suburbs than people realize, for residential areas, cemeteries, golf courses, city parks, campuses, and the like frequently contain old trees with many cavities. The slow, quavering call, uttered on different pitches, may be heard much of the year. Whistled imitations (or the playing of tape recordings) of the call will often induce the calling bird to approach and investigate.

Butler wrote that the screech-owl was an abundant permanent resident of Indiana. It is still common throughout the state and may be locally abundant, as has been shown by some Christmas bird counts. On December 27, 1970, one hundred were recorded at South Bend; eighty-seven were found on December 18, 1976, at Lafayette. Such numbers were found in both instances with the aid of taped screech-owl calls.

The screech-owl may be found wherever there are suitable sites for nesting—tree cavities, buildings, bridges, and the like. Nesting boxes erected for squirrels, wood ducks, and other animals are frequently used by it. Daytime roosts include the same sites chosen for nesting, as well as pine plantations, deciduous trees with foliage, caves, and abandoned buildings.

We know nothing about possible movements of this little owl, but two were found dead along Lake Michigan after the April 16, 1960, storm (Segal, 1960). It is presumed the birds were caught in flight over the water and drowned.

Screech-owls call throughout the year, but are heard most commonly in spring and fall. Many birds are heard in August. Courtship begins in late winter, as it does with most other owls, which helps to explain why so many screech-owls respond to the playing of their taped calls on Christmas counts. Nests contain eggs from at least March 23 to April 24, according to our scanty data. Clutches usually contain four or five eggs, occasionally more. Twelve observations of young either in the nest or recently fledged indicate that three to (rarely) six make up a brood. Most broods, however, contain three to four young. Adults near nests containing young may be quite aggressive toward humans; there are several records of their attacking people who ventured too near.

The food of the screech-owl consists mostly of small mammals and birds; insects, spiders, and crayfish are also eaten. Butler mentioned finding a minnow in one screech-owl he examined and "a quantity of butter" in another. These owls apparently often hunt along roads, for many are killed each year by motor vehicles. Perhaps the owls have found that the small nocturnal mammals and large flying insects upon which they feed are sometimes plentiful along roads.

On sunny days in cold weather, screech-owls can sometimes be seen perched at the opening of their roosting cavities, eyes closed, evidently sunbathing. Stewart (1925) reported that a roost near Dublin, Indiana, was used for nine consecutive winters by a screech-owl. The bird was not banded, so more than a single owl may have been involved.

There has been much interest in the fact that screech-owls exhibit dichromatism—some are gray, others reddish. Both color phases may be present in a single brood. Butler discussed the prevalence of each color phase in Indiana for certain areas, noting that ninety-five percent of the owls in the Wabash River valley were of the red phase (according to Robert Ridgway). Biologists are still conducting research on this phenomenon and several theories have been advanced to account for it. Actually, there are many color variations between the "gray" and the "red" birds. Each of these shades can provide useful camouflage, under the right conditions. One red-phase bird was found perched during the day on a dead branch of a red pine; the branch had broken and fallen to the ground, but was still attached to the tree; the needles were a rusty red that exactly matched the bird's plumage, making it difficult to see. And gray-phase birds, sleeping at the entrances to their roosting holes in trees, are almost invisible because their plumage matches the tree bark so perfectly. The nesting pair illustrated consists of one red-phase and one gray-phase bird.

GREAT HORNED OWL

Bubo virginianus

Big Long-eared Owl, Cat Owl, Horned Owl, Hoot Owl

Snow lay on the ground and the cold wind rattled the dry leaves. According to the calendar it was late March, but it felt like midwinter. On a sandy ridge stood several huge, fire-scarred black oaks, in one of which, about fifteen feet from the ground, just where the massive trunk divided to form three sturdy branches, was a large, snow-covered stick nest. The nest had probably originally been constructed by a red-tailed hawk, but it now contained an adult great horned owl, incubating its eggs. The owl was scarcely visible; it had seen us and lowered itself into the nest cup so that only the top of its head and its ear tufts showed. It was obviously uneasy, and we, fearing it might take flight and leave its eggs unprotected, quickly went on our way. Several weeks later we were happy to see two young owls in this nest.

Butler considered the great horned owl a common permanent resident throughout the state, being the most common large owl in the southeastern portion. We do not know how present-day populations compare with those of the late 1890s, but the great horned owl is still commonly found everywhere in Indiana. Christmas bird count data offer the best index of numbers. As many as twenty-seven great horned owls have twice been recorded on Lafayette counts, and twenty-four were found on a Willow Slough count. More than ten per count have been reported at Richmond and Whitewater.

The presence of trees is the most important component of the habitat of this large owl; it occurs in forests, woodlands, cemeteries, residential areas, and anywhere there are roosting and nesting sites.

Some movements of this owl apparently take place, but we are unable to offer any details. Banded great horned owls have been recovered some distance beyond what would be considered their normal home range.

Although calling evidently occurs throughout the year, there is usually a noticeable increase in September and October. Mating takes place in the fall, for eggs are laid during winter. The eggs are normally deposited in an old nest made by a crow, hawk, or other large bird, and sometimes on top of old squirrel nests. Nesting is not confined to structures among the tree branches; numerous nests are located in the hollows of broken-off trees. One pair nested in a gravel chute at a sand and gravel pit.

We have records of great horned owls observed on nests as early as February 2, but no doubt many birds nest even earlier than that. Eggs have been found in Indiana nests from February 13 to April 2. Eleven of fifteen nests contained two eggs each and four contained three eggs each.

The great horned owl is a powerful, bold predator, taking a wide variety of animals as food. The prey of this owl recorded in Indiana includes insects, mammals ranging in size from the least shrew to the striped skunk, and birds from the size of starlings to turkeys. One landowner lost fifty-nine guinea fowl to great horned owls one fall.

SNOWY OWL

Nyctea scandiaca

White Owl

When they put in one of their periodic winter appearances in Indiana, snowy owls never fail to attract widespread attention. These spectacular birds are not only conspicuous but frequently inhabit areas heavily populated by man, even the center of large cities. Here the owls perch on television antennas, utility poles, or tall buildings, from which they swoop down to attack and feed on domestic pigeons (rock doves). Before the public became more enlightened about conservation, most of these beautiful, unwary owls were shot for trophies or out of curiosity.

A snowy owl was discovered at West Lafayette one January that was seen by many observers. Each evening at about the same time it could be found perched within a small area, where it fed on voles. About every five minutes the owl flew down from its perch (usually a utility pole), deftly caught a vole in the pasture, then returned to its perch and consumed its prey. Some voles were caught as much as seventy-five yards from the owl's perch—it obviously had special sensory adaptations for discerning its prey in the failing light.

Butler wrote that the snowy owl was an irregular winter visitor that was seen almost every winter. He further noted that it was usually rare, but occasionally appeared in some numbers. From what we can infer from early accounts, the snowy owl is considerably more rare today, even though its frequency of occurrence is about the same as in former years. For example, we have records of this owl in Indiana for every year but one (1952)

GREAT HORNED OWL

from 1949 to 1982. Its numbers swell about very four years; this cycle has received much attention and been rather well documented in the literature. Butler mentioned several winters when peak flights were noted, remarking that during the winter of 1905–06 more snowy owls were reported in the state than ever before. Peak flights were subsequently recorded in 1926, 1930, 1934, 1937, 1941, 1945, 1949, 1959, 1978, and 1981. The snowy owl has been recorded from most of the counties in Indiana and can be expected anywhere in the state, although it is most likely to be observed across the northern portion.

Any habitat may harbor snowy owls during invasion years. The birds show no fear of man and choose to remain at almost any site where they can find food. Such sites have included offshore ice floes at Michigan City and downtown Indianapolis.

The earliest arrival date on record is October 8, 1965, when a snowy owl was found in LaPorte County. The latest record is May 15, 1950, in Lake County. There are only a handful of records for October, and the first birds are usually found in November. We have more records for December than for any other month. For some unexplained reason, however, it has been recorded on relatively few Christmas bird counts. There is a considerable decrease in sightings throughout January and February; there are two records after March. A taxidermist in Mishawaka (St. Joseph County) received eighteen dead snowy owls in November 1949; another at Hammond (Lake County) had nine brought in from December 1 to 8, 1926.

This owl feeds on a wide variety of animals. Audubon described how it captured fish at the Falls of the Ohio River. Bluegills caught and left on the ice at Lake Manitou were eaten by snowy owls. Other reported prey includes voles, American coots, and domestic chickens. The remains of a black scoter and a saw-whet owl were found at one of the perching sites of a snowy owl near Lake Michigan.

[NORTHERN HAWK-OWL]

Surnia ulula

American Hawk Owl, Day Owl

This accidental visitor is uncorroborated because none of the several reported sightings meet the requirements for the "official" state list. Our best evidence for the appearance of this northern owl in Indiana is the observation by James E. Landing of one sitting on the ice off Michigan City on February 7, 1965 (Burr, 1966). Although other birders were contacted, none arrived in time to see the owl.

BURROWING OWL

Athene cunicularia

The interesting burrowing owl was not even on Butler's hypothetical list, for in 1898 it seemed very unlikely that this species might occur in Indiana. The first record is a specimen collected April 16, 1924, in Porter County (Hine, 1924). Another was collected in Newton County on April 12, 1942. On July 13, 1980, a burrowing owl was found near Hammond (Lake County); it was seen by many people (and also photographed and banded) through September 24. Yet another was captured in a building under construction at Fort Wayne (Allen County) on April 24, 1981, and taken to the Children's Zoo in that city.

Raymond Grow (1982) picked up a pellet from the resting place of the Hammond burrowing owl; it contained only remains of insects (beetles and grasshoppers). The bird was usually seen among a pile of steel girders lying on the ground.

BARRED OWL

Strix varia

Northern Barred Owl, Hoot Owl, Muley Owl, Big Woods Owl

As a boy in southeastern Illinois, Mumford often went on night fishing expeditions with his father. What he remembers best about those warm, late-summer nights is not the numbers of yellow bullheads caught but the serenades of the barred owls. There he'd be, sitting on the creek bank in the dark, holding his cane fishing pole, waiting for the tug of a catfish, and just about to doze off—despite the buzzing of mosquitoes about his head—when suddenly from a tree overhead would come the startling, loud hooting of a barred owl. The first time this happened (not that he was a bit frightened) it seemed advisable to make a quick check on Dad's whereabouts. Later he learned to imitate the calls, and frequently could induce a distant bird to fly closer and call in response. By pointing a flashlight in the direction of the noise and quickly snapping the switch, he could sometimes catch a brief glimpse of this great bird of the swamps, peering down, before it flew.

The barred owl was a common Indiana resident around 1900, but even then the clearing of much forested land throughout the state was causing a decrease in its numbers. However, they remained common where wooded

BARRED OWL

swamps and woods remained along some of the larger rivers, such as the Kankakee, for some time after 1900. The current status of this fine large owl is probably best assessed by an examination of Christmas bird count records. The maximum numbers reported on single counts (six to eleven) were all from the southern half of Indiana, but the species occurs throughout the state. The largest numbers were recorded on counts at Bloomington, Indianapolis, Lake Monroe, Richmond, Terre Haute, and Whitewater. Eleven were seen on the Whitewater count on December 19, 1976.

The barred owl seems most at home in wooded swamps, floodplain woodlands, and forested river valleys, but it also occurs in upland woods. It appears to prefer having water nearby, as evidenced by its relative abundance in portions of southwestern Indiana and elsewhere about swampy places. In the northern part of the state, it is found primarily along rivers or about marshes and other wetland areas adjacent to woodlands containing large trees.

The courtship of this owl is a noisy performance well known to many rural Hoosiers. Although barred owls call each month of the year, they are particularly vociferous in late fall and early winter when trying to attract mates, and may call persistently throughout the night, especially if there is a full moon. Calling is also quite frequently heard at any time on dark, cloudy days, more rarely, on sunny days. Nests are usually placed in the cavities of large trees, where available, but old nests of crows, hawks, and squirrels are sometimes used. There are few data regarding nesting in Indiana, and we have been unable to find any references to dates on which eggs have been found. Young in one nest had just hatched on April 29. Young have been observed out of the nest by early May; some of these were birds still quite small and unable to fly. Two young per nest is evidently the usual number, but on occasion three are produced.

The barred owl feeds on a variety of animal foods: mice, shrews, red squirrels, Norway rats, birds, and crayfish. At dusk the birds can frequently be found perched fairly close to the ground in trees along a road through the woods. The birds presumably do much of their hunting from such perches, since the openings created by roads provide habitat for prey animals.

The call heard most often from this owl is the eight-syllable *whoo-whoo-whoo-whoo; whoo-whoo-whoo-whoah*, sometimes transcribed *Who cooks for you; who cooks for you-all*, which aptly fits the cadence of the call. At other times, the birds may call *whoo-all* one or several times without uttering the remainder of the eight notes. Loud screams are also part of its repertoire, and the young have other characteristic calls that differ from those of adults.

The barred owl is sometimes active—apparently hunting—on sunless days, especially during the winter. It may be that when the ground is snow-covered the owl finds the hunting better by day than by night because detecting its prey is easier in daylight. And it is known that the small rodents that make up much of this owl's diet tend to become more diurnal in extremely cold weather. In any case, especially under such conditions the owls sometimes seem to find it worth their while to forage by day. Barred owls hunting by day are often attacked by various birds, especially American crows, which appear to delight in mobbing owls. According to Butler, H. K. Coale once saw a barred owl perched in a tree being harassed simultaneously by a wood thrush, a blue jay, a blue-gray gnatcatcher, a great crested flycatcher, a yellow warbler, and an American redstart.

GREAT GRAY OWL
Strix nebulosa

The great gray owl is a large northern species that may have been more common in this region in former years, but is still considered an accidental visitor to Indiana. E. R. Quick reported the capture of one in Franklin County "several years" before 1897. We know of three reports of specimens supposedly collected in the state, all from around the turn of the century: in Franklin County; near Fowler, in Benton County; and at Hovey Lake (Posey County). Although Brayton (1880) reported the great gray owl from northern Indiana, he gave no details. His comments were probably based on the reported presence of this owl in northeastern Illinois.

LONG-EARED OWL

LONG-EARED OWL

Asio otus

American Long-eared Owl, Wilson's Owl, Little Long-eared Owl

One day in late December we were walking through a planting of twenty-year-old white pines in the Morgan-Monroe State Forest. Little understory was present and the pines had been pruned to a height of about fifteen feet, so the walking was easy and silent. Beneath one tree were some white splashings of droppings and a few moist gray pellets—telltale signs that an owl had recently been roosting there. We carefully circled the base of the tree and saw a long-eared owl, its body compressed and elongated, sitting on a small, high branch against the trunk.

After a short time it became uneasy and flew off through the trees, only to alight about thirty yards away. This time it did not allow such a close approach and flew out of sight when it flushed.

This rather silent owl has never been well known in Indiana. It is retiring and, in our experience, calls very little, choosing to roost by day in the dense foliage of pine plantations or deciduous trees and matted clumps of vines. It is found throughout Indiana in winter wherever suitable habitat is present. Maximum numbers on Christmas counts are eighteen at Lafayette, fourteen at Indianapolis. Since this owl is a permanent resident, migration dates are quite difficult to determine. Since it is less common in summer, some migration obviously takes place, but its extent is unknown. We have nesting records from nine counties, Jennings being the southernmost, and there seems little doubt that it breeds in places for which we have no records, especially across the northern third of the state.

The long-eared owl normally lays its eggs in the old nest of a crow (shown in the illustration) or hawk. Most of the nests found have been in pine plantations, but one was in a pin oak in an oak-hickory woods. There are few records for nests with eggs. Three nests held two, three, and six eggs from March 30 to April 27. Downy young were observed in one nest as early as April 9, and some young were observed out of the nest, but unable to fly, on May 11. It is not unusual to find one or more of the larger young out of the nest (either in the nest tree or one nearby) before the smaller young have left the nest.

Charles M. Kirkpatrick, Donald E. Stullken, and Hallock J. Hosford reported some of the calls made by adult long-eared owls while the three men were examining young at a nest. One call was a high-pitched *wook wook wook* and another was somewhat like the barking of a dog—a sort of *wook wook wook wooo o o o*. A third call was a catlike meowing sound. We have heard adults giving similar calls at a nest containing large young.

Considerable research has been done on food habits of the long-eared owl by examination of pellets. The majority of the food remains were of meadow voles, prairie voles, and white-footed mice. Nine species of mammals ranging to the size of a Norway rat were included, as were bird remains, of which only cardinal was identified. Shrews and mice comprised the bulk of the diet.

Depicted tree: Eastern white pine (*Pinus strobus*)

SHORT-EARED OWL

Asio flammeus

Prairie Owl

One of the last sizable stands of native prairie grassland remaining in Newton County was on a sandy site a few miles northeast of Enos. Greater prairie-chickens roosted there and performed their unique courtship on a nearby booming ground each spring. During the summer six-lined racerunners scampered across the sand in the windblown openings of the switch grass. And every autumn several short-eared owls returned to the prairie to spend the winter. They roosted on the ground amid the tall grasses, and during the day you could usually flush several of these tawny owls from their haunts as you walked about. Then they would fly, as silently and buoyantly as huge moths, before alighting again in a distant part of the field. At dusk they could be seen flying low over the field, and occasionally one would perch briefly on a fencepost. Although they were active primarily at night, on gloomy days one or more might be seen foraging.

Butler reported that this owl was a permanent resident "in some numbers" in northern Indiana, but elsewhere it was an irregular winter visitor in varying numbers. During some winters it was not seen; in others, like that of 1886–87, it was very abundant. The single nesting record cited by Butler was for Starke County, about May 6, 1890. Today there are nesting records for eight counties, and this owl is an uncommon to rare winter visitor and a local permanent resident throughout the state. It is still quite variable in numbers from year to year and may be totally absent where the habitat is unsuitable. The largest number reported on a single Christmas bird count was

SHORT-EARED OWL

thirty-five, at Morocco (Newton County), on December 28, 1971 (some of these birds may actually have been in nearby Illinois).

In the past twenty years northern Indiana's wheat and oat stubble fields, which provided excellent winter roosting cover for the short-eared owl, have all but disappeared owing to the increased popularity of fall plowing. Sightings of this owl, especially on the former prairie areas in the northwestern part of the state, have decreased in that region. And prairie grasslands of sufficient size to be used by the birds are now nearly nonexistent. However, there are a few isolated, open areas supporting roosting cover scattered over the state, and, in southern Indiana, a promising development: the reclamation and establishment on lands formerly stripmined for coal of extensive prairielike vegetation (fescue, sweet clover, etc.). Large tracts in Pike and Warrick Counties are becoming prime habitat for this owl, which is now nesting there for the first time.

There is usually an influx of migrating short-eared owls

in Indiana during the fall. Early fall migrants generally appear across northern Indiana the last half of October. August and September sightings may be of birds present all summer, or they may represent early migrants. Most records of the short-eared owl for the state are for mid-winter. Relatively few remain after mid-April.

This is the only owl found in Indiana that nests on the ground. Few nests have been observed here. Ruthven Deane found two nests "in large grass tussocks in the open meadow" at English Lake (Starke County). Homer F. Price mentioned a nest in Allen County that was located on a high spot in marsh grasses on a bushy tract. A recent nest found in Pike County was in a grassy area near the base of a fence post. Eggs have been seen in nests from April 19 to May 6. In four nests, the number of eggs was three, three, five, and six. One nest contained three young and three eggs on April 19.

By far the most common prey item found in the pellets of short-eared owls is the prairie vole, which is sometimes abundant in the owls' habitat. Other mice, shrews, birds, and grasshoppers were also eaten. One pellet contained a trace of eastern cottontail.

The short-eared owl is a comparatively silent bird, except in defense of its nest. Price mentioned that while he was examining a nest the adults flew overhead uttering "their peculiar puppy notes." Once at dusk, happening to find ourselves in a field over which a pair of short-eared owls and several northern harriers were foraging, we began to make squeaking noises. The owls responded instantly, flying overhead and uttering short, explosive barking calls. And one spring we watched a short-eared owl, high in the air, pursuing a northern harrier and flying rings around it. The owl was surprisingly swift; it easily outmaneuvered the hawk, and even struck it twice.

Depicted plant: Elliott beard grass (*Andropogon elliotti*)

NORTHERN SAW-WHET OWL

Aegolius acadicus

Acadian Owl

An Indiana birdwatcher's first encounter with this tame little owl is usually memorable, for it normally shows little fear and can be watched at close range for some time. Several have even been captured by hand. These small round-headed owls are usually found during the winter, in eight- to fifteen-year old Scotch pines planted in upland fields. They often perch not more than six feet above ground and may be quite easily seen when one parts the branches of the pines. Occasionally an owl will be found perched holding a decapitated white-footed mouse in its talons.

Butler listed the saw-whet owl as a "not uncommon" permanent resident in northern Indiana and an irregular winter visitor in the south; it was "rather common locally" in some winters. However, his assessment may have been partially influenced by the reported relative abundance of this owl in the Chicago region. Today this little owl is likely to be found anywhere in Indiana in small numbers throughout the winter. It may be uncommon to rare in most places, but favored sites may harbor several in a small area. Its distribution in summer is poorly known, but it appears that at this season most birds occupy the northern half of the state, and the population is quite sparse.

Although most saw-whet owls are found in pine plantations, the birds also probably inhabit deciduous woodlands, where they are not so easy to locate. Individuals have been seen in a small bush, a small thicket of small oak trees, in a dense tangle of grapevines at the base of a clump of willows and in red cedar trees in an abandoned field. Barton W. Evermann reported the most unusual sighting—one found sitting on the edge of a cradle in a child's bedroom. Favored nesting sites are woodpecker nesting holes and cavities in trees.

The fall influx of migrants is usually first noticed during the last half of October. Most of the non-nesting owls have departed by May 1. We know of no large or conspicuous migrations through Indiana. The largest number

NORTHERN SAW-WHET OWL

reported—eight—was during the winter of 1960–61 near Connersville (Fayette County).

There are no published accounts of finding a nest or eggs of this owl in the state. The relatively few breeding records involve observations of young, in most cases after they had left their nests. One brood had nested near a house in a shade tree on the lawn. Another nest site was a dead elm in an old thicket. The nest in the illustration is in a pine tree; the nesting hole was probably made by a flicker. The saw-whet owl is known to have nested as far south as Richmond (Wayne County). Young have been observed in May, June, and July.

Prey items found in pellets of saw-whet owls from Indiana included shrews, mice, and small birds. The majority of the items identified were remains of either white-footed mice or deer mice. John P. Buck saw a saw-whet owl capture a house sparrow that Buck flushed from under the eaves of his home.

One of the calls of this owl gives the species its name; it suggests the filing of a saw. There are relatively few records of calling by Indiana birds, possibly because during the main calling season there are few present. Some recorded dates for such calls are April 19 and August 19.

COMMON NIGHTHAWK

Chordeiles minor

Eastern Nighthawk, Bull Bat, Night Hawk

The familiar common nighthawk, although seen by most people, is not really very well known because observations are usually of birds flitting overhead at dusk. Many confuse it with its close relative, the whip-poor-will; others think it is some type of hawk, or even mistake it for a large bat. Before man came upon the scene, nighthawks were probably most numerous in rural areas, where they nested on the ground in open places. The birds have now adapted to nesting on the graveled roofs of flat-topped buildings and as a consequence have become common in towns and cities. There is reason to believe that today nighthawks are considerably more abundant and nest over a much larger portion of Indiana than they did around 1900.

Butler reported that it was a common summer resident in northwestern Indiana, locally elsewhere in some numbers, and an abundant migrant (most numerous in fall). Although he noted that it bred in suitable localities, he cited breeding records for only five counties. Its status today is that of a common migrant and summer resident, still seen in greater numbers in fall than in spring; it breeds throughout the state.

In Butler's time, most nighthawks still nested on the ground in fields, but some had been found nesting on buildings in Cincinnati, Detroit, and Chicago. Nowadays the presence of flat-roofed buildings is apparently the most important component of the summer habitat of the species. Migrant birds rest by day on horizontal tree branches, the crossarms of telephone poles, telephone wires, roofs of buildings, television antennas, or (rarely) the ground. Flocks of migrating birds may be seen nearly anywhere, for they often feed as they migrate over wooded or open habitats, cities, and water areas.

Spring migrants appear in most places in late April or in May, but there are three March sightings. Fall migration begins in August; most stragglers have departed by mid-October, and we have two November records. Extreme dates are March 2 and November 21. Spring migration is not particularly spectacular. Arrivals usually appear in small numbers and are usually first noticed at dusk as they come out to feed. The maximum number of migrants recorded in spring was 300 at Lake Waveland (Montgomery County) on May 23, 1976, by Alan W. Bruner. Fall migrations involve huge flocks of milling birds, many of which pass during the day, along with monarch butterflies. Sometimes these flocks contain 2,000 individuals, and there are a number of records of flocks of more than 400. The largest flights are frequently seen moving just ahead of an approaching severe storm, normally in the last week of August or the first week of September.

The courtship of the male nighthawk is a spectacular aerial performance. He will fly about high in the air, uttering an occasional nasal call, then fold his wings and dive toward the ground at great speed, pulling out of the dive at the last moment. The rush of air through his wings and tail produces a peculiar "booming" sound. Males have been observed performing their booming courtship dives as late as August 19. We watched one male call three times in a short period while perched during midday on the branch of a tree.

There are practically no data about egg laying; most nests, being on top of buildings, are inaccessible to observers. According to the few records we have, eggs are present at least from May 26 to July 7, suggesting a prolonged nesting season. Keller examined one young nighthawk, with undeveloped tail and some down on the body, on August 24. Torrential rains sometimes destroy nests containing eggs or young by flooding the nesting sites.

The nighthawk feeds on flying insects, capturing them in flight in its large mouth. Various species of insects are eaten; the stomach of one bird that we examined contained nothing but large beetles. The birds feed during the daytime as well as at night. Atmospheric pressure no doubt has an effect on the elevation at which insects fly, and thus where the birds will hunt, on a particular evening. When the air is "heavy" and insects are flying closer to the ground, nighthawks hunt at low levels, sometimes just skimming over the plants to take insects. Otherwise, feeding generally takes place high in the air. We have noticed that nighthawks are frequently quite actively feeding on evenings when there is a light, warm drizzle, and that they like to feed over lighted areas (such as city streets and parking lots) to which insects are attracted.

The birds are sometimes forced to leave their daytime roosts on roofs by flash floods. After a short but severe cloudburst at Crawfordsville, we once watched more than a hundred nighthawks milling about over the city, evidently put to flight by the sudden flooding of their roosts.

CHUCK-WILL'S-WIDOW

Caprimulgus carolinensis

Giant Goatsucker

The chuck-will's-widow was something of a mystery bird in Indiana until about 1953, when night censuses of singing males revealed that it was actually locally common in Crawford and Harrison Counties. There, among the hills, pastures, and cornfields, this big cousin of the whip-poor-will had evidently been present for some time, unnoticed by the relatively few birders working in that region. A complicating factor was that many southern Indiana residents who had heard the calls of the two species made no distinction between them, referring to both as whip-poor-wills.

Before 1900, the chuck-will's-widow was thought to be a summer resident only in the lower Wabash River valley. Butler reported (without evidence) that it bred there and was "not uncommon." It was next reported from near Mitchell (Lawrence County) in 1907 by Walter L. Hahn, and in the spring of 1908 one was found dead at Indianapolis. During the following fifty years, it was reported from numerous counties in southern Indiana, especially in the south-central hill region. The largest known concentrations of birds were found in 1953 in Crawford and Harrison Counties, where on the nights of June 22, 23, and 24, a total of fifty-three chuck-will's-widows were heard. Although most of the birds appear to be in the southern half of the state, there are records from as far north as Kosciusko, Lake, and Porter Counties. The chuck-will's-widow today is probably rare to uncommon locally in suitable habitats in the southern half of Indiana and rare to absent elsewhere.

There is a single breeding record, for the Willow Slough Fish and Wildlife Area (Newton County), where the first and only nest of this bird ever found in Indiana was discovered by Delano Z. Arvin (1981b). The nesting site was a thinly wooded oak grove with an understory of small oak bushes and pine seedlings from two to eight feet tall bordering a plantation of larger pines. Since no actual nest is constructed by this large goatsucker, the two eggs present on June 7 were lying on oak leaves on the ground. They evidently hatched about June 10.

The Harrison County habitat of the chuck-will's-widow was characterized by rolling hills interspersed with farmland, pastures, homesites, brushy areas, and woodland borders. The birds seemed to prefer this rather open, forest-edge habitat to the more densely wooded forest land and bottomlands used by most whip-poor-wills. Observations of chuck-will's-widows observed elsewhere in the state have generally been in similar areas.

There are relatively few migration data. There appears to be a general pattern of "first" spring dates during May, but singing birds have been heard as early as April 16. It is possible that spring migrants return earlier and simply do not sing. Since the amount of singing decreases greatly during July (our latest record is for July 25), late-departing birds may be silent for some time before they leave the state. Only rarely are chuck-will's-widows found during the daytime; most records are for night-singing birds.

There are dozens of records of singing chuck-will's-widows, but not much information on the perches they use. We have one observation of a male singing from a perch twenty feet above the ground on a horizontal tree branch. No doubt much singing is also done from the ground, in the manner of the whip-poor-will.

In the illustration, note the white in the tail feathers of the male, and also the large mouth. These birds have been known to catch warblers and sparrows as well as insects. The predator is a long-tailed weasel (*Mustela frenata*).

WHIP-POOR-WILL

Caprimulgus vociferus

Eastern Whip-poor-will, Nightjar

To most Hoosiers the whip-poor-will is only a familiar voice in the warm summer night. Relatively few people have ever seen one at close quarters; yet, because of its distinctive call, it is widely known throughout the state. Many of us can remember nights when we were either entertained or kept awake by the seemingly endless calling of the whip-poor-wills. On one warm, moonlit night we actually counted more than seven hundred continuous calls uttered by an individual male; Arline L. Carter heard one give one thousand calls.

At the turn of the century the whip-poor-will was a common summer resident. In the southern forested areas of the state it is still common. In northern Indiana, though widely distributed, it may be locally common, greatly decreased, or absent depending upon the presence of absence of wooded areas. On June 6, 1952, by driving in the hills of Jackson County at dusk and stopping periodically to listen, Mumford located thirty-six singing whip-poor-wills within six miles.

Butler noted that the species preferred "more open woods overgrown with underbrush, or bushy pastures." It also occurs in extensive woodlands, and tends to come out along roads, power line easements, or other open spaces at dusk to sing. Many singing birds are seen on roads, and are usually first conspicuous because of their reddish eyeshine.

Spring migrants normally arrive in early April, but there are a few records for the last week of March. Butler cited a singing male heard March 2, 1897; this was extremely early. Most have left the state by the end of September, but several have been recorded from October 1 to 16. Records indicate that males may be silent for a time immediately after arriving and just before leaving. Singing has been heard from March 2 to September 26.

Although the whip-poor-will breeds throughout Indiana, there are relatively few records of nests and eggs. This is not surprising; nests are very well camouflaged by their placement and the coloring of the incubating parent, which seldom leaves the eggs during the daytime.

Like the chuck-will's-widow, the whip-poor-will constructs no nest as such, but lays the eggs (usually two per clutch) on leaves or grasses on the ground. Small young have been observed as early as May 13 and eggs have been found as late as July 14. Nests were located in deciduous woods, sometimes not far from the edge of old fields, or in upland, abandoned fields where sassafras, hickory, sugar maple, black cherry, or dogwood sprouts and saplings, blackberry briers, and greenbrier were present. One nest was found in "an open shed."

Food, captured on the wing, consists of various insects. The intestinal tract of a whip-poor-will we examined contained four large moths.

Depicted plant: Downy yellow violet (*Viola pubescens*)

CHIMNEY SWIFT

Chaetura pelagica

Chimney Swallow

Chimney swifts are seldom seen except in flight, circling overhead in constant, rapid motion and uttering their chattering calls. They are entirely creatures of the sky, feeding, drinking, and even gathering nesting materials on the wing; it seems miraculous that they can find the energy to remain in flight for so many hours each day. Although normally seen fairly high in the air, on damp, stormy days they may feed just above the ground; some are actually struck by motor vehicles along roads. In autumn, migrating flocks gather at dusk before going to roost in chimneys. At the roosting site large numbers of swifts may congregate, incessantly circling overhead, giving their characteristic calls, and waiting until the time comes to enter the roost. Birds come from all directions and join the swirling mass in close-packed formation, somehow managing to avoid collisions. By some signal, birds begin to drop from the bottom of the group and enter the chimney. Then, in a methodical, circling flight pattern, they all spiral down and disappear into the chimney for the night.

The chimney swift was formerly an abundant summer resident in Indiana, according to Butler, but there are no numerical data with which we can compare today's populations. It is still a common migrant and summer resident throughout the state and may be abundant locally during migration anywhere food and water are present.

Our earliest spring date for migrants is March 23; there are two other records for the last week of March. Most swifts arrive in April and reach a peak of abundance from late April to mid-May; during this period flocks of several hundred may be observed. In the Terre Haute (Vigo County) area, 3,058 were recorded on an all-day count May 11, 1974. From late August to early October, as many as 1,000 birds will sometimes flock at favored roosting chimneys. Many birds leave in September, and most stragglers have departed by mid-October. The latest of three November dates is the 20th.

Before manmade structures were available swifts nested mostly in hollow trees, and a few birds do so even today. A tree nest was found at Turkey Run State Park, in the summer of 1928, in a hollow beech snag. Alan W. Bruner found this swift nesting in hollow sycamore trees in Shades State Park on May 29, 1983. Most swifts now construct their nests in chimneys or on the walls of deserted buildings; outhouses, stables, wood silos, and a dug well lined with stones have also harbored nesting birds. Grant Henderson once observed seven nests on the wall of an old house; they were in a row, about eight inches apart. Some nest sites are occupied year after year. There is little information on nesting dates or clutch size

CHIMNEY SWIFT

for the chimney swift in our files. Eggs were seen in nests from May 26 to June 2, and clutch size in six nests ranged from three to five (average 4.2). Swifts were seen gathering nesting material on April 27. Nests are composed of small dry twigs (which the birds grasp in their feet and break off in flight), held together by a gluey secretion from their salivary glands.

Swifts feed on flying insects, but we have no data on types of prey found in Indiana specimens. Often swifts are still feeding in the evening after bats have emerged. On such occasions the interaction can be fascinating to watch. We have seen a swift and a bat converge on the same insect; we have also seen swifts chase bats and bats chase swifts.

RUBY-THROATED HUMMINGBIRD

Archilochus colubris

Hummer, Hummingbird

This hummingbird was obviously a favorite of Amos W. Butler's, for in 1898 he wrote, "There are many beautiful and interesting birds found throughout our State, but beside this little flying gem all others are as common pebbles beside the ruby." Many others no doubt share his views, for the ruby-throat is indeed a unique member of Indiana's avifauna. We normally see it as it hovers at a showy flower gathering nectar, then buzzes away with incredibly rapid wingbeats to another site. At times, especially on cool mornings, an individual will perch in the top of a shrub or on a dead twig to sunbathe and preen its iridescent feathers. Finding your first hummingbird nest is a noteworthy event, on a par with discovering your first perfect flint arrowhead.

Butler considered the hummingbird a common summer resident, and described a certain sandbar near Brookville, where hundreds gathered in August and early September to feed on a plant he called Bouncing Betty. Although we know of no congregations of this size in recent years, the ruby-throated hummingbird is still found throughout the state during migration and in summer. It is probably considerably less common than it used to be, but during migration it may still be found by the dozens at sites where favorite nectar-bearing plants are blooming in profusion.

The summer habitat of the hummingbird includes woodlands, brushy old fields, wooded stream valleys, residential areas, and cities; in all these places, nests have been observed. Migrants may appear anywhere that flowers upon which the birds feed are present.

Hummingbirds usually arrive in southern Indiana beginning about mid-April, but arrival dates vary from year to year depending upon prevailing weather. Our earliest record is April 8, when one was seen in Monroe County by Val Nolan Jr. The latest stragglers have generally left northern Indiana by mid-October, but a few linger throughout the month in southern Indiana. David A. Manuwal flushed a female hummingbird in a cornfield on November 10, near Wolcott (White County). The bird flew weakly, with its legs and feet hanging down, but it could not be captured by hand. By far the largest numbers of hummingbirds are recorded during fall migration.

Not long after arriving, male ruby-throats may be seen engaged in their spectacular "pendulum" display during courtship. The male flies a deep U-shaped course over and over before the female. Females can be observed hovering at spider webs and gathering spider silk and lichens for their nests. Completed nests have been found by May 12 and eggs have been seen in nests from May 13 to August 8. The nesting season is quite long; young have been seen in the nest until September 1. A clutch usually consists of two eggs, but sometimes only a single egg is laid. The twenty-four nests for which we have height records ranged from five to thirty feet above the ground. It is possible, of course, that the lower nests are more easily found. Nests are frequently placed on tree branches over a road through the woods, along a marsh or stream, along the side of a trail, or even over a city street. Several have been found in apple orchards. Since the male deserts the female after she lays her eggs, the illustration pictures them separately.

Hummingbirds feed primarily on nectar. They are especially attracted to yellow, orange, and red flowers, and visit many species of plants. Some of their favorites are jewelweed (both pale and spotted), trumpet creeper, canna, honeysuckle, and columbine. The birds feed also on gladiolus, nasturtiums, petunias, lilac, and peach,

plum, and buckeye blossoms. One hummingbird hovered about a woman wearing a red head scarf. Feeders containing red sugar water are quite popular with hummingbirds; as many as twenty may be seen at a feeder at one time. Herbert L. Stoddard reported "literally thousands of hummingbirds in the swamps and surrounding territory" between Gary and Mineral Springs on September 10, 1919. A week later, the tamarack swamps in this same area were "still alive" with them, but there were fewer than on his earlier visit. It is not unusual to see forty to fifty of the birds at a large patch of jewelweed in bloom in the early fall.

We once saw a hummingbird chase an osprey that had probably ventured too close to the hummer's nest. Another time we watched a male hummingbird bathing on the perpendicular face of a forty-foot sandstone escarpment over which ran a trickle of water. The damp rock face supported a luxuriant growth of mosses. The bird would fly to a mossy spot, cling to the cliff face, and let the water spray over it.

Depicted plants: Hophornbeam (*Ostrya virginiana*); Leather-flower (*Clematis viorna*)

RUBY-THROATED HUMMINGBIRD

BELTED KINGFISHER

BELTED KINGFISHER

Ceryle alcyon

Eastern Belted Kingfisher

Everyone who has spent much time fishing along the bank of a rocky, shallow stream has seen kingfishers in action. First there is a loud, rattling call, then a shaggy-crested, bluish-gray bird comes flying along the creek, perches on a dead branch overlooking a quiet eddy be-low a riffle, and peers down, waiting for a fish to appear. Suddenly it dives, striking the water with a loud splash, emerges, shaking its wings vigorously, and flies back to its perch with a squirming minnow in its beak. Here it sits, hammering the minnow against its perch until fish scales fly through the air. When the fish is dead, the bird turns it deftly around so it can be swallowed head first. Although this is the usual *modus operandi*, these birds sometimes also dive for fish after hovering in flight above the water. Kingfishers often follow the stream course in their flight, but may take "shortcuts" and fly over land rather than follow each looping meander of the stream.

Butler noted that the belted kingfisher was a permanent resident in southern Indiana and a common summer resident in the northern portion, from which it usually withdrew except in the mildest winters. Today it seems to be a permanent resident throughout the state in small numbers. The maximum number recorded on a single Christmas count, thirty-three, was at Lafayette on December 18, 1976.

Kingfishers frequent any water area containing small fish. They can be seen along streams of all sizes, about ponds and lakes, along roadside ditches and gravel pits, and at fish hatcheries, where they sometimes become a nuisance preying upon goldfish or trout fry being reared in the ponds.

Butler mentioned that migrant kingfishers usually returned to northern Indiana during late March and early April. Since the species is now so widespread throughout the winter, we have little significant information on migration dates. Such data are best obtained after severe winter weather (leaving virtually no open water available) has made it necessary for the birds to migrate southward.

Nests are placed at the end of burrows dug into vertical banks of clay, sand, or gravel. Eroded stream banks are frequently used for nesting sites, as are gravel or sand quarries and roadside cutbanks. Nests may be some distance from water and one can see the adults making relatively long overland flights carrying food to the young. Portions of food not digested by the birds are regurgitated as pellets, which accumulate in the nests. We know very little about the nesting habits of kingfishers, but complete clutches of eggs have been recorded by April 25. It appears that from five to seven eggs are usually laid. Young are capable of flight when they leave the nest.

Under certain conditions, belted kingfishers are partially nocturnal; we have seen one flying and calling in mid-September at 7:15 P.M. Boyd Gill saw an immature bird lying on his lawn, apparently sunbathing. An individual may use a favored perch day after day for weeks at a time.

RED-HEADED WOODPECKER

Melanerpes erythrocephalus

Red-Head

The showy red-headed woodpecker is a well-known bird, for it frequents roadsides, woodlots, and residential areas as well as more remote sites away from humans, and when one flies across an open area, flaunting its tri-colored plumage, it is virtually impossible to miss. It is often seen along country roads, perhaps picking up insects that have been knocked down by motor vehicles, or perched on a fence post or telephone pole, usually sidling around the pole out of sight when a car approaches.

There have always been fluctuations in the numbers of red-headed woodpeckers in Indiana, accompanied by periodic fears that the species is dying out. Undoubtedly it is far less abundant now than it was a hundred years ago, but it is still distributed throughout the state in fairly good numbers. Some years in a particular location it may be plentiful, other years virtually absent, depending mainly on the availability of suitable food in winter. Such fluctuations are evident when we study a series of Christmas bird counts from a given area. For example, on thirty-seven counts at Lafayette (Tippecanoe County), numbers of red-headed woodpeckers seen ranged from one to seventy-six per count, with ten or fewer found on twenty-one counts. The largest number ever tallied on a Christmas count in the state—243—was on December 20, 1980, at the Indiana Dunes National Lakeshore. In that year they were also plentiful at other northwestern Indiana localities. It is no coincidence that 1980 was also a bumper year for nuts and acorns.

In summer, this woodpecker is widely distributed in wooded areas, woodlots, residential areas, and other habitats that support nesting trees. In more open areas, where trees are not plentiful, the birds nest in telephone poles and fence posts. Wintering woodpeckers are likely to be most abundant in oak-hickory woodlands or beechwoods, since these are important sources of food. Old oak woodlots containing overmature trees with many cavities and

RED-HEADED WOODPECKER

dead branches harbor many red-headed woodpeckers in years when the acorn crop is large. Water-killed trees bordering lakes, marshes, and swamps are also favored habitats, and so, until they finally fell, were the many elm trees throughout the state that had succumbed to Dutch elm disease.

Despite the fact that this woodpecker is a permanent resident, a considerable amount of migration occurs, as we have indicated, when food is scarce. One such migration took place on September 20, 1954, near Maumee (Jackson County): between 1:45 P.M. and 4:45 P.M. sixty-two red-heads passed overhead to the south. The birds were moving on a front at least half a mile wide, so there may have been many more that were not seen. Similar movements have been reported in other parts of Indiana from late August to early October. Spring migration, because of the presence of wintering birds, is less obvious.

Most nesting records consist of observations of adults seen entering nesting holes or feeding young in nests. Because of the difficulty in reaching and examining such

nests, we have few data. Egg laying begins by mid-May and probably earlier, and young have been found in nests as late as August 30. Young birds retain their black heads into their first winter season, so each year's young are easily identified.

The diet of the red-headed woodpeckers is quite varied: larval and adult insects, seeds, fruit, corn, and nuts. They are fond of cherries and mulberries, and have been seen busily gathering pecans at Hovey Lake. A considerable amount of food is stored. One observer watched them taking bits of toast from a bird-feeding tray and storing them in holes in telephone poles. The species often engages in flycatching as well. Evermann and Clark (1920) discussed the aerial feeding of red-headed woodpeckers on flying chironomid insects, which sometimes emerged at Lake Maxinkuckee "in untold millions." Around bird feeders they can be quite aggressive; according to William Zimmerman's observations, even the big pileated woodpecker defers to the red-head.

RED-BELLIED WOODPECKER

RED-BELLIED WOODPECKER

Melanerpes carolinus

Guinea Woodpecker, Zebra Woodpecker, Carolina Woodpecker, Checkered Woodpecker

The red-bellied woodpecker is a familiar bird, especially in southern Indiana. It is usually noisy, and so conspicuous that birders, hunters, fishermen, and rural residents all know it well, although some mistakenly but understandably call it a red-headed woodpecker because of its brilliant scarlet cap and nape. Less distinctive is the reddish cast of the breast feathers that is responsible for the species' name. Perhaps a better name (as some have suggested) would be zebra woodpecker, because of the striking black and white markings of the back. The red-bellied can often be found in fairly good numbers along streams, especially where there are oak or beech trees.

Butler reported this woodpecker to be a common resident in the southern third of the state, but "rare northward." It was evidently least abundant along the Kankakee River in northwestern Indiana, where extensive woodlands were absent. It is generally common today throughout most of the state. Northwestern Indiana is still the area of least abundance, but even there it may be common locally. For example, forty-four were recorded on the 1980 Indiana Dunes National Lakeshore Christmas bird count. Despite the wide distribution of the red-belly in the state, there are relatively few nesting records.

Our experience has been that it prefers wooded stream valleys, low-lying woodlands, and swamps. Butler stated that along the Whitewater and Ohio Rivers it was seldom seen in the lowlands. No doubt the major reason for its absence in those regions was the dearth of suitable food trees (beech, oak, hickory). Upland wooded areas also support good populations of this woodpecker. Butler implied that some migration occurred, but we have no data pertaining to this behavior.

Egg laying begins by mid-April and adults have been observed excavating a nesting cavity by March 24. One nest was thought to contain eggs on August 31. Fully grown young are evident by early June.

The red-bellied woodpecker is primarily a vegetarian, consuming many different types of seeds and fruit including beechnuts, acorns, pecans, hickory nuts, corn, apples, and sunflower seeds. The bird frequents corncribs and feeders where corn is available and feeds on waste grain spilled along roads. It is also attracted to suet at feeding stations. One January we watched one gathering shagbark hickory nuts and storing them in a large oak tree. In a Florida orange grove, we have seen red-bellied woodpeckers piercing oranges to get at the juice.

YELLOW-BELLIED SAPSUCKER

Sphyrapicus varius

Sapsucker, Yellow-bellied Woodpecker

We know of a yellow-bellied sapsucker that put in an appearance in a Scotch pine on a certain city lawn every April for nearly ten years. It usually stayed from a few days to a week, feeding on the sap oozing from hundreds of squarish holes it had neatly pecked in a geometrical pattern in the cambium layer of the tree. This sap, a milky resin, hardened in streaks down the tree trunk or formed rough, unsightly blobs. By the following spring the holes had grown over, but many were reopened by the sapsucker on its annual visit. Sapsuckers feed on many kinds of trees. They seem especially attracted to Scotch pine, tulip

tree, apple, hickory, birch, maples, and basswood. Ruby-throated hummingbirds, white-breasted nuthatches, and warblers are among the other birds that frequently feed at sapsucker borings, consuming either the tree sap or the insects attracted to it.

This sapsucker was formerly a common migrant, a rare summer resident in the northern portion of the state, and a winter resident (mainly in southern Indiana) in varying numbers throughout. Since Butler did not give any precise figures, we are unable to make direct comparisons with his data. In our opinion, however, there has been a

YELLOW-BELLIED SAPSUCKER

decrease in the Indiana sapsucker population during the past seventy-five years or so. It is still locally common during migration, and winters in the greatest numbers largely in southwestern Indiana, then north as far as Terre Haute and Indianapolis. The maximum numbers observed on recent Christmas bird counts in the Evansville and Oakland City areas have ranged from ten to eighteen per count. The current nesting status is imperfectly known, but there are indications that more may breed in Indiana than was previously thought.

Sapsuckers are usually quiet and rather inactive, and may be inconspicuous at times. They frequent apple orchards, woodlots, forested areas, wooded stream valleys, cemeteries, golf courses, campuses, and residential areas.

Spring arrivals may be difficult to detect because there is a wintering population throughout the state. Migration peaks have been noted most often during April. At least 141 dead sapsuckers were found on Lake Michigan beaches in Indiana after the April 16, 1960, storm. This date coincides with observed peaks of spring migration in northwestern Indiana in other years. Fall migrants are usually most numerous during late September and early October.

There are relatively few nesting records. Butler reported breeding in Carroll, DeKalb, LaPorte, Porter, and Starke Counties before 1900, but since that date there are only three confirmed records. Young were found in a nest near Kouts (Porter County) in 1910. A pair nested near Goshen (Elkhart County) in 1973, but the nesting cavity was taken over by red-bellied woodpeckers in 1974. A nest was reported in Marshall County in 1982. Sapsuckers have also been observed during June, July, and August, and occasional nesting quite possibly takes place. Most such records are from the northern end of the state. One nest near Waterloo (DeKalb County) contained three eggs on May 13. The two nests for which we have details were in dead trees.

In addition to feeding on tree sap, this woodpecker also eats insects. At feeding stations it has been seen eating bone marrow, suet, bread, cake, and baked potato. One was feeding on persimmons in midwinter.

The usual call note given by the sapsucker (when not courting in spring) is a short mewing sound, similar to that of a domestic cat.

DOWNY WOODPECKER

DOWNY WOODPECKER

Picoides pubescens

Little Spotted Woodpecker, Little Sapsucker, Southern Downy Woodpecker, Northern Downy Woodpecker

This, the smallest and most common North American woodpecker, is the species most likely to be seen throughout Indiana. Although a rather quiet bird, the downy is known to many Hoosiers because it occurs in large numbers and does not shun areas inhabited by humans. It is often a conspicuous member of the "winter flocks" of small birds that forage together in woods or at their borders. Such groups may also contain tufted titmice, chickadees, juncoes, cardinals, and nuthatches, among others. Mixed assemblages seem especially evident during Christmas bird counts; one may walk nearly a mile without seeing a bird, then suddenly come upon one of these active winter groups.

The downy woodpecker has probably always been a common permanent state resident. We know nothing about its movements, although the fact that ten were found dead along Lake Michigan after a severe spring storm indicates that some migration takes place. Breeding occurs throughout the state. More than one hundred downy woodpeckers have been recorded per Christmas count at ten localities widely scattered about Indiana. The largest number for a single count was 309 at Lafayette (Tippecanoe County) on December 20, 1980.

Nearly any habitat with trees supports the downy woodpecker. It can be seen in cities, suburbs, cemeteries, golf courses, fencerows, and other more open areas as well as woodlands and woodlots. Foraging birds may be found in cornfields, dense stands of giant ragweed, and abandoned weed fields and brushy areas. They are easily attracted to backyard feeding stations.

The earliest date for eggs found in a nest is April 23; this particular nest was placed on the rail of a fence. Clutch size usually ranges from three to five. Young have been observed in nests by mid-May and out of the nest by mid-June. Fledged young are sometimes seen being fed by their parents at bird feeding stations. Nests are usually fairly near the ground, but one was recorded as being forty-three feet in height. Both house sparrows and red-headed woodpeckers sometimes take over nesting cavities being excavated by downy woodpeckers.

A considerable amount of insect food is eaten by this woodpecker. It extracts larvae from tree bark, branches, and plant stems, including giant ragweed, cornstalks, and goldenrod. During the winter we have seen them eating persimmons and poison ivy fruits. At bird feeders they take a variety of food items—sunflower seeds, suet, cracked nuts, and the like. Sunflower seeds are sometimes stored, usually in trees; at one site, however, the downies pecked small holes in a nearby house and stored sunflower seeds in the holes.

HAIRY WOODPECKER

Picoides villosus

Big Sapsucker, Big Spotted Woodpecker, Eastern Hairy Woodpecker

Many people confuse this rather retiring bird with its smaller cousin, the downy woodpecker. This is not very surprising, for both have the same general color pattern and are told apart mainly by subtle differences in overall size, relative beak length, and plumage markings. The hairy woodpecker is not found in populated areas quite so regularly as the downy woodpecker, and it tends to be more solitary and less social. Finally, it is much less abundant than the downy everywhere in the state.

Butler thought the hairy woodpecker was more numerous in southern Indiana during migration and winter, but considered it a common permanent resident. He also noted that it was not as numerous as the downy woodpecker. The hairy today is found throughout the state, but usually in small numbers. It is much less common than the downy, which on four selected Christmas bird counts (at Indianapolis, Lafayette, Richmond, and South Bend between 1950 and 1980) outnumbered the hairy about seven to one over the past thirty years. Maxima of twenty or more hairy woodpeckers per count have been recorded at eleven localities. The largest number observed was thirty-nine, at the Indiana Dunes National Lakeshore on December 18, 1976, and at the Pigeon River Fish and Wildlife Area on December 19, 1982.

The hairy woodpecker and the downy woodpecker like the same type of habitat, except that the hairy is not so likely to be found in towns or near human dwellings away from woodlands. The hairy appears to be a bit more numerous in habitats near water, such as wooded stream valleys and about lakes and swamps.

From only a handful of nesting records, it is evident that young are ready to leave the nest by at least mid-May. One nest contained three eggs and another held three young.

The eating habits of the hairy woodpecker are much like those of the downy woodpecker, but the hairy, being larger, can evidently more easily excavate holes in trees to extract the larvae of wood-boring insects. Fruits and seeds of many kinds are eaten, as are ants and numerous other insects.

HAIRY WOODPECKER

BLACK-BACKED WOODPECKER
Picoides arcticus

Arctic Three-toed Woodpecker, Three-toed Woodpecker, American Three-toed Woodpecker, Black-backed Three-toed Woodpecker

This northern woodpecker was first reported from Indiana by Herbert L. Stoddard, who found one at Miller (Lake County) on March 11, 1917 (Stoddard, 1917). Additional birds were found in Lake and Porter Counties in the winters of 1920–21, 1924–25, 1926–27, and 1927–28. Authenticated records have not been obtained since October 16, 1927, although there have been reports of this woodpecker in the same general area

as recently as the winter of 1965–66 and the fall of 1982. We should mention here that immature hairy woodpeckers are sometimes mistaken for black-backed woodpeckers.

All records for this species in Indiana are from October 3 to March 11. The most observed in one day was three, at Millers, on November 26, 1920. Today we classify the black-backed woodpecker as an accidental visitor.

Stoddard's notes contain information on the feeding behavior and calls of the birds he saw. He found the woodpeckers stripping the bark from dying or dead "scrub" jack pines, then digging insect larvae from the tree trunks. One specimen contained the remains of twenty-three wood-boring larvae of *Monohammus (=Monochamus) titillator*.

NORTHERN FLICKER

Colaptes auratus

Yellow-shafted Flicker, Yellowhammer, High Hole, Yarup,
Golden-winged Woodpecker, Wickup, Golden-shafted Woodpecker, Pigeon Woodpecker, High Holder

The noisy, conspicuous flicker, long well known in Indiana, has acquired many local vernacular names, some derived from call notes of the bird and others from its coloration. Where Mumford grew up in southeastern Illinois, it was called yellowhammer, and he has vivid memories of the day one flew into and shattered the windshield of his father's Model A Ford. The flicker feeds to a considerable extent on the ground, where it avidly consumes ants. During courtship, males frequently drum on metal—guttering, downspouts, and transformer boxes are common choices. Such performances may continue for days, much to the consternation of people trying to sleep through the early-morning ruckus.

This flicker was formerly considered to be a very common permanent resident in southern Indiana but rare in the north. It was "common everywhere throughout the warmer parts of the year." It is fairly common today throughout the state, especially during migration and in summer. Fewer winter in northern than in southern Indiana. The largest numbers recorded on single Christmas bird counts have consistently been from the Evansville and Oakland City areas. The maximum of 197 was in Gibson County on December 31, 1977. More than seventy-five per count have been recorded at Berne, Lafayette, Muscatatuck National Wildlife Refuge, Richmond, and Whitewater. At South Bend from 1947 through 1980 from one to thirty have been seen per count. The average is 9.2. The maximum number at South Bend was seen on January 4, 1981—the date of the 1980 Christmas count.

Nearly any habitat with fairly large trees supports this flicker, which seems equally at home in remote wooded tracts or about human dwellings. In more open areas, where they often feed, the birds make use of fenceposts and telephone poles, in which they sometimes nest. Migrating flocks are frequently seen feeding in impoverished old fields with bare soil, close-cropped pastures, golf courses, and similar sites where ants are found.

Spring migrants are evident in southern Indiana during March; throughout the state migration occurs mainly in March and April. James E. Landing observed about 600 flickers at Michigan City on April 6, 1958. A movement of flickers was reported near South Bend on August 16, but most fall migrants are first noticed from mid-September to mid-October. Warren S. Rowe saw about 150 at the Willow Slough Fish and Wildlife Area on September 26. These migrants, often seen in flocks containing as many as fifty birds, feed in grassy pastures, on air strips, in burned-over fields, on lawns and golf courses, and in sparsely vegetated old fields. The birds in these feeding flocks do not form a compact group; rather, individuals are widely scattered on the feeding ground. The stomach of a flicker has been known to contain more than 3,000 ants.

The flicker's fondness for ants explains why it is so much more territorial than the other woodpeckers in Indiana. Close relatives of the northern flicker that occur in South America also feed to a considerable extent on ants. The rather long, curved beak of the northern flicker is an efficient tool for probing for and catching ants, and the long, extensible tongue covered with a sticky mucous aids the birds in capturing prey.

Nests are usually in cavities of dead trees, frequently near the top of a rotting snag, as the painting shows. The birds use natural tree holes or excavate their own. They also next in boxes placed for them. Complete clutches of eggs are laid by the first week of May. Young may remain in the nest until at least July 1. Most nests examined contained from three to six eggs each, but the sample is small. The northern flicker is an indeterminate layer; if one removes eggs from the nest as they are laid the birds may continue laying for weeks. Barton W. Evermann removed thirty-seven eggs from a nest between May 4 and June 22. There is sometimes considerable competition between northern flickers and European starlings for nesting cavities and fierce physical combat (often won by the starling) sometimes results in the death of the woodpecker.

The great numbers of ants eaten during the period of the year when they are available are supplemented at other seasons by seeds, fruits, other insects, and corn. Flickers eat mulberries and fruits of red osier dogwood, hackberry, poison ivy, and Virginia creeper. They sometimes capture insects on the wing.

We have seen a striking specimen that is all white except for the yellow feather shafts, the yellow undersides of the wing and tail feathers, and a red crescent on the nape.

NORTHERN FLICKER

PILEATED WOODPECKER

Dryocopus pileatus

Great Black Woodpecker, Black Woodcock, Logcock, Great Black Logcock, Northern Pileated Woodpecker

Once a male pileated woodpecker has found exactly the right hollow tree branch on which to produce his far-reaching drumming noises, he will return to it day after day to advertise his territorial boundaries to other males and attract a potential mate. On quiet spring mornings his vigorous rapping can be heard at least a mile away. Hoosiers nowadays can, without much difficulty, experience the thrill of seeing one of these great birds, at least in southern Indiana—fifty years ago they were rarely seen.

Most early ornithologists concur that the pileated woodpecker was formerly very common here, but by 1898 it was found only in the more heavily timbered and sparsely populated parts of the state. Though at that time a permanent resident, there were practically no breeding records for the counties in which it was reported to be present. Until the 1930s many feared this woodpecker was becoming extinct in Indiana, but it persisted in the heavily wooded south-central hill region and began expanding its range in about the early 1950s. This expansion still continues; the general movement has been northward, to a great extent along wooded stream valleys. On December 28, 1975, forty-six pileateds were observed on the Nashville (Brown County) Christmas bird count.

The pileated used to be confined mostly to extensive, remote, heavily wooded regions. Thus, some of the refugia where the birds remained after the general decline in numbers included such places as Brown County State Park and the wooded hills of Jackson County. Today the species is apparently much more widely distributed over a more varied range of habitat—woodlots, residential areas, and along stream valleys supporting relatively narrow bands of forest, as well as the deep woods.

This woodpecker excavates nesting cavities in either dead or living trees. Entrances to nests are usually round (feeding excavations are rectangular). Harmon P. Weeks, Jr., examined a nest in Martin County that contained two eggs and two newly hatched young on May 12. Young in another nest fledged on May 28. Honeybees took over the nesting cavity of one pair of woodpeckers. Val Nolan Jr. observed a pilot black snake (black rat snake) enter a tree hole where pileated woodpeckers were thought to be nesting. The male woodpecker attacked (and probably killed) the snake.

As they feed on insect larvae and ants that live in the tree trunks, pileated woodpeckers make distinctive rectangular holes anywhere from three to five inches wide and four to twelve inches long. Sometimes they remove so much wood that the tree is damaged. They seem to prefer sassafras trees, no doubt because they attract a particular type of insect the birds like. Ants are known to be a favorite food of theirs. More difficult to explain are the excavations made by pileateds in creosoted telephone poles and in buildings, where one would judge that food was absent. The birds also eat various fruits, such as poison ivy berries, and at feeding stations take suet and corn. Near Nashville, where pileateds are plentiful, seven of them were in view around a feeder at one time.

IVORY-BILLED WOODPECKER

Campephilus principalis

We know of no extant physical evidence that this large woodpecker ever occurred in Indiana, but on the basis of its former reported range and early reports from Indiana we assume that it was indeed once a part of the state's avifauna. Butler thought that it had once been a local resident in southern Indiana, where it was already then extinct. Rufus Haymond had told him that ivory-bills formerly were present in Bath and Springfield townships, Franklin County, where they lived in swampy woods near the beaver ponds. There was also a report of this woodpecker from Monroe County, and Audubon mentioned its occurrence in Indiana. We hope that someday the remains of this fine woodpecker will be exhumed in some archeological site in the state. But even that could be misleading if Indians here (some tribes highly prized the beaks of ivory-bills) traded for woodpecker parts with Indians in other states.

PILEATED WOODPECKER

OLIVE-SIDED FLYCATCHER

Contopus borealis

Because of its choice of habitat during migration and its scarcity, this interesting flycatcher is relatively little known. Singing birds sometimes call attention to themselves by their distinctive *whip-three-beers* song. Normally the olive-sided flycatcher is a solitary species; it is rare for more than two to be found in a small area. The fluffy whitish patches of feathers on the olive flanks that give the bird its name are not always visible.

At the turn of the century this flycatcher was considered a generally rare migrant in Indiana, most numerous along the south end of Lake Michigan, and known from southern Indiana by a single record at Wheatland (Knox County). It is still an uncommon to rare spring and fall migrant, scarce or absent from numerous areas that lack suitable habitat.

Olive-sided flycatchers seem to prefer trees near water and characteristically perch on a dead branch in the top of a fairly tall tree. Here they watch for insects, darting out to catch them on the wing in the manner of most other flycatchers. The birds may use the same perch for several consecutive days. We have noticed that at the Jasper-Pulaski Fish and Wildlife Area and other sites, perches are frequently in dead trees or snags standing in the water bordering the marshes and swamps. One bird was observed perched briefly on the television antenna of a house near a woods.

Spring migrants probably enter southern Indiana during the last week of April, but most arrival dates are for the first week of May. Our earliest arrival date is April 21. Stragglers remain in northern Indiana until mid-June (one was seen in mid-July in Allen County). During the first week of August southbound migrants begin to appear along the northern border of the state; the latest fall date is October 9.

EASTERN WOOD-PEWEE

Contopus virens

Wood Pewee, Pewee

This drab, retiring pewee usually gives itself away by the plaintive call, usually heard from May to September, for which it gets its name. A nondescript flycatcher that may be confused with similar species, it is not well known, but is often found near human activity. Butler called it a common summer resident and the most abundant flycatcher in Indiana. It is still a common to uncommon migrant and summer resident locally.

In general the wood-pewee is a woodland bird, but it also frequents rather open, wooded places, including city parks and residential areas. It is a solitary species for the most part, although during migrations numerous pewees can be found in fairly close proximity along wooded or brushy roadsides.

In the wooded hills of south central Indiana, especially where we have studied the pewee in Jackson County, one is likely to find it along the dirt roads winding through the forest that are probably used as travel ways by the large flying insects upon which the wood pewee feeds. We have watched it pursue butterflies and dragonflies and have found its nest in such places. It hunts in much the same manner as other flycatchers—perching quietly, watching for passing prey. It darts out, snatches the insect in flight, often with an audible snap of the mandibles, then returns to the same or another perch.

The usual call, *pee-a-wee*, is rather soft and may not carry far in the deep woods. Butler wrote that the pewee's call "has a smooth, soothing sound that speaks of rest and contentment." This is a good analogy, for the pleasant song fits well the general mood of a lazy summer day in a Hoosier forest.

Spring migration normally begins in April (our earliest record is March 22), and reaches its peak in May. Butler noted that the wood pewee arrived at about the same date each year, relatively late in spring when the weather is usually fairly warm. He mentioned, however, that an unusual cold snap on May 20, 1883, killed many wood pewees. Few pewees remain in the state later than mid-October, but there is a November 7 sighting for Wayne County. We suspect that some very early and very late records for pewees may actually have been sightings of eastern phoebes, which may be present in winter.

EASTERN WOOD-PEWEE

The wood-pewee has been observed constructing nests in late May. It is not unusual for a pair to raise two broods in a season, resulting in some late nesting records. Very small young have been seen in the nest on September 4 and fully grown fledglings were being fed by the adults about September 29. Nests are usually saddled on a limb from eleven to fifty feet above the ground. Tree branches overhanging roads through wooded areas are frequently chosen as nesting sites. Dorothy Luther (1967) watched two young fledged from one nest help adults mold their second nest, in which they were fed by the parent birds.

The shallow, lichen-covered nest is well camouflaged and resembles a knot on a tree branch. When the adults are away from the nest it may be quite difficult to locate, even though it is often constructed in a relatively open site.

Much of the pewee's food consists of insects taken on the wing. We watched one capture a large, black swallowtail butterfly, which it swallowed wings and all. Like most other flycatchers, the wood-pewee is quite aggressive in defense of its territory and nesting site. One chased and collided with a white-breasted nuthatch, the two birds flying and clinging together until the nuthatch alighted on a tree trunk. Chases may involve swift dashes through the trees and much bill-snapping and excited calling.

Depicted tree: Pignut hickory (*Carya glabra*)

YELLOW-BELLIED FLYCATCHER

Empidonax flaviventris

Of all the members of the "confusing" genus *Empidonax* that are found in Indiana, this is undoubtedly the least well known. It is also the quietest of the group, and many migrants undoubtedly come and go undetected by birdwatchers. It is most likely to be mistaken for the Acadian flycatcher, especially in the fall, when both species exhibit quite similar plumages. It was formerly considered to be a rare migrant and occasional summer resident, "breeding" in northwestern Indiana. We have been unable to find a record of anyone actually finding a yellow-bellied flycatcher's nest in the state, but E. W. Nelson (1876) wrote, "The first of July, 1873, I found them quite common in a dense,

swampy thicket in northern Indiana, where they had probably nested." We have no way of determining whether Nelson's "nesting" record is valid, for early naturalists and ornithologists had great difficulty in correctly identifying the several small flycatchers of this genus. Today the yellow-bellied is an uncommon to rare spring and fall migrant, usually found in brushy areas, the understory of woodlands, or about marshes and swamps.

Spring migrants have been recorded from May 1 to mid-June. The species is a relatively late spring migrant and there is a queried observation for July 17. Fall migrants appear in northern Indiana about mid-August or slightly earlier, and have mostly departed by October 1. An unusual fall record is that of a singing bird at South Bend on October 8.

ACADIAN FLYCATCHER

Empidonax virescens

Green-crested Flycatcher

In Perry County there is a small hidden valley through which flows a shallow, rocky stream, in summer little more than a trickle. The valley is narrow, with sloping banks containing rocky outcrops; traces of an abandoned road roughly parallel the stream. Scattered along the stream are giant beech trees, interspersed with sycamore, butternut, black walnut, and tulip tree. The entire valley is completely shaded by the canopies of these large trees. Beneath the tree overstory there are various shrubs and spring wildflowers, and, at some spots along the stream, dense stands of jewelweed. In late May, this is a delightful place to walk and listen to the singing of a bird characteristic of such southern Indiana habitat—the Acadian flycatcher.

The Acadian flycatcher was formerly found throughout the state and in many localities was very common. Today, it is generally most common in southern Indiana, and may be locally present in large numbers where habitat is optimum. There are places in central Indiana where it is abundant. Alan W. Bruner found 161 singing males in the south half of Shades State Park in June 1979. It is found throughout the state, but may be locally absent or scarce in former prairie regions or where the forests have been cleared.

This woodland species is most abundant in heavily wooded areas where there are shaded valleys and a fair to good understory. Where extensive forested areas are absent, the birds may be found mostly along wooded stream banks, especially floodplain areas. During migration Acadians may be found "out of habitat," but unless they are singing these individuals are usually difficult to identify.

Spring migrants appear at most localities during May, but a few birds are present by April 15. It is possible that early migrants may not sing for a time after arrival and thus go undetected. Most have departed by mid-September, but there are records as late as September 30. There is considerable singing during early September and at least as late as September 21. The Acadian flycatcher has a dawn song and an evening song, both of which are quite prolonged and differ from the songs heard during the remainder of the day.

The small, untidy-looking nest is usually constructed from eight to twenty feet from the ground on a thin descending branch of a tree or shrub. Beech trees are favorite nesting sites in some areas and in northern Indiana witch hazel provides another commonly used nesting site. Nests are often placed over a trail, road, or stream. Eggs have been found from May 23 to July 7. The usual clutch

ACADIAN FLYCATCHER

NEST OF WILLOW FLYCATCHER

NEST OF LEAST FLYCATCHER

size is three. Twenty-one of the twenty-six nests for which we have data contained three eggs; the remainder contained two each.

This flycatcher feeds primarily on insects, including large dragonflies. Insects are usually taken on the wing, but the birds are capable of hovering and gleaning food from leaves and tree trunks.

An Acadian flycatcher is shown in the illustration; its nest, in a downy serviceberry (*Amelanchier arborea*) has the characteristic long streamers hanging down. The Acadian faces a willow flycatcher's nest in a sandbar willow (*Salix interior*). Below it is the much smaller nest of a least flycatcher, in an American hornbeam (*Carpinus caroliniana*).

ALDER FLYCATCHER

Empidonax alnorum

Traill's Flycatcher, Willow Flycatcher

For many years ornithologists lumped this flycatcher together with the willow flycatcher as a single species, sometimes called Traill's flycatcher, sometimes willow flycatcher. Thus, all records older than 1972 are hopelessly confused and therefore unusable. We now know they are two separate species, and realize that those birds we heard singing "strange songs" some years back were probably alder flycatchers rather than willow flycatchers with aberrant songs. In the field, song is the only way to separate the two species.

It appears that the alder flycatcher is widely distributed throughout Indiana during migration and present in summer (and presumably nesting) over the northern half of the state. To date no nest has been discovered, but twelve singing males were found June 1980 in the Beverly Shores area (Porter County).

The preferred habitat does not differ noticeably from that chosen by the willow flycatcher; it consists mainly of wet areas near bogs and marshes and along ditch banks where there are dense shrubs and thickets. At several locations, the alder and the willow flycatcher occur together. More information is needed to determine whether there are subtle differences in habitat and nest sites between the two species.

Migration dates, based on singing individuals, range from May 7 to July 25. Singing males usually cease their song in late July, and it is difficult to determine how long the birds are here in the fall.

WILLOW FLYCATCHER

Empidonax traillii

Traill's Flycatcher, Little Flycatcher, Alder Flycatcher

We were wading through the cattails around a small pothole marsh in northeastern Indiana searching for least bittern nests. From a bordering sedge meadow dotted with willows, dogwoods, and swamp roses we heard the distinctive *fitz-bew* song of the willow flycatcher. We soon located its nest, which was in the upright fork of a willow near the water. During the same summer, numerous other nests of this species were found in similar places across the northern end of the state.

It was formerly a locally common, generally distributed summer resident, especially in northern Indiana. Although it is still a fairly common to common migrant and may sometimes be a common resident in favored habitat, its overall abundance may have decreased. Lee A. Casebere and Mark A. Weldon found sixty-seven singing males at the Pigeon River Fish and Wildlife Area in the summer of 1977. We do not know if those from southern Indiana reflect a change in breeding distribution or if the species was overlooked by earlier naturalists.

During the nesting season, the willow flycatcher is most often found in shrubby vegetation about the borders of potholes and marshes and along brushy ditch banks. At other locations, it may be found in scrubby overgrown pastures and other similar habitats in upland sites some distance from water. Migrants probably frequent many nonwooded habitats, but the birds are not easily identified during migration unless singing. Migration dates (based on collected specimens and singing birds) range from April 24 to September 18, but further field work will probably reveal both earlier spring arrivals and later fall departures.

Nests are usually placed from three to six feet above the ground, often about thickets or dense clumps of shrubs such as hawthorn, elderberry, box elder, red cedar, sumac, elm, swamp rose, willow, red maple, or multiflora rose. Two to four eggs constitute a clutch; four is the most commonly observed number. Eggs have been seen in nests from June 6 to July 16 and young were still present in one nest on August 7.

Since the Acadian, willow, and least flycatcher are so similar in appearance, only the nest of this species is shown in the illustration.

LEAST FLYCATCHER

Empidonax minimus

Che-bec

One of the May sounds heard in Indiana woodlands is the vigorous, persistent *che-bec* call of the least flycatcher. The singer sits quietly, giving each call with open, uptilted beak and flicking tail. The song does not carry far, for it is rather soft. It is when this small, grayish flycatcher is actively singing and defending its territory that it is most conspicuous. Non-singing migrants can easily be missed, for they do not call attention to themselves.

Butler reported that the least flycatcher was a summer resident "in some numbers" in northern Indiana, but cited a single nesting record. He also listed it as a rather common migrant in the southern part of the state. It appears to us that this flycatcher has increased in numbers since about 1900. It is now a common to fairly common migrant throughout the state and is present in summer (and presumably breeding) across the northern quarter of Indiana. Although there are relatively few data concerning actual nests found, the least flycatcher is present (in some places, common) along the Kankakee River (Jasper, Lake, Newton Counties), in the Indiana Dunes region and in portions of Lagrange and Steuben Counties during summer. There were an estimated twenty-five pairs on the Pigeon River Fish and Wildlife Area in 1979.

Favored summer habitat appears to be rather open woodlands, bordering rivers, marshes or lakes where there are openings and brushy borders. Migrants may appear in other sites, such as on campuses, in city parks, orchards, brushy old fields, and the like.

Most migrants are recorded in May, although early arrivals have been observed by April 20. Most have probably left the state by the end of September, but there are fewer records for fall migrants because of the lack of singing at this season (and the difficulty of identifying silent birds). Stragglers have remained until mid-October (very rarely) and our latest date is October 18. If the weather is right, they may be locally abundant in spring. For example, there were forty-two least flycatchers at Richmond (Wayne County) on May 8, 1979.

Nests have been found in DeKalb, Hamilton, Jasper, Lake, Steuben and Washington Counties. We have reluctantly had to discount some reports of nesting least flycatchers, because we feel they were probably other species. Most nests were rather high; two were situated thirty and thirty-five feet above the ground. There are undoubtedly a few birds nesting in the southern two-thirds of the state, but singing males may be present in June (and, rarely, July). Charles E. Mills found one in Gibson County on July 4, 1982. The nesting record obtained by J. Dan Webster in Washington County in 1961 is remarkable for being so far south in the state. It is hoped that more knowledge of the breeding distribution of this interesting little flycatcher in Indiana will eventually become available.

In the illustration, only the nest of the least flycatcher is shown; Acadian, willow, and least flycatchers are very similar in appearance.

EASTERN PHOEBE

Sayornis phoebe

Flycatcher, Pewee, Bridge Pewee, Bridge Bird, Phoebe-bird, Pewit

On the moss-covered, rocky walls of the sandstone canyons of Shades and Turkey Run State Parks, eastern phoebes nest. Even in midsummer these canyons are cool and damp, for small, spring-fed streams flow through them. The canyon rims, sometimes seventy-five feet or more above the streams, are lined with large deciduous trees and in some places hemlock and yew. Rocky cliff walls were probably the usual nesting sites of this phoebe in Indiana before the settlers arrived and manmade structures became available. Northern rough-winged swallows share the rocky canyon walls with the phoebes during the summer and nest in niches among the outcrops.

Butler did not comment on the numerical status of the eastern phoebe in Indiana, but implied that it was common. From time to time, unseasonally cold spring weather decimates phoebe populations, which may take several years to return to normal. Such an event occurred in 1895 and there have been other striking population fluctuations. In general, this phoebe remains an uncommon to common migrant and summer resident locally. Some may remain all winter, mostly in counties along the Ohio River, but there are winter records for as far north as Tippecanoe County.

The eastern phoebe inhabits wooded areas, especially those with streams, rivers, creeks, rock outcrops, caves, quarries, and buildings. It occurs in non-wooded regions about marshes, at bridges, and about buildings.

It is an early spring migrant, sometimes appearing in southern Indiana by the last week of February. Most have left by November, except for late stragglers and wintering individuals.

Adults have been observed carrying nesting material by March 15 and a nest with five eggs was found April 7. Nests are constructed on bridges and culverts, on cut banks or rock outcrops, at the mouth of caves and mines, in or on buildings, on concrete spillways of dams and in basements of abandoned houses. There is widespread use of bridges as nesting sites throughout Indiana, a habit that was reported as early as 1875. Some pairs have complete clutches of eggs by the time the fire pink has bloomed along the rocky ledges where the birds nest. Two broods are usually raised per season and eggs have been found in nests at least as late as July 23. Weeks (1979) reported that the average number of eggs in 171 complete clutches was 4.7, with 3 to 6 eggs per nest. Territorial singing diminishes, and usually ceases, in late summer. There is some resurgence of singing in the fall and Edna Banta heard a phoebe singing on December 2.

Depicted plant: Fire pink (*Silene virginica*)

[SAY'S PHOEBE]

Sayornis saya

Pitelka (1938) published the sole record of this flycatcher for Indiana. Pitelka, Amy G. Baldwin, and Alfred Lewy observed a Say's phoebe in Porter County on April 4, 1937. This phoebe occasionally strays eastward from its normal range, but is considered an accidental visitor to Indiana.

GREAT CRESTED FLYCATCHER

Myiarchus crinitus

Northern Crested Flycatcher, Crested Flycatcher

This noisy woodland flycatcher is an attractive member of the family and although fairly common may be relatively unknown locally. Its loud *wheep* note carries far and is usually what brings it to notice. A pair of crested flycatchers will sometimes sing antiphonally, uttering alternate notes, producing a song that sounds as though it were rendered by a single bird. Considerable mention has been made in the literature of the fact that this species frequently adds the cast skin of a snake to its nest; sometimes part of the snakeskin hangs out of the nesting cavity.

Formerly the crested flycatcher was considered to be as common as the eastern kingbird, which Butler listed as abundant. It must be pointed out that there was then much more forested land in the state. Today the crested flycatcher remains a common migrant and summer resident, nesting throughout the state where there is available woodland habitat. It may be primarily confined to riparian tree growth in some counties that support relatively little forest, but it also utilizes woodlots, city parks, and other locations where trees are present.

Spring migration usually begins the last half of April, but there is an early record of April 12. The birds are most in evidence during May and June, becoming less vociferous in late summer, then calling again just before departure. Singing has been heard until September 13. The latest fall record is for October 6.

Nests are placed in tree cavities (especially knotholes),

GREAT CRESTED FLYCATCHER

old woodpecker nesting holes in trees and telephone poles, or nesting boxes (and mailboxes). The cylindrical, post-mounted newspaper delivery boxes seen in rural areas frequently serve as nesting sites. Nests have been observed from four to fifty feet from the ground. Most nests are not easily examined, so there is a shortage of data on egg laying dates, clutch size, and hatching dates. Some soft or smooth material is usually present in nests—

hair, feathers, fluffy plant materials, paper, cellophane, or snakeskin. Harmon P. Weeks, Jr., watched a crested flycatcher gathering hair from a dead opossum along the road. Nest construction has been recorded by May 4. The number of eggs per clutch in five nests was five or six, one clutch of five being completed by May 21. Large young have been observed in nests until July 6 and the feeding of young by adults has been reported until August 5.

WESTERN KINGBIRD

Tyrannus verticalis

Arkansas Kingbird

This western species was first reported from Indiana in 1939 by Donald H. Boyd. By the end of 1982, there were eighteen more records. Thirteen of these sightings were in the northwestern portion of the state, four in central Indiana. The birds are usu-

ally seen along roadsides, perched on telephone wires. Dates of occurrence range from May 29 to November 2. Seven were found in September and three each in June and August. There are single records from May, October, and November (one sighting was undated). There are records from ten counties, situated roughly in a line from Lake Michigan southeasterly to Jackson and Ripley Counties.

EASTERN KINGBIRD

EASTERN KINGBIRD

Tyrannus tyrannus

Bee Martin, Bee Bird, Dumb-bird, Kingbird

The red-tailed hawk came flying over the clover field on its way from a woodlot to a perch in an isolated tree. Suddenly, as it crossed an osage orange fencerow, an eastern kingbird flew up and attacked it from above, diving down and striking it on the back. The hawk hurried away. As soon as it left the kingbird's territory, the kingbird ceased its pursuit. Such belligerent and aggressive behavior is characteristic of this well-known flycatcher during the nesting season. People in rural areas are usually glad to have a kingbird around, for its presence helps to discourage hawks from invading their chicken yards. Bee keepers, however, sometimes feel that kingbirds eat too many bees and try to discourage them.

Butler knew the eastern kingbird as an abundant summer resident. Today it is a common migrant and summer resident throughout the state.

This is not a bird of the woodlands; it prefers fencerows, old pastures, orchards, pond, lake, and marsh borders, roadsides, ditch and stream banks, and other relatively open areas. Many nesting sites are located over water at the edges of marshes and ponds.

The eastern kingbird begins to arrive in southern Indiana during the last half of April. There is a very early record of March 21 for Monroe County. Peak numbers, often including relatively large flocks, are reached around mid-May. As many as twenty to fifty may be seen—although infrequently—and we have a record of seventy in such a flock. Fall migration is usually at its peak the last week of August and first week of September and flocks equal in size to those found in spring are present. The latest departure date is October 19, but this is quite unusual. Northern orioles are occasionally found with eastern kingbirds during migration. Ten orioles and fifty kingbirds were observed together in late August.

Nesting evidently begins in May. Ten of the twenty-seven nests for which we have records were built over the water. The overall average height of all nests was 15.2 feet. Ten nests constructed over water averaged 7.8 feet above the water and ranged from 3 to 25 feet. Seventeen nests over dry land averaged 20 feet in height and ranged from 5 to 50 feet. A nest at Hovey Lake was in a cypress tree out in the lake 75 feet from shore. Clutch size for twelve nests ranged from 3 to 4 and averaged 3.4. Nests contained eggs from May 27 to July 10 and young were found in nests until July 20. Two broods are evidently produced by some pairs.

Although much of the food of the eastern kingbird consists of insects, various fruits are also eaten. We have seen it feeding on fruits of sassafras and black cherry. Steven H. Glass and Donald Whitehead made some interesting observations involving eastern kingbirds seen on May 13, 1973, near Bloomington. A dense growth of ragwort (*Senecio*) had grown in a depression in a field. As the observers walked through the field, they were engulfed by swarms of insects. They noticed about thirty kingbirds flying up from the ground in the field and back into the ragwort. Later in the morning seventy kingbirds were counted sitting along a fence bordering the field. All six species of swallows native to Indiana were also feeding over the field.

Depicted tree: Black cherry (*Prunus serotina*)

SCISSOR-TAILED FLYCATCHER

Tyrannus forficatus

This spectacular flycatcher has recently been extending its range eastward and northward in the United States. It was first reported from our state by Karl E. Bartel (1948), who, with others, observed one at Wolf Lake (Lake County) on May 3 and 4, 1947. There have been seven additional sightings in five other counties (Daviess, LaPorte, Marion, Owen, Warren) since then. Dates of occurrence ranged from April 13 to July 28.

A surprising development in the history of this species in Indiana was the discovery on July 3, 1974, of a nest near Montgomery (Daviess County). Howell and Theroff (1976) published the details of this nesting. The nest was twenty-five feet above the ground in an isolated sycamore tree in a cornfield. Young were successfully fledged from this nest. One scissor-tailed flycatcher returned to the site in 1975, but did not remain. A scissor-tail was found in Owen County on May 11, 1976, and two were seen there on July 28, 1976. The remaining reports are of single birds.

HORNED LARK

Eremophila alpestris

Prairie Horned Lark, Shore Lark, American Lark

While driving in the open countryside one often sees sparrow-sized, brownish birds feeding along shoulders, or even on the road. The birds flush, showing pale outer tail feathers, and alight not far away in adjacent fields, where they are often difficult to see, for their coloration blends well with the soil and vegetation. Roadside foraging is a common behavior of horned larks, especially when the ground is covered with snow and roads provide about the only open sites to find weed seeds, spilled grain, and grit. In the summer, unpaved roads are widely used for dusting sites. From late fall to early spring, horned larks may be seen in large flocks, often with Lapland longspurs and snow buntings.

The horned lark is undoubtedly more numerous in Indiana than it used to be, for the cutting of the forests and cultivation of land have been of great benefit to it. Butler noted that it was a permanent resident and common in parts of northern Indiana (probably in the prairie re-

gions). He wrote, "They are evidently gradually extending their range as the country is more and more brought under cultivation." He first saw young in Franklin County in 1891. We consider it a common permanent resident throughout much of the state, but most abundant in northern Indiana, where single Christmas count maxima of more than one thousand have been recorded in Kosciusko, LaPorte, and St. Joseph Counties. Fair numbers also winter in southern Indiana, but most do not remain to breed there.

Horned larks inhabit rather extensive open areas, such as cultivated fields, airports, golf courses, native grasslands, grassy vacant lots, pastures, and the like. When snow is deep they may come (usually in small numbers) to bird feeders and are sometimes found with livestock near barns and in feedlots.

It is difficult to determine migration dates because of the presence of birds throughout the year. Flocks containing more than a hundred birds have been seen in Posey County the last week of February, but there is evidently some movement northward about this time. Summer residents begin to form flocks of more than twenty by at least mid-August. In some years, there is a major influx of fall migrants near Lake Michigan in late October. More than

190 horned larks passed toward the southwest in flocks of fifteen to forty at Geist Reservoir, near Indianapolis, on December 22, 1962.

Males establish their breeding territories early; we have seen them chasing each other as early as January 19. Courtship involves much singing and steep headlong diving flights by the males from high in the air to the ground. Eggs have been found in nests by mid-February; some early nests are destroyed by cold and snow. Young have been reported out of the nest by March. More than one brood may be reared, for eggs have been found in nests as late as July 5. Nests are on or slightly sunken into the ground and placed in clover fields, grassy areas, grain stubble, rough areas on golf courses, and similar sites. One was found on the chalked line of an athletic field. The usual clutch size appears to be four, but ranged from two to five (average: 3.7) in sixteen nests.

Horned larks feed on insects and seeds (especially in winter) and have been found eating foxtail, lamb's-quarters, pigweed, and wheat. They also take cracked corn at feeders, and glean grain from livestock droppings and from manured fields.

Depicted plants: two lichens, British soldiers and reindeer moss (*Cladonia* spp.)

PURPLE MARTIN

Progne subis

Few would argue with the proposition that a summer colony of purple martins nesting nearby is a desirable thing. Not only are they attractive and graceful birds, but they consume vast quantities of flying insects. It is said that the American Indians were the first people to provide nesting structures—theirs were made of gourds—in hopes of attracting them, and the custom continues today in rural areas.

Butler said little about the status of this martin in Indiana, but did mention that it was a well-known summer resident in most localities. He further stated, "In southeastern Indiana they are notably few in numbers, compared with those that summered there before the Sparrows came." The purple martin is still a common migrant and summer resident, but local abundance fluctuates greatly. House sparrows continue to be a problem, and the species is also susceptible to the spring cold snaps that sometimes occur after the birds have reached their breeding grounds. Forced by the cold and the shortage of flying insects to stay inside their houses, many birds die.

The purple martin is a bird of open areas. During migration it may be seen, often with other species of swallows, foraging over fields, lakes, and marshes. Nesting habitats are usually lawns, cemeteries, golf courses, or other similar sites where nesting boxes have been erected for them. Thus, most present-day breeding colonies are near human habitations. Roosting sites include shrubby trees about marshes and large trees in cities, which they frequently share with blackbirds, grackles, cowbirds, and starlings.

Spring migration begins early and martins have reached all parts of the state by the last week in March. Our earliest dates are March 4 (Jay County) and March 8 (LaPorte County). These early sightings are usually of birds seen at martin houses; early arrivals are invariably male "scouts" which often appear early, then leave, other martins coming to the site later. Large flocks are not usually observed in the spring. By mid-July aggregations of hundreds of purple martins have formed. The flocks grow in size, especially at roosts, and from 30,000 to 40,000 were reported at a roost in early August. Flights of hundreds of martins have been seen along Lake Michigan on August 11 and 13. On August 13, 1979, Raymond Grow saw 3,000 pass in Porter County in ninety minutes. Fall migration is evidently rather prolonged; the birds leave the nesting areas quite early. There are numerous records of late

PURPLE MARTIN

stragglers throughout September, but most have departed earlier. The latest sighting is October 12 (Lake County).

Before manmade structures were available, most martins probably nested in holes in trees or possibly about rocky cliffs. We have found a single record for martins nesting in trees in Indiana: Evermann and Clark (1920) reported that a pair apparently nested in a hole in an elm tree at Lake Maxinkuckee (Marshall County) in 1899. Adults were feeding young at the same site in July 1900. Jane L. Hine (1911) observed a pair nesting in a hole in a cornice of an old building "with an English Sparrow's nest on either side" in DeKalb County. No doubt the house (English) sparrow has taken a tremendous toll on nesting martins since it became so numerous in the state. This is still the most common problem with establishing martins in nesting boxes. A single reference to a nest with eggs has been found. The birds were constructing the nest April 25 and the first of four eggs was laid May 9. Young have been observed leaving nests from June 30 to August 17.

This martin feeds primarily on flying insects. A flock of some 2,000 martins was seen in a city park in mid-August. About seventy-five of them were on the bare ground of a baseball diamond, pecking at the soil. Although the observer checked the area, he could not determine what they were picking up. It may have been small bits of gravel.

TREE SWALLOW

Tachycineta bicolor

White-bellied Swallow

In late March, often even before the last of winter's ice has disappeared from lakes and marshes in northern Indiana, groups of tree swallows can be seen foraging for insects over the water. An early migrant, this species is another of the welcome sights of spring. Feeding birds, like other swallows, are almost constantly in motion, hawking insects just above the water or above the stands of cattails and other emergent vegetation. Birds in foraging flocks may be heard giving their "conversational" twittering calls. During late summer and early fall, all of the native species of swallows can be found together in large flocks feeding on some locally abundant insect food.

The tree swallow was formerly most abundant during the nesting season in the northern half of Indiana, where suitable nesting habitat was more prevalent, but it also nested in sloughs along the lower Wabash River valley and probably at other local sites in the southern part of the state. It was locally rare to abundant from area to area throughout its nesting range depending upon the habitat. Butler made no comment about its status during migration, but we assume that it was common. It remains a common spring and fall migrant and no doubt has expanded its breeding range, especially throughout the southern half of Indiana, because of the numerous reservoirs and other impoundments that now provide nesting habitat, particularly stands of dead trees killed by flooding.

During migration, tree swallows may be seen nearly anywhere, feeding over dry or wet areas, resting in great numbers on wires along roadsides, or passing overhead. Flocks tend to form near lakes, marshes, and other feeding and drinking areas. During the nesting season, most birds are found near water and many nests are placed in dead trees or snags standing in water.

Of the swallows that occur in the state, the tree swallow is the earliest spring migrant. It reaches northern Indiana by mid-March in some years. The earliest record is March 4 in Hamilton County. Flocks containing 500 or more may be seen in April or May. Flocks of 100 birds have been observed by mid-July, and by the middle of August groups of 1,000 have been reported. There were 4,000 tree swallows at Geist Reservoir, near Indianapolis, on October 7, 1978. Late stragglers usually leave the state by mid-November. One was at Lake Waveland on November 13. There are two unusual sightings for Gibson County, where singles were seen January 25, 1975, and February 23, 1980.

Nests are usually constructed in woodpecker nesting holes and natural cavities in dead trees, or in bird nesting boxes over or near water. Bluebird houses and other nest-

TREE SWALLOW

ing boxes on dry sites and holes in orchard trees are also used. Nests are lined with feathers, if available, and the birds seem to select white feathers when they have a choice. Nests may be as close to the ground as three feet or as high as seventy feet, but are usually relatively low. Eggs have been seen in nests from May 9 to June 3. Clutch size varied from three to six and averaged 4.3 in nine nests. Tree swallow eggs and wood duck eggs have been observed together in the same nesting structure. One swallow nest contained two eggs and three newly hatched young on May 24. The latest report of young in the nest was July 15. Nesting has been recorded from various counties throughout the state.

Food is normally taken on the wing, but Donald H. Boyd described an occasion when he saw tree swallows roosting in "bur marigolds," and feeding on bees that came to the plants. If the weather becomes inclement after tree swallows have arrived at their breeding grounds, flying insects may be scarce or absent. The unseasonable cold and lack of food weakens the birds and may kill them. Following one such cold spell, Ruthven Deane (1923) wrote: "I have seen hundreds of tree swallows that had collected on the bare limbs of dead trees bordering the Kankakee River at English Lake, Indiana, so benumbed by an exceedingly cold night in early spring, that they were unable to take flight when I struck the limbs with my paddle."

NORTHERN ROUGH-WINGED SWALLOW

Stelgidopteryx serripennis

Bank Swallow

The brown-backed swallows found near bridges during the summer are usually rough-winged swallows, which often nest in drainage pipes and crevices in the concrete bridge abutments. This swallow is also seen along streams and around gravel or sand pits during the nesting season. Rough-wings are also generally present in mixed flocks of migrating swallows in both spring and fall, but in the swirling masses of birds it is sometimes difficult to determine the species of individuals. The rough-wing is slightly larger than its very similar near relative, the bank swallow, but this is difficult to determine in the field.

Butler noted that the rough-wing was a summer resident throughout the state, but rare and in some places absent in the northern part. It was less abundant than the bank swallow. The rough-wing today is a common spring and fall migrant and an uncommon to common summer resident locally. Spring flocks of one hundred or more are occasionally reported and even larger assemblages may be observed in the fall. Five hundred were seen in Dear-born County on September 23, 1979. In most cases, the large numbers are found in company with other swallows. Extreme migration dates are March 27 and November 20.

Nests are usually in a vertical bank of clay, sand, or gravel, often along streams. Gravel and sand pits and stone quarries also provide similar nesting sites, as do rock outcrops created by road cuts. Many birds nest in pipes used for the drainage of bridges or buildings. Crevices in sandstone canyon walls are favored nesting sites for this swallow at both Shades and Turkey Run State Parks. Although it is somewhat unusual for rough-winged swallows to nest in trees, there are two such records for Indiana. In the illustration, the bird is using an old belted kingfisher nest.

Eggs are laid at least by May 10 and have been present in nests until July 2. The clutch size in twenty-seven nests varied from three to eight and averaged 5.3.

BANK SWALLOW

Riparia riparia

Sand Martin

Along the White River north of Martinsville at a place called Blue Bluff, there once were three small colonies of bank swallows, nesting in a stretch of cut bank. The largest housed several dozen birds. Similar breeding colonies have been found along other major Indiana streams in places where the stream banks are vertical. To see large numbers of bank swallows during the summer it is almost necessary to travel along rivers, or else happen on a gravel pit where the birds have congregated to nest.

This swallow was formerly an abundant summer resident and migrant, nesting in suitable habitat throughout Indiana. About 1923 or 1924, it nested by the hundreds in the gravel pits near Winona Lake (Kosciusko County). It is still a common migrant and summer resident, but only where its rather specific nesting sites—cut banks—are available. Migrants may occur almost anywhere there is food and water. All of the swallows may be found con-

gregating along roadsides on telephone wires or feeding in weedy fields.

Spring migrants appear at most places in April, but there are several records for March, the earliest being March 13 (Gibson County). The largest numbers have been reported during the first half of May, when flocks of 500 were recorded. Fall migration has been observed along Lake Michigan as early as July 6 and sometimes thousands of birds are found there in early August. On August 20, as many as 1,000 were seen in Gibson County. Most birds have departed by mid-September, but a few remain until the last week of that month; our latest fall date is October 1.

The birds construct nesting burrows by digging into vertical banks or stored piles of sand or gravel. The numbers of nests per colony in eighteen colonies ranged from two to 260. The three largest contained 101, 250, and

260 nests (therefore pairs) each. The remaining fifteen colonies averaged thirty nests each. Bank swallows and rough-winged swallows frequently nest together in mixed colonies. There are, however, scarcely any details on clutch size and egg-laying dates in reports of bank swallow nests found in Indiana. Nests with eggs have been found from May 30 to July 13 and the number of eggs per clutch varied from three to five. At one colony, all the young had left the nests by July 30; colonies are usually abandoned soon after all the young have fledged.

CLIFF SWALLOW

Hirundo pyrrhonota

Eave Swallow, Square-tailed Barn Swallow, Mud Dauber, Barn Martin

Early Indiana farmers knew cliff swallows well, for the birds built gourd-shaped nests of mud beneath the eaves of unpainted barns. As a rule the birds were usually welcomed; barn owners sometimes even tacked strips of wood on the sides of their barns under the eaves to enable the birds to attach their heavy nests more easily. Then the aggressive house sparrow appeared on the scene (it was first reported from Indiana in New Albany in 1867), and by 1900 its effect on nesting cliff swallows was devastating.

The cliff swallow was evidently quite rare in Indiana until about 1850, but during the next five decades apparently occurred locally throughout the state in some numbers. Butler recalled seeing during his childhood barns that supported "from one to two hundred nests" and wrote in 1913, "Where are the great numbers that formerly built their curious bottle-shaped nests of mud under the eaves of the farmers' barns?" And later (1928) he was prompted to write, "In recent years we have had to change our books regarding this swallow. Formerly it was an abundant migrant and summer resident. Now in many localities it is unknown. Few breed with us. What is their future?" There appears to have been an increase in cliff swallows from about the late 1920s to 1935, but for the period 1935 through 1960 there is only one nesting record. Few colonies were reported in the 1960s, but from 1970 to the present there has been an encouraging increase in the numbers of breeding colonies throughout much of the state. The cliff swallow today is an uncommon spring and fall migrant and a rare to uncommon breeder locally.

Before manmade structures (barns, bridges) were available as nesting sites, the cliff swallow constructed its nest on rocky cliffs, sometimes along rivers. Except for the colonies established at bridges, many current breeding colonies are in upland regions. Migrants, along with other swallows, frequent most habitats, gathering to feed over clover fields and other farmlands, near marshes or lakes, and along rivers. Some roosting sites are situated in stands of cattails about water areas.

The earliest spring record is April 1 (Cedar Lake, Lake County) and there are several other records for the first half of April, but most of the birds are present in May. Flocks of one hundred have been seen about mid-May. Some of the nesting colonies are deserted by mid-July, when the birds begin to flock. By late August at least three hundred have been seen in mixed flocks containing several thousand swallows. Most have departed by the end of September, but a few stragglers remain into early October; our latest record is October 21.

Cliff swallows nested along "the rock bluffs" on either side of the lower Wabash River about 1923 and nests were found on "high cliffs" along Sugar Creek in 1927. We have found no later references to this swallow nesting in these natural sites. Unpainted barns and barns built of rough-sawn lumber were usually chosen for the establishment of nesting colonies in the early years. Painting a barn necessitated the removal of nests and the birds had difficulty in attaching new nests to the freshly painted surfaces. Most of our information about the nesting habits of this bird in Indiana comes from Harmon P. Weeks, Jr., and his students, who since 1970 have been observing cliff swallows that nest under bridges at the Crane Naval Weapons Support Center in Martin County. At Crane, 268 nests were discovered on bridges in 1977. The earliest dates of egg laying were from May 1 to May 10. Second clutches were laid in many cases, the latest being observed from July 20 to 29. The mean clutch size for first clutches was 3.7; for second clutches 3.1. The number of eggs per clutch ranged from one to six (both extremely rare), and was most commonly three or four.

Nesting colonies on barns are sometimes initiated by a single pair of birds. There will be only one nest the first

year, but increasing numbers later. Twenty-eight such colonies averaged twenty-one nests each.

Irwin and Willis Eby have been instrumental in maintaining a cliff swallow nesting colony on a barn in Elkhart County. When swallows first nested there in 1930 they constructed six nests, of which three fell. The Ebys noticed that house sparrows usurped the swallow nests, and since 1930 strict house sparrow control has been practiced. In addition, nests that fell or were washed away by rain were replaced with artificial nests made of dipper gourds. The birds accepted the gourds from the start. When Raymond Grow visited this colony in the summer of 1955, he counted one hundred mud nests and forty-three gourd nests in use.

BARN SWALLOW

Hirundo rustica

Forked-tailed Barn Swallow

Anyone who lives on a farm or once did has seen barn swallows hawking insects over the lawn to feed to their nestlings in the nearby barn. This beautiful, graceful swallow normally constructs its nest of mud and grass lined with feathers in or on buildings. After the young leave the nest, family groups may be seen perched on fences or telephone wires.

Butler considered the barn swallow an abundant sum-

mer resident. Today, it is still a common spring and fall migrant and summer resident, nesting throughout the state. It is locally abundant during migration. Flocks of as many as 1,000 birds have been seen about mid-May and flocks of similar size form at least by late July. Thousands of barn swallows, usually accompanied by other swallows, migrate east to west along Lake Michigan (Lake and Porter Counties) during August and September of some years.

The largest inland concentrations have usually been observed near water, such as Geist Reservoir, but sizable flocks also forage over weedy or crop fields. It is assumed that this swallow also nested formerly on cliffs, but today it has adopted buildings and bridges for nesting sites.

Early migrants arrive in March, the earliest date being March 19 (Clark County), but at most Indiana localities the birds appear in April. Flocks of around twenty have been observed as early as June 30; these probably represent young birds produced by first broods of the season. The large groups have left by October 1, but numerous stragglers have been recorded throughout that month. Of the several November sightings, the latest is November 23.

Most barn swallow nests are in buildings, mostly barns and open sheds. Nests are also constructed on porches of occupied houses, above doors or atop light fixtures and in other sites where the nest can be attached. Many nests are on bridges and some of the bridge colonies may contain forty or more nests. Nests are made of mud and dried grasses and lined with soft materials, such as hair and feathers. Of forty nests at a bridge in Newton County in 1952 twenty-one contained feathers of the greater prairie-chicken, which is now extinct in Indiana. The nest colony was situated at the border of a tract used by the chickens. Domestic chicken, mallard, and great blue heron feathers were also found in these nests. Quite often the nest has some bottom support (such as an I-beam beneath a bridge) but many nests are simply attached to a vertical surface.

Egg laying begins by May 10 and eggs have been seen in nests until July 19. However, since young have been known to leave the nest as late as September 7, eggs must sometimes be present in late August. Clutch size for thirty-four nests ranged from two (complete clutch) to six and averaged 4.2. Two broods are reared per season.

BLUE JAY

Cyanocitta cristata

One of the most common and obvious woodland birds is the beautiful blue jay, which can also be found in residential areas, city parks, cemetaries, and other places near man. Jays are brightly colored, noisy, alert, and aggressive birds. Groups often gambol through the woods like a band of shouting small boys. Little escapes the sharp eye of the blue jay. Squirrel hunters dislike it, for it often sounds a loud alarm call when a human appears on the scene, and feeding jays drop many nuts and acorns that hunters often mistake for squirrel activity. In the fall, jays industriously gather and store acorns by the thousands, seemingly from daylight to dark, screeching and squawking all the while. All this lends a welcome touch of color to the drab landscape that signals the coming of winter.

The blue jay has evidently always been a common and

well-known permanent resident. Butler wrote that in the northern part of the state some of them migrate over winter. There are pronounced migrations evident today in spring and fall, but jays are just as abundant (possibly more so) along the northern border of Indiana in winter as they are elsewhere in the state, according to Christmas bird counts. The only areas reporting more than five hundred jays per count are the Indiana Dunes National Lakeshore and South Bend. In the winter of 1980–81 more than 725 jays were observed at each of these places. The maximum number of blue jays seen on a single count elsewhere in Indiana is 484 (Lake Monroe). The species is common and breeds throughout the state.

Although migration is a common behavior of the blue jay, it passes over silently in loose flocks of from four to fifty birds, and movements may often be missed by the casual observer. Spring migrants have been recorded from April 12 to May 20. The largest numbers have been reported along Lake Michigan, where on April 28, 1981, in a forty-five-minute period Raymond Grow counted about 2,210 jays flying from west to east. Fall migration has been detected from September 19 to October 29. Flock size during the fall seems to be about the same as that in spring; there is, however, one fall report of an unusually large group: 90. Hundreds of blue jays passed at Indianapolis on September 20. Very large flocks are often seen along Lake Michigan in spring, but there are no fall reports of large flocks there. Perhaps the birds congregate there in spring because of their reluctance to fly out over the water, then proceed to migrate along the shore rather than across the length of the lake. We have watched flocks of blue jays at Jeffersonville, on the north bank of the Ohio River, starting to cross the river only to return to shore and attempt it again once or twice before they actually crossed.

The blue jay is an early nester; nest construction has been observed as early as February 20. Nests are normally in various species of deciduous and coniferous trees, and usually from five to twenty feet from the ground, but some are as high as forty-five feet. Many nests are built against the main trunk of the tree. One nest was found between the rafters of a corncrib and another was under the porch roof of a lakeside cottage, both unusual blue jay nesting sites. Clutch size ranged from three to five eggs and averaged 4.4 for twelve nests. Eggs have been observed in nests from April 4 to June 14.

The calls of the blue jay are numerous and varied. They range from a soft song to harsh, raucous notes. One particular call mimics almost perfectly the common call of the red-shouldered hawk and creates confusion among birdwatchers and, perhaps, other birds.

Blue jays eat a wide variety of vegetable and animal foods, ranging from small vertebrates to corn and insects. They can deftly remove hulls from sunflower seeds or capture a flying insect on the wing. We were once releasing banded little brown bats and a blue jay pursued, but did not catch, one of them.

Interesting roosting behavior on the part of blue jays has been observed, mainly on dark, cold winter days. On three different occasions in midafternoon we have found individuals roosting close to the trunks of isolated red cedar trees in old fields. Others have been observed to go roost in the daytime in clumps of dead leaves hanging on a tree. Others were roosting about 2:30 P.M. in Norway spruces, where they remained throughout the night.

Depicted tree: Northern red oak (*Quercus rubra*)

BLACK-BILLED MAGPIE

Pica pica

American Magpie

This showy species has been recorded in Indiana on five different occasions, twice in April (1951, 1956), twice in December (1907, 1959), and once in January (1975). One of the birds found in December evidently remained until the following February. There are at least three additional sightings of this magpie for the state, but it is possible these were escaped cage birds.

Chansler (1910) published the earliest record of occurrence in Indiana: a black-billed magpie was seen near Bicknell (Knox County) on December 24, 1907; there was another sighting there (probably the same bird) on February 10, 1908. It frequented feedlots and slaughter pens and fed on offal. There are records of single birds from Delaware (where a bird was photographed by Robert H. Cooper), Fulton, Kosciusko, and Vanderburgh Counties. The Kosciusko County bird was observed eating house sparrows. Mr. and Mrs. Dale A. Zimmerman saw three magpies flying northward near Evansville on April 2, 1956.

The species should be considered an accidental visitor; no doubt other records will be obtained from time to time.

AMERICAN CROW

Corvus brachyrhynchos

Crow, Eastern Crow, Common Crow

One of the best-known, one might say notorious, birds that live here year-round, the crow, is regarded by many people as a pest, pure and simple. Farmers dislike its fondness for grain (including sprouting corn) and young poultry, and many birdlovers deplore its habit of raiding other birds' nests of eggs or young. But there are some who admire this black ruffian of the jay family for its resourcefulness, wariness, and ability to thrive in the face of persecution over the years. Many people used to have crows as pets, and they made intelligent and entertaining pets indeed. In Indiana, the crow has recently been placed on the game bird list in a move to perpetuate this interesting member of our native fauna.

Butler wrote that this crow was a very common permanent resident throughout the state, being less common in northern Indiana during the winter. Some of the communal roosts were estimated to contain 300,000 birds. There has been a great decline in the Indiana crow population since that was written. Although they are still common everywhere in Indiana, roosts are now much smaller and nesting birds far less numerous. There are few data pertaining to the abundance of crows so we have analyzed Christmas bird count information to assess winter populations. The largest numbers recorded per count are 17,804 (Posey County), 8,849 (Indianapolis), and 6,800 (South Bend). From 1944 to 1980, the number of crows per annual count at South Bend varied from 69 to 6,800. These fluctuations do not appear to follow a pattern and probably prevailing weather, number of birdwatchers in the field per count, and the proximity of large winter roosts all have an effect on the numbers seen per count.

Crows spend a great deal of their feeding and foraging time on the ground, where they obtain the greatest portion of their varied diet. They roost communally in pine plantations or stands of deciduous trees. They utilize all habitats, even coming into residential areas of cities, parks, cemeteries, golf courses, and the like to feed, roost, or nest where there are suitable wooded areas.

We have practically no data regarding migration, but flocks of crows (possibly migrants) have been seen flying south, high in the air, in October and November. However, crows move about over considerable distances during the day from feeding grounds to roosting sites.

Nest construction has been observed as early as March 1, and full clutches of eggs have been found by March 20.

Clutch size in fifteen nests ranged from three to five and averaged 4.3. One nest contained young as late as June 24. Nests are placed in coniferous or deciduous trees in woodlands, woodlots, fencerows (especially osage orange), along streams, in cemeteries, city parks, and orchards. Most nests are from fifteen to forty feet above the ground; one was sixty feet up. Butler mentioned that W. W. Pfrimmer reported a "rookery" near Newton and Demotte (Porter county) that contained five hundred nests within two or three acres. This must have been an unusual situation, for crows usually are not colonial during the nesting season. Edward R. Ford found fourteen crow nests in one day, April 18, 1920, in Porter County, although "no special effort was made to see how many nests could be found." We observed eleven nests along fifteen miles of the Blue River (Shelby County) on April 26, 1951.

Probably one reason for the success of crows is their varied diet, consisting of grain, fruit, seeds and nuts, insects, vertebrate animals, and carrion. They are opportunistic feeders, taking advantage of waste grain in the fields, dead fish along lakes and rivers, pecans and other mast, young and eggs of other birds, young eastern cottontails in the nest, fruits in season, and animals of all sorts killed along roadways. When a flock of crows is feeding, one or more birds act as sentries.

The vocalizations of crows are varied and numerous. There are special calls that signify danger and one that is an "assembly" call. When mobbing hawks and owls, as they often do, crows call persistently and excitedly.

Crows have been utilized for human food. Brennan (1923) wrote, "Crow squab, under the name of Italian Woodcock, is now being tried in some Chicago restaurants. It is said to be good." Some forty-five years ago crowburgers were served at the Illinois State Fair, in an attempt to encourage the destruction of the species.

COMMON RAVEN
Corvus corax

Northern Raven, American Raven, Raven

Between Ellsworth and Dubois (Dubois County), a sandstone cliff seventy-five to eighty feet high was formerly known as Ravens Rock because of the ravens that nested on shelves and crevices in and about its rock face. Ravens also used to be found about five miles south of Shoals (Martin County) at a site known locally as Ravens' Hollow. This general region proved to be the last stand for nesting ravens in Indiana; after 1894 it was evidently no longer used (Wilson, 1910).

Butler reported the raven as a rare resident and still breeding in the state in 1898, although he could cite no nesting records obtained within the past four years. Rufus Haymond (1870), in writing of Franklin County, said, "The raven was once numerous in this section, yet now so rare that I have seen but one during the past twenty years." The raven was reportedly "not uncommon" in Allen County during the winter of 1890–91, and the last record known to Butler for northern Indiana was for Boone County, in 1894. A raven was seen along Lake Michigan in 1919 and in October 1953. We know of no later Indiana records.

Wilson described nests found in Dubois County as "rough, constructed of large weeds, and sticks, and lined with hair and wool." A nest and eggs were reportedly collected in Martin County in 1894.

People living near the former nesting sites considered the ravens a sign of bad luck, and reported that they ate rabbits and took eggs. It is implied that the birds remained fairly close to the nesting sites, although they were observed "five miles from the rock."

BLACK-CAPPED CHICKADEE

Parus atricapillus

Chickadee, Black-capped Titmouse

If a bird popularity poll were taken in northern Indiana, the winner, for its attractiveness and spirit, especially in winter, would probably be this chickadee. It is a welcome visitor to feeding stations and always a pleasure to see or hear in the woods. Chickadees are usually at their peak of coloration in early December, just after they have acquired their winter plumage and before it has become worn from going in and out of the tree holes they roost in. In midwinter one often sees small mixed bands of chickadees, titmice, nuthatches, and other songbirds foraging together.

Where ranges overlap, distinguishing between the black-capped chickadee and the Carolina chickadee in the field can be difficult. Although the black-cap is slightly larger, this is difficult to ascertain. When the birds are in fresh plumage, the greater amount of white in the black-cap's wing feathers is a helpful field mark. Song, long considered the best method of separating the two, has been found unreliable in some places, for each species will sometimes also sing the song of the other.

Butler reported that the black-cap was an abundant permanent resident in the northern part of Indiana and a common winter resident "for a little distance south of the area" where it was found throughout the year. He noted that it was not often seen in southern Indiana, and then only as a winter visitor. Although the same generalization holds today, there have evidently been some local range expansions, especially in the northeastern part of the state, by the Carolina chickadee, into territory formerly occupied solely by the black-cap, and the latter is decreasing at such localities—parts of Adams, Allen, Huntington, and Wells Counties. Annual winter populations of black-caps vary widely, evidently because of periodic migrations, as indicated by the annual Christmas bird counts at South Bend, Fort Wayne, Indiana Dunes National Lakeshore, southern Lake County, and southeastern LaPorte County. For example, at South Bend there have been anywhere from 6 to 385 per count for the period 1951 to 1980; numbers may be very large one year, very small the next. During the winter of 1975–76 385 were recorded there, the largest number of black-capped chickadees for any Indiana Christmas census; the next largest, 361, was at South Bend the following winter. Only at South Bend and the Indiana Dunes National Lakeshore have more than 300 been reported on a single count.

BLACK-CAPPED CHICKADEE

One can expect to find the black-capped chickadee in forested areas, especially along rivers and in floodplain woodlands. It also occurs in brushy fencerows, woodlots, residential areas, and other more or less open tracts with trees suitable for nesting or feeding. Chickadees come readily to bird feeders in town, especially in winter.

Butler's account of the black-capped chickadee implies migratory behavior, for birds were present in winter southward from where they were found in summer. The extent of migration requires further study, especially of banded birds. Like present-day birders, naturalists a hundred years ago doubtless sometimes confused the two species. Butler stated that "in the absence of a series of specimens it is impossible to define the limits of the range" of the black-cap southward or of the Carolina northward. Peter G. Merritt (1977) studied both chickadees in nine counties in northeastern Indiana during the winter and early spring of 1975–76. Winter ranges of the two species overlapped by about 25 kilometers and spring ranges were separated by about thirty kilometers. This hiatus between breeding populations of the two species probably occurs westward through Indiana as well.

Despite the fact that the black-capped chickadee is such a common and familiar bird, nesting data are extremely limited. Chickadees when nesting become quiet and secretive, and are very hard to find. Birds have been seen excavating a nesting hole in a stump on April 21 and carrying food to young on May 2. One nest contained five eggs. Young left one nest on June 24. Nests are constructed in old woodpecker nesting holes or natural cavities of trees, or in bird nesting boxes, usually at no great height. The chickadees are able to excavate their own nesting cavities in partially rotten and other softer woods of stumps and snags. Nesting records thought to be authentic are largely for the northern third of the state, as far south as Madison County. The species may nest farther south occasionally.

Summer food includes insects and other invertebrates, plus seeds and fruits. In winter chickadees eat a wide variety of seeds and have been observed several times eating the fruits of poison ivy. One observer watched this chickadee pecking into the older stems of cattail, presumably to extract insect larvae. The birds take sunflower seed, suet, and numerous other foods provided at feeders.

CAROLINA CHICKADEE

Parus carolinensis

Chickadee

This restless little mite is usually seen busily foraging in wooded or brushy areas. Its rapidly uttered *chick-a-dee-dee* call is faster than the similar call of the larger black-capped chickadee, but it takes a trained ear to detect this. One may see the Carolina busily examining a cluster of dead leaves or hanging upside down on a sweet gum seed ball high in the air. Chickadees are seldom still for long and appear to have boundless energy.

The Carolina chickadee used to be an abundant resident throughout southern Indiana and occurred as far north as Carroll County, where according to Butler it and the black-capped chickadee were both said to be resident. We do not know the exact limits of the original range of the Carolina, for the two species were confused so often it

created a real problem. But it appears that the Carolina has moved northward (and may still be expanding north) in the northeastern section of the state. It is still a common permanent resident in southern Indiana and found throughout the southern two-thirds of the state. It nests north at least to Grant County. More than three hundred have been recorded on single Christmas bird counts in Tippecanoe and Vanderburgh Counties.

Carolina chickadees are found in habitats similar to those that harbor black-capped chickadees. Forested areas, brushy and wooded stream valleys, forest edges and adjacent overgrown fields, woodlots, and residential areas are all suitable.

Although it appears that black-capped chickadees mi-

grate, there is no evidence that Carolinas do. Local seasonal movements probably occur, since birds may move from winter to summer ranges no great distance apart (Merritt, 1977).

Nests are constructed in woodpecker nesting holes and natural cavities in trees or stumps and nesting boxes. One pair nested for two consecutive years in the rotted-out top of a fencepost; another built a nest in a large dead tree in an open field. Butler mentioned a nest in a hole in a fence rail. Nests are frequently lined with hair. Distance from the ground varied from three to thirty feet and averaged about nine. One nest was under construction in late March, but this may be quite early. Full clutches of eggs have been found by April 24. Adults have been observed feeding fledglings out of the nest on August 10. Fifteen clutches of eggs ranged from 4 to 7 per clutch and averaged 6.3.

We have seen Carolina chickadees feeding in winter on the seeds of sweet gum, tulip poplar, flowering dogwood, and staghorn sumac. Butler reported that this chickadee would perch on an apple and extract a worm from within the fruit. It eats a variety of seeds and suet at bird feeders. Where their ranges overlap, both species of chickadees may be found foraging together in small groups.

Depicted plant: Trumpet honeysuckle (*Lonicera sempervirens*)

BOREAL CHICKADEE
Parus hudsonicus

Brown-capped Chickadee, Hudsonian Chickadee

This chickadee was on Butler's hypothetical list. On November 20, 1951, Raymond Grow (1952) obtained the first record for the state when he discovered one in the "pinery" in Porter County feeding on jack pine and goldenrod seeds. At least three more were found in Lake and Porter Counties later in the winter of 1951–52, and two birds lingered near Dunes State Park until at least April 18, 1952. One was banded and photographed near Gary by Mr. and Mrs. Floyd Maffit.

The next record was an individual found at the Fox Island Nature Preserve (Allen County) on May 8, 1976, by several persons. It was photographed by James A. Haw, Jeff S. Moore, and perhaps others, and was last seen there June 1, 1976. Interestingly enough, one (the same?) was reported at Fox Island on January 3, 1977. Thomas Alexander reported a boreal chickadee at his feeding station near Bloomington (Monroe County) on October 31, 1976, a considerable distance south of the other observations.

The boreal chickadee can only be considered an accidental visitor to Indiana.

CAROLINA CHICKADEE

TUFTED TITMOUSE

TUFTED TITMOUSE

Parus bicolor

Peter-Peter, Sugar Bird

In early spring, at about the time when the operators of maple sugar camps start tapping their trees, the woodlands ring with the *peter-peter-peter* calls of the tufted titmouse. In some parts of the Midwest it is known as the sugar bird. Actually, titmice can be heard singing at any time of the year, including warm winter days, but their spring song sounds especially enthusiastic and spirited. A whistled imitation of it will usually get a quick response —the singer comes close and peers at the intruder with its black, beady eyes, nervously hopping about, its expressive crest fully extended, and calling persistently.

At the turn of the century the tufted titmouse was an abundant permanent resident in southern Indiana and occurred in varying numbers throughout much of the northern half of the state. It was reportedly absent around the southern end of Lake Michigan. At many northern localities it was absent some years or parts of some years, evidently because the species was then just beginning to

expand its range. There is certainly no shortage of tufted titmice in northern Indiana today. At the Indiana Dunes National Lakeshore, from 94 to 197 per year have been recorded on annual Christmas bird counts from 1972 to 1982. More than 200 per count have been observed at Evansville, Lafayette, Terre Haute, and South Bend.

Titmice frequent all types of woodlands, woodlots, brushy and wooded stream valleys, residential areas, city parks, wooded cemeteries, and the like. Some observers feel that during the winter this titmouse tends to wander from the deep woodlands to more populated areas, especially where feeding stations are maintained, and to the brushy borders of stream valleys and floodplain forests.

Butler's account of the tufted titmouse implies that some migration was evident in northern Indiana around 1880 to 1890, for at some places birds were present only during a single season of the year.

Nest building has been observed by mid-April and

nests containing young have been seen on May 1. Nests are usually in holes in trees, snags, stumps, wooden posts, hollow iron posts, and nesting houses. We have found no record of a nest with eggs, but from four to six young have been found per nest. Many nests are quite close to the ground (four to eight feet). The birds like to line their nests with soft materials, particularly hair. Titmice have been seen trying to take hair from a human's head, from a sleeping dog, and from a squirrel in a tree. One bird attempted to remove bristles from a shoe brush.

Although throughout most of Indiana one can recognize the song of the tufted titmouse, there are local dialects. One of the most striking is that of the birds at Turkey Run State Park, which visitors familiar with the song of the species often fail to recognize. Martin L. Fisher heard a tufted titmouse singing at night.

Seasonal foods include insects and seeds. Titmice have been seen in winter feeding on the fruits of flowering dogwood (Harmon P. Weeks, Jr.). Sunflower seeds are readily taken and adults sometimes feed them to their fledged young.

RED-BREASTED NUTHATCH

Sitta canadensis

Red-bellied Nuthatch

In mid-September, when flowering dogwood and poison ivy leaves are turning red, spotted jewelweed is in bloom, and monarch butterflies are migrating southward, the forests are fairly quiet. If you watch carefully at this season, you may see migrant red-breasted nuthatches foraging in wooded areas with several species of warblers and other seasonal migrants. The nuthatch is likely to be silently and industriously climbing about on tree trunks searching for food. Its call is higher pitched than that of its larger relative the white-breasted nuthatch, and has been likened to the sound of a small tin horn.

Butler wrote, "The Red-breasted Nuthatch is a bird of very irregular and peculiar distribution." Then as now, its abundance and occurrence apparently varied greatly from year to year. He mentioned a breeding record from Carroll County in 1878 and made reference to possible nesting in the northern part of the state, but gave no details. Winter numbers still fluctuate greatly for any locality, as is evidenced by annual Christmas bird counts; there are flight years, when the species is common, and years when scarcely any appear, but some are always present. The largest number recorded for a single count is forty-seven (December 30, 1965, Warrick County), but thirty or more have been seen at five other localities. In general, the largest numbers are usually seen in the northern half of the state, but in good flight years more than thirty per count have been found in extreme southwestern Indiana. There have been seven nesting records from 1965 to the present.

This nuthatch occurs in most wooded habitats, but, unlike the white-breasted nuthatch, shows a decided preference for coniferous trees, especially in winter. It readily comes to feeding stations and may nest near human dwellings.

Since so few red-breasted nuthatches nest in the state, fall migration is usually evident. It begins the last half of August; an early date is August 8. Throughout most of the state, however, fall migrants first appear in September. Forty were near Baileytown (Porter County) on September 5–6, 1957. Many birds are still present in May and the departure of spring migrants broadly overlaps the dates of nesting. Thus it is difficult to separate possible nesting birds from late migrants. There are several observations for early June (and later) at localities where the species is not yet known to have nested.

After 1878 there were no Indiana reports of nesting by this nuthatch until 1931, when it nested in Howard County. It nested in Elkhart County in 1965, 1966, and

RED-BREASTED NUTHATCH

1980, according to Merle E. Jacobs. Other nestings were as follows: Vigo County (1979); St. Joseph County (1981 and 1982); Marion County (1982). Since the usual breeding range is generally considerably to the north of Indiana, the recent dramatic increase in breeding records, especially so far south, is difficult to explain. Adults were seen excavating a nesting cavity on April 24 and feeding young on May 8 at one nest site. No one has reported a nest containing eggs, but several of the nests under observation fledged young successfully. All nests were in tree holes or nesting boxes and situated from five to fifty feet above the ground. At two nests (one in a natural cavity, one in a nest box), the adults had smeared pitch from coniferous trees around the entrance hole.

Winter foods of the red-breasted nuthatch include seeds of red pine, jack pine, white pine, cantaloupe, honeydew, and sunflower; hickory nut kernels, coconut, lard, and suet. An occasional bird at a feeder will be so tame it can be fed from the hand. One bird stored sunflower seeds on evergreen twigs and on the ground beneath evergreen trees. Another stored white pine seeds.

WHITE-BREASTED NUTHATCH

Sitta carolinensis

Tomtit, White-bellied Nuthatch, Sap Sucker, Carolina Nuthatch

The nasal *yeank, yeank* call of this trim and energetic nuthatch can be heard most of the year, except for the nesting season, when it often becomes quiet and inconspicuous. From its characteristic way of foraging up and down tree trunks and creeping along large branches, even upside down, it might be taken for some kind of woodpecker. But it does not possess the stiffened tail feathers of the woodpecker. Nuthatches are among the few species who can descend a vertical tree trunk head first. They get their names from their habit of holding a seed or small nut in their feet, then hammering it open with their beaks—"hatching" it. The white-breasted nuthatch is often a member of those aggregations of woodland birds that forage together in winter. Butler noted that at this season this nuthatch might be seen "keeping company" with chickadees, tufted titmice, downy woodpeckers, juncos, and tree sparrows, all "moving about for the sake of food and enjoying each other's company."

This nuthatch was formerly a common permanent resident throughout the state, possibly less common in winter than in summer in the northern portion (Butler, 1898a). It enjoys much the same status today wherever there is suitable habitat, but appears now to be equally abundant in winter in all sections. More than one hundred per count have been recorded on Christmas bird counts at Berne, Fort Wayne, Grant County, Lafayette, South Bend, and the Indiana Dunes National Lakeshore. The largest number seen on a count is 282 (South Bend). Winter populations appear to fluctuate from time to time, but whether this is the result of migrations we do not know. For example, on thirty-seven Christmas bird counts at South Bend from 1944 to 1982, an average of 72 were seen. Numbers per count ranged from 14 to 282 (on December 27, 1981). On December 26, 1982, 204 were counted.

All wooded habitats are frequented by the white-breasted nuthatch and its requirements are much the same as those of the red-breasted nuthatch.

Although this nuthatch breeds throughout Indiana, there are relatively few nesting records. Nests are situated in tree cavities and nesting boxes (one was in a house), and their contents are frequently impossible to see without destroying the nesting site. Adults were seen entering and leaving a hole in a tree on March 3, and a nest was built there later in the season. One pair was carrying bits of tree bark to a nesting hole on April 9. A nest containing six eggs on April 2 was composed almost entirely of whitish hair from a pet dog chained nearby. Another nest held six young on May 6. Nests varied in height from four to twenty-five feet.

Nuthatches eat a variety of foods. Sunflower seeds are a favorite at feeding stations, as is suet. One observer watched a male feeding a female shelled sunflower seeds in late February. A white-breasted nuthatch was seen drinking sap from borings made by a yellow-bellied sapsucker. Other foods include beetles, ants, caterpillars, spiders, acorns, and corn.

For some unexplained reason, at Lake Maxinkuckee the vernacular name of this nuthatch was pumpkin-seed.

[BROWN-HEADED NUTHATCH]

Sitta pusilla

This accidental visitor has been reported but once in the state; Butler had it on his hypothetical list. Archie F. Wilson found one in Whiting Park (Lake County) on April 5, 1932, and Donald H. Boyd verified the identification the following day. Wilson took copious notes (now in our files) describing the plumage and calls of this bird, which he observed with binoculars for a long time from a distance of about twenty feet.

BROWN CREEPER

Certhia americana

American Creeper

Along the Wabash River just below Lafayette grow giant eastern cottonwood trees, some of them at least eighty feet tall and four feet in diameter, with deeply furrowed, thick bark. In winter we can always find brown creepers on these trees, for the birds can apparently be assured of getting a good meal here by extracting insects from crevices in the bark. The creepers alight near the base of a tree, climbing upward in a spiral as they forage along the trunk. When near the top, they fly down at a steep angle to alight near the base of a neighboring tree and repeat the whole process. The creeper usually goes silently about its business; its infrequent calls are soft and high-pitched, and do not carry far.

Butler considered this creeper to be a very common migrant throughout the state. It was an irregular winter resident in parts of Indiana, especially the southern part. Butler knew of breeding records for the northeastern section, where he thought the species might be a rare permanent resident. Winter populations are consistently large at Lafayette; forty or more have been seen per count on eleven Christmas bird counts. The largest number seen on a Lafayette count was 193. No other locality has reported as many as forty per count, but twenty or more have been seen at nine places, all in the northern two-thirds of the state. There is only one additional nesting record since 1900.

In addition to the tall trees along streams, the brown creeper occupies many other wooded areas. There are several records of its foraging on the outside walls of buildings and roosting either inside or outside at night. Summer and nesting habitats are usually swampy wooded areas.

Even though the brown creeper is a permanent resident in the state, there are marked spring and fall migrations. Spring migration appears to peak in April. After the April 16, 1960, storm over Lake Michigan, forty-seven dead creepers were found along the lake shore. Thirty creepers were seen in Porter County on April 24. There are relatively few fall records involving large numbers of creepers. The birds begin to appear in northern Indiana in early September and the largest numbers are normally reported on Christmas bird counts. During the first week of October in 1924, Donald H. Boyd of Whiting found that numerous birds were roosting at night both inside and outside buildings and on their outside walls; he captured and banded ten. He remarked on their docility when handled.

R. W. McBride found the nest of a brown creeper near Golden Lake (Steuben County) on May 8, 1882. The nest, under the loose bark of a dead tree, contained six eggs and was four feet above the water in a swampy area. McBride also reported a set of eggs taken from a nest at Fox Lake (Steuben County) in May 1883. Amazingly, it was not until a century later that the next nest was found in Indiana: on June 3, 1982, Jerry M. Skinner and others found a pair of brown creepers in Posey County carrying nesting material. The nest was in a crevice in the bark of a dead cypress tree and was located about eight feet above the water. Neither the contents nor the fate of the nest was determined. Posey County and Steuben County are at the extreme opposite corners of the state.

Brown creepers have been observed in June or July in seven additional counties from 1948 to the present. It is quite likely that the birds nested in some of these places, especially at the Kankakee Fish and Wildlife Area, where they have been seen repeatedly. Five of the counties (Allen, Elkhart, Noble, Porter, St. Joseph) are in the northern one-fourth of Indiana; the others are Johnson, Marion, and Monroe Counties.

To Amos Butler every bit of nature was worth while; a small, unspectacular bird fascinated him as much as one that was large and brilliantly colored. He used the drab little brown creeper as an example in earnestly chiding those unobservant folk who look but never really see the wonders about them:

This Creeper is colored so near the markings on the trees that few people see it, and to most persons it is a rare bird. When its piping notes are known, one realizes that, before, he was often in a woods peopled with interesting birds but beyond occasionally seeing one fly from one tree to another, he did not know of their presence.

Butler had noticed that in the fall brown creepers are sometimes found in "little mixed parties" of chickadees, downy woodpeckers, and other "chosen spirits," but that in the spring (and occasionally in fall as well) their usual associates were golden-crowned kinglets. "I never saw so many birds of these two species as I did on April 12, 1897," he reported. "The woods were alive with them."

Creepers obtain the bulk of their food from tree bark, where they capture beetles, bugs, spiders, and other invertebrate animals. At bird feeders they sometimes eat suet.

ROCK WREN

Salpinctes obsoletus

There is a single record for this western species in Indiana. About October 18, 1977, Robert Farlow found one on a rock pile near his patio, a few miles from Winchester (Randolph County). It remained there, dividing its time between the rock pile and a small pond nearby, until October 21 (Carter, 1978). A number of people saw this accidental visitor and several obtained excellent photographs of it (cover and page 50, *Indiana Audubon Quarterly*, 56, No. 2).

CAROLINA WREN

Thryothorus ludovicianus

Great Carolina Wren, Mocking Wren, Large Wood Wren

While walking along the brushy, wooded bank of a small creek, you will often hear a loud, rollicking song coming from a thicket, a tangle of vines, or a brushpile. If you make a few squeaking sounds by kissing the back of your hand, a large, cinnamon-colored wren may pop out of the tangle, curious about the intruder. The bird may then perch in plain view and give its loud song. This is typical behavior for the Carolina wren.

Butler reported that it was abundant as far north as Franklin and Knox Counties, common at Terre Haute, and fairly common at both Lafayette and Bloomington. He further noted that it was rare in Carroll County and DeKalb County (but increasing), and at Greencastle, Michigan City, Richmond, and Wabash. At several localities in northern Indiana it was known as a seasonal straggler. Reportedly, there were virtually none in extreme northwestern or in east-central portions of the state. Butler wrote, "Ten to fifteen years ago this was the House Wren of the Whitewater Valley. They nested more often about houses and outbuildings than in thickets, brush piles, fence corners, and fallen timber. Now it is changed. Bewick's Wren has appeared upon the scene and has become the domestic Wren."

The winter of 1976–77 will long be remembered as the one that virtually silenced the Carolina wren throughout the state. At nine selected sites with good records, 432 were recorded on the 1976–77 Christmas bird counts;

on the 1977–78 counts 23 were seen; and only 9 were found in 1978–79. An increase has been noted in each of the following three winters, but only 57 were reported in 1981–82 and 151 in 1982–83. Winter kill has happened in the past and no doubt will happen again, for the Carolina wren is best adapted to warmer climates than ours. Until the recent population decline, it was a common permanent resident throughout the southern two-thirds of the state, as far north as Lafayette, where 89 were seen on the 1976–77 Christmas bird count. The largest numbers seen per count were 110 and 104 at Evansville during 1976–77 and 1974–75, respectively.

Little is known about migration, but it is interesting that after the April 16, 1960, storm over Lake Michigan fourteen dead Carolina wrens were found along the beach there.

Butler wrote that "the breeding season appears to extend almost the year around," and cited a report of nesting two consecutive winters at one site, with eggs in the nest about December 1. One wonders whether these were nests in which unhatched eggs remained that birds were using for winter roosts.

Nests are constructed in many places, often in and about buildings. Some of the places where they have been found are a cardboard container; nesting boxes in a chicken house; beneath bridges; in pipes; in windows, nooks, and crannies of buildings; in a cavity in a sand-

CAROLINA WREN

stone cliff; in the roots of a fallen tree; and in a tangle of grapevines. Butler observed a nest built in a sheepskin hanging on a back porch. Nests are usually quite bulky structures of leaves and twigs lined with hair and feathers. Nest building has been observed from March 13 to August 31. The earliest full clutch of eggs was found March 20, and clutch size averaged five eggs (four to six) for thirteen nests. Twelve nests averaged five feet above the ground, and the highest was about ten feet. Earl Brooks (1963) observed four Carolina wrens building a single nest.

Much of the Carolina wren's food is obtained on or near the ground and the birds forage in all types of dark crannies, tangles of brush, and litter on the ground. One was seen inside the hollow base of a tree. It is fond of peanut butter and suet at feeding stations.

This wren sings throughout the year, suddenly bursting forth in song even on cold winter days. It sometimes sings at night. Many people confuse its song with that of the Kentucky warbler, which shares its haunts in summer.

It frequently roosts, especially in winter, in groups of as many as five, in nests of its own species or nests of the eastern phoebe, and about buildings and cave entrances. Two habitually roosted one winter in a hanging flowerpot on a cabin porch.

Depicted plant: Mertensia (*M. virginica*)

BEWICK'S WREN

BEWICK'S WREN

Thryomanes bewickii

Long-tailed House Wren, Long-tailed Wren

The saga of the Bewick's wren in Indiana is an interesting one. It was apparently first detected in the state a few years before 1869, enjoyed a widespread distribution, then began a marked decline about thirty years ago. It is becoming more and more difficult to find it today. We feel confident that many Hoosiers in southern Indiana, where this wren was formerly quite common, did not differentiate between it and the house wren. Amos W. Butler and others have written about the relationships of the Bewick's, Carolina, and house wrens in Indiana, but many details about the relative abundance of these species at particular localities are lacking.

By 1897, said Butler, the Bewick's wren was "a common summer resident throughout the greater part of southern Indiana and in the lower Wabash Valley, at least,

north to Knox County," was a permanent resident. He added that the recent extension of the range of Bewick's was noteworthy. In 1897, he found six pairs nesting in a one-half-mile-by-one-mile area in Franklin County, and the species was recorded northward to Tippecanoe and Wabash Counties. It had reached the northern border of the state (Lake County) by at least 1921.

In the late 1940s and early 1950s it was common and widely distributed in the south-central Indiana hill country. Its loud song could be heard in town after town in the spring, especially in Harrison and Washington Counties. It was observed on twenty-one Christmas bird counts as far north as Adams, Tippecanoe, and Tipton Counties, but was most frequent at Evansville (Vanderburgh County). There are nesting records from throughout the state, but only three are later than 1956. The species has rarely been reported from anywhere in Indiana during the past ten years.

The Bewick's wren formerly was found in open woodlands, fencerows, thickets, and orchards, according to Butler, but it soon adapted to nesting near human dwellings, thus becoming the "house wren" at many places in southern Indiana. Butler noted that at Brookville (Franklin County) by 1897 the Bewick's wren was found mostly near buildings, where the Carolina wren had formerly been present and the house wren was very rare. Our experience and that of many others has been that Bewick's are normally found near buildings, whether inhabited or abandoned. It is possible that the southward expansion of the nesting range of the house wren into many parts of southern Indiana where it was previously known only as a migrant may in some way have influenced the habitat chosen by the Bewick's wren. The eggs in one Bewick's nest were pierced by a house wren.

The Bewick's is an early spring migrant, usually arriving one to two weeks (or more) before house wrens do. In parts of the state where it is not known to spend the winter, spring migrants have been recorded from March 18. Most first appear during the first half of April. The latest fall record is October 21, but there are few observations for this season. Samuel E. Perkins, III, and others recorded nine in the Hovey Lake area on May 13, 1929.

This wren chooses almost any nook or cranny in which to construct its nest: old cars in junkyard, old can on porch, mailbox, lantern hanging on wall, gourd, ball of twine in binder, drawbar of railroad car, old buggy top, grape basket, farm machinery toolbox, bucket hanging in shed, old sack hanging on fence, wood rack near building, bluebird box, and mantelpiece in deserted house. Eggs have been found in nests as early as March 20 and eleven nests contained from four to eight eggs each and averaged 5.7. More than one brood is sometimes reared and nest construction has been noted as late as August 4. At one nest, the adults were feeding their young caterpillars of the catalpa sphinx moth. Three were dusting on a gravel road in late July.

HOUSE WREN

Troglodytes aedon

Short-tailed House Wren, Western House Wren

Judging from the numbers of nesting boxes of all descriptions that one sees throughout the state, the popularity of the house wren among Hoosiers must certainly be high. It is a backyard bird, energetic and a good songster, and many people are pleased to have a pair of "Jenny Wrens" nesting in the yard each summer. Unfortunately, this wren is destructive to other nesting birds, piercing their eggs in the nests and removing eggs and young. Mrs. Charles F. Weigle (1925) reported seeing house wrens remove eggs and young of eastern bluebirds and tufted titmice from nesting boxes and peck out the eyes of some of the young. Some people now make a choice between having nesting bluebirds or house wrens on their property; others simply let nature take its course. Whether pro or con, many have strong feelings about "their wrens."

About 1900 the house wren was known throughout much of southern Indiana only as a migrant. Roughly north of an imaginary line connecting Terre Haute, Greencastle, Indianapolis, and Richmond it was a common breeding bird, but local in distribution around the state.

During the intervening years, it has expanded its breeding range southward and is now a common to fairly common migrant and nester throughout Indiana. It is a winter resident (six records, all since 1969) north to Shades State Park. Large breeding populations may be present in swamps with an abundance of dead trees.

Butler commented that the house wren in southern Indiana was formerly found in thickets, along fences, about drift piles, or in streamside vegetation. It still inhabits such sites, but today is much more commonly found about human dwellings, both rural and in cities. It appears that in much of southern Indiana in earlier years, the house wren was a bird of the lowland swamp and river valleys, but was rare in dry, upland sections (especially in some of the more rugged counties). This was true in Jackson County in the mid-1930s and early 1950s.

Spring migration evidently begins the last half of March; the earliest date (March 9) may have involved a wintering bird. House wrens arrive in most places, however, in April. All ten March records are for the southern half of

HOUSE WREN

the state. The latest date of fall departure (except for wintering records) is November 26 along the northern border of Indiana.

The bulky nest, constructed of sticks and other items and lined with soft materials, may be placed in various nooks and crannies, tree cavities, or nesting boxes. Metal and wire are often used; Harmon P. Weeks, Jr., saw a nest that except for the lining was composed of small, uniform lengths of rusted wire, which resembled dead twigs. Gertrude L. Ward (1963) described a nest made entirely of 120 pieces of wire, metal, and plastic (except for a lining of grasses). The nest weighed 135.3 grams and some individual pieces of the nesting material weighed nearly twenty-three percent as much as an adult house wren. The birds had transported these items to the nest site seven feet above the ground. Nesting sites mentioned by various Indiana observers include holes in trees, outbuildings, "pasteboard oatmeal boxes placed under the roof of a porch," an old buggy top, a pail hanging on a tree, a rural mailbox, a fencepost, a tin can on a fence,

gourds, and nesting boxes. Nest building has been observed by April 25 and a full clutch of six eggs was found May 1. Seventeen nests contained five to eight eggs and averaged 6.9. Nests are usually placed fairly low and all for which we have records were situated from four to thirty feet above the ground. Males build many more nests than are used to lay eggs in. Young left one nest on September 8.

In optimum habitat local breeding populations may be quite large, as they were for many years in the Kankakee Fish and Wildlife Area. On July 5, 1972, the Mumfords counted seventy-five singing males there along a two-mile walk. More than sixty were observed there on June 24, 1978, and June 16, 1979. There are also numerous birds (presumably nesting) along some rivers in April and May. On May 10, 1950, on a float trip down the Salamonie River from Montpelier to Warren, forty-three males were heard. Breeding birds are still much more abundant in northern Indiana than in southern Indiana.

Depicted plant: Turkey-tail (*Trametes versicolor*)

WINTER WREN

Troglodytes troglodytes

Bunty Wren

When deep snow has almost covered the ground, it is sometimes possible to find a winter wren along a stream, where overhanging banks give protection in the form of tangles of roots and debris, or in brushpiles or among fallen logs—wherever it can find a snow-free feeding site. If the wren becomes aware that an intruder is present, it may hop up on top of the tangle, sit there briefly watching the observer, bob up and down a few times on its short legs, and dive back to cover. Persistent pursuit will usually cause it to fly, normally close to the ground, to another hiding place. It is normally silent at this season, but occasionally it bursts into song, a loud, wild, prolonged performance that is remarkable for such a small bird.

Butler considered the winter wren a common migrant and a winter resident throughout the southern half of the state. He thought it was probably found in winter as far north as Wabash County, and its abundance at that season fluctuated greatly. Evermann (1889) thought it nested in Carroll County, but this was probably erroneous. Today, it is a regular but generally uncommon migrant and rare to uncommon winter resident. It has been recorded on Christmas bird counts from forty counties throughout the state. The maximum number per count was fourteen (Indianapolis) on December 26, 1959. Nine were found at Lafayette on January 2, 1954.

As noted by Butler, the winter wren frequents woods, thickets, bushy fencerows, dark ravines and even orchards, outbuildings, and woodpiles. We have noticed that although wooded and brushy stream valleys are good winter habitat, it may also occur in dryer, upland sites, usually where there are logs, debris, or dense clumps of vegetation on or near the ground. It may appear in more open sites during migration.

An unusually early date of fall migration is August 29, for Hancock County. There are numerous sightings throughout September and birds reach Gibson and Vanderburgh Counties by October 10. Wintering birds have left many localities by May 1, but May stragglers have been observed as far south as Monroe County. In general, all have left the state by June 1, but in recent years there have been some interesting summer records from the Indiana Dunes. Kenneth J. Brock and Charles T. Clark heard a singing male at Indiana Dunes State Park (Porter County) on June 9, June 14, and July 7, 1974. On June 12, 1976, Robert C. Tweit found one in the Indiana Dunes.

Several observers reported a migration wave at Michigan City (LaPorte County) on October 4, 1980. During the early morning, many were seen flying in off Lake Michigan and at least twenty were seen in the Michigan City harbor and nearby areas. Thirty-two winter wrens were found dead on Lake Michigan beaches after the storm of April 16, 1960.

SEDGE WREN

Cistothorus platensis

Short-billed Marsh Wren, Short-tailed Marsh Wren

This small wren is normally not easily observed, nor is it likely to be seen outside its preferred habitat. The chattering, staccato song is usually the first indication of its presence, and observations of the bird may be brief and unsatisfactory, as it generally emerges from dense ground cover, flies a short distance, and dives back into hiding. Sedge wrens may sing for long periods at night; many of us were treated to such a serenade in mid-May at Pokagon State Park. There is much to learn about the habits of this secretive wren in Indiana.

Butler had relatively little information about this species, but noted that it was a migrant and summer resident, breeding locally in "some numbers" where habitat was suitable. He reported that it was much more numerous in the northwestern part of the state and had been found nesting as far south as Putnam County. There appears to have been little change in status to the present time, but today its occurrence is known to be more widespread and there are breeding reports southward to Jackson and Monroe Counties. It may be locally common, but in general is uncommon to rare, depending upon available habitat. It appears to be a very rare winter resident.

The sedge wren prefers the damp sedge meadows surrounding marshes or about ponds and lakes. During migration, singing birds have been found in alfalfa, clover, and rye fields. Nesting sites are usually low, damp swales or poorly drained depressions in otherwise drier fields. Vegetation found in such habitats may include sedges, tall grasses, weeds, scattered cattails, buttonbush, and other marsh plants. A large, low-lying field planted to Reed canary grass contained numerous birds in mid-June.

Early spring migrants have been observed by April 2, but most are first noted after mid-April. Since we do not know if the birds sing upon arrival, they may be present

and undetected until heard. It has been noticed that on some breeding areas, singing is not heard until July or August. Practically all have left the state by November 1, but there are records from throughout October. November 24 is a late record (Porter County) and in recent years a few birds have been found in winter. One was reported in Elkhart County on January 22, 1967. Two were seen on the Muscatatuck National Wildlife Refuge on December 31, 1977. One (?) was seen intermittently in Gibson County from December 1980 to April 20, 1981. On May 13, ten were seen at the Jasper-Pulaski Fish and Wildlife Area, fifteen in Lake County. Ten were present on August 21 in Monroe County.

Although numerous nests have been reported from Indiana, most of them were empty. Like other wrens, the sedge wren constructs "dummy nests" which are not used. Most reports give few specifics, but one nest was nine inches and another eighteen inches from the ground. Nest are not normally built over water and may be on dry sites. A nest contained three eggs and two naked young on June 17. Two nests held two and five eggs each on June 30 and another contained seven eggs on July 17. Nests are not normally built over water and may be on dry sites. A nest contained three eggs and two naked pairs of birds. In late May 1916, "about 50" were found in a swale near Lake Michigan. Thirty-five were recorded at the Kingsbury Fish and Wildlife Area on July 3, 1976.

Dorothy M. Hobson (1950) furnished an interesting report on night singing by this wren. On August 20 (in a full moon), a male sang 2,000 complete and 8 incomplete songs between 8:50 and 11:10 P.M. "with the regularity and continuity of the ticking of a clock." Night singing has been heard by others on May 19 and July 9.

Depicted plant: Larger blue flag (*Iris versicolor*)

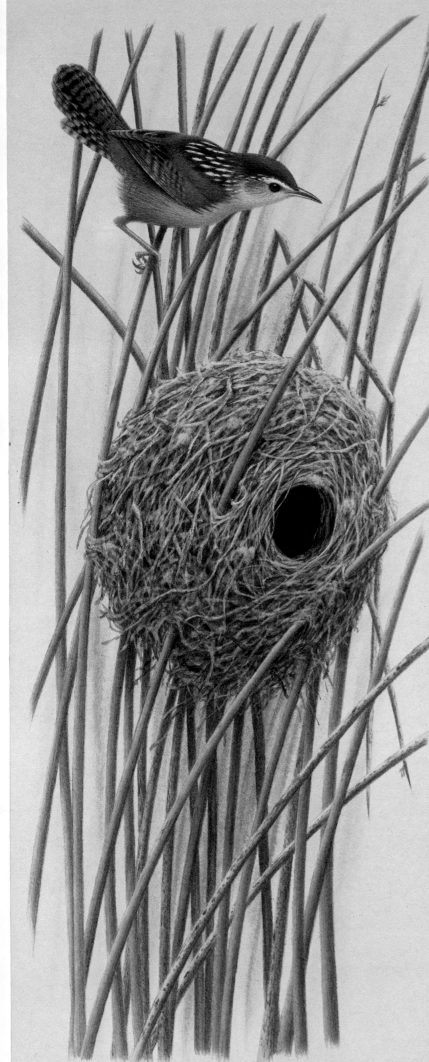

MARSH WREN

Cistothorus palustris

Long-billed Marsh Wren, Prairie Marsh Wren

This marsh-inhabiting species seems most at home in cattail marshes, where it can be found from April to November. Here it nests over the water in the emergent plants, constructing a sphere-shaped nest of woven plant materials gathered nearby. The male builds several nests, often referred to as cock nests or dummy nests, but the female lays her eggs in only one of them. In the spring, when males are on territory, their bubbling songs can be heard from all sides in the larger marshes. A male will often fly up on quivering wings above the cattails and sing in flight, dropping back again into dense cover. The best way to see marsh wrens is to wade into a marsh and search through the emergent vegetation. As you approach the territory of a male, it will frequently come close, sing, and scold, affording you ample time to study it. Like other wrens they never remain long in one spot, but flit from perch to perch, singing, scolding, and chattering all the while.

"The Long-billed Marsh Wren is an abundant resident wherever there are marshes," wrote Butler in 1898. He remarked that elsewhere it was only a migrant and was rarely seen. It reportedly bred "in numbers" throughout the northern part of the state and along the Wabash River valley, in suitable localities. He knew of no wintering records for Indiana. Today, the marsh wren is a locally common to abundant summer resident and migrant across the northern one-third of the state. Its summer abundance diminishes in central and southern Indiana because of lack of habitat, but recent marsh development about newly constructed reservoirs and lakes may eventually change that. It is casual in winter throughout the state. The breeding localities that Butler referred to in the lower Wabash River valley have since disappeared and recent nesting reports have been obtained south to Monroe County.

Seldom does one find the marsh wren in habitats other than marshes. Butler mentioned that he had found them along streams, and it also has been seen in tall weeds and scattered bushes along ditches. Cattail marshes are by far the preferred habitats, although nests may be in cattails, bulrushes, or other tall emergent vegetation.

Spring migration is most in evidence in April and by the end of the first week of that month some marsh wrens

MARSH WREN

in Clark County by D. E. Blackburn, C. J. Schultz, and L. D. Smith.

Gnatcatchers commence building their nests soon after they arrive on the nesting grounds, sometimes within three days. The nests are beautiful—each is a rather deep cup lined with soft materials and covered on the outside with bits of lichens. They look like out-size versions of the nests of ruby-throated hummingbirds. First nests of the season are sometimes accidentally built in dead trees, for the birds nest so early that many trees have not yet leafed out. The birds have been seen to dismantle such nests and rebuild them in other locations. The use of materials from an old nest (or the first nest of the season) to construct another is not unusual. By far the greatest number of gnatcatcher nests reported from Indiana have been found near Buck Creek (Tippecanoe County) by Delano Z. Arvin and his family. The Arvins have observed dozens

of nests and provided the bulk of our nesting data. Nests were found in fourteen species of trees and in multiflora rose. Thirteen nests were in locust trees, eight in black walnut trees, one in a red cedar, and one in a hemlock. Relatively few nests have been examined, because most are so high. The average height of sixty-one nests was 20.5 feet, but heights ranged from 2.25 feet to 70 feet. Forty-three were between twenty and forty feet above ground. Ten were less than nine feet high and three were only 27, 34, and 36 inches from the ground. Clutch size in the ten lowest nests ranged from two (possibly incomplete clutches) to five. Five nests held four eggs each, and three nests three each. Eggs were found in nests from May 7 to July 16, but an adult was incubating April 26 on a nest whose contents were not seen.

Depicted tree: Black locust (*Robinia pseudo-acacia*)

EASTERN BLUEBIRD

Sialia sialis

Blue Bird, Common Bluebird

Who can forget his first encounter with early migrant bluebirds against the white backdrop of a spring snow? The bright blue of the male's plumage as it flies ahead at one's approach reminds us of the oncoming warmer weather and blue skies. Forgotten, for the time being, are thoughts of winter, lead-gray clouds, and the daily hassles of life. It is a cheering sight.

Butler called the bluebird a common summer resident, noting that it was also a permanent resident of irregular occurrence throughout Indiana, but especially in the southern third, and that it had become less numerous in the past twenty to twenty-five years. Bluebird populations are sometimes decimated by unseasonable cold weather in late winter or early spring, as they were in the winter of 1894–95 and again in 1959–60. More recently, three successive severe winters (1976–77, 1977–78, 1978–79) again had an adverse effect on bluebird numbers. In general, the eastern bluebird is a fairly common spring and fall migrant and summer resident. It is a permanent resident throughout the state, but the largest numbers are normally present in the southern part during the winter. Numbers fluctuate greatly from year to year. One hundred or more have been recorded per count on Christmas bird counts at Bloomington, Lake Monroe, Muscatatuck National Wildlife Refuge, Nashville, and Oakland City. The maximum was 183 (Muscatatuck) on January 3, 1976. At Lafayette, from one to fifteen (average five) have been seen on counts between 1943 and 1980; birds were absent on twelve counts. Bluebirds were seen on counts at Evansville and vicinity thirty of the thirty-two years from 1948 to 1980. Numbers per count ranged from none to sixty-five and averaged twenty-one. In contrast, only seven of thirty-two counts at South Bend listed bluebirds. The average per count was 4.4 and numbers ranged from 2 to 14.

Bluebirds like open areas and will nest in old fields, orchards, pastures, young pine plantations, roadside thickets, and other similar habitats. Butler called it "one of the most domestic of birds"; many nest near human habitations.

Although the eastern bluebird is really a permanent resident, there are some noticeable migrations in spring and fall. Spring migrants appear in February and probably reach a peak in numbers during March. One hundred were seen in Lake County on March 20, 1946. Fall migration is not so conspicuous in most years. Family groups, which are evident after the fledging of first broods,

EASTERN BLUEBIRD

merge by mid-September into larger congregations of as many as twenty. Migrants are moving southward in late October and November. On September 22, 1966, about seventy bluebirds were seen at Lake Lemon (Monroe–Brown Counties).

Butler mentioned seeing bluebirds "nest hunting" on March 10 and "nesting" on April 11, but did not elaborate. We have seen birds carrying nesting materials on March 24. Bluebirds normally raise two broods of young per year, occasionally three broods. Maybelle M. Snow observed a female bluebird carrying materials to a nest box on October 23, 1949. Nests are placed in woodpecker nesting holes or natural cavities in trees, fence posts, telephone poles (formerly in rail fences), and in nesting boxes. Butler noted that bluebirds will nest in outbuildings. Two of the more unusual nesting sites were a felt hat hanging on a nail and the open center of a ball of binder twine.

Evermann and Clark (1920) wrote:

During the period of clearing the timbered land in Indiana, say from 1850 to 1870, and before the farmers had done much in the way of removing the stumps, every field contained hundreds of stumps one to three feet high, of oak, maple, elm, sycamore, hickory, ash, walnut, tulip, and other hardwood trees. Many of these were hollow, the hole being often only three to six inches in diameter, and these holes were favorite nesting places for bluebirds. The senior author remembers distinctly one large 18-acre field in which stumps were particularly abundant and in which there were many bluebirds' nests every spring. An estimate of five bluebird nests per acre, or 90 for the field, would be a very conservative one.

Many "bluebird trails" have been established throughout the past years; these consist of a series of nesting boxes (erected along rural roads) which are kept in repair and periodically cleaned of debris by the persons laying out the trail.

Eggs have been reported in nests from April 13 to August 10, but diligent searching would no doubt reveal that eggs are laid both earlier and later. Fifty nests contained from two to six eggs each. There were twenty-two nests with five eggs each and nineteen with four each. Nesting boxes used by bluebirds are also attractive to house wrens, house sparrows, tree swallows, tufted titmice, chickadees, and white-breasted nuthatches, as well as to white-footed mice and (probably) deer mice. Brown-headed cowbirds are known to have parasitized a few bluebird nests. The house wren is quite destructive to bluebird eggs. We once saw a bluebird chase a red-headed woodpecker from a nesting cavity where the bluebird was incubating eggs. Another time, a bluebird pursued a house sparrow from a nesting box.

Bluebirds eat a wide variety of insects during the warmer months, and seeds and fruits at other seasons. We have observations of their feeding on various sumacs, black cherry, Virginia creeper, bittersweet, greenbrier, and red osier dogwood. At one feeding station, bluebirds ate pieces of bread, and at three others came to suet feeders.

Bluebirds sometimes form communal roosts in nesting boxes, possibly because of inclement weather. One box contained thirteen birds in a "state of suspended animation" after a very cold night on February 17–18 (Frazier, 1971). Butler mentioned that dead eastern bluebirds were sometimes found under loose bark of trees or in crevices and cavities after severe weather.

Depicted tree: Redbud (*Cercis canadensis*)

VEERY

Catharus fuscescens

Wilson's Thrush, Willow Thrush, Vera, Tawny Thrush, Tommy Thrush, Nightingale

If you stand at dusk on the bridge over the Pigeon River at the east end of the large tamarack swamp upstream from Mongo (Lagrange County) in June, you will probably hear veeries singing. Here, at the Pigeon River Fish and Wildlife Area, is the largest known concentration of nesting veeries in Indiana, and they find the boggy areas along the river and bordering woods to their liking. When several males are singing simultaneously, their soft, clear, rather bell-like (to some, sad), songs add an addi-tional touch of mystery and fascination to the swampy tamarack stands.

Butler considered the veery a rare migrant that occasionally was present in summer and nested. It was common in some places (e.g., DeKalb County). He cited no nesting record for the state. However, three eggs were collected from a nest at Bluffton (Wells County) on June 15, 1896, and reported by Van Tyne (1936). It is currently a fairly common migrant in small numbers throughout the

state, being recorded more frequently in spring than in fall. There has been a dramatic change in the summer distribution of this thrush since 1898 for reasons unknown. Singing males (some possibly late migrants) have been reported in June as far south as Gibson and Shelby Counties. Nests or broods have been observed south to Marion, Parke, and Putnam Counties.

The veery seems to prefer to nest in low, wet wooded areas with a considerable amount of undergrowth: along rivers, about bogs, swamps, and lakes, and in flat, wet woods. Some birds also nest in upland wooded areas, sometimes where deep ravines are present. During migration, one may find it in the backyard shrubbery or in various types of woods.

Spring migrants normally arrive around mid-April; the earliest date is April 3 (St. Joseph County). Numbers appear to be largest about mid-May. Fifteen were seen in Tippecanoe County on May 17, 1945. September is the month when veeries are most regularly seen during fall migration, but the species is not present in large numbers at that season. The maximum reported was four, on September 7, 1940 (Lake County). The latest fall date is October 22.

Although veeries have been present during the summer in many localities, relatively few nests have been reported; practically all were found since 1976. Most were on the ground, but one nest was 6.5 feet up in the crotch of a willow, over water, one 2.5 feet up in a small hemlock tree, and one 1.5 feet above ground in a clump of multiflora rose. Eggs were seen in nests from May 27 to June 15; two nests had been parasitized by cowbirds. Clutch size varied from two to five, but four nests contained four eggs each and one held five.

The major nesting grounds of the veery in Indiana are located in the northeastern corner. Lee A. Casebere (1978) estimated that fifty pairs were present on the Pigeon River Fish and Wildlife Area during the summer of 1978. The birds have also nested at the Indiana Dunes State Park for many years, at least as early as 1937. Singing males were observed at Pokagon State Park in 1955 and thereafter. The optimum nesting habitat for the veery in Indiana is found across northern Indiana, but the ability it has shown in recent years to adapt to drier, wooded sites may well result in an increasing number of nesting records in counties further south. Robert Ridgway reported its nesting in Gibson and Knox Counties prior to 1897, but we know of no definite records.

Depicted plants: American hazelnut (*Corylus americana*); Showy lady's-slipper (*Cypripedium reginae*)

GRAY-CHEEKED THRUSH

Catharus minimus

Alice's Thrush

There is a group of confusing thrushes that to an inexperienced birder may seem to have been put on earth solely for the purpose of testing his or her identification powers. They all look pretty much alike, are rather shy and quiet, especially during migration, and usually confine their activities to areas of dense vegetation. In general, the gray-cheeked thrush exhibits the least striking features of any of these.

Butler knew the gray-cheeked as an uncommon migrant, noting that his correspondents around the state rated it anywhere from rare to abundant. Since this thrush today is a fairly common to uncommon spring migrant, its status possibly has not changed much since the turn of the century, except for the few recent winter records.

All thrushes are primarily woodland birds, especially during the nesting season. Even during migration the largest numbers are usually found in wooded areas, although they may also appear in city parks and residential areas. It is not unusual during migration to find as many as five different species of thrushes in the same location at these times.

Spring migration generally is first evident in April and peaks during May. April 7 is the earliest sighting, and fifty gray-cheeked thrushes were reported in Lake County on May 11, 1929. Some may linger into late May and early June, the last date being June 3. Fall migrants have appeared as early as August 11, but most pass through the state during September. There are several records for late October and November and three sightings for central and one for northern Indiana between December 19 and January 17.

SWAINSON'S THRUSH

Catharus ustulatus

Olive-backed Thrush

Numbers of migrating thrushes sometimes appear in the woods in May. This is usually the easiest one to identify and the most numerous. Thrushes are noted for their beautiful songs, and in Indiana the opportunity to hear the migrants singing occurs all too seldom. Of the three—gray-cheeked, hermit, and Swainson's—that do not breed here, Swainson's is the one whose song is most likely to be heard.

Around 1900, the Swainson's thrush was a common migrant. Although it was believed that it might nest in northern Indiana, there are no nesting records for the state. Spring migrants do linger into June (and very rarely into July), but we consider them non-breeding birds. It is a common spring and fall migrant and a very rare winter resident. Its habitat is essentially the same as that of the gray-cheeked.

Our earliest date for spring migrants is April 8. By the end of May, most have departed. Twenty-five were seen at Jasper-Pulaski Fish and Wildlife Area May 16, 1975. Thomas C. Stankus found one at Potato Creek Recreation Area (St. Joseph County) June 13–15, 1978. One was seen in Porter County, on July 29, 1962, by Virginia Reuter-skiold, and another in Indiana Dunes State Park, on July 31, 1967, by Laurence C. Binford. Southbound migrants enter extreme northern Indiana during August, in some years as early as August 1. The peak numbers are usually present during September, but fifty were found in Lake County on October 1, 1955. There are sightings for all of October and the first week of November. Although there are six sightings for December and January, the only verified identification is a bird photographed by Kenneth J. Brock on January 31, 1981 (Porter County). The other observations may be reliable, but we need more information about the winter status of this thrush.

Like the gray-cheeked thrush (which has been seen eating pokeberries) and other thrushes, the Swainson's consumes seeds and fruits when insects are not available. It has been observed feeding on the fruits of red osier dogwood, sassafras, bittersweet, and "Florida holly."

HERMIT THRUSH

Catharus guttatus

This shy, furtive inhabitant of the understory of woodlands and brushy tangles and thickets is the famed songster that Walt Whitman was inspired to write about. Fortunate are those who have visited the bird's nesting grounds when the territorial males were in full song, whether it was in the mountains of Arizona or the Upper Peninsula of Michigan. Hoosiers sometimes have the chance to hear the song of the hermit thrush in our state during spring migration.

Butler called this thrush a common migrant and believed it possible that a very few wintered in the lower Wabash River valley. He also suggested that it might be a rare nester, but there is no evidence of this. Today, it is a fairly common spring and fall migrant and winters in small numbers throughout the state, but most abundantly from the latitude of Bloomington southward. The maximum number recorded on a Christmas bird count was seven (Jackson County) on December 24, 1935.

There seems to be little difference in the habitats of this thrush and those of the gray-cheeked and Swainson's thrushes.

Spring migration and dates of arrival of northbound migrants are not always easy to determine because of the possibility of wintering birds. The bulk of the migrants appear to be present in April and the latest spring date is May 26. More than twenty were found in Allen County on April 27, 1976, and a similar number was observed in Porter County on April 17, 1960. After the April 16, 1960, storm, 147 were found dead along Lake Michigan. The earliest arrival date for fall migrants is September 2, but most birds arrive later that month. Twenty-two were recorded in Porter County on September 30, 1972, and twenty in Lake County on October 6, 1942.

Wintering birds feed on various seeds and fruits, such as wild grape and sumacs. Individuals in winter can frequently be called out of hiding by an imitation of a screech owl's call or by *pishing* and squeaking noises. The bird may come up from the ground, where it normally is found during the day, perch and look about alertly, give a low *chuck* note, and move its wings and tail.

Many hermit thrushes spent the winter of 1954–55 in the Harrison State Forest (west of Corydon). At 5:30 A.M. on March 31, 1955, Mumford was conducting a ruffed grouse drumming count in the forest. One of the listening posts on the route was midway down a south-facing slope covered with a heavy growth of young red cedar and oak trees. When he stepped from his Jeep, he became aware of at least four hermit thrushes in song. Ruffed grouse were forgotten for a while in deference to the beautiful voices of these thrushes.

WOOD THRUSH

WOOD THRUSH

Hylocichla mustelina

Amos W. Butler must have liked the wood thrush, for he wrote:

Throughout the denser woodland its ringing metallic notes may be commonly heard from its arrival in spring until July and occasionally into August. Its well-known call, *e-o-lie*, is one of the features of our forests that is passing with the clearing of the land. . . . The song of the Wood Thrush is one of the most beautiful in the forest.

Butler knew this thrush as a common summer resident. It has retained its status as a common summer resident and migrant throughout the state, but we suspect it actually was much more numerous a hundred years ago. Observers have not recorded large numbers during migration. It may be a very rare winter resident.

The wood thrush is a woodland bird, even though it may nest in woods borders and over roads through the forest. Its large eyes are well adapted for gloomy, poorly lit places on the forest floor or in the understory. Still, it does not hesitate to nest near clearings or buildings in wooded areas.

Spring migrants usually arrive in southern Indiana around mid-April, but come earlier in some years, as mentioned by Butler, whose earliest date was April 3. There are two March sightings for the state, but we do not know if they are authentic. The wood thrush seems to be most abundant about mid-May. Twenty-three were seen in Tippecanoe County on May 12, 1962, but some of these may have been on their nesting grounds. Fall migrants linger throughout October and as late as November 11. One was reported December 30, 1972, at Evansville and another December 30, 1978, at Terre Haute. The maximum number recorded in the fall was six, at Indianapolis, on September 8, 1946.

The rather bulky nests are usually constructed in understory shrubs and trees. Thirty-six nests ranged from four to eighteen feet in height and averaged nearly nine. Eight were in beeches, eight in maples, and four in flowering dogwoods. Much of the nesting material is dead leaves, so wood thrush nests are quite easy to identify.

In twenty-one nests, the clutch size varied from two to four; nine nests contained three eggs and seven held two each. Because so many wood thrush nests are parasitized by brown-headed cowbirds, some of these clutches may not have been complete when recorded. Eggs were found in nests from May 6 to July 14, but an adult was seen on one nest on August 8; the contents of this nest are not known. Alan W. Bruner estimated that forty-six pairs of wood thrushes were nesting at Pine Hills Nature Preserve and in Shades State Park during the summer of 1979.

Parks (1908) reported that eleven of twelve wood thrush nests he found near Crawfordsville were parasitized by cowbirds. Harmon P. Weeks, Jr., found cowbird eggs in nine of twenty nests in Martin County and other observers have remarked on the high incidence of cowbird eggs in the nests of this thrush.

The wood thrush is known to eat pokeberries and raspberries; it no doubt eats other fruits, along with its usual summer diet of insects, worms, and other invertebrates. Much time is spent feeding and foraging on the ground.

We recall with much pleasure the wood thrushes that sang on summer evenings at Spring Mill State Park. The inn there has a large, open terrace that overlooks a wooded slope leading down to the lake. Guests would often sit on the terrace in the dusk, enjoying the cool, still evening air and the music of the wood thrush, which would often sing until dark.

Depicted tree: Beech (*Fagus grandifolia*)

AMERICAN ROBIN

Turdus migratorius

Robin, Robin Red Breast, American Red Breast

The American robin is undoubtedly one of the best-known birds in Indiana. It nests and feeds near humans, benefiting from their preoccupation with beautiful lawns and gardens. It probably nested around Indian encampments and was certainly a common bird in the clearings made by early settlers. Hoosiers have long regarded it as a harbinger of spring, although in fact many robins winter here. But spring is still "robin season," and we enjoy those warm, humid April evenings when rain is imminent and the robins are in especially good voice.

Around 1900, robins were considered common summer residents and migrants. They were also irregular winter residents throughout the state, but more regular and most numerous in the southern part. It is quite possible, that the Indiana robin population is even greater nowadays, for man has been creating even more of the sort of habitat they prefer. They are abundant summer residents and migrants and regular winter residents. Winter numbers may fluctuate greatly from year to year. More than 300 per count have been recorded on Christmas bird counts in ten counties from the latitude of Grant and Tippecanoe Counties south. There were 1,051 on the Gibson County count in 1977. From 1945 to 1980, robins were found on counts at South Bend in twenty-nine years; the numbers varied from one to eighty-three and averaged about eleven per count.

There are very few habitats where robins cannot be found at some season or other. Overgrown fields with stands of red cedar are among the favorite wintering and roosting sites in extreme southern Indiana. Spring migrants are plentiful on golf courses and in open fields and pastures, commonly in large, loose flocks foraging amid the remains of winter's snow. Fencerows, borders of ponds, marshes, and lakes, and trees along city streets are all used for nesting sites.

Spring migration is often evident by mid-February, except in years when there are great numbers of wintering birds. In mid-January 1958, flocks of from fifty to seventy-five migrant robins appeared in the South Bend area. The largest numbers are observed in March. James E. Landing found an "uncountable influx" of robins at Michigan City on March 15, 1959. After the storm of April 16, 1960, 437 dead robins were found along Lake Michigan. George W. Pyle observed robins flocking to a roost at Crown Point at the end of July; there were about 1,000 there by the end of August. Keller recorded about 10,000

robins in a roost near Beech Grove (Marion County) on September 13, 1961. Most birds leave the state between late October and mid-November, but the date of departure is quite variable and depends upon weather and the food supply.

Nest building has been observed in March and robins will nest almost anywhere—in many kinds of trees and shrubs, on, in, or about buildings, under bridges, on stumps and rail fences, on abandoned cars and farm machinery, in mailboxes, and (very rarely) on the ground. Fifty-six nests in trees averaged eight feet in height and ranged from 2.5 to 40 feet. Robins' nests have even been found on railroad cars and automobiles that were in frequent use. Kenneth L. Tatlock watched robins completely dismantle a nest of the previous year and transport the materials to a new nest site.

Eggs have been found in nests from at least March 29 to August 18. One robin was first noticed incubating a nest containing three eggs on August 18 and continued to incubate the infertile eggs until October 6. The most common number of eggs per clutch is four, found in thirty-five of sixty-five nests. Twenty-four nests held three eggs each. Some two-egg clutches were evidently complete and two five-egg, one six-egg, and one seven-egg clutch were reported by various observers.

Paul R. Macklin observed birds roosting in his yard in Norway spruces. During a night of freezing rain and sleet, twenty-four robins, six hermit thrushes, two rufous-sided towhees, and one ruby-crowned kinglet took shelter in one tree. In another were an unspecified number of robins, a field sparrow, a dark-eyed junco, and a winter wren. Robins roosted from eighteen inches to twenty feet above the ground, many of them in pairs, sometimes touching.

The robin may be heard singing in every month of the year, but during the non–breeding season low "whisper songs" are heard more often than the full territorial songs of spring. At times, many members of a migrating flock will sing simultaneously.

Earthworms and insects are important items of diet in warm weather. Robins also feed heavily on various fruits and seeds, particularly in fall and winter. Among these are pokeberry, raspberry, barberry, flowering dogwood, red osier dogwood, holly, wild grape, cherry, wild cherry, hackberry, red cedar, multiflora rose, hawthorn, apple, honeysuckle, pear, sumac, persimmon, mulberry, devil's walking stick, and firethorn. Larch sawfly larvae are eaten, as are periodical cicadas (some of them taken by flycatching), and they sometimes eat breadcrumbs at bird feeders.

Depicted tree: Flowering dogwood (*Cornus florida*)

VARIED THRUSH

Ixoreus naevius

This western North American species was not even included on Butler's hypothetical list in 1898. Maybelle M. Snow (1967) published the first Indiana record for this showy winter visitor.

On 9 January 1967 [in Wayne County], Mr. Snow and I had the experience of closely observing a Varied Thrush (*Ixoreus naevius*), of which we had caught a fleeting glimpse on the day of our Christmas Bird Count. . . . [The bird was coming to a feeder and proved to be] a beautifully colored and distinctly marked male, which remained in the area for about five weeks.

Since that date, at least eight other varied thrushes have been seen in the state: in Delaware (1978), Hendricks (1982), Porter (1968, 1979, 1981), Steuben (1977–78), St. Joseph (1976), and White (1982) Counties, all between mid-December and April 27. At least five of the birds were photographed.

Most of them were first noticed at bird feeders, usually near woods or thickets. One bird frequented the undergrowth in a shallow ravine, where it was seen in multiflora rose. Another ate insects, worms, and fruit on a lawn, where it was seen beneath a highbush cranberry.

On the basis of these recent records, the varied thrush is now considered a casual winter visitor.

GRAY CATBIRD

Dumetella carolinensis

Catbird, English Mocking Bird, Carolina Mockingbird

The gray catbird is closely related to the northern mockingbird and the brown thrasher, and like them, it is a talented mimic, although its imitations have neither the verve nor the fidelity of mockingbird and thrasher concerts. Catbird songs are usually more subdued, occasionally whisperlike, and often punctuated with sharp *chuck* notes. Even when the singer is invisible, it is easy to tell which of the three species you are hearing. The mockingbird sings each phrase three or more times in succession, the thrasher usually sings each phrase twice, the catbird doesn't repeat phrases. One can frequently attract hidden catbirds by making squeaking sounds, to which they respond by coming nearer (although often still out of sight) and uttering catlike mewing sounds. Catbirds seem to feel most secure in dense undergrowth, spending much of their time near or on the ground.

Butler made no estimate of its relative abundance in Indiana, simply stating that it was a well-known summer resident. It is currently a common migrant and summer resident and winters in small numbers throughout the state. It was recorded on forty-four Christmas bird counts from 1937 to 1980, but the maximum number per count was three (Vanderburgh County) on December 27, 1958.

Non-wintering birds begin to appear in southern Indiana about mid-April, but in some years birds have arrived by March 26. Certainly, April is the time to watch for migrants anywhere in the state. On May 13, 1961, sixty-two were observed in Marion County. Thirty-three

GRAY CATBIRD

were counted May 12, 1950, during a float trip down the Elkhart River from Ligonier to Benton. Thirty were seen at Indianapolis on September 15, 1946. Most fall migrants have left the state by mid-November, but some remain all winter.

Butler noted that it frequented swamps, thickets, bushy ravines, and other tangles in the wild, but was most abundant in gardens, orchards, berry patches, vineyards, and lawns. This is quite true; to find catbirds one need only search in thickets and dense clumps of vegetation in fencerows, old fields, and ditches or beside ponds, lakes, marshes, or streams. They are commonly found in residential areas and often nest in shrubs next to buildings. There is only one record of a catbird nest in a coniferous tree: it was in a red cedar on a lawn.

Thorn-bearing shrubs and trees like osage orange, multiflora rose, hawthorn, and blackberry are favored nesting sites. Nests are sometimes over water. Besides the usual nesting materials—sticks, grasses, and rootlets—there may be paper, string, excelsior, snakeskin, and other materials. The outside of one nest we observed was constructed mainly of discarded soda pop straws.

Nests are placed fairly low. The average height of seventy nests was 5.4 feet, with a range of 2.3 to 11 feet. Nest building was observed April 30 and the earliest recorded date for eggs in a nest is May 8. At least one nest still held eggs on August 16. The clutch size in seventy-six nests varied from two to five; three-egg clutches in thirty-five nests and four-egg clutches in twenty-nine. During the summer of 1979, Alan W. Bruner estimated that ninety-three pairs of catbirds nested at Pine Hills Nature Preserve and Shades State Park.

In addition to insects, the gray catbird has been seen eating fruits of pokeberry, mulberry, wild cherry, and red osier dogwood. George Cline watched a catbird eating fungi; other birds consumed large numbers of larch sawfly larvae on a Scotch pine. One ate a medium-sized dragonfly. Rufus Haymond reported that the catbird ate the eggs and young of other birds. A catbird with crossed mandibles foraged mainly about garbage cans at a shelter house in a state park.

One adult catbird fed young cardinals in their nest and another catbird fed young house wrens in a nesting box.

Depicted plant: American elder (*Sambucus canadensis*)

NORTHERN MOCKINGBIRD

Mimus polyglottos

Mocker

Of all the songbirds native to our state, we doubt if there is one whose vocal performances have received either such acclaim or such condemnation as the northern mockingbird. Its loud, persistent outbursts may be heard not only throughout the day but on moonlit nights, much to the annoyance of anyone attempting to sleep. This showy and conspicuous species often sings in flight, and likes to jump up from a perch, wings madly fluttering, then return to the perch only to leap up again. Butler was quite taken with the mockingbird's song; he wrote:

At morning or evening, from the top of a tree, a fence stake, or a wheat stack, it begins its marvelous imitations. It may begin with the notes of a Bobwhite, then follow with the song of a Carolina Wren, and succeed these with recognizable productions of the Whip-poor-will, Robin, Wood Thrush, Phoebe, Cardinal, Red-headed Woodpecker, and Flicker. It seems to have practiced on nearly all the bird songs and calls in the neighborhood and confidently undertakes their reproduction.

About 1900, the mockingbird was known to be a permanent resident in the lower Wabash River valley as far north as Terre Haute, but was much more common in summer there. It was a rare summer resident elsewhere in the southern half of Indiana, accidental in the remainder of the state. Butler may not have known about records for Cass County in 1881 and Newton (where it nested) and Starke Counties in 1884. It was seen in Lake County in 1905. Evidently the populations across the northern half of Indiana later largely disappeared and that region was reinvaded during the 1920s. There was a rather spotty distribution in northern Indiana until the 1940s, when a considerable expansion of range occurred. We think much of this was made possible by the widespread planting of multiflora rose, which is ideal for nesting, roosting, feeding, and winter cover. Three successive severe winters from 1976 to 1978 took their toll of mockingbirds, but numbers are again increasing. Today, the mockingbird is common in the southern third of the state, uncommon to rare in the northern third. It still is found in winter throughout the state. It is most abundant in winter in southwestern Indiana; the average number seen on Christmas bird counts in Vanderburgh County from 1971 to 1980 was 130. Numbers per count ranged from 66 (in 1978) to 197. The average number seen statewide on all counts during the same period was 306; the smallest numbers (160, 186) were reported in 1978 and 1979 respectively. Only fifty-seven were found in 1982.

Mockingbirds prefer much the same habitats as gray catbirds and brown thrashers—brushy fencerows, old pastures with scattered clumps of hawthorn, osage orange, and other trees, multiflora rose plantings, orchards, and shrubby or brushy areas near human habitations. Butler noted their fondness for living near farm dwellings.

We know little about migration, but seasonal movements are quite noticeable, for in many places they regularly arrive each spring and leave each fall. At other places, wherever there is a good food supply, birds will come for the winter, but leave in the spring.

Nests are usually found in hedges, multiflora rose fences, brushy fencerows, overgrown pastures, conifer plantings, and shrubs. They have also been found in red cedar trees and in hawthorns. One nest was in a dense clump of honeysuckle that had overgrown a woven wire fence. Seven nests were built from three to eleven feet above the ground.

Eggs have been found in nests from April 14 to July 1, but the sample is small. Clutch size varied from two to five; six nests contained two eggs each, but some clutches may have been incomplete. Three or four eggs per clutch appear to be more common. We have relatively little information about the nesting of mockingbirds in Indiana.

Besides insects, the birds also eat fruits of multiflora rose, pokeberry, yew, apple, and Russian olive. Seeds of sumac are sometimes eaten, as is finely cracked corn. Mockingbirds at bird feeders eat raisins, currants, cracker crumbs, or mixtures of peanut butter, suet, and bird seed. The mockingbird is an aggressive species, often driving other birds from feeders and protecting its nests against intruders, including humans, cats, dogs, crows, and hawks.

Some early settlers kept caged mockingbirds because of their singing powers. Ned Barker told Fred T. Hall that when Barker was a young man in 1884 he and a friend used to catch the birds in Newton County and keep them in cages. In captivity the adults would produce young, and the boys would sell these birds as songsters.

Depicted plant: Trumpet-creeper (*Campsis radicans*)

BROWN THRASHER

Toxostoma rufum

Brown Thrush, Tawny Thrush, Brown Mockingbird, French Mockingbird, English Mockingbird, Sandy Mocking Bird

Many years ago, while still a small boy, Keller was fascinated to discover a pair of brown thrashers nesting in a lilac bush in an Indianapolis park. Despite his frequent visits to the park to check on the nest, the parents managed to raise four young. He still vividly recalls the bright yellow eyes of the adult birds, and their fearlessness. No matter how close he came, they would remain on the nest, scolding with their *smack, smack* calls at the intrusion.

Butler listed the brown thrasher as a common summer resident throughout the state and thought it remained in the extreme southern part all winter. It is still a common migrant and summer resident, and appears to be more common in winter than it used to be. Between 1947 and 1980 it was recorded on ninety-two Christmas bird counts from throughout the state. The maximum number on a count was twenty, at Evansville in 1972. In winter, the largest numbers are consistently found in the Evansville area.

The thrasher is rather shy, and is usually found in thickets and other tangles of vegetation. Not a bird of the deep woods, it prefers bushy open places along woods borders and roads, cleared powerline rights-of-way, and other forest openings. It also likes overgrown fencerows, railroad grades, and ditch banks.

Non-wintering birds arrive in southern Indiana around mid-March and some spring migrants reach the northern border of the state by April 1. Thirty-one were found dead along Lake Michigan after the April 16, 1960, storm. In spring, most thrashers appear during the last half of April; forty-nine were counted in St. Joseph County on May 8, 1976. Most fall migrants have left the state by mid-November, but the presence of wintering birds con-

BROWN THRASHER

fuses departure date records. The largest number reported during fall migration is five, at Indianapolis on September 4, 1954.

Most spring dates are ascertained by observations of singing males, but it is possible that males may not commence singing immediately upon arrival. The following, written some years ago by Mumford, is a typical scenario:

It is late March in Jackson County. The days have become warmer and early bird migrants have been passing through. One steps from the house one fine morning and feels the first warm rays of the sun. Suddenly, he is aware of a new voice that was not there yesterday. It comes from the top of a tall tree a hundred yards away in a fencerow bordering a pasture. There . . . sits a male brown thrasher pouring forth his exuberant song. The singing continues for a prolonged period and one thinks that surely the bird will tire and stop, but somehow he finds the energy to proclaim his territorial rights to all who will listen, day after day.

Nests are normally placed in tangles of bushes, briers, multiflora rose, vines, brushpiles, and other similar, hidden sites. We have five records of nests that were on the ground; one was in an alfalfa field bordering a small pond. Thirty-two elevated nests were at heights ranging from two to 7.5 feet and averaged four feet above the ground.

Egg laying begins by at least April 14. In fifty-three nests, clutch size varied from two to five, but thirty clutches contained four and sixteen clutches contained three each. Young were still present in one nest on July 21.

Like its close relatives the catbird and mockingbird, the thrasher supplements its insect diet with various seeds and fruit. Some of these include mulberry, pokeberry, and red osier dogwood. At one feeder, thrashers learned to extract the kernels from broken sunflower seeds; at other feeders, they ate raisins and peanut butter. Young being raised in captivity attempted to catch butterflies in flight. During an outbreak of periodical cicadas, we saw brown thrashers catching the insects on the wing.

Thrashers delight in dusting and sunbathing. They sprawl out with wings extended and feathers fluffed in the dust beside gravel roads, and they also like sunning themselves in tall trees.

Depicted plant: Blackberry (*Rubus* sp.)

WATER PIPIT

Anthus spinoletta

American Pipit, Pipit, American Titlark, Brown Lark, Louisiana Pipit, Pennsylvania Pipit

This small, sparrowlike bird of the open fields is not well known in Indiana, and is easily overlooked by inexperienced birdwatchers. Butler characterized it well:

The Titlark, familiar to every plowman in early spring, is one of those birds that frequent the wet fields in flocks and give forth a mellow *pee-de, pee-de*, as they rise and when on the wing. They arise from the meadow and frequently fly a long distance, or ascend to a great height, and, after various evolutions, return almost to the spot from which they started. One who is acquainted with their call can recognize them by it as they pass overhead, even when they are out of sight.

This pipit was known to Butler as an abundant migrant and he thought that it might occasionally be a winter resident in the southern part of the state. We consider it to be a common migrant throughout Indiana and a casual winter resident as far north as Tippecanoe County, where it has been recorded on a Christmas bird count. It is possibly an uncommon winter resident in extreme southwestern Indiana, where fifty were seen on December 27, 1953, and thirty on January 1, 1957, in the Hovey Lake area.

In addition to wet, open fields and similar areas, birds also occur in or about golf courses, sewage lagoons, fish hatchery ponds, lake shores, and mudflats.

Away from known wintering areas, spring migrants have been observed from March 2 to May 20. Fall migrants have been seen by September 2, but this is early. (One August 6 sighting may be reliable.) This pipit is usually seen in flocks containing from twenty to a hundred birds, but singles and small groups are also seen. On March 28, 1982, a thousand were seen near Merom (Sullivan County) by Dennis W. Jones. Ruthven Deane reported that on November 16, 1892, hundreds of water pipits were passing in flocks over the marshes at English Lake. Six hundred were observed in Knox County on November 1, 1981.

Although pipits are normally seen on the ground, they sometimes perch on fences and even telephone wires. One, shot and injured, took refuge in a woodchuck burrow.

[SPRAGUE'S PIPIT]

Anthus spragueii

This western species is probably accidental in Indiana, although it may prove to be a casual visitor when we know more about its winter range. It was not on Bulter's hypothetical list.

There have been four Indiana sightings of this pipit, but because of its similarity to the water pipit a museum specimen or good photograph is desirable. One was seen near Walkerton (St. Joseph County) on May 1, 1954, by Janet Kochanowski and Nancy Rea. On March 27, 1966, George Pacenza, Jerome E. Parrot, and Steven W. Rissing observed one in Whitley County. George W. Pyle found one with water pipits in Lake County on October 12, 1968. Five were reported in LaPorte County on April 11, 1973, by Marie Jones and Nancy Rea.

BOHEMIAN WAXWING

Bombycilla garrulus

Northern Waxwing, Black-throated Waxwing, Waxen Chatterer

This beautiful, trim bird, the larger of two species of waxwings that occur in Indiana, is rarely seen. The first record is that of J. E. Beasley, who allegedly shot nineteen at Indianapolis about 1856. We have found none of these specimens. Most of the Indiana sightings were made in the dunes along Lake Michigan. This waxwing was also found at South Bend during four winters from 1954 to 1963. The two southernmost records are for Wayne County and Marion County.

On the basis of available records, we consider this waxwing to be a very rare and irregular winter visitor in the northern third of Indiana. The last sighting was March 15, 1978 (Porter County). Dates of occurrence range from November 24 to May 18. We believe two later May sightings at Indianapolis are incorrect.

Some of the birds seen at South Bend frequented a cemetery and another came to a bird feeder with cedar waxwings. Flocks of cedar waxwings should be carefully studied for the presence of Bohemian waxwings, for the species occur together.

CEDAR WAXWING

Bombycilla cedrorum

Cherry Bird, Cedar Bird, Southern Waxwing

Waxwings get their name from the hardened red tips of their secondary wing feathers, which look like sealing wax. Only adults sport the red feather tips. The cedar waxwing is a comparatively silent bird, most of its vocalizations consisting of faint, lisping notes.

Butler summed up the status of this species in Indiana as follows:

Except during the breeding season, the Cedar Waxwings are gregarious, wandering about the country in flocks, usually of six to twenty-five, sometimes of a hundred or more. They roam at will, being abundant or scarce in a locality as food is plentiful or scanty. They are resident throughout the State, but vary in numbers, being generally most numerous northward in summer, from early May until October, and southward in winter and during the migrations.

In general, this also describes the status today, except that for some reason, wintering birds are frequently most numerous around South Bend (especially on Christmas counts). The maximum number per count, 390, was recorded there in 1964. More than 100 per count have been observed on the grounds of Crane Naval Weapons Support Center in western Gibson County, at Goshen, at Hanover-Madison, and at Indianapolis.

There are few habitats waxwings do not utilize, for in their wanderings they tend to appear wherever food is available, stay until the supply has been exhausted, then move on. They will nest almost anywhere—in deep woods, forest clearings, marshes, creeksides, ditches, old fields with scattered trees, tree nurseries, orchards, residential areas, campuses—even along city streets.

Because they roam so frequently and so freely, it is difficult to pinpoint migration peaks. In 1953 it was estimated that nearly a thousand waxwings were in Marion County from March 8 to March 16. Concentrations of three hundred have been reported at other places in January, February, and May. Several hundred were at Indiana Dunes State Park on June 1, 1947. There were reportedly hundreds in Wells County as early as August 16, 1968, and several hundred in St. Joseph County on September 9, 1952. At several other sites at least two hundred have been observed during November and throughout the winter.

The nesting season of the waxwing is relatively late, the earliest date for a nest with a full clutch being June 1. Active nests can be found for several months thereafter. Young left a nest at Bloomington on October 6. Waxwings usually make their nests in deciduous trees, but one was found in a white pine. Seventeen nests varied in height from 6.5 to 60 feet, and averaged about 21. A few nests were over water. Clutch size in eleven nests ranged from three to five, and averaged four.

Cedar waxwings feed on insects and fruits. Young are given caterpillars and adults often engage in flycatching, especially near water. Flocks may be seen flycatching from the tops of the taller trees. They eat the fruits of many plants, including hawthorn, apple, rose, wild cherry, elderberry, honeysuckle, wild grape, mulberry, cherry, pokeberry, red cedar, persimmon, bittersweet, hackberry, dogwood, and poison ivy.

Feeding flocks may be quite large; they normally move and behave as a unit, perching near each other and flying in close formation. An interesting and common waxwing behavior is food passing. Two or more birds perch on a tree branch; one picks a fruit, passes it to the next, which passes it, and so on down the line. Digestion is extremely rapid—fruit fed to the young may pass through the digestive tract in sixteen minutes, and the messy droppings soon accumulate under the food-bearing trees and on nearby buildings, cars, and sidewalks. Waxwings feeding on rotting or fermenting fruit in late winter or early spring sometimes become intoxicated and fly into buildings, windows, and other obstructions near the feeding site. One winter on the Purdue University campus, more than a dozen waxwings were found dead or injured near several Washington hawthorn trees where they had been feeding.

Depicted tree: Sassafras (*S. albidum*)

NORTHERN SHRIKE

Lanius excubitor

Butcher Bird, Gray Shrike, Great Northern Shrike

In certain winters this northern visitor can be found near Lake Michigan, hunting the songbirds it preys on, in interdunal marshes and brushland with scattered tall trees. Perching in the top of one of these trees, the shrike watches and waits; then it drops sharply and flies rapidly along close to the ground, capturing and killing a small bird, then ascending again to perch in another treetop. At first glance shrikes may be mistaken for mockingbirds, but the real difficulty is in distinguishing between the northern shrike and the loggerhead shrike in the field. This should be done very carefully.

Butler thought the northern shrike was "a tolerably common" winter resident in northern Indiana and an irregular, rare winter visitor to the southern part. Its current status is that of a rare to uncommon winter resident locally in northern Indiana, most numerous in the northwestern corner. It is normally very rare in central Indiana and casual in the southern third of the state, but in some winters there will be more birds than usual. Butler mentioned that this shrike was "quite common" at Brookville during the winter of 1880–81, and a specimen in his collection taken there December 3, 1880, supports this statement.

As mentioned, the northern shrike prefers open areas, brushy sites, and woodland borders or fencerows. It readily comes to bird feeders or bird banding stations and to places where house sparrows may be found. One entered a garage, apparently in search of sparrows.

There used to be a specimen identified as a northern shrike in the Indiana State Museum that supposedly had been collected October 11, 1893, in Brown County. If correct (we have not seen it), this would represent the earliest arrival date on record for the state. The next earliest is October 30, but most birds arrive later in that month. The latest spring departure date is April 13, 1964 (LaPorte County). Four northern shrikes were recorded on the 1956 Michigan City Christmas count. Five were observed in Porter County during the winter of 1953–54, and again on November 15, 1981.

Our meager information on food habits of wintering northern shrikes indicates that birds were eaten more regularly than anything else, although shrikes also feed on small mammals (and, in season, insects). Prey mentioned in the records includes dark-eyed juncos, house sparrows, and Carolina wrens. Merrill Sweet observed a northern shrike "riding herd" on a flock of twenty-six eastern bluebirds in mid-March, and another appeared to show an interest in mourning doves flying past it.

LOGGERHEAD SHRIKE

LOGGERHEAD SHRIKE

Lanius ludovicianus

Migrant Shrike, White-rumped Shrike, Butcher Bird, Common Shrike

One of Mumford's boyhood memories is of climbing up to the first loggerhead shrike's nest found in the neighborhood. It was in an osage orange tree in one of the "living fences" that were once so common throughout the Midwest. Not far from the nest several large grasshoppers were impaled on a strand of barbed wire, a favorite place for the birds to hang their prey. To a young boy bent on expanding his growing egg collection, the discovery of every new bird's nest was a special delight.

Around 1900, this shrike was a common summer resident, most numerous in central and northern Indiana. In some winters it remained in the lower Wabash River valley. Butler wrote: "As the woods are cleared away and hedges are planted, or thorn trees grow, these birds are appearing in new neighborhoods, and most everywhere in the more level portion of the State an increase in numbers is noted."

There has been a drastic decline in the number of loggerhead shrikes in Indiana over the past fifteen years; the expansion of range and population boom the birds experienced after 1900 have now been reversed. Today this shrike is a rare migrant and very rare summer resident. In southern Indiana, where it was formerly an uncommon winter resident, it is now generally rare; elsewhere in the state, it is very rare in winter. The maximum number seen on a Christmas bird count was nine, in the Oakland City area, December 23, 1978. Three were found in 1971 at Evansville and four in 1976 at Oakland City. These are the only localities where more than two per count have been recorded, stressing the importance of extreme southwestern Indiana as a major wintering ground.

The habitat of the loggerhead shrike is much the same as that of the northern shrike. Both are birds of the roadside and open country; loggerheads frequently nest in brushy fencerows, especially those composed of osage orange. Both species often use telephone wires as perches.

Spring migration is more easily detected in northern Indiana, where very few birds winter. Migrants appear in late March and early April, but are not found in large numbers. Charles M. Kirkpatrick saw five while driving in Benton, Tippecanoe, and White Counties on April 8, 1948, and four were seen in Jasper County on April 6, 1950. Most shrike observations involve single birds or pairs; the only groups are adults with fledged young. Fall migrants have generally left northern Indiana by December 1, but stragglers and winter residents are recorded later. Four were seen in Tippecanoe County on September 4, 1959.

One of the favorite nesting sites for the loggerhead shrike is an osage orange "hedgerow," but other brushy fencerows are also used. Old pastures with scattered clumps of osage orange or hawthorn were important nesting areas around Lafayette in the 1950s. Fred T. Hall reported that several pairs nested in a long row of catalpa trees near Crawfordsville. Other nests were found in orchards. A nest was found in a conifer in a suburban backyard (Posey County). Shrikes evidently waste little time after arrival on their nesting grounds before initiating nest construction. Nests are bulky, with a deep cup often thickly lined with soft materials (feathers, wool, hair, etc.). Nine nests ranged from four to twenty feet in height and averaged nearly nine. One nest was used two years in succession. A clutch of six eggs was found in a nest on March 28 and the latest date for eggs in a nest is June 22. In fourteen nests, the average number of eggs per clutch was 5.6, with a range from 4 to 6.

The name butcher bird was given to shrikes because of their habit of killing prey, then impaling it on thorns, sharp twigs, or the barbs of a barbed wire fence—much like old-time butchers, who hung cuts of meat on hooks. Katie M. Roads (1912) wrote of finding mice impaled on thorns all along a hedge fence near a shrike's nest in Dearborn County. The loggerhead shrike eats grasshoppers, other insects, snakes, mice and small birds. Jane L. Hine reported that shrikes came to cornfields in DeKalb County to catch mice that ran from the cornshocks when farmers were opening the shocks. Among birds known to be killed by this shrike are dickcissel, American goldfinch, and field sparrow. Lowell E. Carter (1928) observed a shrike taking food from common grackles. The grackles were following the plow, picking up insects, but the shrike forced the birds to give up their prey, which the shrike then ate. Carter also reported that when he plowed young mice out of the ground one spring he placed them on the tops of fence posts near a shrike's nest. An adult shrike picked them up, swallowing the smaller ones whole and impaling the larger ones.

Depicted plant: Wild rose (*Rosa* sp.)

EUROPEAN STARLING

EUROPEAN STARLING

Sturnus vulgaris

The word opportunistic aptly describes the starling. It has been able not only to cope with introduction into a foreign place but to prosper by taking advantage of local conditions. Although attempts to establish it in the United States were made before 1850, it is generally conceded that it was the birds released in New York City in 1890 and 1891 that initiated the expansion across the continent. In fact, the starling is still increasing its distribution in the New World. This aggressive and adaptable new-comer has become a threat to more desirable birds, with which it competes for nesting sites, food, and roosting places, and has become a noisy, filthy nuisance.

Donald H. Boyd reported the first starlings in Indiana: "A few seen in LaPorte Co. in 1919. On Dec. 15th 8 were feeding at suet cage." This sighting, unpublished until now, predates one in 1924 that has long been considered

the earliest state report. Amos W. Butler (1928) collected considerable information on the spread of the starling in Indiana before 1930 and made the following prophetic statement: "Now we do not look upon the starling as much of a problem. Perhaps in 20 years we shall look upon it otherwise." By 1930, it had been reported in all of Indiana except the southwestern part. Even Butler would no doubt have been surprised to learn that 200,337 star-lings were reported on thirty-one Christmas bird counts during the winter of 1976–77. At Terre Haute there were 131,353 on December 26, 1974. Needless to say, it is now an abundant, permanent resident throughout the state.

Starlings make use of all land habitats and even roost in cattail marshes and nest and feed (mostly by flycatch-ing) over water in aquatic areas. They feed in fields, wood-lands, suburban areas, and cities. Roosting sites are groves of deciduous or coniferous trees, buildings, marshes, or large bridges. Nests are placed almost anywhere above the ground where there is a cranny—tree cavities, crevices in buildings or bridges, woodpecker nesting holes, bird nesting boxes, telephone poles and transformers, billboards, and airport runway markers.

Although the starling is highly migratory, the presence of so many throughout the state all year may mask such movements. Young of the year, easily identified by their plumage, begin flocking in June. A flock of 1,000 young had gathered to roost at Brazil on June 6, 1953. Larger and larger flocks then form. An aggregation of 50,000 was seen November 25, 1954 (Lawrence County). James H. Mason and Amy Mason found an estimated 125,000 starlings roosting under a bridge at Terre Haute. The largest congregations are usually reported during the winter, when they are probably not in migration. Roosts are often shared with common grackles, red-winged blackbirds, rusty blackbirds, and brown-headed cowbirds.

Despite the fact that the starling is one of the most abundant and widespread birds in the state, we have very meager data regarding times of nesting, numbers of eggs per nest, and other aspects of reproduction. Nests range from five to one hundred feet above the ground (or water). Since most nests are hidden in cavities and crevices, relatively few have been examined to determine their contents. Clutch size appears to vary from four to six and eggs are known to have been found by at least April 3.

The first starling nest recorded in Indiana was found April 5, 1927, near Pendleton. It was in a nesting hole made by a northern flicker, about twenty-five feet above the ground in a beech snag. Nests were subsequently found in three other counties in that year.

The food of the starling includes insects, seeds, grain, fruits, and garbage. Fruits eaten include English ivy, poison ivy, dogwoods, persimmon, pokeberry, cherry, mulberry, and grape. Starlings have also been seen eating seeds of sumacs. At bird feeders, they readily come to suet, bread, and other foods. We have seen them feeding with domestic sheep and hogs, birds being seen on the back of both these animals. There are several observations of starlings picking face flies from cattle. Periodical cicadas are eaten, as are unidentified insects taken in flight. Homeowners are sometimes concerned to find that their lawn contains hundreds of small, cone-shaped depressions in the sod; these are made by starlings probing with their beaks for grubs and other insects.

The starling is an accomplished mimic. Listening closely to an individual bird, you can sometimes hear the calls of several other species, including the killdeer and the northern bobwhite. Singing and calling are heard during most of the year and territorial songs may be given in midwinter when there are warm periods.

Hawks—especially accipiters—are sometimes chased by starlings. We have several times seen flocks of starlings pursuing a Cooper's hawk, and once we saw about two hundred starlings harrying a red-tailed hawk.

On cold days it is not unusual to see starlings lined up around the top of a chimney, taking advantage of the rising heat—just one example of the ways in which this bird has learned to adjust to existing conditions.

Depicted tree: Apple (*Pyrus* sp.)

WHITE-EYED VIREO

Vireo griseus

A soft haze hangs over the dense scrub at the edge of an abandoned pasture in southern Indiana. In the depths of the thicket an unseen bird flits furtively from branch to branch, announcing its presence by a characteristic *chip-taweo-chick* song with a strange ventriloquial quality that often causes a novice birder to search in the wrong place. This time the observer is patient, and makes a squeaking sound by sucking air through his lips pressed to the back of his hand. Curious, the white-eyed vireo suddenly pops into view a few feet from the observer, takes a quick look, and retreats to cover.

Butler knew this vireo as a summer resident throughout most of the state. It was locally common in southern Indiana, but generally rare in the northern part and apparently absent from the Lake Michigan region. It remains a common summer resident in southern and central Indiana and an uncommon summer resident farther north, having successfully invaded sections of northwestern Indiana where it was formerly absent. It has probably increased in numbers throughout the northern half of the state since 1900.

As Butler noted, it "frequents thickets, brier patches,

WHITE-EYED VIREO

undergrowth in more open woods and the tangle about ravines in the rougher part of the State" and is often found near water. It is much more often heard than seen.

Spring migrants generally arrive in mid-April, but there is an early record (specimen) of one found dead in a garage in Benton County on March 26, 1950. Most have left Indiana by mid-October; the latest sighting was October 31 (Parke County). Ten were seen in Tippecanoe County on May 17, 1958, and May 12, 1962. The fall maximum was four, September 7, 1952 (Brown County), and September 24, 1972 (Lake Monroe).

Nests are usually fairly close to the ground and well concealed. They have been found in brushy ravines and thickets, in abandoned fields, near swamps, marshes, and ponds, and along roadsides. Specific sites were in a hazelnut-greenbrier tangle, a lilac bush, and a wild plum; on a red cedar branch with blackberry canes overgrowing

it; and in willow, sugar maple, oak, and black cherry sprouts. Eleven nests averaged three feet in height; the range was twenty inches to four feet. Eggs were found in nests from May 5 to July 25 and clutch size was generally three or four, for a small sample of nests. Val Nolan Jr. found that a twelve-acre shrubby field near Bloomington supported three nesting pairs of this vireo. Alan W. Bruner estimated that forty-eight pairs nested at Shades State Park and the Pine Hills Nature Preserve in the summer of 1979.

Singing has been heard as late as September 30. Individual white-eyed vireos sometimes include imitations of other birds in their songs. An atypical song we have heard was a long series of scolding, nasal notes and bird imitations, suggestive of the song of the gray catbird. One such song had a duration of seventeen seconds.

Depicted plant: Wild hydrangea (*H. arborescens*)

BELL'S VIREO

Vireo bellii

John James Audubon discovered Bell's vireo while on his Missouri River expedition in 1843, and named it for his companion, J. G. Bell, who collected the first specimen. This western vireo is a comparative newcomer to Indiana, but it is possible that it was present here for some time before anyone detected it. Its curious, rapid song is quite distinctive, though difficult to transcribe. To some, it sounds like *jiggledy jiggledy jee, jiggledy jiggledy ju*, and is given with much enthusiasm when an observer is near its nest.

Butler included Bell's vireo on his hypothetical list because of its occurrence in Illinois. Donald H. Boyd, a careful observer and notekeeper, found what he identified as Bell's vireos in Springville Township, LaPorte County,

on May 7, 1922. His notes include a description of the song and indicate that he observed ten birds. If correct, this represents the first recorded sighting of this vireo in Indiana. It was seen at Camp Pottawotamie, Tippecanoe River State Park, on July 4, 1943, and apparently nested in Pulaski County in 1945, since adults were seen feeding a young brown-headed cowbird. Mumford (1952) summarized all known records for the state. Since then, Bell's vireo has expanded its range across Indiana, with a large increase in the southwestern portion, especially in Gibson, Pike, and Warrick Counties, where the birds find the old stripmined lands to their liking. The species appears to be absent from the southeastern portion of the state but has been recorded in twenty-nine counties. It is now an uncommon migrant throughout the remainder of Indiana and is locally rare to common in suitable habitat. Twelve singing males were counted in an old stripmined area in Pike County on May 28, 1977. During the summer of 1980, ten were found in various parts of Pulaski County.

The favored habitat of this vireo appears to be old fields or pastures and other similar areas that support a weedy ground cover and scattered clumps of shrubs. When tree growth becomes to dense and the trees too tall, the birds no longer inhabit the sites. Some birds nested in a tree nursery and a few have been found along brushy fencerows. One pair nested in a suburban vacant lot. One migrant was observed in a privet hedge in a suburb.

The earliest date of spring arrival is April 19 and the latest fall sighting was made on September 5. Most birds are first found on their breeding grounds in late April throughout the state. We suspect that earlier migrants are generally overlooked because they do not sing. Singing has been reported from April 24 to September 3.

Nests are similar to those of the white-eyed vireo, although less pointed at the base, and are normally usually at the lower edges of the shrub or tree crown where the branch supporting the nest is partially screened by weeds forming the ground cover. Nests have been found in hawthorns, apple trees, clumps of hazelnut, mulberry, and black locust, in elderberry and wild plum thickets, in clumps of wild rose, blackberry, and sumac, and in sprouts in old fields. Twenty-four nests ranged in height from 1.5 to 12 feet, but only two were more than 3.5 feet above the ground. Excluding the two highest, the average height was about 2.5 feet.

There were eight clutches of three eggs each and sixteen clutches of four each. Some three-egg clutches may have been incomplete due to interference by brown-headed cowbirds, a frequent parasite. Eggs were found in nests from about May 16 to at least July 10. Nolan (1960) reported on the breeding behavior of this vireo in southern Indiana.

Like the white-eyed vireo, Bell's vireo at times, instead of its usual song, renders a longer, more rambling vocalization. Nolan heard such a song that lasted for ten seconds or more. We have noticed that the closer an observer is to the nest, the more frequently the male sings, up to seventeen songs per minute. Frequency of song is thus a rough indication of distance from a suspected nest.

Depicted plant: Buttonbush (*Cephalanthus occidentalis*)

SOLITARY VIREO
Vireo solitarius

Blue-headed Vireo, Blue-headed Greenlet, Solitary Greenlet

A rather quiet, inconspicuous bird with deliberate movements, the solitary vireo may go undetected during migration amid the throng of noisier and more showy woodland birds. Its song is similar to that of the common red-eyed vireo and other species, but once the listener becomes aware of its distinctive traits, it becomes easier to identify.

The solitary vireo is one of those species whose status in Indiana has changed dramatically within the past decade. Butler considered it a regular migrant which was rare to common from year to year. He knew of no nesting records. This status did not change until about 1970, when summer observations began to accumulate. One was seen at Willow Slough Fish and Wildlife Area in June and July 1979. Then came the surprising discovery by Jan Kristin Hammerberg of a nest on May 29, 1980, in Brown County State Park, much farther south than one would expect. A solitary vireo was seen in Huntington County in mid-June 1980. On May 17, 1981, a nest was found at Potato Creek Recreation Area (St. Joseph County). Another summer record for LaPorte County was established on July 23, 1982. Thus there appears to be a recent trend for birds to remain during the nesting season.

Like the red-eyed, yellow-throated, and Philadelphia vireos, the solitary prefers woodlands; it is found on wooded hillsides, in upland woods, on wooded golf courses and campuses, and in cemeteries and residential areas with many trees.

Spring migrants usually appear in late April or early May; the earliest date is April 11. Most have departed by June 1, with the exceptions noted above. An early fall migrant was observed on August 6 and the latest sighting was October 29. Ten solitary vireos were found May 7, 1922, in Lake County, but large numbers are not the rule, especially in the fall. Except for two reported on October 1, 1958 (Wayne County), all fall sightings were of singles. Solitary is an apt name for this vireo.

The nest in Brown County was about twenty feet from the ground in a sassafras tree adjacent to a small stand of conifers and not far from the nature center, where there was considerable human activity. The young had left it by June 15. The nest at Potato Creek was about sixteen to eighteen feet from the ground, in a maple along a path through a beech-maple woods.

YELLOW-THROATED VIREO

Vireo flavifrons

Yellow-throated Greenlet

As it moves about in the upper foliage of the tallest trees this vireo seldom allows the observer more than the briefest glance. Fortunately, vireos are inquisitive birds and will readily investigate a squeaking noise produced by the birder. Keller once lured a brightly plumaged male into a mist net in this way. In the hand, one can appreciate the full beauty of the delicate olive-green back, yellow "spectacles," and bright yellow throat. Such close examination is one of the greatest pleasures of bird banding and no doubt contributes to the appeal of the technique, whether as a semi-hobby or for scientific purposes.

Around 1900, the yellow-throated vireo was a common migrant. It was found in summer "in some numbers" in northern Indiana, but was rarer in the southern por-

tion. Today, it is a fairly common migrant and summer resident, seemingly more evenly distributed throughout the state during the summer than formerly.

Robert Ridgway noted that it was most often found in the luxuriant forests of the southwestern Indiana bottomlands. It may show a slight preference for nesting along rivers and streams in some portions of the state. But it is basically a woodland bird, in general occupying a higher stratum of the canopy than the red-eyed vireo.

Spring migrants arrive in southern Indiana around mid-April, the earliest date being April 14. They are not normally found in large numbers; the maximum noted was eight, on May 16, 1975, at the Jasper-Pulaski Fish and Wildlife Area. It is not unusual for stragglers to remain into October; the latest sighting is for October 19. Six were seen in Brown County on September 7, 1952. Males evidently sing during most of the time they are in the state, for songs have been heard from April 15 to September 25. A singing bird was heard March 30.

There are few nesting data because of the difficulty of reaching and examining the nests, which are on small branches high in the trees. Harmon P. Weeks, Jr., found four vireo eggs and one brown-headed cowbird egg in a nest on May 26. This is our only observation regarding clutch size or laying dates. Another nest fledged three young. The recorded nest height for five nests ranged from twenty-five to fifty, and averaged thirty-six feet. Adults were seen constructing nests from May 6 to June 14. All nests reported were in deciduous woods or along wooded stream banks.

Depicted tree: Sour gum or Black tupelo (*Nyssa sylvatica*)

WARBLING VIREO

Vireo gilvus

Warbling Greenlet

Amos W. Butler often saw this vireo near his home at Brookville. He wrote,

The Warbling Vireo is the first of that family to arrive in southern Indiana, preceding the Red-eyed a few days. It is first observed among the elms, cottonwoods and sycamores along streams, which are choice places for it at all times. A little later it appears in orchards and lawns, and even frequents the well-shaded streets of towns. Its presence is announced by a beautiful song that comes from the top of some tall cottonwood, while the author often is invisible.

It is certainly the persistent, warbling song, sometimes given by the male while he is on the nest, that attracts one's attention to this rather drab treetop dweller, and we can enjoy it throughout the summer.

Butler did not assign a status to the warbling vireo, but today it is a common migrant and summer resident statewide. It shows a decided preference for nesting near water, but is also found in orchards, residential areas, on golf courses, and in open woodlands and their borders during the nesting season. The largest numbers have been recorded along streams and at swampy sites. During migration, the birds may appear in many locations, both rural and urban, where trees are present.

By mid-April, warbling vireos arrive in southern Indiana. Apparently they begin to sing immediately. An early date for arrival is April 5. More than forty warbling vireos were found along the Elkhart River between Ligonier and Benton on May 4, 1949, and twenty-two were recorded on a fourteen-mile float trip down the Tippecanoe River from Leiter's Ford on May 5, 1950. The numbers reported during fall migration are small and give no indication of the peak of movements. From three to four birds have been found in late August or early September in several locations. October 21 is the latest sighting.

Although this vireo is common during the nesting season, there are relatively few data concerning nests and eggs owing to the height of many of the nests. Ten nests placed high in large trees ranged from twelve to seventy feet from the ground and averaged forty-one. But seven nests found in orchards were all less than ten feet from the ground. Five nests were built in cottonwoods, two in willows, and one each in an elm and a silver maple. Alan W. Bruner estimated that sixteen pairs were distributed along Sugar Creek at Shades State Park and the Pine Hills Nature Preserve in 1979. Forty-two warbling vireos were counted at the Kankakee Fish and Wildlife Area on June 2, 1979, where the swampy habitat along the Kankakee and Yellow Rivers must be near optimum for the species in Indiana. Nest building was observed on April 27, and eggs were found in nests from May 19 to July 7. In six nests examined, there were three clutches of three, two of two, and one of one. Another nest fledged three young.

Depicted tree: Common or Eastern cottonwood (*Populus deltoides*)

WARBLING VIREO

PHILADELPHIA VIREO
Vireo philadelphicus

Brotherly Love Vireo, Brotherly Love, Greenlet

By mid-May when the warbler migration is at its peak in central Indiana, the woods and thickets are alive with brightly colored, flitting birds. Among the feathered throng, there is little to call attention to this rather rare, relatively slow-moving vireo, and it may be mistaken for another species of vireo or a Tennessee warbler, or even missed altogether by the casual observer.

This woodland vireo may also be found in brushy areas along streams and borders of marshes, ponds, and lakes. Little has been recorded regarding its habitat in Indiana.

Butler knew it as a generally rare migrant, sometimes "rather common" near Lake Michigan. He listed it as a rare summer resident, partly on the basis of a specimen collected on June 8, 1884, in Starke County, but cited no nesting record. It is still considered to be a rare migrant throughout the state.

Spring migration usually begins in late April, but there is an early sighting for April 17. A few birds evidently linger into June, and there is a possible July record. We consider such birds non-nesters, but perhaps more attention should be paid to summering birds. On May 12, 1979, a reported maximum of five was seen at Shades State Park. Fall migrants reenter the state in late August but are not found in large numbers. The earliest autumn date is August 18. Four were seen in Marion County on August 27, 1972, by Alfred Starling. Two were observed eating sassafras fruits in late September. There are several October sightings, the latest being for the 27th.

RED-EYED VIREO

RED-EYED VIREO

Vireo olivaceus

Red-eyed Greenlet

The steamy mist of an early June morning rises from the forest floor in one of Indiana's state parks. From somewhere high up among the leafy branches of a huge sycamore comes the ceaseless, inquisitive song of the red-eyed vireo; *Who is it? Who did it? Is that you?* and so on, persistently, to the point, one would think, of exhaustion. Butler transcribed this vireo's song as *See it? See it? Who are you? Cheer up.* In a typical deciduous Hoosier forest, this repetitive song is as much a part of the sounds of summer as the raspy barking of the fox squirrel and the hum of the annual cicada.

Butler described the red-eyed vireo as one of the most common woodland birds in the state, especially during spring migration. We assume that it was equally common

during summer and fall, actually abundant in many forested areas, as it remains today, and elsewhere a common summer resident and migrant. It probably is not as numerous today as in earlier years when more forested habitat was available.

The earliest arrival date for spring migrants is April 14. Generally one can expect birds to appear in southern Indiana around mid-April. They may linger throughout October and into November. Of several November records, the latest is November 27, 1970, when Henry C. West banded a red-eyed vireo in Fayette County. The largest spring numbers are normally reported in May. Forty were seen in Tippecanoe County on May 12, 1952. On May 22, 1951, at least twenty-one were observed along nine miles of Pigeon Creek above Yankeetown (Warrick County). Twenty-six were found along seven miles of the Blue River below Milltown (Crawford-Harrison Counties) on May 24, 1951. A fall maximum was fifty, in Monroe County, on September 13, 1949. In migration, it occurs in residential areas, city parks, and cemeteries and on golf courses and similar sites where scattered trees are present.

Nests of this vireo are usually placed at no great height; sixteen nests were an average of about eight feet from the ground and ranged from five to seventeen. Woodlands with a well-developed understory of saplings and shrubs appear to be good nesting habitats. Alan W. Bruner estimated that ninety-five pairs of red-eyed vireos nested at the Pine Hills Nature Preserve and Shades State Park in 1979. Since nearly all of the nests reported in Indiana were parasitized by brown-headed cowbirds, there is a scarcity of data on clutch size. Three nests contained three vireo eggs each, but two of these nests also held a cowbird egg. Another nest contained six vireo eggs. Several nests held nothing but cowbird eggs, sometimes as many as four. Eggs were found in nests from May 25 to July 18. Nest building has been observed by May 17. J. Dan Webster reported a male vireo singing while sitting on a nest.

Depicted tree: Sugar maple (*Acer saccharum*)

BACHMAN'S WARBLER
Vermivora bachmanii

This interesting warbler, now very rare throughout its range, can only be considered an accidental visitor to Indiana. Butler (1900) reported that a specimen was collected at Greensburg (Decatur County) on May 2, 1899. He must have seen it, for he gave a detailed description. For some reason, however, he reported it first as a female, later as a male. The current whereabouts of this specimen is not known. Etta S. Wilson (1918) reported a Bachman's warbler at Indianapolis on May 16, 1917, and later supposedly saw both a male and female there. We think this record may be incorrect.

BLUE-WINGED WARBLER
Vermivora pinus

Blue-winged Yellow Warbler

In late April, when the flowering dogwoods are blooming in central Indiana, we may find this pretty warbler on brushy hillsides and in scrubby pastures. In movements it is more deliberate than most other warblers, and it will sometimes cling to a tree blossom like a chickadee and explore the corolla for insects. The high-pitched, buzzy song is rather insectlike, suggesting an inhaled phrase followed by an exhaled phrase—*swe-e-e-e ze-e-e-e-e*. Territorial males often sing from the top of a tree or tall bush.

Butler noted that the blue-winged warbler was generally common in suitable places in southern Indiana, and rare to uncommon throughout most of northern Indiana, but increasing in numbers. Today, it is a common migrant and fairly common summer resident in the southern two-thirds of the state, and elsewhere a fairly common migrant and uncommon summer resident.

In southeastern Indiana, partially wooded bushy hillsides are favored habitats. The birds also inhabit overgrown fields and pastures and brushy, overgrown clearings (such as former homesites) in forested areas, especially in southern Indiana. Birds that nest in northern Indiana are usually associated with wet sites, such as marsh or lake borders and low, boggy areas.

April 14 is the earliest date of spring arrival; most birds appear in the hill region of south-central Indiana around mid-April. Irving W. Burr found ten in Tippecanoe County on May 13, 1972. An extremely late fall date is October 22, but there are several other sightings for that month.

Eight were recorded in Brown County on September 7, 1952.

Nests are built on the ground or slightly above it; the highest elevated nest was only a foot from the ground. Old, abandoned fields with scattered trees, bushes, and tall grasses or weeds provide nesting sites in southern Indiana. In the Indiana Dunes region, where blue-winged warblers have nested for years, they seem to prefer marshy, boggy, swampy places. Nests are usually constructed in a clump of grass or at its base. Eggs were observed from May 12 to June 24 (possibly a deserted nest) and clutch size ranged from three to six. Four nests contained five eggs each and four or five probably constitutes the normal clutch. Eight to twelve pairs of blue-winged warblers reportedly nested in the Indiana Dunes in 1948 and 1949. Alan W. Bruner estimated that twenty-four pairs nested in Shades State Park and the Pine Hills Nature Preserve during the summer of 1979.

The blue-winged and golden-winged warbler interbreed and produce recognizable hybrids, two of which have been named: Brewster's warbler and Lawrence's warbler. These hybrids have been reported from many places in Indiana. A breeding pair may consist of any combination of the four (or more) morphological types. A bird that sings the song of one type may actually look more like another type, and some birds sing songs that are unlike either "regular" song. The long-term effect of interbreeding may eventually alter the relative abundance of blue-winged and golden-winged warblers in the state.

Depicted plant: Prairie loosestrife (*Lysimachia quadriflora*)

GOLDEN-WINGED WARBLER

Vermivora chrysoptera

Blue Golden-winged Warbler, Golden-winged Swamp Warbler

A century ago almost every large swamp in northern Indiana had its pair of nesting golden-winged warblers. By 1900, however, this beautiful, soft-hued warbler was already beginning to decrease in numbers. Nowadays it is rarely seen, is on the verge of becoming a threatened species, and should be closely monitored.

Butler knew it as a migrant throughout the state, reporting that where conditions were favorable in the northern part of the state it nested "in some numbers," but that it was not abundant anywhere. Today it is an uncommon to rare migrant throughout the state and a very rare summer resident, mostly in the northern third. Throughout the past forty years it has been found most consistently in summer in the Indiana Dunes, but it also occurs eastward across the state in habitat similar to that in which its near-relative the blue-winged warbler (with which it interbreeds) is found: bogs, swamps, marshes, and adjacent overgrown fields. Around Brookville, where Butler lived, he noticed that they preferred wooded hill-tops to river valleys.

Spring migrants have been recorded as early as April 24; most birds arrive in late April or early May. The surprising number of twenty-three was reported at Eagle Creek Reservoir on May 15, 1978, by Timothy C. Keller. Other maximum spring counts are also for mid-May. The latest fall sighting was on October 8. The largest number reported in the fall was three, in Brown County on September 7, 1952.

With two exceptions, all nesting records are from the northernmost three tiers of counties. In Monroe County, Val Nolan Jr. found a female golden-winged warbler that mated with a male blue-winged warbler. Timothy C. Keller observed two adult golden-wings feeding young out of the nest in Brown County on July 9, 1978. Singing males have been found in several other counties in summer. We have only one report of the actual discovery and examination of a nest. It was found on June 3, 1923, near Zulu (Allen County), and contained five eggs. It was well concealed in a tuft of grass under a brier bush (Price, 1935).

Depicted plant: Sensitive fern (*Onoclea sensibilis*)

TENNESSEE WARBLER

Vermivora peregrina

Warbler watching can be quite a challenge after mid-May. When the tree leaves are fairly well developed, so that it is difficult to identify the small birds flitting through the tree crowns by sight alone, a good ear is a great help in identification. At about this season, the Tennessee warbler is often present in numbers and many are singing. The loud, chippering song of this drab little vireolike warbler seems to come from all sides and cannot be ignored. Being so distinctive, it is a good warbler song to begin training one's ear on. To some it sounds like the rapid chatter of an old electric sewing machine running at fairly high speed. As the birds forage among the foliage, now and then they will hang upside down for a moment or hover at a leaf or blossom.

Butler reported this warbler as a regular migrant, usually abundant in the fall, less numerous and frequently rare in spring. It is more abundant in spring today, being a common migrant at that season, as well as in the fall. An occasional bird may remain into winter.

This is essentially a woodland warbler, especially in the spring, but it is also found in many other places, including brushy ravines, brier patches, overgrown fencerows, and weed patches. At times it is common in cemeteries, city parks, and residential suburbs, and on campuses and golf courses.

April 10 is the earliest spring date for a migrant, and birds remain through May. There are three June sightings and one July observation of what were undoubtedly non-nesting birds. Fall migrants have appeared in northern Indiana as early as August 4 and the latest sighting was on November 19. Val Nolan Jr. found two hundred in Monroe County on May 8–9, 1949, and there were fifty in Jackson County on September 20, 1954.

Although insects make up most of the summer food of this warbler, during migration through Indiana it has been seen to pierce cultivated grapes, apparently for the juice, and there are two reports of Tennessee warblers feeding at clusters of elderberry fruits. One warbler drank at a hummingbird feeder.

ORANGE-CROWNED WARBLER

Vermivora celata

Around 1900 this rather large, dull-hued warbler was considered very rare and was known only as a migrant. Butler observed it in Franklin County only four times in nineteen years. It is currently a rare spring and uncommon fall migrant, and casual in winter. But if birders learn to look for it in the sort of habitat it prefers, we may find that it is more numerous than has been supposed. Tangles, thickets, and stands of tall weeds seem to attract the orange-crowned warbler, as do overgrown abandoned fields, scrub at the edge of woods, and willow thickets. We have also seen it in stands of giant ragweed near old homesites. Its orange crown patch is generally not evident, and its behavior is seldom conspicuous, but if it is present it can often be lured into view by means of squeaking noises.

Spring migrants probably return to Indiana in late April; some earlier sightings may represent wintering individuals. The latest spring date is May 27. Returning fall migrants have been reported as early as September 6, but most birds probably pass through between late September and October. They sometimes linger in the fall long after most other warbler species have departed. Wintering birds are likely to visit bird feeding stations. There are at least nine records of sightings between December 2 and March 21, from scattered counties throughout the state. Henry C. West and John M. Satter found six orange-crowns in a hawthorn tree on May 7, 1951. James A. Haw recorded ten on October 10, 1974, in Allen County.

NASHVILLE WARBLER

Vermivora ruficapilla

Little is known about this inconspicuous bird's activities in Indiana. Among the more colorful relatives with which it is found during migration, it is somewhat unobtrusive. Males in full nuptial plumage are striking, but their songs may be mistaken for those of other warblers.

Butler wrote that he usually found these warblers "high in the trees." Other observers also mentioned finding them in the treetops, but some birds were reported in orchards and in "an open blackberry patch." One late fall migrant was in a weedy, brushy patch containing small saplings. During migration this species may occur with other warblers nearly anywhere sufficient tree growth is present.

Butler considered the Nashville warbler a rather rare migrant, "at times" locally common. It appears to be an uncommon spring and fall migrant today. There is one winter record, but it may prove to be casual at that season.

The earliest arrival date for spring migrants is April 15. Most birds have left the state by the end of May, but there are three sightings from June 1 to 10. Twenty-five were seen in Tippecanoe County on May 14, 1950, by Irving W. Burr. Fall migrants have been reported as early as August 16, but most are evidently present in September. Kenneth J. Brock found twenty-five at the Jasper-Pulaski Fish and Wildlife Area on September 7, 1974. An individual remained in a residential area in Tippecanoe County from at least December 24, 1974, to January 12, 1975, according to Pablo Ruiz-Ramon. This bird was seen feeding in pine trees.

NORTHERN PARULA

Parula americana

Blue Yellow-backed Warbler

To see a large "wave" of migrating warblers is an unforgettable experience, and it is most likely to happen on one of those rare spring days when weather conditions are just right—a stalled cold front preceded by unstable air. Then woods, orchards, and even metropolitan parks may teem with warblers. It is a red-letter day when the first northern parula arrives, usually in just such a wave. Finding this feathered jewel in the tree crowns is hard on the neck, but there is always the hope of being rewarded with a close view during one of its infrequent forays nearer the ground.

Butler said little about the parula's status in Indiana except that it was variable—common in some years, absent in others. Modern data show that it is generally rare to very rare in eastern Indiana and uncommon to fairly common in the west-central and southwest portions. It occurs as a spring and fall migrant and summer resident. It may nest throughout the state, but there are few records of actual nests or broods.

In southeastern Indiana, Butler "always found them in the heavier woodlands, where they frequent the higher tree-tops, preferably maple, elm and oak." Migrants may be found in many wooded habitats and even in over-grown old fields with moderately tall trees. During the nesting season, the parula appears to favor riparian trees, often tall sycamores, and well-developed woodlands or their borders. Many summering birds are found near water.

Migrants appear about mid-April. The earliest date is April 14. Migrants are rarely found in large numbers. Delano Z. Arvin saw from one to seven daily from April 28 to May 21, 1975, in Tippecanoe County. The latest fall sighting was on October 14, which is undoubtedly quite late. Two parulas seen in northwestern Indiana on October 12, 1952, represent the largest number recorded on fall migration.

Although Butler indicated that the northern parula had been reported as nesting in DeKalb, Gibson, and Knox Counties, he cited no definite nest records. This is not very surprising, for it is adept at hiding its nest, often very high in large trees. The first nest found in the state that we know of was located by Charles E. Mills, in June 1975, in the "Buckskin Bottoms" region of Gibson County. The nest was about twenty-five feet from the ground, in a tree

at the edge of a swamp beside a railroad grade, and appeared to be constructed mainly of yellowish, stringy material, possibly dried grass. Alan W. Bruner found adults feeding fledged young at the Pine Hills Nature Preserve on July 16, 1976. In May 1976, Arvin found an adult gathering nesting material (willow "fluff") in Tippecanoe County. The species nested again at Pine Hills in 1977, when Bruner watched adults feeding fledglings on June 18. Birds were again seen gathering nesting material (spider silk) in Tippecanoe County on May 15, 1980. On April 18, 1981, several observers watched a nest being built about fifty-five feet from the ground in the top of a sycamore tree in Montgomery County.

Singing northern parulas have been found in various parts of the state during the nesting season and future field work will no doubt reveal more about the summer distribution of this elusive bird. Mills reported that it had been present in the Buckskin Bottoms each summer from 1970 to 1978. Bruner estimated that fifteen pairs were present during the summer of 1979 at Pine Hills and Shades State Park.

Depicted tree: Eastern hemlock (*Tsuga canadensis*)

YELLOW WARBLER

Dendroica petechia

Summer Warbler, Summer Yellow Bird, Golden Warbler, Blue-eyed Yellow Bird

The morning dew was heavy on the foliage of the willows and other riparian plants along a southern Brown County stream. It was early May and the surrounding countryside was cloaked in the fresh green of new leaves. A small, energetic yellow bird moved from willow clump to willow clump, pausing frequently to sing its *sweet-sweet-sweeter-sweet* song. The observer quickly hid in some vegetation along the stream and was rewarded with a close view of the early morning singer—a yellow warbler.

Butler wrote, "The Yellow Warbler is one of our best known and most abundant summer residents. It arrives as the buds on the apple trees are bursting into bloom." It was found throughout the state then as it is today, and it remains a common migrant and summer resident. There is a single winter sighting.

This is a warbler of open areas, not the deep woods. Its favored summer haunts are near water—ditches, marshes,

ponds, lakes, creeks, and rivers—in willows, wild roses, and other wetland plants, although some nest in the scrub in old fields. During migration the yellow warbler may be found in places it uses rarely if at all as nesting habitats, such as orchards and residential areas.

This warbler normally appears in southern Indiana in mid-April. There is an early sighting on April 4 for Brown County. It is probably most numerous in early May. Ted T. Cable found forty at the Willow Slough Fish and Wildlife Area on May 8, 1979. The dearth of fall records supports Butler's comment that "their disappearance is so gradual that few . . . note their going." Two were observed in Marion County on September 3, 1972. It was seen in Allen County on October 15 and in Warren County on October 24.

Nest construction begins in April and full clutches of eggs have been seen in nests from May 1 to June 24. Nests are usually near water in shrubs or fairly small trees, such

as willows, wild rose bushes, maples, pin oaks, button-bushes, sycamores, and blackberry bushes. Birds have also been found nesting in drier sites in multiflora rose, box elder, elderberry, wild plum, elm, pear, lilac, catalpa, and vines. Sixty-one nests ranged from 1.5 to 30 feet above the ground and averaged 5.7 feet. Compactly built of soft materials, with relatively thick walls, they resemble the nests of the American goldfinch. Clutch size in forty-one nests usually ranged from three to five, but was occasionally two. Twelve nests held three eggs and thirteen nests each contained four or five. The brown-headed cowbird often parasitizes yellow warbler nests. In some cases, the birds desert when the cowbird eggs are deposited. There are several records, however, of the warblers' building another story on the nests to cover the offending egg. As many as three stories may be built if cowbirds persist in laying in a particular nest.

In the spring of 1983 William Zimmerman watched from his studio window the building of three nests: an American robin's, a northern oriole's, and a yellow warbler's. The robin was making slow headway—the oriole kept stealing bits from the robin's nest to use in its own. Soon after, Zimmerman was fascinated to see that the yellow warbler was plundering the oriole's nest for materials.

Alan W. Bruner observed a yellow warbler at his bird feeder on December 23 and 25, 1975. The bird fed on suet. This sighting constitutes the only winter record for the species in Indiana.

Depicted tree: Red maple (*Acer rubrum*)

CHESTNUT-SIDED WARBLER

Dendroica pensylvanica

June 15, 1965, was a warm, humid day. By noon in the oak woods bordering Ringneck Lake at the Jasper-Pulaski Fish and Wildlife Area, few birds were singing. Mumford found that if he lingered in a shady spot, he attracted hordes of mosquitos. He was looking for nests, and had been surprised to find one of the least flycatcher. Then he noticed a large nest of sticks not far from the lake with the tail of a red-shouldered hawk extending from it. While watching the hawk, he heard a warbler sing nearby and soon located a male chestnut-sided warbler bringing a mouthful of insect larvae to a young brown-headed cowbird, out of the nest and larger than its foster parent. Soon the female arrived with food. No doubt the birds had raised the cowbird in a nest nearby, but Mumford was not able to find it.

Butler reported that this warbler was a common mi-

grant most years but was sometimes rather rare. It was reportedly a summer resident in the extreme northern part of the state, although no details of nesting were given. Nests have been found in Allen, Marshall, Newton, and Porter Counties, but singing male chestnut-sided warblers have been observed during the nesting season south to a line connecting Montgomery, Marion, and Wayne Counties. A bird (sex not specified) was reported in Spencer County on June 18, 1980. It is possible that the species nests at least as far south as Indianapolis.

Butler knew the chestnut-sided as a migrant that frequented the wooded hillsides and uplands of Franklin County. Although it is found in woodlands during spring and fall migration, its nesting habitat is the more open, brushy clearings and woods borders, frequently near marshes or streams. Migrants may appear in almost any wooded area—suburbs, campuses, golf courses, parks, and the like.

The earliest arrival date for spring migrants is April 18 and birds may appear throughout the state by May 1. Peak numbers have been reported around mid-May. Twenty-three were seen in Marion County on May 13, 1961. Fall migrants usually are evident in August and some linger into October. The maximum recorded was six, in Lake County, on September 7, 1940. There is one sighting for October 17. Data for this and other warblers during the fall migration point up the shortage of information for this season. Most warbler watchers spend little time in the fall studying the birds.

James D. Watson reported that chestnut-sided warblers nested (no details) in the Indiana Dunes State Park in 1948 and 1949 (Ford, 1956). Our earliest report of an actual nest examined is for 1955, when Theodore A. Chandik, Raymond Grow, and Virginia Reuter-skiold lo-cated a nest near Baileytown (Porter County) on June 14. It was under construction on June 14 and held three eggs on June 21. Edward M. Hopkins found a nest with two eggs at the Willow Slough Fish and Wildlife Area (Newton County) on July 7, 1974, and another there with two warbler eggs and two cowbird eggs on June 20, 1975. A nest with four eggs was found June 8, 1978, in Lagrange County by Mark A. Weldon. On June 2, 1979, a nest with one cowbird egg and one warbler egg was found in Allen County.

Observed nests were built in blackberry, honeysuckle, witchhazel, and elderberry. One nest was 3.5 feet from the ground. During each of the summers of 1977, 1978 and 1979, eight singing male chestnut-sided warblers were present on the Pigeon River Fish and Wildlife Area. Five singing males were found in Indiana Dunes State Park in the summer of 1980.

Depicted tree: Red elderberry (*Sambucus pubens*)

MAGNOLIA WARBLER

Dendroica magnolia

Black and Yellow Warbler

Among the more beautiful warblers that migrate through Indiana in spring is the magnolia. This is a comparatively easy warbler to see because it seems to prefer the lower, more open growths of small trees and the lower canopy of woodlands and because its movements are more leisurely than those of many other warblers. Frequently it holds its tail partially spread, cooperatively displaying the diagnostic markings.

The magnolia warbler was reportedly "oftentimes common" during migration in some parts of Indiana about 1900. Butler did not find it so in the Whitewater River valley and wrote little about its status in the state. It is now a common migrant, evidently more abundant in the spring than in the fall, and perhaps a casual summer resident. There are no nesting records. It may prove to also be a casual winter resident.

Many of the woodland warblers are found in similar habitats, often in mixed flocks containing ten or more species. Almost any wooded habitat, rural or urban, is frequented by the magnolia, but it is not a bird of open areas.

April 13 is the earliest spring arrival date, but most birds do not appear until late April or early May. Peak numbers are normally found about mid-May. There were sixty in Tippecanoe County on May 17, 1945. There are at least a half a dozen June sightings, some as far south as Johnson and Vigo Counties. Herbert L. Stoddard found it "rather common" along Lake Michigan on June 2, 1917. A dead (still fresh) magnolia warbler was found on a Lake Michigan beach on July 11, 1978, and a singing male was located in Porter County on July 29, 1961. Fall migrants enter northern Indiana around mid-August. There is an early record for August 10. The maximum number reported in fall was thirty (Monroe County) on September 11, 1950. There are two winter sightings, but neither is backed by physical evidence. One involves three birds reported on the Evansville Christmas bird count, December 27, 1975. Another was of a bird seen near Madison on February 26, 1933.

CAPE MAY WARBLER

Dendroica tigrina

May 6, 1897, at noon, I observed a Cape May Warbler among the cedar and apple trees in my yard at Brookville. It was very deliberate, but very industrious. The apple trees were in full bloom. It went over them from lowest limb to topmost branch, apparently visiting most of the blossoms. If it caught an insect every time it appeared to, it must have taken hundreds. Even the warm mid-day sun did not stop its work, and its little song only sounded the clearer when those of many other birds had ceased. [Butler, 1898a]

Around 1900, this warbler was considered to be rare everywhere in its range. Butler noted, however, that while it was absent in Indiana in some years, in others it was common or even abundant. He considered it a spring and fall migrant, more common during fall. It currently appears to be an uncommon migrant and a casual winter resident.

When the Cape May warbler is here, observers often find it in conifers—on campuses or golf courses or in tree nurseries, pine plantations, or residential areas. Butler remarked on its occurrence in the drier uplands, among the oak woods, where he usually found it in high bushes, small trees, or the lower branches of big trees. He also mentioned that it came into towns, where it was attracted to the blossoms of all types of shade or fruit trees. Fall migrants were found in thickets, brier patches, overgrown fencerows, and weedy roadsides.

The earliest spring arrival is April 22. The Cape May warbler is normally one of the later spring warbler migrants, and has been observed as late as May 31. Alan W. Bruner recorded twenty-four in Montgomery County on May 8, 1982. In May 1961, near Bloomington, Val Nolan Jr. found a female carrying what appeared to be nesting material, but the bird was probably a migrant. The earliest fall arrival is August 10, and stragglers remain throughout October and into early November. In September 1971 as many as seven per day were seen in LaPorte County. There are six sightings for the species between December 9 and March 19 (1960 to 1980).

Cape May warblers, like Tennessee warblers, are known to pierce grapes to obtain the juice. Waldo L. McAtee reported on this behavior in 1904. The warblers fed actively on insects among the grapevines, refreshing themselves from time to time by piercing grapes and drinking the juice. Other observers have seen the Cape May "pricking" elderberry fruits, no doubt for the same purpose. The bird that spent much of February and March 1980 at Spring Mill State Park (Lawrence County) often fed on insects picked from rocks or from the edge of a swiftly flowing stream. Food items were probably aquatic insects.

BLACK-THROATED BLUE WARBLER
Dendroica caerulescens

Each warbler species has its own special appeal. The male black-throated blue warbler has beautiful plumage, and the pleasure of seeing him is all the greater for being so rare.

Butler considered it to be a generally common migrant in southeastern Indiana, but in some years it was rare and in others absent there. He mentioned, however, that in other parts of the state it was thought to be rare. Perhaps something about the habitat or geographic location of the Brookville area attracted it. In our experience, it has been an uncommon migrant in spring, and but little more abundant in fall. A few birds linger through June and there are two December sightings.

The sites in which he had found this warbler in Franklin County were described by Butler as follows:

In the Whitewater Valley I have found they habitually frequent the upland woods, sometimes finding their way into orchards, but generally, if I want to find them, I go among the upland beeches, hickories, oaks and sassafras. There they frequent the lower branches or the taller undergrowth.

We have noticed that brushy hillsides, often near water, and other undergrowth frequently shelter this warbler, which is usually seen fairly close to the ground. One was in some shrubbery on the lawn of a residential area.

April 11 is an early date for spring arrival; most do not appear until May. Six were seen in Tippecanoe County on May 15, 1943. Some of the males that are still here in June are singing. Alfred Starling observed a black-throated blue carrying nesting material at Eagle Creek Park, Indianapolis, on May 21, 1978. Fall migrants appear in northern Indiana as early as August 25; the maximum number reported in the fall was six (Steuben County) on August 28, 1975. One was captured in a classroom at Goshen College on December 9, 1949. An adult male visited a bird feeder at Zionsville (Boone County) from December 16, 1979, to January 30, 1980.

YELLOW-RUMPED WARBLER
Dendroica coronata

Myrtle Warbler, Yellow-crowned Warbler

The major part of the fall warbler migration is generally over by the first week of October. At this season the evenings are becoming cooler, and one may wake some morning to find a light frost on the land. Now, when our attention is focused on the first arriving dark-eyed juncos and white-throated sparrows, the yellow-rumped warblers appear in force. Their presence is easily detected by the often-repeated *check* call note. Most are in dull plumage, but the yellow rump patch is displayed prominently as the birds forage among the leaves, move from tree to tree, or flycatch.

Butler knew this warbler as an abundant migrant and an irregular winter resident north to Brookville, Greensburg, and Bloomington. It remains an abundant migrant in spring and fall, but larger numbers are recorded during fall migration. It now winters throughout the state, varying in numbers from year to year for any one locality. More than twenty-five have been reported on Christmas bird counts in six counties, the northernmost of which is Delaware. One hundred were observed at the Muscatatuck National Wildlife Refuge on December 18, 1976.

During migration, this warbler may be found in nearly any habitat where there is sufficient tree growth, including remote woodlands as well as city parks and residential areas. Many frequent riverbank trees and tangles during the spring. Wintering birds may be attracted to conifers, where they may roost and feed.

Spring migration sometimes peaks in late April. One hundred yellow-rumps were seen in Tippecanoe County on April 27, 1943, and in Marion County on April 22, 1967. Forty-seven were found dead along Lake Michigan after the April 16, 1960, storm. Most have departed from the state by June, but there are sightings from the northernmost two tiers of counties as late as June 27. Early fall migrants have appeared by August 22, but the bulk of them come later and reach a peak in October. Donald H. Boyd found a thousand in Lake County on October 7, 1949.

Although this warbler is primarily an insect eater during the warmer months of the year, even doing considerable flycatching, wintering birds feed heavily on poison ivy and poison sumac fruits, frozen apples, and fruits of red cedar. In some winters, yellow-rumped warblers, cedar waxwings, purple finches, and American robins are seen in the stands of red cedars in Harrison County. One warbler ate bits of suet dropped by European starlings at a feeding station.

[BLACK-THROATED GRAY WARBLER]
Dendroica nigrescens

This western species was seen on September 27, 1983, at Indiana Dunes State Park by Helen Michalik. She watched the bird for four or five minutes at a distance of ten to fifteen feet under good viewing conditions. Direct comparison was made at the time with a nearby black-and-white warbler, and the yellow lores of the black-throated gray were distinctly noted.

[TOWNSEND'S WARBLER]
Dendroica townsendi

On April 30, 1979, James H. Campbell and Willard N. Gray observed a singing male warbler they identified as this species in Warrick County. Jay Kendall found a Townsend's warbler at Indiana Dunes State Park on May 1, 1983. The next day Kenneth J. Brock located this bird and wrote a detailed description of it. This western species is accidental in Indiana.

BLACK-THROATED GREEN WARBLER
Dendroica virens

At the east entrance to Eagle Creek Park (Marion County), tall conifers line the road for about a quarter of a mile. Here each spring and fall a host of migrating warblers can often be found searching through the tree foliage at various heights from near ground level to sixty feet. Among the more common species of warbler is the black-throated green, which seems adept at foraging for food in all parts of the tree—needles, cones, bark, and branches. It will flutter mothlike at the end of a cone or even creep around the trunk.

"The Black-throated Green Warbler is a very common migrant," wrote Butler in 1898. He continued, "Few among the Wood Warblers, perhaps none, are as well known as this." It is still a common spring and fall migrant.

In common with several other species of warblers, the black-throated green may be found in most wooded areas. Butler found it in forests and "wood pastures," and it frequents parks, cemeteries, golf courses, residential areas, and similar habitats. It is often found in conifers during migration and some of the males that linger into June have been found singing in sites where some conifers were present. The first nesting record was obtained in 1983.

The earliest date for spring migration is March 25, 1975, when Nathalee D. Stocks found one at Evansville. A singing male was at the Jasper-Pulaski Fish and Wildlife Area on April 4, 1959. Two were singing in Marion County on April 4, 1956. These are unusually early dates, however, and most migrants arrive later in April and reach a peak of abundance the first half of May. Twenty each were seen on May 7, 1972, at Jasper-Pulaski, and on May 14, 1946, in Tippecanoe County. There are at least eight sightings for June and three for July. One bird spent most of the summer of 1950 at Shades State Park. Singing males were found in Brown County State Park during June in 1981, 1982, and 1983. Circumstantial evidence of nesting was finally obtained in 1983 when an adult was seen carrying food and what sounded like calls of young begging for food were heard. A female was seen carrying nesting material near Beverly Shores (Porter County) on June 15, 1983, by Fred Kase. On July 10 and 11, 1983, Kase, Helen Dancey, and Kenneth J. Brock watched a pair of adult black-throated green warblers feeding a fledgling out of the nest. This constitutes the first proof of nesting in the state.

Along the northern border of the state, fall migrants have appeared as early as August 6 and the fall migration extends over a long period. One was seen in LaPorte County on November 22, 1959. The maximum number recorded at this season is twenty-two (Wayne County) on October 7, 1949. There is a reported sighting for February 26, 1933, near Madison.

BLACKBURNIAN WARBLER
Dendroica fusca

This beautiful little warbler is named for Anna Blackburne, an English botanist of the eighteenth century who kept a museum of American birds in her home in Lancashire. The specimens she had were sent to her by her brother, who lived in the American colonies. Bent (1953) wrote, "Blackburnian seems to be a doubly appropriate name, for its upper parts are largely black and its throat burns like a brilliant orange flame amid the dark foliage of the hemlocks and spruces. A glimpse of such a brilliant gem, flashing out from its sombre surroundings, is fairly startling." This is an apt observation, and doubtless there are many people who became forever hooked on warbler watching when they saw their first Blackburnian. Like most other members of the family, it is an active bird, flying from branch to branch, fluttering, and flycatching, in nearly constant motion. It occasionally pauses to sing its high-pitched song from some high twig, often exposing the fiery flash of its orange throat.

This warbler was a regular, generally common, migrant around 1900. In some years it was abundant. Butler thought that it might be found nesting in Indiana, but that has not happened to date. It remains a fairly common migrant throughout the state. There have been occasional sightings in June and July in the past sixty years.

The habitat of the Blackburnian warbler is little different from that of the black-throated green: wooded areas of all kinds. Birds are likely to appear nearly anywhere during migration. The Blackburnian seems to spend most of its time fairly high in the trees.

An early arrival date is April 15, but numbers usually peak around mid-May. There were fifty in Madison County on May 11, 1924. Most have left the state by June 1, but there are observations for June and July from the Indiana Dunes, Fox Island County Park (Allen County), Pigeon River Fish and Wildlife Area, and the Pine Hills Nature Preserve. Fall migrants have been found as early as August 8 and the latest sighting is for November 18. There were twenty-five in Brown County on September 7, 1952.

YELLOW-THROATED WARBLER

YELLOW-THROATED WARBLER

Dendroica dominica

Sycamore Warbler, White-browed Warbler

In vistas of the leafless woods, it is easy to tell where the streams run. Creekside sycamores make ribbons of white, cream, and beige in the otherwise somber landscape. Seeing them in early spring always reminds us that the songs of yellow-throated warblers will soon be ringing through them. No other Indiana bird is so closely associated with sycamores as this handsome warbler. It seems to spend most of its time in them, and all of the nests reported from the state were found in sycamores.

According to Butler, the sycamore warbler—as it was then called—was "resident along the streams of southern Indiana, where timber containing sycamore trees is found." It was rare along the upper Wabash River and had not been found in the Kankakee River valley, or north of it, in the state. Today, it is a common summer resident and migrant throughout most of the southern

half of Indiana. In the northern half, it may be present or absent, but is generally distributed throughout the region, even being recorded along the Kankakee River and in the Indiana Dunes, both areas where it formerly was very rare or absent. During migration this warbler has been found not only in its favorite habitat, but in residential areas, and even shade trees along streets in towns.

John C. Kirkpatrick found a yellow-throated warbler at Madison on March 30, 1938. There are numerous sightings for the first week of April, for it is an early spring migrant. Ten were found at McCormick's Creek State Park on April 29, 1972. The latest date of fall departure is November 27, but there are relatively few records after October 1. On September 18, 1902, "it seemed that every shade tree in [Bloomington] contained five or six of these birds," wrote W. L. McAtee.

The first nests of the yellow-throated warbler reported in Indiana were evidently those observed by Mrs. Harry Bucklin of Brazil. She gave nesting data to Amos W. Butler that dated at least from 1924. We have records of eleven nests, but no information on clutch size or numbers of young in nests. This is not surprising since these nests were from thirty-five to eighty feet from the ground, most of them on small branches. The average height was about sixty-five feet. Nest building has been observed from April 26 to June 13. An adult yellow-throated warbler was seen feeding a fledgling on August 9.

Alan W. Bruner found forty-two singing males along Clifty, Indian, and Sugar Creeks (Montgomery County) in June 1979.

The "Sutton's warbler," once thought to be a distinct species, is now considered a hybrid of the yellow-throated and northern parula. In April 1980, Mr. and Mrs. Dolph E. Ulrich found a warbler of this type at their rural home near the border of Warren and Tippecanoe Counties. The bird was seen in association with a female northern parula. Many people saw this unusual hybrid, which was netted and photographed for detailed studies (*American Birds* 34:784). It chased a yellow-throated warbler from a bird feeder.

Depicted tree: Sycamore (*Platanus occidentalis*)

PINE WARBLER

Dendroica pinus

Pine-creeping Warbler

Some of the most spectacular topographical features of the Clark State Forest are the knobs, which rise more than 1,000 feet above sea level and several hundred feet above the surrounding terrain. The tops of the knobs support a mixed forest of Virginia pine, chestnut oak, and other deciduous trees. Here, in late March, one can often find male pine warblers in full song and evidently on territory. The species has probably nested here at least since the summer of 1903; the area may represent one of the best examples of native nesting habitat left in Indiana.

Butler remarked that this warbler was in general a rare migrant, but in a few localities small numbers of birds spent the summer. The only valid nesting record was that of E. W. Nelson, who found "a large number of these birds, with young just old enough to follow their parents" in a site locally called "The Pinery" (Lake County), on July 1, 1874. The species also was said to nest in Gibson and Knox Counties and to be present in summer in LaPorte County. Its current status may be about the same as around 1900, but we feel that the additional pine plantings in southern Indiana may have brought about an increase in the numbers of birds nesting there. In contrast, there are now fewer (and smaller) native pine stands near Lake Michigan, where pine warblers used to nest in some numbers, and few do so today.

The pine warbler is a woodland-inhabiting species which is not necessarily always found near conifers. However, it prefers to nest where pines are present, generally being found away from pines only during migration.

It is probably the most misidentified warbler that occurs in the state. Beginning birders confuse it with vireos or other warblers in spring and fall. This makes it necessary to evaluate sightings of "out of season" birds and unusual numbers with caution. It is not unusual to find pine warblers the last half of March; Alan W. Bruner found one as far north as Montgomery County on March 19, 1979. A few may winter in the state. Two were singing in Clark County on February 27, 1981. In areas where it does not nest, most have departed by the last week of May. Few remain in the fall by mid-October, but some have been found in November.

One was captured and banded at Marion (Grant County) from November 28 to December 1, 1979. One was seen on December 7, 1980, in Clark County; another on December 21, 1969, across the Ohio River from Louisville, Kentucky. Large numbers are never reported. Eight were seen in Marion County on May 17, 1946. On September 27, 1949, ten were recorded in Lake County.

Charles P. Smith found adult pine warblers feeding young out of the nest in Clark State Forest on July 20,

PINE WARBLER

1903. A nest was found in a Virginia pine in the same area about 1940, according to Floyd S. Carpenter. J. Dan Webster found a nest with three young in this forest May 12, 1977. It was twenty feet from the ground in a Virginia pine. These meager records sum up the information on nesting in the state.

Birds have been found during the nesting season in south-central Indiana, in an area bounded by Gibson, Morgan, and Clark Counties. Most of this region is in the unglaciated part of the state. There are a few recent summer records from about the southern end of Lake Michigan and St. Joseph County. Otherwise, the birds appear to be absent in the breeding season from the northern two-fifths of the state. No doubt there are isolated sites within this large area where the species will eventually be found at this season.

Depicted tree: Virginia or Scrub pine (*Pinus virginiana*)

KIRTLAND'S WARBLER
Dendroica kirtlandii

This fine warbler, on the rare and endangered lists for some years, nests only in a relatively small area in Michigan. Since its only known wintering grounds are in the Bahamas, migrants have at times been found in Indiana, where it is casual to accidental. Butler knew of two specimens (which we have examined), both collected by William O. Wallace at Wabash (Wabash County). One, sex not specified, was taken May 1, 1893, and another, a male, on May 7, 1895.

The first specimen was found in a thicket, where it was actively flycatching. The second was heard singing in a plum thicket. Between 1918 and 1983, nine additional sightings of this warbler were reported for Indiana. Only two were verified by physical evidence. One was photographed at Chesterton (Porter County) and seen by many on May 17 and 18, 1981. Kenneth J. Brock (1982), who found this bird, described the event. It foraged most of May 17 in a planting of Scotch pines and was remarkably tame. The other, a singing male, was found at Michigan City on May 22 and 23, 1983; many persons observed this bird, and it was also photographed.

Other observations were reported from Hamilton, Marion, Porter, Randolph, and Wayne Counties. All records are for May, ranging from the 1st to the 25th.

PRAIRIE WARBLER

Dendroica discolor

By early June in overgrown old fields in southern Indiana, the oxeye daisy is blooming profusely and thickets of blackberry are starred with white flowers. The early morning dew hangs heavy on the weedy vegetation; the absence of any wind indicates that by midday it will be quite warm. As you walk in the rolling fields, which support clumps of sassafras, scattered redbud, and other sprouts or bushes, the thin, ascending song of the prairie warbler may be heard. In these dry, hot, upland fields, it remains throughout the summer as one of the characteristic birds of the community. Among its nesting associates are the yellow-breasted chat, field sparrow, and indigo bunting.

Butler considered the prairie warbler a rare migrant and summer resident, but knew of no actual nesting records for Indiana. Robert Ridgway found it in Knox County on April 15, 1881, and by 1897 it had been sighted in Boone, Gibson, Monroe, Starke, and Wabash Counties.

A male was seen in the Indiana Dunes (near Miller) on May 16, 1909. During the summer of 1910, Philip Baker found prairie warblers in Brown County, where they undoubtedly nested that year. On May 8, 1916, Baker found the first Indiana nest of this species there (Butler, 1917). The prairie warbler has greatly increased in Indiana since the early 1900s and probably nests (or has nested) in at least sixty counties. It may nest in every county in the southern half of the state. In addition, birds still nest along the Lake Michigan dunes (Lake and Porter Counties), in Wabash County, and possibly in Huntington, Lagrange, and Tippecanoe Counties in northern Indiana. The major breeding range is south of a line connecting Montgomery and Wayne Counties.

Val Nolan Jr. (1978) conducted his classic study of the prairie warbler near Bloomington (Monroe County). The habitat there was rather typical of good prairie warbler nesting habitat in south-central Indiana, consisting of abandoned, overgrown, upland agricultural fields with scattered shrubs and small trees. This warbler has also been found nesting in old stripmined lands, overgrown orchards, Christmas tree plantings, and shrubby, rather open, sandy areas along the shores of Lake Michigan. It prefers open areas with high ground cover and relatively few large trees. At Nolan's study areas, much of the ground cover was composed of broomgrass, other grasses, pussytoes, daisy, goldenrod, blackberry, and raspberry. The commonest trees were redbud, sassafras, American elm, flowering dogwood, shining sumac, sugar maple, black cherry, ashes, and red cedar.

Spring migrants normally arrive in April. The earliest arrival date is April 11, at Bloomington, where the median arrival date from 1952 to 1967 was about April 18. Fall migrants linger into October and Nolan found the latest in his study area on October 10. Boyd Gill recorded a prairie warbler at the Muscatatuck National Wildlife Refuge on November 19, 1976. Most prairie warblers are seen on their nesting grounds; there are few data regarding migrants elsewhere.

Nolan found approximately 750 nests, which were constructed in about forty species of trees or shrubs, plus vines. About fifty-one percent of the nests were in American elms, which comprised only twenty-five percent of all trees in the study area. Sugar maple, hawthorn, and flowering dogwood each accounted for more than five percent of the nests. Sugar maples and dogwoods were selected as nesting sites approximately in proportion to their numbers. Nest heights ranged from 9.4 inches to about 44.5 feet, but the mean height was about 7.4 feet for 608 nests.

Eggs were found in nests from May 2 to at least July 25. Fourteen clutches contained five eggs each; one hundred and thirty-nine held four each; thirty-five contained three each. The average number of eggs per clutch was 3.9. Young left one nest on August 15.

In the sand dunes along Lake Michigan during nesting season, sixty pairs of prairie warblers per one hundred acres were found by Holly Reed Bennett. Nolan reported nineteen to twenty-three pairs per one hundred acres on his study areas near Bloomington. Alan W. Bruner estimated that forty pairs nested in the Shades State Park-Pine Hills areas in the summer of 1979.

Practically all of the food consumed on the breeding grounds is animal, mainly insects. Nolan found that prairie warblers obtained food by various methods, including gleaning, flycatching, hovering, clinging to vertical stems, hanging upside down, and even feeding on the ground.

Depicted plant: Sweet crabapple (*Pyrus coronaria*)

PALM WARBLER

Dendroica palmarum

Red-poll Warbler

Among the eighteen species of warblers of the genus *Dendroica* that occur in Indiana are birds of diverse habits. Some stay mostly in the treetops—the Blackburnian, bay-breasted, black-poll, and cerulean. Other forage and spend much time at moderate heights—the yellow, black-throated blue, and chestnut-sided. The palm warbler is one of those that feed on or near the ground. It may be seen there or flitting from weed top to bush; when perched, it engages in its characteristic tail-wagging, a good field mark.

Butler knew the palm warbler as a migrant that was very common (often very abundant) in the original prairie region of the state. It was much more numerous in spring than in fall. From most other places in Indiana, it was reported to be rare to "tolerably common," but in the southeastern half it was of irregular occurrence and seldom common. Today it is a generally common migrant throughout the state and at times is quite abundant along Lake Michigan in the fall. It is a very rare winter resident.

Habitats include open fields, fencerows, roadsides, thickets, and wooded areas. We have noticed it near marshes, in overgrown fields, in city parks, and similar sites, and about pine plantations. It has been seen foraging on plowed ground.

Non-wintering birds usually appear in April and normally are found throughout the state by the middle of that month. A hundred were seen in Monroe County on April 26, 1951. The latest spring date is May 27. An early fall migrant was observed August 22. It is not too unusual to see a hundred or more in a day in northwestern Indiana in late September or early October. Several hundred were probably present along Lake Michigan on October 18–19, 1980. Stragglers remain throughout the fall and into winter. There are at least eleven records for December and January and more birds may winter than is known at present. Wintering individuals may be found anywhere in the state, although most records are for the southern half.

BAY-BREASTED WARBLER

Dendroica castanea

Butler wrote the following about this pretty warbler, which arrived in spring a little later than the chestnut-sided warbler near his home at Brookville.

These two Warblers are always associated in my mind because the first specimen of each I shot were taken almost at the same hour, one spring morning, when almost all birds were new to me. They were new discoveries to a boy, to whom the high branches above became filled with flitting wings and a repetition of *t-sep* notes that plainly told of a world among the treetops, peopled by beautiful forms, unknown to the common run of mankind, who, though they have eyes and ears, neither see nor hear the inhabitants of that land. Their sight has not been quickened to see the unseen, nor their ears attuned to nature's harmony. She speaks not to them, because they have no communion with her. These associations, these discoveries, that come to each one of us, are a part of life that mean nothing to anyone save the individual concerned.

About 1900, the bay-breasted warbler was considered to be a very rare spring migrant, but was much more common in the fall. No doubt this summed up its status near Brookville, for Butler mentioned that in other parts of Indiana the species had been reported as common in spring. Its current status is that of a fairly common spring migrant and common fall migrant throughout the state.

It seems to prefer more open woodlands and open groves of trees to dense forest habitat. Like many other warblers, migrants may appear nearly anywhere that trees are present, so many birds are found in parks and residential areas, on campuses and golf courses, and in shrubby woods borders.

There are only a handful of April sightings, the earliest of which is for the 24th. The bay-breasted normally does not appear before early May and most leave the state by the end of that month. There is a June 4 record. August 9 is the earliest fall sighting and November 1 the latest. On May 17, 1946, Keller found forty-three in Marion County. Fifty-five were seen in Lawrence County on September 20, 1954, among 107 warblers of sixteen species.

Insects make up most of the food of this warbler, but migrants have been seen pecking at pokeberries and wild grapes. They may have been obtaining juice from these fruits.

BLACKPOLL WARBLER

Dendroica striata

This trim black and white warbler is a favorite of many. Males in spring are so unlike males in fall that casual observers might think two different species were involved. Many birders find it hard to tell fall-plumaged blackpolls from bay-breasted warblers, which are quite similar in appearance. Earlier ornithologists relied heavily on the shotgun in identifying the confusing fall warblers; they accepted little in the way of sight records.

Butler knew the blackpoll as a generally rare irregular migrant that was common in some years and usually more common in fall than in spring. It is now a fairly common spring migrant and a fairly common to common fall migrant throughout most of the state. It is not unusual for numbers to vary annually and locally.

The blackpoll warbler may be found in nearly any type of wooded habitat. In residential areas it may show a preference for evergreen trees. In general, it frequents the higher portions of the foliage.

The earliest date of spring arrival is April 26, but most do not arrive until May. Numerous birds may remain into the first week of June. Herbert L. Stoddard found blackpolls "common" on June 2, 1917, along Lake Michigan, and one was reported on June 6. James B. Cope found a singing male at Richmond on June 24, 1954. An early fall migration date is August 8; the latest is October 26. Spring migration usually peaks around mid-May. Fifty blackpolls were found in Owen County on May 13, 1951. Fall numbers appear to peak in late September. A total of thirty dead blackpolls were found beneath some television towers near South Bend on September 25 and 26, 1962.

CERULEAN WARBLER

Dendroica cerulea

Blue Warbler

This beautiful warbler inhabits the forest canopy, where two of its common bird neighbors in the summer are the red-eyed vireo and the eastern wood-pewee. Its wheezy song is what usually alerts the birder to its presence. Once the trees have leafed out, it is hard to get a good look at a cerulean. But they sometimes come to the ground to bathe or drink or to gather spider silk and other nesting materials; at close range, the pleasing blue of their plumage can be fully appreciated.

Butler thought that the cerulean warbler might be the most common tree-inhabiting warbler in the rougher land of southern Indiana during the summer and at migration times. It was a summer resident throughout most if not all of the state, but was possibly locally absent or rare. Today this warbler is in general a fairly common summer resident and migrant throughout the state in suitable habitat. It appears to be rare in some areas. The rugged, forested hill country of south-central Indiana still seems to contain the largest summer populations, but fairly large numbers are found elsewhere.

This typical woodland-inhabiting species is usually found in that habitat at all seasons that it is present, although during migration birds may appear out-of-habitat in less forested areas.

CERULEAN WARBLER

It has been observed in southern Indiana as early as April 11, but most migrants arrive during the last half of April or early May over the state as a whole. On May 16, 1964, sixteen were found in Tippecanoe County. Fall sightings are rather sparse; the latest record is for October 4. Our fall records reveal no more than two individuals seen in any one day. The cerulean is another of those woodland birds that quietly slips away after the nesting season and little has been recorded of its autumn movements.

Nest construction has been reported by May 5. Nests are normally placed high in large trees, sometimes over water. Eleven nests ranged in height from fifteen to eighty feet and averaged forty-five feet. They were all in deciduous trees, such as oak, elm, black walnut, and sycamore. There is a single record of the examination of a nest with eggs. Homer F. Price found a nest containing four warbler eggs and one brown-headed cowbird egg on May 28, 1933, near Zulu (Allen County). Small young just out of the nest were being fed by adults on June 23. An estimated forty-three pairs of cerulean warblers nested at the Shades State Park and Pine Hills Nature Preserve during the summer of 1979, according to Alan W. Bruner.

Depicted tree: White oak (*Quercus alba*)

BLACK-AND-WHITE WARBLER

BLACK-AND-WHITE WARBLER

Mniotilta varia

Black and White Creeper, Black and White Creeping Warbler, Variegated Creeper

Although most species of warblers that we see in Indiana in spring are transients, eager to get to their nesting grounds farther north, there are others that are in no hurry because they choose to nest in the state. One of the latter is the perky little black-and-white warbler, which because of its habits may sometimes be overlooked among the throng. But there it is, clinging to a large tree branch, climbing about searching crevices in the bark for insects, somewhat in the manner of a nuthatch, and living up to one of its vernacular names, "creeping warbler." Its high-pitched, monotonous song is soft, and can be difficult to hear above the songs of the louder species that may accompany it.

Butler implied that this warbler was common, at least during spring migration, and wrote that a few always nested throughout the state. It is currently a fairly common migrant and very rare summer resident in all sections of Indiana. There is a single winter record.

The black-and-white warbler is essentially a woodland-inhabiting species, although it may be observed during migration in other places where fairly large trees are present. It is regularly found in summer throughout the forested hill country of south-central Indiana and may be a regular but rare summer resident locally in other wooded sections of the state.

It is one of the earliest spring migrants, frequently arriving during the first half of April. There are sightings for March 27 (Tippecanoe County) and March 30 (Vanderburgh County). Irving W. Burr found thirty in the Lafayette area on May 17, 1945. Eight were seen in Brown County on September 3, 1950. Some birds linger until mid-October and as late as October 19. One black-and-white warbler was seen at Geist Reservoir on December 25 and 29, 1974.

Although this warbler may be found during the nesting season anywhere in suitable habitat in the state, there are few actual nesting records. Nests are on the ground and are usually quite well concealed. One contained four eggs, another six eggs, and a third held four young. A nest with six eggs was found near Lafayette on April 30, 1897; this appears to be an early date for a full clutch of eggs. One nest found by Keller was at the base of a small sassafras tree next to a logging trail in a mixed secondary forest. It was dome-shaped and lined with fine hairs and grasses. Another, found in a deciduous woods, was lined with deer hair. Val Nolan Jr. found ten singing male black-and-white warblers in the Morgan-Monroe State Forest during the summer of 1949.

Butler transcribed the song of this warbler as *easy-easy-easy-easy-easy*. This rendition is most often heard from the males in spring, but the singer is sometimes hard to locate because of the ventriloquial nature of the vocalizations.

Depicted plant: Three-lobed violet (*Viola triloba*)

AMERICAN REDSTART

Setophaga ruticilla

Redtail

This New World warbler obtained its name from early settlers who came from Europe or England, where a small member of the thrush family resembling the American bird was called a redstart. It was not unusual for Europeans who settled in North America to give Old World names to birds and mammals that reminded them of similar species at home. The American redstart is the most active of the warblers that grace Indiana. It appears to be constantly in motion, opening and closing its brightly colored tail as it flits from branch to branch, darts from side to side, or makes a sudden movement upward or downward, with drooping wings and ever-moving tail. It can scarcely be missed. Butler suggested that "little fantail" would be a good name for it.

Around 1900, it was considered generally common and was abundant in the northern part of the state. Butler implied that it nested throughout the state where there were wooded areas, but he actually provided little information on its breeding distribution. It is generally a common migrant and fairly common summer resident today, being most abundant in summer in the more heavily forested areas, which supply the best nesting habitats. It no doubt nests throughout Indiana.

It may be found in nearly any wooded habitat during migration, including shrubbery and lawns in towns and cities. In the forest it forages at all levels, but is often seen near the ground. In some parts of the state, large numbers of redstarts are present during the summer in wet or swampy woodlands. Nests have been found in forests, woodland borders, and old, overgrown fields, especially near streams.

April 12 is the earliest date for spring migration and redstarts are usually most abundant during May. There were fifty in Tippecanoe County on May 19, 1956. September is the peak of fall migration. Bruce A. Fall observed forty-three in Tippecanoe County on September 18, 1960. Most have left the state by mid-October, but there is one sighting for October 22. A live redstart was seen at Terre Haute in early December 1978.

Nest construction evidently begins in May, and one nest was about two-thirds complete on May 14. Twenty-nine nests were found to range from 4.5 to 35 feet above the ground; the average was 18.5 feet. Some were in small saplings, others on horizontal branches of large trees. Most were in deciduous woods, sometimes near a trail or along a creek. Delano Z. Arvin found more than two

AMERICAN REDSTART

dozen nests near Buck Creek (Tippecanoe County) from 1975 to 1980. Several of them were in box elder trees in fallow fields bordering woodlands.

Eggs were found in nests from May 21 to June 22. The clutch size in twenty-six nests ranged from two to four, and thirteen nests contained three eggs each. Some of the seven two-egg clutches may have been incomplete. In the summer of 1979, Alan W. Bruner found an estimated thirty pairs of redstarts nesting at Pine Hills Nature Pre-

serve and Shades State Park. Many of these pairs were inhabiting second-growth woodlands dominated by black locust. Sixty-eight redstarts were recorded at the Kankakee Fish and Wildlife Area on June 16, 1979. In 1924, Donald H. Boyd observed twenty-eight nests in a wooded tract containing from seventy-five to one hundred acres of "heavy timber" on the east side of Tippecanoe Lake (Kosciusko County).

Depicted plant: Mountain laurel (*Kalmia latifolia*)

PROTHONOTARY WARBLER

Protonotaria citrea

Golden Swamp Warbler

Golden swamp warbler is an apt name for this beautiful bird, which makes an unforgettable impression as it flies, now in shadow, now in sunlight, among the buttonbushes and cypresses of old river bayous, sloughs, and swamps in southwestern Indiana. The eminent Massachusetts ornithologist William Brewster (1878) wrote glowingly of seeing this warbler in that area in the spring of 1878 when he accompanied Robert Ridgway to some choice birding spots in Illinois and Indiana. According to Butler, Brewster's was the first report of its occurrence in Indiana.

Butler reported that it was a local summer resident, common in some places. It was found mainly in the Wabash River valley and along the Kankakee River, but was thought to be absent in summer from the Ohio River valley upstream from the mouth of the Wabash River. There were reports of local abundance in Lagrange County and of birds at other widely scattered locations in the northern half of the state. Butler wrote, "In the remainder of the State, east and south of the valley of the Wabash River, it is practically unknown." Today, it is a common to locally abundant summer resident in good habitat. It appears to be quite rare in migration away from its nesting grounds, but probably migrates along watercourses to a great extent, and has been observed throughout the state.

Swampy backwaters, sloughs, cypress swamps, and stream or river courses are the major habitats of this showy warbler. Favored nesting sites are holes in trees and branches (especially those that are dead) over water. It is unusual to find it far from water.

Spring migrants usually arrive in southern Indiana around mid-April, and the earliest sighting was April 10. Although Butler apparently never saw this warbler at Brookville, fourteen were seen on April 25, 1950, along the Whitewater River between Brookville and Cedar Grove. There were more than twenty-five at Hovey Lake on August 9, 1950. Most summering birds and migrants have departed by October 1, but one was found dead beneath a television tower in Floyd County on October 7. One was shot by a hunter near Newburgh (Warrick County) on November 27, 1959. This bird had sustained a fracture of the left radius and possibly was unable to fly when shot.

Many nests are placed in dead willow stems, which are

often abundant in flooded areas. Old woodpecker nesting holes or natural cavities are both used. Dead snags, stumps, nesting boxes, posts or even buildings are used for nesting sites on land. More unusual nesting locations were an empty tin can in a refuse container on a houseboat, a mailbox on a hotel's main door, a vent pipe, a water pipe, and an old pail suspended beneath the raised porch of a shack by a stream. Eighteen nests ranged from two to twenty feet in height above the water or land, and averaged nearly six feet. Flash floods sometimes destroy the lower nests.

Eggs have been observed in nests from May 13 to July 3. Clutch size data for eight nests include one clutch of two, two clutches of three, two of four, and three of five eggs. Two of the nests with five-egg clutches had a sixth, brown-headed cowbird egg.

Charles T. Clark estimated that one hundred pairs of prothonotary warblers were present on the Kankakee Fish and Wildlife Area on June 6, 1973. Before World War II, he had found only one or two pairs there. In 1954, Keller found about fifty pairs at Hovey Lake, and he saw fifty birds in Warrick County during June and early July 1981. Along about thirteen miles of Pigeon Creek above Yankeetown, an estimated fifty were observed on May 22, 1951.

The bird collected November 27 had insect remains of orders Hemiptera and Homoptera in its stomach, according to Nixon A. Wilson.

WORM-EATING WARBLER

Helmitheros vermivorus

Worm-eating Swamp Warbler

In Montgomery County where Indian Creek flows into Sugar Creek in the area known as Pine Hills, there is a series of spectacular hogback ridges that were formed by the erosive action of water on the sandstone over eons of time. A typical summer bird there is the worm-eating warbler, which was common in the general area as early as 1887. This scenic habitat is shared by the northern rough-winged swallow, yellow-throated warbler, northern parula, and summer tanager, among others. Many worm-eating warblers probably go undetected on their breeding grounds, because their songs are both difficult to hear and often mistaken for those of the chipping sparrow.

Around 1900 the worm-eating warbler was a common summer resident in suitable places in southern Indiana. Butler wrote that it was "one of the most abundant woodland species" in certain parts of the Whitewater River valley. It was also reportedly common in the lower Wabash River valley and at sites in Montgomery and Parke Counties. In general it was evidently absent to uncommon throughout most of northern Indiana, with local exceptions (DeKalb County). Butler knew of no records for northwestern Indiana north of the Wabash River. It is still locally common in optimum habitat throughout south-central Indiana and in parts of Montgomery and Parke Counties. It appears to be relatively rare during migration, but has been observed throughout the state. It probably nests wherever suitable habitat is found, even in northwestern Indiana. At Turkey Run State Park it was fairly common during the summer of 1948, but was apparently absent in the early 1960s. An estimated twelve pairs nested in the Pine Hills–Shades State Park area in 1979, but twenty-one pairs were found there in 1980.

Butler noted that this was a warbler of the "denser woodlands, especially in rough country, on hillsides and ravines, where down timber and underbrush" were plentiful. He mentioned that a "wind fall" was a favorite site. In our experience, it is a bird of rather heavily wooded hillsides where there are often steep slopes, ravines, and small streams. Alan W. Bruner found that many of the birds in the Pine Hills–Shades State Park area were on dry wooded slopes steeper than 50 degrees. It is found in deciduous woodlands and in mixed deciduous and coniferous areas.

The earliest spring record in April 15 (Clark County), and it arrives at most nesting areas during that month. Six males were singing at Clark State Forest on April 24, 1954. Although fall migrants are not reported from many areas, some birds linger as late as October 7. There is one sighting for November 5. The maximum number reported in the fall appears to be two, August 16, 1953

WORM-EATING WARBLER

(Vigo County), and August 31, 1952 (Brown County). Relatively few observers frequent the nesting areas of this warbler during the fall, thus the lack of data.

The nest is placed on the ground; two were in clumps of fern. Another was within three feet of the edge of a little-used gravel road. Eggs have been found from May 12 to July 4. In six nests clutch size ranged from three to six. Four nests each contained three eggs, one had five warbler eggs and two brown-headed cowbird eggs, and one had six warbler eggs and one cowbird egg.

Depicted plant: Wild ginger (*Asarum canadense*)

[SWAINSON'S WARBLER]
Limnothlypis swainsonii

Whether this warbler has in fact ever been seen in Indiana is not clear. Butler mentioned that Robert Ridgway had found the species in Knox County in 1878 and reported it as breeding there, but the two published sources Butler cited are not entirely persuasive. In Ridgway (1878), an account of the birds found in Illinois and Indiana, Swainson's warbler is listed with question marks preceding it. Indiana is not specifically mentioned, and from the writing it is impossible to determine which state he was talking about. Ridgway (1889) discussed the distribution of this warbler, including southwestern Indiana with a question mark. He may have given Butler additional information thereafter, but years later he stated only that it probably occurred in Indiana. Since then, sightings have been reported in Marion and Porter Counties, but we are not sure of their validity.

OVENBIRD

Seiurus aurocapillus

Golden-crowned Thrush, Golden-crowned Wagtail

The stillness of a late spring or early summer morning stroll through an Indiana woodland may be broken by the sharp, ascending staccato *teacher-teacher-TEACHER-TEACHER-TEACHER* song of the ovenbird. It is a distinctive song, although some have mistaken it for that of the Kentucky warbler or Carolina wren. The ovenbird is a bird of the forest floor, where it walks about in the gloom in search of insects and constructs its "Dutch oven" type nest, which is responsible for the bird's vernacular name. Golden-crowned thrush is also an apt name, for (except for its golden crown) the ovenbird resembles a small wood thrush in color and body proportions.

Butler considered the ovenbird a common summer resident in the denser woodlands of the state, noting that it was very abundant throughout the rougher, forested areas of southern Indiana. The widespread cutting of timber and other habitat changes have caused the ovenbird to be today a fairly common summer resident and common migrant statewide. It may be common to absent locally, however, and unless there is suitable wooded habitat birds may be scarce. During the nesting season, it appears to be quite rare in extreme southwestern Indiana.

Butler wrote that the ovenbird frequented "such land as the Worm-eating Warbler likes—the cool, dark shades of the quiet forest, where amid the thick undergrowth, the fallen trees and broken limbs, man nor anything that belongs to him comes to disturb its life." Alan W. Bruner found that in the Pine Hills–Shades State Park area of west-central Indiana, nesting ovenbirds favored the dry mature and second-growth woodlands with little undergrowth. Migrants, like so many other species, may appear out-of-habitat in other wooded or partially wooded areas.

The earliest date of spring arrival is March 31 at Indianapolis. Arrival dates for other southern counties fall around mid-April. Ovenbirds remain throughout October and into the first week of November. Sightings were made November 9 in Porter County and November 10 in Allen County. The single winter record is for a bird seen at Richmond on December 26, 1965. Irving W. Burr estimated fifty ovenbirds in Tippecanoe County on May 15, 1943. The fall peak was ten, seen in Marion County by Val Nolan Jr. on September 21, 1948.

Nests are placed on the ground and are usually quite well concealed by available ground cover and by the fact that they are domed over on top, with a side entrance. One was found beside a fallen log. Full clutches of eggs have been seen as early as May 13; a nest investigated on June 24 contained two eggs and a naked young. Young just out of the nest were seen July 12. Clutch size varied from four to six for the few nests recorded in our files. A nest observed at regular intervals in Warren County by Dolph E. Ulrich and Susan H. Ulrich eventually contained nine brown-headed cowbird eggs and no ovenbird eggs. During the summer of 1979, an estimated twenty-four pairs of ovenbirds nested at the Pine Hills–Shades State Park complex, according to Alan W. Bruner.

The flight song of the ovenbird is not often heard. The singing bird will rise above the ground, sometimes to the treetops, then flys about beating its wings in a high arc over its back, while warbling a pleasing series of notes. We have heard this song in April and May at dusk and in early September at dawn.

Depicted plant: Wild geranium (G. maculatum)

NORTHERN WATERTHRUSH

Seiurus noveboracensis

Small-billed Water Thrush, Water Wagtail, Grinnell's Water Thrush,
Short-billed Water Thrush, Water Thrush

The Muscatatuck River from where it crosses Route 39 to Sparksville is meandering and rather sluggish. Along its banks are sloughs and small swamps where willows and buttonbushes grow in profusion. On May 6, 1954, a number of northern waterthrushes were singing along this section of the river. To the bird's many vernacular names one could add the additional one of swamp waterthrush, for it is often observed in bushes or trees over the water.

It appears to have been a rather rare migrant throughout the state about 1900 and Butler thought (without evidence) that it nested in the northern section. This waterthrush today appears to be a fairly common migrant and a casual summer resident locally in northeastern Indiana. There is one nesting record and one winter observation. Much confusion exists among birders regarding the correct identification of the northern waterthrush and the Louisiana waterthrush in the field.

Northerns occur along streams and on the borders of lakes, marshes, and other water areas where there is good cover. Some of the birds found recently during June have been in swamps, where they may have been nesting. Tangles of willows and other vegetation at the water's edge seem to be favorite foraging sites.

The earliest spring arrival was reported on March 27, but most of the birds appear during April. Most have departed northward by June 1, but there are a few exceptions. Fall migrants have appeared as early as August 5 and remained as late as October 16. Again, we are citing these records with the assumption that the species was correctly identified. One was recorded at Lafayette on December 26, 1966. Spring migration usually reaches its peak around mid-May. Nineteen northern waterthrushes were observed along the Salamonie River between Montpelier and Warren on May 10, 1950. Smaller numbers are reported in the fall; the maximum appears to be three each in Lake County (September 1, 1929) and Marion County (September 4, 1972).

There are reports of nesting in DeKalb County before 1898 and in Kosciusko County in 1902. Neither record can be verified. Singing males were present at the Pigeon River Fish and Wildlife Area in June during the late 1970s and the species was seen in Huntington County in June 1980. Henry C. West banded a waterthrush he identified as an immature of this species at the Mary Gray Bird Sanctuary (Fayette County) on June 14, 1975. Finally, D. Peter Siminski located a nest at Pigeon River during the summer of 1982. We clearly need further information on the occurrence of this interesting warbler in Indiana during the nesting season.

LOUISIANA WATERTHRUSH

Seiurus motacilla

Large-billed Water Thrush, Water Wagtail

The loud, ringing song of the Louisiana waterthrush may be heard along small, rocky streams in the hills of south-central Indiana so early in the spring that the woodlands still present a winter aspect. Spring migrants return early to their rather special habitats, where they can be seen walking on the rocks with tails wagging, or foraging at streamside with tails tilted upward. When disturbed, the birds give a loud *chink* call that resembles metal striking metal. From time to time the males will burst into their wild, distinctive songs, sometimes given in flight.

Butler knew this waterthrush as a common summer resident in southern Indiana in suitable localities, but mentioned that it was less common northward. He thought that it was rare in the Kankakee River valley northward in northwestern Indiana. It remains a fairly common migrant and summer resident where habitat conditions are right throughout most of the southern half of the state. In northern Indiana, it is in general an uncommon migrant and rare summer resident, with some local exceptions.

Butler remarked that woodland streams, springs, and ponds attracted this warbler. The Louisiana waterthrush seems to prefer to nest along small streams, some of which may be intermittent. It is seldom found very far from water.

Spring migrants can be expected in late March; Palmer D. Skaar found one in Monroe County on March 20, 1948. Birds have been found as far north as the Pine Hills Nature Preserve by March 21. A maximum of twenty was reported in Marion County on May 12, 1934. Most have left the state by the end of September, but there are a few sightings for October and an extremely late one for November 5, 1953, by Eugene Hollinger at Goshen (Elkhart County). Ten were seen near Bedford on September 20, 1954.

Nests are usually placed beside flowing streams or in cut banks of intermittent streams and ravines in wooded areas. Most of them are on the ground among roots and leaves under overhanging banks. One nest was on the ground about eight feet above a stream. Others were found among the roots of a fallen tree over the water, in a cavity of a huge rotten stump, and at the rocky entrance to a cave, high up on a limestone ledge.

Sixteen nests contained from three to six eggs each and averaged 4.6 per nest. Six nests held four each; five nests contained five each. Eggs were found in nests as early as May 2. One pair of waterthrushes was building a nest on June 9, and there were young in another nest on June 20. Alan W. Bruner estimated that twenty-three pairs nested in Pine Hills and Shades State Park in the summer of 1979. He knew the nests were nearby when he found large numbers of fecal sacs deposited by the birds in the wet stream bed.

Depicted plant: Wild stonecrop (*Sedum ternatum*)

KENTUCKY WARBLER

Oporornis formosus

Most warblers of the genus *Oporornis* are noted for being secretive. Yet there are rare opportunities when conditions are just right for viewing one of these shy species. A bright ray of sunlight may penetrate the gloom of the forest floor and illuminate a singing male Kentucky warbler perched on a small sapling. Or one may see this yellowish bird with its yellow "spectacles" walking about in the leaves under blooming Mayapples, appearing reluctant to allow the observer a clear view. The loud two- or three-noted song may be mistaken for that of the Carolina wren or the ovenbird. One rendition sounds to us like *giddy-ap, giddy-ap, giddy-ap*.

Around 1900, the Kentucky warbler was considered to be a common summer resident throughout the southern two-thirds of Indiana, but was seldom reported north of Lafayette. It remains a common migrant and summer resident, where habitat is suitable, throughout the state except the northern third. However, the Kentucky warbler has been observed, and probably nests, in all parts of Indiana. It may be locally absent to common.

Robert Ridgway found this warbler most abundant in the lower Wabash River valley in the "rich woods of the bottom lands." Butler noted that in the Whitewater River valley, where there were few bottomland woods, the Kentucky warbler was found in dark, damp woods. But it is also found in rugged, dry, upland woods. It is seldom seen away from well-wooded areas.

Spring migrants arrive in southern Indiana in April; the earliest date is April 13. Abundance peaks are reached in May; fifteen Kentucky warblers were seen in Tippecanoe County on May 16, 1942. There are practically no fall data for migrants. The birds evidently slip away from their summer haunts relatively early in the fall migratory season. A few have been recorded in September, and Butler mentioned an observation of six in Boone County, on October 11, 1894, by J. E. Beasley. This is quite late and is also the largest fall number reported.

Nests are either on the ground or elevated as much as a foot above it. One nest was at the base of a small tree, another in ferns, and one was in the grasses that had grown up in an old logging road. The clutch size for ten nests ranged from three to five and averaged slightly more than four eggs per nest. Three of the three-egg nests, however, also contained cowbird eggs and may have been incomplete clutches. Seven nests each contained four eggs. Eggs were found in nests from May 25 to June 16. The latest occupied nest was seen on June 19, at which time it held four young.

At Fox Island Park (Allen County), about twelve Kentucky warblers were present during the summer of 1976. This is an unusual number for a locality so far north. It was estimated that thirty-one pairs nested in the Shades State Park–Pine Hills area during the summer of 1979.

Depicted plant: Spiderwort (*Tradescantia virginiana*)

CONNECTICUT WARBLER
Oporornis agilis

It was a partly cloudy, warm afternoon in late May. The mature woods not far from Scottsburg contained many large beech, tulip, poplar, sweet gum, sycamore, and other trees typical of a low, flat region bordering a stream. As we walked among the huge trees (often wading through standing pools of water), we were continually pushing aside branches of spicebush, which grew profusely. As the newly emerged spicebush leaves were crushed, they gave off their characteristic "spiced soap" odor. An Acadian flycatcher was building a nest in a large beech tree, wood thrushes were singing, and we had found a migrant gray-cheeked thrush. Not far ahead, we heard a bird song we did not immediately recognize, although it sounded familiar. We squatted down in the undergrowth and made a few *pishing* sounds. The singer hopped up from its perch near the ground onto a twig, peering about for the cause of the disturbance, and we got a good look at him: a Connecticut warbler.

Butler knew this warbler as a generally very rare migrant and wrote that he had seen it only three of nineteen years at Brookville. He did, however, find it "rather common" there from May 22 to 25, 1882. Elsewhere in the state, its status appears to have been about the same, birds being reported northeastward to Wabash County. It is now a rare spring migrant and very rare fall migrant, in our experience. The extreme difficulty of identifying immature Connecticut warblers in the fall should lead to caution when evaluating observations made at that season.

It is a shy bird that prefers rather dense ground cover and underbrush, especially in low, damp places, and spends most of its time on or near the ground.

This warbler generally arrives in May, but there are a few late April sightings, the earliest being for the 27th. It is not unusual for some birds to remain into early June. There are sightings for June 1 to 4 from several counties, the southernmost being Marion and Wayne. A very late straggler was found in Marion County on June 23, 1955. Irving W. Burr found ten in Tippecanoe County on May 23, 1959. The earliest fall migrant was reported on August 25. There are several October sightings, of which the latest is for the 9th. A dead Connecticut warbler was found beneath a television tower in Floyd County on October 7. At another television tower near South Bend, three were found dead each morning on September 25 and 26, 1962.

MOURNING WARBLER
Oporornis philadelphia
Philadelphia Warbler

Alexander Wilson named this warbler for its black bib, which he thought made the bird look as though it were in mourning. This is another elusive denizen of the woodland floor. It is generally less difficult to observe than its near relative, the Connecticut warbler, which it sometimes accompanies on migration. We know of a spot in a second-growth woods on the floodplain of the Wabash River where by late May a profusion of poison ivy completely covers the ground. If we search here assiduously during the last week of May, we can usually be assured of finding the mourning warbler. At times we have seen as many as three or more in the ivy patch. But anyone sensitive to poison ivy is barred from seeking this beautiful warbler in such haunts.

Around 1900, this warbler was described as a rare migrant whose abundance varied somewhat from year to year at a given locality. Butler thought it might possibly nest in northern Indiana, but there is still no record of its doing so, although there have been numerous sightings during the nesting season. It currently appears to be an uncommon spring migrant and a rare fall migrant, but birders should be on the lookout for nesting birds across the northern end of Indiana.

The mourning warbler uses much the same habitat as the Connecticut warbler: low, damp patches with dense ground cover. It can also be seen in woods or marsh borders where there is sufficient brushy cover.

Spring migrants normally appear in May, but there is an April 24 sighting for Allen County. There are early June records for nearly a dozen counties, the southernmost of which is Posey; evidently many birds are stragglers during spring migration. The presence of singing males in late June suggests the possibility of nesting. Mark A. Weldon found two males singing at the Pigeon River Fish and Wildlife Area on June 21, 1979. A male was singing in Porter County on June 29, 1955, and Emma B. Pitcher banded a mourning warbler in that county on July 4, 1975. From May 13 to June 18, 1961, Virginia Reuterskiold observed sixty mourning warblers near Baileytown (Porter County). Twelve were seen on May 30, 1963, in Tippecanoe County. An early fall migrant was found in Allen County on August 22. There are several October sightings, the latest of which is for the 31st. Again, one should exercise caution in identifying immatures in the fall. The maximum number noted in autumn was two, on September 17, 1978, in Lake County.

[MACGILLIVRAY'S WARBLER]
Oporornis tolmiei

For many years it was believed that this western United States species had once been found in Indiana. On June 1, 1879, a bird of the genus *Oporornis* was collected in Lake County. The specimen was sent to the British Museum, where R. B. Sharpe (1885) identified it as a MacGillivray's warbler. Butler evidently questioned the accuracy of this identification, as did others, including Robert Ridgway. But the record stood until reexamination of the specimen showed that the bird was actually a mourning warbler. This was recently confirmed by Peter R. Colston of the British Museum (letter to Keller, June 23, 1982).

Earl A. Brooks (1925) reported the banding of a MacGillivray's warbler near Noblesville on May 29, 1924. However, from what we now know of plumages, Brooks's basis for the identification (the incomplete eye-ring) was insufficient to separate MacGillivray's warbler from mourning warbler. He may have been correct, but we must consider the record uncorroborated.

COMMON YELLOWTHROAT

Geothlypis trichas

Black-masked Warbler

In some ways, this striking little marshland dweller looks more like a wren than a warbler. It announces its presence with a *witchity-witchity-witchity* song, which may be rendered from a hidden spot in the lush vegetation or a higher, exposed site such as a telephone wire. An observer wandering in the marshy border of a pothole pond during the nesting season may suddenly be scolded soundly by an excited pair of yellowthroats. The birds come near, fluttering out of the vegetation to utter sharp chipping notes and excitedly moving around. It is at such times that one can best observe this showy species, and careful searching may reveal a nest or young nearby.

Butler knew the yellowthroat as a common summer resident throughout the state. Its status is much the same today, except that there is now sufficient evidence to state that it is also a very rare winter resident. One was recorded at Richmond on December 21, 1952. From 1971 to the present, twelve additional winter records from eleven other counties scattered about the state have accumulated in our files.

The yellowthroat frequents "the tall grasses, sedges and shrubbery about the swamps and damp places and along the valleys of streams," wrote Butler, who also noted that "some wander away to the hillsides and uplands." This warbler is usually found near water and may be quite abundant near larger marshes. Birds are also found in drier, upland sites in old fields. Migrants may appear in habitats which they do not use during the nesting season.

Spring migrants have been found in southern Indiana as early as April 15. A peak of fifty was noticed at the Willow Slough Fish and Wildlife Area on May 15 and 16, 1979, by Ted T. Cable. Despite its apparent absence from many areas by the end of October, some yellowthroats linger throughout November and December. There were twelve at Willow Slough on September 20, 1952. Males seldom sing after July and the birds remaining on the nesting grounds are then harder to find.

COMMON YELLOWTHROAT

Most nests are placed on or near the ground (or water), usually slightly above it. Practically all of the nests for which we have records were within three to eighteen inches of the ground and were in clumps of grasses or other vegetation. One unusual nest was three feet above the water in a stand of cattails, and two others were over water in mixed stands of cattails and grasses. Edgar R. Quick found a three-story nest, each additional layer having been built to cover a brown-headed cowbird egg.

Full clutches of eggs were observed as early as May 7 and eggs were present in one nest on July 28. Clutch size ranged from three to five and averaged 4.2 eggs per nest. Nine of nineteen nests each contained four eggs and seven contained five eggs each. Another nest held five yellow-throat and two cowbird eggs. During the summer of 1979, an estimated forty pairs of yellowthroats nested in Shades State Park.

Michael P. Kowalski conducted research on vocalizations of the yellowthroat in southern Indiana. A male observed on April 27, 1970, uttered 255 songs in one hour. Territorial males sang most persistently early in the morning in late April, early May, and the first half of July. Part of the repertoire of the yellowthroat is a flight song, given most often between four and six in the evening in late June. Charles E. Keller and Timothy C. Keller heard a male singing an unusual insectlike buzzing song, somewhat like that of the blue-winged warbler.

Depicted plant: Black-eyed Susan (*Rudbeckia hirta*)

HOODED WARBLER

Wilsonia citrina

Hooded Fly-catching Warbler

We were searching for morels in one of our favorite spots, a remote, wooded section of the Morgan-Monroe State Forest, in late April. It was a warm, still morning and a ruffed grouse occasionally drummed in the distance. Box turtles were out and we had picked one up to admire its beautifully designed protective shell. From the top of a partially rotted log that lay on the hillside an eastern chipmunk scolded then dashed, chattering, into its burrow when we came too near. Then we heard the clear *weeta—weeta—wee tee o* of a male hooded warbler that had probably just arrived on its nesting grounds. A few minutes later we watched it walking around among the Christmas ferns on the forest floor. It was a beautiful bird in a pleasant setting, and for a few minutes we forgot about morels.

This warbler was a generally rare summer resident in Indiana about 1900, being common in parts of the lower Wabash River valley and very rare in the northern part of the state (with local exceptions). Butler remarked that it was more numerous everywhere during migration. It is still a fairly common migrant and summer resident in certain parts of southern and central Indiana. Northward, it may be locally fairly common to absent. There are summer and nesting records from throughout the state and this warbler probably nests in suitable habitat statewide. However, the bulk of the nesting population is south of the latitude of Indianapolis.

This is a woodland species, most likely to be found in forested areas with well-developed understory and ground cover. Some of the best habitat appears to be the wooded hill country of south-central Indiana, where hooded warblers have been found regularly in fairly good numbers for at least thirty-five years.

The earliest date for a spring migrant is March 25, 1954, when Theodore A. Chandik found an adult male at Whiting. This is quite early, but there is also an April 14, 1931, sighting for the same place. The earliest observation for southern Indiana is April 16, at Greensburg. There were six singing males in the Harrison State Forest on May 20, 1959. Although fall records are relatively few (and all are of single birds), some of them are for October. The latest sightings were made on October 20, which is undoubtedly quite late. Most have departed by mid-September.

We know little about the nesting habits of the hooded warbler and have reports of few nests. All were in wooded areas. One was two feet from the ground in a crotch formed by a maple-leaved viburnum sprout and a green-brier. It contained three warbler eggs and a brown-headed cowbird egg on May 29. Another was in a greenbrier three feet from the ground. One nest contained three young on June 8 and another held six young on May 27. Another, 28.5 inches off the ground in a viburnum, held three young on June 23.

HOODED WARBLER

At least fifteen singing male hooded warblers were present in the Morgan-Monroe State Forest during the summer of 1949. One northern area of local abundance during the summer is the Pigeon River Fish and Wildlife Area, where four singing males were present in 1977, six in 1978, and at least eight pairs were estimated in 1979.

Depicted plants: Elm (*Ulmus sp.*); Columbine (*Aquilegia canadensis*)

WILSON'S WARBLER
Wilsonia pusilla

Black-capped Flycatching Warbler, Green Black-capped Fly-catching Warbler, Black-capped Yellow Warbler, Pileolated Warbler

After most of the other warblers have arrived in spring, and many have moved northward out of the state, we watch for one of our favorites—Wilson's warbler. In most cases a bird of the understory like the other members of the genus, it appears to prefer willows for foraging, whether they are growing about a marsh, along a ditchbank, or near ponds. The male is a striking bird, with a jet-black skull cap and beady black eyes. One early May morning in a brushy woodlot we watched one bathing in the dew that had collected on a large buckeye leaf.

Butler wrote that it occurred throughout the state as a migrant, but was more common in fall than in spring. It now appears to be an uncommon spring migrant and fairly common fall migrant. It may be locally common for brief periods or be very rare to absent. It frequents the undergrowth of woodlands, and is often found near water, but may appear in many habitats. One was feeding in giant ragweeds along a creek.

The Wilson's generally arrives in May throughout the state (there is an April 22 sighting), and it is not unusual for individuals to remain into June; most of these are males, some of which sing rather persistently at this season. One was seen as late as June 12. An early fall date is August 4. Most migrants enter northern Indiana during the last ten days of August. Four were recorded in Marion County on September 7, 1960. A few stragglers linger into October, for there are several records for the first half of the month and two for the last half, and even one sighting for November 9.

CANADA WARBLER

CANADA WARBLER

Wilsonia canadensis

Canadian fly-catching Warbler

Those of us who have searched for nesting birds in the Indiana Dunes State Park during the summer know what a frustrating experience it can be. There are numerous swampy places with almost impenetrable vegetation and black, knee-deep muck. In the heat you sweat so much that your insect repellent washes off, leaving you vulnerable to the hordes of ravenous mosquitos. Yet there is much to attract the interested birder. It is the only place we know of where it is possible to stand in one place and hear both the Canada warbler and its southern cousin, the hooded warbler, singing simultaneously—the avifauna of the dunes offer a curious mingling of north and south. We and others have tried for many years to locate the nests of the Canada warbler here, but the birds have always eluded us.

Butler reported that this warbler was a "tolerably common migrant" that varied in numbers from year to year and was usually more common in fall than in spring. He made no mention of the possibility of nesting in Indiana and listed no sightings later than May 26. Today it is in general a fairly common migrant and a rare, local summer resident across the northern end of the state, and probably nests in places other than those for which we have records.

Spring migration usually occurs mostly in May, although Robert Ridgway collected a specimen in Knox County on April 18, 1881. Since the Canada warbler is a relatively late spring migrant, birds (many of them singing males) linger into early June. There are June sightings from as far south as southeastern Monroe County, where a female was seen on June 11, 1978. Irving W. Burr saw twenty in Tippecanoe County on May 23, 1954. Fall migrants appear in northern Indiana in August and one was found as far south as Knox County on August 17. Raymond J. Fleetwood saw six in Elkhart County on August 28, 1932. October 9 is the latest fall record.

Favored habitats are the undergrowth and borders of wooded areas, edges of swamps and marshes, damp woods, and thickets along streams. During the summer most birds are found (sometimes with veeries) in wet areas such as swamps or low, wet woods.

There are only two actual nesting records for Indiana and a single nest has been found. Herbert L. Stoddard found a Canada warbler at Tremont (Porter County) on July 15, 1917, and wrote that it "acted like it might be a nesting bird." It was found in this general area during the summers of 1956 and 1957, and Raymond Grow found adults feeding a fledgling cowbird (out of the nest) in 1958. Canada warblers have been present in the dunes regularly since then. Birds were seen carrying nesting material in 1975, and Kenneth J. Brock found an adult with an immature (out of the nest) on July 23, 1979.

The first nest was found on the Pigeon River Fish and Wildlife Area on June 16, 1978, by Lee A. Casebere, D. Peter Siminski, and Mark A. Weldon. Canada warblers have been found here in summer since at least 1974. Casebere (1979) described finding this nest and summarized previous records for the area. The nest was in a tamarack swamp containing such other woody vegetation as red maple, elm, poison sumac, spicebush, and juneberry. Herbaceous vegetation included skunk cabbage, marsh marigold, meadowrue, dwarf raspberry, horsetail, sedges, and grasses. Many root tangles and mossy clumps were present. The nest was built into the side of a mossy clump near the bases of a small dogwood and a swamp rose. It contained one egg and two young on June 16 and three young the following day.

There are June or July sightings for the Canada warbler from twelve counties, and diligent searching will no doubt reveal additional nests in the future, especially in extreme northern Indiana, where the most suitable habitat is present.

Depicted plant: Toothed wood fern (*Dryopteris spinulosa*)

YELLOW-BREASTED CHAT

Icteria virens

To some who know the chat, it seems a bit odd that it is classified as a warbler, for its behavior is more like that of a mimic thrush—especially a mockingbird. It scolds the intruder from a hiding place in a dense thicket or brier patch with a series of harsh clucks, whistles, squeaks, squawks, and other vocal efforts difficult to describe. It may fly from one bushy clump to another over a considerable distance, all the while slowly flapping its wings, pumping its tail, dangling its legs, and singing. At times the chat even sings throughout the night. Butler wrote,

Everyone who is acquainted with brier patches, thickets and bushy clearings, knows this bird. If they do not know its name, they know it as the bird which fills the thicket with such sounds as no other bird ever dreamed of. It is more often heard than seen. Were it not that occasionally its yellow breast comes into view, we should think it but a voice among the bushes. They are great ventriloquists. Often a person unacquainted with their habit will look long in the direction from which the sound seems to come and not see the author, who is elsewhere. They have quite a variety of notes, which, with their strange antics, render them the most interesting summer birds among the bushes. At mating time they devote much time to aerial evolutions, which are always interesting because of their oddity, but at times become exceedingly ludicrous. While performing these various evolutions they give voice to a multitude of strange sounds, that seem to come from here, there and everywhere, except the throat of the odd and awkward bird descending towards the clump of bushes near by.

Butler knew the chat as a common summer resident in the southern half of the state. In northern Indiana, it was reported locally common in Madison, Tippecanoe, and Wayne Counties, uncommon at Wabash, and rare in Allen, DeKalb, Elkhart, and Starke Counties. Before 1893 it was almost unknown in the northwestern portion of the state, but there was evidently a considerable range extension northward in 1894. Its abundance at certain places has fluctuated greatly over the years, the birds being sometimes common, sometimes rare. Its present status is about the same as described by Butler, except

YELLOW-BREASTED CHAT

that there are now different areas of local abundance in northern Indiana. It evidently breeds throughout the state where it can find the correct habitat. It was abundant in overgrown stripmined land in eastern Gibson County and western Pike County in 1980. There is a single winter record.

There is an extremely early spring sighting on April 6, 1928, from northwestern Indiana. The next earliest observations were made on April 19 (Harrison and Vanderburgh Counties). At most locations, the birds first arrive during May. Fifteen each were seen in Tippecanoe County (May 30, 1963) and the Willow Slough Fish and Wildlife Area (May 29, 1977). The maximum number reported in the fall was two, September 24, 1979, at South Bend. Most depart by the end of September, but there are sightings for October 7 and 12. Butler collected one (probably at Brookville) on December 1, 1881. One was reported at Evansville on December 28, 1955.

The chat is a bird of old, overgrown fields, where there are grasses, weeds, brier patches, clumps of bushes, small trees, and thickets. Most of the nest records for which habitat is mentioned refer to shrubby or brushy old fields; an occasional nest is found about the brushy edges of wet or swampy places. The birds will nest in multiflora rose where it is available to them. In abandoned agricultural fields near Bloomington, most nests were in small elm trees. Numerous nests have been found in blackberry briers. Nests are not far from the ground and placed in various types of bushes, briers and small trees. Twenty-one nests near Bloomington ranged from six inches to four feet above the ground and averaged thirty-five inches. Twenty-eight others were from eighteen inches to four and three-quarters feet off the ground and averaged about thirty-two inches.

Eggs were found in nests from May 12 to July 24. Clutch size ranged from three to six and averaged 3.6 for sixty-two nests. Thirty-three nests contained four eggs each, twenty-six held three each; there were two clutches of five and one of six. Thompson and Nolan (1973) reported on the population ecology of the chat near Bloomington; some of the above data are from their study.

Alan W. Bruner estimated that one hundred pairs of chats nested at Pine Hills Nature Preserve and Shades State Park in the summer of 1979. Eight singing males were present on the Pigeon River Fish and Wildlife Area in 1978.

Depicted tree: Roughleaf dogwood (*Cornus drummondi*)

SUMMER TANAGER

SUMMER TANAGER

Piranga rubra

Summer Redbird, Red Bee-bird, Rose Tanager

Many southern Indiana residents know this tanager by the name summer redbird. But many more do not know it at all, for, like the scarlet tanager, it spends considerable time concealed in tree foliage. Males do frequently sing from the tops of tall trees or telephone poles near woodland borders or clearings and along wooded roadsides, and they are then more conspicuous. Their song is similar to that of the scarlet tanager, but not so harsh.

Around 1900 the summer tanager was considered a common summer resident over "a good portion" of southern Indiana, and Butler had records from as far north as "Shades of Death" (Shades State Park, Parke County). Currently it is a fairly common summer resident and migrant in the southern third of the state, a very rare and irregular migrant and summer resident in the northern third.

Although usually found in wooded areas, the summer tanager seems a little less restricted than the scarlet tanager to dense forest, for it also frequents more open areas, sometimes nesting near houses, especially those in forest clearings or at woodland edges.

The earliest spring record is April 1, but in most places the birds appear in late April or early May. Summer tanagers apparently have not been reported in large numbers anywhere, nor do they flock, as the scarlet tanager does at times. Our latest fall record for the summer tanager is October 15 and there are other October sightings, but most have departed by then.

Nests are often on horizontal tree branches, frequently over a road or other opening in the forest, or in bushes and small trees. Distance from the ground varied from six to forty feet for ten nests, averaging about sixteen.

Clutches apparently consist of four to five eggs, but there are few data on summer tanager nests in Indiana. Eggs have been found in nests from May 19 to July 13. Two nests had been parasitized by the brown-headed cowbird; one contained nothing but three cowbird eggs. Nesting has been reported north to Howard and Tippecanoe Counties.

To the experienced listener the calls of the summer tanager are distinctive, but they may be confused with those of the scarlet tanager on occasion. During the summer of 1947 a male sang every day at Spring Mill State Park from its perch high in a tall tree on the lawn at the inn. One out-of-state visitor, who was suffering mightily from chigger bites at the time, swore that its calls could be transcribed *chick chick chigger belly*—a good description of the cadence. Calling has been heard as late as October 11.

One of the vernacular names of the summer tanager—red bee bird—comes from its predilection for eating wasps, bees, and hornets. We once watched a female taking honeybees on the wing in rapid succession as they flew near their nest in a tall forest tree, and have seen a male singing while holding a large yellow and brown wasp in its beak.

Depicted tree: Sweetgum (*Liquidambar styraciflua*)

SCARLET TANAGER

Piranga olivacea

Black-winged Redbird

A glimpse of the brilliant plumage of a male scarlet tanager must surely have transformed more than one casual observer into a dedicated birdwatcher. When a patch of sunlight strikes him as he perches among the dark leaves, he seems to glow. It is amazing to us that such a brightly colored bird can be so difficult to locate when singing from a well-shaded perch. Its song is likely to be confused with that of the summer tanager, American robin, or rose-breasted grosbeak, and for that reason its presence may go unnoticed.

According to Butler, this tanager was a common summer resident throughout the state. Today it is a fairly common migrant in all sections of Indiana, but most abundant (and fairly common) during the breeding season in the northern third. Elsewhere, especially in extreme southern Indiana, it appears to be an uncommon summer resident.

Scarlet tanagers occupy much the same habitats as summer tanagers, perhaps utilizing deep woodlands a bit more. Both are partial to the drier upland wooded areas and may be found about clearings and woodland borders. Nesting habitats are also similar, but the scarlet tanager tends to nest at a higher level.

Spring migrants begin appearing in mid-April, some reaching the northern border of the state by April 13, our earliest date. A number remain into October; our latest fall date is October 23. They are never seen in large groups; fifteen in a single day is the maximum number in our records. Samuel W. Witmer noticed that on cool May mornings several male tanagers might be seen perched on plowed ground at the edge of a woods, where they may have been feeding or sunning.

Nests of both the summer and scarlet tanagers are rather loosely constructed, saucer-shaped structures; one can sometimes count the eggs by looking up through the bottom of the nest. Nests are frequently placed on the fork of a horizontal tree limb, usually some distance from the trunk, and may be above a clearing or a road. Twelve scarlet tanager nests varied from nine to forty feet above the ground and averaged about twenty-five. Eggs have been found in nests on May 20, but there are few records from which we can determine laying dates or clutch size. One nest contained three eggs; another, five; and yet another, four tanager and three cowbird eggs. One nest was in a red cedar; all the others were in deciduous trees.

The food of the scarlet tanager consists mostly of insects and their larvae. During the infestation of periodical cicadas in southern Indiana in 1953, this tanager (like many other species of birds) took advantage of this extra source of food. One tanager was seen eating pokeweed berries.

Depicted tree: Yellowwood (*Cladrastis lutea*)

SCARLET TANAGER

[WESTERN TANAGER]

Piranga ludoviciana

A small number of birds have been "identified" as western tanagers in Indiana, but it is difficult to determine how many of these records are valid. The confusion results from the plumage changes that occur in late summer in both scarlet and summer tanagers. The head can remain red, while the body turns yellowish with dark wings; certain birds may superficially resemble western tanagers. In any event, the western tanager would be an accidental visitor to the state.

Among the possibly reliable sightings are the following: August 4, 1960, a female at Geist Reservoir, near Indianapolis; all field marks were noted by the observers, Robert F. Buskirk, William H. Buskirk, and Bruce A. Fall. A male was reported at Jeffersonville (Clark County) on May 7, 1962 (Monroe, 1976). Joy Underborn described a male seen on May 7, 1977, in Lake County.

NORTHERN CARDINAL

Cardinalis cardinalis

Redbird, Virginia Cardinal, Cardinal Grosbeak

The "redbird," always a favorite of Hoosiers, was chosen as the official state bird in 1933. There is hardly a resident of Indiana who has not been thrilled at some time or other by the brilliantly colored cardinal. Both males and females are talented singers. People are most familiar with the loud, whistled *cheer, cheer, cheer, cheer,* but there are many variations of song. Cardinals occasionally sing at night and are among the earliest birds to sing at dawn. On late winter days, the ringing song of the male cardinal is especially appreciated; it signals that spring is coming.

During the nineteenth century, many Hoosiers kept caged cardinals. A. W. Brayton had this to say in 1880: "A loud whistling singer, much sought as a cage bird; the nest is easily found as it is low, and the male in his pride readily leads to it; the farmer's lads get the young, and about Indianapolis sell them for $2.00 a pair."

In 1898, the cardinal was resident throughout the state and very common as far north as Warren County, Indianapolis, and Connersville. It was rare in some parts of northern Indiana, and absent some winters at particular sites. Cardinals were very rare and of irregular occurrence northwest of the Wabash River valley. They were more common in northeastern Indiana, increasing in numbers, and extending their range. Since 1900 cardinals have increased in range and numbers in northern Indiana. Many think of the species as nonmigratory, but banding recoveries reveal movements of two hundred miles. Some cardinals evidently move northward from Indiana in spring,

for two were among the many dead birds found after a severe storm over Lake Michigan on April 16, 1960. In the annual Christmas bird counts in Indiana since 1962, Terre Haute had the highest average number of cardinals per count (437), followed by the counts at Evansville, South Bend, Lafayette, Indianapolis, and Richmond. The smallest numbers since 1957 were tallied in southeastern LaPorte County and southern Lake County, in the northwestern section, much of which was originally prairie and a less favorable cardinal habitat.

Cardinals live in urban, suburban, and wilder areas—from backyards to brushy, weedy stream bottoms or heavily vegetated woodland borders. In winter most cardinals seek more protected habitats, such as creek valleys, fallow fields with thickets and tall weeds, and the brushy tangles of shrubs and vines of the understory of woodlands. Patches of giant ragweed that have grown rank along streams are favorite winter haunts, and it is not unusual to see thirty or more in a flock in such places. In residential areas and cities, an abundance of winter food concentrates the birds (one February Delano Z. Arvin counted forty-five cardinals at his feeder near Buck Creek). Roosts are often in dense shrubs or trees, frequently conifers, such as scattered red cedars in overgrown fields.

Part of the courtship behavior is the feeding of the female by the male (shown in the illustration). Nest building begins in late March or early April, and the breeding season is quite long. Eggs have been found in nests from April 10 to September 1. The average number of eggs in

NORTHERN CARDINAL

fifty-seven nests was three (one to six). We have seven records of brown-headed cowbird eggs in cardinal nests. Young are known to occupy the nest until October 15. The average height of sixty-seven nests was 5.4 feet (2 to 12 feet). Nests were usually placed in dense shrubs or trees, including multiflora rose, often close to houses. In the countryside, nests were in abandoned orchards, woodlands, old pastures, and brushy woodland borders; along ditch and stream banks (some over water); in tangles of vines and shrubs in old fields; in pine plantations; and along shrubby fencerows. Cardinals frequently use strips of wild grape vine bark to line their nests.

Cardinals eat insects and many types of seeds, grains, and fruit, including pokeberry, poison ivy fruit, elm buds, box elder seeds, ragweed seeds, sunflower seeds, muskmelon seeds (at feeders), and corn. The birds often forage along roadsides (probably for both food and grit), and many are killed by automobiles. In winter, cardinals feed with mixed flocks of dark-eyed juncos, American tree sparrows, purple finches, rufous-sided towhees, and other seed-eating species.

Depicted tree: Red cedar (*Juniperus virginiana*)

ROSE-BREASTED GROSBEAK

ROSE-BREASTED GROSBEAK

Pheucticus ludovicianus

During June, wooded areas in the lake country of northeastern Indiana are likely to contain fair numbers of nesting rose-breasted grosbeaks. The males, which help to incubate the eggs, often sing while sitting on their nests, and a dawn serenade by several birds on adjacent territories is delightful to hear. The song is like that of a robin, but more prolonged and usually with shorter, fewer pauses between notes and phrases.

Butler reported that this grosbeak was a summer resident "in most places" throughout northern Indiana; elsewhere in the state it was an irregular migrant, in some years very common and in others rare or absent. Nowadays it is a common migrant throughout Indiana. It is most common in summer in the northern third of the

state, less common in the central, and rare to absent locally in the southern third. As a nesting species it may be locally common; breeding has been reported as far south as Daviess County. It is casual to very rare in winter.

Primarily a forest bird, the rose-breasted grosbeak has adapted to man's activities and can also be found in brushy woodland borders, woodlots, city parks, wooded cemeteries, campuses, residential areas, and old fields overgrown with brushy thickets and trees.

Spring migrants usually begin to appear throughout Indiana during the last half of April, frequently in mixed flocks with indigo buntings. There is one sighting for March 30, 1981, in St. Joseph County, where one was also recorded during the winter of 1980–81. On an all-day bird count in the Lake Waveland (Montgomery County) area on May 10, 1980, 215 grosbeaks were reported. From May 7 to 12, 1966, large numbers—as many as 100—were seen in Fayette, Marion, and Wayne Counties. There were "dozens" in Montgomery County on September 19, 1953, and thirteen were found on September 27, 1975, in Allen County. A few stragglers linger until mid-November; our latest record is November 20. A male appeared at a bird feeder at Evansville on February 12, 1978, and stayed "for the remainder of the winter," according to Mariana Wilke, who photographed him. A male was found dead at Notre Dame during the winter of 1980–81.

Rose-breasted grosbeaks build their nests in shrubs and trees. We have records for six nests that ranged from five to twelve feet above the ground; a seventh was thirty-two feet from the ground. Full clutches of eggs have been found as early as May 21. In twelve nests the number of eggs per clutch varied from 3 to 5; the average was 3.7. Alan W. Bruner estimated that at least twenty pairs of grosbeaks nested in the black locust–elm–hawthorn stands around Lake Waveland in 1981. This appears to be a significant concentration of breeding birds so far south. Many of the nests, he reported, were parasitized by cowbirds. Sidney R. Esten, who studied nesting grosbeaks, found that the adults fed mostly caterpillars and seeds to the young. We have three records of the birds eating mulberries. In spring, grosbeaks do considerable budding, especially of elm, oak, and maple trees. One wintering individual patronized a feeder filled with sunflower seeds. There is still much to learn about the breeding distribution, habits, and abundance of this showy bird in Indiana.

Depicted tree: Quaking aspen (*Populus tremuloides*)

[BLACK-HEADED GROSBEAK]

Pheucticus melanocephalus

This accidental western visitor has been reported a few times from Indiana, but, since field identification is frequently quite difficult, sightings should be evaluated with caution. The first Indiana report was of one that frequented a bird feeder in Lake County between December 23, 1968, and March 20, 1969. It was seen by many competent observers, but never successfully photographed. Thomas A. Potter reported one near Martinsville (Morgan County) on October 24, 1979. Michael Dani and Frank Dani found one at Schneider (Lake County) on September 12, 1980. And adult male was seen at Beverly Shores (Porter County) on October 3, 1980, by Nancy J. Gruse and Robert Wyhoff. James B. Cope saw one in Wayne County on September 22, 1982.

BLUE GROSBEAK

Guiraca caerulea

A hundred years ago there was a single Indiana record for the blue grosbeak; Robert Ridgway had seen one in Knox County in the spring of 1881. About fifty years elapsed, then came a few more sightings—from Madison and Morgan Counties in 1930, Posey County in 1939, and Vanderburgh County in 1951. By 1953 there were seven more. This southern grosbeak was next reported from Porter County in 1960 and 1961, from LaPorte County in 1960 and 1978, from Perry County in 1970 (with an unconfirmed report of a nest), and from Wells County, also in 1970.

Since 1972 there has been a dramatic increase in the number of sightings. If all reports are valid, the blue grosbeak has now been recorded from about twenty counties scattered throughout the state. Most of the records, however, are from the southern half. Unfortunately, overenthusiastic birders sometimes misidentify indigo buntings as blue grosbeaks, so a completely accurate assessment of distribution both past and present is impossible; but the breeding range does appear to be expanding northward, into southwestern and possibly south-central Indiana. Nonetheless, it is still a rare and local summer resident in those regions. Throughout the northern two-thirds of the state it is a rare migrant; in the northwestern corner of the state it is a casual local nester.

Our earliest date of spring arrival is April 14; our latest

BLUE GROSBEAK

date of fall departure is October 4. Most sightings have been in May and June.

Blue grosbeaks are found in old overgrown fields where there are briers, thickets, and dense growths of bushes and shrubs. They also like the shrubby borders of woodlands along roadsides, overgrown railroad rights-of-way, and thick, brushy fencerows. A nest found in Pike County (four miles east of Somerville) in 1976 was in an overgrown field bordering abandoned, stripmined land (Mills and Smith, 1976). The female was carrying nesting material to the site on June 11. The nest, in a thicket of poison ivy and sassafras about three feet above the ground, contained three eggs on June 20; these hatched between June 27 and July 1. Two immatures and two adults were observed in Warrick County on August 6, 1978, by James H. Campbell and Willard N. Gray. Young grosbeaks were found in Newton County during the summer of 1979. A nest discovered at the Atterbury Fish and Wildlife Area on June 13, 1980, contained young on June 25, according to Boyd Gill. There is an unconfirmed report of nesting in LaPorte County in 1960. Some of the breeding-season sightings in other counties were undoubtedly of nesting birds.

Depicted plant: Poison ivy (*Rhus radicans*)

[LAZULI BUNTING]

Passerina amoena

This accidental visitor has been reported from Indiana twice: once in Marion County in the spring of 1934, after "the dust storm that blew in from the West and carried dust as far as New York"; and once at a bird feeder at Holliday Park, Indianapolis, from December 8, 1946, to February 9, 1947. This bird, an immature male, was seen by at least twenty-five people from a distance of four feet (Hadley, 1947).

INDIGO BUNTING

Passerina cyanea

Indigo Bird, Indigo Finch

When the "dog days" of August set in, the male indigo bunting can still be heard along country roads. Day after day, ever since his arrival in late April or early May, he has been singing, expending incredible amounts of energy. During this time, most of the common roadside wildflowers have bloomed and set seed—goatsbeard, daylily, Bouncing Bet, Queen Anne's lace, chicory. Most nesting birds have ceased to sing, but nothing, not even the oppressive damp heat of late summer, subdues the male indigo.

The indigo bunting was a common summer resident throughout Indiana in the late 1890s. The clearing of much forested area in the state has been of benefit to this species, and it is now abundant in summer and during migration nearly everywhere. It is casual in winter.

Forest edges, old weedy fields, shrubby areas, brushy and weedy roadsides and railroad rights-of-way, brushy ravines and creek bottoms, and overgrown, relatively open waste places are the habitats of this familiar bird. It is sometimes found in forested places, especially where there are openings such as roads, streams, and cleared power line rights-of-way.

In the spring, migrants arrive at most localities after mid-April, but there are two March sightings, the earliest being March 7. Peak spring numbers are usually seen the last week of April or first half of May. On May 13, 1961, 105 were seen (Marion County), and 100 were observed in Tippecanoe County on May 8, 1950. Although fall migration begins considerably earlier, a number remain throughout most of October. There is one record for November 5. Seventy-five were found in Marion County on September 3, 1972 and a flock of forty-seven was there on September 20, 1953. Individuals have been observed December 3, 1978 (Allen County), and December 29,

1979 (Muscatatuck National Wildlife Refuge). One was banded at Mooresville (Morgan County) on January 18, 1960, and it remained until at least February 28, according to Robert S. Gregory. Another was seen in Starke County on January 29, 1907. An incapacitated bird died while being examined by James H. Campbell and Willard N. Gray on February 14, 1981, in Warrick County.

Old fields overgrown with briers, scattered sprouts and bushes, and tall weeds and the shrubby borders of wooded areas are excellent places to search for nests of the indigo bunting. Nests are often placed in raspberry, blackberry, wild rose, greenbrier, or multiflora rose. Others are constructed in tall weeds, bushes, tree sprouts, and tangles of vines (especially where vines grow over a bush). There is one report of a nest in a Virginia pine.

Thirty-four nests were placed from eight inches to seven and one half feet above the ground; the average height was two and one-half feet. The average clutch size in forty nests was 3.5; complete clutches contained from three to five eggs, but a single nest contained as many as five. Eggs were found in nests from May 21 to August 21 and Val Nolan Jr. watched a nest from which young departed on September 14. Many nests were parasitized by the brown-headed cowbird; some of these were subsequently abandoned by the buntings. Nathalee D. Stocks counted thirty-five indigo buntings along twenty miles of gravel road in Warrick County on June 18, 1969.

Besides the usual territorial song, the indigo bunting also has a flight song, which is most likely to be heard at dusk; one male performed it three times from 8 P.M. (sundown) to 8:20 P.M., when he ceased singing for the day. We have heard the flight song as late as September 26.

Depicted plant: Hawthorn (*Crataegus* sp.)

PAINTED BUNTING

Passerina ciris

We initially felt obliged to include this species because of the existence of an adult male specimen in the collection of the California Academy of Science that, according to the label, was taken April 12, 1886, at Indianapolis by Fletcher M. Noe. It is strange that Butler did not mention this specimen, for he published many of Noe's other bird records. In any case, it has been proved that Noe falsified some of his data, so this record too may be invalid.

But after we had written the preceding paragraph, Robert F. Buskirk found a dead male next to the City-County Building in Indianapolis on May 5, 1983. The specimen was prepared and placed in the Joseph Moore Museum at Earlham College. Recently there have been a number of extra-limital records of the painted bunting in the Midwest; this gorgeous bird may be expanding its range.

DICKCISSEL

Spiza americana

Black-throated Bunting, Little Meadow Lark

The delightful little dickcissel reminds us of hot summer days, weedy pastures, new-mown hay, and country roads. In this type of habitat males habitually perch on telephone wires and fences and sing their names over and over again. A car cruising slowly along the road, far from disturbing them, seems to stimulate them to sing all the more.

Butler wrote, "In most localities the Dickcissel is an abundant summer resident. However, it is a recent introduction into our fauna. Mr. E. J. Chansler says he can remember when it was rare in Knox County, where its numbers now are perhaps exceeded by no other bird. It appeared in Franklin County some time between 1869 and 1879. . . . As is to be supposed, it is rare in the more heavily timbered portion of southern Indiana." It was becoming more common in Carroll County in 1886, and was first seen in DeKalb County in 1887. The dickcissel is currently an uncommon to common migrant and summer resident throughout the state and may be quite irregular in occurrence from year to year—locally abundant in "dickcissel years," virtually absent at other times. Since the dickcissel was relatively new to the avifauna of Indiana during Butler's time, he could not have been aware of these fluctuations. It is a casual winter resident.

Typical dickcissel habitats are meadows, pastures, grasslands, hayfields (and other cultivated fields), airports,

DICKCISSEL

and other grassy or weedy open areas—the same kinds of places in which the grasshopper sparrow is found.

The first dickcissels of spring usually arrive during the last half of April, the earliest date being April 17. Forty were observed in Tippecanoe County on May 17, 1950, and twenty-six were counted at Indianapolis on May 13, 1961. Fall migration is seldom evident; the birds simply leave their nesting grounds and slip away, largely unnoticed. Several have been reported in late September and early October; the latest fall departure date is October 23. More attention should be paid to flocks of house sparrows along roadsides during late fall, for dickcissels sometimes occur in such flocks. Most wintering birds have been seen at feeders, usually with house sparrows. One dickcissel was at Terre Haute for about three weeks in November and December of 1971. Another was seen in Terre Haute on December 27, 1972, and still another—or the same bird—several days later elsewhere in the town. One, observed from December 15, 1979, to January 21, 1980, at Fort Wayne, was banded on January 2. One visited a feeder at Greenfield on January 4 and 5, 1980. Another was at Evansville on December 20, 1980.

Nests are constructed on or near the ground. Distances from the ground for three nests were one inch, two inches, and one foot. One was in a clump of *Spirea* in a pastured old field near a marsh, one in a clump of blackberry briers in an old field, and one in a patch of clover in an old field. Nests have also been found in hayfields. Ten nests contained from three to six eggs per clutch (average 4.2). Eggs were seen in nests from May 18 to July 10 and young were still in one nest on August 11.

In "dickcissel years," ten or fifteen males may be found singing in a single clover field or hayfield from late May to early July. Charles E. Mills counted twenty-five males along a ditch and levees around a fifteen-acre area in Gibson County on July 25, 1980. The latest date for singing males was August 6.

Depicted plant: Butterfly weed (*Asclepias tuberosa*)

[GREEN-TAILED TOWHEE]
Pipilo chlorurus

This western species has been reported from Indiana on two occasions and can only be considered an accidental visitor. One was observed in Goshen (Elkhart County) from November 1952 into the spring of 1953 (Witmer, 1969). Between April 19 and May 2, 1973, one was seen in the yard of a home at South Bend, and at least fifteen observers identified it. It usually fed in deep shade under a yew bush and therefore could not be satisfactorily photographed, according to Mr. and Mrs. Russell S. Dufendach, who discovered it.

RUFOUS-SIDED TOWHEE

Pipilo erythrophthalmus

Chewink, Ground Robin, Towhee Bunting, Jewee, Joree, Marsh Robin, Swamp Robin, Towhee, Red-eyed Towhee

Hikers making their way along the border of a wooded area will sometimes hear a noisy scuffling in the dead leaves on the floor of a thicket. Expecting to see a squirrel or chipmunk, or even some larger mammal, they are surprised to find it is only a towhee, vigorously scratching away in search of food. Towhees spend much of their time on the ground, but in spring territorial males may sing from treetops, sometimes as high as fifty feet from the ground. The familiar loud *drink-your-tea* song is a favorite of many spring birdwatchers.

At the turn of the century this towhee was a common permanent resident in southern Indiana and as far north as Vincennes and Brookville. In some winters it could be found over most of the southern half of the state, and in mild winters a few remained throughout Indiana. Today it is a permanent resident throughout the state, but much more common in winter in the southern third, as Christmas counts attest. It appears to be a common summer resident, with local exceptions, wherever suitable habitat is present. There are no estimates of breeding populations. The largest numbers of wintering birds have been recorded from Bloomington southward. The largest number for a single Christmas bird count was eighty-four; this was at Lake Monroe on December 19, 1976.

Rufous-sided towhees are birds of brushy areas—overgrown old fields, shrubby fencerows, thickets, tangles of briers and brush, and open deciduous woodlands and their borders. Most often found in drier sites, they also frequent marsh borders, low, wet woods, and other moist places, and, especially in winter, may appear at bird feeders.

Nests are usually either on the ground (especially early in the season) or in bushes and trees. Fifteen of thirty-six nests were on the ground. Above-ground nests ranged from 2 to 17.5 feet above the ground and were placed in bushes, trees, brier tangles, and vines (especially vines overgrowing shrubs). One nest was in a pine tree, another in a red cedar. Ground nests are usually in a grassy tussock or at the base of a sprout.

Nests containing eggs have been observed from April 15 to August 20. Nineteen nests held from 3 to 6 eggs each and averaged 3.6 eggs per clutch. Many nests were parasitized by brown-headed cowbirds; two were destroyed by a "black snake."

Sidney R. Esten observed adults feeding nestlings over an extended period. Foods fed included caterpillars, moths, dragonflies, mosquitos, crane flies, beetles, mulberries, and seeds. Towhees have been seen eating raspberries and apples. One bird, at a feeder, fed on sunflower seed but appeared to be having considerable difficulty. Another fed regularly on corn at a corncrib.

Mrs. Max D. Parker reported the presence of twenty towhees in her yard in the Harrison State Forest on October 11, 1952. The house was in a clearing in the forest and was surrounded by a considerable amount of brushy habitat. In December we found a flock of twenty-three towhees in a wild plum thicket, just inside the border of a deciduous woods (Clay County). An odd song was heard from this group, not the typical song one hears during the remainder of the year.

Depicted plant: Partridge-pea (*Cassia fasciculata*)

RUFOUS-SIDED TOWHEE

BACHMAN'S SPARROW

Aimophila aestivalis

Pine-woods Sparrow, Oak-woods Sparrow

South-central Indiana used to contain many overgrown, partially eroded old fields, originally forested, that were created when pioneer farmers cleared the high, more level ridge tops in order to plant corn and other crops. Where the terrain was uneven, erosion gulleys eventually formed. These gradually enlarged until in some cases the fields could no longer be farmed. Once cultivation ceased, scattered stands of broom grass, weeds, briers, sassafras, tulip tree, sumac, persimmon, red cedar, and other trees and shrubs sprang up on the worn-out soil. In the early 1950s there were many such places in the Hoosier National Forest, and the Bachman's sparrow was present over a wide range. Although not conspicuous, its distinctive *theee lut lut lut* song could be heard in county after county. Bachman's sparrow shared the habitat with the prairie warbler and the blue-winged warbler in many places—all three species finding certain fields that satisfied their needs during the breeding season. Unfortunately, present-day birdwatchers almost never see or hear Bachman's sparrow in Indiana; most of its former habitats have grown up to planted pines and forest trees and are no longer suitable for the birds.

Butler wrote that this sparrow was a summer resident in the southwestern quarter of the state, but usually was not common. For some reason he failed to mention his own record for Franklin County in 1896 (Butler, 1897). It was first reported from Indiana by Robert Ridgway on April 26, 1881, near Wheatland (Knox County). Butler knew of records from as far north as southern Warren County. It was recorded in Tippecanoe County in 1904 and in Pulaski County in 1947. The northernmost record was established on April 4, 1939, when Amy Baldwin found one in the dunes of Porter County. In southern Indiana before 1950 it was increasing and expanding its range, especially on abandoned land in the south-central hill area. Between 1950 and 1955 it was recorded in twenty counties and as far north as Tippecanoe County. There were reports from only seven counties from 1956 to 1966. The next sightings were in 1976 (Orange County), 1978 (Knox County), 1979 (Johnson and Warrick Counties), and 1980 (Johnson County).

The decline of this sparrow, then, has been dramatic. Recent records indicate that it is now probably a very rare and local summer resident in the southern half of the state. It has been reported from the northern half only once since 1963 and may be casual or absent there. Undoubtedly a major reason for the decrease in the state is the disappearance of suitable habitat—the abandoned cultivated fields that once supplied the bird's needs—coupled with its inability to adapt to changing conditions.

March 19 is the earliest spring date; most "first" dates are for April or May. Singing males have been heard as late as September 12. Butler collected a specimen on September 22 and the latest fall date is September 24 (Posey County). One was reported at a feeder at Fort Wayne on December 21, 1968. Most records are of singing birds; if not singing they are practically impossible to locate.

There are nesting records for at least eight counties, the northernmost of which is Tippecanoe. Van Nolan Jr. has probably collected more data on nesting Bachman's sparrows in Indiana than anyone else, for it nested in areas where he was conducting his research on prairie warblers near Bloomington. Nests were on the ground, some domed over the top, others not. Each of seven nests found between May 15 and July 7 contained four eggs. Nolan (1953) described the courtship singing (sometimes while in flight), distraction displays, and other interesting behavior of adults around nests containing eggs or young.

Depicted plant: Pasture rose (*Rosa carolina*)

AMERICAN TREE SPARROW

Spizella arborea

Arctic Chippie

One of the pleasant sounds of winter is the soft, tinkling chorus of dozens of tree sparrows feeding in a snow-covered field. Busily the birds move about, often in the company of dark-eyed juncos, in weed fields where erect stems of evening primrose, buffeted by the wind, shed their tiny black seeds. The flock forages across the field, then settles down for a loafing period in a sheltered, sunny spot along a brushy fencerow. In northwestern Indiana in spring, tree sparrows are present in great numbers, swarming along weedy field borders and fencerows, probably staging for their northward flight.

This sparrow has always been a common winter visitor throughout the state, although in severe winters fewer are present in extreme northern Indiana. From year to year, however, numbers at a particular locality may fluctuate greatly. Christmas bird counts reveal that more tree sparrows are present in the northwestern quarter of the state than elsewhere during winter. More than one thousand per count have been recorded in southeastern LaPorte County, Lafayette, and South Bend.

The largest average number seen per count is for southeastern LaPorte County. On January 2, 1982, there were 2,242 there. The only other locality where one thousand have been observed is New Castle. In extreme southwestern Indiana, annual counts have yielded numbers ranging anywhere from 1 to nearly 500 at Evansville and from about 40 to 480 in Gibson County.

Tree sparrows are partial to weedy and grassy fields, brushy waste areas, and overgrown fencerows, in short, wherever there are seed-bearing plants.

Dates of arrival of fall migrants can vary greatly from year to year. In northern Indiana, many tree sparrows appear in October, but some arrive as early as September 12. Elsewhere in the state, none may be seen until November. The amount of snow cover and availability of weed seeds no doubt determine both movements and local abundance. By the last week of March, thousands of tree sparrows have been observed in Newton County. After the April 16, 1960, storm, 331 dead tree sparrows were counted along the beaches of Lake Michigan. Stragglers have been reported at Indianapolis on April 28 and in St. Joseph County on May 20, our latest date. Before the birds depart in the spring, there is often an opportunity for Hoosiers to hear their clear spring song that has replaced the short call notes of winter.

CHIPPING SPARROW

CHIPPING SPARROW

Spizella passerina

Chippy, Hair Bird, Chip Bird, Eastern Chipping Sparrow

Truly a sociable species, the trim little chipping sparrow seems to prefer to nest near human dwellings and is therefore frequently seen foraging on lawns. Many do not know its simple, trilling song, for it is quite soft and may be drowned out by other neighborhood noises. The nickname hair bird comes from its predilection for lining its nest with horsehair when available. Years ago in rural areas almost every nest we examined had its characteristic horsehair lining, often of a dark color that made a pleasing background for the beautiful bluish eggs with dark markings. Butler noted that the chipping sparrow preferred black horsehair to line its nest.

Although Butler said nothing specific about the abundance of this sparrow in his day, we infer that it was common. It is currently a common migrant and summer resident throughout the state, probably more abundant now than in Butler's time. Although there are numerous winter reports, we suspect that most of them are the result of misidentifications of other sparrows. The chippy appears to be a casual to very rare winter resident, especially in southern Indiana, but more data (and critical identifications) are needed to determine its true status at this season.

What kind of habitats chipping sparrows used before man came on the scene is unknown. No doubt they were present in forest openings, brushy fields, and fencerows, where they now may be found during migration (and, occasionally, nesting). But today this sparrow is closely associated with man and nests almost exclusively near human habitations.

Since an unknown number of chipping sparrows may winter locally in the state, dates of first arrival in spring may be subject to error. However, it appears that most first appear from March 10 to the end of that month. Large numbers are not usually seen, but Palmer D. Skaar found 110 in Monroe County on April 23, 1950. Departure dates in the fall are difficult to determine, for misidentifications are frequent at this season as well as in winter. The largest fall numbers we know about are for September 4 and 24, 1972, when Alfred Starling saw twenty-five chipping sparrows each day in Marion County. Several birds linger into November and there are a few records for early December. Some individuals (at least one of which was captured and banded) have remained at feeding stations for part or most of the winter.

Nest construction has usually begun by April 15 and full clutches of eggs are present by April 25. Twenty-five nests were built from two to twenty feet (average seven) above the ground. About half of the nests for which we have data were in conifers, mostly ornamentals near homes, but one nest was in a pine plantation. One nest was in a "bush in a field," one in a tangle of vines along a small stream, and one in a peach tree. The remainder were near houses or other buildings on lawns, campuses, and the like. One pair built their nest in a hanging Boston fern beneath the eaves of a rural house. Another unusual site was inside a large pen, constructed of poultry netting and posts, that had been built for ring-necked pheasants. The sparrows' nest was in a false buckwheat vine growing up the side of one of the pen partitions, thirty-five feet inside the pen.

Nests were located in a variety of deciduous trees and shrubs. In larger trees, both deciduous and coniferous, the nest is usually placed near the end of a horizontal branch; in smaller trees, bushes, and shrubs, it is more in the interior.

Where horsehair was not available, nests were lined with hair from woodchucks, eastern cottontails, or other mammals. Jane L. Hine reported this sparrow lining its nests with human hair.

Clutch size in 26 nests ranged from 2 to 4 and averaged 3.5. Some of the two-egg clutches may not have been complete. The latest date for young in the nest was September 4.

Singing has been heard from at least March 30 to October 26.

Depicted plant: American bittersweet (*Celastrus scandens*)

CLAY-COLORED SPARROW

Spizella pallida

Ashy-Nape, Shattuck

Relatively few birdwatchers have seen this sparrow in Indiana. Its identification in the field has always been the bane of ornithologists because of the difficulty in separating chipping sparrow and clay-colored sparrow sightings, particularly in the fall. Since records are not always reliable, our knowledge of the true status of this species remains incomplete. Butler knew of a single record for the state, a specimen collected near Terre Haute on September 27, 1890, but thought it might be a rare, local summer resident. We do not know the whereabouts of this specimen and cannot vouch for it. The next record is that of a female collected in Porter County on May 25 or 26, 1919; another was taken in the same county in May 1924. James B. Cope collected one near Richmond in the spring of 1973. There are about a dozen additional records for the state, mostly for the spring, all from Owen County northward, throughout the northern two-thirds of Indiana. The three fall records are for Lake, LaPorte, and Vigo Counties, the western side of the state. This sparrow is apparently a casual migrant, possibly more abundant than records now indicate. During the summer of 1933 one reportedly remained throughout the summer on the prairie south of Whiting (Lake County).

Spring migrants have been seen as early as April 6. Fall sightings were made between September 15 and October 26. One was reported by James A. Haw on December 21, 1980, in Lagrange County; another was reported from Huntington County on January 1, 1981.

FIELD SPARROW

Spizella pusilla

Old-field Sparrow

Sometimes during unusually warm periods in February, the plaintive song of the field sparrow can be heard. Such singing is done by wintering birds, no doubt stimulated by the unseasonable springlike weather, since migrants have not yet returned to their haunts. Although the field sparrow is not widely known among Hoosiers, it is a common species. It is drab and rather retiring, but to those who know it and listen each year for its song, it is an early harbinger of spring.

Although Butler commented that the field sparrow was "much more numerous than the Chipping Sparrow" he failed to assign a numerical status to the latter. He reported that the field sparrow was a common summer resi-

dent throughout the state and occasionally wintered as far north as Vincennes. Today it is probably more numerous than during Butler's period of field work; we consider it an abundant migrant and summer resident in all sections of Indiana. It also winters in all regions, most commonly in the southern third. Thus over much of the state it is really a permanent resident. In the northern half it may be rare or absent locally from year to year.

As the name implies, the field sparrow prefers old fields and other grassy, weedy, and shrubby openings. It is not as likely to be seen in residential or suburban areas as the chipping sparrow or the song sparrow, but an individual may occasionally come to a feeder in winter. Where it is known primarily as a migrant, spring arrival is usually in March. It lingers into November in many areas during the fall, even where it may not winter. The largest numbers of spring migrants are usually reported the last week of March or first week of April. In Marion County, forty-two were seen on April 4, 1970. Maximum numbers of fall migrants are usually reported in September and October; we have reports of thirty-three in Elkhart County on September 4, 1932, and thirty in Jackson County on October 7, 1952. The largest number of field sparrows are recorded on various Christmas bird counts, but we cannot vouch for the authenticity of all these since other wintering sparrows are often confused with field sparrows. Two hundred were reported at the Muscatatuck National Wildlife Refuge on December 18, 1976, and 170 in Warrick County on December 24, 1966.

Most nests have been found in the typical old field habitats, and nest building has been recorded as early as April 25. The earliest date for a full clutch of eggs is April 30. The nesting season is long and multiple broods are reared. Val Nolan Jr. watched a nest from which the young departed on September 18. Four seems to be the most common number of eggs per nest. In ninety-one nests, there were five clutches of two, thirty-four of three, fifty of four, and two of five.

Many nests built early in the season are on the ground, for nesting may be begun before shrubs and other field vegetation has fully leafed out. But later in the nesting season, relatively few nests are placed on the ground; elevated nests in weeds, vines, shrubs, and trees are the rule. Fifty-two elevated nests ranged from one inch to 9.7 feet above the ground; the average was 1.5 feet. Ground nests are usually placed in a grass tussock or at the base of a sapling, weed, or sprout. Nests have been found in a wide variety of plants, mostly deciduous, but also in red cedar and pine trees.

Singing has been heard from February 25 to September 14. The field sparrow sometimes sings at night; in one case, a male burst into song in response to the slamming of a car door. Night singing has been recorded between 11:45 P.M. and 3:00 A.M. on several occasions, all in June or July. One of the nights was warm and there was a full moon.

Depicted plant: Rose-pink (*Sabatia angularis*)

VESPER SPARROW

Pooecetes gramineus

Bay-winged Bunting, Ground Bird, Grass Finch, Eastern Vesper Sparrow

In spring this early migrant and sometime winter resident is one of the first sparrows to be heard singing in the open fields. There, often perched on telephone wires, they loudly declare their territorial rights with distinctive songs. We know these rather large sparrows with white outer tail feathers well, for we usually saw and heard them in early April during expeditions to the original prairie tracts of northwestern Indiana in search of greater prairie-chickens.

Butler reported that it was quite common throughout Indiana from March to November and that it had been found in winter in Knox County. The vesper sparrow today is a fairly common migrant and summer resident in the northern two-thirds of the state, an uncommon summer resident in the remainder. In winter it is very rare throughout the state, but most likely to be found in the southern portion at that season.

Vesper sparrows inhabit open fields (both cultivated and uncultivated), pastures, airports, and grassy roadsides. They are frequently seen on country roads, where they probably obtain some food and grit and find dusting sites. We have seen them sprawled out in the dust on a gravel road in midsummer.

Spring migrants may appear in late February, but it is sometimes not possible to differentiate between early migrants and wintering birds. Throughout the state as a whole, the birds first appear during the last half of March. A "migration of about 300" in St. Joseph County was reported during the spring of 1950. Many birds remain into the late fall and early winter, so that departure

dates are often not evident. In northern counties, most have left by mid-October or November 1, but there are reports of stragglers as late as mid-November.

Nests are on the ground, in grassy areas. Eggs were seen in nests from April 25 to June 9 and one nest contained two young on July 3. Two to five eggs constitute a clutch; in sixteen nests clutch size averaged 3.5.

Depicted plant: Prickly-pear (*Opuntia humifusa*)

LARK SPARROW

Chondestes grammacus

Lark Finch

This handsome sparrow may be more common then many birders realize, and it is well worth searching for. Most are found along roadsides; when they fly up from the ground or fence as a car approaches, the white-spotted tip of the tail is a good field mark. The song of the lark sparrow is often given from a fairly high perch. To some, it is rather brown thrasher-like; it reminded Amos Butler of that of the indigo bunting.

The lark sparrow was at one time quite rare in Indiana.

As the forests were cut away it extended its range greatly. It appears now to be locally rare as a migrant and summer resident throughout the state, being perhaps most abundant in the southern one-third. In our files are sight records from forty-five counties, nesting records from only fourteen. Suitable habitat is evidently what mostly determines the presence of lark sparrows in a given area. It is probably a casual winter resident.

The lark sparrow prefers open areas with bare patches

of soil. It thus frequents old pastures, cultivated fields, stripmined land, grassy roadsides and railroad rights-of-way, and other weedy, grassy areas (sometimes with scattered briers or shrubs). In the northwestern section of the state, it is frequently associated with bare blowsand areas along roadsides or ditches and in fields. The birds forage in soybean or newly disked cultivated fields, along roadsides, on golf courses, and the like.

Spring arrival dates are mostly for April and May, but there are sightings for March 11 and 26. Most birds have departed by October; the latest record is for November 20. Two were reported on the 1954 Lafayette Christmas bird count. Another was seen at a bird feeder in Mishawaka from February 4 to 6, 1977.

Nest building has been reported as early as April 18. All recent nests for which we have data were on the ground. However, Butler, who found four pairs of lark sparrows nesting along less than a mile of public highway near Brookville (Franklin County), wrote that "the nests are placed in bushes, in a thicket or along a fence." Nest sites were in impoverished pastures, old fields, and other open areas of low grasses and weeds. Several nests were placed at the base of a plant, partially hidden and shaded by the lower leaves. Some nests were less concealed. Seven contained 3 or 4 eggs each and averaged 3.6 per nest. Newly hatched young were seen on May 12 and eggs were found in one nest June 27.

Depicted plant: Birdfoot violet (*Viola pedata*)

LARK BUNTING
Calamospiza melanocorys

An accidental visitor, this western species has been reported from Indiana four times. Mr. and Mrs. Joel W. Hadley saw one near Indianapolis on April 30, 1950. On May 10, 1950, Aaron Nigh reported a sighting near Morristown (Shelby County).

James E. Landing watched one at Michigan City on April 18, 1956. Kenneth J. Brock found a singing male near the Beaver Lake Prairie Chicken Refuge (Newton County) on June 7, 1978. In the next two days many others saw and photographed it (see cover, *Indiana Audubon Quarterly*, 57, No. 3). It frequently sang its aerial courtship song and appeared to be on territory (Brock, 1979b).

SAVANNAH SPARROW

Passerculus sandwichensis

It is easy to overlook this little grassland sparrow; its habits are such that it is not exposed to view most of the time, and its song is a rather weak, buzzy, insectlike rendition that can go unnoticed. During the peaks of spring or fall migration, however, savannah sparrows may be fairly numerous in meadows near marshes. As you walk through the tall grass the birds run ahead, reluctant to fly. When one does flush, it usually flies close to the ground for a short distance, then drops back into the grass. You can search for it at the spot where it alighted to no avail; it has already run farther on. During the nesting season, when it perches on roadside fences, it is more visible.

Butler evidently had very little information about this inconspicuous sparrow. He mentioned that it was a rare resident, in some seasons, in the lower Wabash River valley, wintering in Knox County, and cited no nesting records. It is now a fairly common migrant throughout the state and may be locally common. It apparently nests south to Jefferson County along the eastern and Sullivan County on the western side of the state, but may be absent in summer from much of the southwestern corner. More intensive field work is needed throughout the Ohio River valley to determine its true summer status. In winter, it is probably a casual resident throughout the northern two-thirds of Indiana, more common in the southern third.

The savannah sparrow is usually found in open fields and the drier portions of sedge meadows and grassy areas bordering marshes (particularly in migration). Fields, both cultivated and fallow, are used for nesting, as are grassy roadsides and moderately grazed pastures. At times it is fairly abundant on the former prairie region of northwestern Indiana.

Although wintering birds are widely scattered, most spring migrants apparently arrive during the last half of March and probably reach their greatest abundance in April. At least fifty were found dead along Lake Michigan after the April 16, 1960, storm. Fall migration is not so obvious in many areas, but local concentrations may occur. Fifty were found around the borders of a small pond near Orleans (Orange County) on October 4 and 5, 1954. It appears that more savannah sparrows than was formerly known winter in extreme southwestern Indiana. From twenty to forty-eight have been recorded on Christmas bird counts in western Gibson County.

The few savannah sparrow nests found in Indiana were all on the ground; one was in grasses and weeds along the shoulder of a sand road, another in a bluegrass area in a pasture. Five nests contained from three to five eggs (average four). A sixth nest held three young. From 1957 until at least 1965, this sparrow nested in fairly large numbers around Shallow Lake, a rather extensive marl lake and surrounding marshy tract in the Pigeon River Fish and Wildlife Area (Steuben County). It was also fairly common in summer throughout the former prairie areas, especially in Newton County, during this same period. Singing males were much in evidence at both sites, some of them perched in trees as high as thirty feet from the ground. Most territorial males, however, sing from fences, tall weeds, or lower tree perches.

Depicted plant: Goat's rue (*Tephrosia virginiana*)

SAVANNAH SPARROW

GRASSHOPPER SPARROW

Ammodramus savannarum

Yellow-winged Sparrow, Cricket Sparrow

This is another of the little nondescript, buzzy-voiced sparrows of open fields; its grasshopper- or cricketlike song has given it its common name. Although it is a persistent singer, the song does not carry far. The best way to see these birds is to drive slowly along roads beside pastures and hayfields where they are nesting, and watch for them perched on fences. Butler said: "A favorite position is on a fence, where they will often permit one in a buggy to pass within 10 or 15 feet of them." On the ground, the birds are skulkers and difficult to see.

Butler considered this sparrow a common summer resident over most of the state and noted that it had been gradually increasing in numbers and extending its range. Although rare anywhere in the lower Whitewater River Valley about 1882, by 1897 it was "the most common meadow bird on the uplands" there. Today it is a fairly common migrant and summer resident throughout the state—sometimes locally abundant, sometimes rare, depending upon habitat—and possibly a casual winter resident.

Hayfields, prairies, cultivated grain fields (and stubble), pastures, and other open, grassy areas are favorite habitats of the grasshopper sparrow, especially the drier, upland sites. In recent years it has become a common breeding bird on reclaimed stripmined lands in southwestern Indiana.

March 14 is the earliest spring date: four singing males were seen in Gibson County (Nathalee D. Stocks). There are a few other dates for the last half of March, but most birds arrive in April. This sparrow is evidently a fairly late fall migrant and we have several records for early November.

It will come as no surprise to those who have spent considerable time searching for the nest of this elusive sparrow that we have records of only three nests in Indiana. Nests are on the ground. One, found in a prairie remnant July 10, contained five young ready to leave the nest. Another nest fledged five young on July 5. A nest with an unreported number of eggs was found June 6.

The amount of cover in chosen nesting fields often undergoes drastic changes, for the birds like to nest in clover, alfalfa, and timothy fields, all of which are mown periodically. James H. Campbell conducted a census of singing grasshopper sparrows along a ten-mile stretch of road through reclaimed stripmined land in Warrick County on July 18, 1980, stopping every tenth of a mile and tallying singing birds. He found thirty on this route.

Depicted plant: Daisy fleabane (*Erigeron anuus*)

HENSLOW'S SPARROW

Ammodramus henslowii

Henslow's Bunting

This little, secretive sparrow of damp meadows is not well known in Indiana. Unless it is perched and singing, it can be difficult to locate and identify. The song, a short, hiccoughlike utterance sometimes transcribed *flee-sic* or *tsee-slick*, is not loud, and can easily go unnoticed or be mistaken for the noise of an insect. We and several others have heard this sparrow singing on warm, still summer nights.

Butler knew of records only for northern Indiana, where it nested locally. He mentioned that C. E. Aiken obtained the first state record when he shot one while hunting prairie-chickens in Lake County in August, 1869. The specimen was not preserved. It is now found throughout Indiana during the summer and is known to nest south to Jefferson County. It probably also nests in Gibson, Spencer, and Warrick Counties, where it is present during the breeding season. For the state as a whole it is probably an uncommon summer resident and migrant, but under suitable conditions it may be locally common or even abundant. Even now it is more abundant in northern than in southern Indiana in summer. It appears to be a casual winter visitor everywhere in the state.

Low-lying weedy and grassy fields, especially with seasonally damp areas, are good habitats for the Henslow's sparrow. It also occurs about hay meadows and similar grassy areas bordering marshes and other bodies of water. It may be found in old pastures and weedy fields with scattered bushes and sprouts in more upland (drier) locations.

Spring migrants have been observed April 2 (Jasper-Pulaski Fish and Wildlife Area), but no doubt appear earlier in southern Indiana. Throughout most of the state, birds are first recorded in spring during April. There is a dearth of data regarding fall migration: because the birds are then silent, they are quite difficult to locate. October 7 is our latest date. Thirty-two dead Henslow's sparrows were found along Lake Michigan after the April 16, 1960, storm. Geoffrey E. Hill estimated that one hundred were singing on the Muscatatuck National Wildlife Refuge on May 9, 1981. One was found there on December 20, 1980. Raymond J. Fleetwood (1934) collected one on December 24, 1933, in Jackson County. One was reported on the southeastern LaPorte County Christmas bird count, December 22, 1963.

Relatively few nests have been found in Indiana. They are placed on or near the ground, usually in dense cover, and are difficult to locate. Three eggs and one newly hatched young were found in one nest on May 20 (there were four young on May 23). This is the earliest date for eggs in a nest. The nesting season is evidently quite long, for a bobtailed young out of the nest was captured by hand on September 23. Six nests contained from three to five eggs each; four nests held four each.

Depicted plants: Purple-headed sneezeweed (*Helenium nudiflorum*); Horse-nettle (*Solanum carolinense*)

LE CONTE'S SPARROW
Ammodramus leconteii

For many years, Le Conte's sparrow was relatively unknown in Indiana. Its secretive behavior, choice of habitat, and silence during its migrations through the state allowed it to pass essentially unnoticed. Also, it can be mistaken for several other species of sparrows that often occur with it. But over the past twenty-five years, as birders have learned to watch for it and know more about when and where to look, the number of sightings has increased greatly.

Butler knew the bird only as a rare migrant and obtained the first specimen for the state near Brookville, on March 12, 1884. He mentioned four records of occurrence in Indiana. Le Conte's sparrow today is probably a rare to very rare migrant throughout the state and locally a casual to rare winter resident in the southernmost two tiers of counties. It may be considerably more common than current records indicate.

It prefers damp meadows and marsh borders, as well as other weedy (and drier) sites. It has been observed in areas that are subject to periodic flooding. Wintering birds have been found in upland, dry stubble fields, in broom grass near a pond in a weedy, upland pasture, and at airports. Marsh borders are likely places to find them during migration, but they may also occur in weedy old fields, occasionally along fencerows.

Birds thought to be migrants have been observed as early as March 12 and as late as May 13. Twenty-two were found on March 1, 1980, in Gibson County, where the species is known to winter. Twelve were at Lake Monroe on April 5 and ten at the Willow Slough Fish and Wildlife Area on April 2. Ten were found dead along Lake Michigan after the April 16, 1960, storm. Fall migration evidently begins in August, for a dozen birds were found at Indianapolis on August 15 and others were seen in Warren County on August 19. The bulk of fall records are for October. On October 17, 1982, nineteen were recorded in Sullivan County. There are winter observations or specimens from Gibson, Jefferson, Posey, Vanderburgh, Warrick, and Washington Counties.

Although this little sparrow prefers to spend most of its time on the ground, we have noticed that if a bird can be induced to move to the edge of dense cover it will frequently hop up into a bush several feet above the ground, which permits better observation, and sometimes perch for several minutes, as though deciding what to do next. On the ground they scurry about rapidly like mice, avoiding small pools of standing water, and it is seldom possible to get more than a glimpse of them.

SHARP-TAILED SPARROW
Ammodramus caudacutus

Nelson's Sparrow, Nelson's Sharp-tailed Finch, Sharp-tail Finch

If all of the species of sparrows that occur in Indiana were entered in a beauty contest, this one would certainly finish high on the list. A striking bird, it never fails to impress those lucky enough to get a good look at it among the cattails. One reason it is not better known in our area is probably that it prefers wet habitat, near marshes, away from which it is seldom seen. It also appears to be present on spring migration only for a short period, being more abundant in the fall.

Only two records were known to Butler who listed the species as a migrant and "possibly a summer resident locally in the northwestern part of the State." We doubt that this sparrow ever nested in Indiana. It is currently thought to be a rare to very rare migrant throughout the state. At times it may be locally common at a suitable site. For example, at least twenty-five (and undoubtedly many more) were at the Willow Slough Fish and Wildlife Area on September 27, 1958.

The sharp-tailed sparrow is usually found in marshes or bordering ponds and lakes in cattails and other vegetation. It may sometimes be found foraging in drier sites, such as sedge meadows, but usually seeks cover among the vegetation of wetter places when disturbed. At Willow Slough, the birds were in a wet meadow about 150 yards wide and 300 yards long and bounded on three sides by the lake. Its drier central portion was covered with a uniform stand of cutgrass, *Bidens*, and other plants about two feet tall. At the edges of this field, were fringes of mudflats sparsely covered with arrowhead, and beyond this, toward the lake, stands of cattails. Most of the birds were flushed from the central portion, but sought the cattails as escape cover. At another site, in Orange County, the birds were found in a dense stand of *Polygonum*, *Bidens*, and other moist-soil plants around the weedy borders of a pond. They also were seen in a patch of wild millet there.

All of the spring dates of observations are for May 7 to 29, suggesting that the birds may be present only during a short period at that season. Fall migrants appear along northern Indiana by September 12. Sharp-tails are much more abundant in the fall. The number of sightings in September is about equal to that in October; several birds have been observed during the last week of October and there are records for November 11 and 30, which is quite late.

While in Indiana, this sparrow is usually silent, although some give high-pitched, weak calls and others a chip note.

When pursued, the birds run rapidly along the ground for distances of at least twenty or thirty feet, zigzagging to dodge plant stems in their paths. They run with their heads and necks stretched out along the plane of their bodies, at times pausing with upraised heads to watch the observer. They frequently hop up onto a plant stock and perch momentarily just before flying.

FOX SPARROW

Passerella iliaca

Fox-colored Sparrow

This large, rusty sparrow is a striking bird, so large it is sometimes mistaken for a hermit thrush. We see this distinctive bird all too infrequently, and even more rarely do we hear its song. Often we only become aware of its presence while watching a mixed flock of sparrows and other birds about thickets or tall weeds; a big sparrow with a reddish tail may suddenly hop up and fly into dense nearby cover.

Butler, who termed the fox sparrow an aristocrat among sparrows, reported the species as a common spring and fall migrant, noting that it wintered as far north as Putnam County in mild winters. It is now a fairly common migrant and rare winter resident throughout the state, being most abundant in winter from about Bloomington southward.

The fox sparrow inhabits thickets, brushy areas, overgrown fields with weeds and brush, shrubby fencerows and roadsides, and marsh borders with thick willows, briers, or other similar vegetation. Wintering individuals are occasionally seen in pines.

Most wintering birds and spring migrants have left the state by May 1, but there are several records for the first half of May and one as late as May 25 (Lake County). There must have been a exodus of migrants from the state on April 16, 1960, for 198 dead fox sparrows were picked up along the Lake Michigan beaches after the storm of that date. The earliest fall migrant was reported September 19 (Porter County). More than ten birds per count have been recorded on Christmas bird counts at Evansville, in Gibson County, and at Lake Monroe and the Muscatatuck National Wildlife Refuge. The maximum for a single count is twenty in Gibson County on December 23, 1978.

Singing birds have been heard both in spring and fall, in March, April, October, and November. Flocks of as many as 25 fox sparrows have been observed in late March, April, and late October. Forty were recorded on April 23, 1946, in Lake County, but the observer did not state whether they were in a single group.

SONG SPARROW

Melospiza melodia

The record for longest annual song period may be held by this common and familiar sparrow: it may be heard any day of the year, and sometimes it even sings at night. The only serious challenger is the northern cardinal. Both are especially appreciated on bleak winter days. Although the song sparrow's song is variable, it is usually easy to recognize. Margaret M. Nice (1945) reported a male in the Indiana Dunes State Park that sang ten different songs. A frequent visitor to bird feeders, it often nests near houses, adding its voice in summer to the backyard chorus.

Butler reported that these birds were resident throughout Indiana, although in the northern portion of the state most departed during the severest part of the winter. It was rare in summer in the extreme southwestern portion, being found south to Jefferson and Knox Counties. Rob-

ert Ridgway (1915) wrote, "Up to 1890, at least, the Song Sparrow was unknown as a summer resident in the Lower Wabash Valley; it was a common winter resident, coming with the White-throats and Juncos about the middle of October, and departing with them late in April or early in May." We now consider it a common to abundant (at least locally) permanent resident throughout Indiana, and still least numerous in extreme southwestern Indiana during the summer. More than 300 have been recorded on single Christmas counts at Fort Wayne, Lafayette, Richmond, and Terre Haute, and 200 per count at Bloomington, Evansville, Muscatatuck National Wildlife Refuge, New Castle, and South Bend. The largest number per count was 443, at Terre Haute, on December 29, 1973. There appeared to be more song sparrows than usual at many localities during the severe winters of 1975–76 and 1976–77.

The favorite habitats of the song sparrow are probably brushy areas along streams, ditches, and about the borders of marshes, lakes, and other water areas. It also can be found in many other places at various seasons, but shuns the woodlands. Rural people know it as a garden or backyard bird; even in the suburbs it may be present throughout the year, nesting in shrubbery foraging on the lawn, and coming to the feeder in the winter.

There are few details concerning the migration of song sparrows in Indiana because they are present at all seasons, but it is known that they migrate long distances. After the storm of April 16, 1960, over Lake Michigan, forty-seven dead song sparrows were found along the beach. Butler mentioned that migrants returned to northern Indiana in February and March.

The song sparrow nests in old fields, about the shrubby borders of water areas, in young pine plantations, along roadside fencerows and ditches, and about human dwellings. Nests are either on the ground or a relatively short distance above it. Eighteen elevated nests were from two inches to nine feet above the ground; the average was slightly more than two feet.

Full clutches of eggs have been found from April 24 to July 27, but adults have been observed feeding young out of the nests much later. Harmon P. Weeks, Jr., found an unusual nest that was completely covered and had a tunnel through the grass leading to it. The number of eggs in forty-two nests varied from two to six and averaged four. One nest contained five sparrow and three brown-headed cowbird eggs. Another nest contained ten eggs, but the observer did not mention whether they were all song sparrow eggs.

Depicted plant: Spotted touch-me-not; Jewelweed (*Impatiens capensis*)

LINCOLN'S SPARROW

Melospiza lincolnii

Lincoln's Finch

Lincoln's sparrow is easily overlooked in Indiana. It is extremely shy, and, during most of its stay here, silent. However, it has been heard singing during spring and fall migrations, and the song, which has been likened to that of the house wren, is a pleasing one.

Butler listed this sparrow as a rare but regular migrant throughout most of the state, generally seen in May or October. It is an uncommon and regular spring and fall migrant and a casual winter resident today.

This trim sparrow is most likely to be found hiding near the ground in thickets, bushes, and other vegetation near marshes and other water areas. Brushy and weedy ditch banks are also used by the bird, and we have seen it in dense patches of poison ivy and nettles in woodlands bordering rivers. The drier sites from which it has been recorded include a rural garden, wheat stubble, clover fields, a residential area in town, and a tree nursery. Its choice of habitat is much the same as that of the song, swamp, and sharp-tailed sparrows. Because of its plumage and choice of habitat, it may be mistaken for some of the other species of sparrows which are found with it.

There is much to learn about the migration periods of this rather shy species. It would also be interesting to have more information regarding its presence in winter, for we cannot vouch for all of the winter records. It has been reported in late February twice (possibly these were wintering birds rather than early spring migrants) and a few times in March. There are numerous April sightings, but most of the birds are reported during May. Our latest date is May 28. Fall migrants appear as early as September 2 in northern Indiana. They are present throughout the state in late September and throughout most of October. Relatively few remain into November, but there is a November 9 record for Lafayette. The species has been reported on Christmas bird counts and during the winter at several localities north to South Bend.

Lincoln's sparrow is usually present in small numbers, but on occasion it is quite numerous in suitable habitat or during migration peaks. Herbert L. Stoddard found it "very common" on September 17 and "unusually abundant" on September 24, 1919, between Millers and Mineral Springs, along Lake Michigan, but unfortunately gave no specific numbers observed on these dates. Eleven were found in Marion County on October 5, 1953, and Henry C. West found eight singing males there on October 13, 1957. Singing has also been reported in late February and during May.

SWAMP SPARROW

Melospiza georgiana

Southern Swamp Sparrow

This nondescript, marsh-dwelling sparrow is relatively unknown except to people who make the effort to visit its haunts. It is most easily found in spring when it is singing, but the song is similar to that of other species and may not be recognized. Even outside of the nesting season swamp sparrows confine most of their activities to marshes, although they do appear in old fields and woodland borders, especially along streams. Their summer bird neighbors are other marsh-dwellers—song sparrows, marsh wrens, least bitterns, common yellowthroats, and red-winged blackbirds.

Around 1900 the swamp sparrow was a regular migrant throughout most of Indiana and in some localities in the northern part an abundant summer resident. Butler noted that in this region it bred in greater numbers than did the song sparrow. He thought that some might remain all winter in the lower Wabash River valley. It is still a common spring and fall migrant, and nests across northern Indiana, but we have no evidence that it is abundant anywhere in summer. Current nesting records are all for the northern quarter of the state, but references (with no specifics) mention nesting as far south as Marion County. Much remains to be learned about summer distribution. Wintering birds are found throughout the state, but are most numerous in the southern third. The maximum number seen on a Christmas bird count, 268, was at the

Muscatatuck National Wildlife Refuge on December 31, 1977. Large numbers also occur in winter in Gibson County.

The swamp sparrow is a bird of marsh borders, wet sedge meadows, old, low-lying fields, and (in winter) shrubby borders of lowland woodlands. During migration it may be found in drier fields, but is usually not far from water.

Spring migrants appear to reach their peak of abundance in late March and early April. More than one hundred were at Willow Slough from March 25 to April 2, 1953. A large flight evidently occurred the night of April 16, 1960, when the storm over Lake Michigan killed so many birds. At least 633 swamp sparrows were found dead along the lake after the storm. There were literally hundreds at Willow Slough on October 8, 1954: more than two hundred were recorded during one field trip, but it appeared that thousands could have been found there.

Relatively few swamp sparrow nests have been reported from Indiana. Nests are usually in a plant tussock in wet places, over water. One was in grasses surrounded by arrowhead and yellow water lily; the nest was ten inches above the water, which was three feet deep. Another nest was eight to ten inches above the water of a marsh, in a grass tussock. Clutch size in three nests was three, three and five. Another nest contained three sparrow and three brown-headed cowbird eggs. Eggs were found in nests from May 9 to June 3.

Depicted plant: Grass pink (*Calopogon pulchellus*)

WHITE-THROATED SPARROW
Zonotrichia albicollis

Peabody Bird

The plaintive, easily recognized song of this attractive, rather large sparrow may be heard in Indiana during spring and fall migrations and even in winter. When you come across a group of birds foraging on the ground in a brushy area where there are tangles of briers, fallen trees, and thickets, stop and make some *pishing* or squeaking sounds; if there are white-throats, they will begin popping into view, coming higher into the vegetation to get a good look at what is causing the disturbance, and often giving their metallic call notes.

Butler knew this sparrow as a very abundant migrant, but had no winter records. He also wrote, "Often they are seen mating, and some years, when they lingered long, they have been observed carrying sticks, as though they had thought to begin nest building." The white-throat today remains an abundant to common migrant throughout Indiana. It also is found everywhere in winter, but is most abundant during that season in the southern half of the state. There are no nesting records, but several birds have been observed (some of them singing) in June and July.

The white-throated sparrow frequents all types of brushy places, both upland and about marsh borders and low-lying forested areas. The birds can be seen in open areas such as overgrown fields, brushy fencerows, and the like, and also in woodlands where brush and other dense vegetation is present. During migration they occur in such places as city parks, cemeteries, residential areas, and campuses, and occasionally come to bird feeders.

Since Butler had no records of wintering birds, his migration dates are of interest. He noted that this sparrow was generally seen in March, April and early May and from September to November. He also reported the collecting of a specimen on July 23, 1887, at Berry Lake (Lake County). It appears that larger numbers are now found in the fall than in the spring. There were 204 observed on an all-day count in St. Joseph County, May 8, 1976, and 130 were seen on April 28, 1966 (Wayne County). Peak numbers were also recorded at other places in late April or early May. During the fall, white-throats are most abundant in October. Donald H. Boyd hiked from Hobart to the dunes along Lake Michigan on October 1, 1928, and reported 800 white-throated sparrows on this trip. More recently, 150 or more have been observed in several counties during the first week of October. More than 200 have been found on Christmas bird counts at Evansville and the Muscatatuck National Wildlife Refuge, and more than 100 per count were tallied in Gibson County, New Castle, Richmond, southern Lake County, and Warrick County.

There are numerous records for the northern half of Indiana for the last week of May. Of greater interest are the various observations of birds that lingered into the summer. Birds have been found from June 6 to 24 in Fayette, Johnson, Newton, and Wabash Counties. A male sang from a clump of evergreens on the Bloomington campus of Indiana University throughout June and until July 13, 1951. Another was seen in the Indiana Dunes on June 5 and July 31, 1965. Fall migrants sometimes appear in northern Indiana as early as September 2. There is a report of three birds in Lake County on August 17, which is very early.

McAtee (1905) included the following quote from Gertrude Hitze, who presumably made the observation near Bloomington. "April 30, 1902, in a brush heap, in an old orchard, I found a White-throated Sparrow building a nest. The bottom of the nest was made of twigs, but every time she carried any material to the nest, a Catbird would fly down and take it away. The Catbird fought and chased the Sparrows until they left the nest unfinished."

[GOLDEN-CROWNED SPARROW]
Zonotrichia atricapilla

On February 21, 1982, Timothy C. Keller, Mark C. Rhodes, and Nancy [Wiesman] Frass saw a bird at Shades State Park (Montgomery County) that they identified as a golden-crowned sparrow. This is the only report of this accidental visitor from the west.

WHITE-CROWNED SPARROW

Zonotrichia leucophrys

"I always associate this beautiful bird," wrote Amos Butler in 1898, "with the fragrance of apple blossoms, for they come together." We too find the white-crowned sparrow pleasant to look at, particularly in mid-May when it shows up on the lawn to eat dandelion seeds.

Butler called it a common migrant and occasional winter resident (in Knox County). He mentioned that stragglers had been found in Wabash County as late as June 6 and 10. Today it is a fairly common to locally common migrant and a winter resident throughout the state. The largest numbers of wintering birds are found in the southern half of Indiana; at least 200 have been recorded on Christmas bird counts both at the Muscatatuck National Wildlife Refuge and at Terre Haute. More than 300 were seen at Muscatatuck on three different counts; the largest number was 381, on December 30, 1978. There are records for June 3, 1979 (Adams County) and June 19, 1941 (Lake County). Virginia Reuter-skiold observed one from July 17 to August 21, 1967, at Rolling Prairie (LaPorte County).

The white-crowned sparrow is usually found in brushy woods borders, thickets, clumps of weeds, bushy fencerows, brier patches, and old field borders. Butler mentioned that it inhabited swampy woods and thickets during the winter. An important factor in the northward extension of its wintering range in Indiana appears to be the proliferation of multiflora rose hedges and fences, a source both of good cover and of food. Many winter sightings throughout the state are made at multiflora rose plantings. During migration, white-crowns also come into towns and visit backyard bird feeders in both urban and rural areas.

Most have left by June 1 (we have listed exceptions earlier), but during the last half of May some can be expected anywhere in the state. The peak of spring migration is usually during the first half of May. On May 8, 1976, 191 white-crowned sparrows were recorded on an all-day count in St. Joseph County. Fall migrants have been detected as early as September 14 and some reach southwestern Indiana by September 29. Fall migration evidently peaks about mid-October and on October 14, 1949, forty were found in Marion County. Numbers appear then to increase on the wintering grounds until the maximum numbers of birds are present in midwinter.

Singing has been heard in spring and in late December, but in general white-crowns sing less during migration and throughout the winter than do white-throated sparrows. White-crowns are attracted to cracked corn and other seeds at bird feeders and have also been seen eating suet rubbed on tree trunks, as well as multiflora rose hips, pokeberries, and insects. We have seen one fly to the vertical trunk of a large tree, cling momentarily to the bark, and pick insects out of crevices.

HARRIS' SPARROW

Zonotrichia querula

This rather large but shy and elusive sparrow is to be watched for mainly in spring and fall, in the company of other sparrows, juncos, cardinals, goldfinches, and other seed-eating birds in brushy places. One of our early observations was along a country road that bordered a patch of giant ragweed near a small marsh. As we drove past this spot, we noticed various birds actively feeding. We stopped the car but remained inside, and squeaked a few times. Up from the dense clump of ragweed came a handsome Harris' sparrow, which perched momentarily on a stalk and then flew to a distant part of the field.

This western species was unknown in Indiana in 1897. The first state record came on May 4, 1907, when one was collected near Sheridan (Hamilton County) by Ernest P. Walker (Butler, 1909). Before that, the species was on Butler's hypothetical list for Indiana. Although quite a few additional records have accumulated over the years, this sparrow is still a very rare spring and fall migrant and casual winter resident throughout most of the state.

It seems to prefer brushy fencerows and overgrown old field borders and dense tangles of vegetation about marsh borders and along small creeks. Here it forages on the ground, but as mentioned above can sometimes be enticed to come up into the open to investigate some disturbance. One, seen in early December, was with white-crowned sparrows and song sparrows along a fencerow grown up with poison ivy, elm sprouts, and giant ragweed. When flushed it flew into a thick growth of ragweed, willow, cattail, and wild grape about the border of a small marsh. Individuals appear at bird feeders occasionally, sometimes with white-crowned sparrows. One was found along a planting of multiflora rose.

Fall migrants have been observed in northwestern Indiana as early as September 20 (there is one August 30 sighting that may be reliable), but most birds at this season occur in October. Birds are then reported throughout the winter, and the latest spring date is May 17 (Lake County). Most records are for single birds, but James E. Landing found eight near Michigan City on October 20, 1957.

DARK-EYED JUNCO

Junco hyemalis

Slate-colored Junco, Snowbird, Black Snowbird, Oregon Junco, Shufeldt's Junco, Pink-sided Junco, Northern Junco

The snowbird, as it is still known to most older Hoosiers, has undergone a number of name changes. (One of them, black snowbird, was used to differentiate this junco from the snow bunting, or white snowbird). But by any name, this is one of our commonest and best-known winter birds.

Although Butler did not comment on the abundance of the junco in the state, we think it was probably common in his time. It is currently an abundant spring and fall migrant and winter resident throughout Indiana. The largest numbers have been recorded on Christmas bird counts. More than 1,000 per count have been reported from Indianapolis, LaPorte County, Lafayette, Terre Haute, and South Bend. The maximum was 2,436 at South Bend on December 28, 1975. Throughout the southern half of the state, from 600 to more than 900 have been found at several localities on these counts.

The dark-eyed junco may be found in old fields, brushy fencerows and woodland borders, thickets and other tangles of vegetation along streams, and other places where weed seeds are plentiful. It also comes into residential areas, parks, and other suburban places, where it is easily attracted to feeders. But during migration it seems to prefer the overgrown fencerows and old field borders, where it is often found with American tree sparrows, American goldfinches, and other seed-eating birds.

Juncos sometimes enter northern Indiana on their fall migration as early as September 5 (an August 29 sighting is very early). They may reach the southernmost counties of the state by October 1. Large numbers appear during October and locally flights have been reported in late November or early December. On October 28, 1978, there were 500 at Indianapolis. There is considerable northward movement during late March and April. Hundreds of birds may be found in the brushy areas of northwestern Indiana from the last week of March on. A thousand were observed on April 7, 1951, in Porter County. After the April 16, 1960, storm, 1,039 dead juncos were counted along Lake Michigan. Some linger into early May nearly everywhere in the state, but by the end of the month all are normally gone. John M. Louis found one in Lake County on June 10, 1956, another visited a feeder in Indianapolis until June 21, 1971.

Wintering juncos eat many weed seeds and have also been seen feeding on the fruits of poison ivy, flowering dogwood, and wild grape. One bird was flycatching in late March. Singing has been heard from at least February 10 until the last spring migrants depart.

Evermann and Clark (1920) commented on the "widespread belief" in central and northern Indiana that juncos change to song sparrows in the spring, then back again in the fall.

[MCCOWN'S LONGSPUR]

Calcarius mccownii

There are at least three sightings of this western longspur in Indiana, but its status here is probably accidental, as far as we now know. It was on Butler's hypothetical list.

Carmony and Brattain (1971) reported it near Lafayette (Tippecanoe County) on January 2, 1971, in a mixed flock of Lapland longspurs, horned larks, and snow buntings. On February 4, 1979, Timothy C. Keller identified a McCown's longspur feeding with Lapland longspurs and snow buntings at Atterbury Fish and Wildlife Area. Alan W. Bruner found one McCown's with thousands of Lapland longspurs in Montgomery County on April 6, 1982. A possible earlier sighting (not previously recorded) is that of Richard L. Zusi, who saw a bird with the McCown's longspur tail pattern in a flock of 300 Lapland longspurs and horned larks, near Medaryville (Pulaski County) on December 2, 1956.

Clearly, more attention should be paid to the large flocks of longspurs and associated birds that appear in western Indiana. McCown's longspur may well occur here more frequently than our current records indicate.

LAPLAND LONGSPUR

Calcarius lapponicus

During early spring, in the extensive grasslands and cultivated fields of western Indiana, it is sometimes possible to see single flocks of Lapland longspurs that contain a thousand birds. On windy, overcast days, they seem restless and may suddenly flush, fly up and mill about, then circle back and alight near where they left the ground, or fly to a distant field. Quite often the longspurs are accompanied by horned larks and snow buntings. When deep snow covers the usual feeding grounds, the birds go foraging along country roads and highways which

have been cleared of snow. It is easier to see them here than in grassy fields or corn stubble, where they can crouch down out of the wind. Before the last migrants have departed in the spring, many males have acquired most of their bright nuptial plumage and begun to sing.

Butler noted that the Lapland longspur was an irregular winter visitor throughout most of Indiana; around the southern end of Lake Michigan it was sometimes seen in great numbers. It was common locally in certain years at other northern Indiana localities. Today it is an irregular and uncommon migrant throughout the eastern half of the state, at times locally common. It seems to be most regular and abundant in the northwestern quarter of Indiana, especially in former prairieland, but there is a recent record (November 13, 1977) of 1,000 in extreme southwestern Indiana (Gibson County).

Longspurs prefer open fields where grain or weed seeds are available: picked cornfields, soybean stubble, plowed fields, hayfields, short grass pastures, and anywhere there is sparse, low vegetation.

Single Lapland longspurs have been seen in Lake County on September 19 and 30, but these dates are quite early. Most birds arrive there in October and later throughout the rest of the state—in much of southern Indiana not before November. Relatively small numbers have been seen on Christmas counts, the maximum being 283 at Lafayette on December 20, 1975. A flock of 5,000 was seen in Porter County on January 29, 1928.

After mid-April there are few sightings, but longspurs have been observed from May 10 to 13 (50 birds, Newton County) in extreme northwestern Indiana (Lake, LaPorte, and Newton Counties). Butler referred to a specimen collected June 14, 1889, at Sheffield in Lake County. The collector reported that this bird appeared rather tame and was probably a cripple.

The largest flocks reported in northwestern Indiana have been found in late March and early April, when as many as 5,000 birds were found in a day. But the most interesting observation was made by Alan W. Bruner and others in Parke County in the spring of 1982. On April 6 Bruner found approximately 4,000 Lapland longspurs, and estimated that four times that many may have passed through the area on April 6 and 7.

SMITH'S LONGSPUR

Calcarius pictus

Painted Longspur

This buffy longspur was apparently overlooked by many early ornithologists in Indiana, partly because it frequently occurred in small numbers with large flocks of Lapland longspurs and/or horned larks, where it went unnoticed, and also perhaps because most of the birds that migrate through Indiana appear to move along the western side of the state, a sparsely populated area at that time. Even today, the number of sightings may be smaller than its numbers warrant, for it frequents terrain not often used by birders. The open fields it likes can be very inhospitable places on early spring mornings with an icy wind whipping through the dried stalks—most birders prefer a more varied (and more sheltered) habitat.

Butler reported the species as a rare migrant that was "sometimes common in the vicinity of Lake Michigan," but of unusual occurrence elsewhere in the state, citing a single record of two collected near Greencastle (Putnam County) on March 29, 1894. Smith's longspur was then reported from Elkhart County in 1928 and 1938, Tippecanoe County in 1932, and Newton County in 1934. In the late 1940s and early 1950s, many birders (notably members of the Chicago Ornithological Society) visited the area around Enos (Newton County) each spring to see the greater prairie-chickens. It soon became apparent that during early April Smith's longspur could be seen regularly in that region, and records began to accumulate. Current records are mostly for counties along the western third of Indiana, from Lake Michigan to Gibson County. Records for Elkhart, Hamilton, and Wayne Counties are the only ones from the eastern two-thirds of Indiana.

Like other longspurs, Smith's longspur is found in open fields, including wheatfields, corn and soybean stubble, pastures, prairie grasslands, and grassy roadsides. Certain fields in Newton County in the early 1950s always seemed to harbor the birds at the correct season; there must have been some particular food plant there that attracted them.

It is unknown when fall migrants arrive, but the earliest recorded data is November 7 (Knox County). Smith's longspurs have been found on four Christmas counts between December 19 and 28, but there are no sightings for January and only one for February. Spring records range from March 7 to April 29 and most observations have been made during April, undoubtedly the month of greatest abundance. Future field work should shed more light on the seasonal occurrence of this interesting bird.

Flock size varies considerably, from 3 or 4 individuals to groups of 150. Flocks containing only Smith's longspurs (rarely more than 30 birds) may be found. Mixed flocks of Smith's and Lapland longspurs are not uncommon, and from time to time such a mixed flock will also contain horned larks.

SNOW BUNTING

Plectrophenax nivalis

Snowflake, White Snowbird

Southern Indiana birders enjoy making periodic winter visits to the Lake Michigan area, an excellent place to see many interesting northern birds. If the time is right, the parking lot at Michigan City harbor often contains a small flock of snow buntings, and others can be found along the nearby beaches. En route, driving through the open country of northwestern Indiana, this bunting can sometimes be seen along the roadside or with horned larks in fields.

Butler considered the snow bunting an irregular winter visitor, varying greatly in numbers from year to year. In some years it was reportedly absent, in others it was "very abundant" at certain sites in the northern portion of the state. He thought it was rare in southern Indiana. The status of this species is little changed today, except that there are now more records for the southern half of the state and additional sightings throughout Indiana. It is still most abundant and most regular in the three northernmost tiers of counties. On Christmas bird counts in these counties, maxima of 300 to 1,200 have been reported on single counts. The largest number (1,790) was seen in LaPorte County on January 2, 1982.

The snow bunting occurs in open fields (especially those free of deep snow), pastures, corn stubble, along the beaches of Lake Michigan, on sandbars bordering water areas, and along roadsides. The birds will also come to feeding sites provided for them in open areas.

The earliest report of a fall migrant is October 7. Many birds arrive later in October, but the greatest flights are in November. Flocks containing as many as 400 birds have been observed in November and on November 24, 1979, 1,000 to 2,000 buntings passed at Michigan City in one hour. Most of the birds have left the state by late March, but a few remain until at least April 3 (Porter County).

Snow buntings occur quite frequently with horned larks, but have also been found with larks and Lapland longspurs. One bunting was found with a flock of water pipits. Many flocks, however, are composed entirely of buntings. Along Lake Michigan, buntings forage on the sandy beaches, at the water's edge, and back among sparse vegetation. One individual was hopping about on the large chunks of riprap at the Michigan City harbor, apparently feeding on something (possibly aquatic insects) on the bases of the concrete slabs, which were kept moist by the waves. When disturbed while foraging, some birds will perch on stumps or even telephone wires.

BOBOLINK

Dolichonyx oryzivorus

White-winged Blackbird, Ricebird, Reedbird

Around May 1, on warm mornings, as you drive along a country road bordering a weedy pasture or hay field, it is sometimes possible to hear the song of the bobolink. The males perch on fence wires or perform their fluttering courtship flights (accompanied by singing) low over the meadows, where the females are often hidden from view. When the males molt from their summer finery to the drab winter plumage, they resemble the females, and both can be mistaken for large, tan sparrows. The birds begin to flock relatively early in summer, sometimes congregating in standing corn, where they are difficult to see.

About 1900 the bobolink was a rare but regular mi-

BOBOLINK

grant in southern Indiana and a common (locally abundant) summer resident in northern Indiana. Butler wrote, "At the time of the settlement of the country by white men it was probably found in summer about the lower end of Lake Michigan, extending westward some distance into Illinois and south into the prairies of the Kankakee basin and as far east as Rochester in Indiana, thence northward to, and, possibly, into southwestern Michigan." By 1897, it was thought to nest throughout northern Indiana south to Union, Decatur, and Vigo Counties. The bobolink is today a common migrant throughout Indiana, a common summer resident across the northern third, and apparently an uncommon and local summer resident throughout the central portion of the state. Birds have been seen in June and July as far south as a line connecting Greene, Gibson, Bartholomew, and Franklin Counties. The bobolink probably nests in small numbers in these counties, but we have no definite nesting records south of the breeding area mentioned by Butler.

The bobolink likes grasslands, weedy and grassy pastures, hayfields, grassy marsh borders and meadows, and similar areas. It usually nests in dry upland fields, but occasionally may be present in damp sedge meadows. Migrants appear to make considerable use of standing corn or weedy and brushy areas near water.

Bobolinks normally appear during spring migration the last half of April or early May throughout the state. The earliest spring date is April 6, at Brookville and Gary,

but this is extremely early. Birds move off the nesting grounds in summer and form flocks. There are few data concerning the major exodus of fall migrants, for they are not as visible during that season and many are heard passing over but do not alight. Stragglers linger into October, the latest departure date being October 17 (Knox County).

The largest numbers of spring migrants are observed in May, when as many as 250 have been reported in a small area. Many flocks were migrating along Lake Michigan, with vast numbers of swallows and other species, on May 18, 1953. One pasture in Montgomery County contained more than 100 bobolinks on May 12, 1980. Some birds leave their nesting grounds by mid-June, but the usual departure date is about a month later. Flocking has been detected as early as July 1, when males were still in summer plumage, but observers have reported birds in winter plumage by July 24. From late July until the birds depart, flocks of from 15 to 70 (averaging about 40) are found. Nearly a hundred bobolinks, all in winter plumage, were seen in Porter County on August 14, 1954.

Bobolinks nest in hayfields, marsh borders, weedy pastures, and weed fields. The nests are usually on the ground or a few inches above it, well hidden and difficult to find. Nineteen nests containing eggs from May 27 to June 26 averaged five eggs per clutch and ranged from three to six. Young were last seen in a nest on July 18.

Depicted plant: Field milkwort (*Polygala sanguinea*)

RED-WINGED BLACKBIRD

Agelaius phoeniceus

Redwing, Marsh Blackbird, Swamp Blackbird

We have noticed that many people with little or no interest in birds often express great fondness for the red-winged blackbird. One non-birding friend always listens rapturously to the males' spring song. Another says they are her favorite birds. And at a dinner party, a New York City couple raved about the "most beautiful bird" they had seen that day along a southern Indiana country road, and described in enthusiastic terms not a northern cardinal, or a wood duck, or an indigo bunting, or an Ameri-

can goldfinch—but a male redwing! Serious birders would probably find it easier to share in this appreciation if the species were not quite so common and so ubiquitous.

Butler knew it as an abundant summer resident in swamps and other wet places, but noted that it was rare (except in migration) in other habitats. There were indications as early as 1897 that this blackbird was beginning to expand its summer range to various nonaquatic sites. Butler also mentioned that some redwings remained in the southern part of the state in winter. There has been a dramatic change in the breeding distribution since Butler's time. Red-winged blackbirds now nest in many dry sites, at distances from any water, and are thriving in these places. Large numbers are also found nearly every winter at scattered localities throughout the state. More than 10,000 were at Michigan City on December 26, 1955, and 12,704 were seen on the Posey County Christmas count on December 31, 1982. The redwing is an abundant migrant and summer resident, locally rare to abundant in winter.

During migration, redwings are found in all habitats, including cities. The largest numbers still nest in marshes where there are extensive stands of emergent vegetation (usually cattails). Most nests are in emergent vegetation over the water. But hayfields, weedy pastures, fallow fields, roadside ditches, and other upland sites now provide alternative habitat. Its ability to adapt to these drier situations has undoubtedly been one reason for its success as a species.

Despite the redwings that are permanent residents in Indiana, spring migration is usually quite evident. Males arrive several weeks before the female (sometimes as early as late January) and soon begin to appear on territories where they will later nest. It is not unusual to find males singing on territories in late February or early March, when ice still covers the ponds and ditches. There is usually a large northward movement during late February and birds continue to arrive through March. Large flocks are found in late March and in April. An estimated one million red-winged blackbirds were in Lake County on April 24, 1961. Fall flocking occurs quite early; males may even flock to communal roosts during the nesting season. Congregations of at least 200,000 may form roosts in the fall. These large groups of redwings may be found with other blackbirds, European starlings, common grackles, and brown-headed cowbirds, so that the total numbers in some roosts are surprisingly large.

Of 286 red-winged blackbird nests, 143 were within three feet of the water or ground, while only twenty-five were more than three feet above ground. The highest was thirteen feet. Eggs were found in nests from May 3 to July 29. Clutch size ranged from two to five eggs per nest, but there were four eggs each in 117 of 265 nests and only eight nests contained as many as five. Most held three or four.

Redwings eat a wide variety of food. Insects make up a large proportion of the diet in warm weather, but in winter the birds will eat grains, seeds, and other foods. During a severe infestation of periodical cicadas, red-winged blackbirds were seen taking the cicadas in flight.

Territorial males will chase crows, herons, other birds and even white-tailed deer that intrude on the nesting areas. Males have been known to strike humans on the head.

Depicted plant: Common cattail (*Typha latifolia*)

EASTERN MEADOWLARK

Sturnella magna

Meadow Lark

The eastern meadowlark was once the only species of meadowlark in the state, and if a Hoosier saw a familiar plump, yellow-breasted bird sitting on a fence along the roadside there was never a doubt about its identity. Then, in the 1920s, the western meadowlark expanded its range into Indiana. Both species occur in the same type of habitat, and look very much alike. To make it even more confusing, in the parts of the state where both nest together, individuals have been known to learn the songs of both species. But the call notes are inherited and are quite different for each species. The call notes of the western is *chupp* or *chuck*, of the eastern *weet* or *dzert*.

The eastern meadowlark was an abundant summer resident around 1900 and in some years spent the winter throughout the state; in other winters, most were absent. Over the southern part of Indiana, it was a permanent resident. Today, it appears to be a common summer resident throughout most of northern Indiana and fairly common at that season in other parts of the state. It has been reported from throughout Indiana on Christmas bird counts and may be locally common or absent in a given year. The largest numbers winter regularly in the southern third, especially in extreme southwestern Indiana (Gibson, Posey, Vanderburgh Counties). The maxi-

EASTERN MEADOWLARK

mum number reported on a single count was 305; this was at the Muscatatuck National Wildlife Refuge, on December 14, 1974. This meadowlark, like the western, is a bird of pastures and fields, both cultivated and fallow. It was probably once quite abundant on the native prairie grasslands and expanded its range into other parts of the state as the forests were cut away.

Although wintering birds may be present anywhere, there is usually a noticeable increase of spring migrants in late January and during February. Waldo L. McAtee mentioned a flock of fifty flying northward, high in the sky, on January 21, 1903, at Bloomington. It is not unusual to see flocks of thirty or forty in spring and fall. The birds remain flocked during the winter and sometimes mixed groups of meadowlarks and European starlings are found. Fall migration is usually less evident than spring migration.

Singing may be heard at almost any time of the year. On warm winter days, groups of birds may be found perched in a tree and many will be singing. During the courtship season, males sing from exposed perches on fences, posts, trees, or wires, or even while standing on the ground. Flight songs are also common, as they are in many other species that nest in open country where singing perches may be scarce.

Nests are on the ground in grassy or weedy fields, hayfields, along grassy roadsides and similar places. Eggs are laid as early as April 11 and have been seen in nests until July 17. Twenty-nine nests contained from three to six eggs each and averaged five. Many nests are lost to mowing operations.

Wintering flocks feed in corn stubble and other farmed fields or overgrown fields that provide grain and weed seeds. The birds frequently feed with hogs and cattle and a small group of meadowlarks was seen feeding in a railroad yard where straw and other litter had been discarded from boxcars.

The first fishing fly Mumford tied when he was a young boy was a few yellow breast feathers of a meadowlark tied to a small hook with a piece of the red-and-white twisted string used by grocers. The fly was a killer for green sunfish in a pond near the house.

WESTERN MEADOWLARK

Sturnella neglecta

Western Meadow Lark

On April 7, 1924, William B. Van Gorder found a singing western meadowlark near Albion (Noble County). On July 29 of that year he wrote the U.S. Department of Agriculture: "This is the first time I have ever seen this bird here. I have seen them in Minnesota, Western Iowa and Eastern Kansas in June 1918." This is the earliest reference to this species in Indiana, although Butler carried the species on his hypothetical list. Unfortunately, there is one difficulty with records of singing birds. Some individuals sing both the western and the eastern meadowlark songs. This was discovered by Samuel W. Witmer, who watched and listened to one singing both songs in 1937 near Goshen (Elkhart County). Thus, since all records prior to the collecting of the first specimen from the state on February 17, 1950 (Posey County), were of singing birds, we cannot determine which is actually the earliest valid one. There is also a question about most subsequent records based only on singing birds. By the late 1940s it was evident that there were a number of western meadowlarks in the former prairie region of northwestern Indiana. Donald H. Boyd had previously reported it from Lake County in 1935. It is currently an uncommon to rare summer resident throughout the northern half of the state and is still probably most numerous in the northwestern fourth. Over the southern half of Indiana, it is very rare to absent in summer and during migration. It has been reported in June or July as far south as Marion and Wayne Counties. There appear to be no records for most of southeastern Indiana. Winter distribution is largely unknown, but it is highly possible that some meadowlarks listed on Christmas bird counts as easterns were in fact westerns. One was collected January 11, 1964, in LaPorte County, and there have been sightings (some perhaps not reliable) from December to February for Lake, Newton, St. Joseph, and Wells Counties. Critical study of wintering flocks would no doubt increase the number of sightings. In fact, we urge birders to spend more time studying meadowlarks at all seasons.

We know practically nothing concerning migration of the western meadowlark in Indiana. Most singing birds are heard from February to May. Five were found dead after the April 16, 1960, storm over Lake Michigan, indicating some movement at that time.

No nest has been found in the state, despite the fact that the species has been present for a great many years and probably has an extensive breeding range. Wesley E. Lanyon (1956) studied the distribution of both species of meadowlarks in the north-central states (including Indiana). He conducted a singing male census over sixty square miles of McClellan and Colfax townships, in Newton County, in early May 1954. At sixty-four listening stations, he heard eighty-one eastern and ten western meadowlarks.

YELLOW-HEADED BLACKBIRD

Xanthocephalus xanthocephalus

Nature played a trick on birders when she created this gorgeous creature of the marshes and then gave it such an unpleasant and insignificant song. On seeing this species for the first time, one admires the bright coloring; but when the bird sings, its song is a rasping croak, and—to a human, if not to a potential mate—the illusion of beauty is somehow reduced. Even so, a male yellow-headed blackbird perched on a swaying cattail in mid-May is a fine sight.

Butler knew the yellow-head as a local summer resident in northwestern Indiana, where Charles E. Aiken found it "breeding abundantly" along the Calumet River (Lake County) in 1871. Aiken reportedly collected over a hundred eggs from this colony. By 1900 its numbers had greatly decreased, and for the next several decades little was reported of it. It nested near Whiting (Lake County) until at least 1940, and there was an unsuccessful nesting attempt in 1975 at the Willow Slough Fish and Wildlife Area. Delano Z. Arvin (1981*a*) found two nests with eggs on May 21, 1980, at Gleason Park (Lake County), where the species continued to nest through 1982. Yellow-heads may have nested at Willow Slough in 1980; they definitely did so in 1981 and 1982. The nests were fastened to cattail stems and placed from one and one-half to two feet above the water. Three nests contained four eggs each, one held two. Three young were found in another nest. Nests with eggs were observed from May 17 to June 17.

This blackbird, then, is currently a rare and local nesting species in Lake and Newton Counties. Throughout the rest of the state it is a casual to very rare spring and fall migrant and winter resident.

Although migrating yellow-headed blackbirds may be

seen near various types of water areas or even in non-aquatic sites (and at feeding stations), they prefer to nest in cattail marshes. Transient and wintering individuals may be found with mixed flocks of other blackbirds, brown-headed cowbirds, and common grackles.

Spring migrants usually appear in April; most fall migrants have departed by November 1. There are sightings for each month of the year. On July 22, 1977, Lee A. Casebere and Mark A. Weldon found about twenty yellow-headed blackbirds in a mixed blackbird flock. Three yellow-heads were reported on the December 14, 1974, Christmas bird count in the Indiana Dunes.

Depicted plant: Narrow-leaved cattail (*Typha angustifolia*)

RUSTY BLACKBIRD

Euphagus carolinus

Rusty Grackle

Sometimes in late March or early April, noisy flocks of rusty blackbirds may be found foraging in wet, brushy places along streams or ditch banks and about the edges of marshes. Here they feed in the shallow water and mud, frequently in sites well screened by willows, buttonbushes, or other shrubs. Many members of resting flocks will sometimes be found singing on warm spring days, and it is often their squeaky songs that first call attention to such groups. In spring the males' slightly rust-colored feather edgings are not conspicuous, but in fall the birds truly appear to be dusted with rust.

Butler suspected this blackbird was really a common migrant, but one usually overlooked by observers. It was a rare winter resident in southern Indiana. Today it is a fairly common and regular spring and fall migrant and a rare winter resident throughout the state. Especially in the northwestern part of Indiana, it may be locally common during migration. About forty years ago, as many as 1,000 were reported from Lake County in late March, early April, late September, and early October. Such numbers do not appear to be present now. In the vicinity of Michigan City, 435 were recorded on December 28, 1948.

About 153 were present in a Vigo County roost during the winter of 1972–73, and 100 were seen on the 1976 Eagle Creek Park Christmas bird count (Marion County).

Mixed flocks of migrating icterids including rusty blackbirds, may be found in cultivated fields, along brushy fence-rows, and in other upland sites. Occasionally rusty blackbirds appear at bird feeders. We found a flock of thirty in a tamarack swamp on February 2, 1960, at the Pigeon River Fish and Wildlife Area.

The rusty blackbird is an early migrant; it is not unusual to find flocks moving into northern Indiana in late February. Peak numbers are usually reached around the first of April and few remain in the state after mid-May. The latest departure date is May 23 (Lake County), but that is unusual. We also have a report of one seen in Warren County on July 30, 1977, by Susan H. Ulrich. Fall migrants appear in northern Indiana the first half of September. A sighting of forty in Lake County on August 20, 1940, is our earliest record. Birds linger throughout the late fall and small numbers remain in winter.

Rusty blackbirds eat weed seeds, grain, and insects. Evermann and Clark (1920) watched them feeding at Lake Maxinkuckee in early October "on the casts of *Chironomus* larvae that had washed up on the shore in great quantities," and on adult *Chironomus* insects, which they picked "from the limbs and trunks of the trees on Long Point."

BREWER'S BLACKBIRD

Euphagus cyanocephalus

This is another western species that invaded Indiana after the turn of the century. It was first recorded from Lake County on April 8, 1949, near Dyer, and it was here that the first nests in Indiana were found in 1952. It is quite likely that this blackbird had been in that region for years, for it closely resembles the much more common rusty blackbird that sometimes migrates through northwestern Indiana in large numbers. Once observers learned to watch for the Brewer's, the number of observations increased greatly. It is relatively easy to scan mixed flocks of blackbirds looking for the brown-eyed female Brewer's, which stand out from the pale-eyed rusty blackbird females. Separating spring-plumaged male Brewer's and rustys is more difficult but close observation reveals the different colors of the body feathers.

Since the initial report in 1949, Brewer's blackbird has been observed somewhere in Indiana each year except 1971. It appears to be a regular but rare spring and fall migrant and casual winter resident throughout the state. It is still possibly a rare summer resident in northwestern Indiana, but no nest has been reported since 1965. As many as eighty were found in the Willow Slough area in

early April 1965 and 300 were seen at a turf farm in St. Joseph County on September 24, 1972. The maximum number on a single Christmas bird count was two hundred, on December 18, 1982, at Evansville.

This blackbird is usually found in grassy cultivated and uncultivated fields and about the borders of marshes, borrow pits, and other water areas. During migration and in winter it may appear almost anywhere—along roadsides, in brushy fencerows, or at bird feeders. Wintering Brewer's blackbirds are normally found in small numbers, often with other blackbirds. Spring arrivals usually reach the northern edge of the state in March (as early as March 9), but the largest numbers are evidently present during the first week of April. The peak of fall migration may occur from late September to the first week of November.

The first nesting colony discovered in Indiana was located in the drier portions of a seasonally wet natural prairie remnant of about twelve acres. The date was May 11, 1952. Switch grass was one of the major plants in drier sections of the area. In wet depressions in the field iris and bulrush were growing, and two cottonwood trees and two dense thickets of quaking aspen were near. One

nest was in a dense stand of switch grass; four others were in partially barren fields that had been cultivated the year before and were now soybean stubble and weeds. A nest in Porter County was in an alfalfa field. A small colony of birds in LaPorte County nested in a grass–clover meadow. The fourth nest site was a partly barren cinder flat (resulting from the filling of a marsh), which supported a sparse weedy growth and scattered shrubs. All nests found in the state were on the ground and were in Lake, LaPorte, and Porter Counties.

Three of the five nests found on May 17, 1952, each contained three eggs; one contained a single egg; the fifth held two eggs and three young. Another nest held an egg and five young on May 23. Four young were in a nest found on June 28. Nests were placed in clumps of vegetation, such as switch grass, goldenrod, and sweet clover.

The adult Brewer's blackbirds on the Dyer breeding grounds were feeding mainly in corn stubble and soybean stubble from the previous year and on freshly plowed ground. Pools of rainwater were present in all of these fields and the birds were carrying large numbers of what appeared to be insects to young in the nest. A mixed flock of Brewer's, brown-headed cowbirds, and red-winged blackbirds, seen in late March, was feeding in a newly planted field and later roosting in a dense, dry stand of switch grass. In August, a group of Brewer's was seen drinking, sunbathing, preening, and loafing on the bare sand and gravel at the edge of a borrow pit.

Depicted plant: Scouring-rush (*Equisetum hyemale*)

BREWER'S BLACKBIRD

COMMON GRACKLE

COMMON GRACKLE

Quiscalus quiscula

Blackbird, Crow Blackbird, Bronzed Grackle, Purple Grackle, Common Blackbird

This big, large-tailed glossy species is the well-known "blackbird" of the Hoosier State; relatively few people here call it a grackle. It is an aggressive visitor at feeding stations, where in the spring one can witness at close range the interesting courtship displays of the males. The birds sometimes take over other birds' nests and kill their young. The grackle has a propensity for forming large communal roosts (usually with other species) that may become a nuisance or a health hazard to humans. Because the common grackle has adapted so well to changing patterns of land use, it continues to be successful.

Butler knew the grackle as a common summer resident that was most numerous in spring and fall and sometimes spent the winter (usually in small numbers). There has been a notable increase in its numbers in Indiana since 1900: it is now an abundant spring and fall migrant and summer resident and a locally uncommon to abundant winter resident. The largest numbers in winter are usually found in the southern part of Indiana.

During migration, grackles may be found in nearly any rural or suburban habitat. Butler noted that in the Whitewater River valley they preferred to nest in groves of cottonwoods, sycamores, and other trees near water courses. Common grackles spend considerable time near water areas, wading about and feeding in shallow water.

The vanguard of spring migrants arrive in Indiana no later than early February and by the middle of that month they have reached the northern border. Local wintering populations may be confused with early spring migrants. Large mixed flocks of other icterids and grackles are common. Fall flocks begin forming in July and we have a record of a flock of 250 coming to a roost as early as July 22. But the numbers are increased tremendously by migrants arriving from farther north later in the fall. Huge groups are reported, although there are practically no data on estimated numbers in such flocks. For example, on November 16, 1970, at Evansville, Mr. and Mrs. Eugene Stocks described such a grackle flight: ". . . thousands and thousands flying in a continuous ribbon from 10 to 50 birds deep and as far as we could see north and south as we watched from a hilltop. This stream of birds continued to pass over for 30 minutes." An inherent problem of counting birds in such flocks is that they are often made up of grackles, several species of blackbirds, brown-headed cowbirds, and European starlings. More than 10,000 grackles per count have been recorded on Christmas bird counts at Bloomington, Evansville, Indiana Dunes, and Indianapolis. There were 31,000 at Evansville on December 26, 1959, and 24,909 in Posey County on December 31, 1982.

Not too long after arrival in spring, groups of males and females gather at potential nesting sites and an active courtship period begins. Chosen sites are frequently stands of conifers or clumps of trees bordering marshes and other water areas. Grackles usually nest in colonies. Full clutches of eggs have been found by April 15 as far north as Lafayette, and eggs are present in nests until at least June 4. Nests have been found from 1.5 to 60 feet above the water. Most nests over dry land range from five to twenty feet in height, with considerable variation. Robert Kern has reported that, from about twenty acres of pines being grown for Christmas trees near Rochester (Fulton County), he and his helpers removed 404 grackle nests in the spring of 1968. The nests were removed to prevent the adults from perching on and damaging the growing tips of the pines, thus rendering them less salable.

Grackles eat a wide variety of foods, including insects, grains, small birds and eggs, and acorns. We have two observations of a grackle pursuing a house sparrow, forcing it to the ground, then killing and eating it. One sparrow was killed by a sharp peck in the back of the head. Grackles were also seen pecking at a young ovenbird. We once saw two grackles chase an adult red squirrel for at least three minutes around a pine tree; the birds actually struck the squirrel several times. A bobtailed young grackle was nearby. Several times we have seen grackles take dry bread (and, in one case, dry Kix cereal) to a bird bath, place the food in the water, then eat it. One bird took about a dozen snake eggs, one at a time, and placed them in the water of a bird bath (Thompson, 1972).

Depicted plant: Smooth blackhaw (*Viburnum prunifolium*)

BROWN-HEADED COWBIRD

Molothrus ater

Cowbird, Cow Bunting, Blackbird

It is difficult to find anything good to say about the cowbird, but we must admit we marvel at the skill with which it manages to locate nests of foster parents in which to lay its eggs. We have seen female cowbirds skulking about in many different habitats searching for nests. In Indiana they parasitize at least forty-nine species, ranging in size from the blue-gray gnatcatcher to the eastern meadowlark, some of which construct very well-hidden nests that are difficult for humans to locate. Many people remove cowbird eggs from other birds' nests whenever they can, but its success has nonetheless been so great that it now appears something more may have to be done to control its numbers, especially where it is having an impact on endangered species.

At the beginning of the current century, the brown-headed cowbird was an abundant summer resident throughout Indiana and remained in some winters in the southern part. It is still an abundant spring and fall migrant and summer resident statewide, and locally common to rare during the winter. In recent years, the largest numbers recorded on Christmas bird counts have been at Terre Haute, where 6,045 were present on December 27, 1972, but more than 1,000 per count have been observed at Fort Wayne, Indianapolis, Richmond, and Shelbyville.

This cowbird inhabits nearly all habitats today, but it was once apparently more or less confined to the prairie areas, moving into formerly wooded sections when the forests were cut. Large flocks may be found in open areas, sometimes in association with other icterids and European starlings. Huge roosting congregations may use pine plantations, cattail marshes, bridges, or stands of deciduous trees (even in cities). During the summer, cowbirds may be expected nearly anywhere that other species of birds are nesting.

The peak of spring migration apparently occurs in late March, when flocks containing as many as 1,000 have been observed. Some spring flocks are composed almost entirely of males, while others contain about equal numbers of males and females. In early August as many as 500 cowbirds may be seen, for flocking takes place quite early. A group of 400 was seen feeding together on August 23, and flocks containing 1,000 or more birds have been reported from mid-October to early November. Hundreds of the birds seen in large flocks in October are sometimes singing in chorus.

During early spring, courting parties of male and female cowbirds are quite evident. Such groups usually contain from three to ten birds, usually with males outnumbering females. These assemblages remain together into the summer, for the cowbird has a long egg laying season (at least April to July). Female cowbirds often remove host eggs from the nests prior to depositing their own. It is difficult to determine how many eggs a female cowbird may lay in a season and it appears that two or more may lay their eggs in the same nest.

Foster species react differently to the presence of cowbird eggs in their nests. Some desert the nest; others remove the cowbird eggs; many rear the young cowbird; several build a new nest layer (or multiple layers) over the cowbird egg.

Female cowbirds sometimes show considerable interest in nests of a previous year. For example, on April 17, 1955, Mumford watched a male and three female cowbirds at the nest of a northern cardinal that had been used the summer before. Two female cowbirds were standing on either side of the nest rim; one, then the other, took several turns sitting briefly in the nest before the entire group flew. Among nests parasitized by cowbirds in Indiana have been fifteen species of warblers, six species of sparrows, and five species of vireos. Cowbirds sometimes appear to have a local preference for laying their eggs in nests of a certain species. (An egg of the pictured pair can be seen in the nest of the chestnut-sided warbler.)

Wintering cowbirds readily come to bird feeders; sometimes 200 or more will be present. They also feed with livestock (mostly hogs and cattle) and gather to eat corn stored on the ground at grain elevators. They have been seen eating periodical cicadas, and in summer they consume large quantities of other insects.

Depicted plant: Pussy willow (*Salix discolor*)

ORCHARD ORIOLE

Icterus spurius

Of the two species of orioles that nest in Indiana, this—the smaller and less conspicuous—is probably overlooked by many because of its subdued coloration and more secretive nature. But in southern Indiana during the nesting season, it is possible to hear the song of the orchard oriole at many places. It is of interest that the males mate and breed successfully in their first spring plumage, which is more like that of the adult female than of second year, and older, adult males.

Butler considered the orchard oriole a common summer resident in most counties of the state, but mentioned that it was steadily increasing in numbers, even in extreme northern Indiana where it had been locally rare or absent prior to the early 1880s. In the spring of 1897, the orchard oriole outnumbered the northern oriole ten or fifteen to one in the Brookville area, where a few years before the northern had been much more abundant. Although today the orchard oriole is present during migration and summer throughout the state, it is generally most common in the southern third and uncommon elsewhere.

As the name implies, this oriole was formerly associated with orchards. Butler wrote, "The orchard is its home, and not the deep woods." It is truly a bird of open areas, nesting not only in orchards, but in scattered trees in and bordering old fields and along roadsides, as well as on lawns. In Indiana, unlike the northern oriole, it does not appear to have an affinity for nesting near water.

Early spring migrants usually are observed around mid-

April, but there are sightings as early as April 2. Butler remarked that the orchard oriole came in the spring "with the blooming of the Buckeye" and early migrants frequented thickets where this tree was found. Fall migration begins quite early. Birds simply leave their nesting sites during July and quietly slip away; one day we realize we have not seen them for a time. Family groups consisting of adults and their fledged young are quite noticeable during July, but most have departed the state by September 1. A few linger into the last half of September and there is a single October record for the 10th, but this is extremely late. Large flocks are not reported, but a group of six was seen in spring and three males were found together on May 18.

Nests are semi-hanging or hanging structures, usually placed near the ends of drooping branches or in the tops of trees. Most of those we have seen were made of green grasses and thus well camouflaged among the tree foliage. Nest heights varied from about eight to thirty feet. Eggs have been found in a small sample of nests from April 24 to June 10; the number per nest ranged from three to six.

Depicted tree: Wild plum (*Prunus* sp.)

NORTHERN ORIOLE

Icterus galbula

Baltimore Oriole, Hang-nest Bird, Golden Robin, Hangbird

One of the most pleasing sights of an Indiana spring is the brilliant orange and jet-black plumage of the flashy bird formerly known as the Baltimore oriole. It and its western counterpart, the Bullock's, are now considered to be a single species, which has been given the name northern oriole. Because of its persistent singing, preference for open habitat, and bright plumage, it is well known.

In Indiana it has been a common migrant and summer resident for the past hundred years, casual in winter. However, shortly after 1900, some writers reported a noticeable decrease, perhaps attributable to the large numbers collected for their plumage, primarily on its wintering grounds in Central America. It occurs throughout the state, except in areas lacking suitable habitat.

This oriole shows a decided preference for living near water and in summer for nesting in various open habitats where tall trees are present. On May 10, 1950, thirty-three northern orioles were seen along the Salamonie River from Montpelier to Warren (15 miles). On May 12, 1950, seventeen males (no females) were observed along the Little Elkhart River between Ligonier and Benton (11 miles). It was a treat in the early 1950s to drive slowly along North River Road from West Lafayette in May. Huge American elms and giant sycamores overhung the road, which parallels the Wabash River. For about two miles orioles were numerous, nesting primarily in the long, drooping branches of the elms. In winter, even more nests were exposed to view that had been hidden in summer. But here, as elsewhere, the orioles' favorite nesting trees succumbed to Dutch elm disease, and they seem now to nest more and more in sycamore, cottonwood, and other tall trees near lakes and ponds, along woodland borders, on golf courses and cemeteries, in small clumps of trees in open fields, along creeks and streams, and in residential areas.

Spring migration begins about mid-April in southern Indiana and continues through the remainder of that month in the central and northern regions. At some localities the first arrivals consistently appear on or about the same date year after year. Fall departure is not well documented, for the birds become increasingly inconspicuous and silent after June, then, beginning in August, slip quietly away before one is aware of it. Most birds have left the state by mid-October. On August 23, 1951, near Lafayette, at least ten orioles and fifty eastern kingbirds were seen together in trees at dusk. We do not know if this was a chance association, but Alexander F. Skutch mentioned northern orioles, "migrating kingbirds," and other species roosting together in Honduras.

Courtship begins in mid-May. The male perches near a female and spreads and flashes his tail and wings. Males jealously guard their territories; a whistled imitation of

NORTHERN ORIOLE

their song will usually elicit an immediate response from the resident male. The beautifully woven, pendant nests are normally placed rather high and usually overhang an opening (a road, field, or lawn). Recorded nest heights ranged from 11 to 80 feet (average 33). The female builds the nest, but the male visits it frequently, chases rival males from the site, and vigorously scolds humans and animals who come too near. Nest construction begins at least as early as April 27. In one instance, orioles arrived May 8 and began nest construction three days later. Jane L. Hine saw a nest woven entirely of black horsehair except for one piece of black twine. The long, silvery strands from milkweed stems are often used in nests. Bird banders sometimes catch female orioles by baiting traps with lengths of twine, yarn, or other potential nesting

materials. Nests are so high and the males so vigilant that we have only one record of eggs in the nest (June 1), but in one nest incubation evidently began May 24. Young probably leave the nest from at least mid-June to early July.

Northern orioles eat a variety of animal and vegetable foods. Young are fed large quantities of insect larvae. Adults feed on grapes, apples, pears, strawberries, and black cherries. They also take insects from pokeberry flowers and from clusters of pine needles, and eat bees. They visit flowering quince; in one case the birds were reportedly eating the flowers. At feeders they eat cake crumbs, blackberries, dried fruit, orange slices, and the honey and water mixture provided for hummingbirds.

Depicted tree: Tulip tree (*Liriodendron tulipifera*)

PINE GROSBEAK
Pinicola enucleator

During the infrequent winters that this grosbeak migrates to Indiana, it always attracts much attention. One such winter was 1951–52. A number of them appeared along the southern shore of Lake Michigan, and it was then that some of us got our first look at these beautiful northern finches. The birds were on the ground only six feet away from us, reaching up to pick shriveled fruits from the nightshade (*Solanum*) plants projecting from the snow. They also exhibited their characteristic tameness at another site, calmly perching and eating fruits from a privet hedge with onlookers barely five feet away.

Butler knew of only three records of occurrence in Indiana (Allen, Lake, LaPorte Counties) and listed it as an irregular or accidental winter visitor. We have records of birds being seen in sixteen different winters from 1913 to 1981; thus it still remains an irregular winter resident. The largest number recorded for a single locality was twenty-five; this was at Pines (Lake County) on December 18, 1977. Most records refer to sightings of from one to nine birds. Most of the pine grosbeaks seen in the state have been found in the three counties bordering Lake Michigan, and in St. Joseph County. The southernmost observation was made at Indianapolis; the remainder of the records are from scattered places in the northern half of the state. The earliest fall record is October 22 and the latest spring sighting is April 29.

In addition to nightshade and privet fruits, pine grosbeaks have been seen to eat the fruits of bush honeysuckle and highbush cranberry, as well as jack pine buds and seeds and ash seeds.

PURPLE FINCH
Carpodacus purpureus

Sometimes in early spring several dozen male purple finches will perch together in a tree for an impromptu choral performance. Mumford made his first acquaintance with this colorful finch more than forty years ago when he encountered such a group. He heard the singing, followed the sound, and located the birds some two hundred yards away. There were fifty or more of them, sitting in the top of a leafless tree in a rolling field and singing loudly and persistently. As he walked away through the fields, he could still hear the singing in the distance. It was a memorable event. Those seeing a male of this species for the first time may wonder why it was ever given the name purple finch when it is not purple at all, but rosy. As for the females,

their plumage is so different from the males that many people do not recognize them when they appear alone at bird feeders.

Butler reported this finch as a regular migrant in varying numbers and an irregular winter resident throughout Indiana. He mentioned the possibility that it might occasionally be found in the northern part of the state during the summer. He found them most common in March and April when migrating. Today it is an uncommon to common, somewhat irregular migrant and winter resident anywhere in the state. It is quite variable in occurrence and numbers during the winter, some years being noted for its abundance and distribution. The winter of 1948–49 was such a winter, when more than one hundred each were found on Christmas bird counts at Lafayette and in the Michigan City area.

Butler remarked that the purple finch might be found "wherever elms grow" and that it preferred less dense woods or the straggling trees along smaller waterways. It frequents brushy fencerows, stands of tall weeds and brush along streams, and brushy tangles about woods borders. During the winter, the birds readily come to bird feeders in both rural and urban areas.

So many birds remain throughout the winter that it is difficult to determine when spring migration begins. As in Butler's time, most migrants at that season are probably present in March and April. Individuals linger into late May. One was present at Goshen (Elkhart County) in June and into July (no year given). A male was found on July 30, 1982, at Beverly Shores (Porter County). It is of interest that an immature was found at the same spot on August 8, 1981, according to Kenneth J. Brock. In Lafayette, John H. Miller observed a male, which he identified as this species, come to his bird feeder with a young bird and feed it on June 14, 1980. It appears that more attention should be paid to the species in summer to investigate the possibility of nesting in the state.

Fall migrants have been noted as early as August 2 in LaPorte County, and "hundreds" were seen in that county on October 21, 1956. In general, the largest numbers are recorded on Christmas bird counts.

Purple finches have been seen feeding on a wide variety of vegetable matter: buds of Chinese elm, red elm, white elm and American beech, catkins of big-toothed aspen, seeds of box elder, white ash, sweet gum, sycamore, tulip tree, staghorn sumac, giant ragweed and sunflower, and the fruits of red cedar, honeysuckle, multiflora rose, hackberry, black haw, and osage orange (crushed). At bird feeders, the birds also eat "thistle" seeds and other seeds and grain.

Singing has been heard at various seasons, but mostly in spring. One bird was uttering a soft "whisper song" on September 8. In addition to the warbling song, this species sometimes sings a different one that resembles that of a vireo, especially the yellow-throated or solitary. One bird sang this song in midwinter.

HOUSE FINCH

Carpodacus mexicanus

This western finch reached Indiana by an unusual route: it invaded the state not from the west, but from the east. The ancestors of these invaders were evidently a population of house finches released and established on Long Island, New York, in the early 1940s. Recently the range of these eastern house finches has been expanding at an accelerated rate into the Midwest. James E. Landing sighted a house finch with some purple finches at Michigan City (LaPorte County) on November 16, 1958; this is our earliest record. Apparently, however, most Indiana birders did not take this record too seriously, and a considerable number of years passed before the species was next reported in the state.

On March 28, 1976, a male was photographed at Indianapolis by Thomas Field and observed by many people. Since then house finches have been recorded in the state each year, but the most noticeable increase was in 1981, when they were reported from twelve counties. They nested in Adams and Allen Counties in 1981, in Johnson and Huntington Counties in 1982 and in Tippecanoe County in 1983. There are now sightings from twenty-four counties throughout Indiana.

It is expected that the status of the house finch in Indiana will vary from year to year until some type of equilibrium in the population is reached. For the present, it has established itself as a member of the avifauna of the state.

On May 9, 1981, a nest found on a porch at Decatur (Adams County) contained small young; the following day it was determined that there were four or five young in the nest. It was thought that four young left this nest by May 19. A nest with eggs was located May 25, 1981, at Fort Wayne (Allen County), about nine feet up in an evergreen tree. On August 24, 1981, two adults brought four young to a bird feeder there. The Tippecanoe County nest was inside an overhead light fixture on a Lafayette front porch. It contained five eggs in mid-May. Many of the birds were first seen at feeders, where they ate thistle (niger) seed, milo, and other grain and seeds provided for them. As many as fourteen birds were visiting a feeder in Bloomington in 1981.

HOUSE FINCH

RED CROSSBILL

RED CROSSBILL

Loxia curvirostra

American Crossbill

Red crossbills feed, parrotlike, in coniferous trees, hanging upside down and negotiating the branches by means of beaks as well as feet. Close inspection will reveal the crossed mandibles, wonderfully adapted for extracting the seeds from cones of evergreens. Crossbills are frequently quite tame and allow observers to approach to within a few feet. Val Nolan Jr. had an interesting experience with a flock of them one sunny afternoon. This group had been extremely active, wild, and restless, and had not permitted him to come near. But later they flew by twos and threes to a solitary jack pine about fifteen feet tall. After a few minutes Nolan investigated and found the birds scattered throughout the tree, some with beaks tucked under the feathers of their backs and eyes closed, others awake but resting, and so tame he could

get within two feet of them. Several of us once saw three crossbills on a telephone wire; one of them was hanging upside down by its feet.

Butler aptly called the red crossbill "a very erratic bird," but noted that it was generally present in Indiana as a winter visitor or migrant. It was not here every year, but might be seen almost any month, and a few had been reported nesting in the state. It is still a rare to irregular winter visitor and migrant throughout the state, but has been recorded in each month of the year. Most records are for the period November through April; there are only six reports of birds observed during July, August, and September. One nesting record has been added since 1897.

Practically all of our reports of red crossbills are of birds found in conifers, although some frequent bird feeders and may be seen eating sunflower seeds in gardens. The species occurs in remote woodlands and also near cities and human dwellings, wherever suitable cone-bearing trees are present. Cemeteries, city parks, and campuses often provide the necessary trees, as do pine plantings.

The red crossbill is a noted wanderer, seemingly on the move much of the time and likely to appear nearly anywhere in the state at any time. There are more reports for November than for any other month, but December runs a close second. Then, after a decreased number of sightings for January and February, March and April observations point to a migration peak during those months. There are four June reports from 1970 to 1980, July records for 1961 and 1973 and a single August record in 1966. This crossbill is normally seen in small groups, but an estimated seventy-five were seen in Clark County on

November 11, 1981, and about fifty were present in mid-May 1961, in Porter County. Butler mentioned that red crossbills reportedly nested at Bloomington and West Lafayette in 1885. No details regarding these nestings can be found in the literature, although young were said to have been collected at West Lafayette. In the spring of 1973, a red crossbill nest with one egg was found at Richmond. The nest was later abandoned, according to James B. Cope. Birders should be aware of the possibility of this crossbill nesting again in the state.

The seeds of larch, spruces, firs, hemlock, and pines have been reported as food of the red crossbill in Indiana. It also has been observed eating sunflower seed and ragweed seed. Feeding flocks can sometimes be heard some distance away as they pry apart the scales of cones to reach the seeds.

Depicted tree: Jack pine (*Pinus banksiana*)

WHITE-WINGED CROSSBILL
Loxia leucoptera

This is the more strikingly plumaged and rarer of the two species of crossbills that occur in Indiana. Both species have similar habits and are sometimes found together. They may also exhibit the same tameness when feeding. The white-winged, however, seems to show more of a preference for the seeds of hemlock cones than does the red crossbill in Indiana.

Butler mentioned that the red crossbill was the commoner of the two species, but that both were irregular visitors. Today, the white-winged crossbill is an irregular and generally rare migrant and winter visitor throughout the northern two-thirds of Indiana. In the southern part of the state it is very rare to casual in occurrence. There are no sightings for July and August. It occurs in smaller groups than does the red crossbill; a flock of twenty is the maximum number reported. It was reportedly present in the summer of 1869, and was reported June 26, 1884, at Michigan City and June 24, 1886, at Bloomington; we know of no additional June records. Recent sightings all fall within the period from September 14 to May 9.

Both crossbills utilize the same habitats, generally where there are cone-bearing trees, and readily come to bird feeders.

Most of the records of white-winged crossbills in Indiana are for November through March. There are few reports (only eleven) for the remaining seven months. Flocks of from fifteen to twenty have been reported in early October, late December, and early February.

The birds have been observed feeding on seeds of the cones of Douglas fir, hemlock, blue spruce, tamarack, Scotch pine, and jack pine. They have also been seen feeding either on fruits or buds of hackberry in early May. It is not unusual to see white-winged crossbills feeding on hemlock cones that have fallen to the ground.

COMMON REDPOLL
Carduelis flammea
Redpoll, Redpoll Linnet

During certain winters, in the snowbelt section of northwestern Indiana, common redpolls appear in large numbers. Where they can find tall weeds that retain their seeds and stand above the snow, the birds often congregate. David A. Easterla (1978) encountered such a place in LaPorte County on February 26, 1972, and found a flock of 4,000 redpolls. Michael R. Brown found a flock of similar size in LaPorte County on February 17, 1978. It is thought that these were the largest two flocks of common redpolls ever recorded in the United States. Other birders who visited the sites were also treated to this unusual spectacle. On cloudy, windy, overcast winter days, the feeding birds may be quite restless. They will feed for a time, then a few will take flight, causing other groups to fly, and soon there is a milling mass of birds overhead. After a short time they often return to the field and continue feeding, only to repeat the performance again and again.

The common redpoll was considered an irregular winter visitor by Butler, who mentioned that in some years it occurred in immense numbers in northern Indiana. It was rare in the southern part of the state. Today, this redpoll remains an irregular winter visitor to Indiana, being much more abundant and most regular in the northwesternmost counties bordering Lake Michigan. From 1940 to 1982, there are only five years for which we have no records. It is rare to uncommon locally in the northern one-third of Indiana, rare to very rare in central, and casual in the southern one-third. The largest numbers are usually reported on Christmas bird counts. There were 2,587 in southeastern LaPorte County on December 28, 1969, and 944 at South Bend on January 1, 1970.

Redpolls prefer open, overgrown fields where there are weeds that provide winter food. The large flock reported by Easterla was feeding in a twenty-acre field that had evidently been planted to corn the year before but had been allowed to lie fallow; herbaceous plants had formed a rather dense cover. The taller, dominant plants were rough pigweed and lamb's-quarters, upon which the redpolls mainly fed. The understory plants were mostly switch grass, foxtail, and smartweed. This field was an island of good cover surrounded by a deciduous woodlot, plowed fields, and soybean stubble, and harvested cornfields. Many of the birds in this field were also seen feeding on the ground on a cold, windy day in early March with light snow swirling about. Redpolls have also been found feeding in harvested soybean fields and about the edges of swamps and marshes where alder, birch, and other food plants were present. They are attracted to birch trees in residential areas, city parks, and the like, and also come to bird feeders.

Fall migrants have been recorded as early as October 26 and the latest spring date for stragglers is April 20. Herbert L. Stoddard observed many hundred migrating northwest along Lake Michigan on March 11, 1917. In general, the greatest numbers are usually present from mid-November to March.

Weed seeds of various species are consumed by this redpoll and constitute much of its winter food in Indiana. The birds also eat seeds of sycamore and alder and the catkins of birch. They are attracted to thistle feeders and also glean grass seeds from lawns on occasion.

HOARY REDPOLL
Carduelis hornemanni

From time to time, among the flocks of common redpolls that winter in Indiana, there will be a few of the paler hoary redpolls. The latter probably went largely undetected throughout earlier years, for there is a single record prior to 1953. Since then, the species has been reported (mostly sightings) a dozen times. Although there is some danger in accepting sight records of this rare redpoll, careful, close scrutiny under good lighting conditions may enable it to be identified.

Butler carried the hoary redpoll on his hypothetical list. The first state record was established on December 23, 1916, when Herbert L. Stoddard (1917) collected one of "four or five" seen feeding with common redpolls at Mineral Springs (Porter County). Current records indicate that the hoary redpoll is an irregular, casual winter visitor, primarily in the northwestern corner of the state. Nine of the dozen records are for the three counties bordering Lake Michigan; there are sightings from Allen, Marion, and St. Joseph Counties. Dates of occurrence range from December 23 to April 12, but by far the most birds were recorded in February.

David A. Easterla saw five (and collected four) hoaries in a mixed flock of about 3,000 common and hoary redpolls on February 20, 1972, in LaPorte County. He obtained another hoary specimen there the following week. There were five pale-colored birds thought to be hoary redpolls in a flock of 4,000 redpolls near Westville, February 18, 1978. Numerous other sightings are of single birds or smaller groups.

The habits and habitats of the hoary redpoll are similar to those of the common redpoll. Future careful field work may reveal more information about the status and distribution of the hoary in the state.

PINE SISKIN

Carduelis pinus

Pine Finch, Pine Linnet, Siskin

"November 17, 1882, I found them everywhere along the Whitewater River bottoms in countless numbers. Roadsides, fencerows, weedy banks and thickets, corn and stubble fields, all were alive with their fluttering wings, while the crackling of weed seeds and their peculiar note added voice to the scene. They were present in great numbers throughout the winter." Thus did Butler describe an abundance of pine siskins at a site near Brookville (Franklin County). We too have had the pleasure of experiencing a winter—1977–1978—when siskins for some reason were unusually plentiful.

Butler reported the pine siskin as a more or less regular winter migrant and rare winter resident. It sometimes was abundant and occasionally associated with American goldfinches in winter and with purple finches in spring. The pine siskin is currently an irregular migrant and winter resident throughout the state, but usually most numerous in the northern two-thirds. At a given locality, it may be absent or abundant from year to year. More than one hundred have been found on Christmas bird counts at Fort Wayne, Grant County, Indiana Dunes, Indianapolis, South Bend, and southeastern LaPorte County. There were 206 at the latter site on December 31, 1977, and 245 at South Bend on December 27, 1981.

Pine siskins are usually found in old fields where weed seeds are plentiful with American goldfinches and other seed-eating birds. They are also attracted to bird feeders, especially to thistle (niger) seed; in some winters it appears that most of the wintering population is sustained mainly by feeders.

During the autumn migration pine siskins begin to appear in Indiana the last week of September, the earliest date being the 24th. On October 9, 1919, Herbert L. Stoddard observed "many thousands" in Porter County and Ted T. Cable found a flock of 1,000 there on November 1, 1980. Birds linger into May, and even June, from time to time, and in the summer of 1978 some siskins remained and nested. There are a handful of sightings for June and July for the years 1966 to 1982, but in general most have departed by June 1. Smaller numbers are generally reported in the spring than in the fall.

During the winter of 1977–78, pine siskins appeared at bird feeders nearly everywhere. A hundred came to a feeder in Porter County and seventy to a feeder in Tippecanoe County. Many of these lingered through May, 1978. On all-day counts at sixteen localities throughout the state, 442 pine siskins were observed on May 13. Mr. and Mrs. John D. Goodman (1978) saw siskins carrying nesting material at Anderson (Madison County) on March 27. Eggs were later deposited in this nest, which was destroyed. This was the first nesting record of the pine siskin for Indiana. Reports were received of other siskin nests, five of which were found at West Lafayette (Weeks and Mumford, 1981). By the end of the breeding season there were nesting records for Lake, Madison, Marion, Tippecanoe, and Wayne Counties. In addition, birds were seen transporting nesting material or nests were partially built in Delaware, Monroe, and Porter Counties. We have no doubt that siskins nested in other places during that season.

The eight nests found were all in conifers (pines and spruces) in residential areas. One nest contained three eggs on April 27; another held 3 newly hatched young and one egg on May 12. Three nests each contained three young the first half of May.

Winter foods of the pine siskin (in addition to thistle seed) include seeds of sweet gum, white birch, jack pine, arborvitae, hemlock, box elder, tulip tree, "locust," wild sunflower, evening primrose, and aster. Siskins frequently eat dandelion seeds in spring.

Depicted tree: American larch, Tamarack (*Larix laricina*)

AMERICAN GOLDFINCH

Carduelis tristis

Wild Canary, Eastern Goldfinch, Lettuce Bird, Salad Bird, Yellow Bird, Thistle Bird, Goldfinch

In summer, the yellow and black male "wild canary" is a familiar bird to residents of Indiana, but many apparently do not recognize him in his more somber winter plumage, for people have told us they have American goldfinches around their homes in summer, but not in winter. Old fields bordered by shrubby fencerows or tall stands of giant ragweed may harbor large flocks of goldfinches during the fall and winter. Often they are with American tree sparrows, dark-eyed juncos, pine siskins, eastern bluebirds, redpolls, purple finches, or other seed-eating birds. And during midwinter it is not unusual to find goldfinches, purple finches, pine siskins, and Carolina chickadees feeding together on the seed balls of sweet gum trees. But it is the noisy singing of late spring flocks of American goldfinches that catch the ear (and eye) of

the casual observer, for then the males are in their bright breeding plumage and their canarylike courtship songs become part of the sounds of spring.

Butler knew the American goldfinch as a permanent resident that was rare in some winters in northern Indiana. We assume that the species was then common to abundant, although he made no statement concerning its numerical status. Because a greater proportion of Indiana was forest then, it is possible that the goldfinch is more plentiful now than it was around 1900. It remains an abundant migrant and summer resident throughout the state, and is common in most sections of Indiana during the winter, although numbers vary considerably from year to year. Three hundred or more have been recorded on Christmas bird counts in nine widely scattered localities, from Lake Monroe northward to the Michigan border. Maximum numbers were present at Indiana Dunes (329), Lake Monroe (630), and South Bend (598) in December 1976. This was the first of three extremely severe winters in succession. There were 800 goldfinches at Eagle Creek Reservoir (Marion County) on January 25, 1970, according to Alfred Starling, and 893 were seen on the Lake Monroe Christmas bird count on December 21, 1980. The largest numbers are normally recorded during the winter censuses. The quantity of year-round residents makes it rather difficult to determine migration dates. Flocks containing as many as 250 goldfinches may be seen during spring and fall migration and in winter.

The American goldfinch inhabits fields, open areas near marshes and lakes, the shrubby borders of woodlands, and overgrown fencerows. Migrants and wintering birds readily come into towns to visit bird feeders and many nest in residential areas in trees on lawns.

Although there is much singing and courtship during the spring, goldfinches appear to be in no hurry to nest, delaying their nest constuction until at least June, and usually later. An early date for eggs in the nest is June 4. The nesting season is quite long; eggs have been found as late as mid-September. Nests are usually in rather open areas, often overgrown fields or their borders. Nest height ranges from about four to seventy feet, but most nests are placed from four to twelve feet above the ground. Seventeen of twenty-eight nests found near Bloomington one season were in sassafras trees in old fields. Nests are placed in various species of trees, sprouts, bushes, or even tall weeds. The average number of eggs in thirty nests was five; clutch size varied from three to six, but nineteen nests each contained five eggs. The number of young in ten other nests ranged from three to six and averaged 4.3. Young unable to fly well were found out of the nest on October 2.

Young goldfinches are fed insects; adults eat seeds of milkweed, thistle, ragweed, sunflower, marigolds, trumpet creeper, dandelion, evening primrose, sweet gum, and sycamore. The birds also eat elm buds, the fruits of privet, the crushed fruits of osage orange, and beet leaves. Goldfinches have been seen feeding at maple blossoms and one bird was eating webworms. As many as a hundred may be present at a thistle feeder at one time.

Depicted plants: Field thistle (*Circium discolor*); Red-osier dogwood (*Cornus stolonifera*)

EVENING GROSBEAK
Coccothraustes vespertinus

It was one of those periodic winters when this large, showy finch invaded Indiana. Several box elder trees in a residential area had produced a large seed crop; their branches hung heavy with the winged seeds. Each day at about the same time a small flock of evening grosbeaks visited the trees, fed quietly for a while, then departed. Birders hearing of these visits began coming to watch the grosbeaks maneuver about in the trees, snipping off the samaras and then separating the seeds from the winged portions, which were allowed to flutter to the ground. When the flock had eaten all the box elder seeds, it moved on.

This grosbeak was a very irregular winter visitor to Indiana around 1900, but "every few years" it occurred in the state, sometimes in numbers. The status today remains that of an irregular winter visitor throughout the state. Some years it is totally absent; other years it may be locally abundant. In general, it is most common in northern (especially extreme northwestern) Indiana, being present in smaller numbers southward. But in some invasion years the birds reach the Ohio River valley in considerable numbers. The winters of 1961–62 and 1977–78 were noted for the numbers of evening grosbeaks. There were 451 seen on the Christmas bird count at Michigan City, December 30, 1961. On December 17, 1977, 379 were seen on the Indiana Dunes count and 125 in the Oakland City area.

The evening grosbeak may appear in almost any habitat supporting tree growth where food is available. It has also been found in overgrown fencerows bordering old fields, but woodlands are its favored habitats. Hundreds come to bird feeders in both urban and rural residential areas, often in mid-city locations. The winter flocks move about wherever food is present, locating a good food source, depleting it, and moving on. They may linger for weeks at a well-supplied bird feeder, consuming sunflower seed in such quantities that the proprietor of the feeder, initially thrilled, may begin to fear for his birdseed budget.

Our earliest record of fall migration is of three birds seen in Marion County on September 24, 1972. This is quite early: most arrivals appear in October. Birds then remain throughout the winter and in some years many linger into late May. Delano Z. Arvin reported eight in Tippecanoe County as late as May 24 (our latest departure date). One hundred were present at Lake Monroe in mid-May and birds were still present in Orange County on May 19. As many as 104 came to a feeder in Starke County during the winter of 1961–62.

Although evening grosbeaks show a decided preference for sunflower seeds at bird feeders, one of their favorite winter foods is box elder seeds. They also eat the seeds of poison sumac, fragrant sumac, staghorn sumac, and ash and the fruits of flowering dogwood, mountain ash, pyracantha, bittersweet, and hawthorn. They sometimes extract and eat the seeds of crabapples, and they have also been seen eating pin oak acorns and oak buds.

HOUSE SPARROW

Passer domesticus

English Sparrow, European House Sparrow

This introduced species is a streetwise little ruffian, so adaptable that it will probably always be with us. The house sparrow's first appearance in Indiana was in 1867 at New Albany. Several hundred were reportedly brought to Indianapolis in 1871 and 1872; others were released at Evansville in 1873 and at Lafayette in 1874. The following is from the *Lafayette Daily Journal* for April 27, 1874:

The English sparrows ordered by Colonel Behm and other of our citizens arrived in good order on Wednesday afternoon. Those of Colonel Behm were put into the bird-cottage which had been prepared for them on Wednesday night, so that the darkness would deter them from immediately flying off again. The plan succeeded, as the birds at once cuddled down and went to sleep. A plentiful supply of food was sprinkled around

their house to await their awakening. It is to be trusted they may be permitted to increase and multiply until our city shall swarm with their lively and useful progeny.

Such was the enthusiasm for the establishment of this foreigner in the state. We can now attest all too well to its phenomenal success.

By 1897, the house sparrow was a permanent resident "found in suitable localities in every part of the state," a status that it still maintains. There are no population figures for the state as a whole, so we do not know how present-day numbers compare with those of around 1900, but it is abundant statewide. The largest number reported on a Christmas bird count, at Lafayette on December 31, 1956, was 5,100. More than 3,000 per count have been reported at seven localities and more than 1,000 at twenty-one other sites.

There is hardly a habitat that this resourceful bird does not utilize. House sparrows thrive in both the country and the city, and in both places they are usually most abundant near manmade structures. Flocks of them are often seen along roadsides.

Surprisingly few Indiana data on nesting are available. Evidently because the species is thought of mainly as a nuisance and pest, people take little interest in it. Therefore, although many nests are destroyed by humans each year, dates of egg laying, clutch size, and the like have seldom been recorded. Practically all our nesting data were collected by Harmon P. Weeks, Jr., near Lafayette.

The house sparrow may well nest throughout the year. Certainly its nesting season is quite long. Birds have been seen adding nesting material to a nest in November and there are unverified reports of nesting in midwinter. Full clutches of eggs have been observed as early as February 20. Nests contain from three to nine eggs. Thirty-four nests studied by Weeks were all in nesting boxes. Clutch sizes ranged from three to six, but sixteen nests contained five eggs each and nine held six eggs each. Eggs were present in nests from April 18 to August 8. House sparrow nests have been found in just about every place imaginable—eaves, street lights, transformer boxes on telephone poles, ivy on buildings, bird nesting boxes, other birds' nests, bridges, water towers—even trees. Writer Henry Mitchell has said they "will nest everywhere except in the exhaust of a jet."

The food of the house sparrow is quite varied, which is no doubt one of the reasons for its success. It eats a variety of grain, such as corn, oats, wheat, barley, and rye, and the leaves or sprouts of lettuce, cabbage, peas, radishes, and beets. Butler noted that it ate apple blossoms and wrote about its destructiveness to grapes, apples, strawberries, cherries, and pears. It consumes dandelion seeds and has learned to extract thistle seed from feeders. Bread scraps and other discarded human food items are readily eaten. In some places, it eats many insects, including insect larvae, flying moths, and periodical cicadas. We have seen this sparrow, roosting on lighted porches of supermarkets, actively feeding throughout the night on flying moths attracted to the lights. Some authors have speculated that one reason why the house sparrow population may have decreased in certain eastern states is because the automobile has replaced the horse. The birds originally depended to a large extent on the food they gleaned from horse droppings, even in the cities.

Attempts have been made locally to decrease house sparrow numbers, with little success in the long run. Tearing down their nests, shooting them, gassing them at night as they roost, and placing a bounty on them have all been tried. The Tippecanoe County Fish, Game and Bird Protection Association placed a two-cent bounty on house sparrows in 1921. The success of a large nesting colony of cliff sparrows in Elkhart County has been made possible by eliminating house sparrows that tried to take over the nests. Such measures may be necessary locally to protect more desirable birds about one's premises.

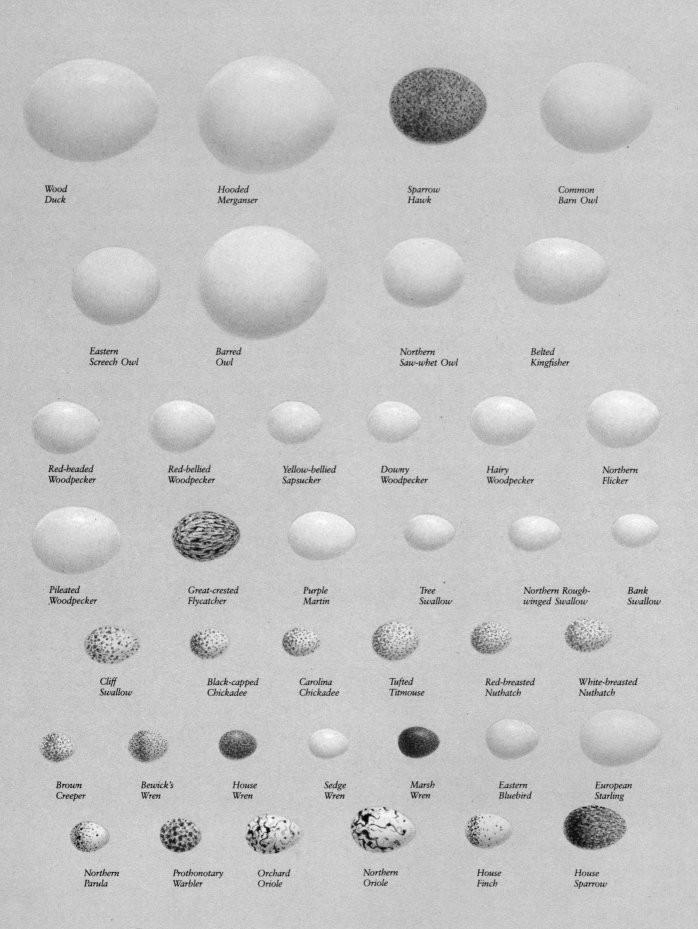

Wood
Duck

Hooded
Merganser

Sparrow
Hawk

Common
Barn Owl

Eastern
Screech Owl

Barred
Owl

Northern
Saw-whet Owl

Belted
Kingfisher

Red-headed
Woodpecker

Red-bellied
Woodpecker

Yellow-bellied
Sapsucker

Downy
Woodpecker

Hairy
Woodpecker

Northern
Flicker

Pileated
Woodpecker

Great-crested
Flycatcher

Purple
Martin

Tree
Swallow

Northern Rough-
winged Swallow

Bank
Swallow

Cliff
Swallow

Black-capped
Chickadee

Carolina
Chickadee

Tufted
Titmouse

Red-breasted
Nuthatch

White-breasted
Nuthatch

Brown
Creeper

Bewick's
Wren

House
Wren

Sedge
Wren

Marsh
Wren

Eastern
Bluebird

European
Starling

Northern
Parula

Prothonotary
Warbler

Orchard
Oriole

Northern
Oriole

House
Finch

House
Sparrow

OCCURRENCE CHART

This chart is intended as a handy reference, a graphic summary of information given in greater detail and broken down by region in the species accounts. It shows when each species is likely to be at its height of abundance in the state. A thin line extending from the first quarter of January through the last quarter of December denotes that the species is usually present throughout the year. Periods of peak abundance are marked by darker lines. (In a few cases, peaks are unmarked because of insufficient data.) When a species has been sighted in the state only a few times, dots are placed to show in which quarter of the month a sighting occurred. Extirpated and extinct species are marked by asterisks (*) and daggers (†), respectively. The names of uncorroborated species are in brackets, as in the main text.

The reader should bear in mind that the chart has been adjusted to apply to the state as a whole. Thus, seasonal abundance is shown for species that occur in only some parts of the state (the Black-Capped Chickadee and the Carolina Chickadee are examples). Likewise, because departure and arrival dates for migrating species may vary from region to region, the extreme dates of migration given in the text are not represented in the chart. For precise information about dates, localities, and relative (as well as seasonal) abundance, the species accounts should be consulted.

SPECIES	J F M A M J J A S O N D
Red-throated Loon	
Arctic Loon	
Common Loon	
Pied-billed Grebe	
Horned Grebe	
Red-necked Grebe	
Eared Grebe	
Western Grebe	
Band-rumped Storm-Petrel	
Northern Gannet	
American White Pelican	
Brown Pelican	
Double-crested Cormorant	
Anhinga	
Magnificent Frigatebird	
American Bittern	
Least Bittern	
Great Blue Heron	

SPECIES	J F M A M J J A S O N D
Great Egret	
Snowy Egret	
Little Blue Heron	
Tricolored Heron	
Cattle Egret	
Green-backed Heron	
Black-crowned Night-Heron	
Yellow-crowned Night-Heron	
White Ibis	
Glossy Ibis	
[White-faced Ibis]	
Roseate Spoonbill	
Wood Stork	
[Fulvous Whistling-Duck]	
Tundra Swan	
Trumpeter Swan*	
Mute Swan	
Greater White-fronted Goose	

SPECIES	J F M A M J J A S O N D
Snow Goose	
[Ross' Goose]	
Brant	
Canada Goose	
Wood Duck	
Green-winged Teal	
American Black Duck	
Mallard	
Northern Pintail	
Blue-winged Teal	
Cinnamon Teal	
Northern Shoveler	
Gadwall	
Eurasian Wigeon	
American Wigeon	
Canvasback	
Redhead	
Ring-necked Duck	
[Tufted Duck]	
Greater Scaup	
Lesser Scaup	
[Common Eider]	
King Eider	
Harlequin Duck	
Oldsquaw	
Black Scoter	
Surf Scoter	
White-winged Scoter	
Common Goldeneye	

SPECIES	J F M A M J J A S O N D
Barrow's Goldeneye	
Bufflehead	
Hooded Merganser	
Common Merganser	
Red-breasted Merganser	
Ruddy Duck	
Black Vulture	
Turkey Vulture	
Osprey	
American Swallow-tailed Kite	
Black-shouldered Kite	
Mississippi Kite	
Bald Eagle	
Northern Harrier	
Sharp-shinned Hawk	
Cooper's Hawk	
Northern Goshawk	
Red-shouldered Hawk	
Broad-winged Hawk	
[Swainson's Hawk]	
Red-tailed Hawk	
Ferruginous Hawk	
Rough-legged Hawk	
Golden Eagle	
American Kestrel	
Merlin	
Peregrine Falcon	
Prairie Falcon	
Gray Partridge	

SPECIES	J F M A M J J A S O N D
Ring-necked Pheasant	
Ruffed Grouse	
Greater Prairie-Chicken*	
[Sharp-tailed Grouse]	
Wild Turkey	
Northern Bobwhite	
Yellow Rail	
Black Rail	
King Rail	
Virginia Rail	
Sora	
Purple Gallinule	
Common Moorhen	
American Coot	
Sandhill Crane	
Whooping Crane*	
Black-bellied Plover	
Lesser Golden-Plover	
[Snowy Plover]	
Semipalmated Plover	
Piping Plover	
Killdeer	
[Black-necked Stilt]	
American Avocet	
Greater Yellowlegs	
Lesser Yellowlegs	
Solitary Sandpiper	
Willet	
Spotted Sandpiper	

SPECIES	J F M A M J J A S O N D
Upland Sandpiper	
Eskimo Curlew*	
Whimbrel	
Long-billed Curlew	
Hudsonian Godwit	
Marbled Godwit	
Ruddy Turnstone	
Red Knot	
Sanderling	
Semipalmated Sandpiper	
Western Sandpiper	
Least Sandpiper	
White-rumped Sandpiper	
Baird's Sandpiper	
Pectoral Sandpiper	
Purple Sandpiper	
Dunlin	
Curlew Sandpiper	
Stilt Sandpiper	
Buff-breasted Sandpiper	
Ruff	
Short-billed Dowitcher	
Long-billed Dowitcher	
Common Snipe	
American Woodcock	
Wilson's Phalarope	
Red-necked Phalarope	
Red Phalarope	
[Pomarine Jaeger]	

SPECIES	J F M A M J J A S O N D
Parasitic Jaeger	bar Aug–Sep
Long-tailed Jaeger	• Jul • Aug •• Sep • Nov
Laughing Gull	bar May–Aug
Franklin's Gull	bar Apr–May; bar Oct–Nov
Little Gull	bar Jan–Feb; bar Oct–Nov
[Common Black-headed Gull]	• Jun •• Jul
Bonaparte's Gull	bar Mar–Apr; bar Sep–Nov
Ring-billed Gull	bar Feb–Jun; bar Aug–Nov
California Gull	• Jun • Oct
Herring Gull	bar Jan–May; bar Aug–Dec
Thayer's Gull	bar Jan–Mar; bar Oct–Dec
Iceland Gull	bar Jan–Apr; bar Oct–Dec
Lesser Black-backed Gull	• Jan • Mar • Aug • Dec
Glaucous Gull	bar Jan–Apr; bar Oct–Dec
Great Black-backed Gull	bar Feb–Mar; • Aug; bar Oct–Nov
Black-legged Kittiwake	bar Oct–Nov
[Ross' Gull]	• Mar
Sabine's Gull	bar Sep–Oct
Caspian Tern	bar Apr–May; bar Jul–Sep
[Royal Tern]	• Apr
Roseate Tern	• Jul
Common Tern	bar Apr–May; bar Jul–Sep
[Arctic Tern]	• Apr
Forster's Tern	bar Apr–May; bar Aug–Oct
Least Tern	bar Jun–Aug
[White-winged Tern]	• Jul
Black Tern	bar Apr–May; bar Jul–Aug
[Black Skimmer]	• Aug
Thick billed Murre	• Feb; bar Dec

SPECIES	J F M A M J J A S O N D
Marbled Murrelet	• Nov
[Kittlitz's Murrelet]	• Jan
Ancient Murrelet	• Nov
Rock Dove	bar Jan–Dec
Band-tailed Pigeon	bar Jan
Ringed Turtle-Dove	bar Jan–Dec
Mourning Dove	bar Jan–Dec
Passenger Pigeon†	(none)
Common Ground-Dove	• Sep •• Nov–Dec
Monk Parakeet	bar Jan–Dec
Carolina Parakeet†	(none)
Black-billed Cuckoo	bar Apr–May; bar Jul–Aug
Yellow-billed Cuckoo	bar Apr–May; bar Jul–Aug
[Smooth-billed Ani]	• Oct
Groove-billed Ani	• Oct • Nov
Common Barn-Owl	bar Jan–Dec
Eastern Screech-Owl	bar Jan–Dec
Great Horned Owl	bar Jan–Dec
Snowy Owl	bar Jan–Mar; bar Nov–Dec
[Northern Hawk-Owl]	• Jan
Burrowing Owl	•• Mar; bar Jun–Aug
Barred Owl	bar Jan–Dec
Great Gray Owl	(none)
Long-eared Owl	bar Jan–Dec
Short-eared Owl	bar Jan–Mar; bar Oct–Dec
Northern Saw-whet Owl	bar Jan–Apr; bar Oct–Dec
Common Nighthawk	bar Apr–May; bar Aug–Sep
Chuck-will's-widow	bar Apr–Jun
Whip-poor-will	bar Apr–Aug

SPECIES	J F M A M J J A S O N D
Chimney Swift	
Ruby-throated Hummingbird	
Belted Kingfisher	
Red-headed Woodpecker	
Red-bellied Woodpecker	
Yellow-bellied Sapsucker	
Downy Woodpecker	
Hairy Woodpecker	
Black-backed Woodpecker	
Northern Flicker	
Pileated Woodpecker	
Ivory-billed Woodpecker†	
Olive-sided Flycatcher	
Eastern Wood-Pewee	
Yellow-bellied Flycatcher	
Acadian Flycatcher	
Alder Flycatcher	
Willow Flycatcher	
Least Flycatcher	
Eastern Phoebe	
[Say's Phoebe]	
Great Crested Flycatcher	
Western Kingbird	
Eastern Kingbird	
Scissor-tailed Flycatcher	
Horned Lark	
Purple Martin	
Tree Swallow	
Northern Rough-winged Swallow	

SPECIES	J F M A M J J A S O N D
Bank Swallow	
Cliff Swallow	
Barn Swallow	
Blue Jay	
Black-billed Magpie	
American Crow	
Common Raven*	
Black-capped Chickadee	
Carolina Chickadee	
Boreal Chickadee	
Tufted Titmouse	
Red-breasted Nuthatch	
White-breasted Nuthatch	
[Brown-headed Nuthatch]	
Brown Creeper	
Rock Wren	
Carolina Wren	
Bewick's Wren	
House Wren	
Winter Wren	
Sedge Wren	
Marsh Wren	
Golden-crowned Kinglet	
Ruby-crowned Kinglet	
Blue-gray Gnatcatcher	
Eastern Bluebird	
Veery	
Gray-cheeked Thrush	
Swainson's Thrush	

SPECIES	J F M A M J J A S O N D
Hermit Thrush	
Wood Thrush	
American Robin	
Varied Thrush	
Gray Catbird	
Northern Mockingbird	
Brown Thrasher	
Water Pipit	
[Sprague's Pipit]	
Bohemian Waxwing	
Cedar Waxwing	
Northern Shrike	
Loggerhead Shrike	
European Starling	
White-eyed Vireo	
Bell's Vireo	
Solitary Vireo	
Yellow-throated Vireo	
Warbling Vireo	
Philadelphia Vireo	
Red-eyed Vireo	
Bachman's Warbler	
Blue-winged Warbler	
Golden-winged Warbler	
Tennessee Warbler	
Orange-crowned Warbler	
Nashville Warbler	
Northern Parula	
Yellow Warbler	

SPECIES	J F M A M J J A S O N D
Chestnut-sided Warbler	
Magnolia Warbler	
Cape May Warbler	
Black-throated Blue Warbler	
Yellow-rumped Warbler	
[Black-throated Gray Warbler]	
[Townsend's Warbler]	
Black-throated Green Warbler	
Blackburnian Warbler	
Yellow-throated Warbler	
Pine Warbler	
Kirtland's Warbler	
Prairie Warbler	
Palm Warbler	
Bay-breasted Warbler	
Blackpoll Warbler	
Cerulean Warbler	
Black-and-white Warbler	
American Redstart	
Prothonotary Warbler	
Worm-eating Warbler	
[Swainson's Warbler]	
Ovenbird	
Northern Waterthrush	
Louisiana Waterthrush	
Kentucky Warbler	
Connecticut Warbler	
Mourning Warbler	
[MacGillivray's Warbler]	

SPECIES	J F M A M J J A S O N D
Common Yellowthroat	
Hooded Warbler	
Wilson's Warbler	
Canada Warbler	
Yellow-breasted Chat	
Summer Tanager	
Scarlet Tanager	
[Western Tanager]	
Northern Cardinal	
Rose-breasted Grosbeak	
[Black-headed Grosbeak]	
Blue Grosbeak	
[Lazuli Bunting]	
Indigo Bunting	
Painted Bunting	
Dickcissel	
[Green-tailed Towhee]	
Rufous-sided Towhee	
Bachman's Sparrow	
American Tree Sparrow	
Chipping Sparrow	
Clay-colored Sparrow	
Field Sparrow	
Vesper Sparrow	
Lark Sparrow	
Lark Bunting	
Savannah Sparrow	
Grasshopper Sparrow	
Henslow's Sparrow	

SPECIES	J F M A M J J A S O N D
Le Conte's Sparrow	
Sharp-tailed Sparrow	
Fox Sparrow	
Song Sparrow	
Lincoln's Sparrow	
Swamp Sparrow	
White-throated Sparrow	
[Golden-crowned Sparrow]	
White-crowned Sparrow	
Harris' Sparrow	
Dark-eyed Junco	
[McCown's Longspur]	
Lapland Longspur	
Smith's Longspur	
Snow Bunting	
Bobolink	
Red-winged Blackbird	
Eastern Meadowlark	
Western Meadowlark	
Yellow-headed Blackbird	
Rusty Blackbird	
Brewer's Blackbird	
Common Grackle	
Brown-headed Cowbird	
Orchard Oriole	
Northern Oriole	
Pine Grosbeak	
Purple Finch	
House Finch	

SPECIES	J F M A M J J A S O N D
Red Crossbill	
White-winged Crossbill	
Common Redpoll	
Hoary Redpoll	

SPECIES	J F M A M J J A S O N D
Pine Siskin	
American Goldfinch	
Evening Grosbeak	
House Sparrow	

Arvin, Delano Z. 1981a. *Xanthocephalus* (the yellow-headed blackbird) returns to Indiana. Ind. Aud. Quart., 59:56–58.

———. 1981b. A first for Indiana: a chuck-will's-widow nest. Ind. Aud. Quart., 59:86–91.

Audubon, John J. 1840–1844. The birds of America. Dover reprint edition. 1967. 7 volumes.

Baczkowski, Frank. 1955. Whooping cranes in Porter County 50 years ago. Ind. Aud. Quart., 33:43–44.

Baker, Mrs. H. A. 1955. 24. Two hay fields and grazed creek pasture. *In* Nineteenth breeding-bird census. Aud. Field Notes, 9:423–424.

Ball, Timothy H. 1900. Northwestern Indiana from 1800 to 1900. Donahue & Henneberry, Chicago. 570 pp.

Banks, Richard C. 1977. The decline and fall of the Eskimo curlew, or why did the curlew go extaille? American Birds, 31:127–134.

Barce, Elmore, and Robert A. Swan. 1930. History of Benton County, Indiana. Fowler, Ind.: Benton Review Shop. 242 pp.

Barnes, William B. 1941. Statewide wildlife survey, game management, and demonstration project. Quarterly Progress Rep. Wildl. Res., Federal Aid to Wildlife Restoration Act, 2:49–72.

———. 1947. The distribution of Indiana's bobwhite quail. Outdoor Indiana, October 1947, 3 pp.

Bartel, Karl E. 1948. Scissor-tailed flycatcher in the Chicago area. Auk, 65:614.

Bellrose, Frank C. 1976. Ducks, geese and swans of North America. Stackpole Books. 544 pp.

Bent, Arthur C. 1926. Life histories of North American marsh birds. U.S. National Museum Bulletin no. 135. 392 pp.

———. 1927. Life histories of North American shorebirds, part 1. U.S. National Museum Bulletin no. 142. 420 pp.

———. 1929. Life histories of North American shorebirds, part 2. U.S. National Museum Bulletin no. 146. 412 pp.

———. 1937. Life histories of North American birds of prey, part 1. U.S. National Museum Bulletin no. 167. 409 pp.

———. 1953. Life histories of North American wood warblers. U.S. National Museum Bulletin no. 203. 734 pp.

Birch, Jesse S. 1928. History of Benton County and historic Oxford. Oxford: Crow & Crow, Inc. 386 pp.

Brayton, Alembert W. 1880. A catalogue of the birds of Indiana with keys and descriptions of the groups of greatest interest to the horticulturist. Trans. Ind. Horticulture Soc. 1879. pp. 89–166.

Brennan, George A. 1918. Sharp-tailed grouse at Tremont, Indiana. Auk, 35:75–76.

———. 1923. The wonders of the dunes. Indianapolis: Bobbs-Merrill Co., 326 pp.

Brewster, William. 1878. The prothonotary warbler (*Protonotaria citrea*). Bulletin Nuttall Ornithological Club, 3:153–162.

Brock, Kenneth J. 1979a. Birdlife of the Michigan City area, Indiana. Ind. Aud. Quart., 57:94–113.

———. 1979b. The lark bunting; a summer Indiana record. Ind. Aud. Quart., 57:186.

———. 1980. Indiana's first record of the curlew sandpiper. Ind. Aud. Quart., 58:120–122.

———. 1982. The Roxana Street white-winged black tern: July 1979—an Indiana first. Ind. Aud. Quart., 60:5–6.

———. 1983. Indiana's first white-winged black tern: an inland sight record. American Birds, 37:109–111.

Brock, Kenneth J., Peter B. Grube, and Edward M. Hopkins. 1978. The black-headed gull: an Indiana record. Ind. Aud. Quart., 56:1–2.

Brock, Kenneth J., and Ted T. Cable. 1981. A first band-tailed pigeon record for Indiana. Ind. Aud. Quart., 59:116–120.

Brock, Kenneth J., Ted T. Cable, and Russell E. Mumford. 1979. Indiana: first tufted duck. Ind. Aud. Quart., 57:234–236.

Brodkorb, Pierce. 1926a. The season. Chicago region. Bird-Lore, 28:214–215.

———. 1926b. The season. Chicago region. Bird-Lore, 28:347–348.

Brooks, Earl. 1925. MacGillivray's warbler in Indiana. Auk, 42:277.

———. 1963. Socialistic Carolina wrens. Ind. Aud. Quart., 41:78–79.

Burr, Irving W. 1966. Northern region—winter, 1964–1965. Ind. Aud. Quart., 44:43–44.

Buskirk, William H. 1962. Sparrow hawk feeds on earthworms. Ind. Aud. Quart., 40:46.

———. 1964. A study of a winter population of white-crowned sparrows. Ind. Aud. Quart., 42:66–71.

Butler, Amos W. 1897. Some additions to the Indiana bird list, with other notes. Proc. Ind. Acad. Sci., 6:244–246.

———. 1898a. The birds of Indiana. 22nd Annual Report, Ind. Dept. Geology and Natural Resources. pp. 575–1187.

———. 1898b. Notes on Indiana heronries. Proc. Ind. Acad. Sci., 7:198–201.

———. 1900. Notes on Indiana birds. Proc. Ind. Acad. Sci., 9:149–151.

———. 1906. Some notes on Indiana birds. Auk, 23:274.

———. 1909. An addition to the birds of Indiana. Proc. Ind. Acad. Sci., 18:49.

———. 1913. Further notes on Indiana birds. Proc. Ind. Acad. Sci., 22:59–65.

———. 1917. Further notes on Indiana birds. Proc. Ind. Acad. Sci., 26:457–458.

———. 1928. Some interesting Indiana bird records. Proc. Ind. Acad. Sci., 37:481–489.

———. 1935. Black vultures in Indiana. Auk, 52:303–304.

———. 1936. The prairie falcon (*Falco mexicanus*) in Indiana. Auk, 53:77.

———. 1937. Common tern and Wilson's phalarope nesting in northern Indiana. Auk, 54:390.

Cable, Ted. T. 1980. A study of a rail population in northern

Indiana. Master's thesis, Purdue Univ., December 1980. 59 pp.

———. 1981. Nest of redhead duck in Newton Co.: First state nesting record. Ind. Aud. Quart., 59:4–5.

Carmony, Duane, and Robert M. Brattain. 1971. McCown's longspur on the Lafayette Christmas count. Ind. Aud. Quart., 49–29.

Carpenter, Floyd S. 1964. Important observations from the Ohio River region. Ind. Aud. Quart., 42:61.

Carter, Larry. 1978. Rock wren in Indiana: a new state bird. Ind. Aud. Quart., 56:50–51.

Carter, Lowell E. 1928. Ten summers with loggerhead shrikes. Bird-Lore, 30:119–120.

Casebere, Lee A. 1978. Nesting records for the veery in Lagrange County. Ind. Aud. Quart., 56:158–161.

———. 1979. Nesting record for the Canada warbler in Lagrange County. Ind. Aud. Quart., 57:113–117.

Chansler, E. J. 1910. Magpie in Knox County, Indiana. Auk, 27:210.

———. 1912. Mississippi and swallow-tailed kites in Knox Co., Ind. Auk, 29:239.

Coffin, Lucy V. Baxter. 1906. A tragedy. Bird-Lore, 8:68.

Cope, James B. 1949. Rough-legged hawk feeds on shrews. J. Mammal., 30:432.

———. 1951. Pacific loon in Indiana. Wilson Bulletin, 63:41.

Cox, Alta R. 1937. Black rail breeding in Indiana. Auk, 54:100–101.

Craigmile, Esther A. 1935. Three rare records. Audubon Annual Bulletin, Nos. 24 and 25:45–46.

Crankshaw, William B., J. A. Smith and Ralph D. Kirkpatrick. 1969. Woodcock singing ground descriptions for two Indiana sites. Proc. Ind. Acad. Sci., 78:241–244.

Deam, Charles C. 1940. The flora of Indiana. Ind. Dept. Cons., Div. Forestry. 1236 pp.

Deane, Ruthven. 1905. The ruff (*Pavoncella pugnax*) in Indiana. Auk, 22:410–411.

———. 1923. The tree swallow (*I.b.*) affected by sudden cold. Auk, 40:332.

DuMont, P. A. and E. K. Smith. 1946. Middle-western region. Aud. Mag. Suppl., 48:7–8.

Easterla, David A. 1978. Mixed flocks of common and hoary redpolls in northern Indiana. Ind. Aud. Quart., 56:51–53.

Eifrig, C. W. G. 1919. Notes on birds of the Chicago area and its immediate vicinity. Auk, 36:513–524.

———. 1927. Notes from the Chicago area. Auk, 44:431–432.

Esten, Sidney R. 1931. Birds of Greene and Noble Counties (from William Van Gorder notes). Proc. Ind. Acad. Sci., 40:323–333.

———. 1933. Check list corrections and additions. Ind. Aud. Soc. Yearbook 1933:15.

Evermann, Barton W. 1889. Birds of Carroll County, Indiana. Auk, 6:22–30.

———. 1917. A century of zoology in Indiana. Proc. Ind. Acad. Sci., 26:214–217.

———. 1921. Notes on the birds of Carroll, Monroe, and Vigo counties, Indiana. Proc. Ind. Acad. Sci., 30:315–401.

Evermann, Barton W., and Howard W. Clark. 1920. Lake Maxinkuckee. A physical and biological survey. Vol. 1. Ind. Dept. Conservation. 660 pp.

Fleetwood, Raymond J. 1934. Western Henslow's sparrow wintering in Indiana. Auk, 51:388.

Forbush, Edward H. 1916. A history of the game birds, wildfowl and shore birds of Massachusetts and adjacent states. Mass. State Bd. Agriculture. 636 pp.

Ford, Edward R. 1956. Birds of the Chicago region. Special Publ. No. 12. Chicago Acad. Sci. 117 pp.

Frazier, Mrs. Anita. 1971. Bluebirds in communal roosts. Ind. Aud. Quart., 49:29–30.

Ginn, William E. 1947. Band returns from Indiana club-reared pheasants. J. Wildl. Mgmt., 11:226–231.

———. 1954. American egret nesting in Indiana. Ind. Aud. Quart., 32:2.

Goodman, John D., and Jeanne M. Goodman. 1978. Pine siskins nest in Indiana, 1978. Ind. Aud. Quart., 56:179–180.

Gordon, Robert B. 1931. Records of the white ibis in southern Indiana. Wilson Bulletin, 43:309.

———. 1936. A preliminary vegetation map of Indiana. Amer. Midl. Nat., 17:866–877.

Grow, Raymond. 1952. Rare and semi-rare winter visitants in northern Indiana. Ind. Aud. Quart., 30:31–34.

———. 1978. Kleptoparasitic action by Bonaparte's gulls on yellowlegs. Ind. Aud. Quart., 56:178–179.

———. 1982. Analysis of an Indiana burrowing owl pellet. Ind. Aud. Quart., 60:13–14.

Hadley, Joel W. 1947. An unusual bird visitor. Ind. Aud. Soc. Yearbook 1947:37.

Harris, A. Trevenning. 1936. Nests found in 1934. The Oologist, 53:68–9.

Haymond, Rufus. 1870. Birds of Franklin County, Indiana. 1st Annual Rept. Geol. Survey. pp. 209–235.

Hine, Ashley. 1924. Burrowing owl in northern Indiana. Auk, 41:602.

Hine, Jane L. 1911. Game and land birds of an Indiana farm. Biennial Rep. Ind. Commissioner Fisheries and Game. pp. 295–470.

Hobson, Dorothy M. 1950. Night singing of the short-billed marsh wren. Ind. Aud. Quart., 28:58–59.

Hohn, E. O. 1969. The phalarope. Scientific American, 220:104–111.

Hosford, Hallock J. 1955. Nesting and migration of the mourning dove in northern Indiana. Ind. Aud. Quart., 33:3–10.

Howell, David and Ed Theroff. 1976. Scissor-tailed flycatcher breeding in southwestern Indiana. Auk, 93:644–645.

Hull, Edwin D. 1913. The predicament of a pied-billed grebe. Bird-Lore, 15:180.

Hush, Anthony. 1934. Nesting Wilson snipe. Bird-Lore, 36:237–238.

Johnson, George. 1965. Ruffed grouse hunting season survey—1965. Ind. Pittman-Robertson Wildl. Res. Rept., 26:40–56.

———. 1966. Ruffed grouse hunting season survey—1966. Ind. Pittmann-Robertson Wildl. Res. Rept., 27:44–50.

Keller, Charles E. 1958. The shorebird families: Charadriidae, Scolopacidae, Recurvirostridae, and Phalaropidae of Indiana. Part 4. Ind. Aud. Quart., 36:2–39.

———. 1962. Behavior of the buff-breasted sandpiper in Indiana. Ind. Aud. Quart., 40:50–52.

———. 1966. Status of the ciconiiformes in Indiana. Ind. Aud. Quart., 44:56–86.

Keller, Charles E., Shirley A. Keller, and Timothy C. Keller. 1979. Indiana birds and their haunts. A checklist and finding guide. Bloomington: Ind. Univ. Press. 214 pp.

Keller, Timothy C. 1983. First Indiana record of the California gull (*Larus californicus*). American Birds, 37:120.

Kirkpatrick, Ralph D., M. R. Roy, G. A. Wise, and L. L. Hardman. 1972. Contents of southern Indiana wild turkey droppings. Proc. Ind. Acad. Sci., 81:165–168.

Langdon, Frank W. 1877. A catalogue of the birds in the vicinity of Cincinnati. Naturalists' Agency. 18 pp.

Lanyon, Wesley E. 1956. Ecological aspects of the sympatric distribution of meadowlarks in the north-central states. Ecology, 37:98–108.

Lindsey, Alton A. 1961. Vegetation of the drainage-aeration classes of northern Indiana soils in 1830. Ecology, 42:432–436.

Lindsey, Alton A., William B. Crankshaw, and S. A. Qadir. 1965. Soil relations and distribution map of the vegetation of pre-settlement Indiana. Botanical Gazette, 126:155–163.

Littell, Clarence G. 1903. The birds of Winona Lake. Proc. Ind. Acad. Sci., 12:134–158.

Luther, Dorothy. 1967. Eastern wood pewee fledglings help parents mold a nest. Ind. Aud. Quart., 46:88–92.

———. 1973. A history of an old heronry in Montgomery County, Indiana. Ind. Aud. Quart., 51:16–19.

———. 1979a. An intensive study of parental behavior in the mourning dove. Ind. Aud. Quart., 57:232.

———. 1979b. Behavior of mourning doves during a 133-day incubation period. Ind. Aud. Quart., 57:232–234.

McAtee, Waldo L. 1905. Ecological notes on the birds occurring within a radius of five miles of the Indiana University campus. Proc. Ind. Acad. Sci., 14:65–202.

McKeever, Otto D. 1944. Waterfowl population studies. Pittman-Robertson Wildl. Res. Rep., 5:1–20.

Merritt, Peter G. 1977. Gap formation: a reproductive isolating mechanism for *Parus atricapillus* and *P. carolinensis* in northern Indiana. Master's thesis. Western Michigan Univ., August 1977. 80 pp.

Mills, Charles and Marietta Smith. 1976. A blue grosbeak nest in Pike County. Ind. Aud. Quart., 54:110–111.

Monroe, Burt L., Sr., and Burt L. Monroe, Jr. 1961. Birds of the Louisville region. Kentucky Warbler, 37:23–42.

Monroe, Burt L., Jr. 1976. Birds of the Louisville region. Kentucky Warbler, 52:61.

Mumford, Russell E. 1952. Bell's vireo in Indiana. Wilson Bulletin, 65:224–233.

———. 1953. White-rumped sandpiper in Indiana. Wilson Bulletin, 65:44–45.

———. 1956. Little gull taken in Indiana. Wilson Bulletin, 68:321.

———. 1964. Cattle egret in Indiana. Ind. Aud. Quart., 42:79.

———. 1966. A Ross's goose in Indiana. Ind. Aud. Quart., 44:114.

———. 1982. The marbled murrelet in Indiana. Ind. Aud. Quart., 60:190–191.

Mumford, Russell E., and Charles R. Danner. 1974. An Indiana marsh hawk roost. Ind. Aud. Quart., 52:96–98.

Mumford, Russell E., and Larry E. Lehman. 1969. Glossy ibis taken in Indiana. Wilson Bulletin, 81:463–464.

Mumford, Russell E., and Warren S. Rowe. 1963. The lesser black-backed gull in Indiana. Wilson Bulletin, 75:93.

Mumford, Russell E., and John O. Whitaker, Jr. 1982. The mammals of Indiana. Indiana Univ. Press. 537 pp.

Nelson, E. W. 1876. Additions to the avi-fauna of Illinois, with notes on other species of Illinois birds. Bulletin Nuttall Ornithological Club, 1:39–44.

Newman, James E. 1966. Bioclimate. *In* Natural features of Indiana, A. A. Lindsey, editor. Ind. Acad. Sci., pp. 171–180.

Nice, Margaret M. 1945. How many times does a song sparrow sing one song. Auk, 62:302.

Nolan, Val Jr. 1949. Three hundred loons in one flock at Oaklandon Reservoir. Ind. Aud. Soc. Yearbook 1949:30–31.

———. 1953. Notes on the Pine-woods sparrow near Bloomington, Indiana. Ind. Aud. Quart., 31:26–28.

———. 1958. Middlewestern prairie region. Aud. Field Notes, 12:415–417.

———. 1960. Breeding behavior of the Bell vireo in southern Indiana. The Condor, 62:225–244.

———. 1978. The ecology and behavior of the prairie warbler *Dendroica discolor*. Ornithological monographs No. 26, A.O.U. 595 pp.

Nuner, Robert D. 1950. Kittiwake gull. Ind. Aud. Quart., 28:61–62.

Parks, W. C. 1908. The wood thrush. The Oologist, 25:170.

Perkins, Samuel E., III. 1935. Double-crested cormorants breeding in Posey County, Indiana. Auk, 52:74–75.

Petty, Robert O., and Marion T. Jackson. 1966. Plant communities. *In* Natural features of Indiana, A. A. Lindsey, editor. Ind. Acad. Sci. pp. 264–296.

Pitelka, Frank A. 1938. Say's phoebe in northern Indiana. Auk, 55:280–281.

Price, Homer F. 1935. The summer birds of northwestern Ohio. The Oologist, 52:26–36.

Reeves, Maurice C. 1955. Bobwhite quail. *In* Ind. Pittman-Robertson Wildlife Restoration 1939–1955. Ind. Dept. Conservation., Pittman-Robertson Bulletin No. 3. pp. 117–138.

Ricker, William E. 1942. Purple sandpiper in Indiana. Wilson Bulletin, 54:250.

Ridgway, Robert. 1878. Notes on birds observed at Mt. Carmel, southern Illinois, in the spring of 1878. Bulletin Nuttall Ornithological Club, 3:162–166.

———. 1889. The ornithology of Illinois. Natural History Survey of Illinois, Vol. 1:121–122.

———. 1915. Bird-life in southern Illinois. IV. Changes which have taken place in half a century. Bird-Lore, 17:191–198.

Roads, Katie M. 1912. Notes from Moore's Hill, Indiana. Wilson Bulletin, 24:157–159.

Robbins, Chandler S., Bertel Bruun, and Herbert S. Zim. 1966. A guide to field identification Birds of North America. Golden Press. 340 pp.

Russell, Robert. 1973. The extirpation of the piping plover as a breeding species in Illinois and Indiana. Illinois Aud. Bulletin, No. 165:46–48.

Schneider, A. F. 1966. Physiography. *In* Natural features of Indiana, A. A. Lindsey, editor. Ind. Acad. Sci. pp. 40–56.

Schorger, A. W. 1944. The prairie chicken and sharp-tailed grouse in early Wisconsin. Trans. Wisconsin Acad. Sci., Arts and Letters, 35:1–59.

———. 1964. The trumpeter swan as a breeding bird in Minnesota, Illinois, and Indiana. Wilson Bulletin, 76:334–336.

Segal, Simon. 1960. Bird tragedy at the dunes. Ind. Aud. Quart., 38:23–25.

Sharpe, R. Bowdler. 1885. Catalogue of the passeriformes or perching birds in the collection of the British Museum, etc. Vol. 10:305, London.

Sieber, Jesseeka. 1932. Black crowned night heronry near Michigantown. Ind. Aud. Soc. Yearbook 1932:90–91.

Smith, Harry M. 1936. Notes on the birds of the Calumet and dune regions. Mimeographed paper. 40 pp.

———. 1950. Notes on the birds of the Chicago region. Auk, 67:109–110.

Snow, Mabelle M. 1967. Two visitors from the west. Ind. Aud. Quart., 46:65–66.

Stewart, M. E. F. 1925. A screech owl in its winter retreat. Bird-Lore, 27:398.

Stoddard, Herbert L. 1916. The long-tailed jaeger in Indiana. Auk, 33:75.

———. 1917. Rare winter visitants in northern Indiana. Auk, 34:487.

Sutherland, D. E. 1971. A 1965 waterfowl population model. Bur. Sport Fisheries and Wildlife, Flyway Habitat Mgmt. Unit Proj., Rept. 4, 11 pp.

Thompson, Charles F., and Val Nolan Jr. 1973. Population ecology of the yellow-breasted chat (*Icteria virens* L.) in southern Indiana. Ecological Monographs, 43:145–171.

Thompson, Mildred T. 1972. Was the grackle fooled? Ind. Aud. Quart., 50:76–77.

Thwaites, R. G., Ed. 1906. Early western travels 1748–1846. Arthur H. Clark Co., pp. 163–197.

Van Tyne, J. 1936. Bird eggs from Indiana in the collection of E. B. Williamson. Ind. Aud. Soc. Yearbook 1936: 30–35.

Visher, Stephen S. 1944. Climate of Indiana. Ind. Univ. Publ. Sci. Series No. 13:511 pp.

Ward, Gertrude L. 1963. A house wren's unusual nest. Ind. Aud. Quart., 41:62–63.

Wayne, William J. 1956. Thickness of drift and bedrock physiography of Indiana north of the Wisconsin glacial boundary. Ind. Dept. Conserv. Geol. Surv. Rept. of Progress No. 7. 70 pp.

Webster, J. Dan. 1980. Scattered field notes from southern Indiana. Ind. Aud. Quart., 58:139–142.

Weeks, Harmon P., Jr. 1970. Courtship and territorial behavior of some Indiana woodcocks. Proc. Ind. Acad. Sci., 79:162–171.

———. 1979. Nesting ecology of the eastern phoebe in southern Indiana. Wilson Bulletin, 91:441–454.

———. 1980. Unusual egg deposition in mourning doves. Wilson Bulletin 92:258–260.

Weeks, Harmon P., Jr., and Russell E. Mumford. 1981. First recorded breeding of pine siskins in Indiana. Ind. Aud. Quart., 59:5–9.

Weigle, Mrs. Charles F. 1925. Bad habits of the house wren. Wilson Bulletin, 37:160–163.

Williamson, E. B. 1900. Biological conditions of Round and Shriner Lakes, Whitley County, Ind. Proc. Ind. Acad. Sci., 8:151–155.

———. 1913. Actions of nesting red-shouldered hawks. Auk, 30:582–583.

Wilson, Alexander. 1812. American ornithology, vol. 6. Bradford & Inskeep.

Wilson, Etta S. 1918. Bachman's warbler and solitary sandpiper in Indiana. Auk, 35:228–229.

Wilson, G. R. 1910. History of Dubois County, from its primitive days to 1910. Publ. by the author.

Witmer, Samuel W. 1969. Observation notes on birds. When, where and how we saw some birds. 93 pp. (Mimeo.)

Woodruff, Frank M. 1907. The birds of the Chicago region. Bulletin No. 6 of the Natural History Survey. Chicago Acad. Sci. 221 pp.

Wright, Vernon L. 1966. Status of the gray partridge in Indiana. Master's thesis. Purdue Univ., June 1966. 64 pp.

SPONSORS AND DONORS

This seems the appropriate place to explain to the world at large the unique funding approach behind the publication of this magnificent book, to acknowledge publicly the individuals and organizations who helped and, above all, to thank the sponsors and donors who had confidence in this project long before it became a reality. First and foremost, we wish to acknowledge Ruth and Dick Johnson of Columbus, Indiana, who, by purchasing the art (and thus the artist's time), are directly responsible for all of the original paintings that make this book so special. The money necessary to subsidize the manufacturing costs, which is to say the money that has made it possible to publish a quality book at a relatively low price, has come from individuals and a few organizations in the state of Indiana as well as some people outside the state. The support of the state Audubon chapters was essential, but what has been especially gratifying and unusual is that this has been primarily the work of individuals talking to other individuals. No professional fundraising organization was involved. No foundation or agency put up the money. What has happened is that bird lovers and book lovers in the state of Indiana have formed a kind of community to support this project. Our approach was to seek sponsorship of all the nesting species, 165 in number. In some cases two sponsors were required for an individual bird as two paintings were involved. Additional funds were sought in the form of general donations up to a hundred in number. At the time the volume went to press all 165 of the nesting species had found sponsors and 72 individuals had made general donations. Several corporations provided matching grants to the contributions made by their employees.

Mr. Thomas Potter, the President of the Indiana Audubon Society when this project was conceived, deserves a special thank you from all of us for his support, encouragement, and the very major effort he made personally on behalf of the fundraising. Other individuals who made singular contributions by organizing fundraising events or by the diligence of their personal search for sponsors and donors are: Delano Z. Arvin, Eleanor and Jeffery Auer, DeVere Burt (Cincinnati Museum of Natural History), Helen and Lynton K. Caldwell, Larry and Linda Cronkleton, Robert Fischgrund, Carol Halsey and Pat Palmer, Ruth and Dick Johnson, John and Marcia Munshower, and Tad Wilson.

Finally, the publisher wishes to thank the authors and the artist for their above-and-beyond-the-call-of-duty efforts on behalf of funding. Their various contributions are so much greater than is customary that it is hard to acknowledge them adequately.—John Gallman, Director, Indiana University Press

SPONSORS

PIED-BILLED GREBE
Mr. and Mrs. Frank R. Stewart, Spencer

DOUBLE-CRESTED CORMORANT
Patricia Newforth, Spencer

AMERICAN BITTERN
Mr. and Mrs. Hugh R. Sullivan, Jr., Indianapolis

LEAST BITTERN
Mr. and Mrs. Sanford L. Cooper, Cincinnati, Ohio

GREAT BLUE HERON
William Paul Kafoure, Hayward, California

GREAT EGRET
Dr. and Mrs. Charles F. White, Zionsville

GREEN-BACKED HERON
Kay F. Koch, North Salem

BLACK-CROWNED NIGHT-HERON
Dr. and Mrs. Nicholas M. Timm, New Carlisle

YELLOW-CROWNED NIGHT-HERON
Elaine Ewing Fess, Zionsville

CANADA GOOSE
Mr. and Mrs. John R. Carpenter, West Lafayette

WOOD DUCK
John and Beth Gallman, Bloomington

GREEN-WINGED TEAL (MALE AND FEMALE)
Samuel G. Johnson, Lenoir City, Tennessee

AMERICAN BLACK DUCK
Mr. and Mrs. Brad Brim, Monticello

MALLARD (MALE AND FEMALE)
James and Judith Burhans, Bloomington

BLUE-WINGED TEAL (MALE AND FEMALE)
Mr. and Mrs. C. W. Long, Indianapolis

NORTHERN SHOVELER (MALE)
Mr. and Mrs. Gary R. Norris, Columbus

NORTHERN SHOVELER (FEMALE)
Mr. and Mrs. A. E. McCain, Jackson, Wyoming

REDHEAD (MALE AND FEMALE)
Thomas W. and F. Carolyn Beers, West Lafayette

RING-NECKED DUCK (MALE AND FEMALE)
Bunger, Harrell and Robertson, Bloomington

HOODED MERGANSER (MALE)
Mark and Charlene Braun, Bloomington

HOODED MERGANSER (FEMALE)
Mr. and Mrs. Stanley L. Thomas, Spencer
Mr. and Mrs. Charles Neumeyer, Spencer
Mr. and Mrs. Tad Wilson, Spencer

RUDDY DUCK
Mr. and Mrs. Don W. Bilyeu, Assumption, Illinois

BLACK VULTURE
Tad and Shirley Wilson, Spencer

TURKEY VULTURE
Andrew John Potter, Indianapolis
Gregory Allen Potter, Indianapolis
(From Their Father)

OSPREY
Rita and John Grunwald, Bloomington

BALD EAGLE
Roger W. Jewett, Indianapolis

NORTHERN HARRIER
Dr. and Mrs. Mark D. Jacobi, Michigan City

SHARP-SHINNED HAWK
C. A. Smith, II, Greenville, South Carolina

COOPER'S HAWK
Ruth and Charlie Miller, West Lafayette

RED-SHOULDERED HAWK
Pauline S. and James L. Rowe, Indianapolis

BROAD-WINGED HAWK
Mr. and Mrs. Elliott Hickam, Spencer

RED-TAILED HAWK
Dr. and Mrs. David G. Frey, Bloomington

AMERICAN KESTREL
Dr. and Mrs. David G. Frey, Bloomington

GRAY PARTRIDGE
Jane and Frank Walker, Indianapolis

RING-NECKED PHEASANT (MALE)
K. B. Zumdome, Indianapolis

RING-NECKED PHEASANT (FEMALE)
Mr. and Mrs. Robert B. Deahl, Syracuse

RUFFED GROUSE
Joan E. and Edward L. Whalen, Bloomington

WILD TURKEY
Lynton K. and Helen W. Caldwell, Bloomington

NORTHERN BOBWHITE
S. G. Johnson, Jr., Nashville

KING RAIL
Donna Polyak, Beverly Shores

VIRGINIA RAIL
Virginia B. Ball, Muncie

SORA
Francis and Elizabeth Kummeth, Goshen
Richard and Ina Strasser, Goshen

COMMON MOORHEN
Mr. and Mrs. Robert Galm,
Brian, Christopher, and Patrick, Nashville

AMERICAN COOT
Hackett Publishing Company, Inc., Indianapolis

SANDHILL CRANE
Tim and Kathy Keller, Indianapolis
Bernadette Keller, Indianapolis

KILLDEER
Mr. and Mrs. E. B. Bryan, Bloomington

SPOTTED SANDPIPER
Anonymous

UPLAND SANDPIPER
Marjorie and Victor Riemenschneider, South Bend

COMMON SNIPE
Jack and Janet Leffert, Logansport

AMERICAN WOODCOCK
Nancy Frass, Martinsville

BLACK TERN
Mrs. J. M. Studebaker III, South Bend

ROCK DOVE
Mrs. William H. Nebergall, Sr., Bloomington

MOURNING DOVE
Shell Oil Company, Indianapolis

BLACK-BILLED CUCKOO
Paul and Mary Jane Curry, Columbus

YELLOW-BILLED CUCKOO
Leora M. Thomas, Columbus

COMMON BARN-OWL
Sears and Villa Crowell, Bloomington

EASTERN SCREECH-OWL
Michael Sacopulos, Terre Haute

GREAT HORNED OWL
Bernard and Marjorie Clayton, Bloomington

BARRED OWL
South Bend Audubon Society, South Bend

LONG-EARED OWL
Margaret S. Dietz, Columbus

SHORT-EARED OWL
Ruth E. Hickam, Bloomington

NORTHERN SAW-WHET OWL
Eleanor Byrnes, Bloomington

COMMON NIGHTHAWK
Mr. and Mrs. James M. Diehl, Bloomington

CHUCK-WILL'S-WIDOW
Ted and Sue Ulrich, Otterbein

WHIP-POOR-WILL
Joan Doak Steele, Leroy

CHIMNEY SWIFT
Jeffrey Belth, Bloomington

RUBY-THROATED HUMMINGBIRD
Bernard and Marjorie Clayton, Bloomington

BELTED KINGFISHER
John and Susan Barnard, Greenwood

RED-HEADED WOODPECKER
William N., Nancy J., and Christopher D. Doemel, Crawfordsville

RED-BELLIED WOODPECKER
Richard L. Johnson, Jr., Columbus

YELLOW-BELLIED SAPSUCKER
Dr. and Mrs. Lyle B. Anderson, Bloomington

DOWNY WOODPECKER
Elaine Caldwell Emmi, Salt Lake City, Utah

HAIRY WOODPECKER
Thomas and Lavetta Stankus, South Bend

NORTHERN FLICKER
Donald E. and Donna L. McCarty, Indianapolis

PILEATED WOODPECKER
Robert L. and Mavis C. Siebenthal, Bloomington

EASTERN WOOD-PEWEE
Mrs. Maurice C. Reeves, Bloomington

ACADIAN FLYCATCHER, WILLOW FLYCATCHER, LEAST FLYCATCHER
M. Phil and Margaret E. Hathaway, Bloomington

EASTERN PHOEBE
Shirley and John McCord, Indianapolis

GREAT CRESTED FLYCATCHER
Edward and Ruth Erickson, Terre Haute

EASTERN KINGBIRD
Ralph and Margaret Richards, Carmel, in memory of Cole Porter

HORNED LARK
Clifford L. and Mary R. Gough, New Castle

PURPLE MARTIN
Untamed Art Gallery, Indianapolis

TREE SWALLOW
John and Rose Parli, Indianapolis

NORTHERN ROUGH-WINGED SWALLOW
In memory of C. Burritt Bryan

BANK SWALLOW
Jane Rodman, Bloomington

CLIFF SWALLOW
The Audubon Society of Ohio

BARN SWALLOW
Hazel Mitchell, Bloomington

BLUE JAY
Gary and Sandy Sojka, Bloomington

AMERICAN CROW
Nancy Ann Miller, Bloomington

BLACK-CAPPED CHICKADEE
Thomas A. and Joann Walker, Bloomington

CAROLINA CHICKADEE
Henry and Alice Gray, Bloomington

TUFTED TITMOUSE
Carl E. Weber, Indianapolis

RED-BREASTED NUTHATCH
Mr. and Mrs. Charles Moulin, Indianapolis

WHITE-BREASTED NUTHATCH
Hazel K. Bartholomew, Bloomington

BROWN CREEPER
Wesselman Park Nature Center Society, Evansville

CAROLINA WREN
Mr. and Mrs. Maurice A. David, Columbus

BEWICK'S WREN
Mr. and Mrs. Philip L. Guilford, Mishawaka

HOUSE WREN
Earl C. Floyd, Bloomington

SEDGE WREN
Dr. and Mrs. W. L. Dalton, Shelbyville

MARSH WREN
Lena Dunn Lo and Irving Lo, Bloomington

BLUE-GRAY GNATCATCHER
Sycamore Audubon Society, West Lafayette

EASTERN BLUEBIRD
Jenny Johnson, Columbus

VEERY
Bill and Pat Burton, Nashville

WOOD THRUSH
Sallie McConnell Potter, Martinsville

AMERICAN ROBIN
Mr. and Mrs. Peter A. Saurer, Nashville

GRAY CATBIRD
Mr. and Mrs. Robert S. Baker, Indianapolis

NORTHERN MOCKINGBIRD
Governor's Residence Library, State of Indiana

BROWN THRASHER
Frances D. Winslow, Bloomington

CEDAR WAXWING
Betty Blumberg Polley, Bloomington

LOGGERHEAD SHRIKE
Mr. and Mrs. W. William Weeks, Indianapolis

EUROPEAN STARLING
Wilma and Henry West, Greenfield

WHITE-EYED VIREO
Dr. and Mrs. William L. Hoover, West Lafayette

BELL'S VIREO
G. Paul McCord, Indianapolis

YELLOW-THROATED VIREO
Mr. and Mrs. Richard Allison, Columbus

WARBLING VIREO
Jerilyn James, Martinsville

RED-EYED VIREO
Mr. and Mrs. C. Harvey Bradley, Jr., Zionsville

BLUE-WINGED WARBLER
Patrick O'Meara, Bloomington

GOLDEN-WINGED WARBLER
Henry and Cecilia Wahl, Bloomington

NORTHERN PARULA
Irene S. Herlocker, Munster

YELLOW WARBLER
Frances Dodson Rhome, Indianapolis

CHESTNUT-SIDED WARBLER
Mr. and Mrs. Henry W. Schick, Frontenac, Missouri

YELLOW-THROATED WARBLER
David L. and Ruth H. Eiler, North Manchester

PINE WARBLER
Barbara Feucht Randall, Bloomington

PRAIRIE WARBLER
Ray and Ginny Berg, Indianapolis

CERULEAN WARBLER
John and Carol Rumple, Columbus

BLACK-AND-WHITE WARBLER
Herman E. and Barbara K. Weidner, Morgantown

AMERICAN REDSTART
Mr. and Mrs. Kenneth J. Galm, Nashville

PROTHONOTARY WARBLER
Robert Menke, Huntingburg

WORM-EATING WARBLER
Gordon and Cheryl McLaughlin, Indianapolis

OVENBIRD
Ethel Horton, Valparaiso

LOUISIANA WATERTHRUSH
Bullskin Creek Bird Club, Wilmington, North
Carolina

KENTUCKY WARBLER
Mr. and Mrs. Howard F. Wright, Indianapolis

COMMON YELLOWTHROAT
Robert Howard Weir, Nashville

HOODED WARBLER
Clara and Henry Kuebler, West Lafayette

CANADA WARBLER
Dr. and Mrs. Mitchell Steinberg, Indianapolis

YELLOW-BREASTED CHAT
Emma B. Pitcher, Chesterton

SUMMER TANAGER
Judson and Jane Mead, Bloomington

SCARLET TANAGER
John and Dorothy Osmun, West Lafayette

NORTHERN CARDINAL
Thomas A. Sebeok and Jean Umiker-Sebeok,
Bloomington

ROSE-BREASTED GROSBEAK
Susie and Robert Dewey, Terre Haute

BLUE GROSBEAK
Jeffery and Eleanor Auer, Bloomington

INDIGO BUNTING
President and Mrs. John Ryan, Indiana University

DICKCISSEL
Dr. and Mrs. Forest K. Paul, Indianapolis

RUFOUS-SIDED TOWHEE
Ann and Don Clark, Bloomington

BACHMAN'S SPARROW
Mr. and Mrs. W. W. Gasser, Jr., Ogden Dunes

CHIPPING SPARROW
Dr. and Mrs. Mark W. Dick, Bloomington

FIELD SPARROW
Dr. and Mrs. Thomas A. Stump, Indianapolis

VESPER SPARROW
Clara S. Nagel, Prescott, Arizona

LARK SPARROW
Mr. and Mrs. V. J. Shiner, Jr., Bloomington

SAVANNAH SPARROW
Hellen Ochs Bird Club, Columbus

GRASSHOPPER SPARROW
Mr. and Mrs. Joseph W. Taylor, Honeoye Falls,
New York

HENSLOW'S SPARROW
Joe Dial, Bloomington

SONG SPARROW
Bernard Perry, Bloomington

SWAMP SPARROW
Mr. and Mrs. Joseph H. Head, Jr., Cincinnati, Ohio

BOBOLINK
Ken and Pearl Eslinger, Terre Haute

RED-WINGED BLACKBIRD
Indiana Heritage Arts, Inc., Nashville

EASTERN MEADOWLARK
Marian Armstrong, Bloomington

YELLOW-HEADED BLACKBIRD
Clayton E. and Dea J. Wiggins, Marion

BREWER'S BLACKBIRD
Carol and J. A. Franklin, Jr., Bloomington

COMMON GRACKLE
Mr. and Mrs. F. G. Summitt, Bloomington

BROWN-HEADED COWBIRD
Judy Figg Davis, Bloomington

ORCHARD ORIOLE
Susan, Dennis, and Kate Wolkoff, Beverly,
Massachusetts

NORTHERN ORIOLE
Dr. and Mrs. H. Sheldon Pattison, Nashville

HOUSE FINCH
Mr. and Mrs. Hugh M. Newsom, Columbus

RED CROSSBILL
Stephen W. Fess, Zionsville

PINE SISKIN
Mr. and Mrs. James William Breeden, Columbus

AMERICAN GOLDFINCH
William G. and Frances Kafoure, Nashville

HOUSE SPARROW
Mr. and Mrs. Leon E. Blume, Marion, in memory
of Kenneth H. Carpenter

EGG PLATE
Dr. and Mrs. James DeVore Lytle, Cincinnati, Ohio

DONORS

Amos W. Butler Chapter (Indianapolis) NAS, in appreciation

Robert D. Arnold, M.D., Indianapolis

Mr. and Mrs. Richard W. Arter, Bloomington

Dr. Delano Z. and Marjory M. Arvin, Lafayette

Kevin D. Arvin, Lafayette

Kyle W. Arvin, Lafayette

Mark C. Arvin, Lafayette

Scott B. Arvin, Lafayette

Francis H. Balcom, M.D., Anaheim, California

Thomas Robert and Leslie Kafoure Baas, and Kelly, Noblesville

John and Peggy Bender, Bloomington

Victoria M. Brock, Chesterton

Steve and Channa Beth Butcher, Martinsville

Joan and Marvin Carmack, Bloomington

Mr. and Mrs. Norris Gary Chumley, Bloomington

Mr. and Mrs. Jonathan J. Cook, South Bend

Luther and Jean Coumbe, Nashville, in memory of Mr. and Mrs. Roy Coumbe and Mr. and Mrs. Thomas Campbell

Dr. and Mrs. John I. Cronkhite, Bloomington

James and Gail Crowe, Plainfield

Dale and Mary Lou Deardorff, Mishawaka

Douglas and Susan Duff, Mishawaka

Dr. and Mrs. Sherman L. Egan, South Bend

Mr. and Mrs. W. K. Estes, Cambridge, Massachusetts

Dr. and Mrs. Stephen W. Fess, Zionsville

Mr. and Mrs. Richard W. Fessenden, South Bend

Robert J. and Florence F. Fischgrund, South Bend

Mr. and Mrs. Raymond Gray, Nashville

Jack W. and Katherine A. Hopkins, Bloomington

Indiana Audubon Society, Inc.

Indiana Historical Society

Joni L. James, Martinsville

Carol A. Jewett, Indianapolis

Ronald and Teri Jonas, Bloomington

Steven G. Kafoure, San Diego, California

Raymond F. and Jane M. Kauffman, Indianapolis

William B. and Janice F. Lacefield, Indianapolis

Alton A. and Elizabeth S. Lindsey, West Lafayette

Dr. and Mrs. Gordon C. McLaughlin, Jr., Terre Haute

Dr. and Mrs. Paul T. Maier, West Lafayette

Metropolitan Printing Service, Inc., Bloomington: Mr. and Mrs. Stanley L. Thomas, Mr. and Mrs. Charles Neumeyer, and Mr. and Mrs. Tad Wilson

Ken Miller, Monticello

Dr. and Mrs. Ernest G. Mishler, Greenwood

Dr. and Mrs. Noel T. Moore, Hagerstown

Dr. and Mrs. William Moores, Indianapolis, in memory of Mr. and Mrs. Ward J. Rice

John and Marcia Munshower, Indianapolis

Mrs. Roland Nobis, Bloomington

E. Jane Peden, Indianapolis

Dr. and Mrs. Willis W. Peelle, Kokomo

John and Peg Percifield, Percifield's Radiator and Auto Air Conditioning Service, Columbus

Mr. and Mrs. William Bradford Perrin, Bloomington

Jennifer Sue Potter, Indianapolis (From Her Father and Sallie)

Robert G. Reed and Carlene R. Reed, Indianapolis

Mildred A. Reeves, Columbus

Ralph and Margaret Richards, Carmel, in memory of James O. Cole III

Mr. and Mrs. Merrill L. Ridgway, Scottsdale, Arizona

Dr. and Mrs. Merrill A. Ritter, Indianapolis

Dr. and Mrs. John A. Robb, Indianapolis

Onnalee C. Rose, Nashville

Mr. and Mrs. Larry Sartin, Nashville

Cal Sawyier, Chicago, Illinois

Dr. and Mrs. Herbert A. Schiller, South Bend

Mr. and Mrs. Loren E. Shahin, Columbus

Howard and Judy Shook, Auburn

Frank C. Springer, Jr., Indianapolis

Elvis J. Stahr, Jr., Greenwich, Connecticut

Jack, Evelyn, and Jenna Lynn Stephenson, Indianapolis

Nancy S. and Jerry F. Tardy, Bloomington

R. Q. and Lou Thompson, Greenwood

John Lloyd and Helen Van Camp, Greenwood

Herman B Wells, Bloomington

Wild Birds Unlimited, Indianapolis

Mr. and Mrs. John R. Womer, Valparaiso

Thomas I. Wood, Carmel

Matching gifts were provided by the following companies, corporations, and foundations:

Atlantic Richfield Foundation, Los Angeles, California

International Minerals and Chemical Corporation, Northbrook, Illinois

Eli Lilly and Company, Indianapolis, Indiana

Page numbers for nesting species, which are accompanied by illustrations, appear in boldface. Non-nesters are indicated by regular type. Page references other than those for the main species accounts are in italic.

THE BIRDS OF INDIANA
Russell E. Mumford and Charles E. Keller
Original Paintings by William Zimmerman

editor: Roberta L. Diehl
designer: Edward D. King
typeface: Sabon
typesetter: G & S Typesetters, Inc.
printer: Dai Nippon Printing Company, Ltd.
paper: Royal Art
binder: Dai Nippon Printing Company, Ltd.
cover material: Mafu V natural finish